ONCE UPON A TIME IN FRANCE

D0925935

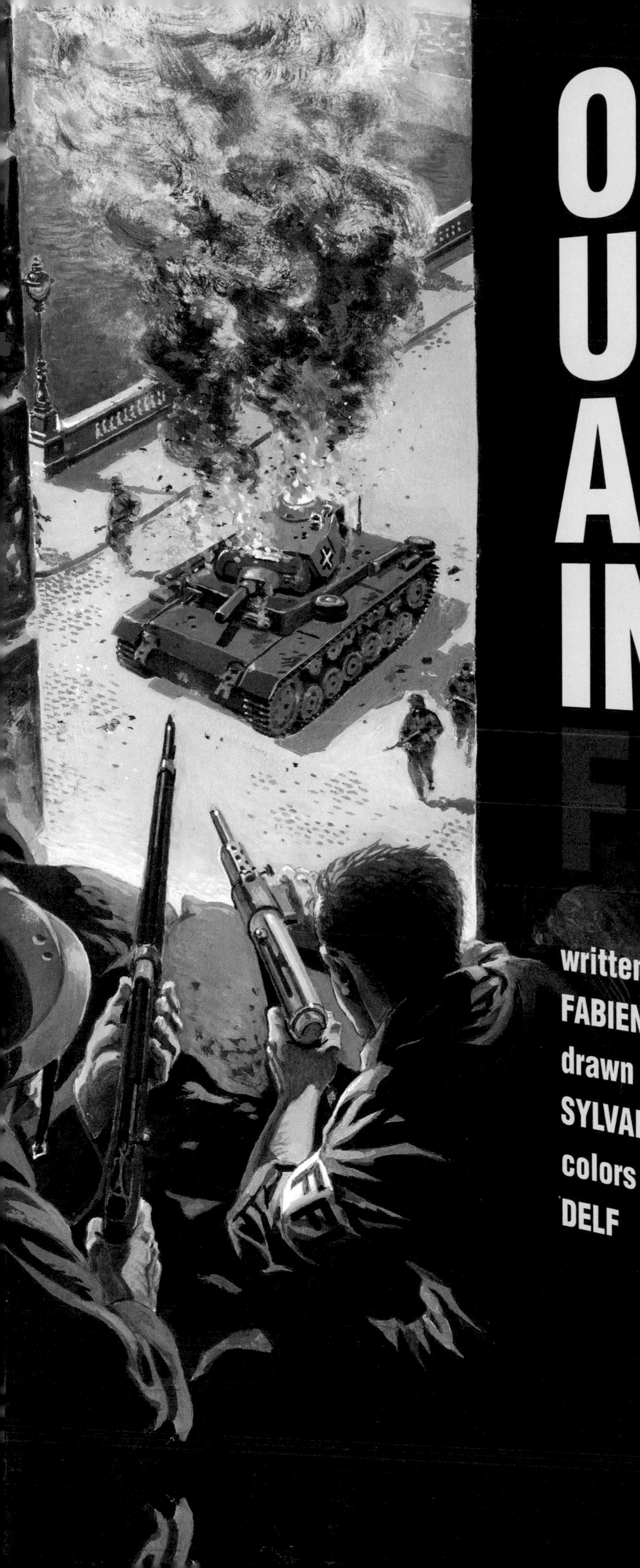

ONCE UPON A TIME IN FRANCE

written by
FABIEN NURY
drawn by
SYLVAIN VALLÉE
colors by
DELF

translated by
IVANKA HAHNENBERGER
lettered by
HALEY ROSE-LYON

WARNING

Although this history is inspired by real events, it is nonetheless fiction: authentic incidents, suppositions, and pure invention are freely mixed. The historical characters exist alongside composite beings and others who are entirely imaginary; their appearances, behaviors, and expressions are made by the authors.

Published by Dead Reckoning
291 Wood Road
Annapolis, MD 21402

First published in French as *Il Était une Fois en France* by F. Nury
and S. Vallée

Names: Nury, Fabien, author. | Vallée, Sylvain, date, illustrator. |
  Hahnenberger, Ivanka, translator.
Title: Once upon a time in France / written by Fabien Nury ; drawn by Sylvain
  Vallée ; translated by Ivanka Hahnenberger.
Other titles: Était une Fois en France. English
Description: Annapolis, MD : Naval Institute Press, [2019] | Although this
  history is inspired by real events, it is nonetheless fiction: authentic
  incidents, suppositions, and pure invention are freely mixed. The
  historical characters exist alongside composite beings and others who are
  entirely imaginary; their appearances, behaviors, and expressions are made
  by the authors. |
Identifiers: LCCN 2019017380 (print) | LCCN 2019019090 (ebook) | ISBN
  9781682474839 (ePDF) | ISBN 9781682474839 (ePub) | ISBN 9781682474716
  (pbk. : alk. paper) | ISBN 9781682474839 (ebook)
Subjects: LCSH: Joinovici, Joseph, 1905-1965–Fiction. | World War,
  1939-1945–Collaborationists–France–Fiction. | Capitalists and
  financiers–France–Fiction.
Classification: LCC PN6747.N87 (ebook) | LCC PN6747.N87 E8313 2019 (print) |
  DDC 741.5/944–dc23
LC record available at https://lccn.loc.gov/2019017380

♾ Print editions meet the requirements of ANSI/NISO z39.48-1992 (Permanence of Paper).

Printed in the United States of America.

27 26 25 24 23 22 21 20 19   9 8 7 6 5 4 3 2 1

First printing

CONTENTS

Mr. Joseph's Empire   1

The Black Flight of Crows   57

Honor and Police   115

To Arms, Citizens!   171

The Little Judge from Melun   235

The Promised Land   295

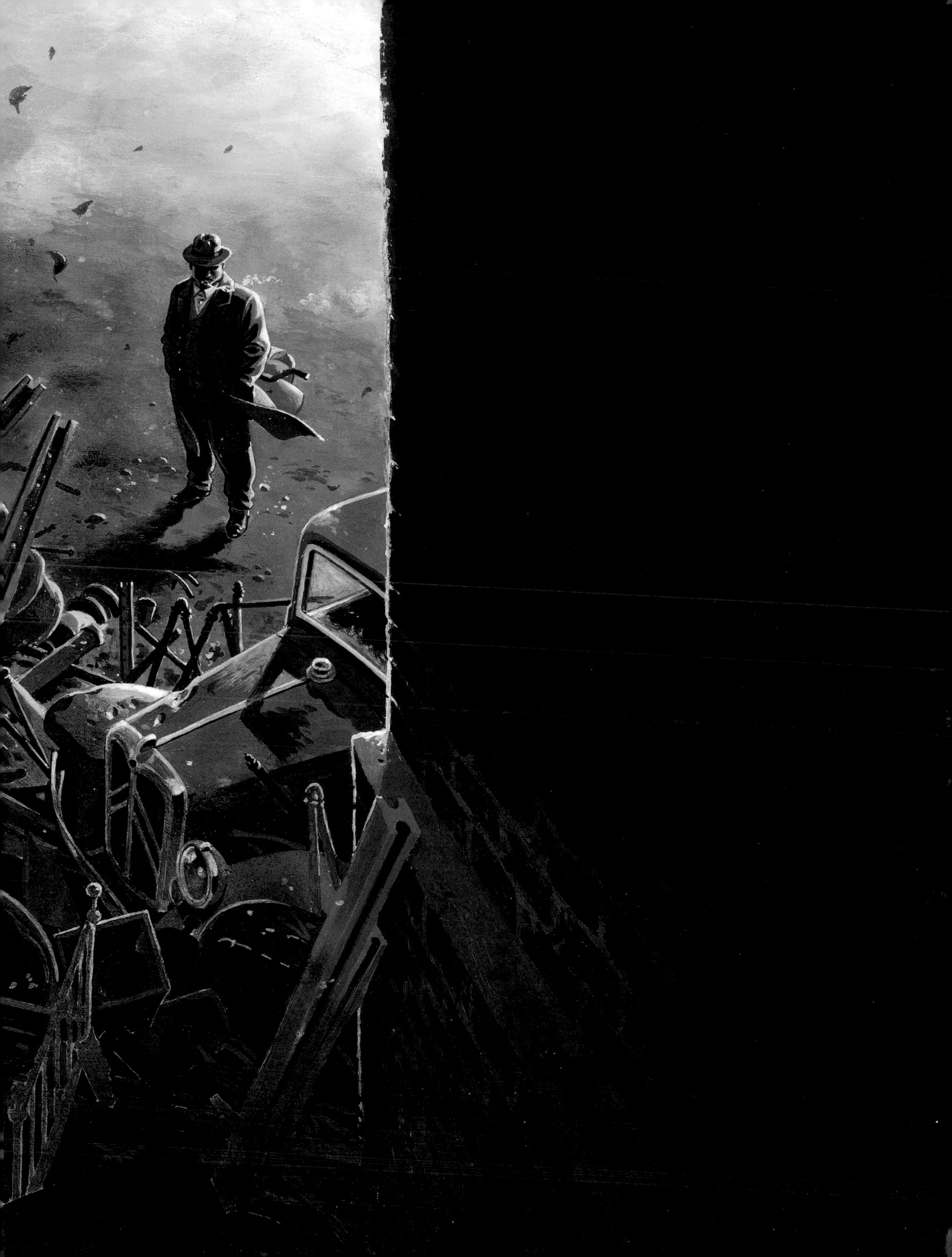

"Go through the ghetto, cast your eyes on the children of the Jews from every country, and you will be able to contemplate all the peoples of the world."

SAMUEL ORNITZ

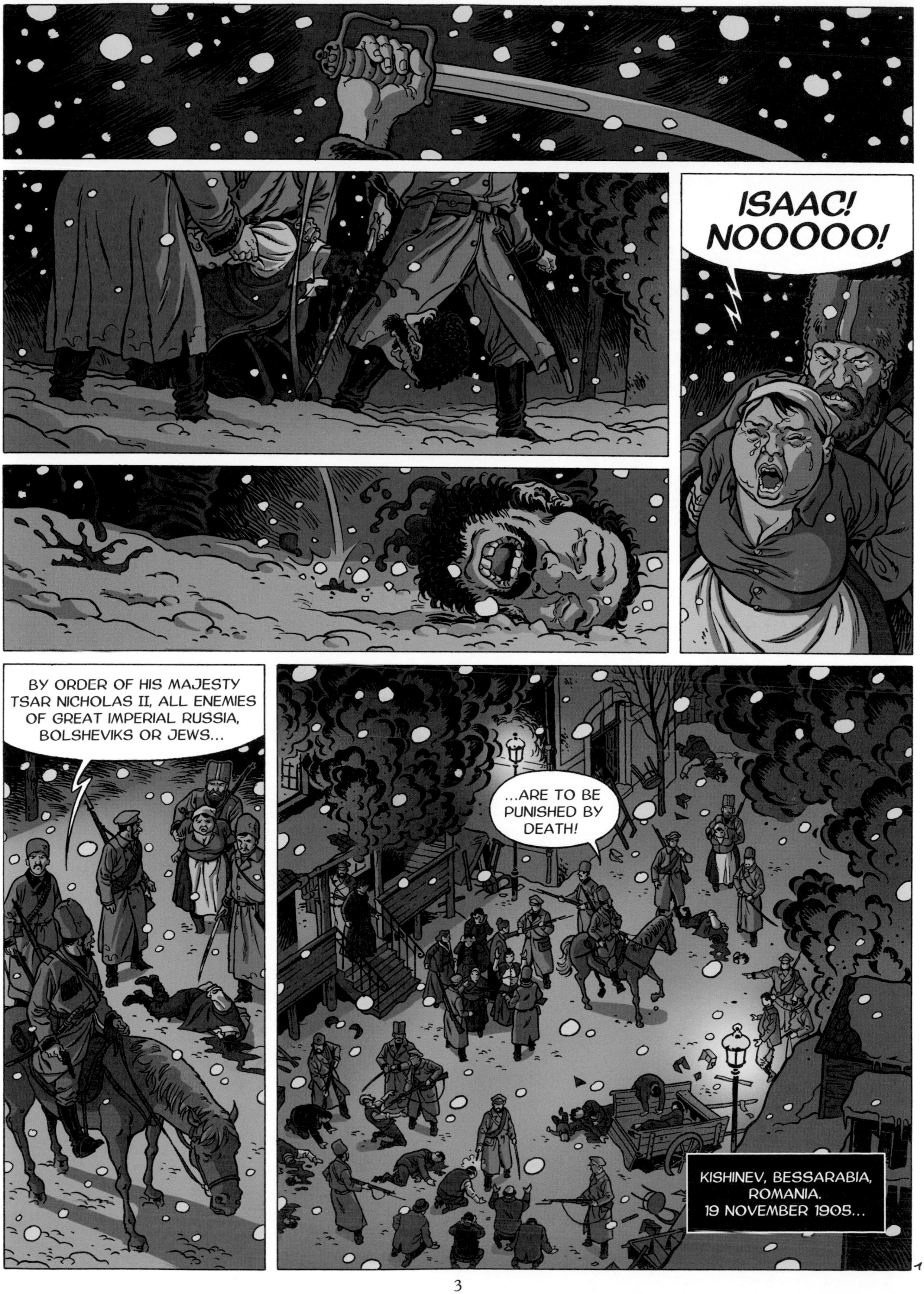
ISAAC! NOOOOO!
BY ORDER OF HIS MAJESTY TSAR NICHOLAS II, ALL ENEMIES OF GREAT IMPERIAL RUSSIA, BOLSHEVIKS OR JEWS...
...ARE TO BE PUNISHED BY DEATH!
KISHINEV, BESSARABIA, ROMANIA. 19 NOVEMBER 1905...

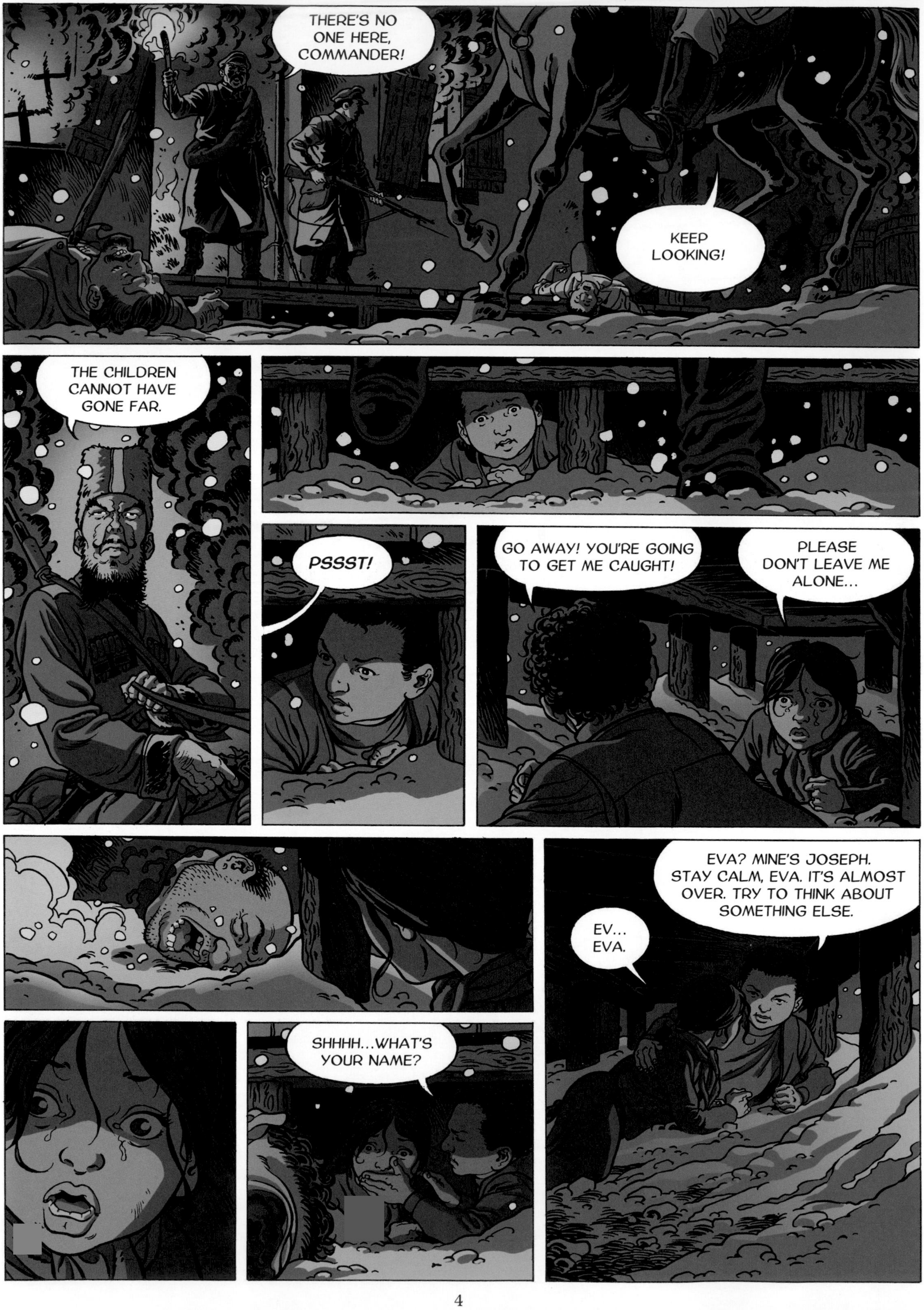
THERE'S NO ONE HERE, COMMANDER!
KEEP LOOKING!
THE CHILDREN CANNOT HAVE GONE FAR.
PSSST!
GO AWAY! YOU'RE GOING TO GET ME CAUGHT!
PLEASE DON'T LEAVE ME ALONE...
SHHHH...WHAT'S YOUR NAME?
EV... EVA.
EVA? MINE'S JOSEPH. STAY CALM, EVA. IT'S ALMOST OVER. TRY TO THINK ABOUT SOMETHING ELSE.

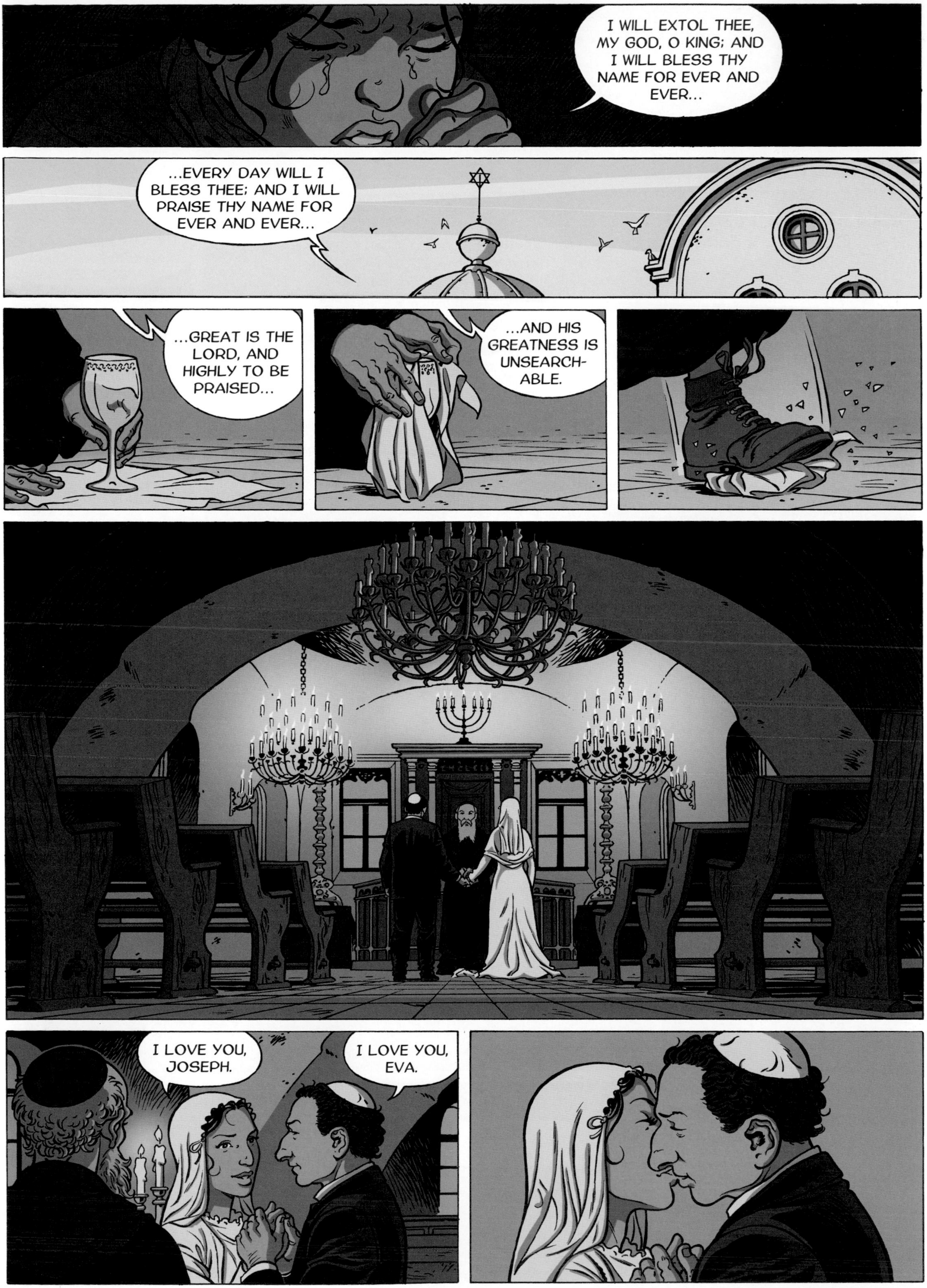
I WILL EXTOL THEE, MY GOD, O KING; AND I WILL BLESS THY NAME FOR EVER AND EVER...
...EVERY DAY WILL I BLESS THEE; AND I WILL PRAISE THY NAME FOR EVER AND EVER...
...GREAT IS THE LORD, AND HIGHLY TO BE PRAISED...
...AND HIS GREATNESS IS UNSEARCH-ABLE.
I LOVE YOU, JOSEPH.
I LOVE YOU, EVA.
3

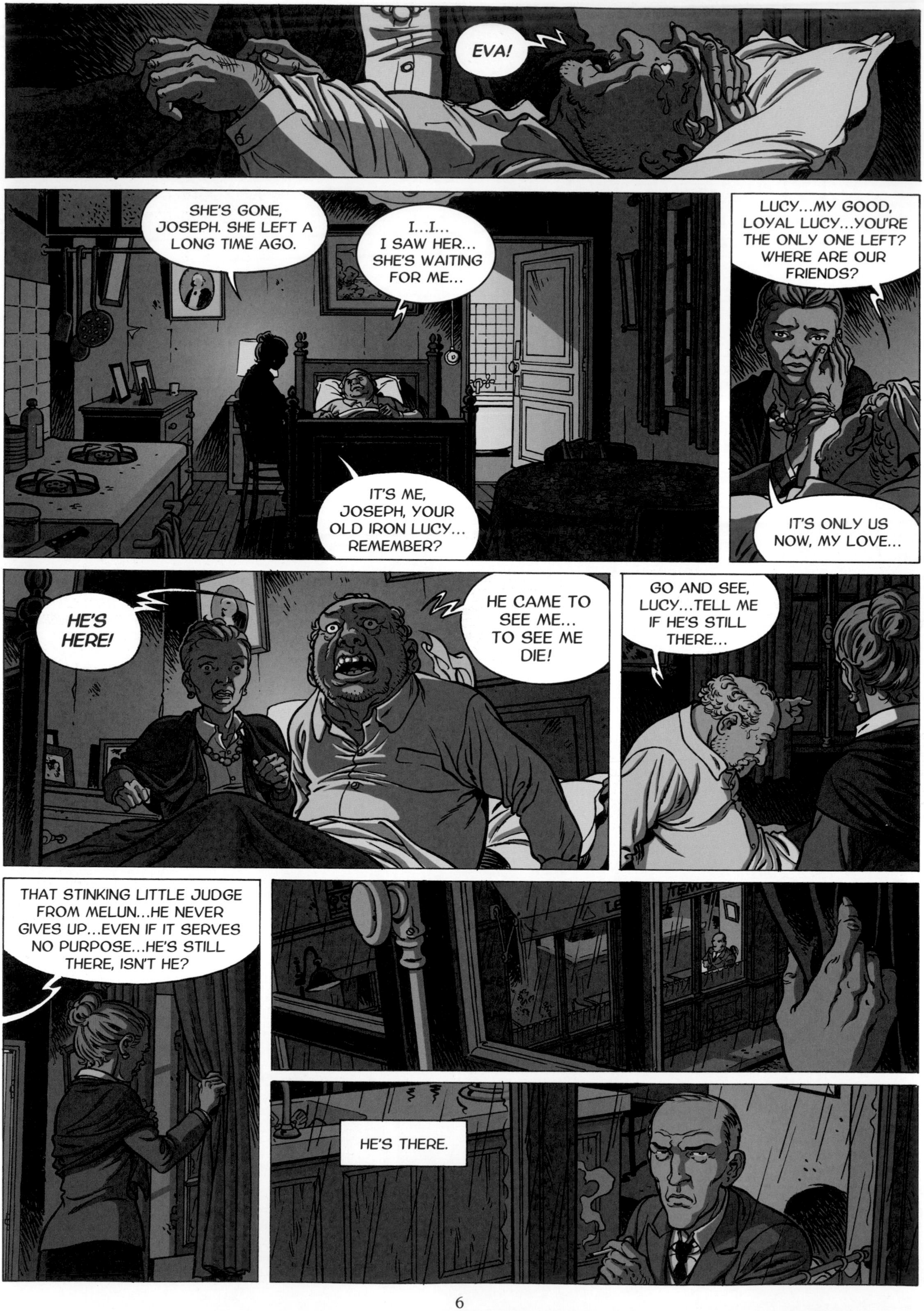
EVA!
SHE'S GONE, JOSEPH. SHE LEFT A LONG TIME AGO.
I...I... I SAW HER... SHE'S WAITING FOR ME...
IT'S ME, JOSEPH, YOUR OLD IRON LUCY... REMEMBER?
LUCY...MY GOOD, LOYAL LUCY...YOU'RE THE ONLY ONE LEFT? WHERE ARE OUR FRIENDS?
IT'S ONLY US NOW, MY LOVE...
HE'S HERE!
HE CAME TO SEE ME... TO SEE ME DIE!
GO AND SEE, LUCY...TELL ME IF HE'S STILL THERE...
THAT STINKING LITTLE JUDGE FROM MELUN...HE NEVER GIVES UP...EVEN IF IT SERVES NO PURPOSE...HE'S STILL THERE, ISN'T HE?
HE'S THERE.
4

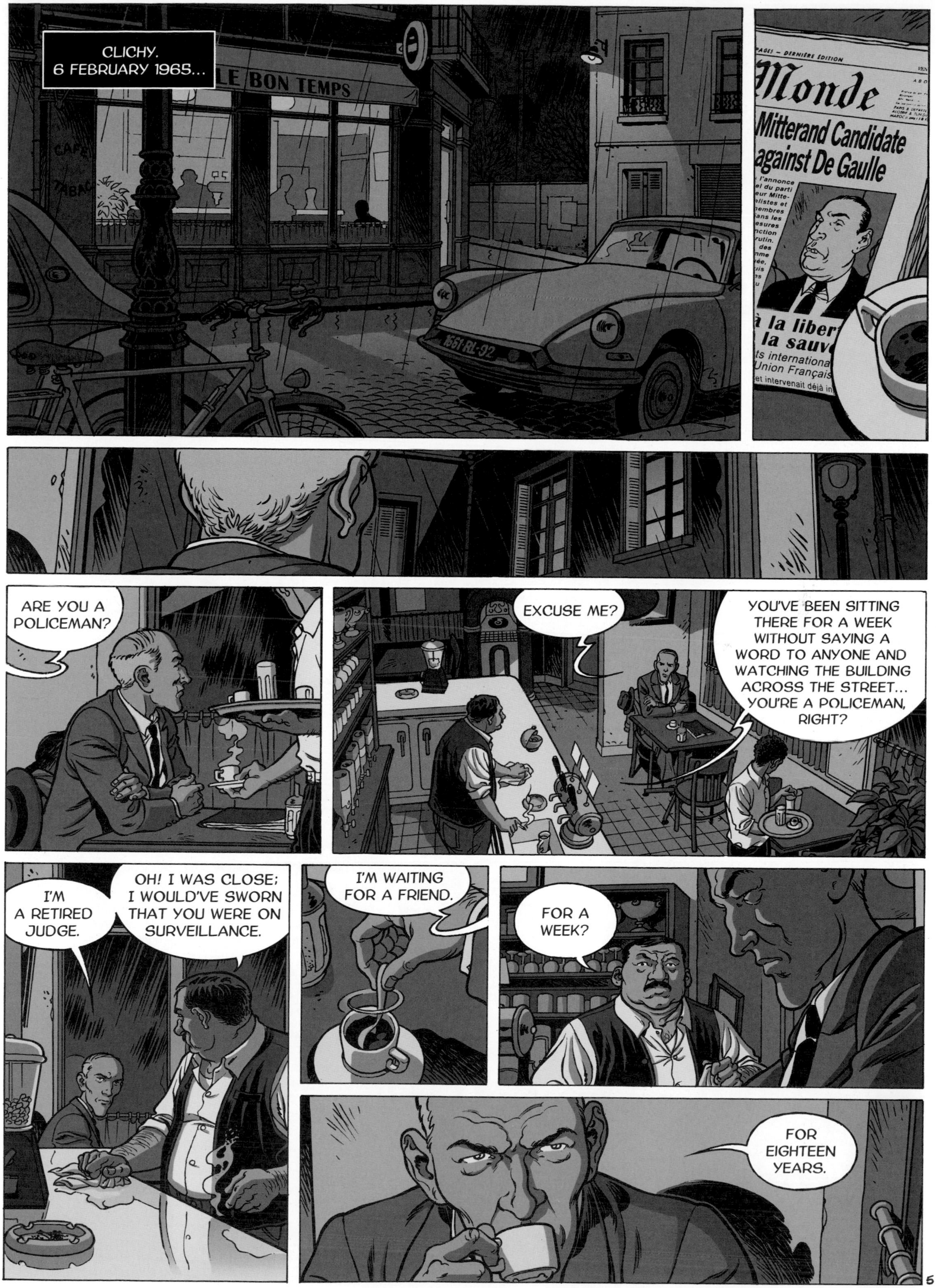
CLICHY.
6 FEBRUARY 1965...
LE BON TEMPS
CAFÉ
TABAC
Monde
Mitterand Candidate against De Gaulle
ARE YOU A POLICEMAN?
EXCUSE ME?
YOU'VE BEEN SITTING THERE FOR A WEEK WITHOUT SAYING A WORD TO ANYONE AND WATCHING THE BUILDING ACROSS THE STREET... YOU'RE A POLICEMAN, RIGHT?
I'M A RETIRED JUDGE.
OH! I WAS CLOSE; I WOULD'VE SWORN THAT YOU WERE ON SURVEILLANCE.
I'M WAITING FOR A FRIEND.
FOR A WEEK?
FOR EIGHTEEN YEARS.
5

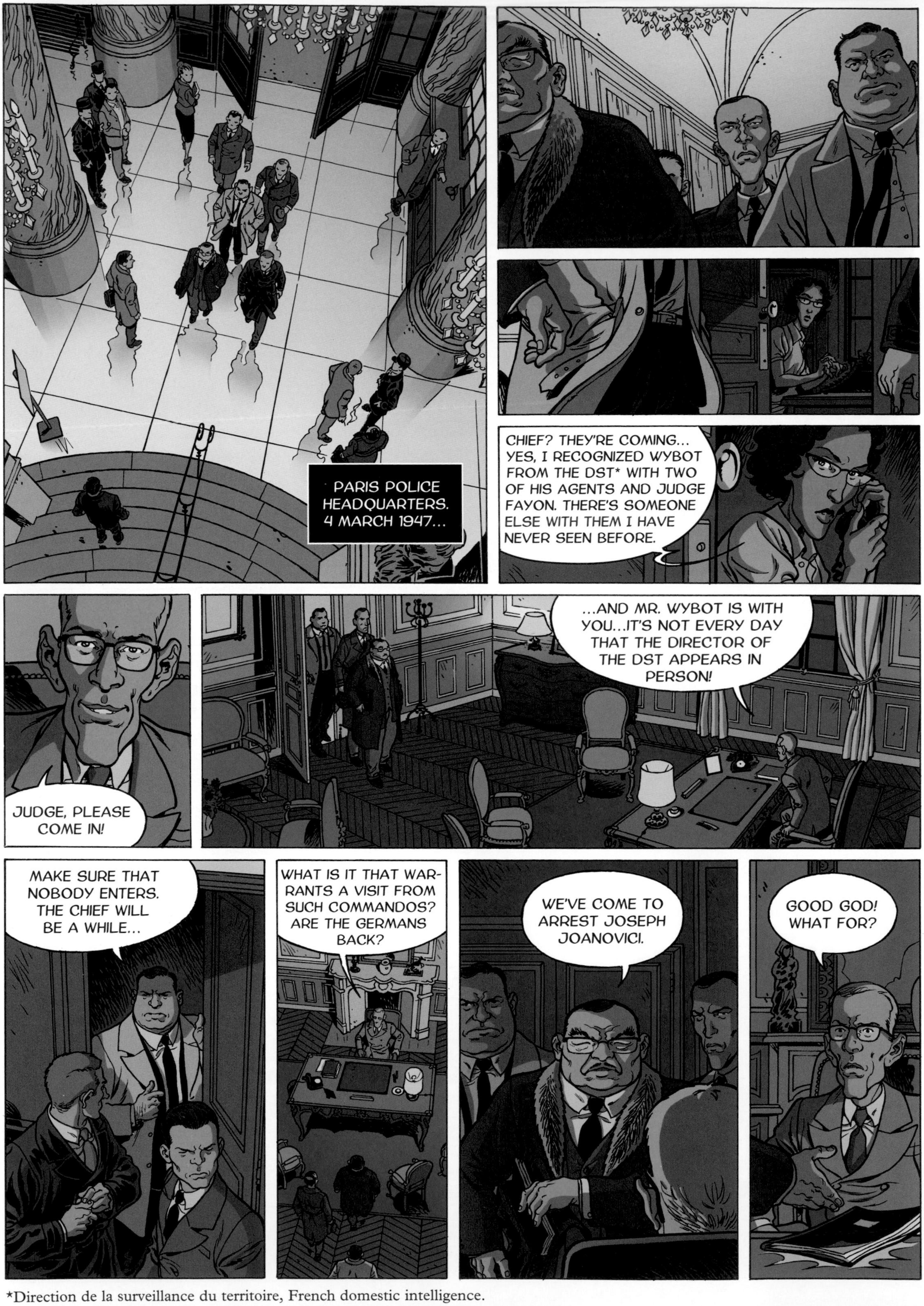
PARIS POLICE HEADQUARTERS. 4 MARCH 1947...
CHIEF? THEY'RE COMING... YES, I RECOGNIZED WYBOT FROM THE DST* WITH TWO OF HIS AGENTS AND JUDGE FAYON. THERE'S SOMEONE ELSE WITH THEM I HAVE NEVER SEEN BEFORE.
JUDGE, PLEASE COME IN!
...AND MR. WYBOT IS WITH YOU...IT'S NOT EVERY DAY THAT THE DIRECTOR OF THE DST APPEARS IN PERSON!
MAKE SURE THAT NOBODY ENTERS. THE CHIEF WILL BE A WHILE...
WHAT IS IT THAT WARRANTS A VISIT FROM SUCH COMMANDOS? ARE THE GERMANS BACK?
WE'VE COME TO ARREST JOSEPH JOANOVICI.
GOOD GOD! WHAT FOR?

*Direction de la surveillance du territoire, French domestic intelligence.

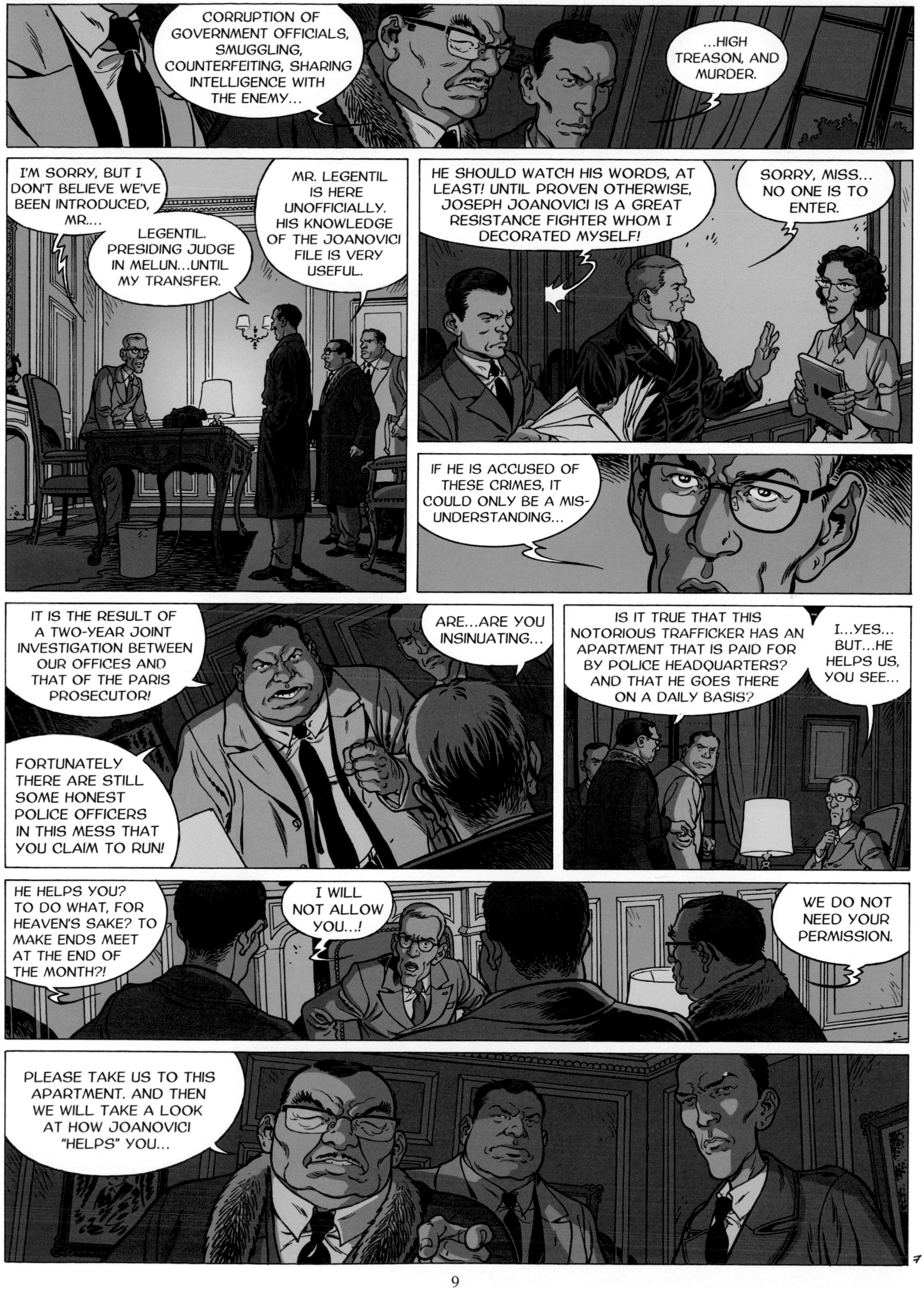
CORRUPTION OF GOVERNMENT OFFICIALS, SMUGGLING, COUNTERFEITING, SHARING INTELLIGENCE WITH THE ENEMY...
...HIGH TREASON, AND MURDER.
I'M SORRY, BUT I DON'T BELIEVE WE'VE BEEN INTRODUCED, MR....
LEGENTIL. PRESIDING JUDGE IN MELUN...UNTIL MY TRANSFER.
MR. LEGENTIL IS HERE UNOFFICIALLY. HIS KNOWLEDGE OF THE JOANOVICI FILE IS VERY USEFUL.
HE SHOULD WATCH HIS WORDS, AT LEAST! UNTIL PROVEN OTHERWISE, JOSEPH JOANOVICI IS A GREAT RESISTANCE FIGHTER WHOM I DECORATED MYSELF!
SORRY, MISS... NO ONE IS TO ENTER.
IF HE IS ACCUSED OF THESE CRIMES, IT COULD ONLY BE A MIS-UNDERSTANDING...
IT IS THE RESULT OF A TWO-YEAR JOINT INVESTIGATION BETWEEN OUR OFFICES AND THAT OF THE PARIS PROSECUTOR!
ARE...ARE YOU INSINUATING...
FORTUNATELY THERE ARE STILL SOME HONEST POLICE OFFICERS IN THIS MESS THAT YOU CLAIM TO RUN!
IS IT TRUE THAT THIS NOTORIOUS TRAFFICKER HAS AN APARTMENT THAT IS PAID FOR BY POLICE HEADQUARTERS? AND THAT HE GOES THERE ON A DAILY BASIS?
I...YES... BUT...HE HELPS US, YOU SEE...
HE HELPS YOU? TO DO WHAT, FOR HEAVEN'S SAKE? TO MAKE ENDS MEET AT THE END OF THE MONTH?!
I WILL NOT ALLOW YOU...!
WE DO NOT NEED YOUR PERMISSION.
PLEASE TAKE US TO THIS APARTMENT. AND THEN WE WILL TAKE A LOOK AT HOW JOANOVICI "HELPS" YOU...
7

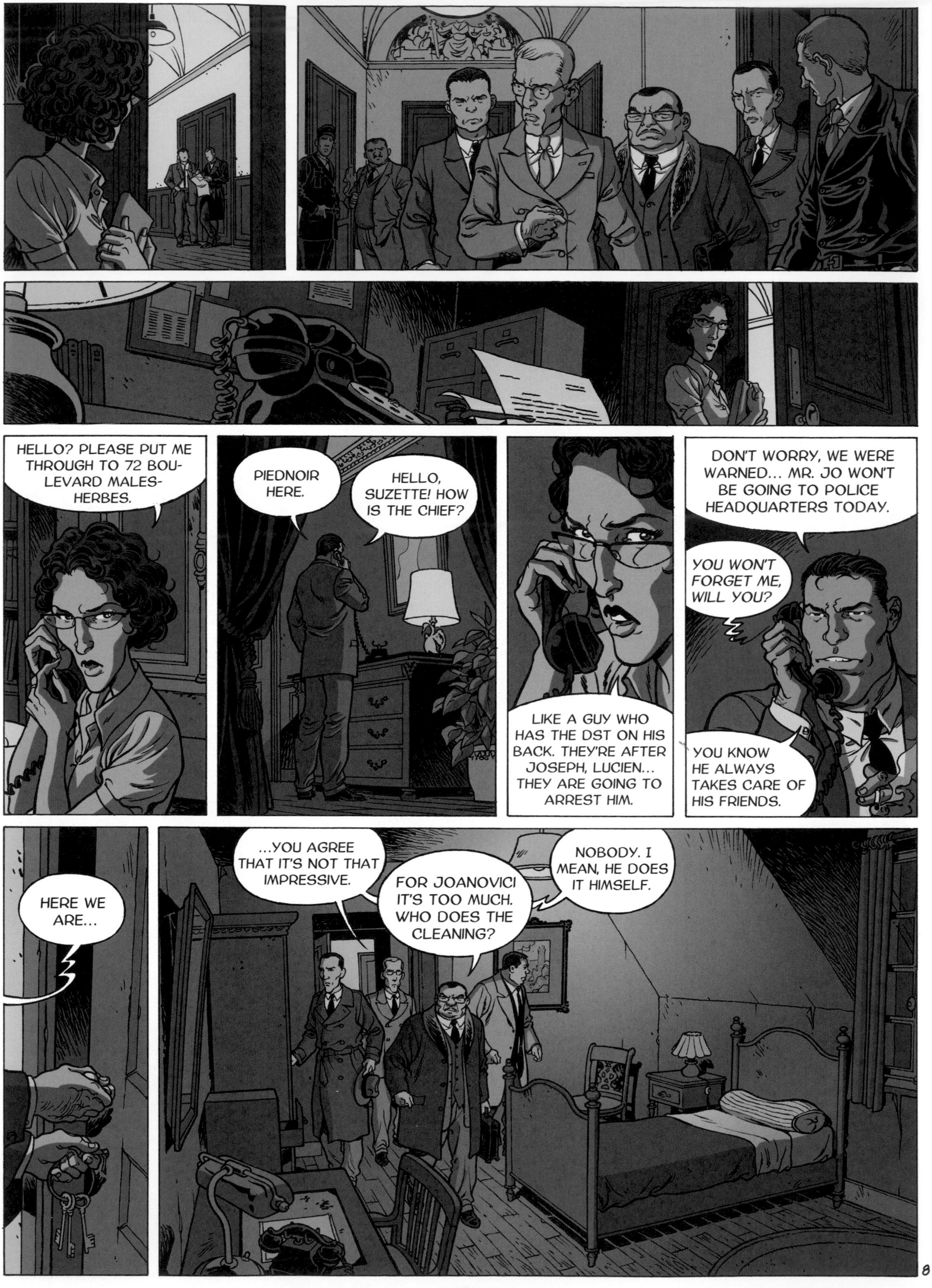
HELLO? PLEASE PUT ME THROUGH TO 72 BOULEVARD MALESHERBES.
PIEDNOIR HERE.
HELLO, SUZETTE! HOW IS THE CHIEF?
LIKE A GUY WHO HAS THE DST ON HIS BACK. THEY'RE AFTER JOSEPH, LUCIEN... THEY ARE GOING TO ARREST HIM.
DON'T WORRY, WE WERE WARNED... MR. JO WON'T BE GOING TO POLICE HEADQUARTERS TODAY.
YOU WON'T FORGET ME, WILL YOU?
YOU KNOW HE ALWAYS TAKES CARE OF HIS FRIENDS.
HERE WE ARE...
...YOU AGREE THAT IT'S NOT THAT IMPRESSIVE.
FOR JOANOVICI IT'S TOO MUCH. WHO DOES THE CLEANING?
NOBODY. I MEAN, HE DOES IT HIMSELF.
8

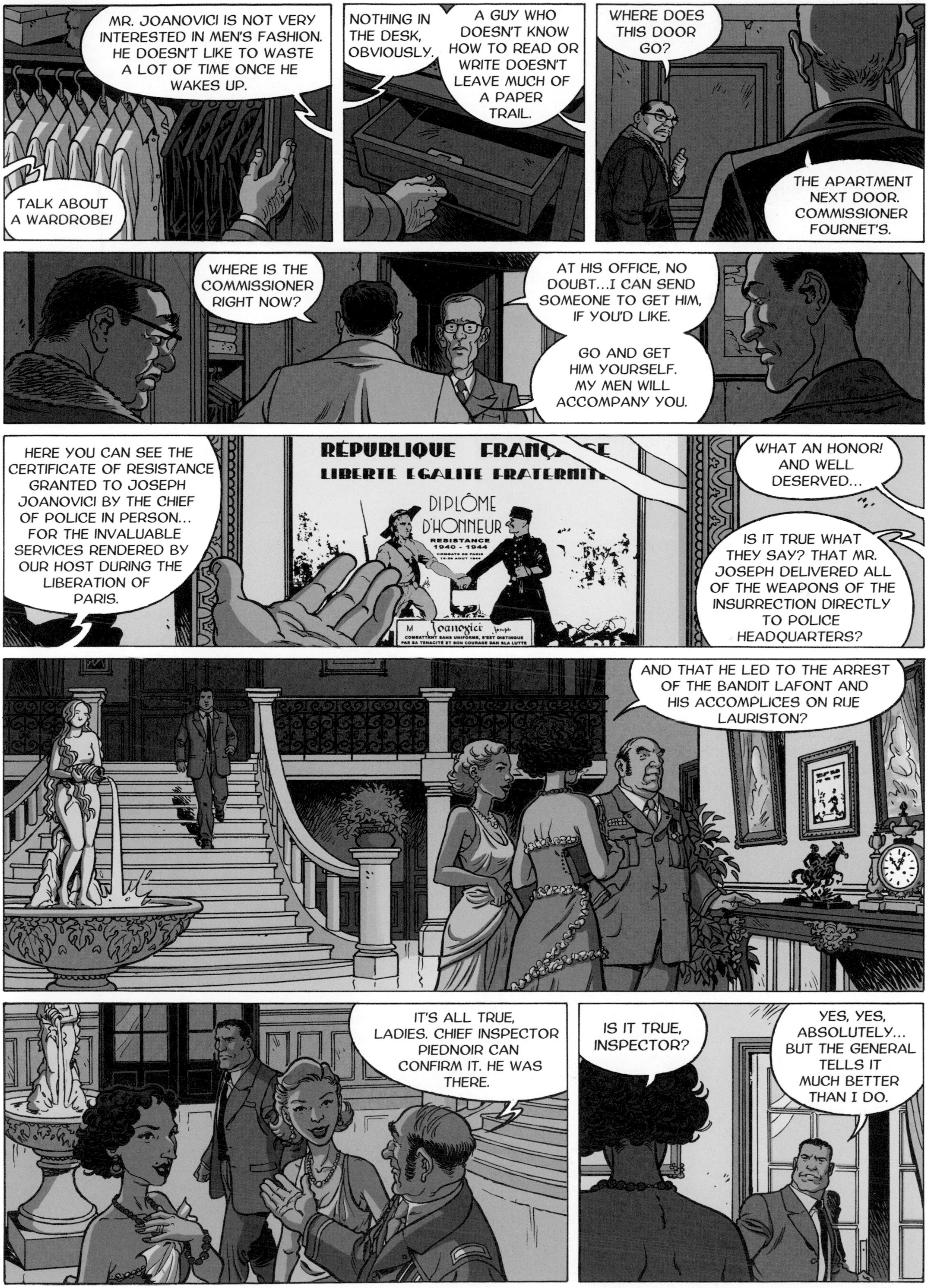
MR. JOANOVICI IS NOT VERY INTERESTED IN MEN'S FASHION. HE DOESN'T LIKE TO WASTE A LOT OF TIME ONCE HE WAKES UP.
TALK ABOUT A WARDROBE!
NOTHING IN THE DESK, OBVIOUSLY.
A GUY WHO DOESN'T KNOW HOW TO READ OR WRITE DOESN'T LEAVE MUCH OF A PAPER TRAIL.
WHERE DOES THIS DOOR GO?
THE APARTMENT NEXT DOOR. COMMISSIONER FOURNET'S.
WHERE IS THE COMMISSIONER RIGHT NOW?
AT HIS OFFICE, NO DOUBT...I CAN SEND SOMEONE TO GET HIM, IF YOU'D LIKE.
GO AND GET HIM YOURSELF. MY MEN WILL ACCOMPANY YOU.
HERE YOU CAN SEE THE CERTIFICATE OF RESISTANCE GRANTED TO JOSEPH JOANOVICI BY THE CHIEF OF POLICE IN PERSON... FOR THE INVALUABLE SERVICES RENDERED BY OUR HOST DURING THE LIBERATION OF PARIS.
RÉPUBLIQUE FRANÇAISE
LIBERTE EGALITE FRATERNITE
DIPLÔME D'HONNEUR
RESISTANCE
1940 - 1944
WHAT AN HONOR! AND WELL DESERVED...
IS IT TRUE WHAT THEY SAY? THAT MR. JOSEPH DELIVERED ALL OF THE WEAPONS OF THE INSURRECTION DIRECTLY TO POLICE HEADQUARTERS?
AND THAT HE LED TO THE ARREST OF THE BANDIT LAFONT AND HIS ACCOMPLICES ON RUE LAURISTON?
IT'S ALL TRUE, LADIES. CHIEF INSPECTOR PIEDNOIR CAN CONFIRM IT. HE WAS THERE.
IS IT TRUE, INSPECTOR?
YES, YES, ABSOLUTELY... BUT THE GENERAL TELLS IT MUCH BETTER THAN I DO.
9

WHERE ARE WE?

80,000 DOWN. THE MAYOR OF CLICHY ALONE IS DOWN THREE GRAND.

DO YOU WANT US TO CONTINUE TO FRONT HIM?

NO, HE CAN LOSE A LITTLE FOR A CHANGE.

...I KNOW HOW MUCH I OWE TO YOU, JOSEPH. IF IT WEREN'T FOR YOU I'D BE IN BUCHENWALD.

...AND I AM NOT TALKING ABOUT YOUR GENEROSITY. I MEAN, THE POKER GAMES THAT YOU ORGANIZE EVERY THURSDAY... IT'S THE ONLY GAME THAT I KNOW OF WHERE THE GUESTS WIN ALL THE TIME.

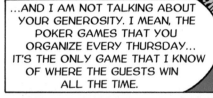

...OF COURSE, I DON'T WANT TO IMPLY THAT YOU ARE OFFERING BRIBES...BUT PEOPLE TALK... AND OUR FRIENDS...

WHAT? THEY'RE AFRAID THE TAP'S BEEN TURNED OFF BECAUSE THEY'VE HEARD THEIR BENEFACTOR IS HEADED FOR JAIL?

HMMM... GOOD EVENING, INSPECTOR. NO, THAT'S NOT WHAT I MEANT, BUT YOU UNDERSTAND...

...WHEN IT WAS ONLY THE LITTLE JUDGE FROM MELUN WE DIDN'T HAVE TO WORRY, BUT THE DST IS ON THE CASE NOW, AS WELL AS JUDGE FAYON...AND I'M AFRAID I CAN'T SMOOTH THIS ONE OVER WITH THOSE WHO... DOUBT.

10

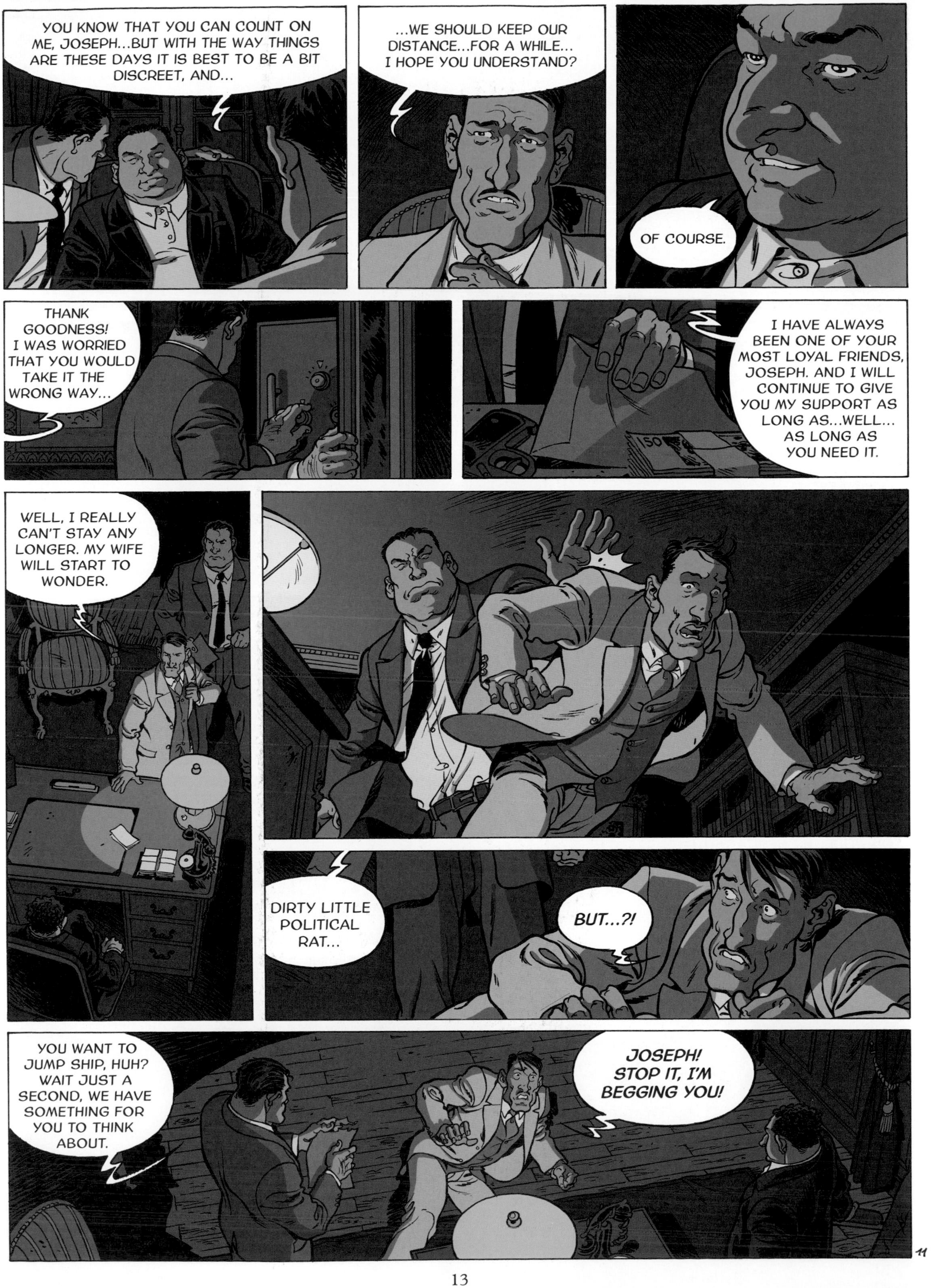
YOU KNOW THAT YOU CAN COUNT ON ME, JOSEPH...BUT WITH THE WAY THINGS ARE THESE DAYS IT IS BEST TO BE A BIT DISCREET, AND...
...WE SHOULD KEEP OUR DISTANCE...FOR A WHILE... I HOPE YOU UNDERSTAND?
OF COURSE.
THANK GOODNESS! I WAS WORRIED THAT YOU WOULD TAKE IT THE WRONG WAY...
I HAVE ALWAYS BEEN ONE OF YOUR MOST LOYAL FRIENDS, JOSEPH. AND I WILL CONTINUE TO GIVE YOU MY SUPPORT AS LONG AS...WELL... AS LONG AS YOU NEED IT.
WELL, I REALLY CAN'T STAY ANY LONGER. MY WIFE WILL START TO WONDER.
DIRTY LITTLE POLITICAL RAT...
BUT...?!
YOU WANT TO JUMP SHIP, HUH? WAIT JUST A SECOND, WE HAVE SOMETHING FOR YOU TO THINK ABOUT.
JOSEPH! STOP IT, I'M BEGGING YOU!
11

DO YOU SEE THESE?

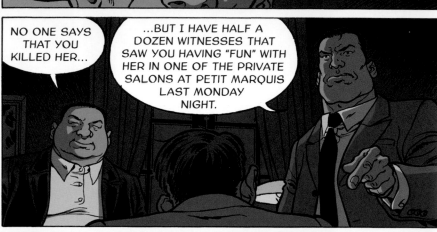

HER NAME IS CECILE KLEIN. SHE WAS ELEVEN YEARS OLD. WE FOUND HER BODY ROLLED UP IN AN OLD CARPET IN A DUMPSTER.

OH, NO... MY GOD, NO...

NO ONE SAYS THAT YOU KILLED HER...

...BUT I HAVE HALF A DOZEN WITNESSES THAT SAW YOU HAVING "FUN" WITH HER IN ONE OF THE PRIVATE SALONS AT PETIT MARQUIS LAST MONDAY NIGHT.

YOU ARE GOING TO CONTINUE SINGING OUR PRAISES, COUNSELOR. YOU WILL CONTINUE TO TELL ALL YOUR FELLOW MEMBERS OF THE BAR THAT JOSEPH JOANOVICI IS THE GREATEST RESISTANCE FIGHTER THAT YOU EVER MET, AND THAT HE SAVED YOUR LIFE AS HE DID THE LIVES OF HUNDREDS OF OTHERS... AND IF YOU HAD TO SWEAR TO IT UNDER OATH, YOU WOULDN'T HESITATE.

IF IT WERE UP TO ME I'D STICK HIM STRAIGHT IN LA SANTÉ PRISON...AND LET THE INMATES KNOW WHAT THE COUNSELOR DOES TO LITTLE GIRLS.

AH, FORGET HIM! HE CERTAINLY WON'T BE FOR- GETTING YOU SOON...

THEY'RE GOING TO GET YOU, JO. YOU MAY BE ABLE TO DELAY IT, BUT YOU WON'T BE ABLE TO AVOID IT.

I KNOW.

PUT ME THROUGH TO POLICE COMMISSIONER FOURNET'S APARTMENT.

12

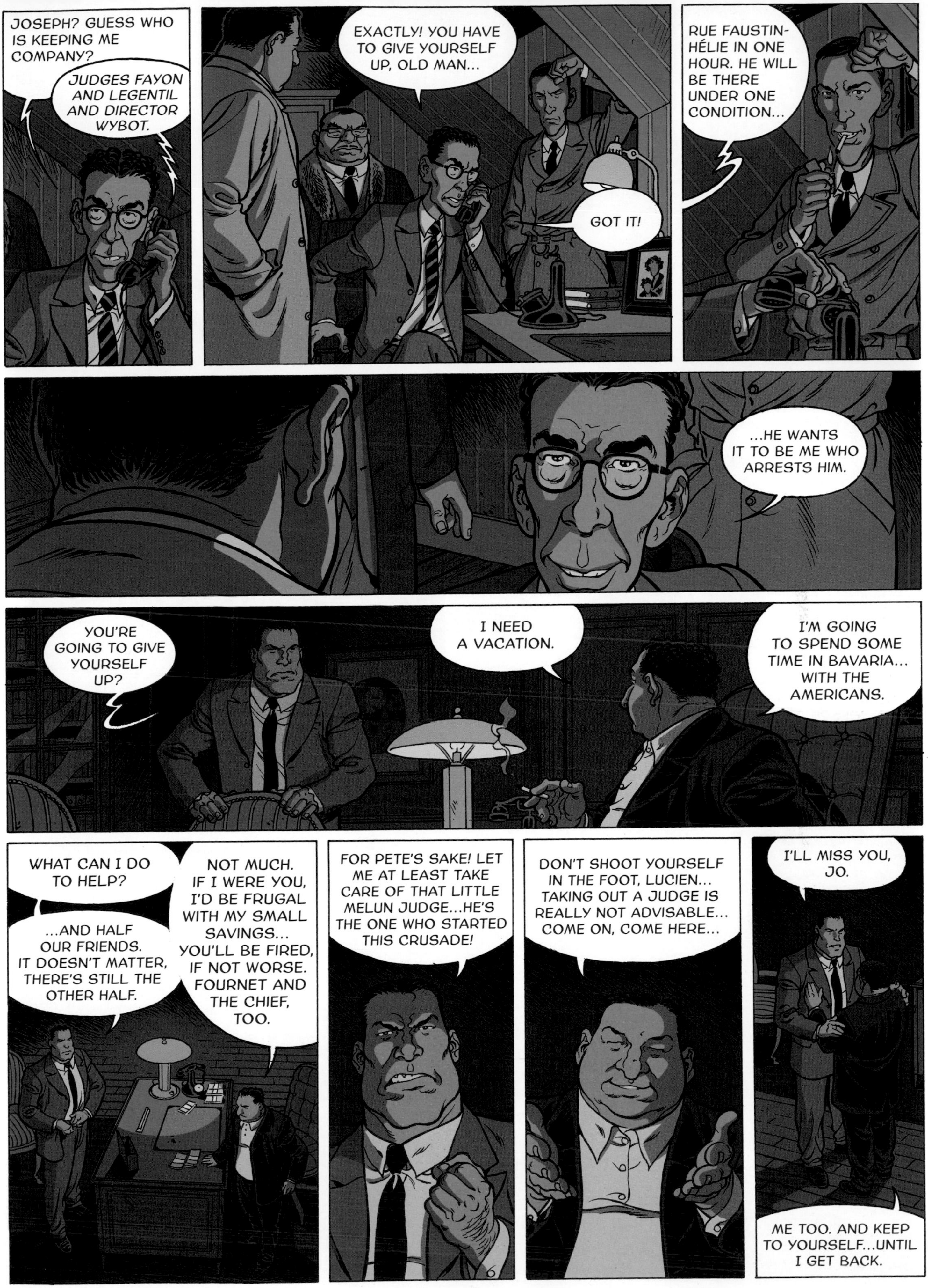
JOSEPH? GUESS WHO IS KEEPING ME COMPANY?
JUDGES FAYON AND LEGENTIL AND DIRECTOR WYBOT.
EXACTLY! YOU HAVE TO GIVE YOURSELF UP, OLD MAN...
GOT IT!
RUE FAUSTIN-HÉLIE IN ONE HOUR. HE WILL BE THERE UNDER ONE CONDITION...
...HE WANTS IT TO BE ME WHO ARRESTS HIM.
YOU'RE GOING TO GIVE YOURSELF UP?
I NEED A VACATION.
I'M GOING TO SPEND SOME TIME IN BAVARIA... WITH THE AMERICANS.
WHAT CAN I DO TO HELP?
...AND HALF OUR FRIENDS. IT DOESN'T MATTER, THERE'S STILL THE OTHER HALF.
NOT MUCH. IF I WERE YOU, I'D BE FRUGAL WITH MY SMALL SAVINGS... YOU'LL BE FIRED, IF NOT WORSE. FOURNET AND THE CHIEF, TOO.
FOR PETE'S SAKE! LET ME AT LEAST TAKE CARE OF THAT LITTLE MELUN JUDGE...HE'S THE ONE WHO STARTED THIS CRUSADE!
DON'T SHOOT YOURSELF IN THE FOOT, LUCIEN... TAKING OUT A JUDGE IS REALLY NOT ADVISABLE... COME ON, COME HERE...
I'LL MISS YOU, JO.
ME TOO. AND KEEP TO YOURSELF...UNTIL I GET BACK.

-13

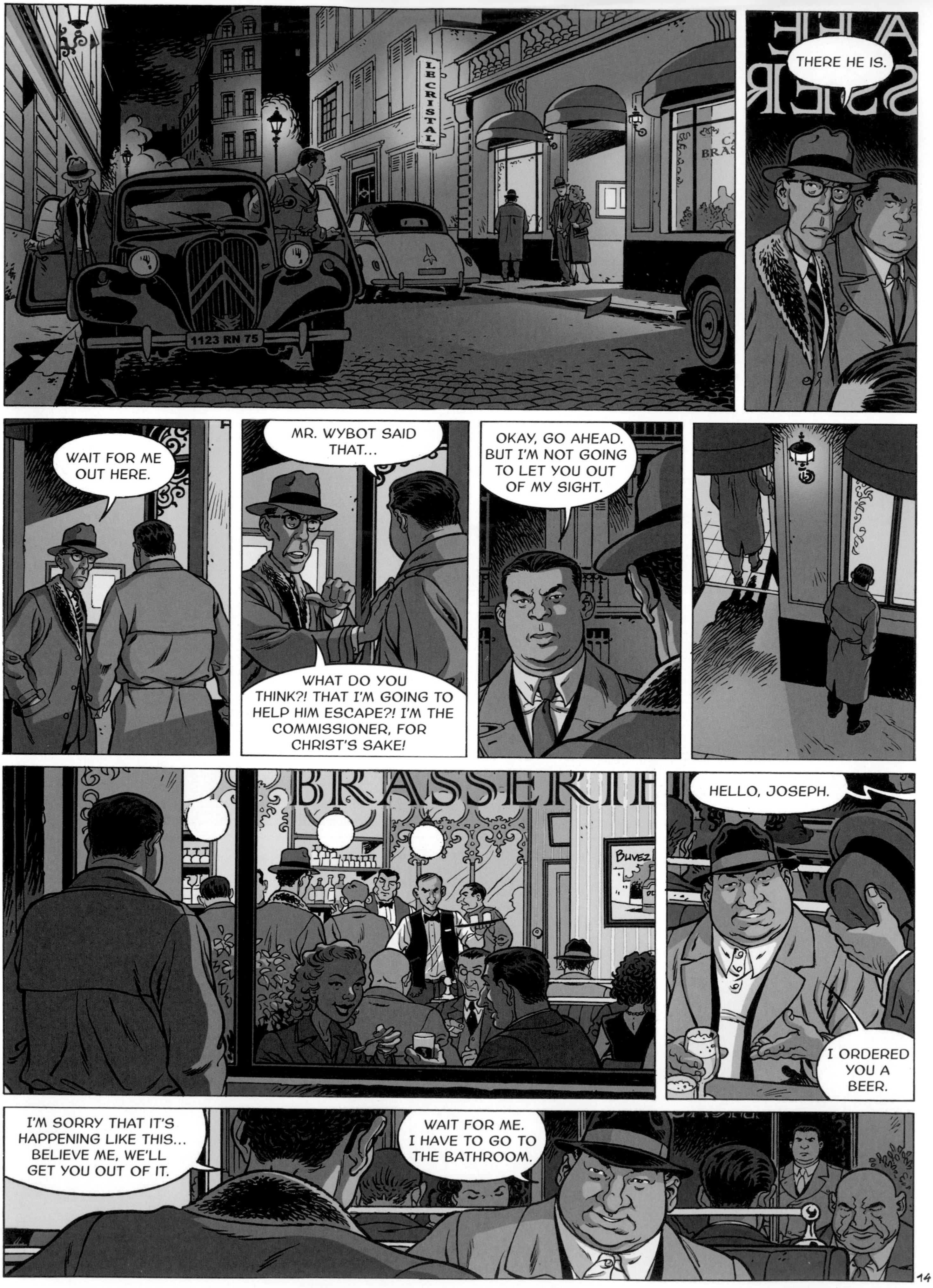

LE CRISTAL
1123 RN 75
THERE HE IS.
WAIT FOR ME OUT HERE.
MR. WYBOT SAID THAT...
WHAT DO YOU THINK?! THAT I'M GOING TO HELP HIM ESCAPE?! I'M THE COMMISSIONER, FOR CHRIST'S SAKE!
OKAY, GO AHEAD. BUT I'M NOT GOING TO LET YOU OUT OF MY SIGHT.
BRASSERIE
BUVEZ
HELLO, JOSEPH.
I ORDERED YOU A BEER.
I'M SORRY THAT IT'S HAPPENING LIKE THIS... BELIEVE ME, WE'LL GET YOU OUT OF IT.
WAIT FOR ME. I HAVE TO GO TO THE BATHROOM.
14

WHAT...?

YOUR FRIEND IS WAITING FOR YOU AT THE BACK DOOR, BY THE TOILETS.

AREN'T YOU GOING TO DRINK YOUR BEER?

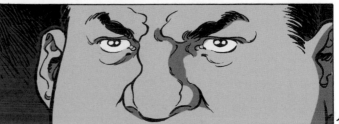

15

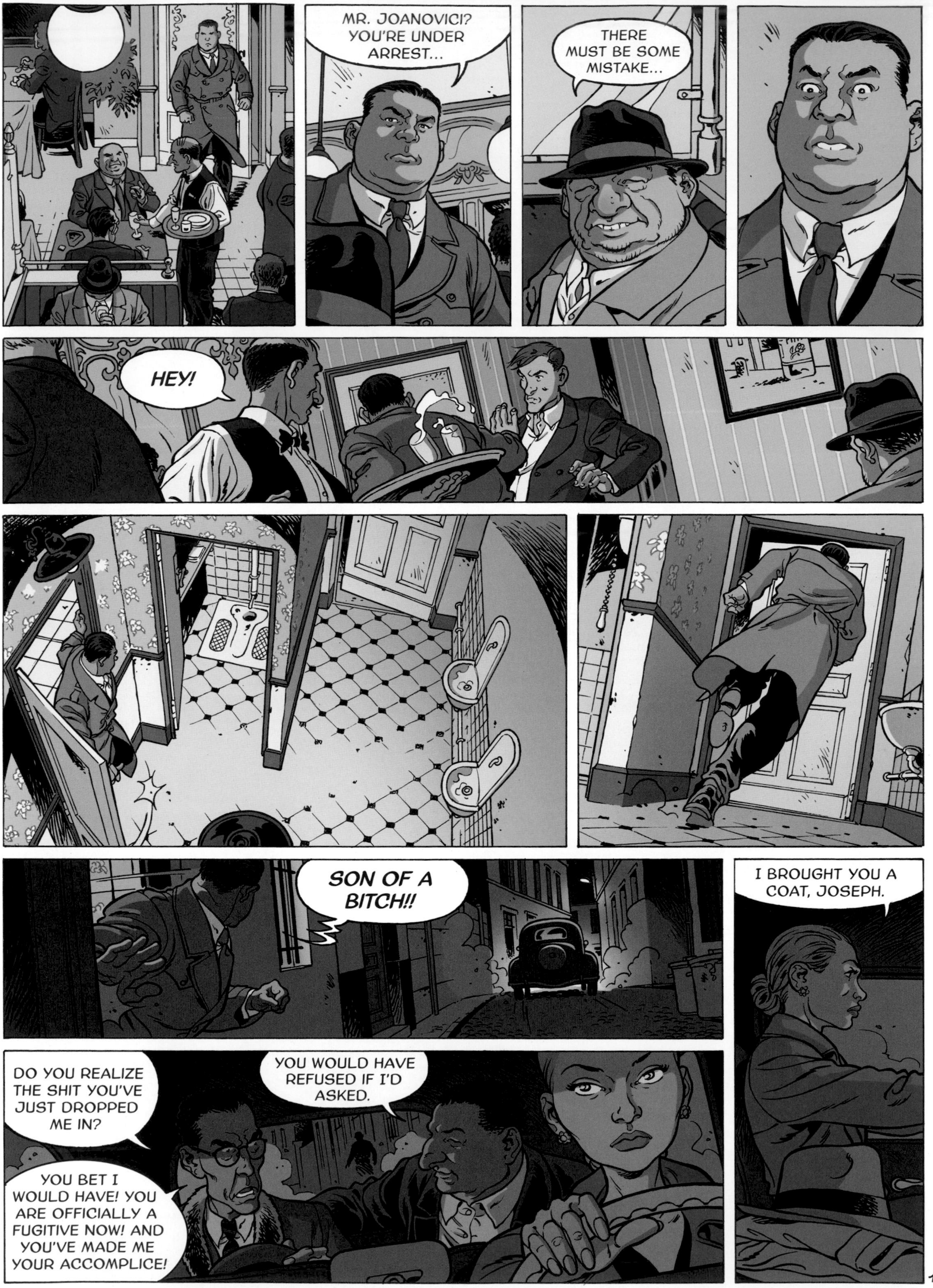
MR. JOANOVICI? YOU'RE UNDER ARREST...
THERE MUST BE SOME MISTAKE...
HEY!
SON OF A BITCH!!
I BROUGHT YOU A COAT, JOSEPH.
DO YOU REALIZE THE SHIT YOU'VE JUST DROPPED ME IN?
YOU WOULD HAVE REFUSED IF I'D ASKED.
YOU BET I WOULD HAVE! YOU ARE OFFICIALLY A FUGITIVE NOW! AND YOU'VE MADE ME YOUR ACCOMPLICE!
16

THANK YOU, LUCY. YOU ALWAYS THINK OF EVERYTHING.

THEY'LL DISMISS ME. THEY'LL CHARGE ME!

FOR WHAT? CALL THEM AND TELL THEM THAT I AGREED TO COME IN...BUT I WANTED TO SEE MY FAMILY FIRST AND YOU HAD TO COME WITH ME.

WHEN SHOULD I CALL THEM?

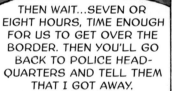
AS SOON AS WE DROP YOU OFF.

THEN WAIT...SEVEN OR EIGHT HOURS, TIME ENOUGH FOR US TO GET OVER THE BORDER. THEN YOU'LL GO BACK TO POLICE HEAD-QUARTERS AND TELL THEM THAT I GOT AWAY.

WHAT AM I GOING TO DO? I HAD A GOOD JOB, A SALARY, AN APARTMENT PAID FOR BY THE PRINCESS... WHAT AM I GOING TO DO NOW?

OH, COME ON, CHEER UP. A YEAR OR TWO IN LA SANTÉ ISN'T A VACATION...

...BUT IT'S NOTHING COMPARED TO TWELVE BULLETS AT DAWN.

GET OUT.

WHAT DO I TELL THEM? HOW DID YOU GET AWAY?

IMPROVISE. I DON'T KNOW...

...JUST SAY THAT YOU FELL ASLEEP.

17

19

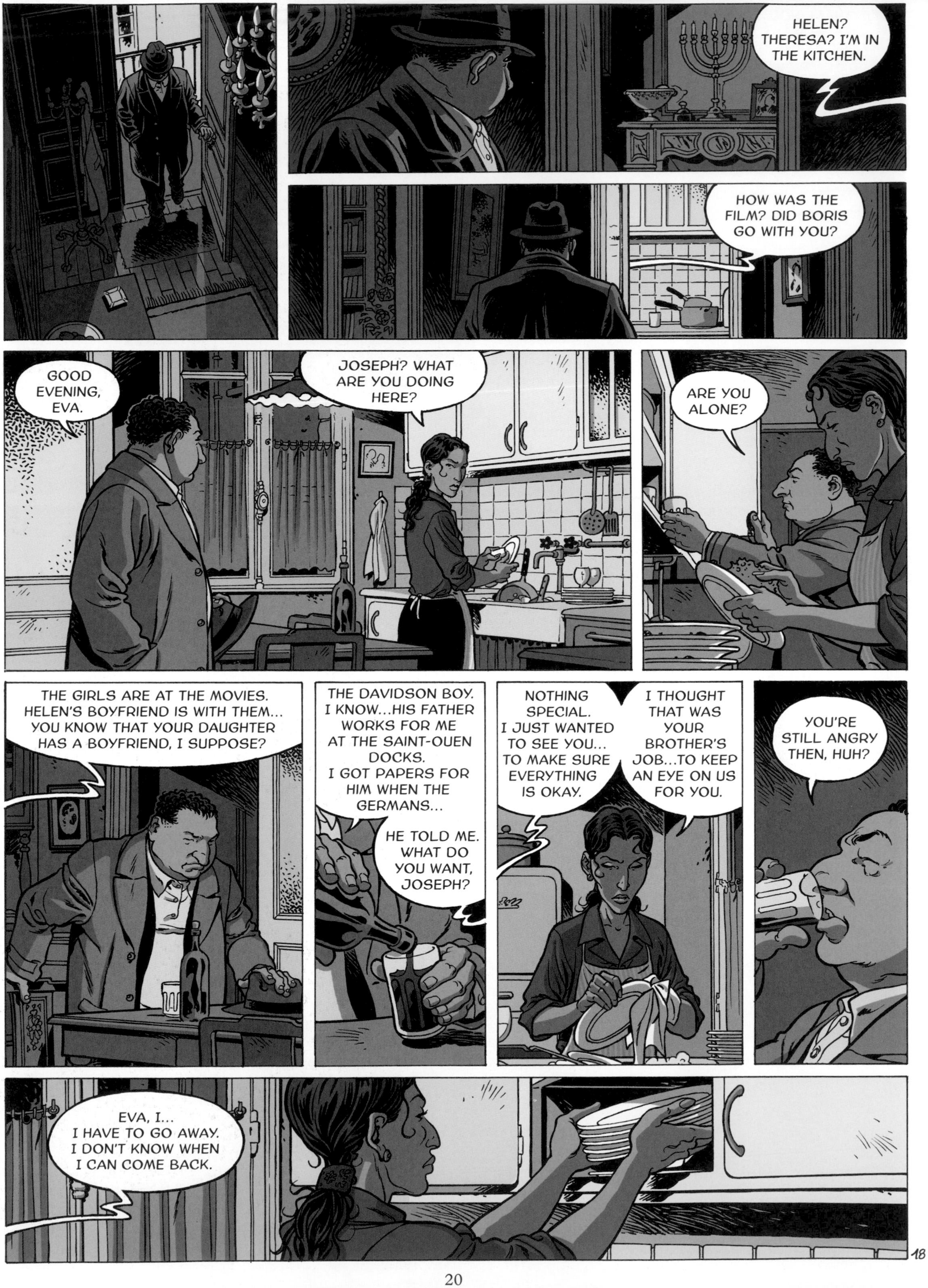
HELEN? THERESA? I'M IN THE KITCHEN.
HOW WAS THE FILM? DID BORIS GO WITH YOU?
GOOD EVENING, EVA.
JOSEPH? WHAT ARE YOU DOING HERE?
ARE YOU ALONE?
THE GIRLS ARE AT THE MOVIES. HELEN'S BOYFRIEND IS WITH THEM... YOU KNOW THAT YOUR DAUGHTER HAS A BOYFRIEND, I SUPPOSE?
THE DAVIDSON BOY. I KNOW...HIS FATHER WORKS FOR ME AT THE SAINT-OUEN DOCKS. I GOT PAPERS FOR HIM WHEN THE GERMANS...
HE TOLD ME. WHAT DO YOU WANT, JOSEPH?
NOTHING SPECIAL. I JUST WANTED TO SEE YOU... TO MAKE SURE EVERYTHING IS OKAY.
I THOUGHT THAT WAS YOUR BROTHER'S JOB...TO KEEP AN EYE ON US FOR YOU.
YOU'RE STILL ANGRY THEN, HUH?
EVA, I... I HAVE TO GO AWAY. I DON'T KNOW WHEN I CAN COME BACK.
18

THAT DOESN'T SEEM TO MATTER TO YOU?

WHAT DID YOU EXPECT? I HAVEN'T SEEN YOU IN A YEAR, JOSEPH. AS FAR AS I'M CONCERNED YOU LEFT A LONG TIME AGO.

AND THE GIRLS?

HELEN HAS HER OWN LIFE. THERESA...SHE LOVES HER FATHER AND IS HAVING A HARD TIME WITHOUT HIM AROUND.

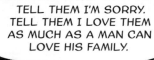

TELL THEM I'M SORRY. TELL THEM I LOVE THEM AS MUCH AS A MAN CAN LOVE HIS FAMILY.

THEY KNOW THAT.

THEY WILL PROBABLY HEAR A LOT OF THINGS ABOUT ME IN THE NEXT FEW WEEKS... UNPLEASANT THINGS.

THEY'LL UNDERSTAND... OR THEY WON'T. EITHER WAY, YOU WON'T BE HERE TO EXPLAIN IT TO THEM.

TELL THEM ANYWAY... PLEASE.

I'VE NEVER SEEN YOU LIKE THIS...

LIKE WHAT?

SCARED.

I HAVE TO GO. LUCY'S WAITING FOR ME.

SHE STAYS WITH YOU NO MATTER WHAT!

I LOVE YOU, EVA.

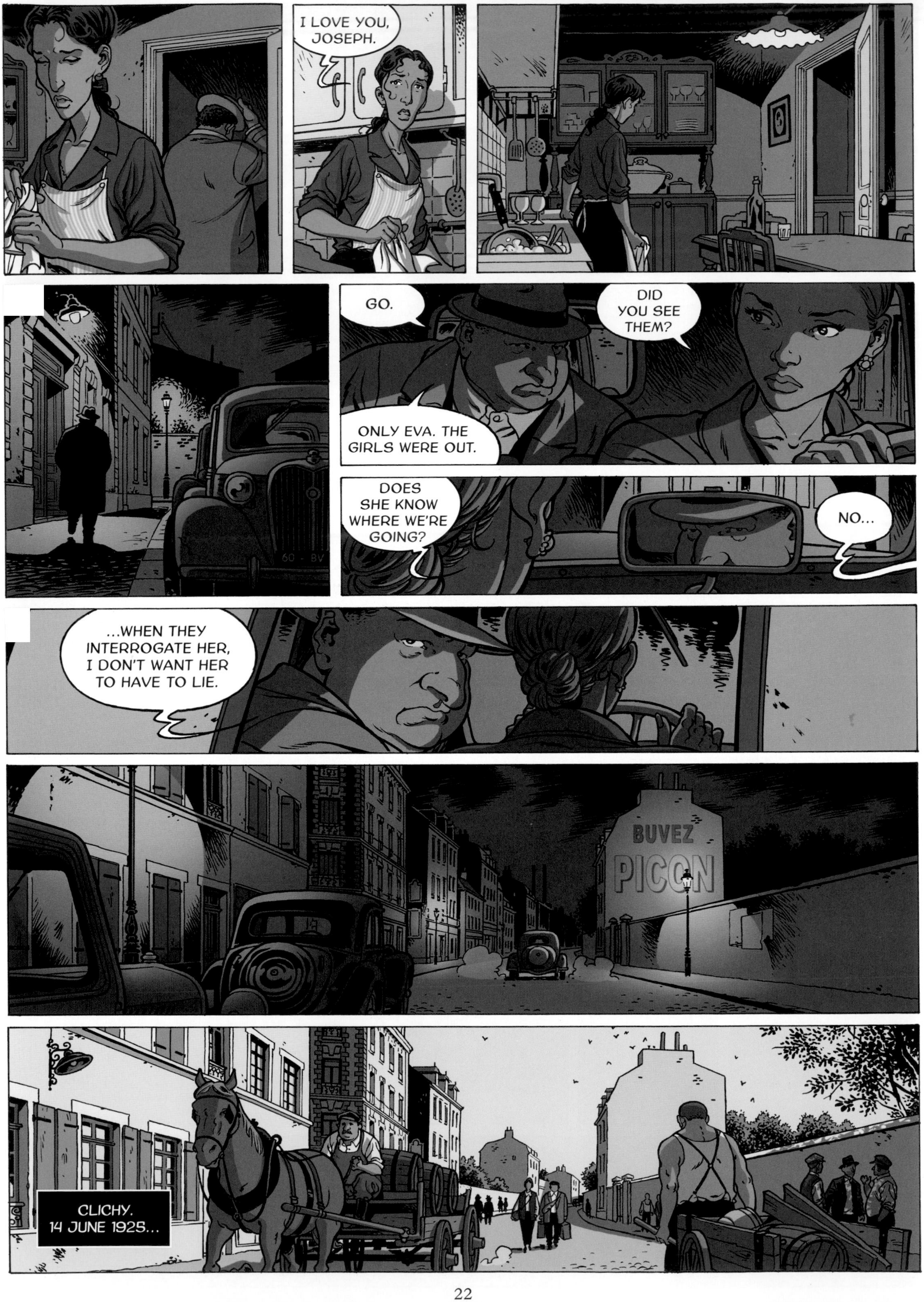
I LOVE YOU, JOSEPH.
GO.
DID YOU SEE THEM?
ONLY EVA. THE GIRLS WERE OUT.
DOES SHE KNOW WHERE WE'RE GOING?
NO...
...WHEN THEY INTERROGATE HER, I DON'T WANT HER TO HAVE TO LIE.
BUVEZ PICON
CLICHY. 14 JUNE 1925...
20

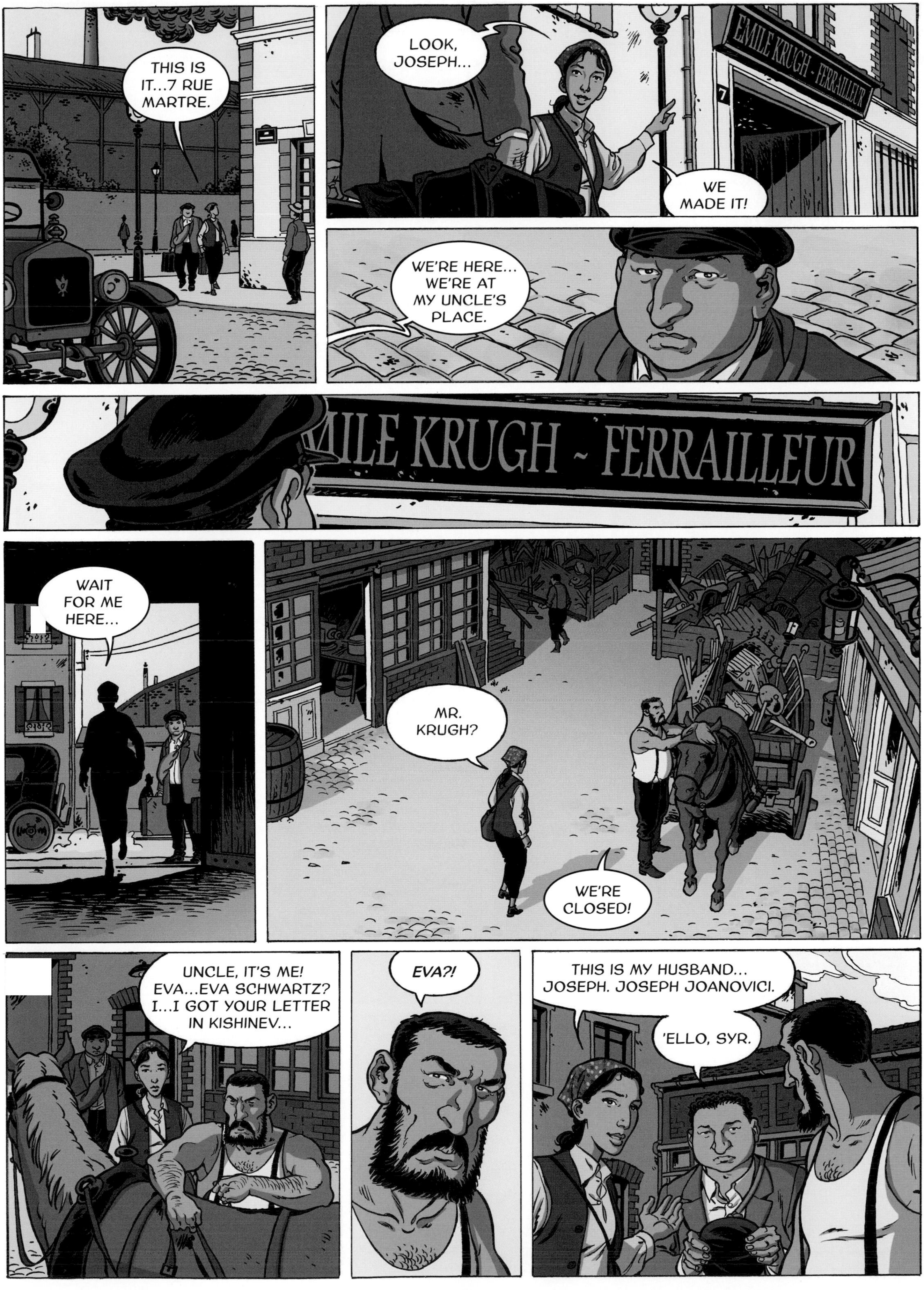
THIS IS IT...7 RUE MARTRE.
LOOK, JOSEPH...
EMILE KRUGH - FERRAILLEUR
7
WE MADE IT!
WE'RE HERE... WE'RE AT MY UNCLE'S PLACE.
MILE KRUGH ~ FERRAILLEUR
WAIT FOR ME HERE...
MR. KRUGH?
WE'RE CLOSED!
UNCLE, IT'S ME! EVA...EVA SCHWARTZ? I...I GOT YOUR LETTER IN KISHINEV...
EVA?!
THIS IS MY HUSBAND... JOSEPH. JOSEPH JOANOVICI.
'ELLO, SYR.
21

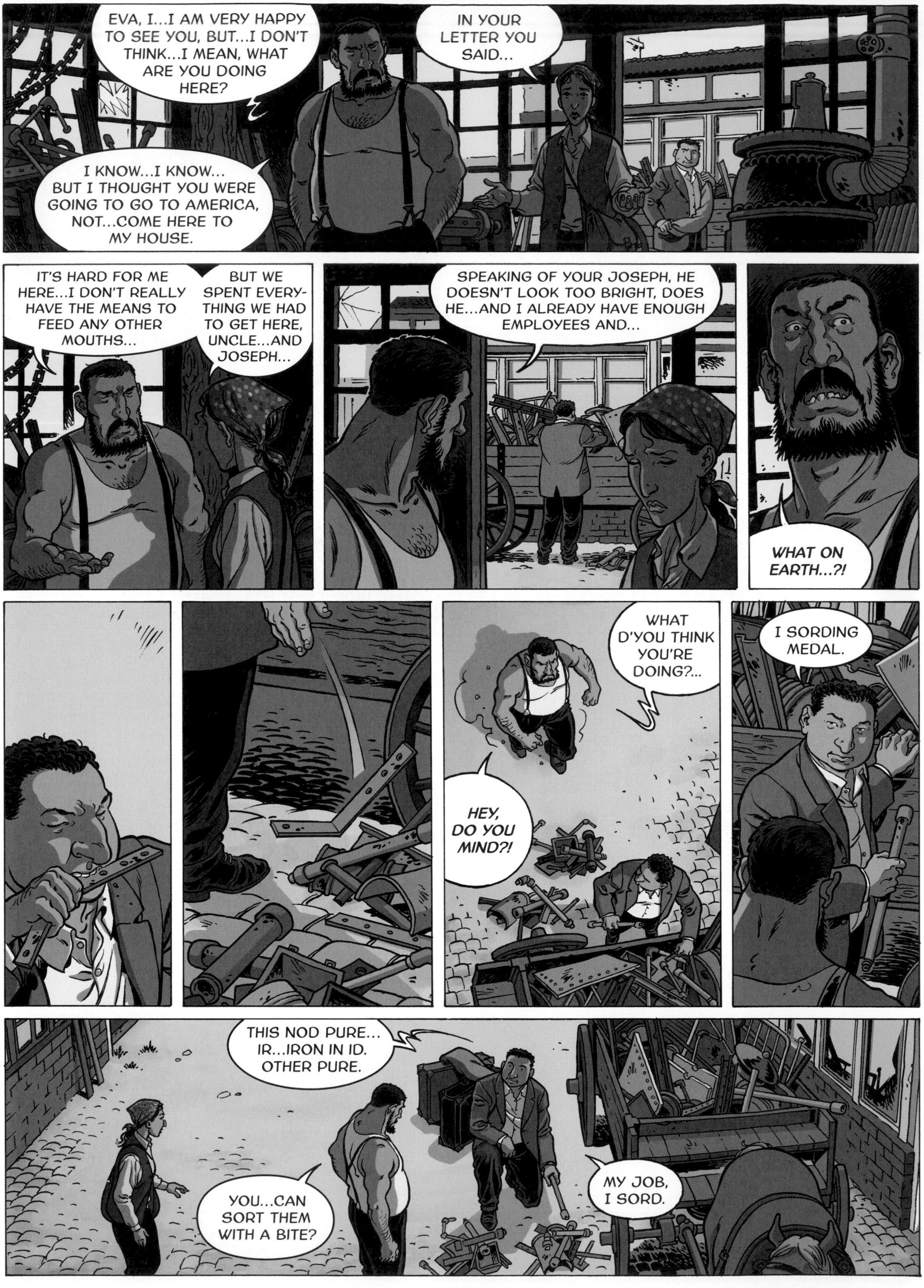
EVA, I...I AM VERY HAPPY TO SEE YOU, BUT...I DON'T THINK...I MEAN, WHAT ARE YOU DOING HERE?
IN YOUR LETTER YOU SAID...
I KNOW...I KNOW... BUT I THOUGHT YOU WERE GOING TO GO TO AMERICA, NOT...COME HERE TO MY HOUSE.
IT'S HARD FOR ME HERE...I DON'T REALLY HAVE THE MEANS TO FEED ANY OTHER MOUTHS...
BUT WE SPENT EVERY-THING WE HAD TO GET HERE, UNCLE...AND JOSEPH...
SPEAKING OF YOUR JOSEPH, HE DOESN'T LOOK TOO BRIGHT, DOES HE...AND I ALREADY HAVE ENOUGH EMPLOYEES AND...
WHAT ON EARTH...?!
WHAT D'YOU THINK YOU'RE DOING?...
HEY, DO YOU MIND?!
I SORDING MEDAL.
THIS NOD PURE... IR...IRON IN ID. OTHER PURE.
YOU...CAN SORT THEM WITH A BITE?
MY JOB, I SORD.
22

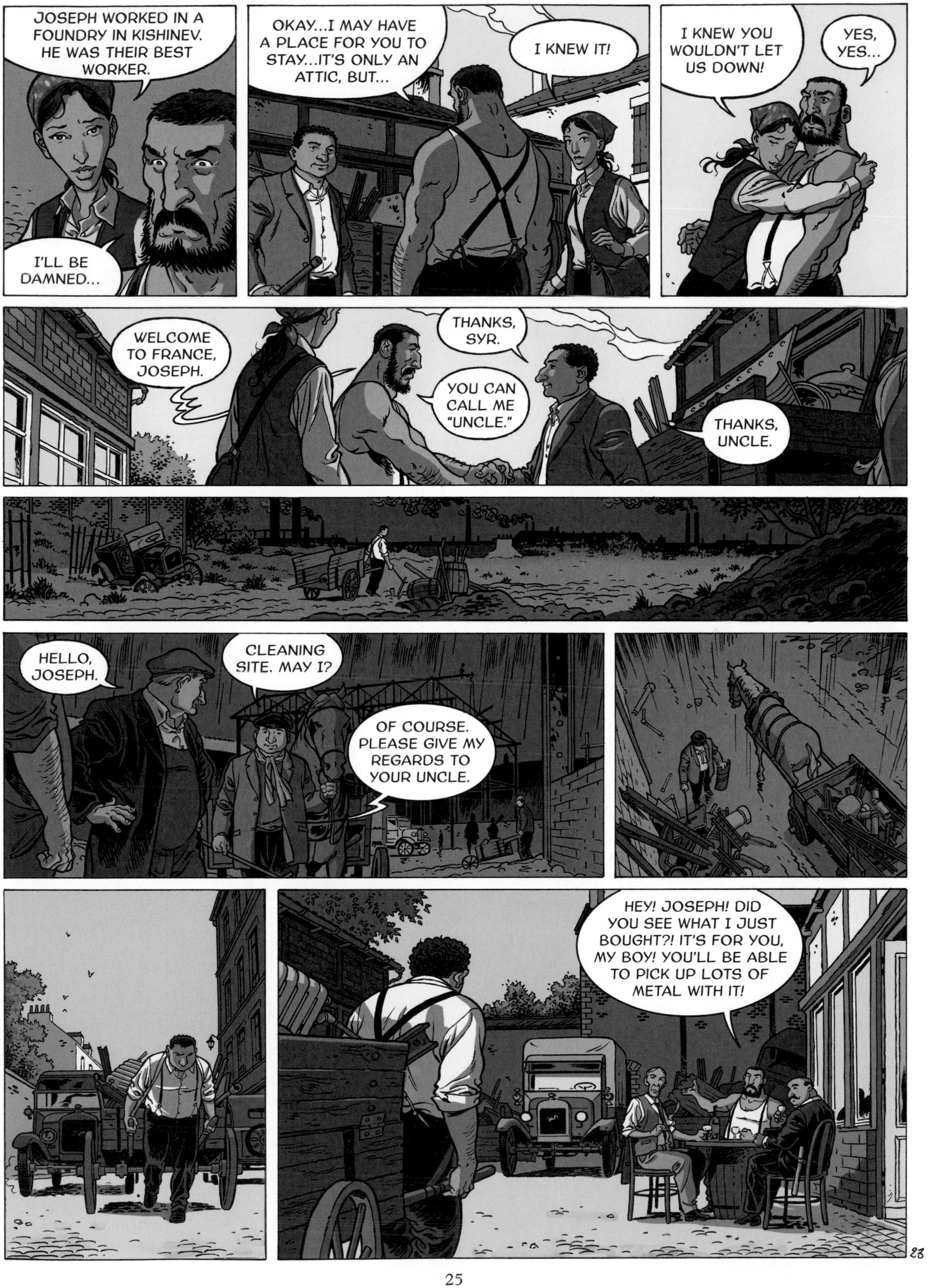
JOSEPH WORKED IN A FOUNDRY IN KISHINEV. HE WAS THEIR BEST WORKER.
I'LL BE DAMNED...
OKAY...I MAY HAVE A PLACE FOR YOU TO STAY...IT'S ONLY AN ATTIC, BUT...
I KNEW IT!
I KNEW YOU WOULDN'T LET US DOWN!
YES, YES...
WELCOME TO FRANCE, JOSEPH.
THANKS, SYR.
YOU CAN CALL ME "UNCLE."
THANKS, UNCLE.
HELLO, JOSEPH.
CLEANING SITE. MAY I?
OF COURSE. PLEASE GIVE MY REGARDS TO YOUR UNCLE.
HEY! JOSEPH! DID YOU SEE WHAT I JUST BOUGHT?! IT'S FOR YOU, MY BOY! YOU'LL BE ABLE TO PICK UP LOTS OF METAL WITH IT!
23

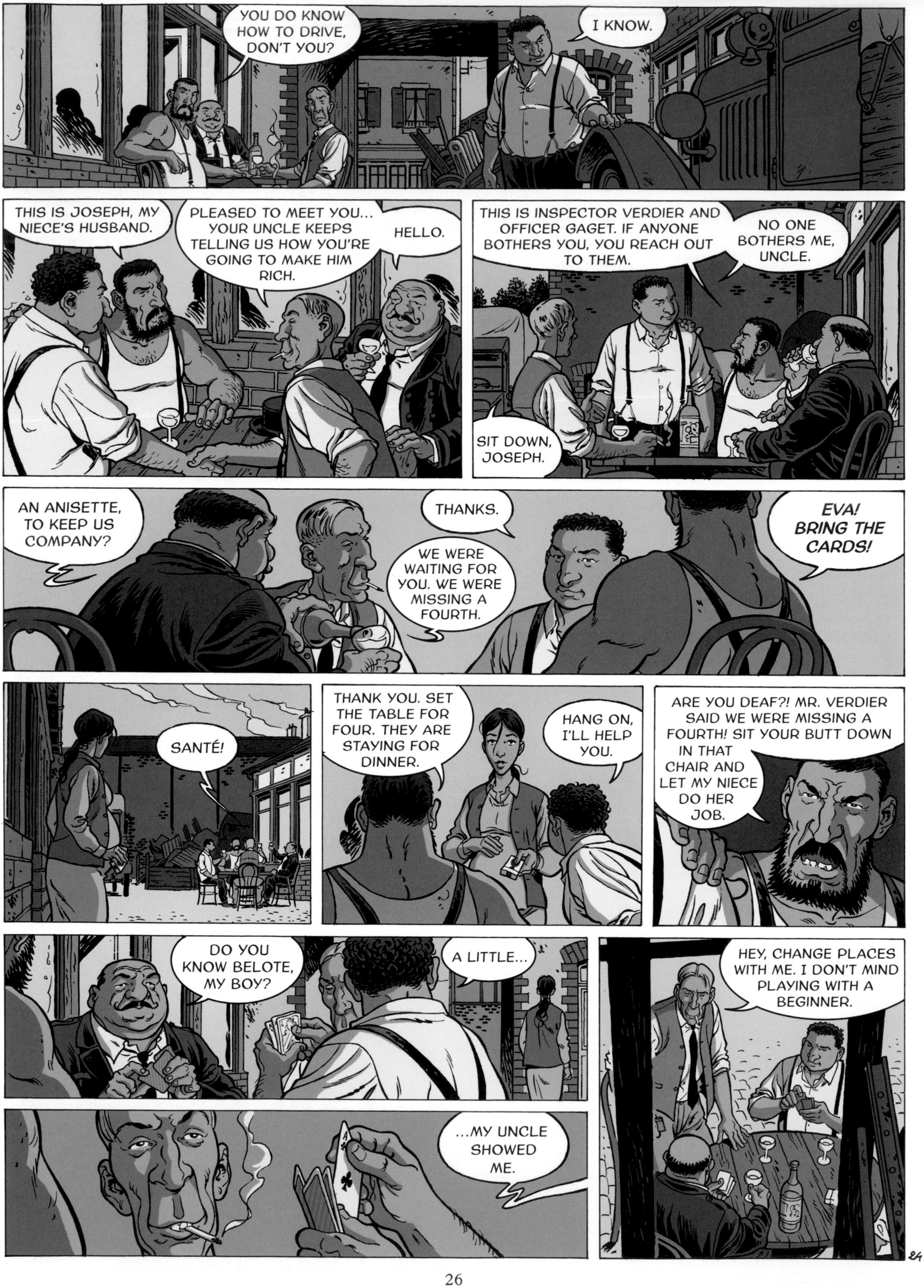
YOU DO KNOW HOW TO DRIVE, DON'T YOU?
I KNOW.
THIS IS JOSEPH, MY NIECE'S HUSBAND.
PLEASED TO MEET YOU... YOUR UNCLE KEEPS TELLING US HOW YOU'RE GOING TO MAKE HIM RICH.
HELLO.
THIS IS INSPECTOR VERDIER AND OFFICER GAGET. IF ANYONE BOTHERS YOU, YOU REACH OUT TO THEM.
NO ONE BOTHERS ME, UNCLE.
SIT DOWN, JOSEPH.
AN ANISETTE, TO KEEP US COMPANY?
THANKS.
WE WERE WAITING FOR YOU. WE WERE MISSING A FOURTH.
EVA! BRING THE CARDS!
SANTÉ!
THANK YOU. SET THE TABLE FOR FOUR. THEY ARE STAYING FOR DINNER.
HANG ON, I'LL HELP YOU.
ARE YOU DEAF?! MR. VERDIER SAID WE WERE MISSING A FOURTH! SIT YOUR BUTT DOWN IN THAT CHAIR AND LET MY NIECE DO HER JOB.
DO YOU KNOW BELOTE, MY BOY?
A LITTLE...
...MY UNCLE SHOWED ME.
HEY, CHANGE PLACES WITH ME. I DON'T MIND PLAYING WITH A BEGINNER.
24

...AND TEN FROM HIS, WHICH MAKES 134. WE GOT IT!

WELL DONE, JOSEPH! STARTING WITH DIAMONDS WAS EXCELLENT!

THANKS.

JUST A RUN OF GOOD LUCK FOR THE LITTLE ROMANIAN.

LUCK! WE WHIP YOU EVERY WEEK. WE'RE BETTER, THAT'S ALL!

2,960 FOR YOU...AND WE HAVE...NO, IT'S MORE THAN THAT, I MADE A MISTAKE...

OH, I'M SICK OF THIS! IT'S ALWAYS ME WHO HAS TO KEEP SCORE!

YOU?! YOU DON'T EVEN KNOW HOW TO WRITE!

I CAN KEEP SCORE.

I CAN COUNT.

WHAT THE HELL IS THAT??!!...

IT'S MY ACCOUNTING SYSTEM...

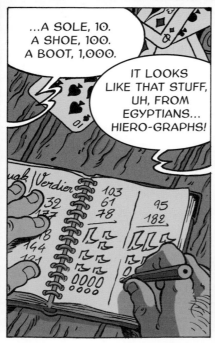

...A SOLE, 10. A SHOE, 100. A BOOT, 1,000.

IT LOOKS LIKE THAT STUFF, UH, FROM EGYPTIANS... HIERO-GRAPHS!

...ARE YOU SCREWING WITH ME WITH YOUR STUPID LITTLE DRAWINGS?!

...GO BACK TO SCHOOL. AND STOP BEING A WISEASS!

NO TIME, UNCLE. TOO MUCH WORK.

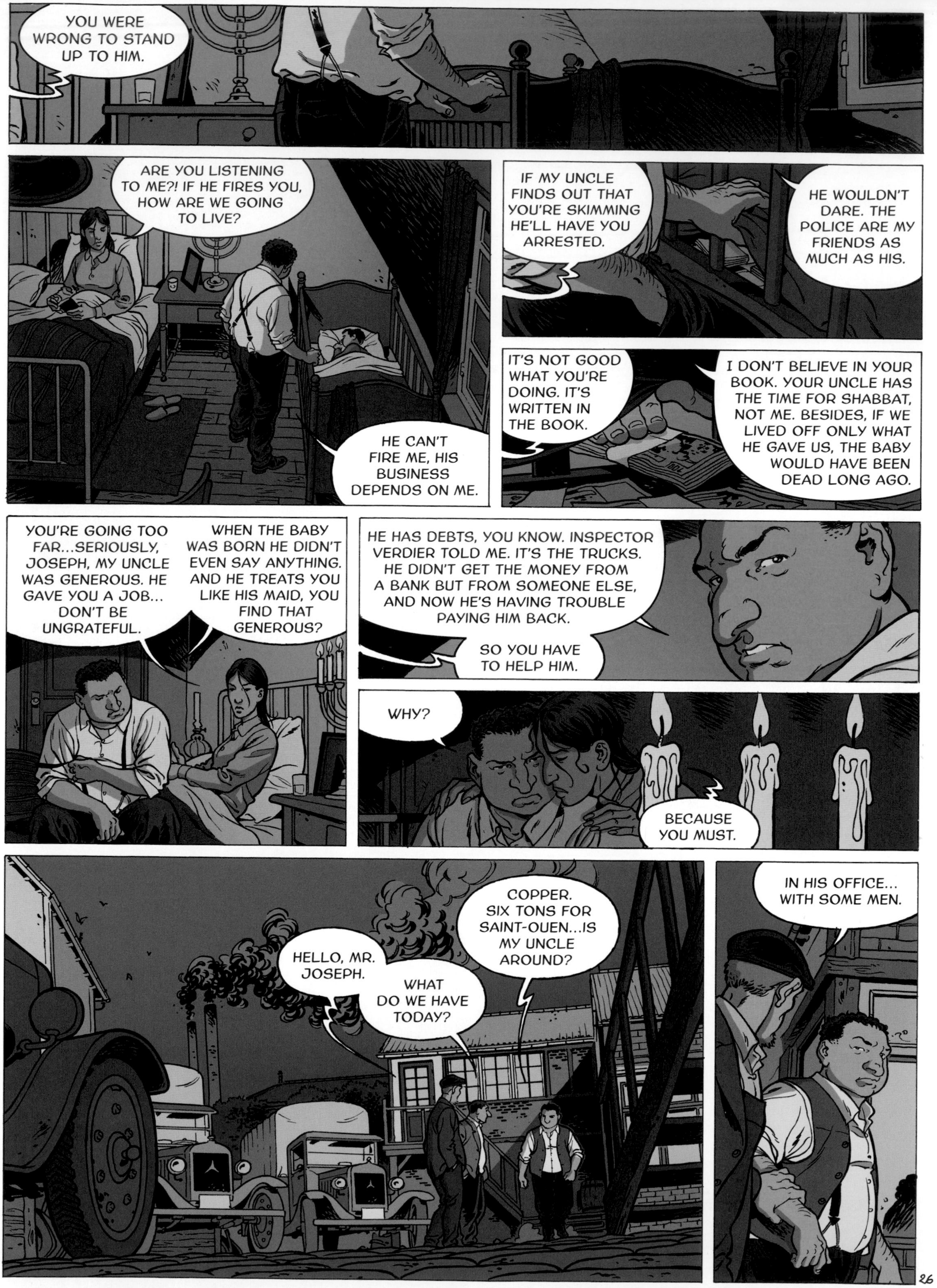
YOU WERE WRONG TO STAND UP TO HIM.
ARE YOU LISTENING TO ME?! IF HE FIRES YOU, HOW ARE WE GOING TO LIVE?
HE CAN'T FIRE ME, HIS BUSINESS DEPENDS ON ME.
IF MY UNCLE FINDS OUT THAT YOU'RE SKIMMING HE'LL HAVE YOU ARRESTED.
HE WOULDN'T DARE. THE POLICE ARE MY FRIENDS AS MUCH AS HIS.
IT'S NOT GOOD WHAT YOU'RE DOING. IT'S WRITTEN IN THE BOOK.
I DON'T BELIEVE IN YOUR BOOK. YOUR UNCLE HAS THE TIME FOR SHABBAT, NOT ME. BESIDES, IF WE LIVED OFF ONLY WHAT HE GAVE US, THE BABY WOULD HAVE BEEN DEAD LONG AGO.
YOU'RE GOING TOO FAR...SERIOUSLY, JOSEPH, MY UNCLE WAS GENEROUS. HE GAVE YOU A JOB... DON'T BE UNGRATEFUL.
WHEN THE BABY WAS BORN HE DIDN'T EVEN SAY ANYTHING. AND HE TREATS YOU LIKE HIS MAID, YOU FIND THAT GENEROUS?
HE HAS DEBTS, YOU KNOW. INSPECTOR VERDIER TOLD ME. IT'S THE TRUCKS. HE DIDN'T GET THE MONEY FROM A BANK BUT FROM SOMEONE ELSE, AND NOW HE'S HAVING TROUBLE PAYING HIM BACK.
SO YOU HAVE TO HELP HIM.
WHY?
BECAUSE YOU MUST.
HELLO, MR. JOSEPH.
WHAT DO WE HAVE TODAY?
COPPER. SIX TONS FOR SAINT-OUEN...IS MY UNCLE AROUND?
IN HIS OFFICE... WITH SOME MEN.
26

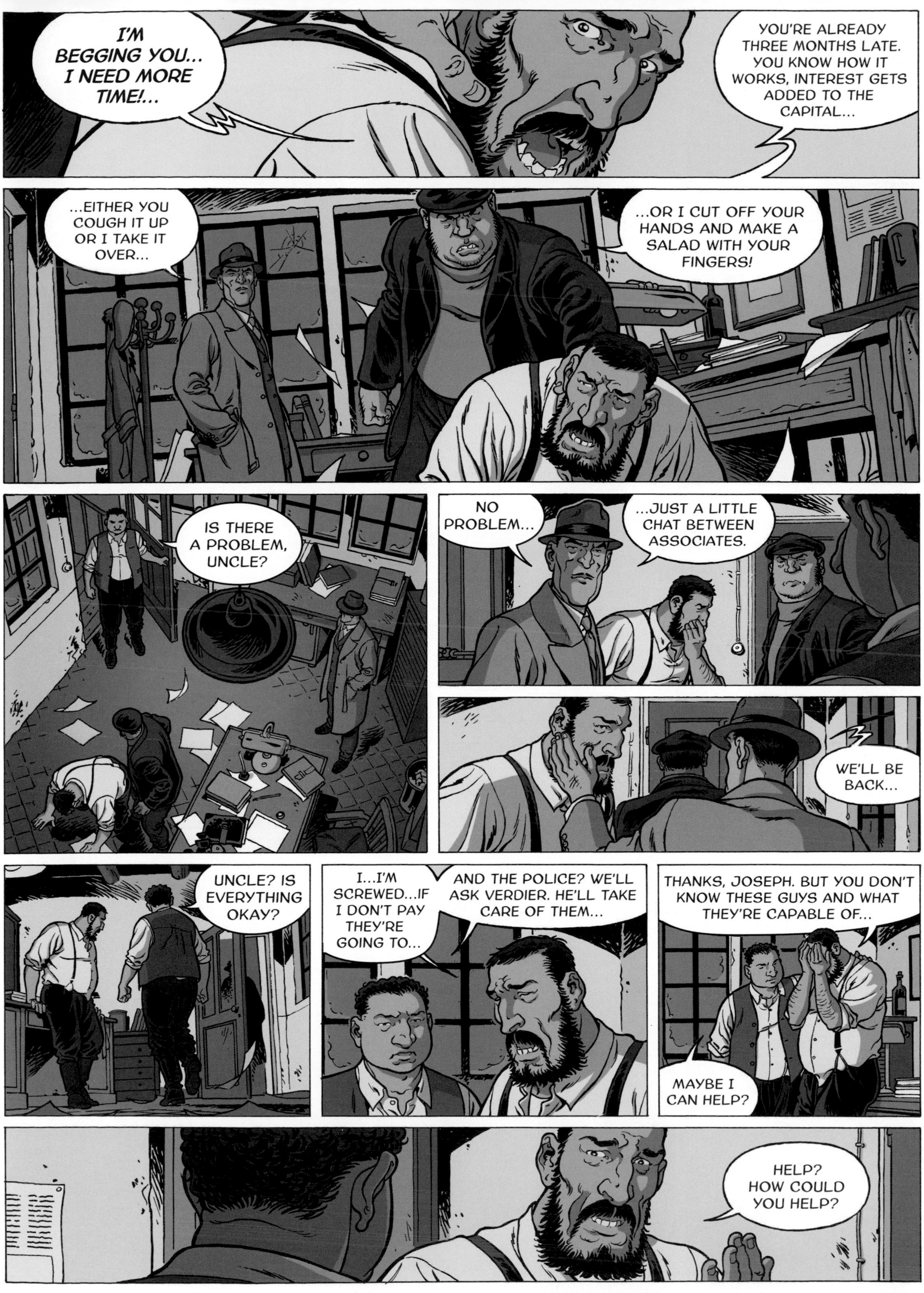
I'M BEGGING YOU... I NEED MORE TIME!...
YOU'RE ALREADY THREE MONTHS LATE. YOU KNOW HOW IT WORKS, INTEREST GETS ADDED TO THE CAPITAL...
...EITHER YOU COUGH IT UP OR I TAKE IT OVER...
...OR I CUT OFF YOUR HANDS AND MAKE A SALAD WITH YOUR FINGERS!
IS THERE A PROBLEM, UNCLE?
NO PROBLEM...
...JUST A LITTLE CHAT BETWEEN ASSOCIATES.
WE'LL BE BACK...
UNCLE? IS EVERYTHING OKAY?
I...I'M SCREWED...IF I DON'T PAY THEY'RE GOING TO...
AND THE POLICE? WE'LL ASK VERDIER. HE'LL TAKE CARE OF THEM...
THANKS, JOSEPH. BUT YOU DON'T KNOW THESE GUYS AND WHAT THEY'RE CAPABLE OF...
MAYBE I CAN HELP?
HELP? HOW COULD YOU HELP?
27

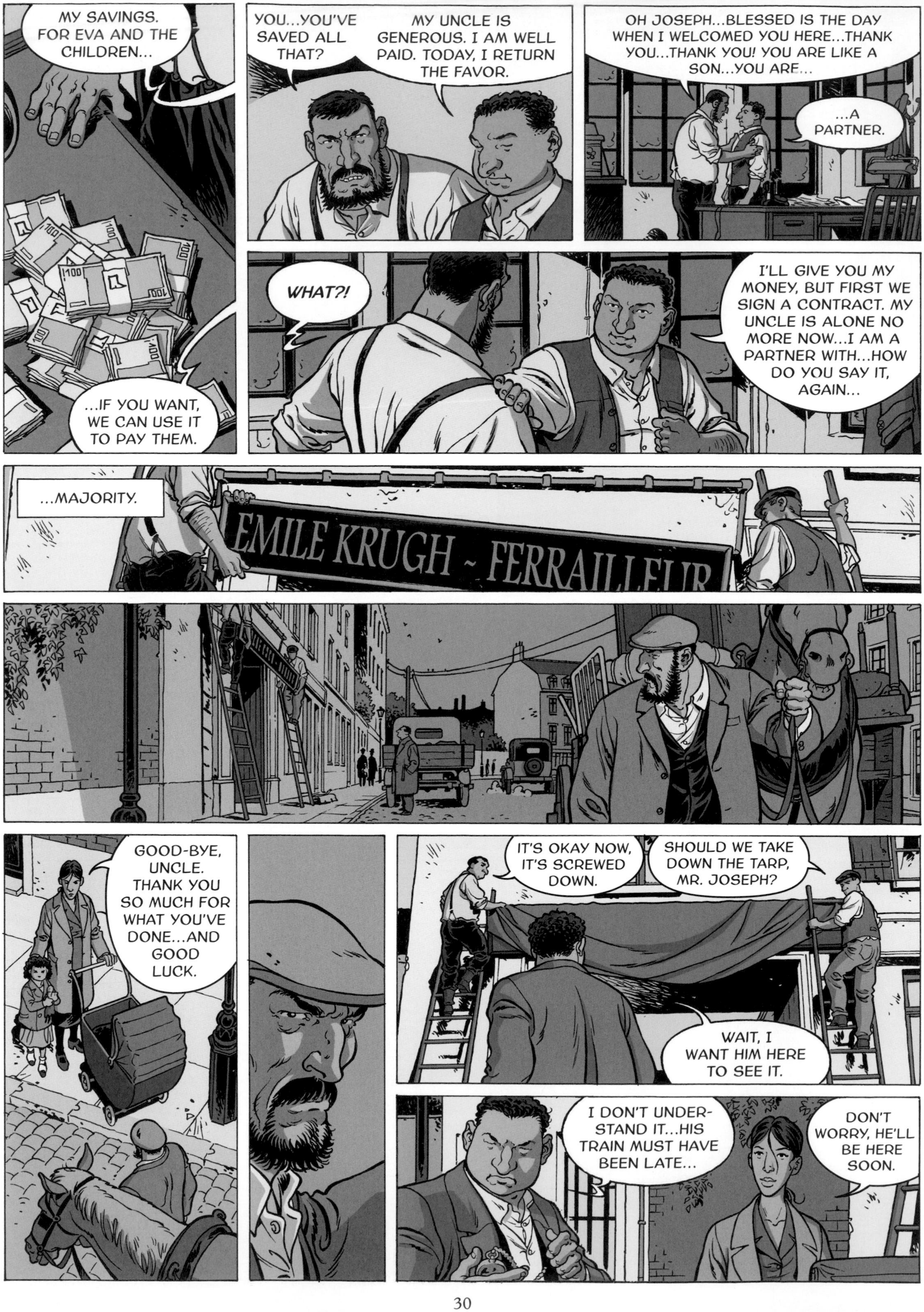
MY SAVINGS. FOR EVA AND THE CHILDREN...
...IF YOU WANT, WE CAN USE IT TO PAY THEM.
YOU...YOU'VE SAVED ALL THAT?
MY UNCLE IS GENEROUS. I AM WELL PAID. TODAY, I RETURN THE FAVOR.
OH JOSEPH...BLESSED IS THE DAY WHEN I WELCOMED YOU HERE...THANK YOU...THANK YOU! YOU ARE LIKE A SON...YOU ARE...
...A PARTNER.
WHAT?!
I'LL GIVE YOU MY MONEY, BUT FIRST WE SIGN A CONTRACT. MY UNCLE IS ALONE NO MORE NOW...I AM A PARTNER WITH...HOW DO YOU SAY IT, AGAIN...
...MAJORITY.
EMILE KRUGH ~ FERRAILLEUR
GOOD-BYE, UNCLE. THANK YOU SO MUCH FOR WHAT YOU'VE DONE...AND GOOD LUCK.
IT'S OKAY NOW, IT'S SCREWED DOWN.
SHOULD WE TAKE DOWN THE TARP, MR. JOSEPH?
WAIT, I WANT HIM HERE TO SEE IT.
I DON'T UNDERSTAND IT...HIS TRAIN MUST HAVE BEEN LATE...
DON'T WORRY, HE'LL BE HERE SOON.
28

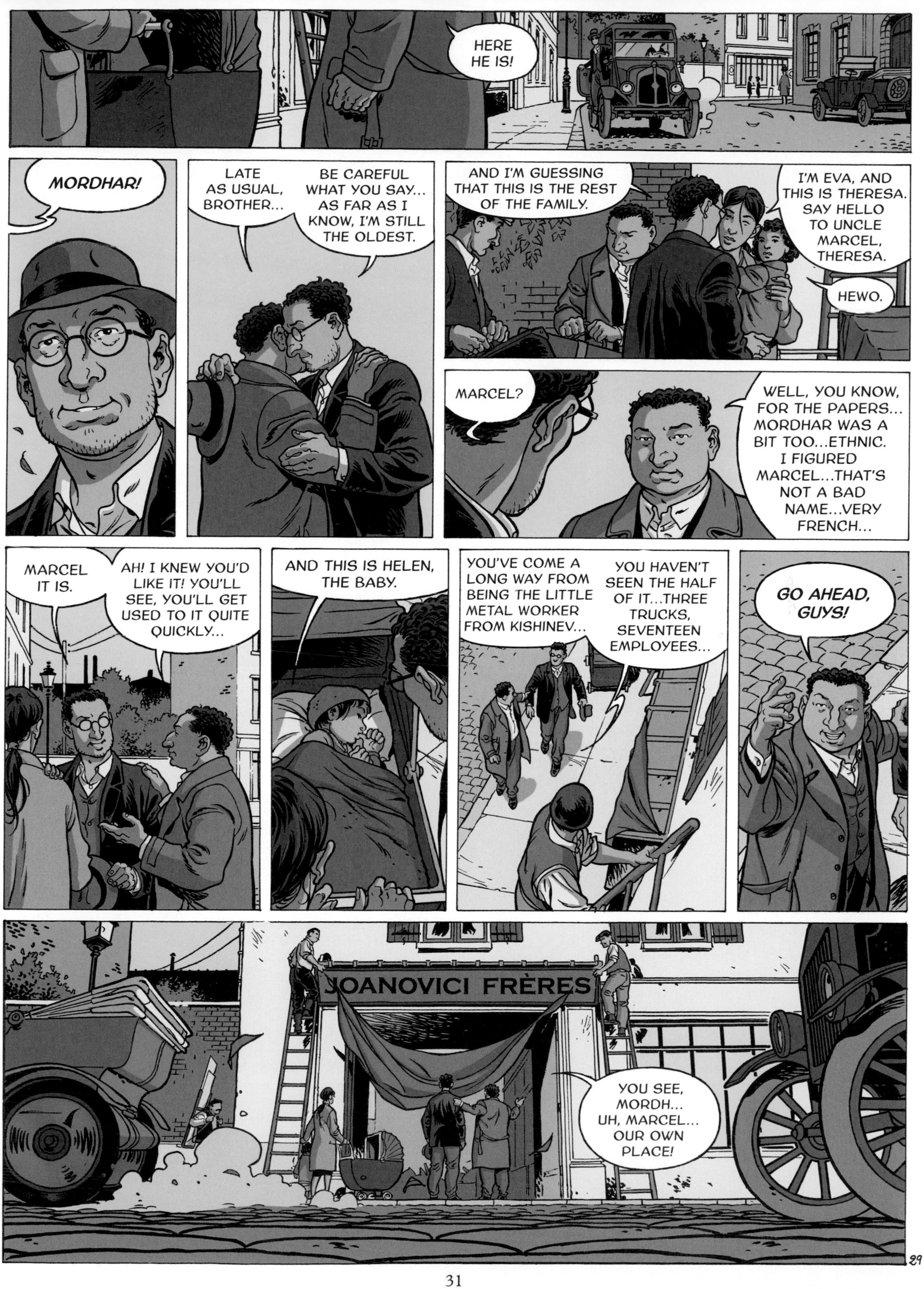
HERE HE IS!
MORDHAR!
LATE AS USUAL, BROTHER...
BE CAREFUL WHAT YOU SAY... AS FAR AS I KNOW, I'M STILL THE OLDEST.
AND I'M GUESSING THAT THIS IS THE REST OF THE FAMILY.
I'M EVA, AND THIS IS THERESA. SAY HELLO TO UNCLE MARCEL, THERESA.
HEWO.
MARCEL?
WELL, YOU KNOW, FOR THE PAPERS... MORDHAR WAS A BIT TOO...ETHNIC. I FIGURED MARCEL...THAT'S NOT A BAD NAME...VERY FRENCH...
MARCEL IT IS.
AH! I KNEW YOU'D LIKE IT! YOU'LL SEE, YOU'LL GET USED TO IT QUITE QUICKLY...
AND THIS IS HELEN, THE BABY.
YOU'VE COME A LONG WAY FROM BEING THE LITTLE METAL WORKER FROM KISHINEV...
YOU HAVEN'T SEEN THE HALF OF IT...THREE TRUCKS, SEVENTEEN EMPLOYEES...
GO AHEAD, GUYS!
JOANOVICI FRÈRES
YOU SEE, MORDH... UH, MARCEL... OUR OWN PLACE!
29

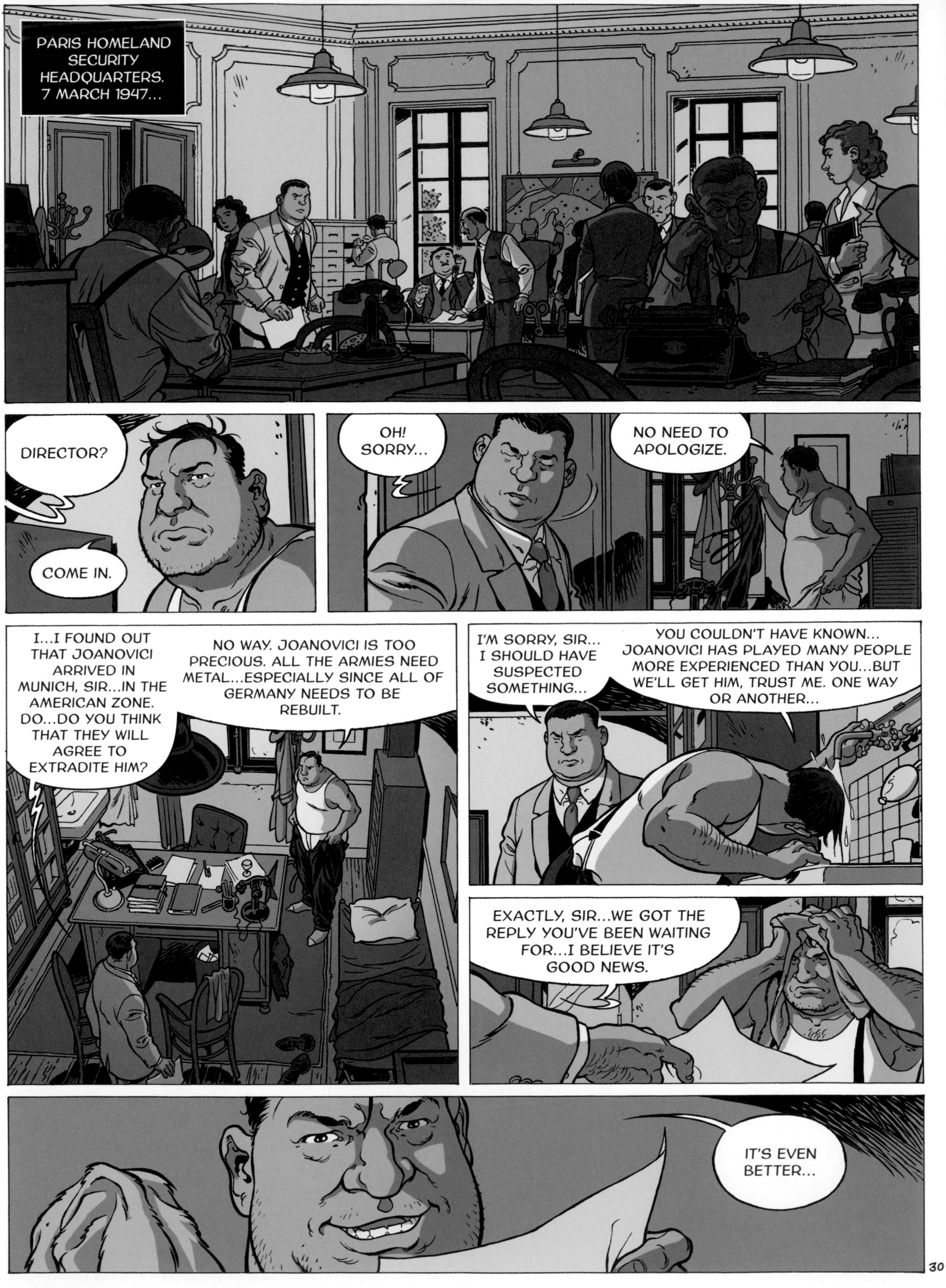

PARIS HOMELAND SECURITY HEADQUARTERS. 7 MARCH 1947...
DIRECTOR?
COME IN.
OH! SORRY...
NO NEED TO APOLOGIZE.
I...I FOUND OUT THAT JOANOVICI ARRIVED IN MUNICH, SIR...IN THE AMERICAN ZONE. DO...DO YOU THINK THAT THEY WILL AGREE TO EXTRADITE HIM?
NO WAY. JOANOVICI IS TOO PRECIOUS. ALL THE ARMIES NEED METAL...ESPECIALLY SINCE ALL OF GERMANY NEEDS TO BE REBUILT.
I'M SORRY, SIR... I SHOULD HAVE SUSPECTED SOMETHING...
YOU COULDN'T HAVE KNOWN... JOANOVICI HAS PLAYED MANY PEOPLE MORE EXPERIENCED THAN YOU...BUT WE'LL GET HIM, TRUST ME. ONE WAY OR ANOTHER...
EXACTLY, SIR...WE GOT THE REPLY YOU'VE BEEN WAITING FOR...I BELIEVE IT'S GOOD NEWS.
IT'S EVEN BETTER...
30

FELL ASLEEP?! YOU REALLY EXPECT ME TO BELIEVE THAT?!

BELIEVE IT OR NOT, I DON'T CARE. IT'S THE SIMPLE TRUTH. IT WAS LATE, I WAS TIRED, AND I DIDN'T HAVE ANY REASON TO BELIEVE THAT HE WOULD GIVE ME THE SLIP.

AND WHILE YOU TOOK YOUR LITTLE NAP, JOANOVICI DRIVES OVER THE BORDER. HOW CONVENIENT!

YOU THINK THAT DID ME ANY FAVORS? I WOULD HAVE PRE-FERRED THAT HE HAD GIVEN HIMSELF UP, FOR GOD'S SAKE! IF HE HAD, I WOULDN'T BE HERE GETTING GRILLED LIKE SOME TWO-BIT SUSPECT...

OH, YOU AREN'T SOME TWO-BIT SUSPECT, BELIEVE ME! YOU ARE THE BACKBONE OF THE LARG-EST RING OF ORGANIZED CORRUPTION THAT I HAVE SEEN IN MORE THAN 100 YEARS OF POLICE HISTORY!

WHY? WHAT DID I DO WRONG? OKAY, I ADMIT THAT JOANOVICI IS A FRIEND. HE SAVED ME FROM THE GESTAPO...

YOU CAN COUNT ON ME TO RID POLICE HEADQUARTERS OF ALL THE TRASH LIKE YOU!

OKAY, I'LL ALSO ADMIT THAT JOANOVICI OWNS THE HAIR SALON WHERE MY WIFE WORKS...I DIDN'T KNOW THAT THAT WAS SUCH A SERIOUS OFFENSE.

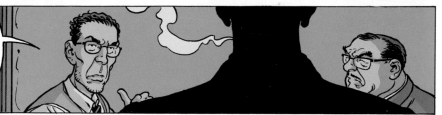

BUT LET ME TELL YOU WHAT I THINK OF MR. JOSEPH...IT'S THANKS TO HIM THAT WE HAD THE WEAPONS FOR THE RESISTANCE. DITTO FOR THE CLOTH FOR THE FFI* ARMBANDS... DITTO FOR YOUR POLICE PATROL CARS! WHAT DO YOU WANT? FOR THE POLICE TO GET AROUND ON BICYCLES?

MR. JOSEPH SAVED AT LEAST 150 PEOPLE FROM THE CAMPS...NOT EVERYONE CAN SAY THAT!

OKAY, SO HE DID BUSINESS WITH THE KRAUTS...AND HE SCREWED THEM BIG-TIME! AND IT'S TRUE THAT HE MADE THE COL-LABORATORS BELIEVE THAT THEY WERE HIS FRIENDS...HE HAD TO DO IT TO SURVIVE! MY GOD, CONSIDERING HIS RELIGION, THE FACT THAT HE GOT OUT ALIVE...YOU SHOULD HAVE SOME RESPECT FOR HIM!

HE WAS IN IT UP TO HIS NECK...HE TOOK HUGE RISKS...AND YOU...THE ONE WHO IS ACCUSING HIM...WHERE WERE YOU WHEN ALL THIS WAS GOING ON? HIDING IN YOUR LITTLE GOVERNMENT OFFICE, SAFE AND SOUND IN MELUN.

31

*The FFI (French Forces of the Interior) was the French resistance inside France toward the end of the war. Those who carried the armbands after the war were protected.

HEY, FOURNET, DO YOU KNOW HOW TO READ... I MEAN, YOU'RE NOT LIKE YOUR BOSS?

OBVIOUSLY I KNOW HOW TO READ. WHY, YOU WANT TO TAKE DOWN MR. JOSEPH FOR BEING ILLITERATE?

LAUGH. GO AHEAD AND LAUGH...

HEY!

YOU'LL BE LAUGHING A LOT LESS WHEN YOU READ THIS!

WHAT IS IT...?

A LETTER ROGATORY. EVEN A CHARLATAN LIKE YOU SHOULD KNOW WHAT THAT IS...AND YOU'LL SEE THAT THERE IS A GERMAN NAME INVOLVED...

HERMANN BRANDL?... DON'T KNOW HIM.

SURE, FOURNET...YOU DON'T KNOW THE MOST IMPORTANT OF ALL OF MR. JOSEPH'S ASSOCIATES?

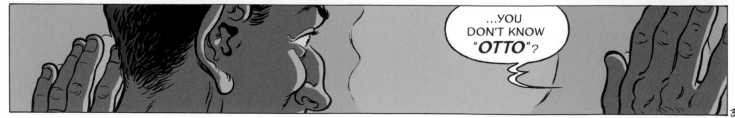

...YOU DON'T KNOW "OTTO"?

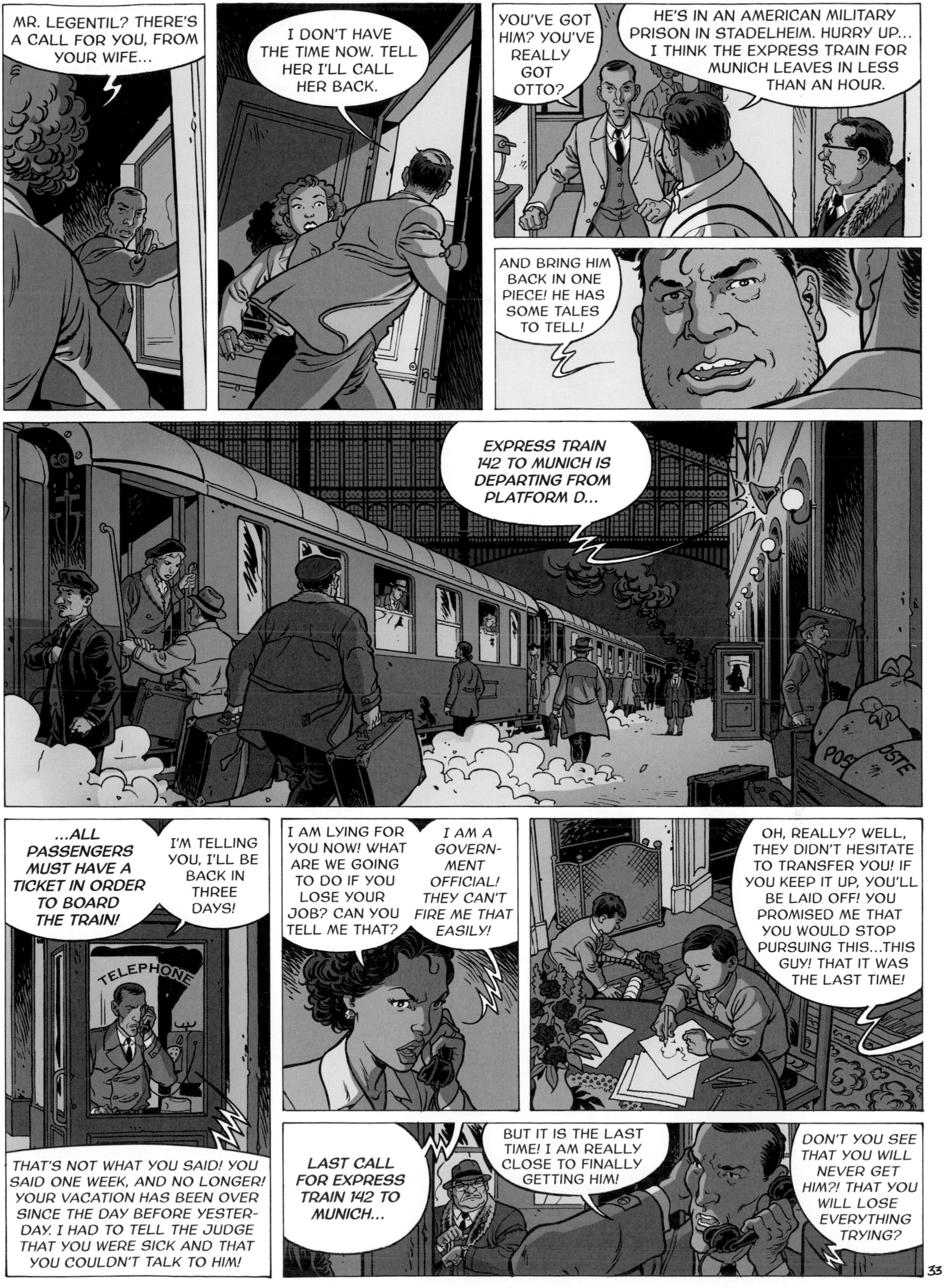
MR. LEGENTIL? THERE'S A CALL FOR YOU, FROM YOUR WIFE...
I DON'T HAVE THE TIME NOW. TELL HER I'LL CALL HER BACK.
YOU'VE GOT HIM? YOU'VE REALLY GOT OTTO?
HE'S IN AN AMERICAN MILITARY PRISON IN STADELHEIM. HURRY UP... I THINK THE EXPRESS TRAIN FOR MUNICH LEAVES IN LESS THAN AN HOUR.
AND BRING HIM BACK IN ONE PIECE! HE HAS SOME TALES TO TELL!
EXPRESS TRAIN 142 TO MUNICH IS DEPARTING FROM PLATFORM D...
POS
OSTE
...ALL PASSENGERS MUST HAVE A TICKET IN ORDER TO BOARD THE TRAIN!
I'M TELLING YOU, I'LL BE BACK IN THREE DAYS!
TELEPHONE
THAT'S NOT WHAT YOU SAID! YOU SAID ONE WEEK, AND NO LONGER! YOUR VACATION HAS BEEN OVER SINCE THE DAY BEFORE YESTERDAY. I HAD TO TELL THE JUDGE THAT YOU WERE SICK AND THAT YOU COULDN'T TALK TO HIM!
I AM LYING FOR YOU NOW! WHAT ARE WE GOING TO DO IF YOU LOSE YOUR JOB? CAN YOU TELL ME THAT?
I AM A GOVERNMENT OFFICIAL! THEY CAN'T FIRE ME THAT EASILY!
OH, REALLY? WELL, THEY DIDN'T HESITATE TO TRANSFER YOU! IF YOU KEEP IT UP, YOU'LL BE LAID OFF! YOU PROMISED ME THAT YOU WOULD STOP PURSUING THIS...THIS GUY! THAT IT WAS THE LAST TIME!
LAST CALL FOR EXPRESS TRAIN 142 TO MUNICH...
BUT IT IS THE LAST TIME! I AM REALLY CLOSE TO FINALLY GETTING HIM!
DON'T YOU SEE THAT YOU WILL NEVER GET HIM?! THAT YOU WILL LOSE EVERYTHING TRYING?
33

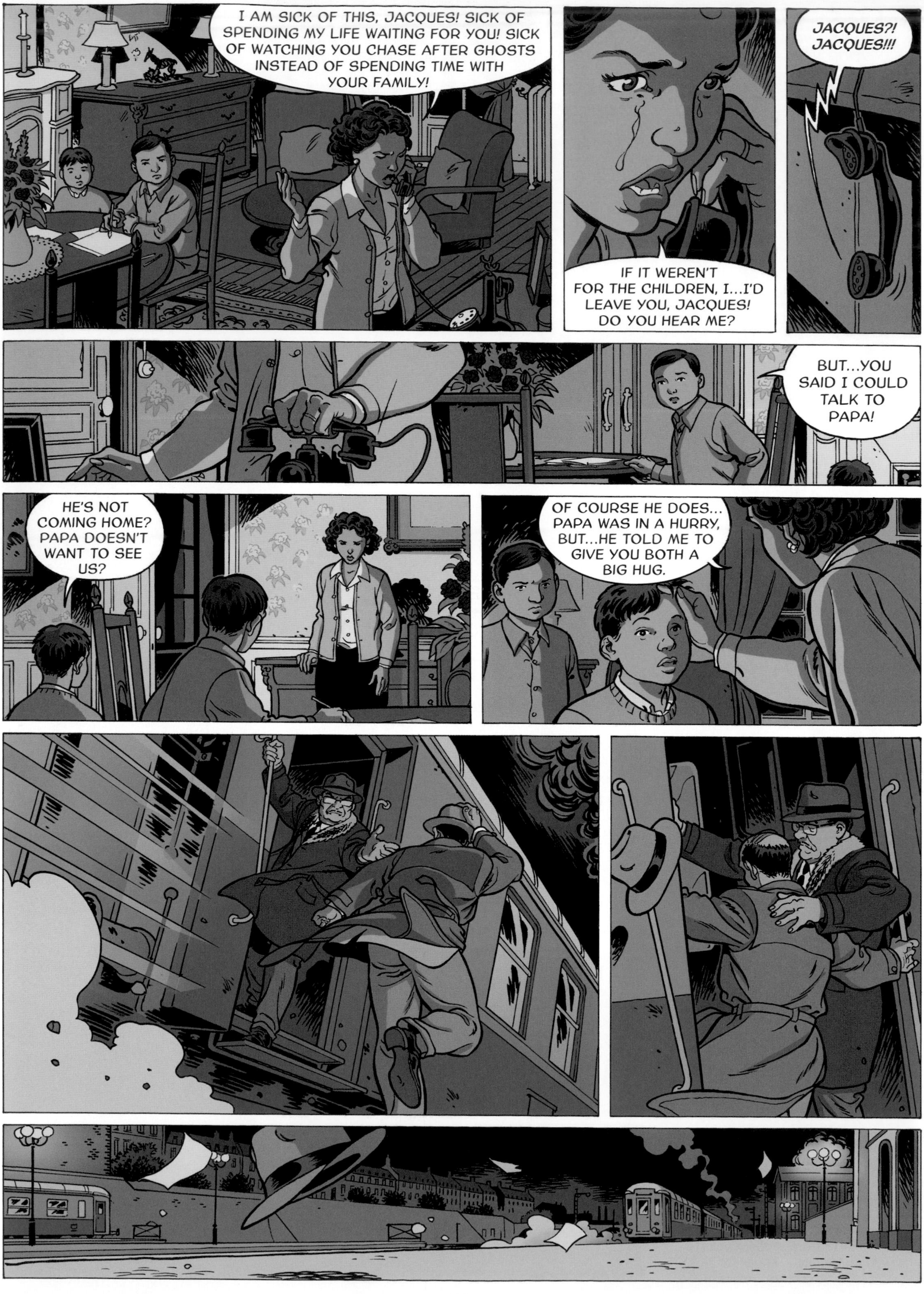
I AM SICK OF THIS, JACQUES! SICK OF SPENDING MY LIFE WAITING FOR YOU! SICK OF WATCHING YOU CHASE AFTER GHOSTS INSTEAD OF SPENDING TIME WITH YOUR FAMILY!
IF IT WEREN'T FOR THE CHILDREN, I...I'D LEAVE YOU, JACQUES! DO YOU HEAR ME?
JACQUES?! JACQUES!!!
BUT...YOU SAID I COULD TALK TO PAPA!
HE'S NOT COMING HOME? PAPA DOESN'T WANT TO SEE US?
OF COURSE HE DOES... PAPA WAS IN A HURRY, BUT...HE TOLD ME TO GIVE YOU BOTH A BIG HUG.
34

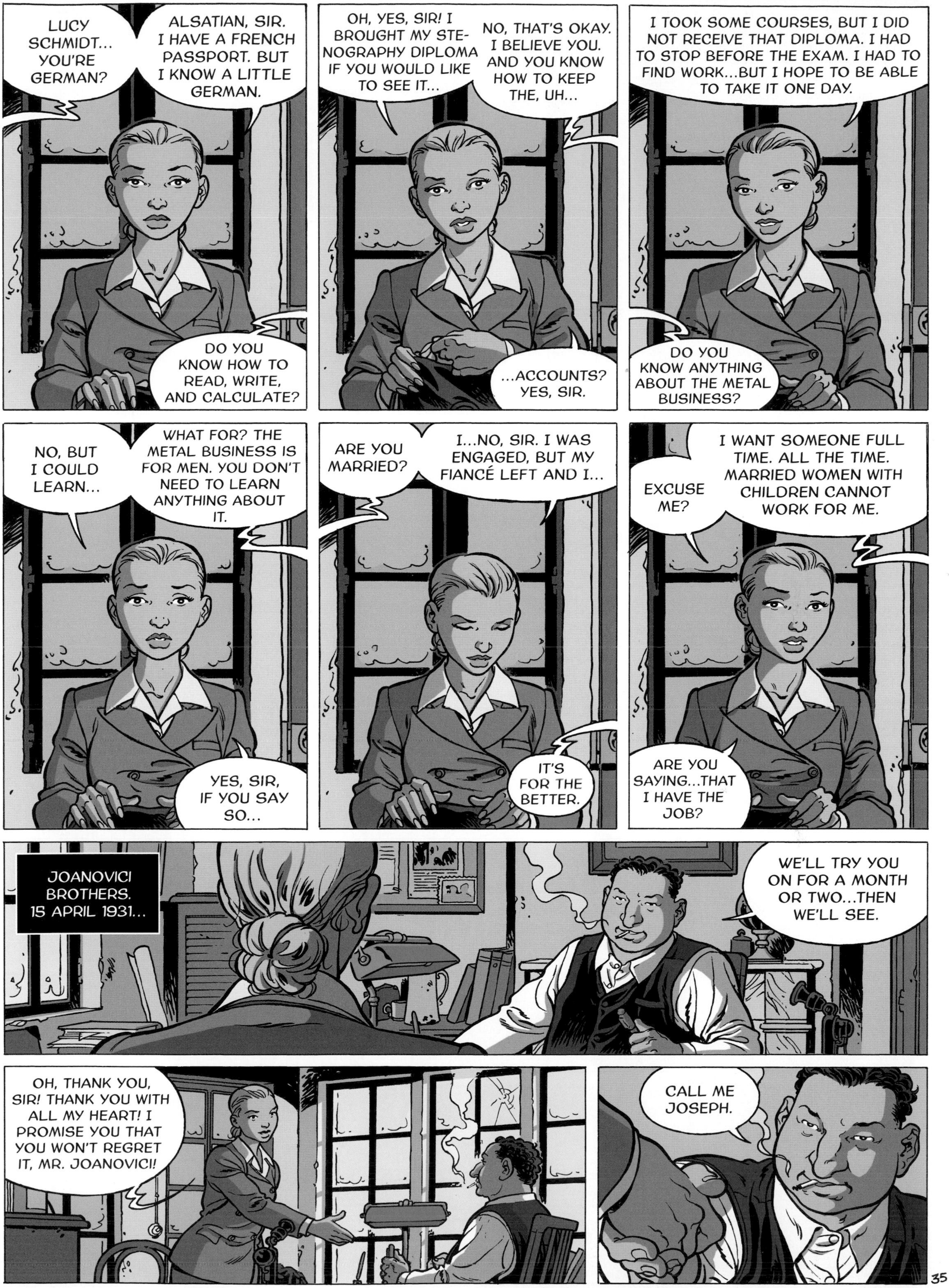
LUCY SCHMIDT... YOU'RE GERMAN?
ALSATIAN, SIR. I HAVE A FRENCH PASSPORT. BUT I KNOW A LITTLE GERMAN.
DO YOU KNOW HOW TO READ, WRITE, AND CALCULATE?
OH, YES, SIR! I BROUGHT MY STENOGRAPHY DIPLOMA IF YOU WOULD LIKE TO SEE IT...
NO, THAT'S OKAY. I BELIEVE YOU. AND YOU KNOW HOW TO KEEP THE, UH...
...ACCOUNTS? YES, SIR.
I TOOK SOME COURSES, BUT I DID NOT RECEIVE THAT DIPLOMA. I HAD TO STOP BEFORE THE EXAM. I HAD TO FIND WORK...BUT I HOPE TO BE ABLE TO TAKE IT ONE DAY.
DO YOU KNOW ANYTHING ABOUT THE METAL BUSINESS?
NO, BUT I COULD LEARN...
WHAT FOR? THE METAL BUSINESS IS FOR MEN. YOU DON'T NEED TO LEARN ANYTHING ABOUT IT.
YES, SIR, IF YOU SAY SO...
ARE YOU MARRIED?
I...NO, SIR. I WAS ENGAGED, BUT MY FIANCÉ LEFT AND I...
IT'S FOR THE BETTER.
EXCUSE ME?
I WANT SOMEONE FULL TIME. ALL THE TIME. MARRIED WOMEN WITH CHILDREN CANNOT WORK FOR ME.
ARE YOU SAYING...THAT I HAVE THE JOB?
JOANOVICI BROTHERS. 15 APRIL 1931...
WE'LL TRY YOU ON FOR A MONTH OR TWO...THEN WE'LL SEE.
OH, THANK YOU, SIR! THANK YOU WITH ALL MY HEART! I PROMISE YOU THAT YOU WON'T REGRET IT, MR. JOANOVICI!
CALL ME JOSEPH.
35

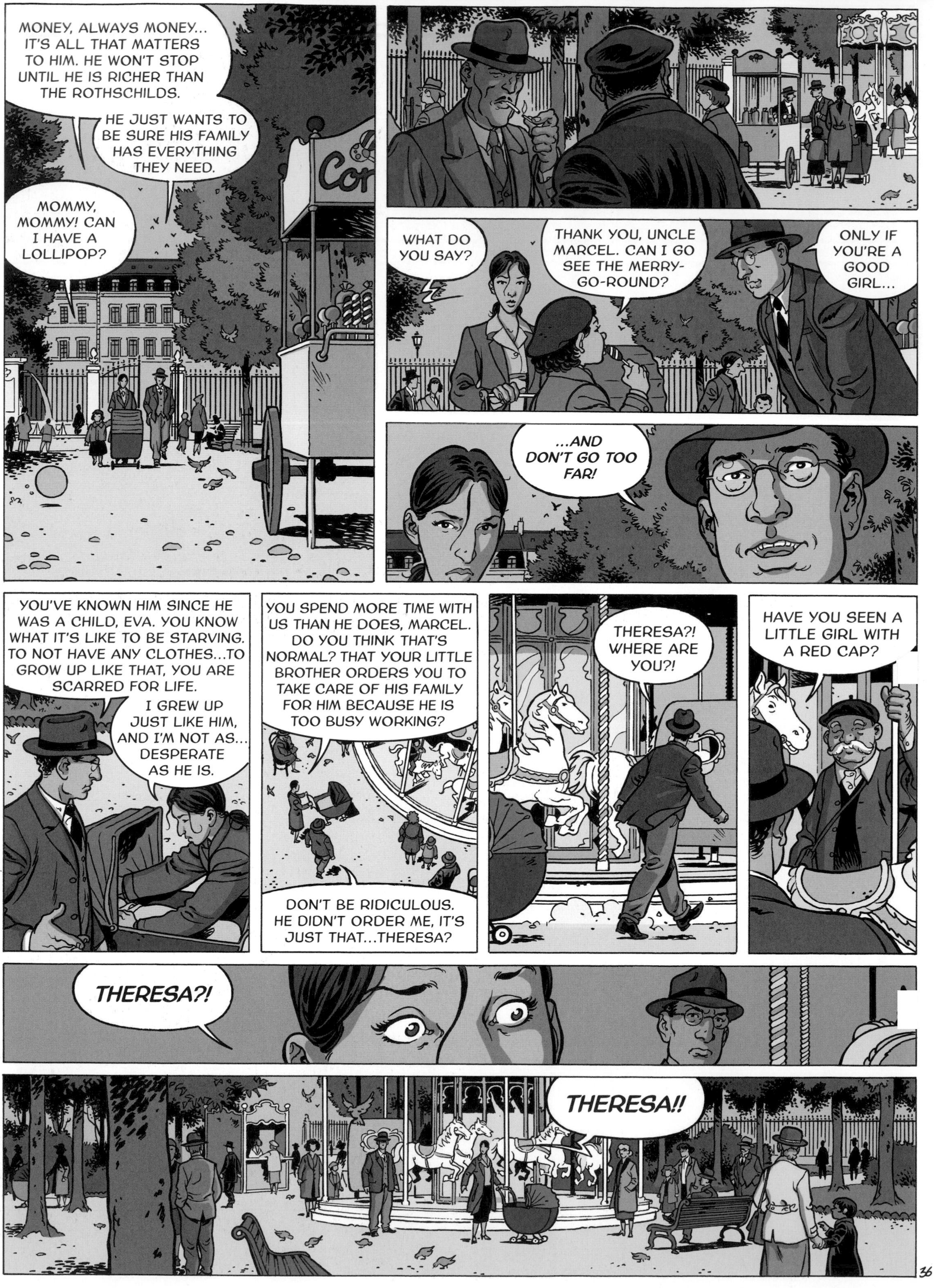
MONEY, ALWAYS MONEY... IT'S ALL THAT MATTERS TO HIM. HE WON'T STOP UNTIL HE IS RICHER THAN THE ROTHSCHILDS.
HE JUST WANTS TO BE SURE HIS FAMILY HAS EVERYTHING THEY NEED.
MOMMY, MOMMY! CAN I HAVE A LOLLIPOP?
WHAT DO YOU SAY?
THANK YOU, UNCLE MARCEL. CAN I GO SEE THE MERRY-GO-ROUND?
ONLY IF YOU'RE A GOOD GIRL...
...AND DON'T GO TOO FAR!
YOU'VE KNOWN HIM SINCE HE WAS A CHILD, EVA. YOU KNOW WHAT IT'S LIKE TO BE STARVING. TO NOT HAVE ANY CLOTHES...TO GROW UP LIKE THAT, YOU ARE SCARRED FOR LIFE.
I GREW UP JUST LIKE HIM, AND I'M NOT AS... DESPERATE AS HE IS.
YOU SPEND MORE TIME WITH US THAN HE DOES, MARCEL. DO YOU THINK THAT'S NORMAL? THAT YOUR LITTLE BROTHER ORDERS YOU TO TAKE CARE OF HIS FAMILY FOR HIM BECAUSE HE IS TOO BUSY WORKING?
DON'T BE RIDICULOUS. HE DIDN'T ORDER ME, IT'S JUST THAT...THERESA?
THERESA?! WHERE ARE YOU?!
HAVE YOU SEEN A LITTLE GIRL WITH A RED CAP?
THERESA?!
THERESA!!
36

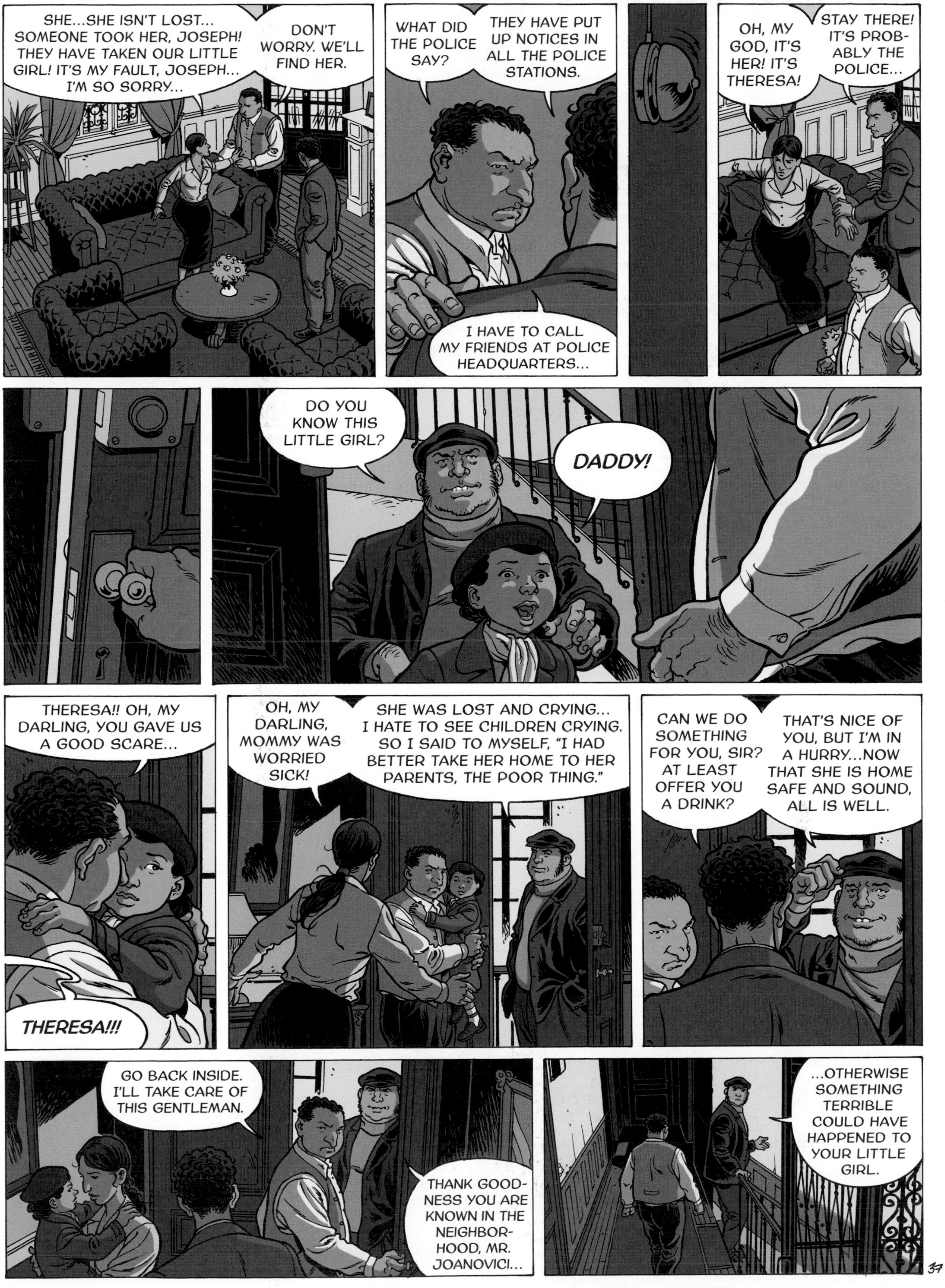
SHE...SHE ISN'T LOST... SOMEONE TOOK HER, JOSEPH! THEY HAVE TAKEN OUR LITTLE GIRL! IT'S MY FAULT, JOSEPH... I'M SO SORRY...
DON'T WORRY. WE'LL FIND HER.
WHAT DID THE POLICE SAY?
THEY HAVE PUT UP NOTICES IN ALL THE POLICE STATIONS.
I HAVE TO CALL MY FRIENDS AT POLICE HEADQUARTERS...
OH, MY GOD, IT'S HER! IT'S THERESA!
STAY THERE! IT'S PROBABLY THE POLICE...
DO YOU KNOW THIS LITTLE GIRL?
DADDY!
THERESA!! OH, MY DARLING, YOU GAVE US A GOOD SCARE...
THERESA!!!
OH, MY DARLING, MOMMY WAS WORRIED SICK!
SHE WAS LOST AND CRYING... I HATE TO SEE CHILDREN CRYING. SO I SAID TO MYSELF, "I HAD BETTER TAKE HER HOME TO HER PARENTS, THE POOR THING."
CAN WE DO SOMETHING FOR YOU, SIR? AT LEAST OFFER YOU A DRINK?
THAT'S NICE OF YOU, BUT I'M IN A HURRY...NOW THAT SHE IS HOME SAFE AND SOUND, ALL IS WELL.
GO BACK INSIDE. I'LL TAKE CARE OF THIS GENTLEMAN.
THANK GOODNESS YOU ARE KNOWN IN THE NEIGHBORHOOD, MR. JOANOVICI...
...OTHERWISE SOMETHING TERRIBLE COULD HAVE HAPPENED TO YOUR LITTLE GIRL.
37

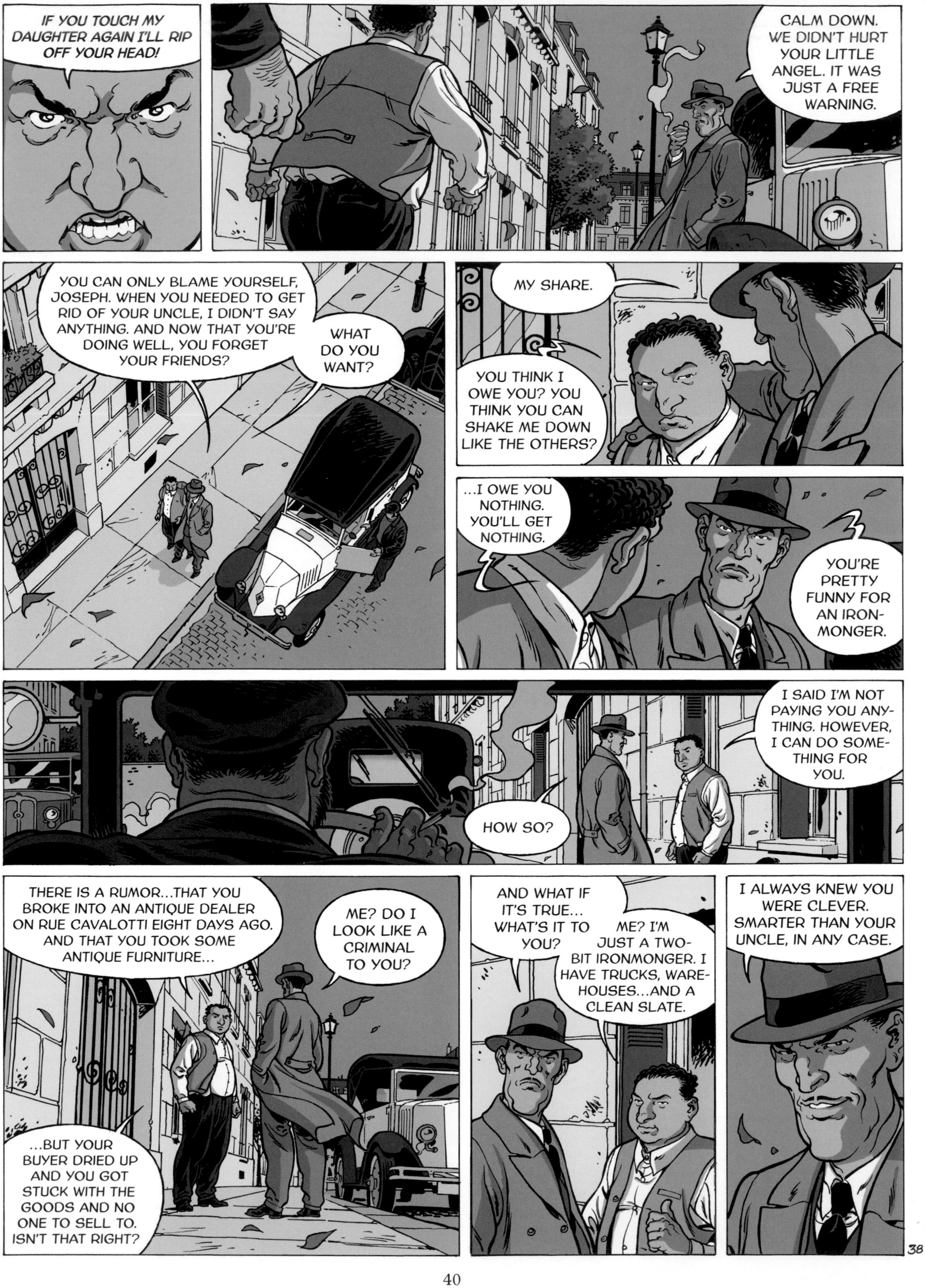
IF YOU TOUCH MY DAUGHTER AGAIN I'LL RIP OFF YOUR HEAD!
CALM DOWN. WE DIDN'T HURT YOUR LITTLE ANGEL. IT WAS JUST A FREE WARNING.
YOU CAN ONLY BLAME YOURSELF, JOSEPH. WHEN YOU NEEDED TO GET RID OF YOUR UNCLE, I DIDN'T SAY ANYTHING. AND NOW THAT YOU'RE DOING WELL, YOU FORGET YOUR FRIENDS?
WHAT DO YOU WANT?
MY SHARE.
YOU THINK I OWE YOU? YOU THINK YOU CAN SHAKE ME DOWN LIKE THE OTHERS?
...I OWE YOU NOTHING. YOU'LL GET NOTHING.
YOU'RE PRETTY FUNNY FOR AN IRON-MONGER.
I SAID I'M NOT PAYING YOU ANY-THING. HOWEVER, I CAN DO SOME-THING FOR YOU.
HOW SO?
THERE IS A RUMOR...THAT YOU BROKE INTO AN ANTIQUE DEALER ON RUE CAVALOTTI EIGHT DAYS AGO. AND THAT YOU TOOK SOME ANTIQUE FURNITURE...
ME? DO I LOOK LIKE A CRIMINAL TO YOU?
...BUT YOUR BUYER DRIED UP AND YOU GOT STUCK WITH THE GOODS AND NO ONE TO SELL TO. ISN'T THAT RIGHT?
AND WHAT IF IT'S TRUE... WHAT'S IT TO YOU?
ME? I'M JUST A TWO-BIT IRONMONGER. I HAVE TRUCKS, WARE-HOUSES...AND A CLEAN SLATE.
I ALWAYS KNEW YOU WERE CLEVER. SMARTER THAN YOUR UNCLE, IN ANY CASE.
38

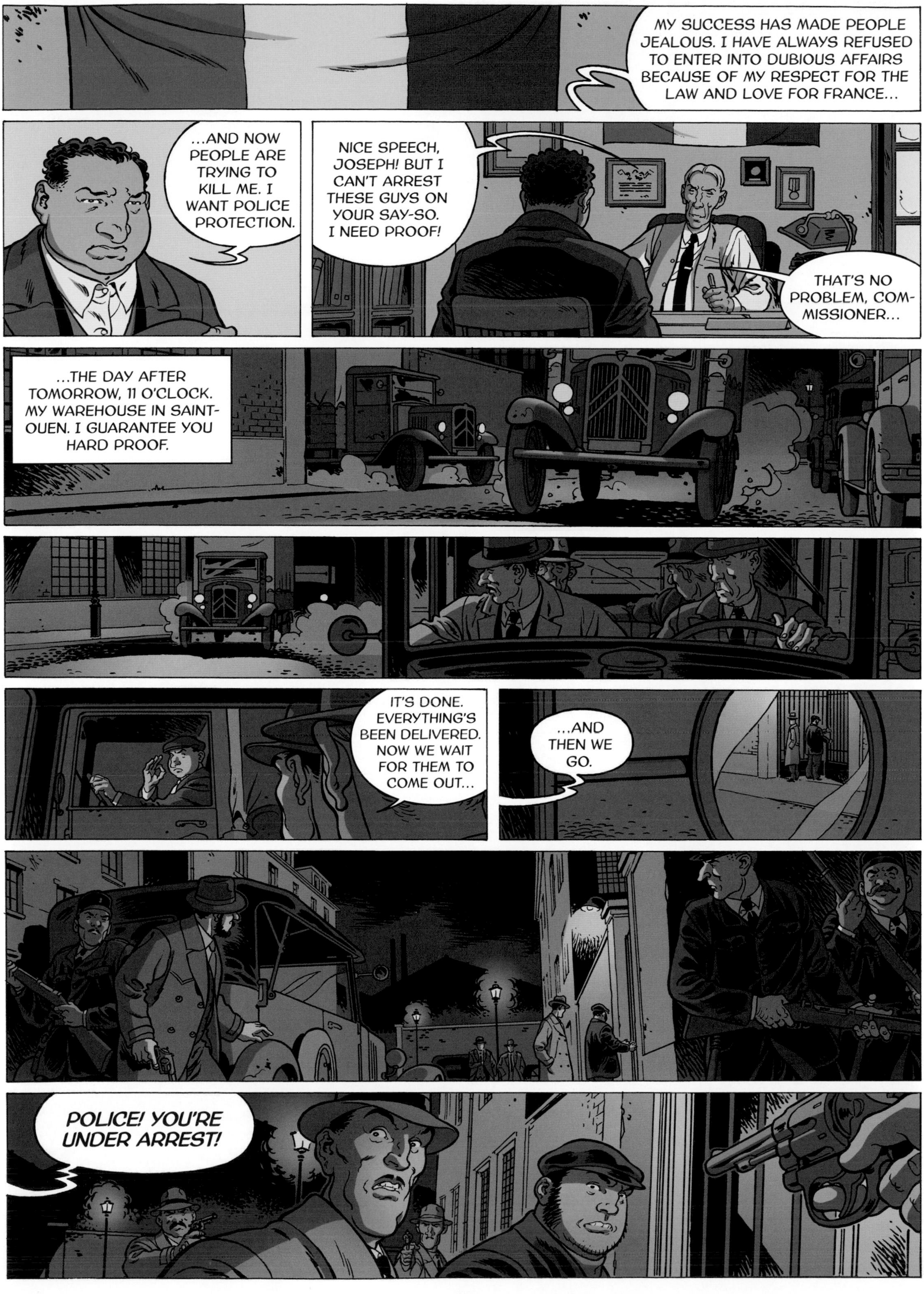
MY SUCCESS HAS MADE PEOPLE JEALOUS. I HAVE ALWAYS REFUSED TO ENTER INTO DUBIOUS AFFAIRS BECAUSE OF MY RESPECT FOR THE LAW AND LOVE FOR FRANCE...
...AND NOW PEOPLE ARE TRYING TO KILL ME. I WANT POLICE PROTECTION.
NICE SPEECH, JOSEPH! BUT I CAN'T ARREST THESE GUYS ON YOUR SAY-SO. I NEED PROOF!
THAT'S NO PROBLEM, COMMISSIONER...
...THE DAY AFTER TOMORROW, 11 O'CLOCK. MY WAREHOUSE IN SAINT-OUEN. I GUARANTEE YOU HARD PROOF.
IT'S DONE. EVERYTHING'S BEEN DELIVERED. NOW WE WAIT FOR THEM TO COME OUT...
...AND THEN WE GO.
POLICE! YOU'RE UNDER ARREST!
39

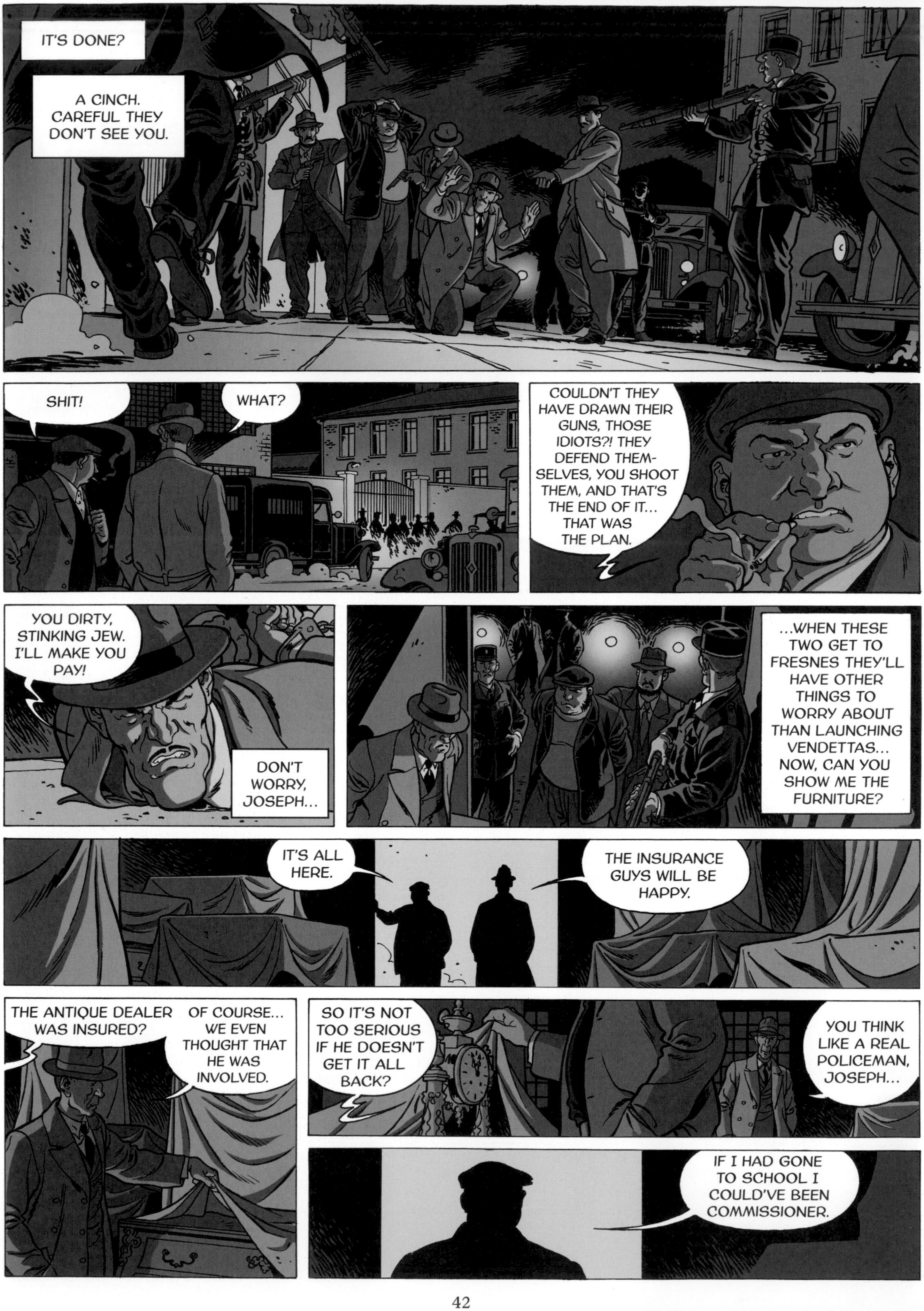
IT'S DONE?
A CINCH. CAREFUL THEY DON'T SEE YOU.
SHIT!
WHAT?
COULDN'T THEY HAVE DRAWN THEIR GUNS, THOSE IDIOTS?! THEY DEFEND THEM-SELVES, YOU SHOOT THEM, AND THAT'S THE END OF IT... THAT WAS THE PLAN.
YOU DIRTY, STINKING JEW. I'LL MAKE YOU PAY!
DON'T WORRY, JOSEPH...
...WHEN THESE TWO GET TO FRESNES THEY'LL HAVE OTHER THINGS TO WORRY ABOUT THAN LAUNCHING VENDETTAS... NOW, CAN YOU SHOW ME THE FURNITURE?
IT'S ALL HERE.
THE INSURANCE GUYS WILL BE HAPPY.
THE ANTIQUE DEALER WAS INSURED?
OF COURSE... WE EVEN THOUGHT THAT HE WAS INVOLVED.
SO IT'S NOT TOO SERIOUS IF HE DOESN'T GET IT ALL BACK?
YOU THINK LIKE A REAL POLICEMAN, JOSEPH...
IF I HAD GONE TO SCHOOL I COULD'VE BEEN COMMISSIONER.
40

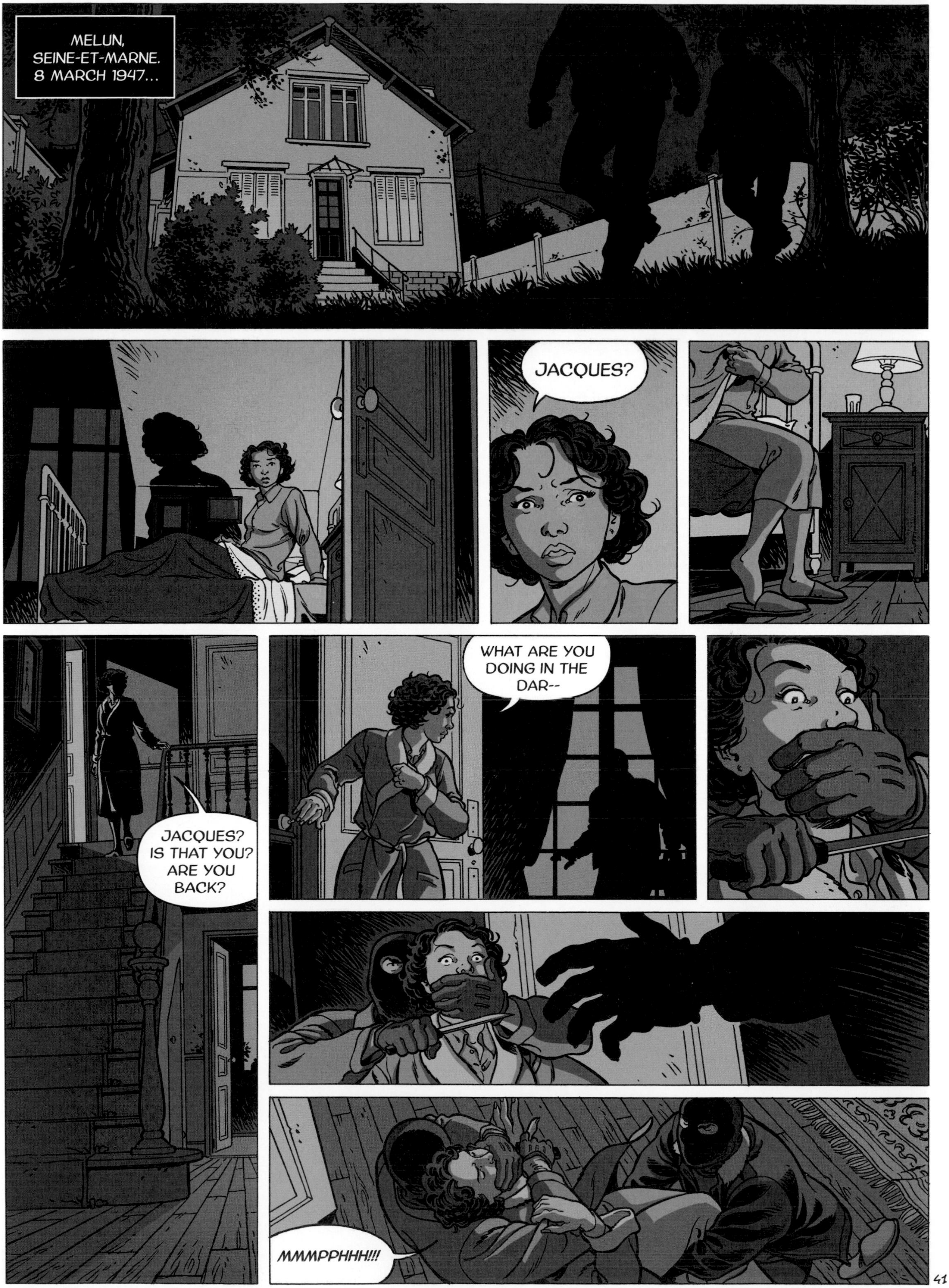
MELUN, SEINE-ET-MARNE. 8 MARCH 1947...
JACQUES?
JACQUES? IS THAT YOU? ARE YOU BACK?
WHAT ARE YOU DOING IN THE DAR--
MMMPPHHH!!!
41

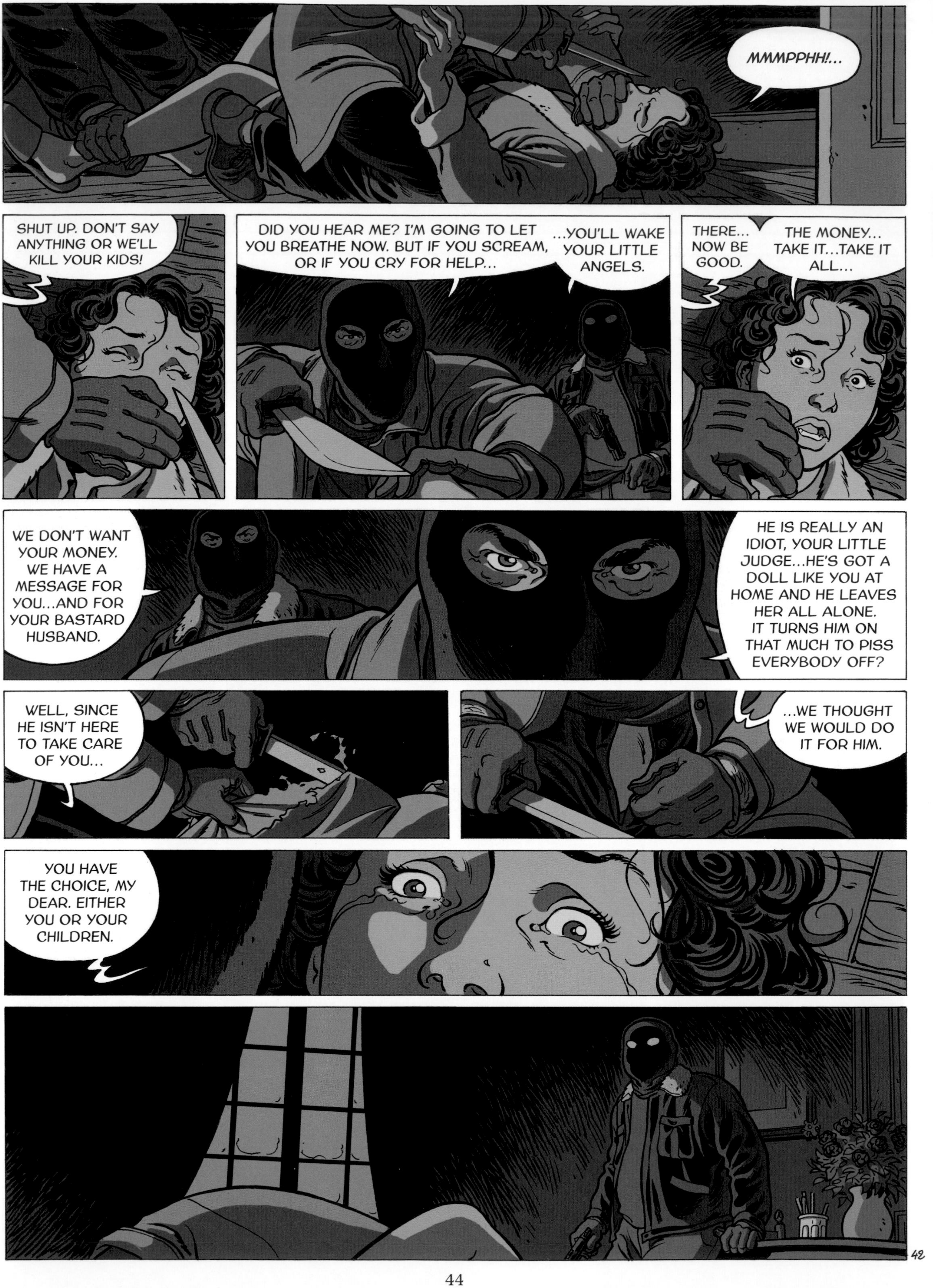
MMMPPHH!...
SHUT UP. DON'T SAY ANYTHING OR WE'LL KILL YOUR KIDS!
DID YOU HEAR ME? I'M GOING TO LET YOU BREATHE NOW. BUT IF YOU SCREAM, OR IF YOU CRY FOR HELP...
...YOU'LL WAKE YOUR LITTLE ANGELS.
THERE... NOW BE GOOD.
THE MONEY... TAKE IT...TAKE IT ALL...
WE DON'T WANT YOUR MONEY. WE HAVE A MESSAGE FOR YOU...AND FOR YOUR BASTARD HUSBAND.
HE IS REALLY AN IDIOT, YOUR LITTLE JUDGE...HE'S GOT A DOLL LIKE YOU AT HOME AND HE LEAVES HER ALL ALONE. IT TURNS HIM ON THAT MUCH TO PISS EVERYBODY OFF?
WELL, SINCE HE ISN'T HERE TO TAKE CARE OF YOU...
...WE THOUGHT WE WOULD DO IT FOR HIM.
YOU HAVE THE CHOICE, MY DEAR. EITHER YOU OR YOUR CHILDREN.
42

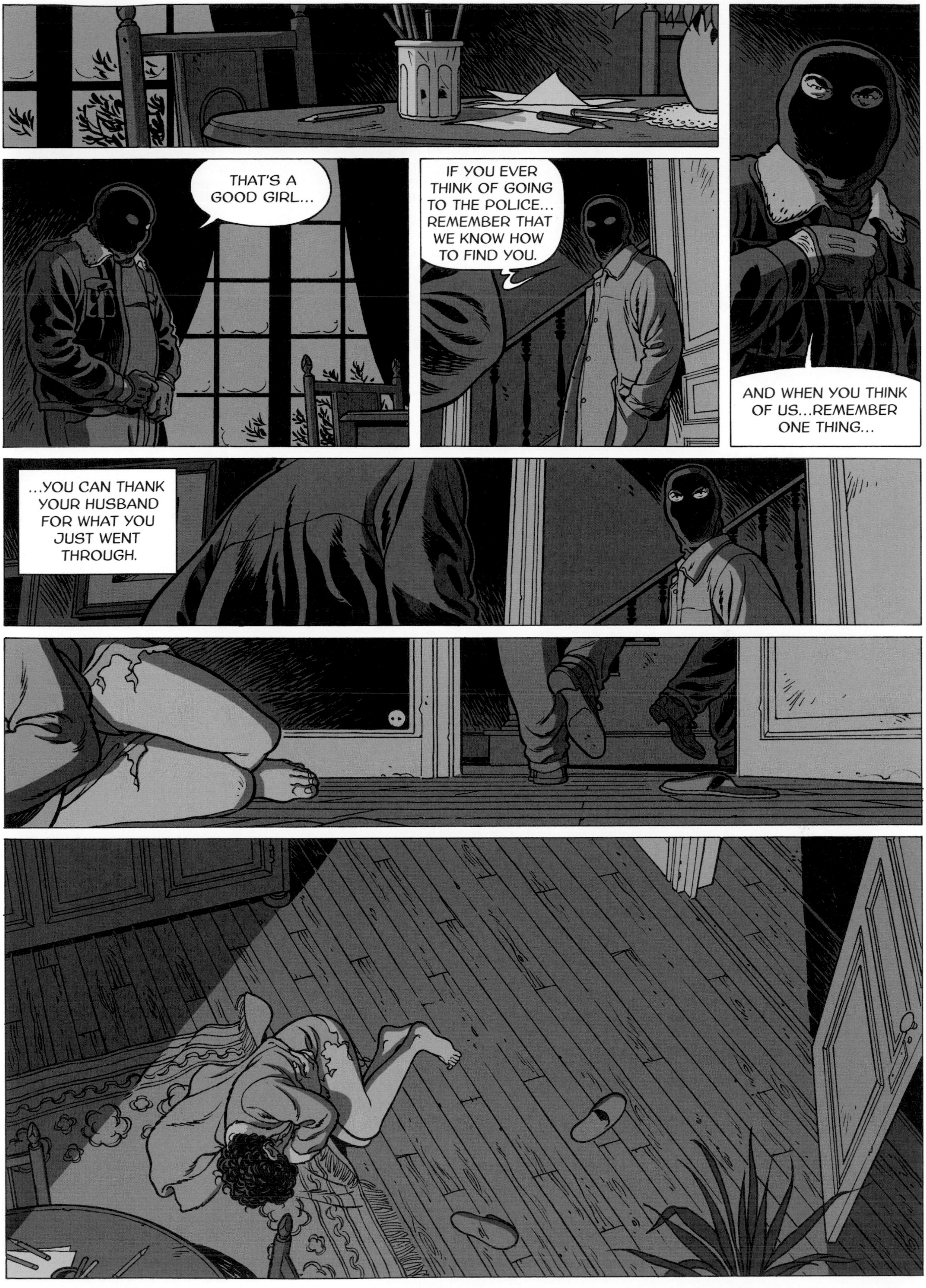
THAT'S A GOOD GIRL...
IF YOU EVER THINK OF GOING TO THE POLICE... REMEMBER THAT WE KNOW HOW TO FIND YOU.
AND WHEN YOU THINK OF US...REMEMBER ONE THING...
...YOU CAN THANK YOUR HUSBAND FOR WHAT YOU JUST WENT THROUGH.

43

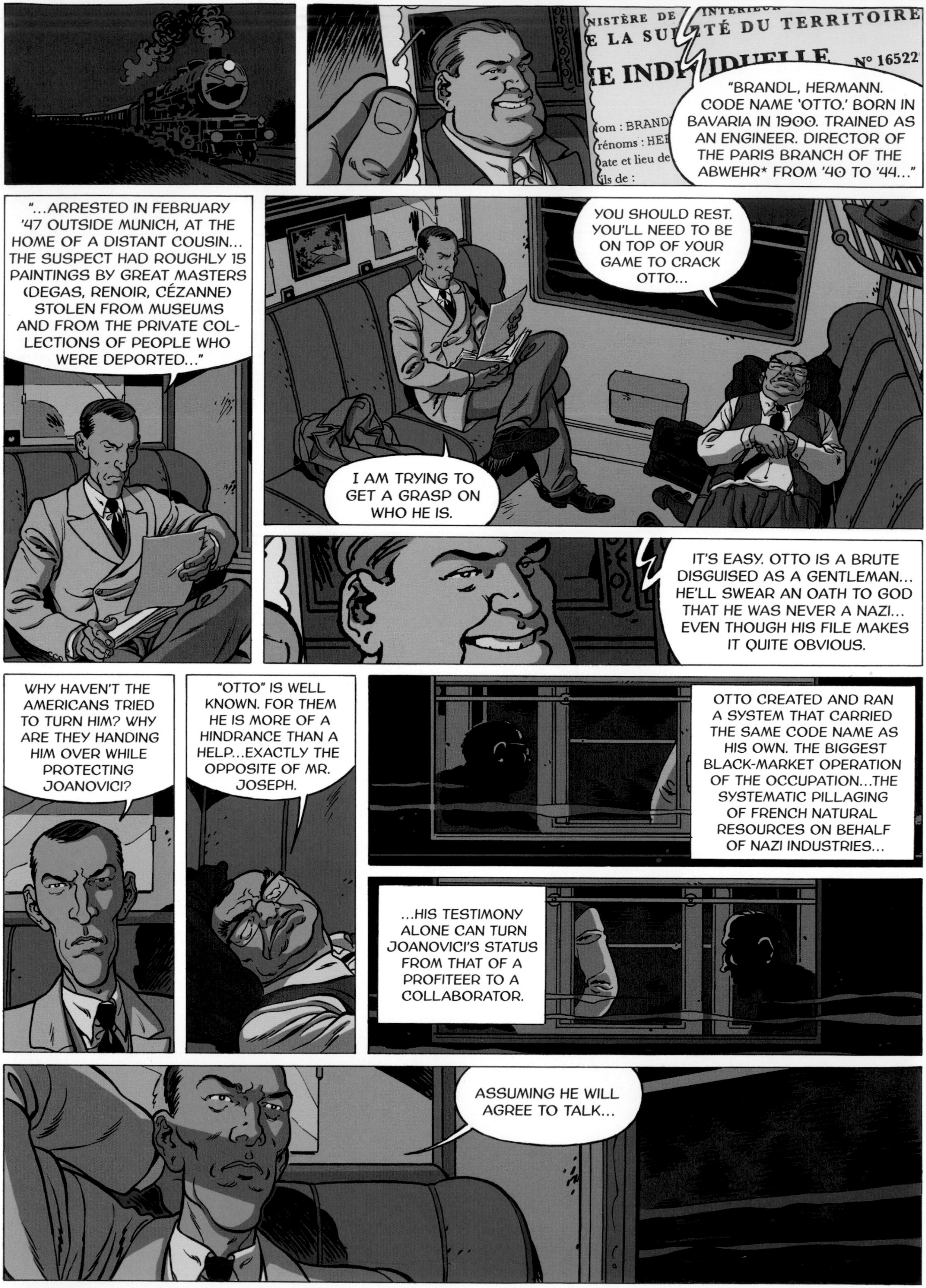
NISTÈRE DE INTÉRIEUR
E LA SÛRETÉ DU TERRITOIRE
E INDIVIDUELLE Nº 16522
om : BRAND
rénoms : HE
ate et lieu de
ils de :
"BRANDL, HERMANN. CODE NAME 'OTTO.' BORN IN BAVARIA IN 1900. TRAINED AS AN ENGINEER. DIRECTOR OF THE PARIS BRANCH OF THE ABWEHR* FROM '40 TO '44..."
"...ARRESTED IN FEBRUARY '47 OUTSIDE MUNICH, AT THE HOME OF A DISTANT COUSIN... THE SUSPECT HAD ROUGHLY 15 PAINTINGS BY GREAT MASTERS (DEGAS, RENOIR, CÉZANNE) STOLEN FROM MUSEUMS AND FROM THE PRIVATE COLLECTIONS OF PEOPLE WHO WERE DEPORTED..."
YOU SHOULD REST. YOU'LL NEED TO BE ON TOP OF YOUR GAME TO CRACK OTTO...
I AM TRYING TO GET A GRASP ON WHO HE IS.
IT'S EASY. OTTO IS A BRUTE DISGUISED AS A GENTLEMAN... HE'LL SWEAR AN OATH TO GOD THAT HE WAS NEVER A NAZI... EVEN THOUGH HIS FILE MAKES IT QUITE OBVIOUS.
WHY HAVEN'T THE AMERICANS TRIED TO TURN HIM? WHY ARE THEY HANDING HIM OVER WHILE PROTECTING JOANOVICI?
"OTTO" IS WELL KNOWN. FOR THEM HE IS MORE OF A HINDRANCE THAN A HELP...EXACTLY THE OPPOSITE OF MR. JOSEPH.
OTTO CREATED AND RAN A SYSTEM THAT CARRIED THE SAME CODE NAME AS HIS OWN. THE BIGGEST BLACK-MARKET OPERATION OF THE OCCUPATION...THE SYSTEMATIC PILLAGING OF FRENCH NATURAL RESOURCES ON BEHALF OF NAZI INDUSTRIES...
...HIS TESTIMONY ALONE CAN TURN JOANOVICI'S STATUS FROM THAT OF A PROFITEER TO A COLLABORATOR.
ASSUMING HE WILL AGREE TO TALK...

*German military intelligence.

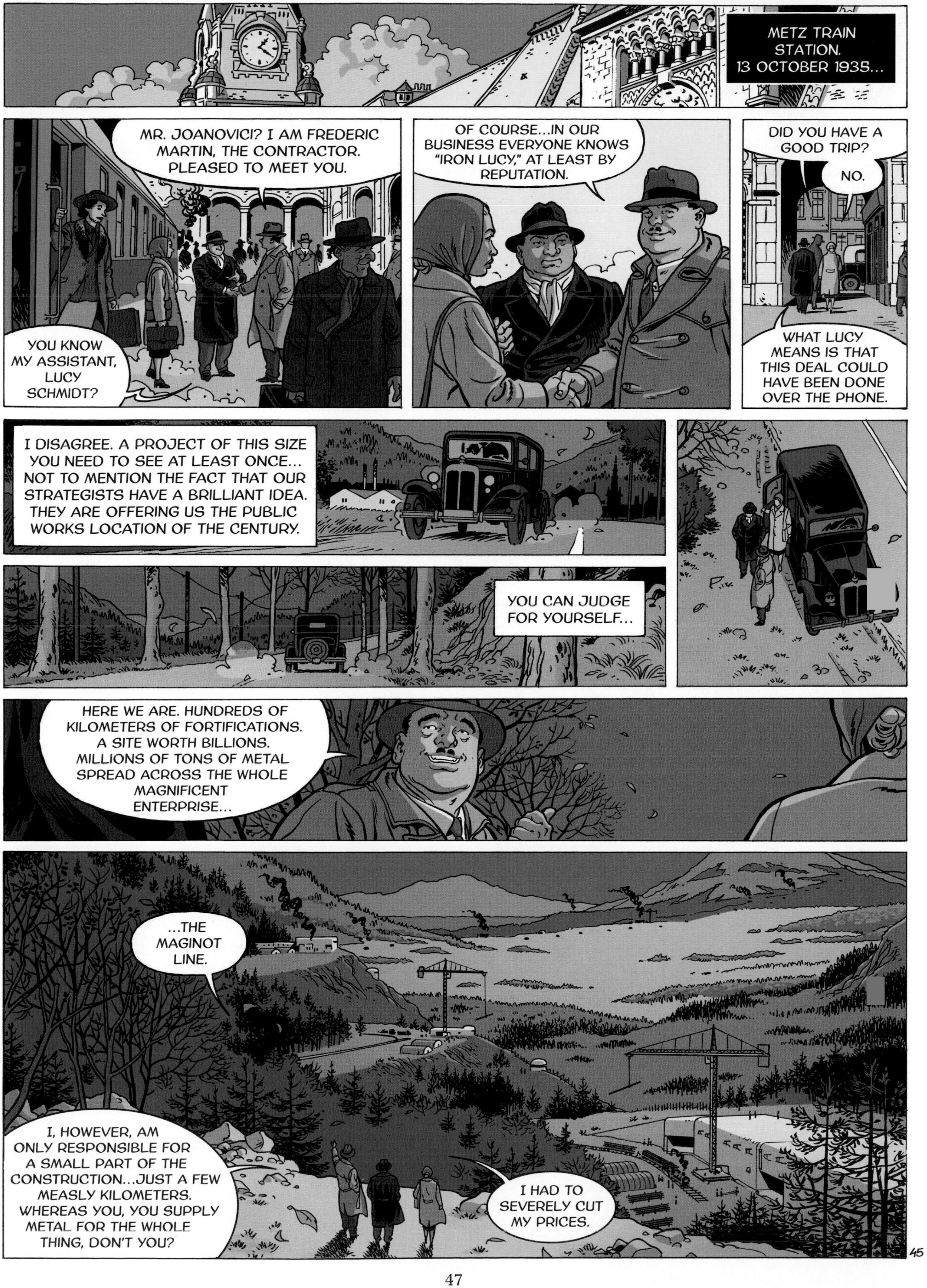
METZ TRAIN STATION. 13 OCTOBER 1935...
MR. JOANOVICI? I AM FREDERIC MARTIN, THE CONTRACTOR. PLEASED TO MEET YOU.
YOU KNOW MY ASSISTANT, LUCY SCHMIDT?
OF COURSE...IN OUR BUSINESS EVERYONE KNOWS "IRON LUCY," AT LEAST BY REPUTATION.
DID YOU HAVE A GOOD TRIP?
NO.
WHAT LUCY MEANS IS THAT THIS DEAL COULD HAVE BEEN DONE OVER THE PHONE.
I DISAGREE. A PROJECT OF THIS SIZE YOU NEED TO SEE AT LEAST ONCE... NOT TO MENTION THE FACT THAT OUR STRATEGISTS HAVE A BRILLIANT IDEA. THEY ARE OFFERING US THE PUBLIC WORKS LOCATION OF THE CENTURY.
YOU CAN JUDGE FOR YOURSELF...
HERE WE ARE. HUNDREDS OF KILOMETERS OF FORTIFICATIONS. A SITE WORTH BILLIONS. MILLIONS OF TONS OF METAL SPREAD ACROSS THE WHOLE MAGNIFICENT ENTERPRISE...
...THE MAGINOT LINE.
I, HOWEVER, AM ONLY RESPONSIBLE FOR A SMALL PART OF THE CONSTRUCTION...JUST A FEW MEASLY KILOMETERS. WHEREAS YOU, YOU SUPPLY METAL FOR THE WHOLE THING, DON'T YOU?
I HAD TO SEVERELY CUT MY PRICES.
45

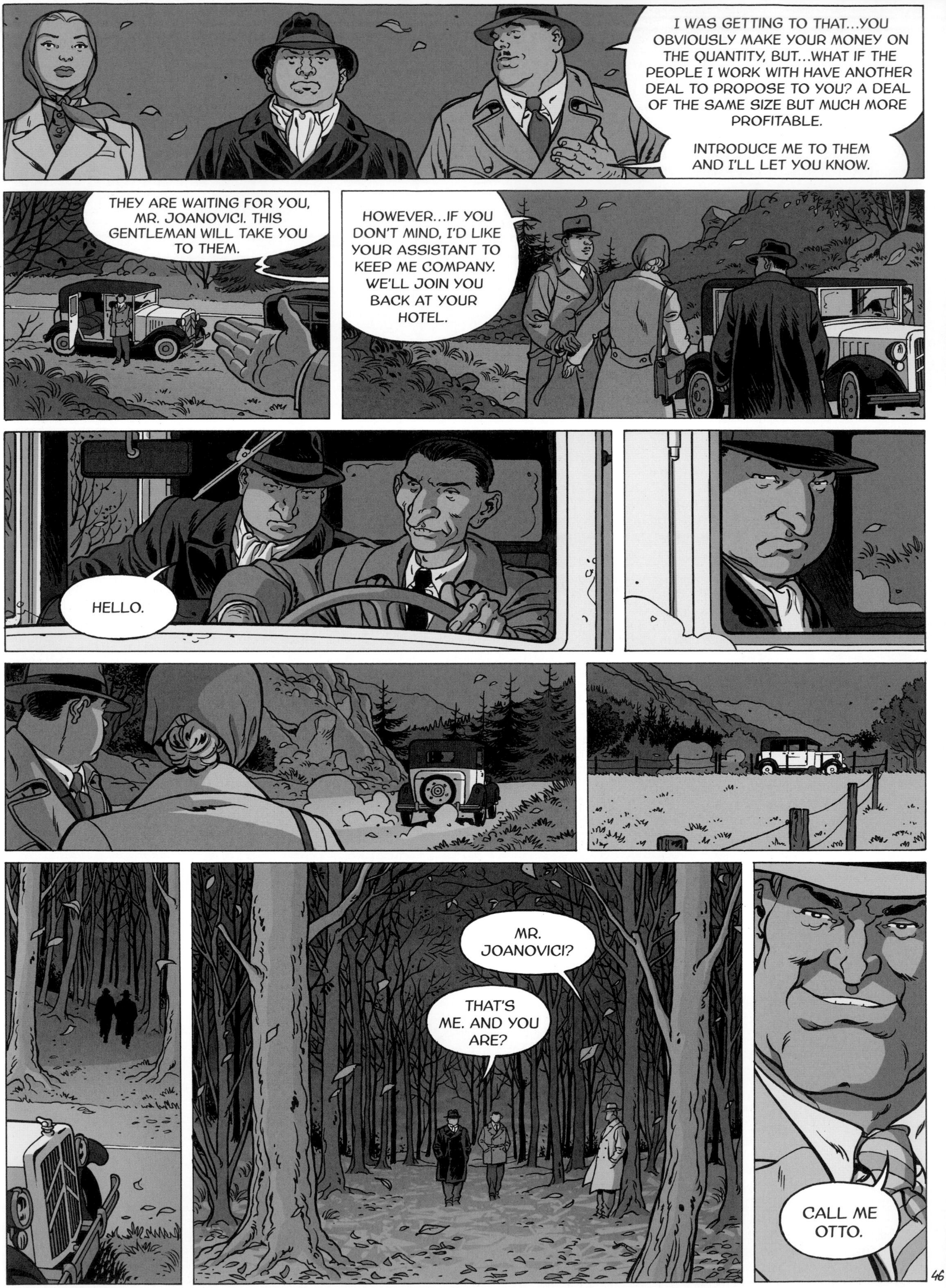
I WAS GETTING TO THAT...YOU OBVIOUSLY MAKE YOUR MONEY ON THE QUANTITY, BUT...WHAT IF THE PEOPLE I WORK WITH HAVE ANOTHER DEAL TO PROPOSE TO YOU? A DEAL OF THE SAME SIZE BUT MUCH MORE PROFITABLE.
INTRODUCE ME TO THEM AND I'LL LET YOU KNOW.
THEY ARE WAITING FOR YOU, MR. JOANOVICI. THIS GENTLEMAN WILL TAKE YOU TO THEM.
HOWEVER...IF YOU DON'T MIND, I'D LIKE YOUR ASSISTANT TO KEEP ME COMPANY. WE'LL JOIN YOU BACK AT YOUR HOTEL.
HELLO.
MR. JOANOVICI?
THAT'S ME. AND YOU ARE?
CALL ME OTTO.
46

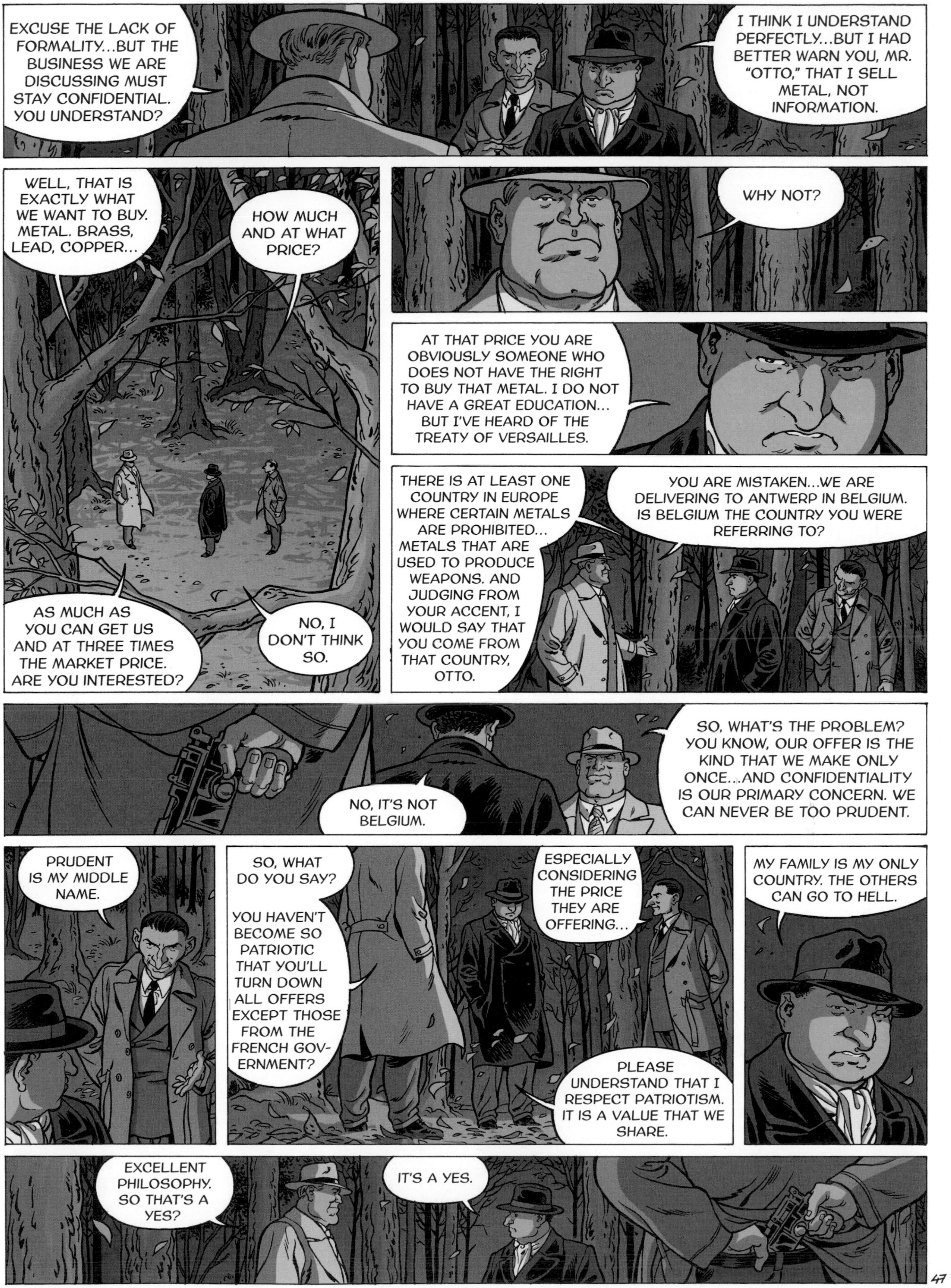
EXCUSE THE LACK OF FORMALITY...BUT THE BUSINESS WE ARE DISCUSSING MUST STAY CONFIDENTIAL. YOU UNDERSTAND?
I THINK I UNDERSTAND PERFECTLY...BUT I HAD BETTER WARN YOU, MR. "OTTO," THAT I SELL METAL, NOT INFORMATION.
WELL, THAT IS EXACTLY WHAT WE WANT TO BUY. METAL. BRASS, LEAD, COPPER...
HOW MUCH AND AT WHAT PRICE?
AS MUCH AS YOU CAN GET US AND AT THREE TIMES THE MARKET PRICE. ARE YOU INTERESTED?
NO, I DON'T THINK SO.
WHY NOT?
AT THAT PRICE YOU ARE OBVIOUSLY SOMEONE WHO DOES NOT HAVE THE RIGHT TO BUY THAT METAL. I DO NOT HAVE A GREAT EDUCATION... BUT I'VE HEARD OF THE TREATY OF VERSAILLES.
YOU ARE MISTAKEN...WE ARE DELIVERING TO ANTWERP IN BELGIUM. IS BELGIUM THE COUNTRY YOU WERE REFERRING TO?
THERE IS AT LEAST ONE COUNTRY IN EUROPE WHERE CERTAIN METALS ARE PROHIBITED... METALS THAT ARE USED TO PRODUCE WEAPONS. AND JUDGING FROM YOUR ACCENT, I WOULD SAY THAT YOU COME FROM THAT COUNTRY, OTTO.
NO, IT'S NOT BELGIUM.
SO, WHAT'S THE PROBLEM? YOU KNOW, OUR OFFER IS THE KIND THAT WE MAKE ONLY ONCE...AND CONFIDENTIALITY IS OUR PRIMARY CONCERN. WE CAN NEVER BE TOO PRUDENT.
PRUDENT IS MY MIDDLE NAME.
SO, WHAT DO YOU SAY?
YOU HAVEN'T BECOME SO PATRIOTIC THAT YOU'LL TURN DOWN ALL OFFERS EXCEPT THOSE FROM THE FRENCH GOVERNMENT?
ESPECIALLY CONSIDERING THE PRICE THEY ARE OFFERING...
PLEASE UNDERSTAND THAT I RESPECT PATRIOTISM. IT IS A VALUE THAT WE SHARE.
MY FAMILY IS MY ONLY COUNTRY. THE OTHERS CAN GO TO HELL.
EXCELLENT PHILOSOPHY. SO THAT'S A YES?
IT'S A YES.
47

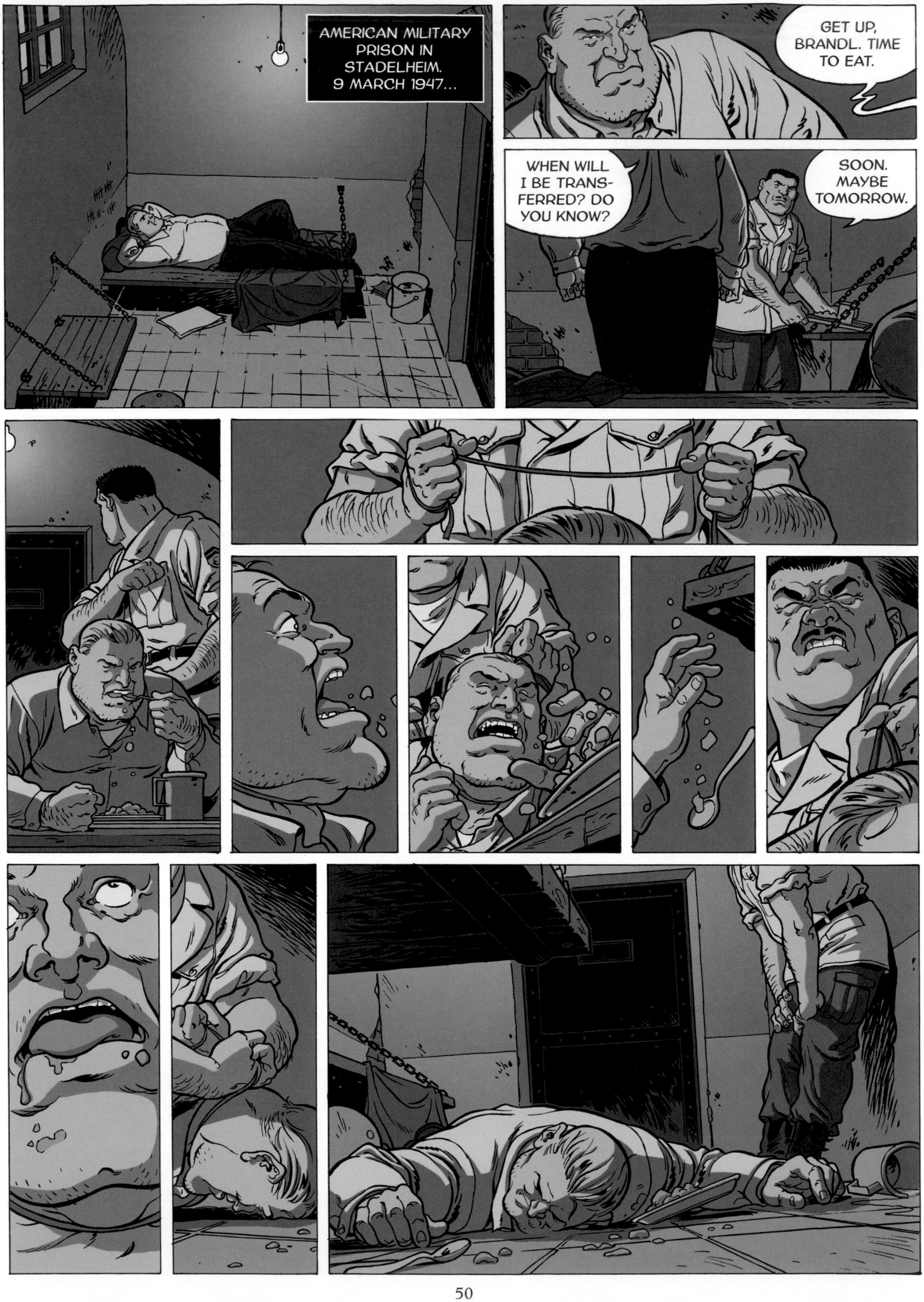
AMERICAN MILITARY PRISON IN STADELHEIM. 9 MARCH 1947...
GET UP, BRANDL. TIME TO EAT.
WHEN WILL I BE TRANS-FERRED? DO YOU KNOW?
SOON. MAYBE TOMORROW.

48

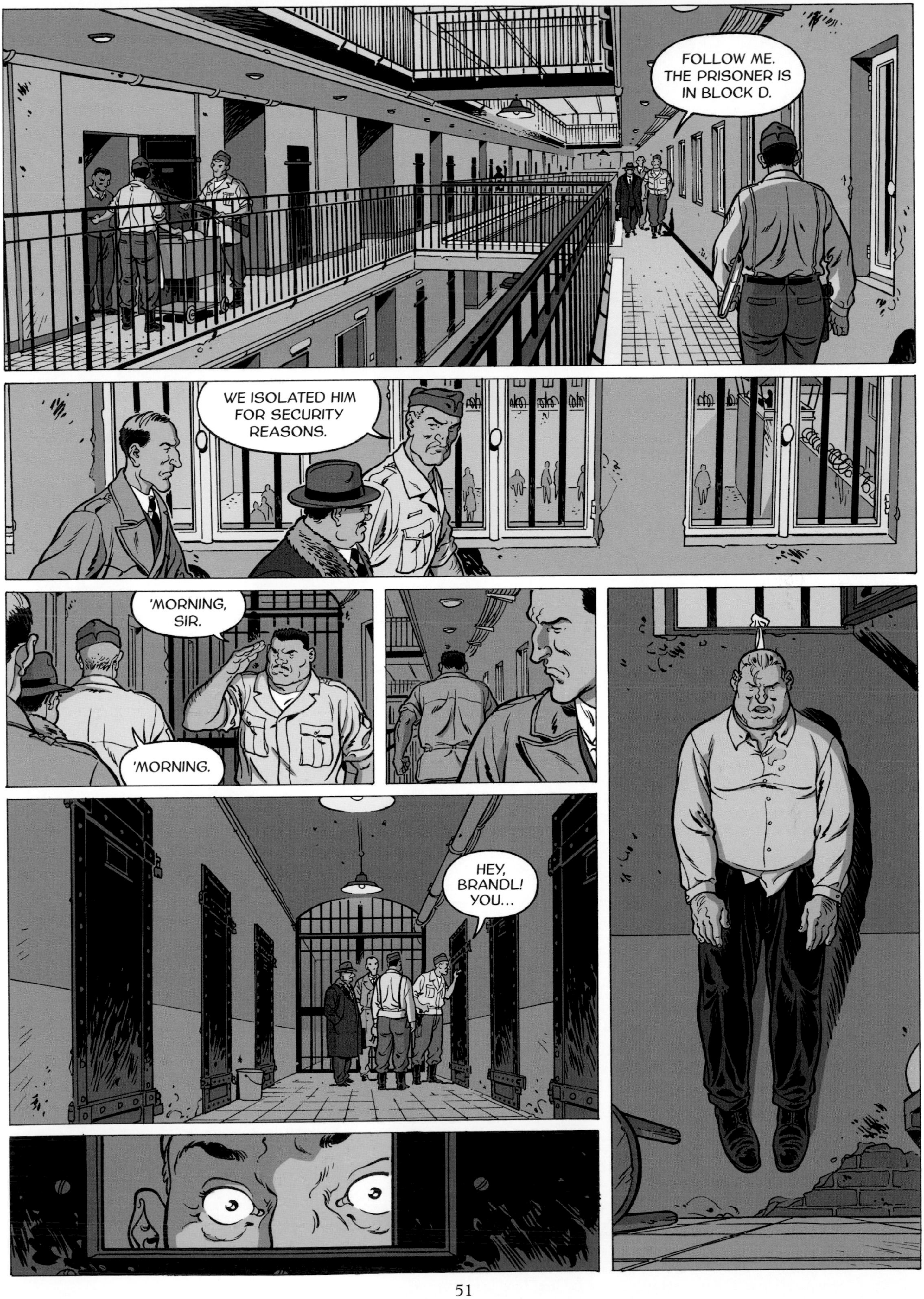
FOLLOW ME. THE PRISONER IS IN BLOCK D.
WE ISOLATED HIM FOR SECURITY REASONS.
'MORNING, SIR.
'MORNING.
HEY, BRANDL! YOU...

49

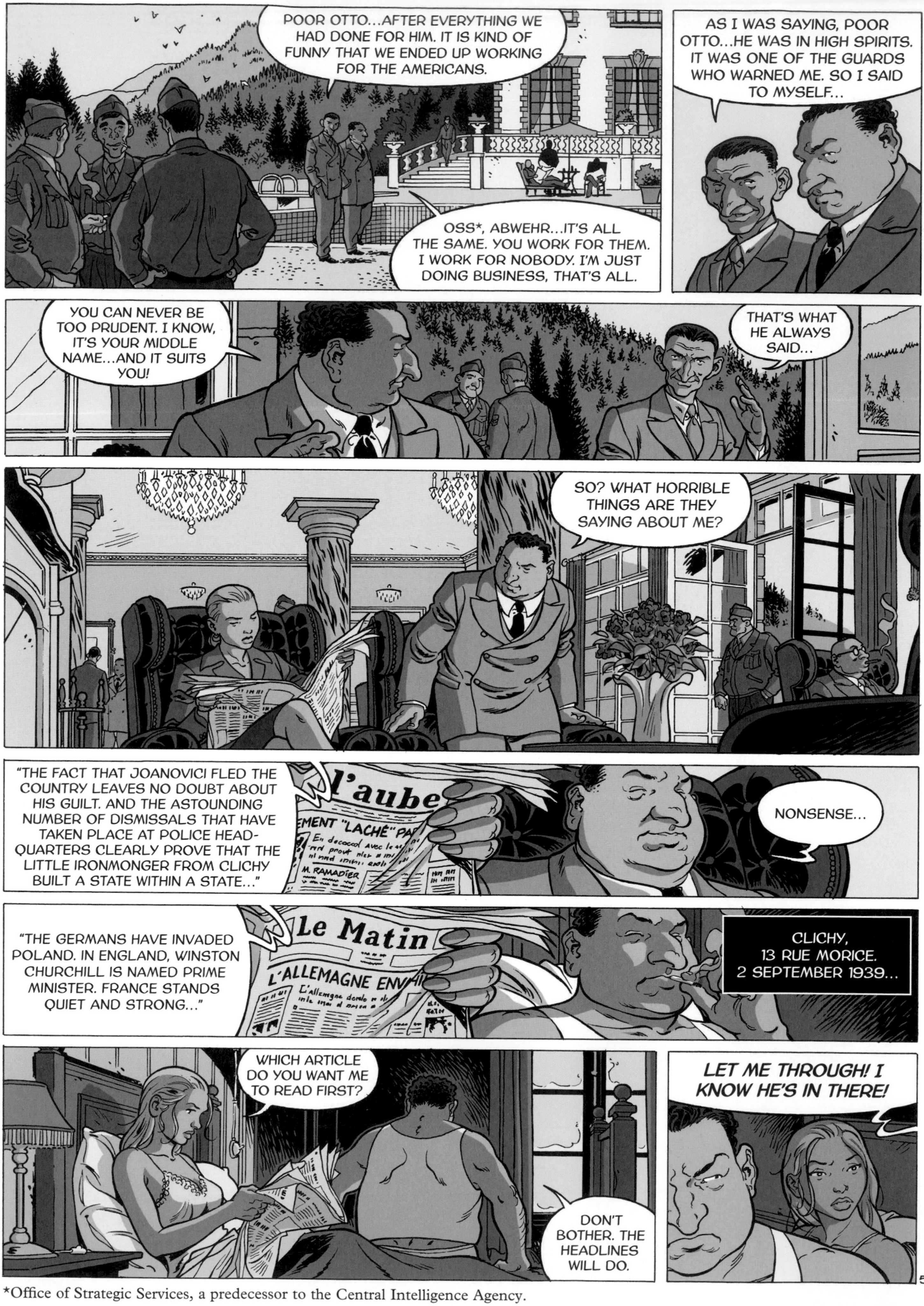
POOR OTTO...AFTER EVERYTHING WE HAD DONE FOR HIM. IT IS KIND OF FUNNY THAT WE ENDED UP WORKING FOR THE AMERICANS.
OSS*, ABWEHR...IT'S ALL THE SAME. YOU WORK FOR THEM. I WORK FOR NOBODY. I'M JUST DOING BUSINESS, THAT'S ALL.
AS I WAS SAYING, POOR OTTO...HE WAS IN HIGH SPIRITS. IT WAS ONE OF THE GUARDS WHO WARNED ME. SO I SAID TO MYSELF...
YOU CAN NEVER BE TOO PRUDENT. I KNOW, IT'S YOUR MIDDLE NAME...AND IT SUITS YOU!
THAT'S WHAT HE ALWAYS SAID...
SO? WHAT HORRIBLE THINGS ARE THEY SAYING ABOUT ME?
"THE FACT THAT JOANOVICI FLED THE COUNTRY LEAVES NO DOUBT ABOUT HIS GUILT. AND THE ASTOUNDING NUMBER OF DISMISSALS THAT HAVE TAKEN PLACE AT POLICE HEAD-QUARTERS CLEARLY PROVE THAT THE LITTLE IRONMONGER FROM CLICHY BUILT A STATE WITHIN A STATE..."
l'aube
EMENT "LACHÉ" PA
M. RAMADIER
NONSENSE...
"THE GERMANS HAVE INVADED POLAND. IN ENGLAND, WINSTON CHURCHILL IS NAMED PRIME MINISTER. FRANCE STANDS QUIET AND STRONG..."
Le Matin
L'ALLEMAGNE ENVH
CLICHY, 13 RUE MORICE. 2 SEPTEMBER 1939...
WHICH ARTICLE DO YOU WANT ME TO READ FIRST?
DON'T BOTHER. THE HEADLINES WILL DO.
LET ME THROUGH! I KNOW HE'S IN THERE!

*Office of Strategic Services, a predecessor to the Central Intelligence Agency.

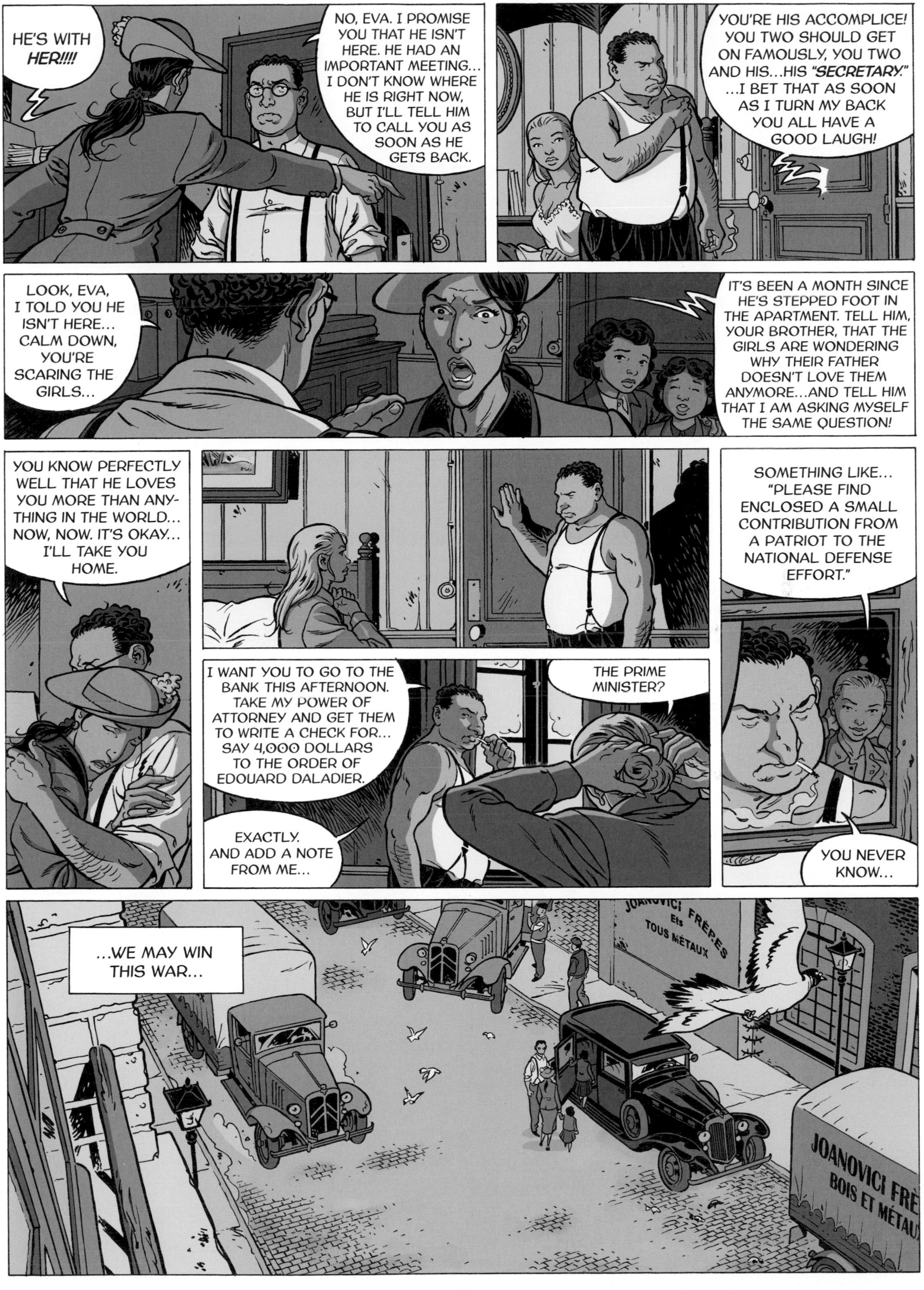
HE'S WITH **HER!!!!**
NO, EVA. I PROMISE YOU THAT HE ISN'T HERE. HE HAD AN IMPORTANT MEETING... I DON'T KNOW WHERE HE IS RIGHT NOW, BUT I'LL TELL HIM TO CALL YOU AS SOON AS HE GETS BACK.
YOU'RE HIS ACCOMPLICE! YOU TWO SHOULD GET ON FAMOUSLY, YOU TWO AND HIS...HIS **"SECRETARY."** ...I BET THAT AS SOON AS I TURN MY BACK YOU ALL HAVE A GOOD LAUGH!
LOOK, EVA, I TOLD YOU HE ISN'T HERE... CALM DOWN, YOU'RE SCARING THE GIRLS...
IT'S BEEN A MONTH SINCE HE'S STEPPED FOOT IN THE APARTMENT. TELL HIM, YOUR BROTHER, THAT THE GIRLS ARE WONDERING WHY THEIR FATHER DOESN'T LOVE THEM ANYMORE...AND TELL HIM THAT I AM ASKING MYSELF THE SAME QUESTION!
YOU KNOW PERFECTLY WELL THAT HE LOVES YOU MORE THAN ANYTHING IN THE WORLD... NOW, NOW. IT'S OKAY... I'LL TAKE YOU HOME.
I WANT YOU TO GO TO THE BANK THIS AFTERNOON. TAKE MY POWER OF ATTORNEY AND GET THEM TO WRITE A CHECK FOR... SAY 4,000 DOLLARS TO THE ORDER OF EDOUARD DALADIER.
THE PRIME MINISTER?
EXACTLY. AND ADD A NOTE FROM ME...
SOMETHING LIKE... "PLEASE FIND ENCLOSED A SMALL CONTRIBUTION FROM A PATRIOT TO THE NATIONAL DEFENSE EFFORT."
YOU NEVER KNOW...
...WE MAY WIN THIS WAR...
JOANOVICI FRÈRES
Ets
TOUS MÉTAUX
JOANOVICI FRÈ
BOIS ET MÉTAU
51

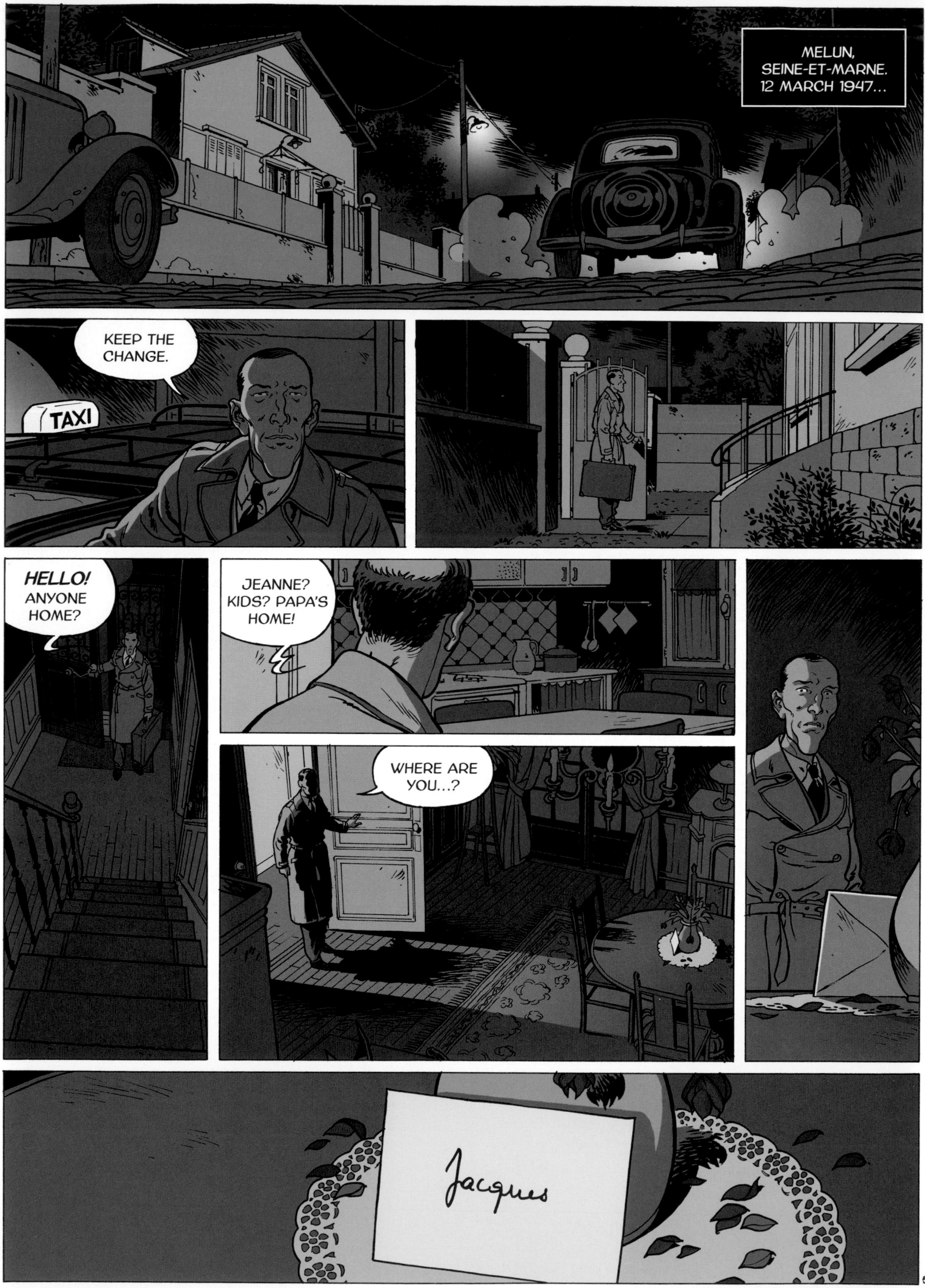
MELUN, SEINE-ET-MARNE. 12 MARCH 1947...
KEEP THE CHANGE.
TAXI
HELLO! ANYONE HOME?
JEANNE? KIDS? PAPA'S HOME!
WHERE ARE YOU...?
Jacques

52

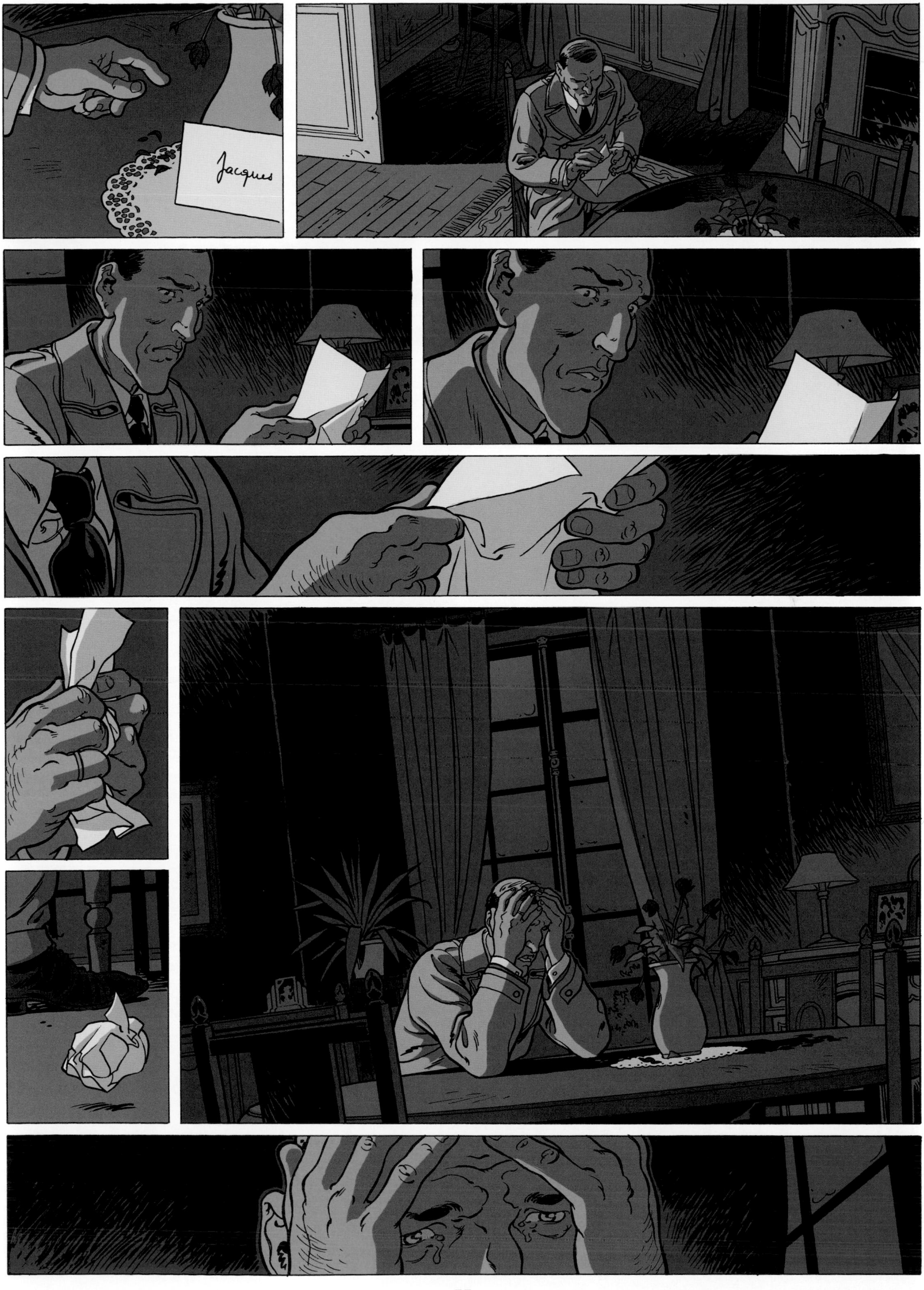
Jacques

53

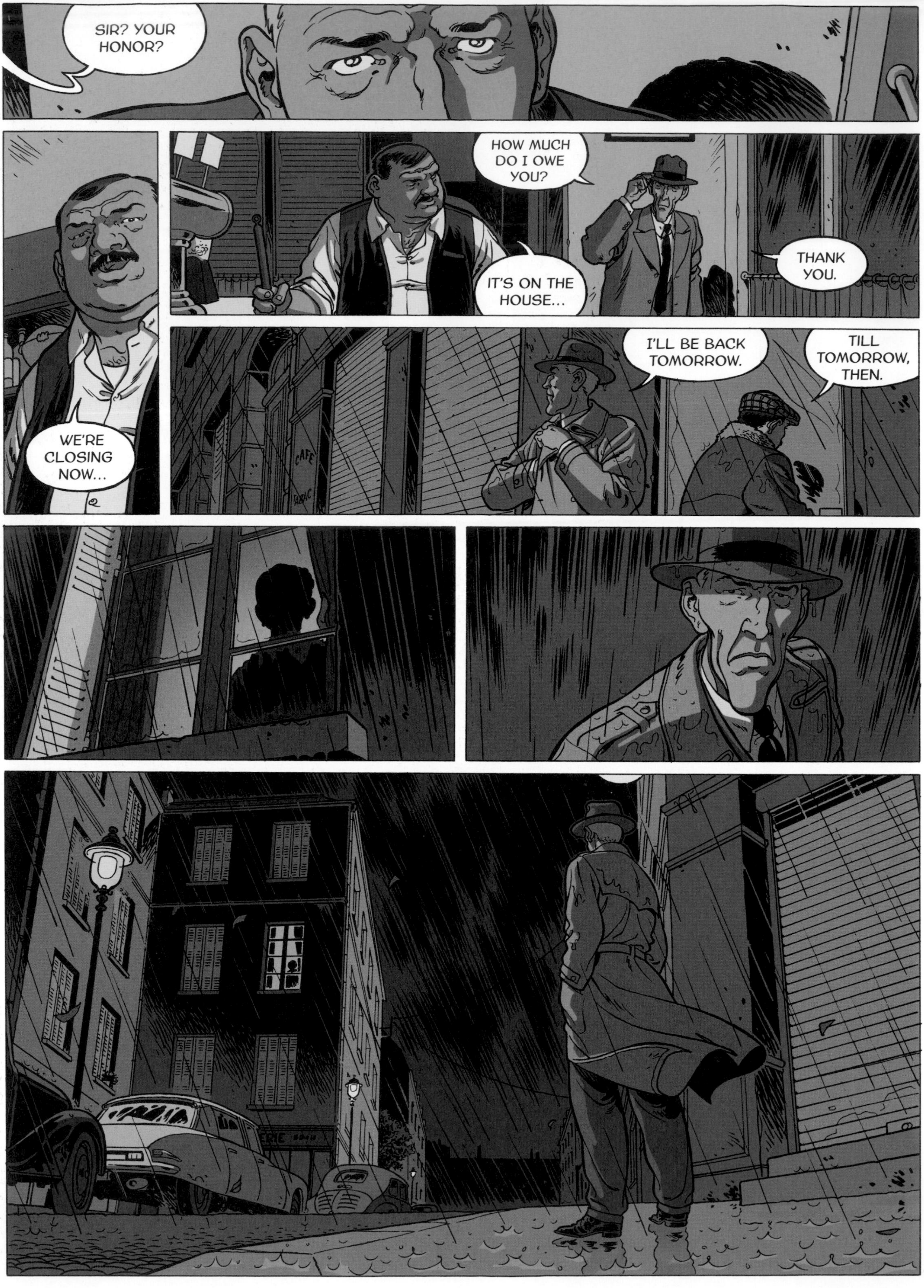
SIR? YOUR HONOR?
WE'RE CLOSING NOW...
HOW MUCH DO I OWE YOU?
IT'S ON THE HOUSE...
THANK YOU.
I'LL BE BACK TOMORROW.
TILL TOMORROW, THEN.
54

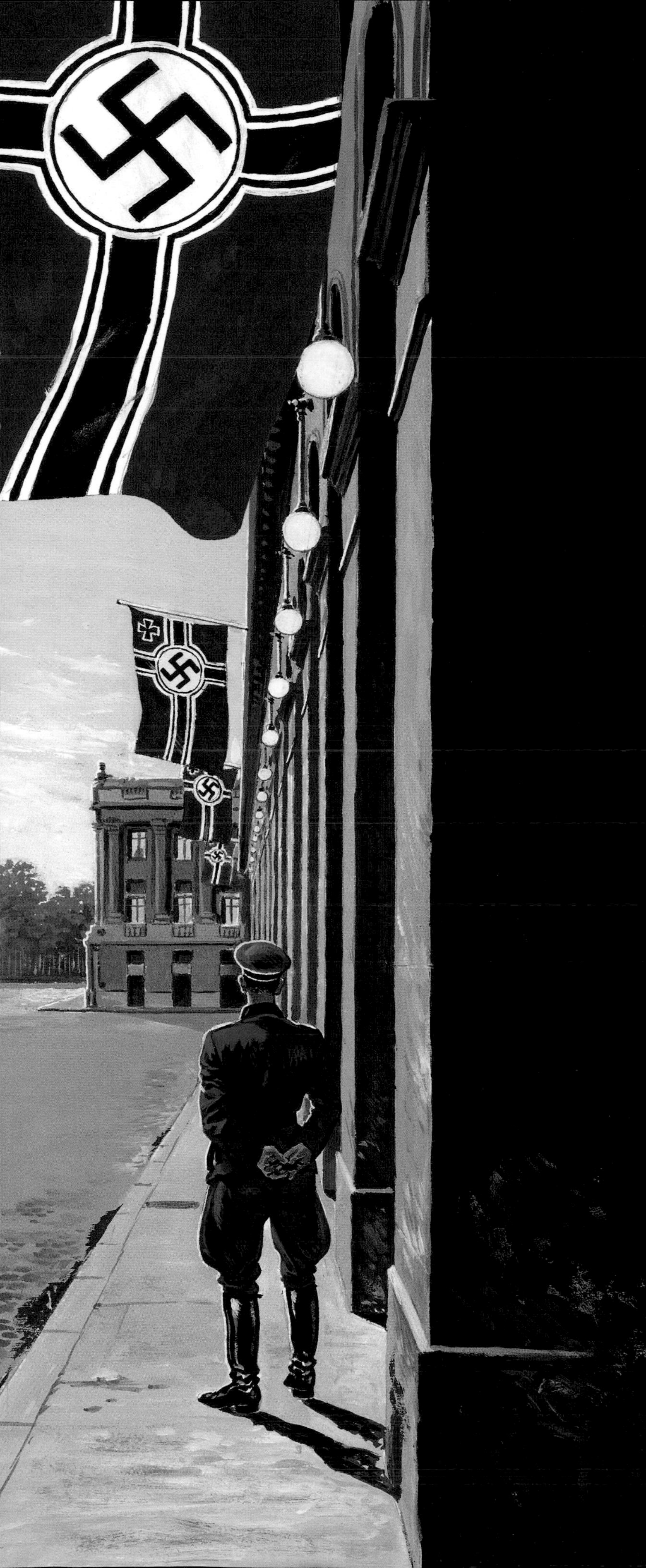

"Friend, do you hear the black flight of the crows over our plains?
Friend, do you hear the dull cries of the country enchained?"

THE PARTISANS' SONG

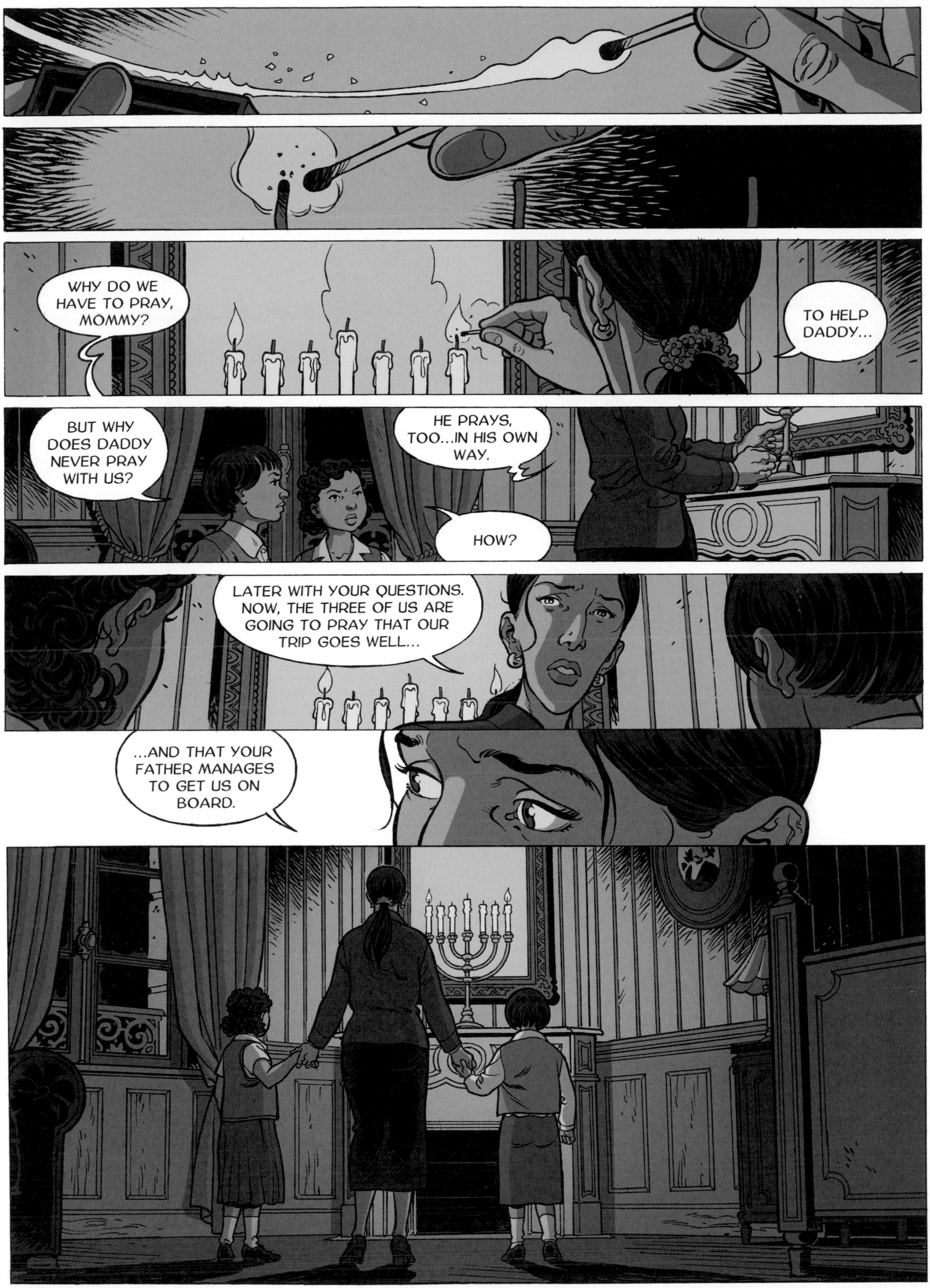
WHY DO WE HAVE TO PRAY, MOMMY?
TO HELP DADDY...
BUT WHY DOES DADDY NEVER PRAY WITH US?
HE PRAYS, TOO...IN HIS OWN WAY.
HOW?
LATER WITH YOUR QUESTIONS. NOW, THE THREE OF US ARE GOING TO PRAY THAT OUR TRIP GOES WELL...
...AND THAT YOUR FATHER MANAGES TO GET US ON BOARD.

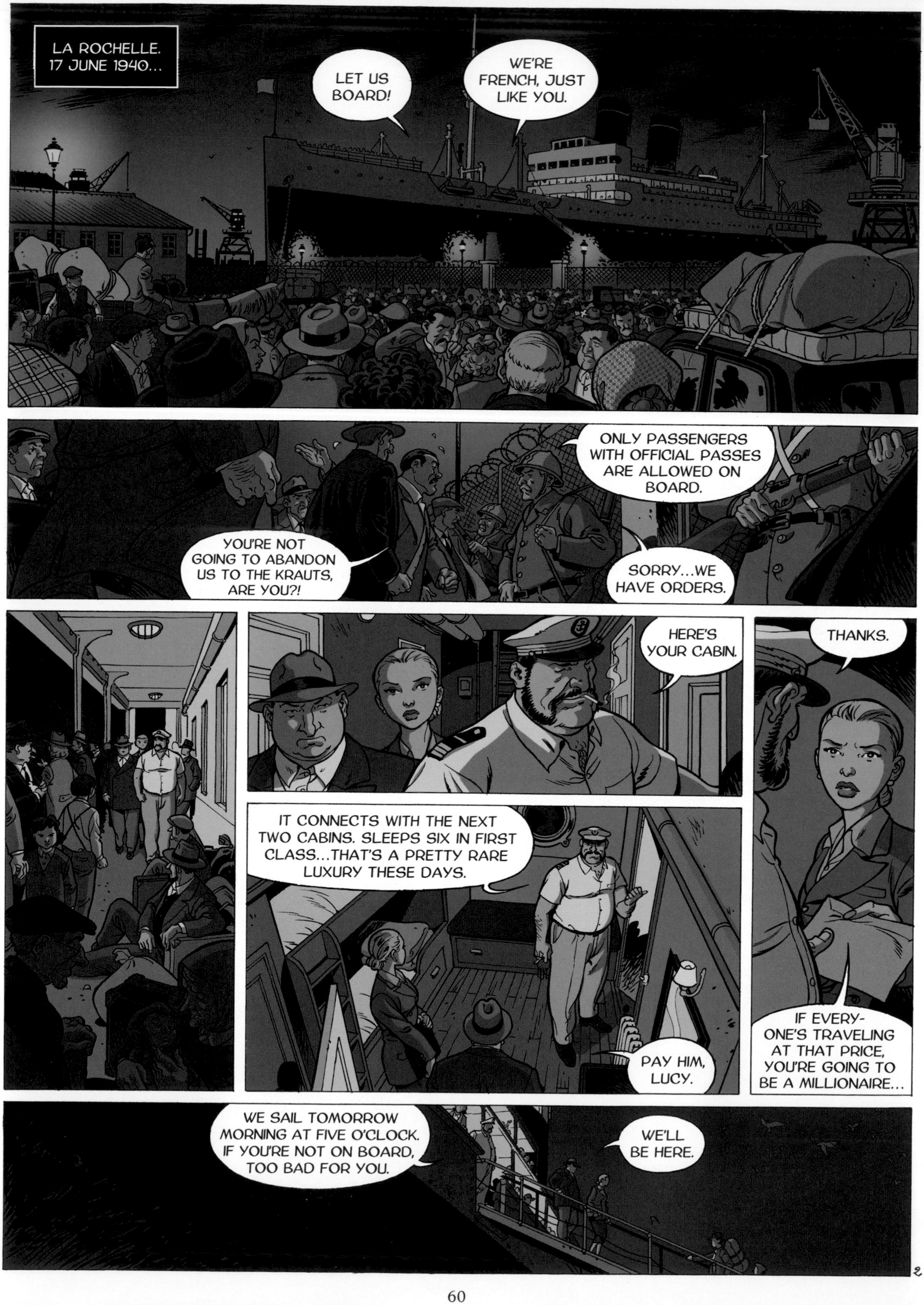
LA ROCHELLE. 17 JUNE 1940...
LET US BOARD!
WE'RE FRENCH, JUST LIKE YOU.
ONLY PASSENGERS WITH OFFICIAL PASSES ARE ALLOWED ON BOARD.
YOU'RE NOT GOING TO ABANDON US TO THE KRAUTS, ARE YOU?!
SORRY...WE HAVE ORDERS.
HERE'S YOUR CABIN.
IT CONNECTS WITH THE NEXT TWO CABINS. SLEEPS SIX IN FIRST CLASS...THAT'S A PRETTY RARE LUXURY THESE DAYS.
PAY HIM, LUCY.
THANKS.
IF EVERY-ONE'S TRAVELING AT THAT PRICE, YOU'RE GOING TO BE A MILLIONAIRE...
WE SAIL TOMORROW MORNING AT FIVE O'CLOCK. IF YOU'RE NOT ON BOARD, TOO BAD FOR YOU.
WE'LL BE HERE.
2

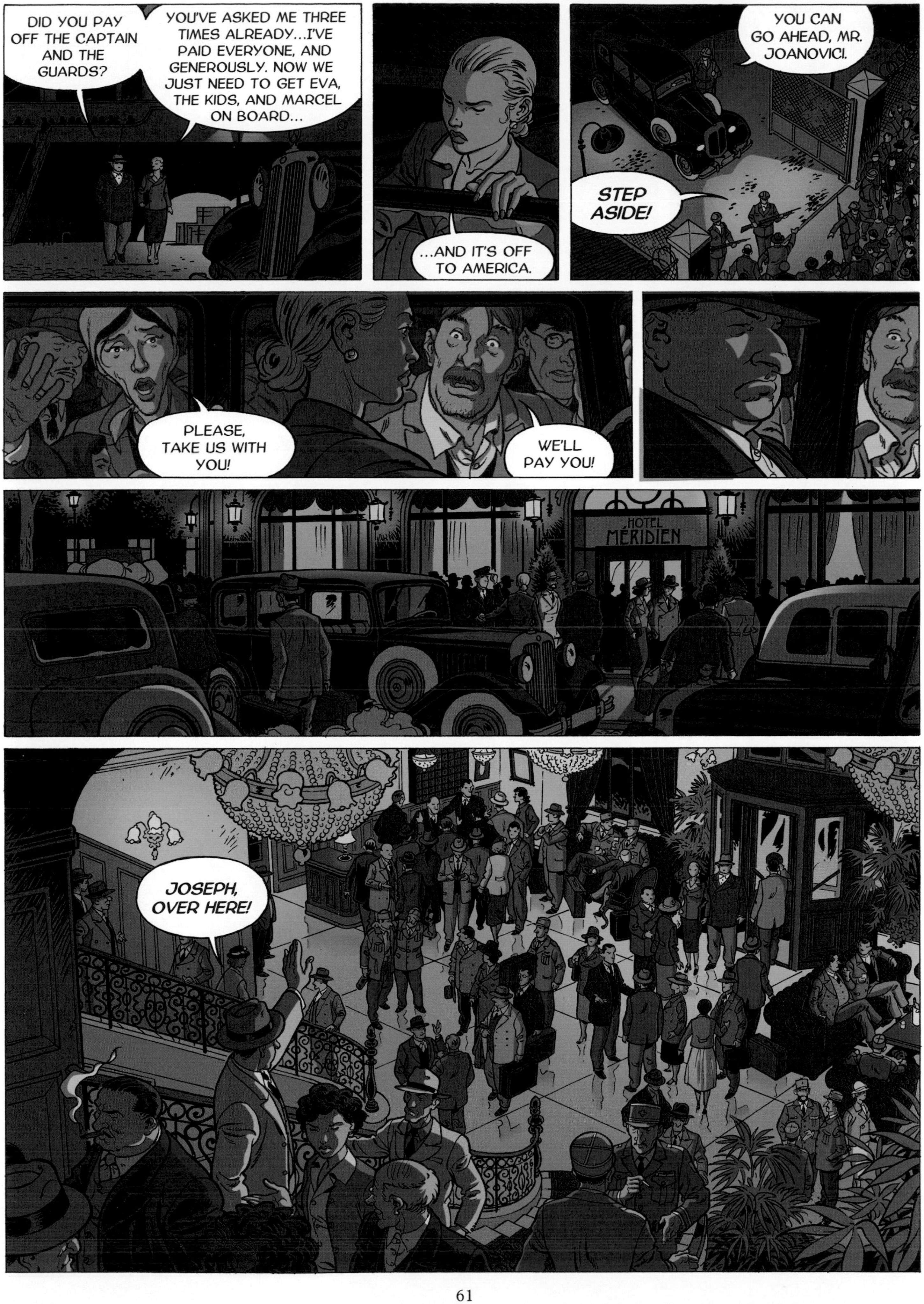
DID YOU PAY OFF THE CAPTAIN AND THE GUARDS?
YOU'VE ASKED ME THREE TIMES ALREADY...I'VE PAID EVERYONE, AND GENEROUSLY. NOW WE JUST NEED TO GET EVA, THE KIDS, AND MARCEL ON BOARD...
...AND IT'S OFF TO AMERICA.
YOU CAN GO AHEAD, MR. JOANOVICI.
STEP ASIDE!
PLEASE, TAKE US WITH YOU!
WE'LL PAY YOU!
HOTEL MÉRIDIEN
JOSEPH, OVER HERE!
3

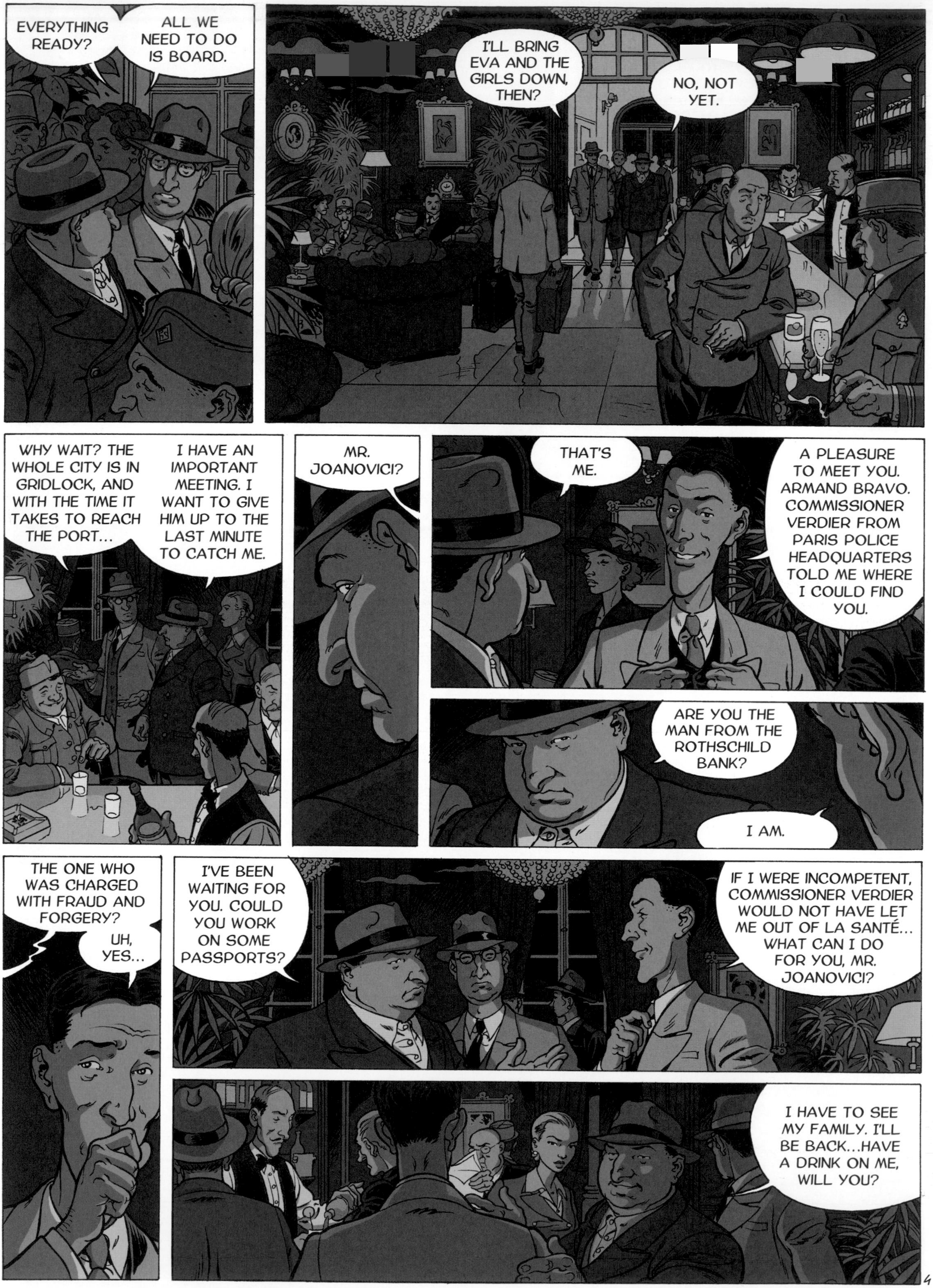

EVERYTHING READY?
ALL WE NEED TO DO IS BOARD.
I'LL BRING EVA AND THE GIRLS DOWN, THEN?
NO, NOT YET.
WHY WAIT? THE WHOLE CITY IS IN GRIDLOCK, AND WITH THE TIME IT TAKES TO REACH THE PORT...
I HAVE AN IMPORTANT MEETING. I WANT TO GIVE HIM UP TO THE LAST MINUTE TO CATCH ME.
MR. JOANOVICI?
THAT'S ME.
A PLEASURE TO MEET YOU. ARMAND BRAVO. COMMISSIONER VERDIER FROM PARIS POLICE HEADQUARTERS TOLD ME WHERE I COULD FIND YOU.
ARE YOU THE MAN FROM THE ROTHSCHILD BANK?
I AM.
THE ONE WHO WAS CHARGED WITH FRAUD AND FORGERY?
UH, YES...
I'VE BEEN WAITING FOR YOU. COULD YOU WORK ON SOME PASSPORTS?
IF I WERE INCOMPETENT, COMMISSIONER VERDIER WOULD NOT HAVE LET ME OUT OF LA SANTÉ... WHAT CAN I DO FOR YOU, MR. JOANOVICI?
I HAVE TO SEE MY FAMILY. I'LL BE BACK...HAVE A DRINK ON ME, WILL YOU?

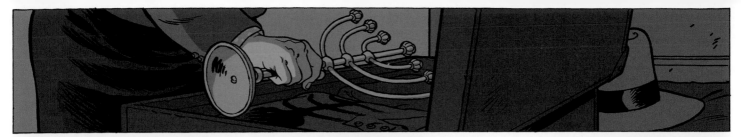

THE GIRLS ARE READY AND THE BAGS ARE PACKED. ALL WE NEED TO DO NOW IS GO DOWN-STAIRS...

WE'RE NOT GOING.

Y...YOU'RE KIDDING?!

MARCEL WILL STAY WITH YOU. I AM GOING BACK TO PARIS TO GET THINGS UP AND RUNNING AGAIN. WHEN ALL IS CALM... I'LL COME BACK FOR YOU.

WHEN DID YOU DECIDE THIS?

JUST NOW.

YOU'RE COMPLETELY CRAZY!...

...DO YOU REALIZE WHAT THE NAZIS ARE GOING TO DO TO US IF WE STAY? YOU MUST HAVE SOME IDEA, DON'T YOU?!

I KNOW THE GERMANS. I'VE BEEN WORKING WITH THEM FOR YEARS. THEY'VE ALWAYS BEEN REASONABLE.

5

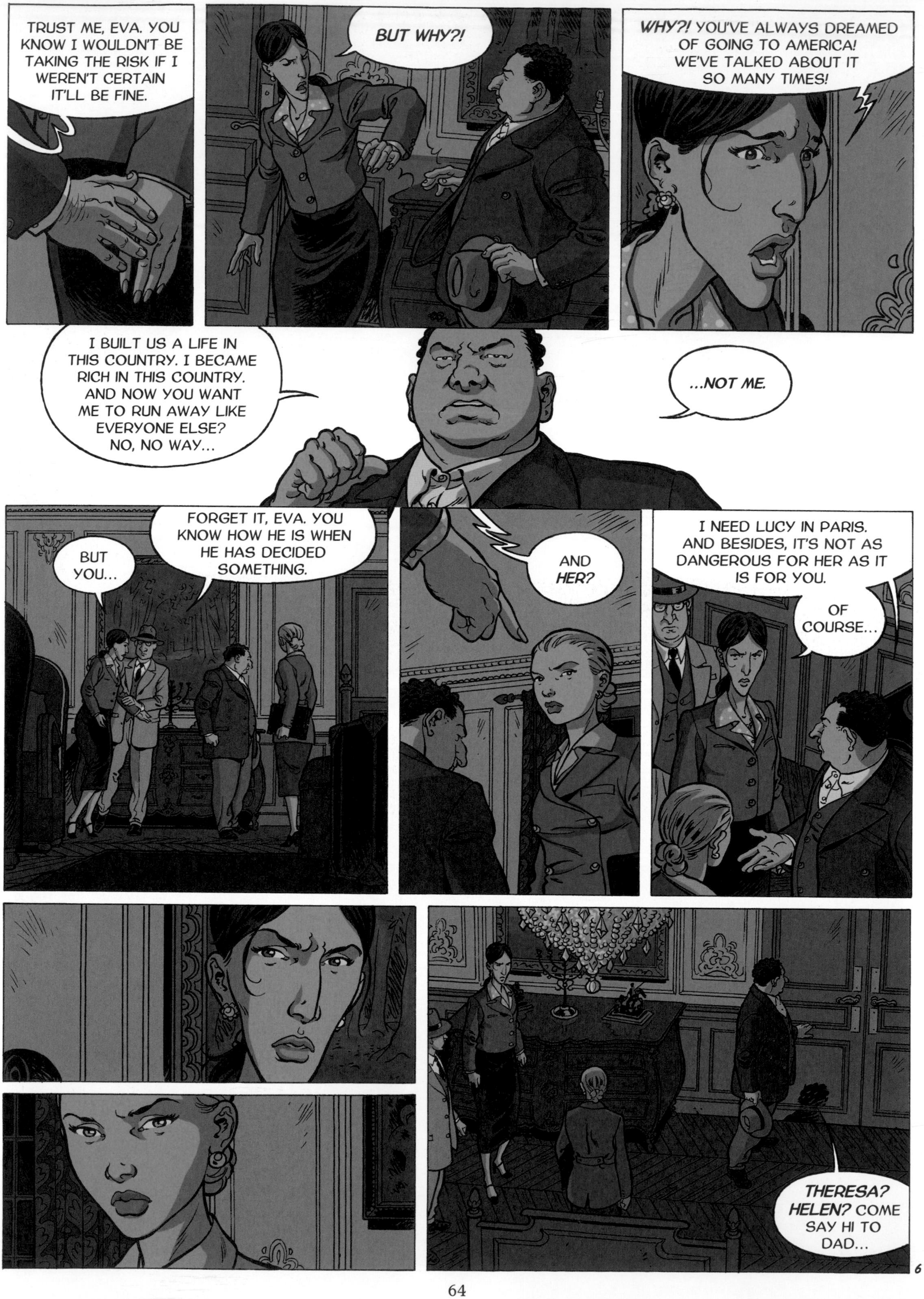
TRUST ME, EVA. YOU KNOW I WOULDN'T BE TAKING THE RISK IF I WEREN'T CERTAIN IT'LL BE FINE.
BUT WHY?!
WHY?! YOU'VE ALWAYS DREAMED OF GOING TO AMERICA! WE'VE TALKED ABOUT IT SO MANY TIMES!
I BUILT US A LIFE IN THIS COUNTRY. I BECAME RICH IN THIS COUNTRY. AND NOW YOU WANT ME TO RUN AWAY LIKE EVERYONE ELSE? NO, NO WAY...
...NOT ME.
BUT YOU...
FORGET IT, EVA. YOU KNOW HOW HE IS WHEN HE HAS DECIDED SOMETHING.
AND HER?
I NEED LUCY IN PARIS. AND BESIDES, IT'S NOT AS DANGEROUS FOR HER AS IT IS FOR YOU.
OF COURSE...
THERESA? HELEN? COME SAY HI TO DAD...
6

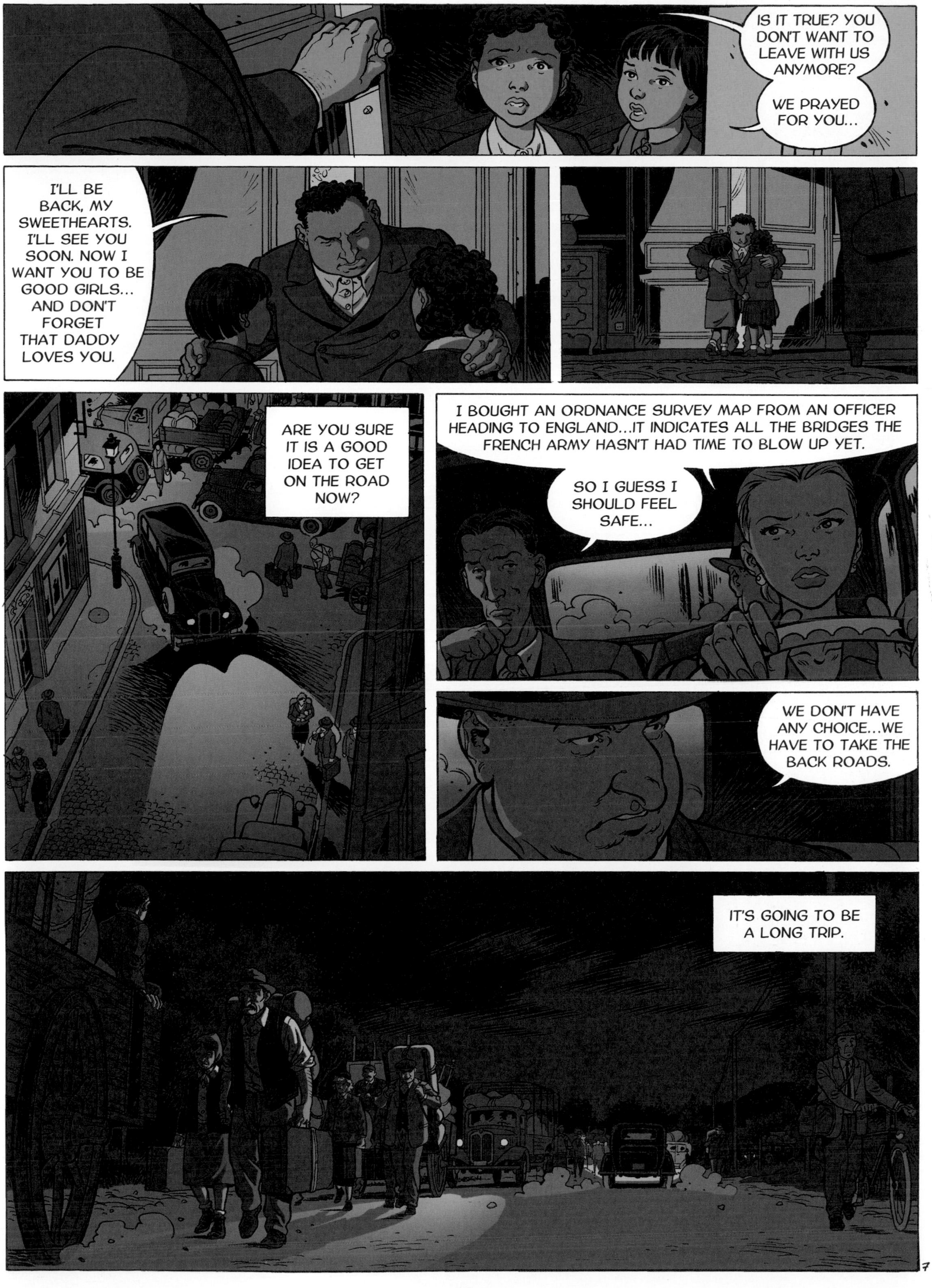
IS IT TRUE? YOU DON'T WANT TO LEAVE WITH US ANYMORE?
WE PRAYED FOR YOU...
I'LL BE BACK, MY SWEETHEARTS. I'LL SEE YOU SOON. NOW I WANT YOU TO BE GOOD GIRLS... AND DON'T FORGET THAT DADDY LOVES YOU.
ARE YOU SURE IT IS A GOOD IDEA TO GET ON THE ROAD NOW?
I BOUGHT AN ORDNANCE SURVEY MAP FROM AN OFFICER HEADING TO ENGLAND...IT INDICATES ALL THE BRIDGES THE FRENCH ARMY HASN'T HAD TIME TO BLOW UP YET.
SO I GUESS I SHOULD FEEL SAFE...
WE DON'T HAVE ANY CHOICE...WE HAVE TO TAKE THE BACK ROADS.
IT'S GOING TO BE A LONG TRIP.
7

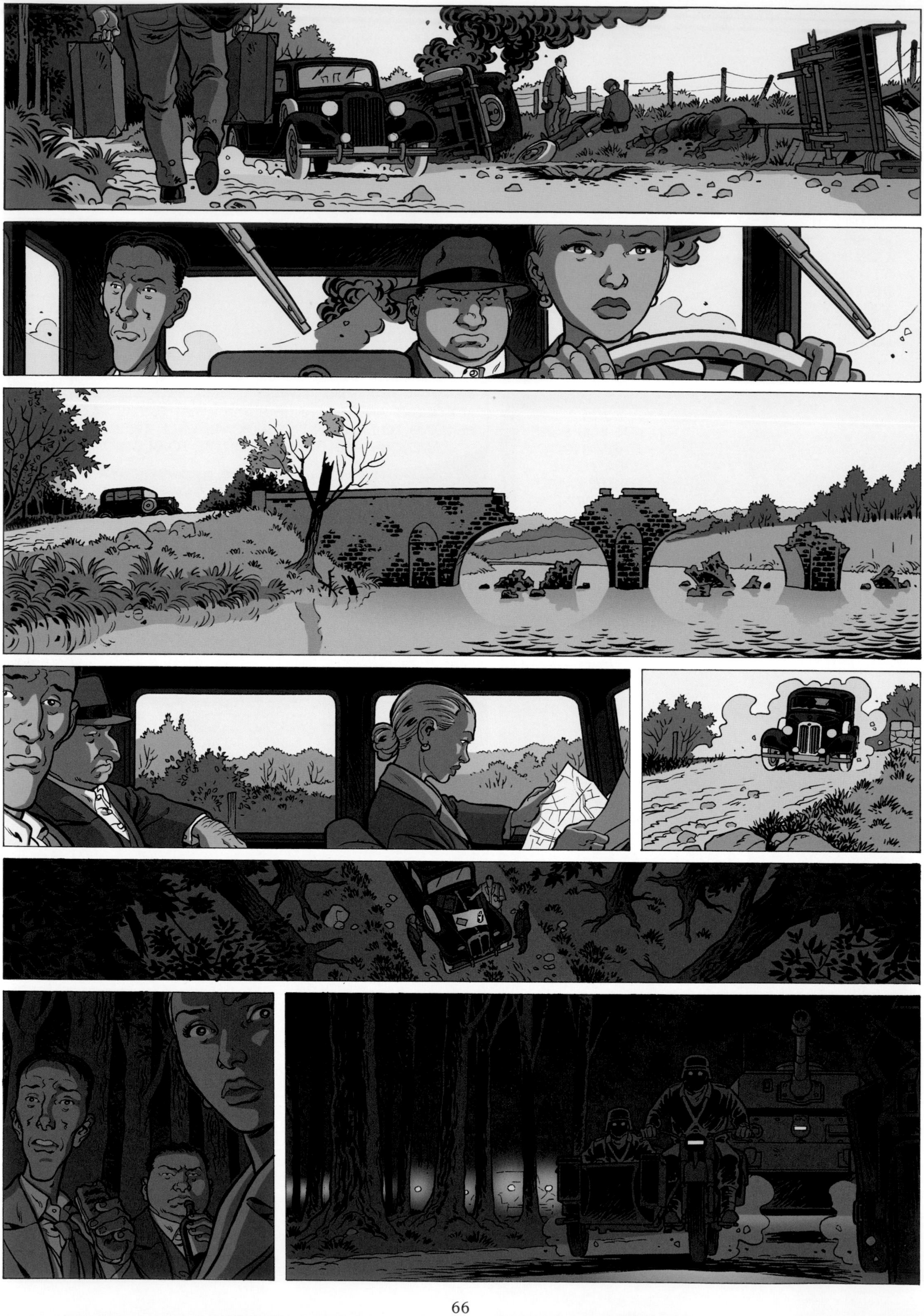

8

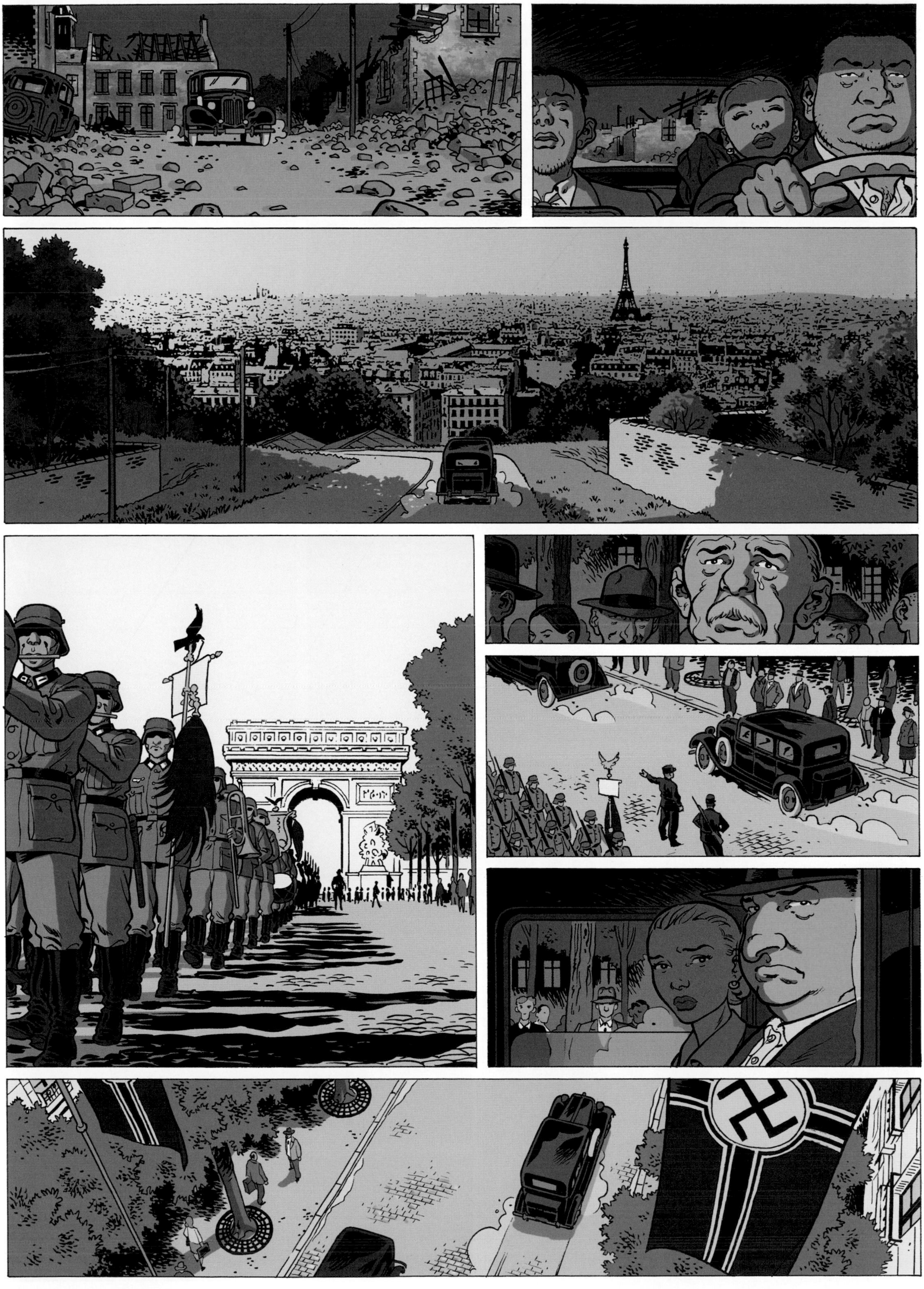

9

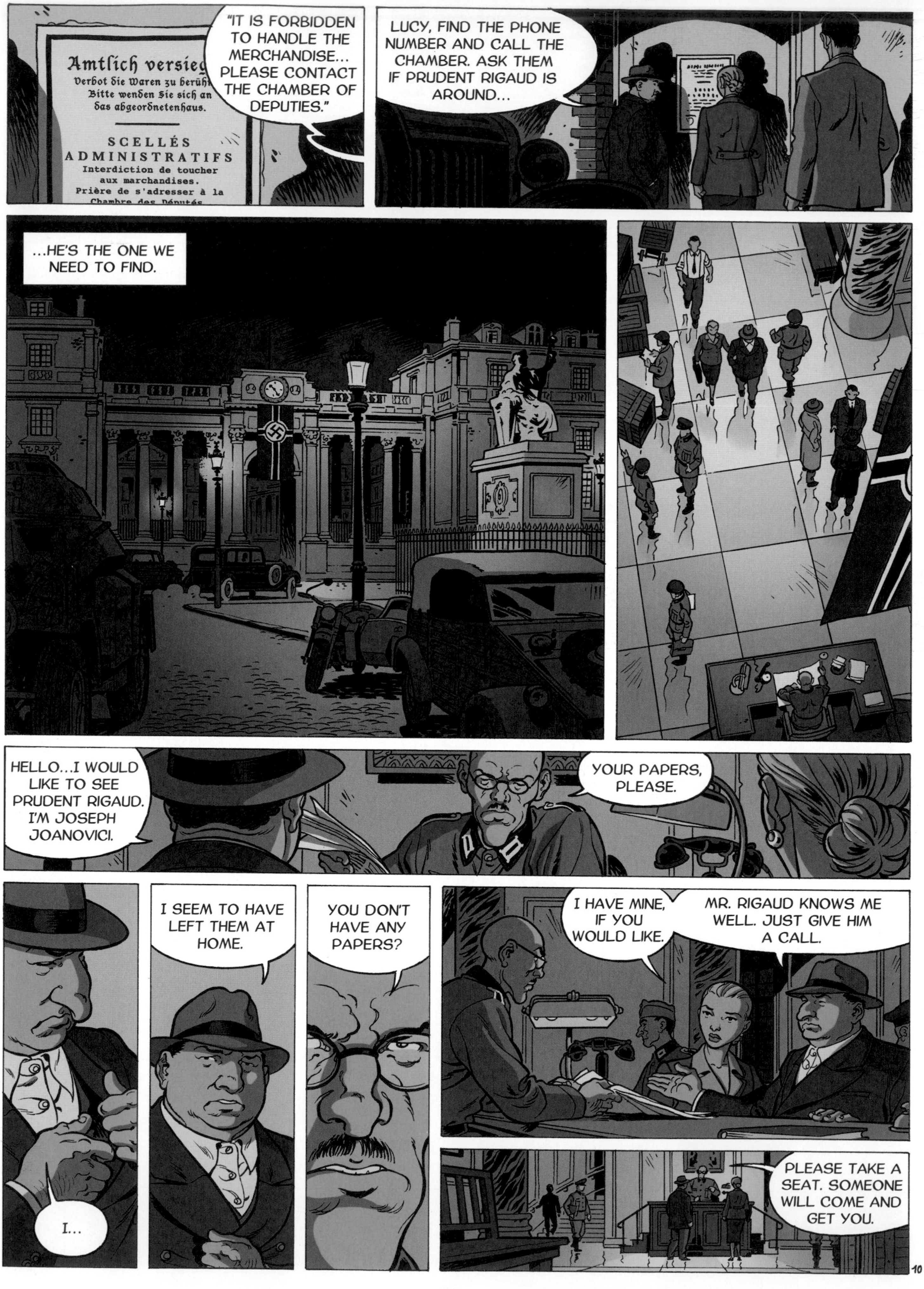
Amtlich versieg
Verbot die Waren zu berühr
Bitte wenden Sie sich an
das abgeordnetenhaus.
SCELLÉS
ADMINISTRATIFS
Interdiction de toucher
aux marchandises.
Prière de s'adresser à la
"IT IS FORBIDDEN TO HANDLE THE MERCHANDISE... PLEASE CONTACT THE CHAMBER OF DEPUTIES."
LUCY, FIND THE PHONE NUMBER AND CALL THE CHAMBER. ASK THEM IF PRUDENT RIGAUD IS AROUND...
...HE'S THE ONE WE NEED TO FIND.
HELLO...I WOULD LIKE TO SEE PRUDENT RIGAUD. I'M JOSEPH JOANOVICI.
YOUR PAPERS, PLEASE.
I...
I SEEM TO HAVE LEFT THEM AT HOME.
YOU DON'T HAVE ANY PAPERS?
I HAVE MINE, IF YOU WOULD LIKE.
MR. RIGAUD KNOWS ME WELL. JUST GIVE HIM A CALL.
PLEASE TAKE A SEAT. SOMEONE WILL COME AND GET YOU.
10

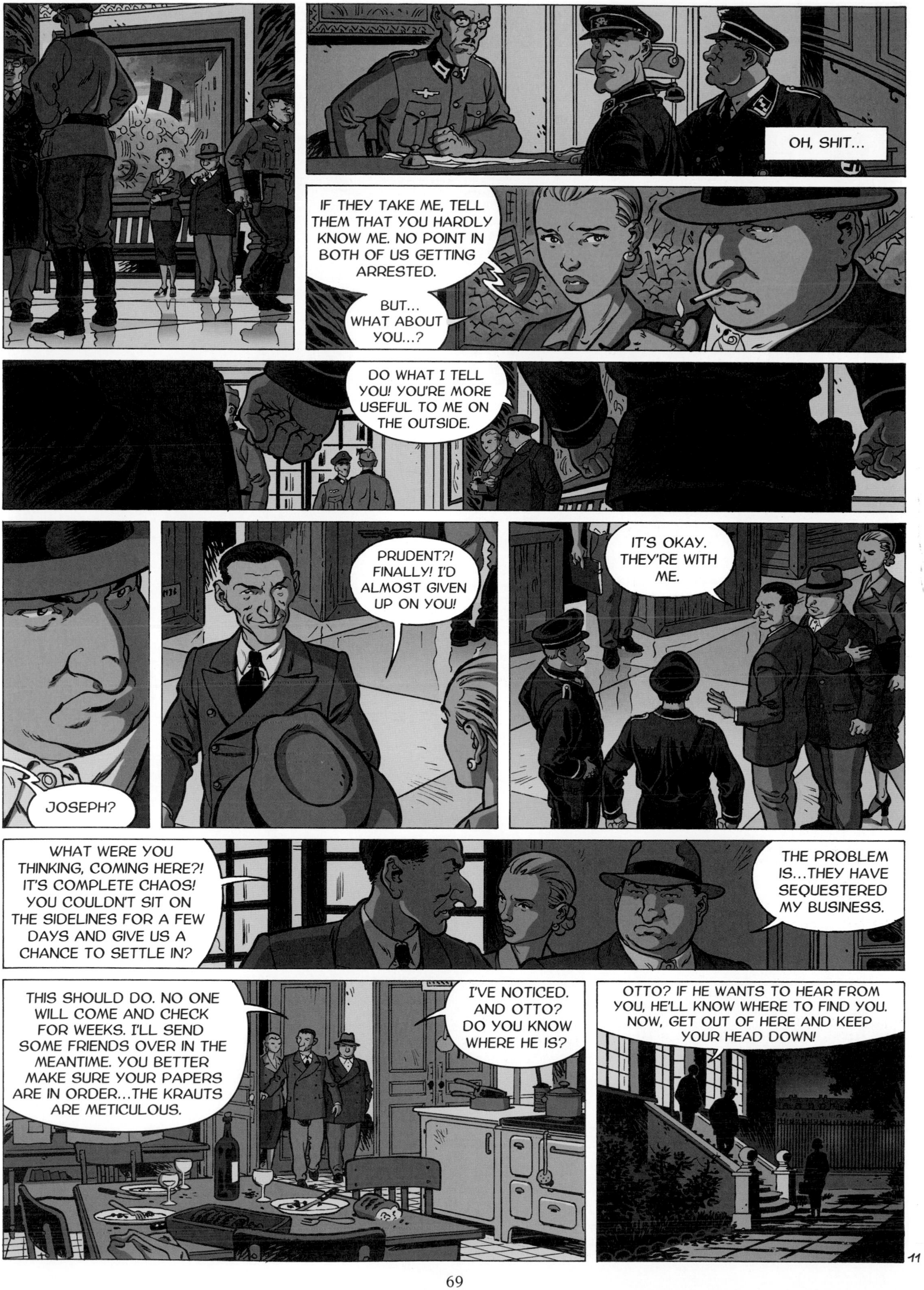

OH, SHIT...
IF THEY TAKE ME, TELL THEM THAT YOU HARDLY KNOW ME. NO POINT IN BOTH OF US GETTING ARRESTED.
BUT... WHAT ABOUT YOU...?
DO WHAT I TELL YOU! YOU'RE MORE USEFUL TO ME ON THE OUTSIDE.
JOSEPH?
PRUDENT?! FINALLY! I'D ALMOST GIVEN UP ON YOU!
IT'S OKAY. THEY'RE WITH ME.
WHAT WERE YOU THINKING, COMING HERE?! IT'S COMPLETE CHAOS! YOU COULDN'T SIT ON THE SIDELINES FOR A FEW DAYS AND GIVE US A CHANCE TO SETTLE IN?
THE PROBLEM IS...THEY HAVE SEQUESTERED MY BUSINESS.
THIS SHOULD DO. NO ONE WILL COME AND CHECK FOR WEEKS. I'LL SEND SOME FRIENDS OVER IN THE MEANTIME. YOU BETTER MAKE SURE YOUR PAPERS ARE IN ORDER...THE KRAUTS ARE METICULOUS.
I'VE NOTICED. AND OTTO? DO YOU KNOW WHERE HE IS?
OTTO? IF HE WANTS TO HEAR FROM YOU, HE'LL KNOW WHERE TO FIND YOU. NOW, GET OUT OF HERE AND KEEP YOUR HEAD DOWN!
11

IT'S BEAUTIFUL WORK, WOULDN'T YOU SAY?

WELL?

HE'S RIGHT. NO ONE WOULD SUSPECT A THING.

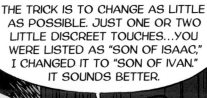

THE TRICK IS TO CHANGE AS LITTLE AS POSSIBLE. JUST ONE OR TWO LITTLE DISCREET TOUCHES...YOU WERE LISTED AS "SON OF ISAAC," I CHANGED IT TO "SON OF IVAN." IT SOUNDS BETTER.

HERE, WHILE YOU'RE WARMED UP...

MY BROTHER'S AND MY WIFE'S. THE GIRLS ARE ON EVA'S...BE CAREFUL WITH THAT ONE.

NO REST FOR THE ARTIST, I SEE...

HERE YOU GO! AN IDENTITY CARD HOT OFF THE PRESS FROM THE FOREIGN SERVICE OFFICE. JOSEPH IS A CITIZEN OF RUSSIAN ORIGIN AND HIS RELIGION IS LISTED AS ORTHODOX...

I HOPE I WON'T NEED TO STUDY THE BIBLE!

INITIAL EACH PAGE OF THE CONTRACT AND THEN SIGN THE LAST PAGE.

SURE, I'VE ALWAYS WANTED TO BE THE PRESIDENT OF A COMPANY. ...AND ME, MAJORITY SHAREHOLDER.

THIS IS YOUR PLACE, GENTS. OFFICIALLY, I'M JUST AN EMPLOYEE.

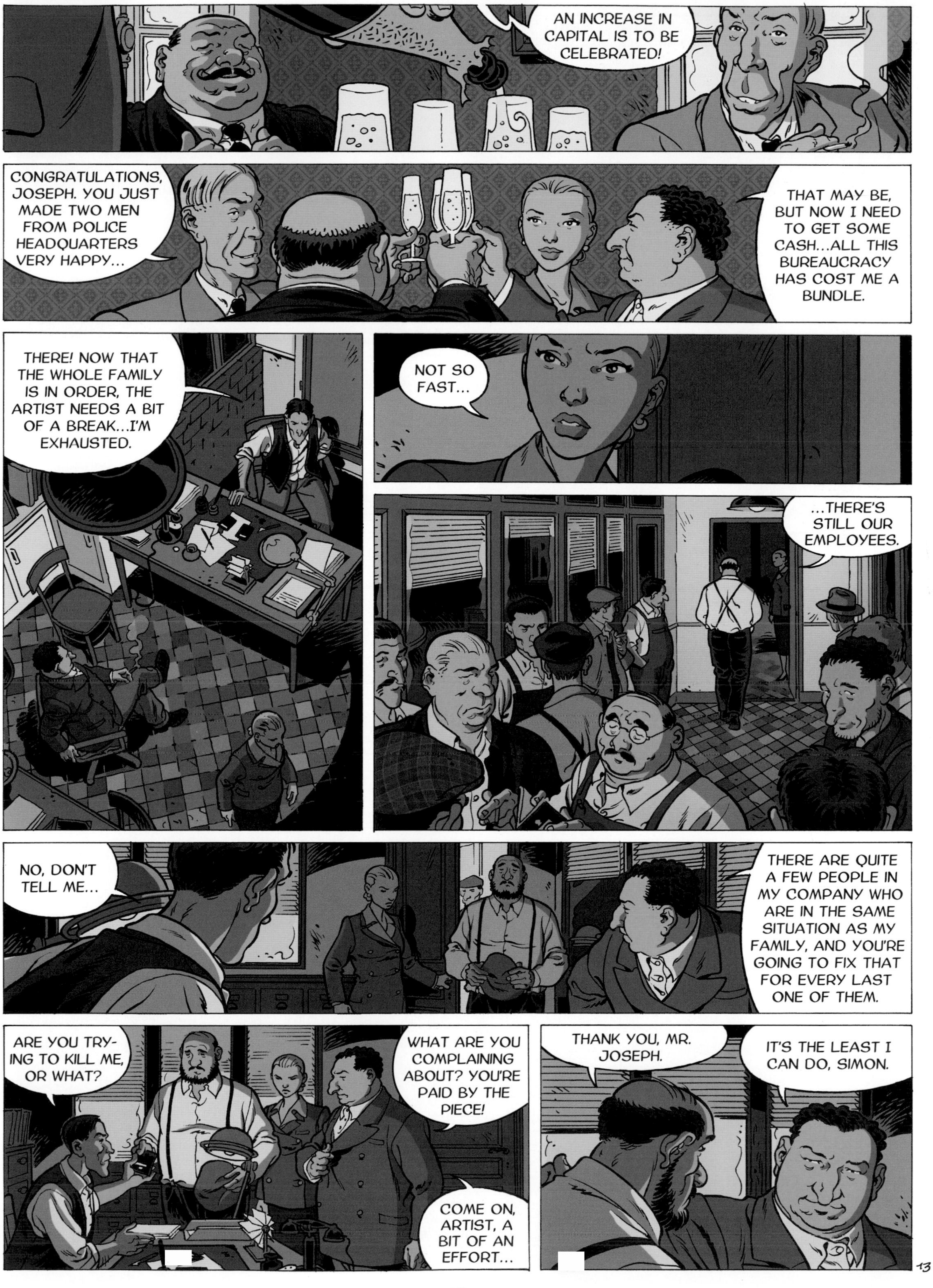
AN INCREASE IN CAPITAL IS TO BE CELEBRATED!
CONGRATULATIONS, JOSEPH. YOU JUST MADE TWO MEN FROM POLICE HEADQUARTERS VERY HAPPY...
THAT MAY BE, BUT NOW I NEED TO GET SOME CASH...ALL THIS BUREAUCRACY HAS COST ME A BUNDLE.
THERE! NOW THAT THE WHOLE FAMILY IS IN ORDER, THE ARTIST NEEDS A BIT OF A BREAK...I'M EXHAUSTED.
NOT SO FAST...
...THERE'S STILL OUR EMPLOYEES.
NO, DON'T TELL ME...
THERE ARE QUITE A FEW PEOPLE IN MY COMPANY WHO ARE IN THE SAME SITUATION AS MY FAMILY, AND YOU'RE GOING TO FIX THAT FOR EVERY LAST ONE OF THEM.
ARE YOU TRY-ING TO KILL ME, OR WHAT?
WHAT ARE YOU COMPLAINING ABOUT? YOU'RE PAID BY THE PIECE!
COME ON, ARTIST, A BIT OF AN EFFORT...
THANK YOU, MR. JOSEPH.
IT'S THE LEAST I CAN DO, SIMON.
13

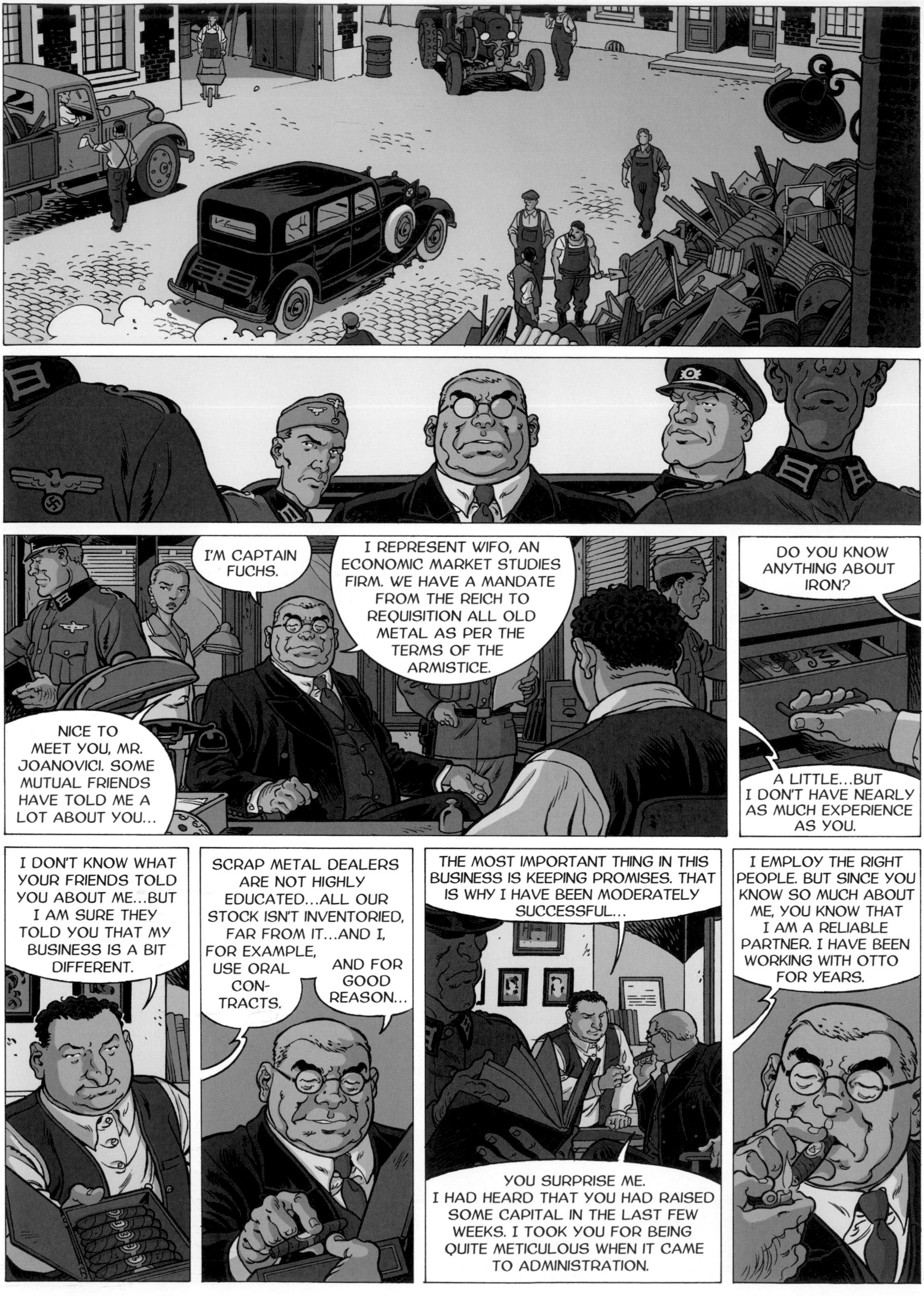
I'M CAPTAIN FUCHS.
I REPRESENT WIFO, AN ECONOMIC MARKET STUDIES FIRM. WE HAVE A MANDATE FROM THE REICH TO REQUISITION ALL OLD METAL AS PER THE TERMS OF THE ARMISTICE.
NICE TO MEET YOU, MR. JOANOVICI. SOME MUTUAL FRIENDS HAVE TOLD ME A LOT ABOUT YOU...
DO YOU KNOW ANYTHING ABOUT IRON?
A LITTLE...BUT I DON'T HAVE NEARLY AS MUCH EXPERIENCE AS YOU.
I DON'T KNOW WHAT YOUR FRIENDS TOLD YOU ABOUT ME...BUT I AM SURE THEY TOLD YOU THAT MY BUSINESS IS A BIT DIFFERENT.
SCRAP METAL DEALERS ARE NOT HIGHLY EDUCATED...ALL OUR STOCK ISN'T INVENTORIED, FAR FROM IT...AND I, FOR EXAMPLE, USE ORAL CON-TRACTS.
AND FOR GOOD REASON...
THE MOST IMPORTANT THING IN THIS BUSINESS IS KEEPING PROMISES. THAT IS WHY I HAVE BEEN MODERATELY SUCCESSFUL...
YOU SURPRISE ME. I HAD HEARD THAT YOU HAD RAISED SOME CAPITAL IN THE LAST FEW WEEKS. I TOOK YOU FOR BEING QUITE METICULOUS WHEN IT CAME TO ADMINISTRATION.
I EMPLOY THE RIGHT PEOPLE. BUT SINCE YOU KNOW SO MUCH ABOUT ME, YOU KNOW THAT I AM A RELIABLE PARTNER. I HAVE BEEN WORKING WITH OTTO FOR YEARS.
14

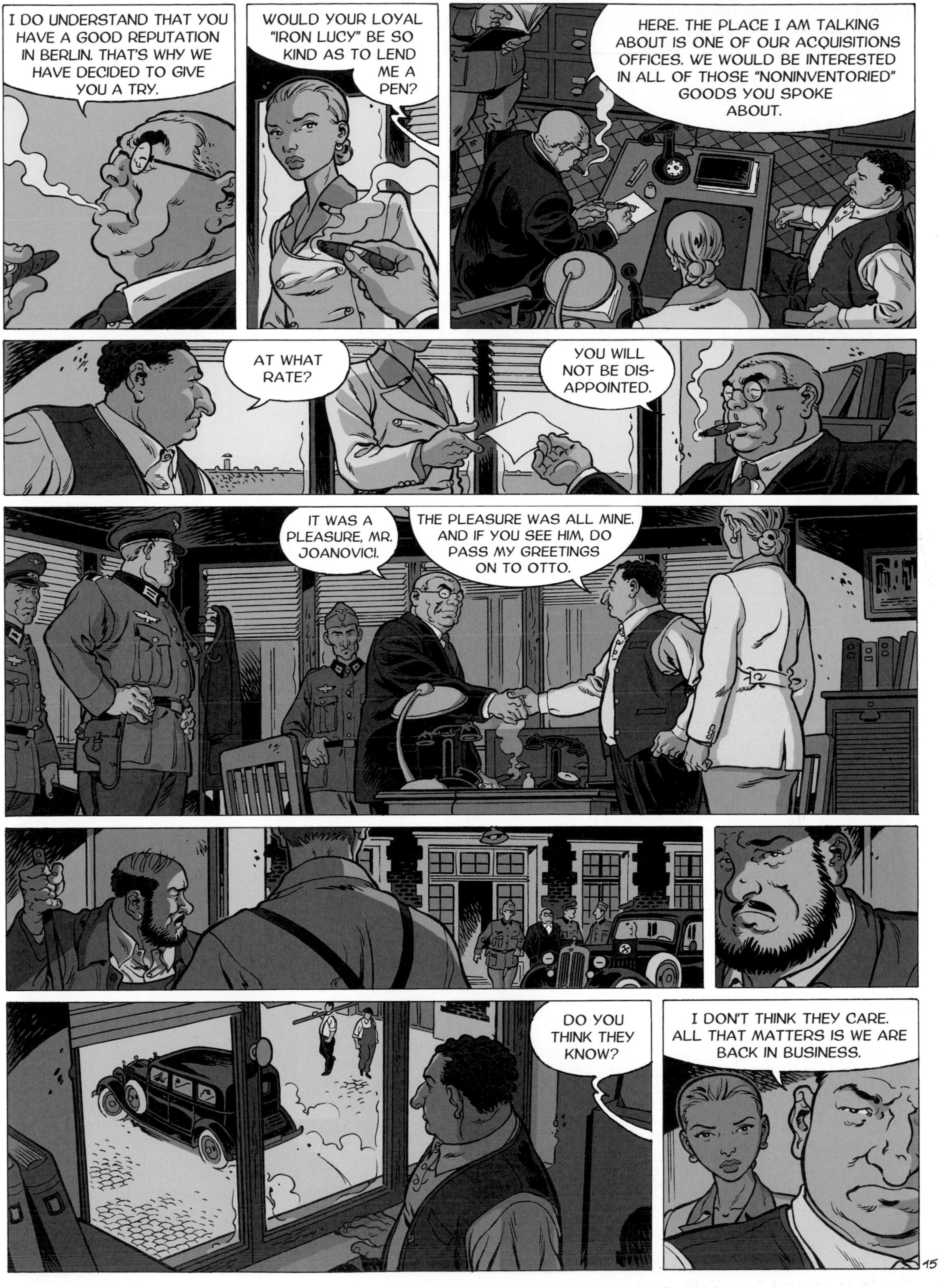
I DO UNDERSTAND THAT YOU HAVE A GOOD REPUTATION IN BERLIN. THAT'S WHY WE HAVE DECIDED TO GIVE YOU A TRY.
WOULD YOUR LOYAL "IRON LUCY" BE SO KIND AS TO LEND ME A PEN?
HERE. THE PLACE I AM TALKING ABOUT IS ONE OF OUR ACQUISITIONS OFFICES. WE WOULD BE INTERESTED IN ALL OF THOSE "NONINVENTORIED" GOODS YOU SPOKE ABOUT.
AT WHAT RATE?
YOU WILL NOT BE DIS-APPOINTED.
IT WAS A PLEASURE, MR. JOANOVICI.
THE PLEASURE WAS ALL MINE. AND IF YOU SEE HIM, DO PASS MY GREETINGS ON TO OTTO.
DO YOU THINK THEY KNOW?
I DON'T THINK THEY CARE. ALL THAT MATTERS IS WE ARE BACK IN BUSINESS.
15

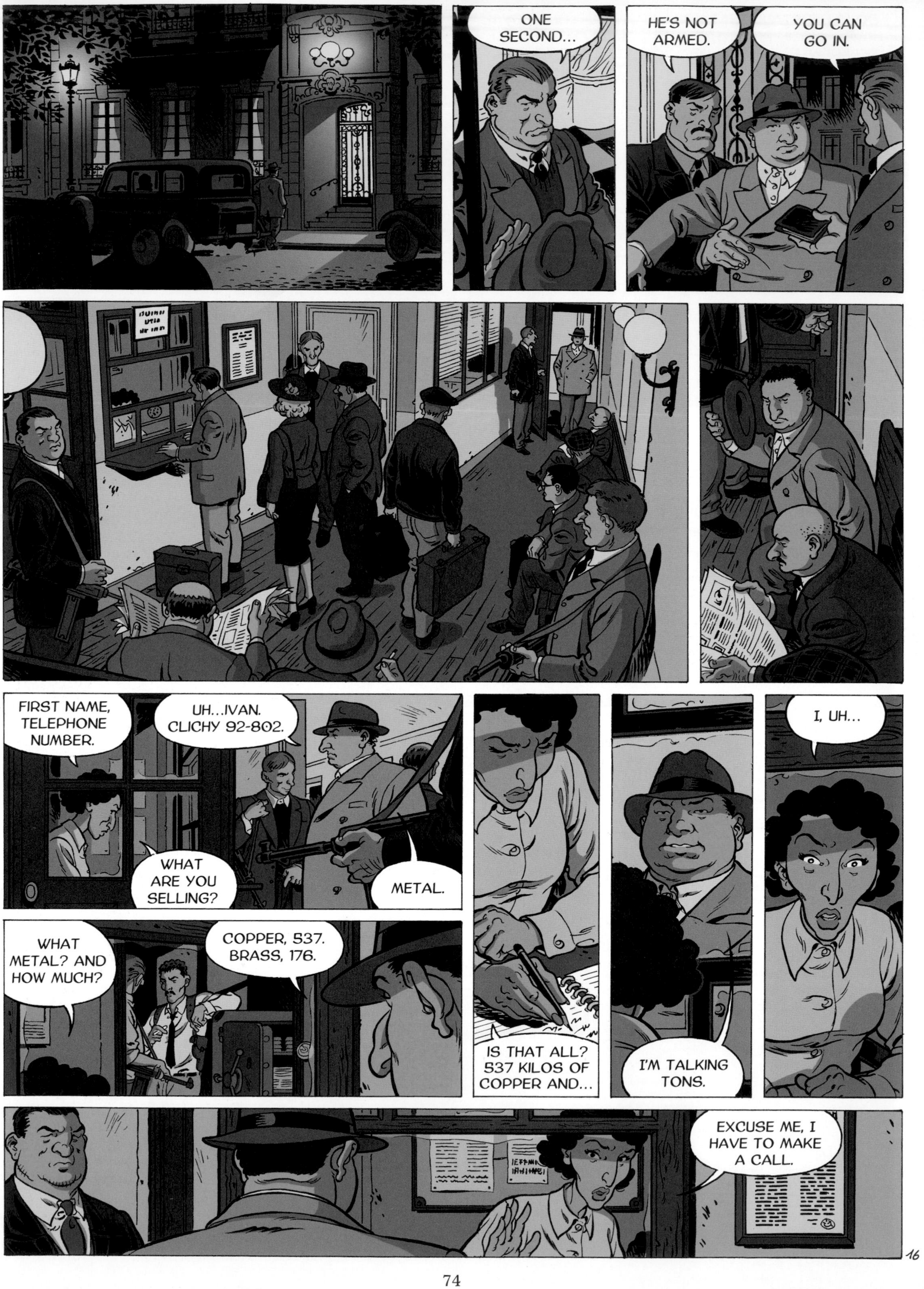
ONE SECOND...
HE'S NOT ARMED.
YOU CAN GO IN.
FIRST NAME, TELEPHONE NUMBER.
UH...IVAN. CLICHY 92-802.
WHAT ARE YOU SELLING?
METAL.
WHAT METAL? AND HOW MUCH?
COPPER, 537. BRASS, 176.
IS THAT ALL? 537 KILOS OF COPPER AND...
I'M TALKING TONS.
I, UH...
EXCUSE ME, I HAVE TO MAKE A CALL.
16

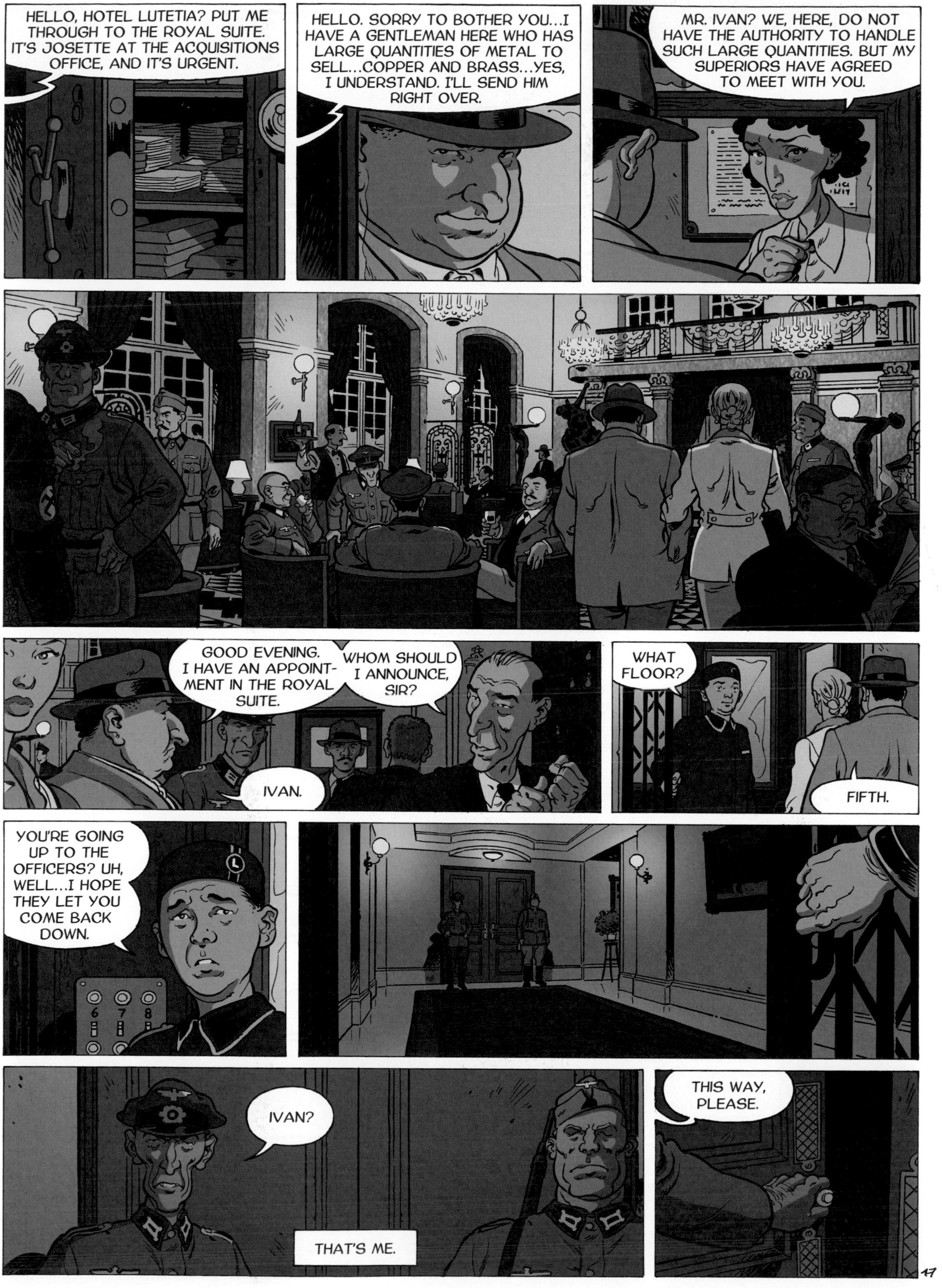
HELLO, HOTEL LUTETIA? PUT ME THROUGH TO THE ROYAL SUITE. IT'S JOSETTE AT THE ACQUISITIONS OFFICE, AND IT'S URGENT.
HELLO. SORRY TO BOTHER YOU...I HAVE A GENTLEMAN HERE WHO HAS LARGE QUANTITIES OF METAL TO SELL...COPPER AND BRASS...YES, I UNDERSTAND. I'LL SEND HIM RIGHT OVER.
MR. IVAN? WE, HERE, DO NOT HAVE THE AUTHORITY TO HANDLE SUCH LARGE QUANTITIES. BUT MY SUPERIORS HAVE AGREED TO MEET WITH YOU.
GOOD EVENING. I HAVE AN APPOINTMENT IN THE ROYAL SUITE.
WHOM SHOULD I ANNOUNCE, SIR?
IVAN.
WHAT FLOOR?
FIFTH.
YOU'RE GOING UP TO THE OFFICERS? UH, WELL...I HOPE THEY LET YOU COME BACK DOWN.
IVAN?
THAT'S ME.
THIS WAY, PLEASE.
17

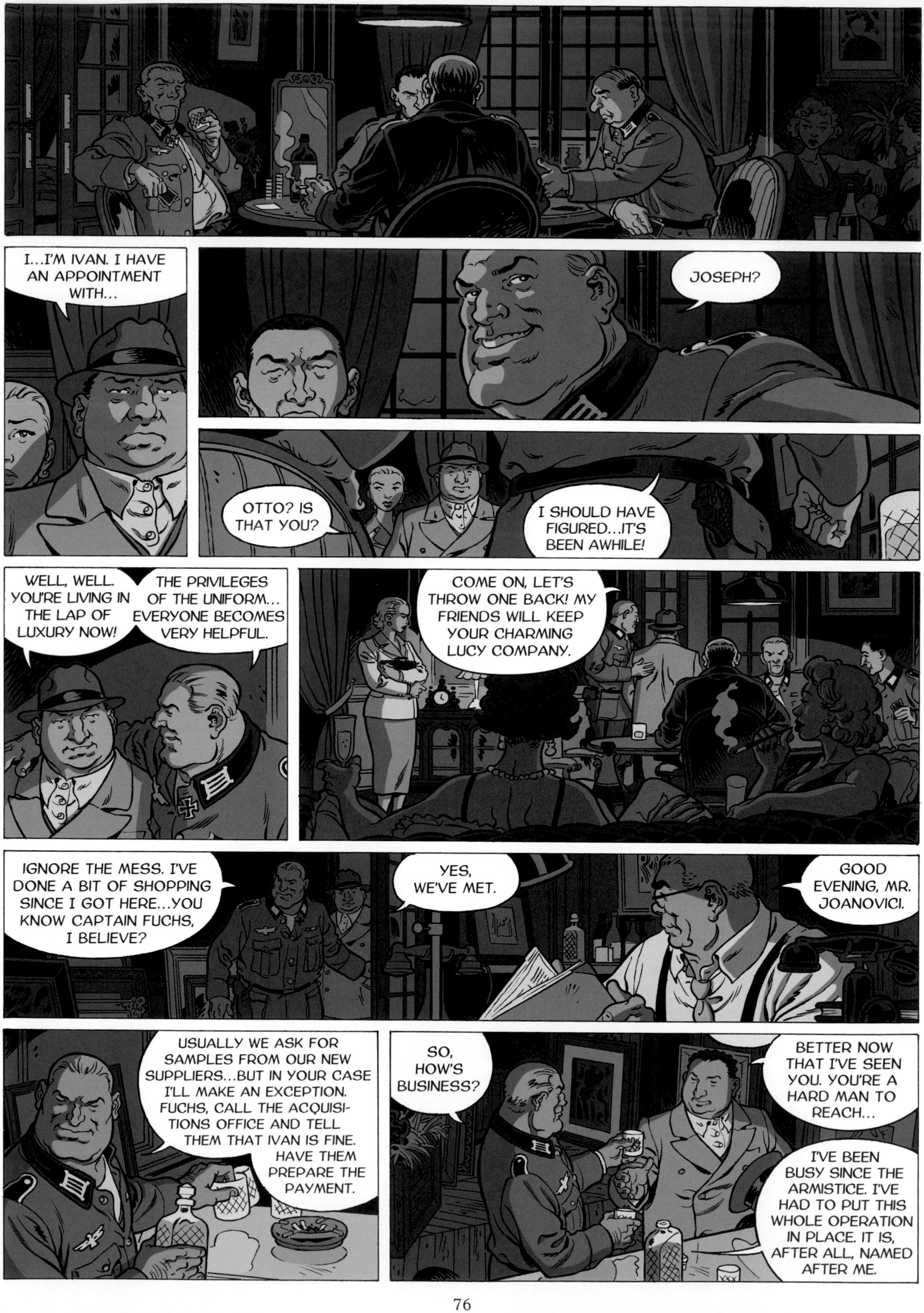
I...I'M IVAN. I HAVE AN APPOINTMENT WITH...
JOSEPH?
OTTO? IS THAT YOU?
I SHOULD HAVE FIGURED...IT'S BEEN AWHILE!
WELL, WELL. YOU'RE LIVING IN THE LAP OF LUXURY NOW!
THE PRIVILEGES OF THE UNIFORM... EVERYONE BECOMES VERY HELPFUL.
COME ON, LET'S THROW ONE BACK! MY FRIENDS WILL KEEP YOUR CHARMING LUCY COMPANY.
IGNORE THE MESS. I'VE DONE A BIT OF SHOPPING SINCE I GOT HERE...YOU KNOW CAPTAIN FUCHS, I BELIEVE?
YES, WE'VE MET.
GOOD EVENING, MR. JOANOVICI.
USUALLY WE ASK FOR SAMPLES FROM OUR NEW SUPPLIERS...BUT IN YOUR CASE I'LL MAKE AN EXCEPTION. FUCHS, CALL THE ACQUISITIONS OFFICE AND TELL THEM THAT IVAN IS FINE.
HAVE THEM PREPARE THE PAYMENT.
SO, HOW'S BUSINESS?
BETTER NOW THAT I'VE SEEN YOU. YOU'RE A HARD MAN TO REACH...
I'VE BEEN BUSY SINCE THE ARMISTICE. I'VE HAD TO PUT THIS WHOLE OPERATION IN PLACE. IT IS, AFTER ALL, NAMED AFTER ME.
18

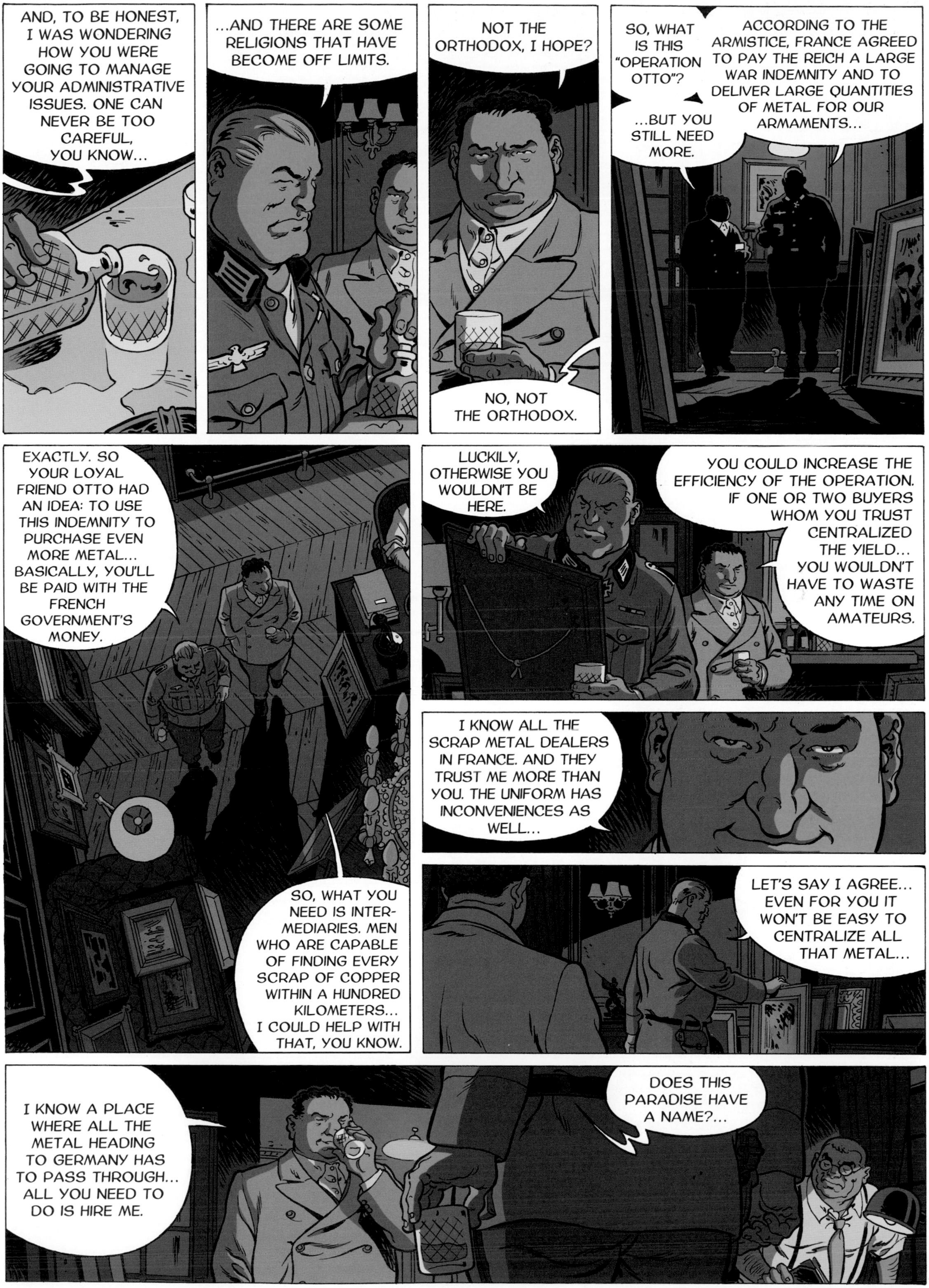
AND, TO BE HONEST, I WAS WONDERING HOW YOU WERE GOING TO MANAGE YOUR ADMINISTRATIVE ISSUES. ONE CAN NEVER BE TOO CAREFUL, YOU KNOW...
...AND THERE ARE SOME RELIGIONS THAT HAVE BECOME OFF LIMITS.
NOT THE ORTHODOX, I HOPE?
NO, NOT THE ORTHODOX.
SO, WHAT IS THIS "OPERATION OTTO"?
ACCORDING TO THE ARMISTICE, FRANCE AGREED TO PAY THE REICH A LARGE WAR INDEMNITY AND TO DELIVER LARGE QUANTITIES OF METAL FOR OUR ARMAMENTS...
...BUT YOU STILL NEED MORE.
EXACTLY. SO YOUR LOYAL FRIEND OTTO HAD AN IDEA: TO USE THIS INDEMNITY TO PURCHASE EVEN MORE METAL... BASICALLY, YOU'LL BE PAID WITH THE FRENCH GOVERNMENT'S MONEY.
SO, WHAT YOU NEED IS INTER-MEDIARIES. MEN WHO ARE CAPABLE OF FINDING EVERY SCRAP OF COPPER WITHIN A HUNDRED KILOMETERS... I COULD HELP WITH THAT, YOU KNOW.
LUCKILY, OTHERWISE YOU WOULDN'T BE HERE.
YOU COULD INCREASE THE EFFICIENCY OF THE OPERATION. IF ONE OR TWO BUYERS WHOM YOU TRUST CENTRALIZED THE YIELD... YOU WOULDN'T HAVE TO WASTE ANY TIME ON AMATEURS.
I KNOW ALL THE SCRAP METAL DEALERS IN FRANCE. AND THEY TRUST ME MORE THAN YOU. THE UNIFORM HAS INCONVENIENCES AS WELL...
LET'S SAY I AGREE... EVEN FOR YOU IT WON'T BE EASY TO CENTRALIZE ALL THAT METAL...
I KNOW A PLACE WHERE ALL THE METAL HEADING TO GERMANY HAS TO PASS THROUGH... ALL YOU NEED TO DO IS HIRE ME.
DOES THIS PARADISE HAVE A NAME?...
19

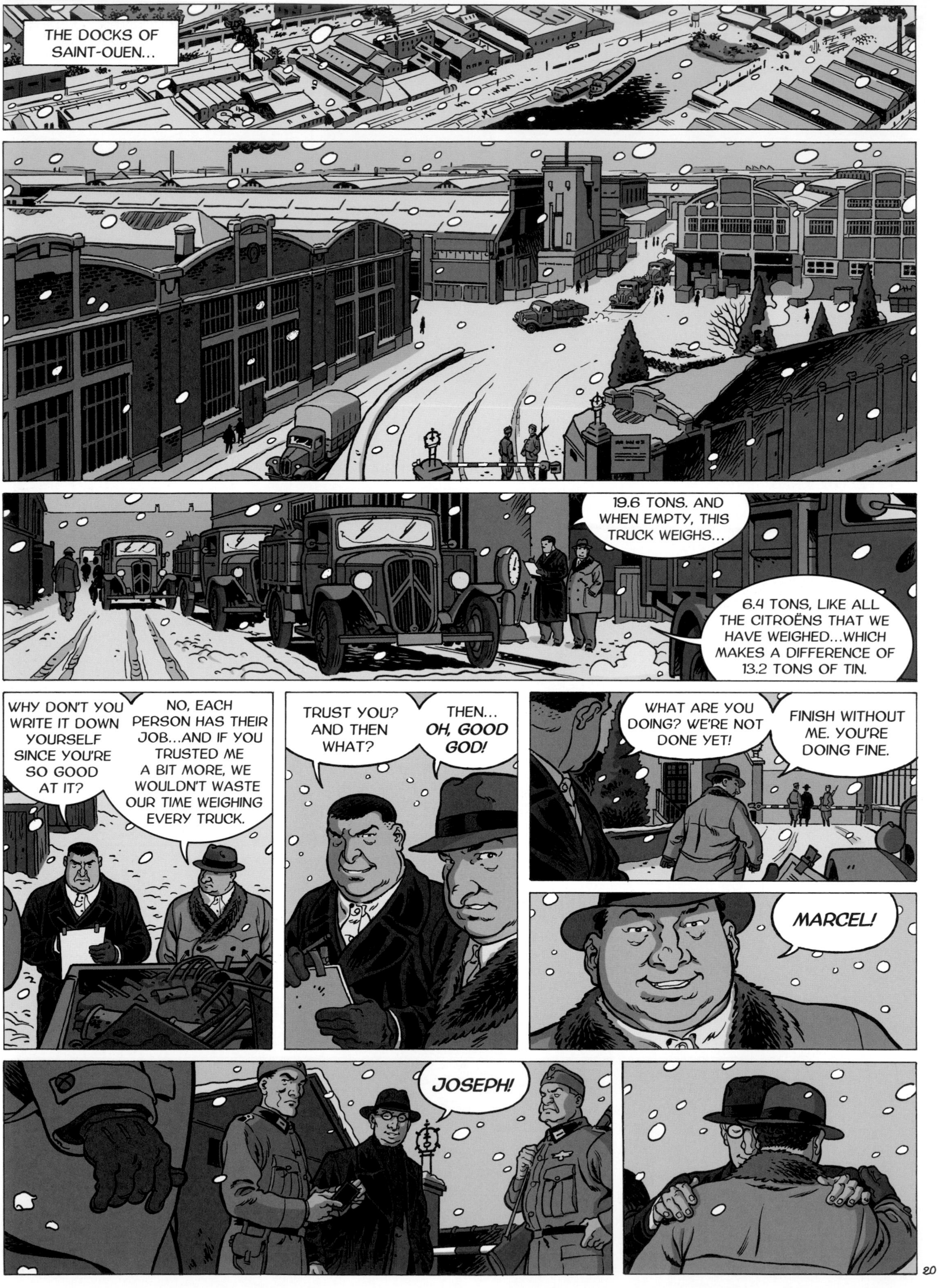
THE DOCKS OF SAINT-OUEN...
19.6 TONS. AND WHEN EMPTY, THIS TRUCK WEIGHS...
6.4 TONS, LIKE ALL THE CITROËNS THAT WE HAVE WEIGHED...WHICH MAKES A DIFFERENCE OF 13.2 TONS OF TIN.
WHY DON'T YOU WRITE IT DOWN YOURSELF SINCE YOU'RE SO GOOD AT IT?
NO, EACH PERSON HAS THEIR JOB...AND IF YOU TRUSTED ME A BIT MORE, WE WOULDN'T WASTE OUR TIME WEIGHING EVERY TRUCK.
TRUST YOU? AND THEN WHAT?
THEN... OH, GOOD GOD!
WHAT ARE YOU DOING? WE'RE NOT DONE YET!
FINISH WITHOUT ME. YOU'RE DOING FINE.
MARCEL!
JOSEPH!
20

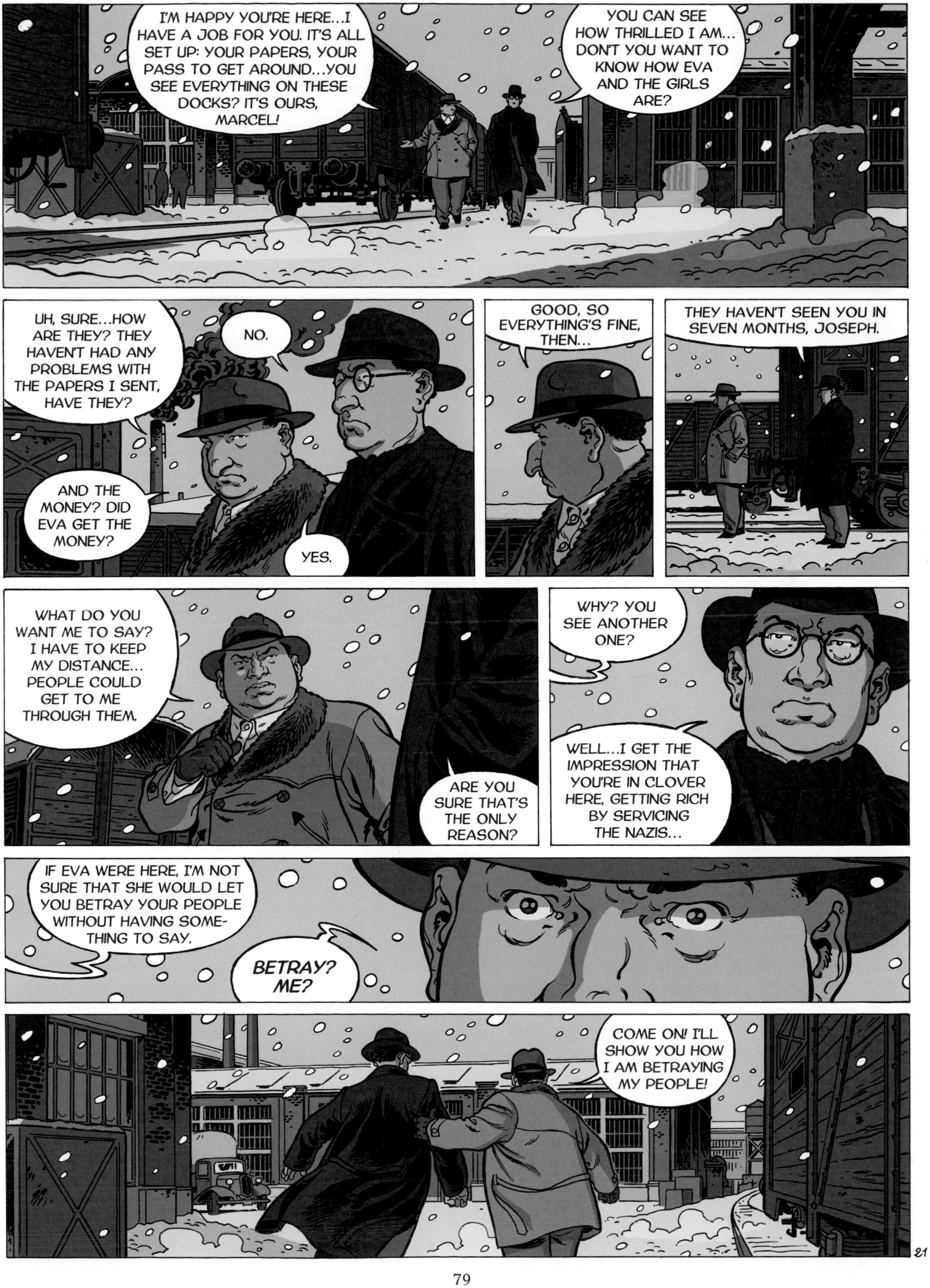
I'M HAPPY YOU'RE HERE...I HAVE A JOB FOR YOU. IT'S ALL SET UP: YOUR PAPERS, YOUR PASS TO GET AROUND...YOU SEE EVERYTHING ON THESE DOCKS? IT'S OURS, MARCEL!
YOU CAN SEE HOW THRILLED I AM... DON'T YOU WANT TO KNOW HOW EVA AND THE GIRLS ARE?
UH, SURE...HOW ARE THEY? THEY HAVEN'T HAD ANY PROBLEMS WITH THE PAPERS I SENT, HAVE THEY?
NO.
AND THE MONEY? DID EVA GET THE MONEY?
YES.
GOOD, SO EVERYTHING'S FINE, THEN...
THEY HAVEN'T SEEN YOU IN SEVEN MONTHS, JOSEPH.
WHAT DO YOU WANT ME TO SAY? I HAVE TO KEEP MY DISTANCE... PEOPLE COULD GET TO ME THROUGH THEM.
ARE YOU SURE THAT'S THE ONLY REASON?
WHY? YOU SEE ANOTHER ONE?
WELL...I GET THE IMPRESSION THAT YOU'RE IN CLOVER HERE, GETTING RICH BY SERVICING THE NAZIS...
IF EVA WERE HERE, I'M NOT SURE THAT SHE WOULD LET YOU BETRAY YOUR PEOPLE WITHOUT HAVING SOME-THING TO SAY.
BETRAY? ME?
COME ON! I'LL SHOW YOU HOW I AM BETRAYING MY PEOPLE!
21

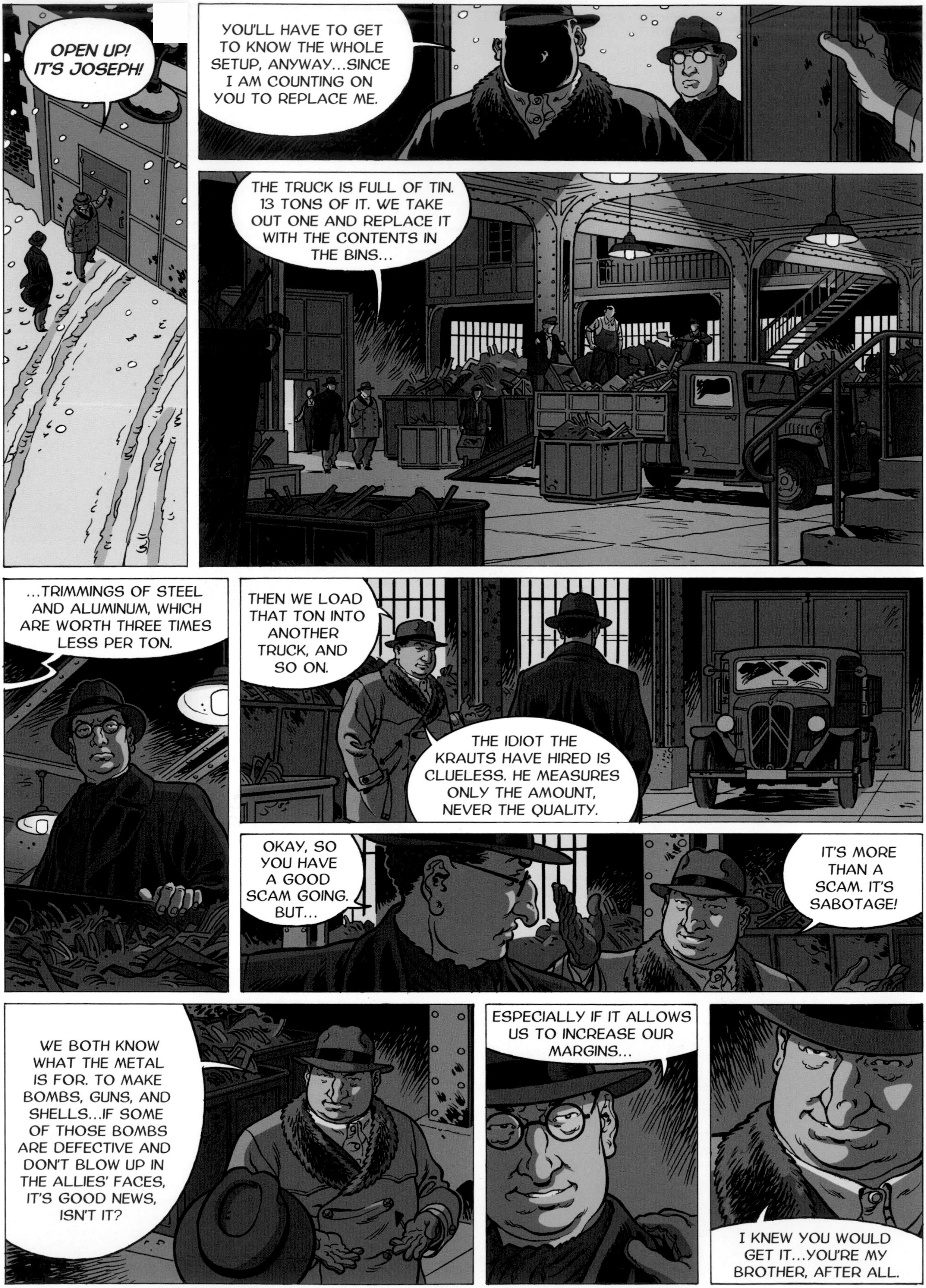
OPEN UP! IT'S JOSEPH!
YOU'LL HAVE TO GET TO KNOW THE WHOLE SETUP, ANYWAY...SINCE I AM COUNTING ON YOU TO REPLACE ME.
THE TRUCK IS FULL OF TIN. 13 TONS OF IT. WE TAKE OUT ONE AND REPLACE IT WITH THE CONTENTS IN THE BINS...
...TRIMMINGS OF STEEL AND ALUMINUM, WHICH ARE WORTH THREE TIMES LESS PER TON.
THEN WE LOAD THAT TON INTO ANOTHER TRUCK, AND SO ON.
THE IDIOT THE KRAUTS HAVE HIRED IS CLUELESS. HE MEASURES ONLY THE AMOUNT, NEVER THE QUALITY.
OKAY, SO YOU HAVE A GOOD SCAM GOING. BUT...
IT'S MORE THAN A SCAM. IT'S SABOTAGE!
WE BOTH KNOW WHAT THE METAL IS FOR. TO MAKE BOMBS, GUNS, AND SHELLS...IF SOME OF THOSE BOMBS ARE DEFECTIVE AND DON'T BLOW UP IN THE ALLIES' FACES, IT'S GOOD NEWS, ISN'T IT?
ESPECIALLY IF IT ALLOWS US TO INCREASE OUR MARGINS...
I KNEW YOU WOULD GET IT...YOU'RE MY BROTHER, AFTER ALL.
22

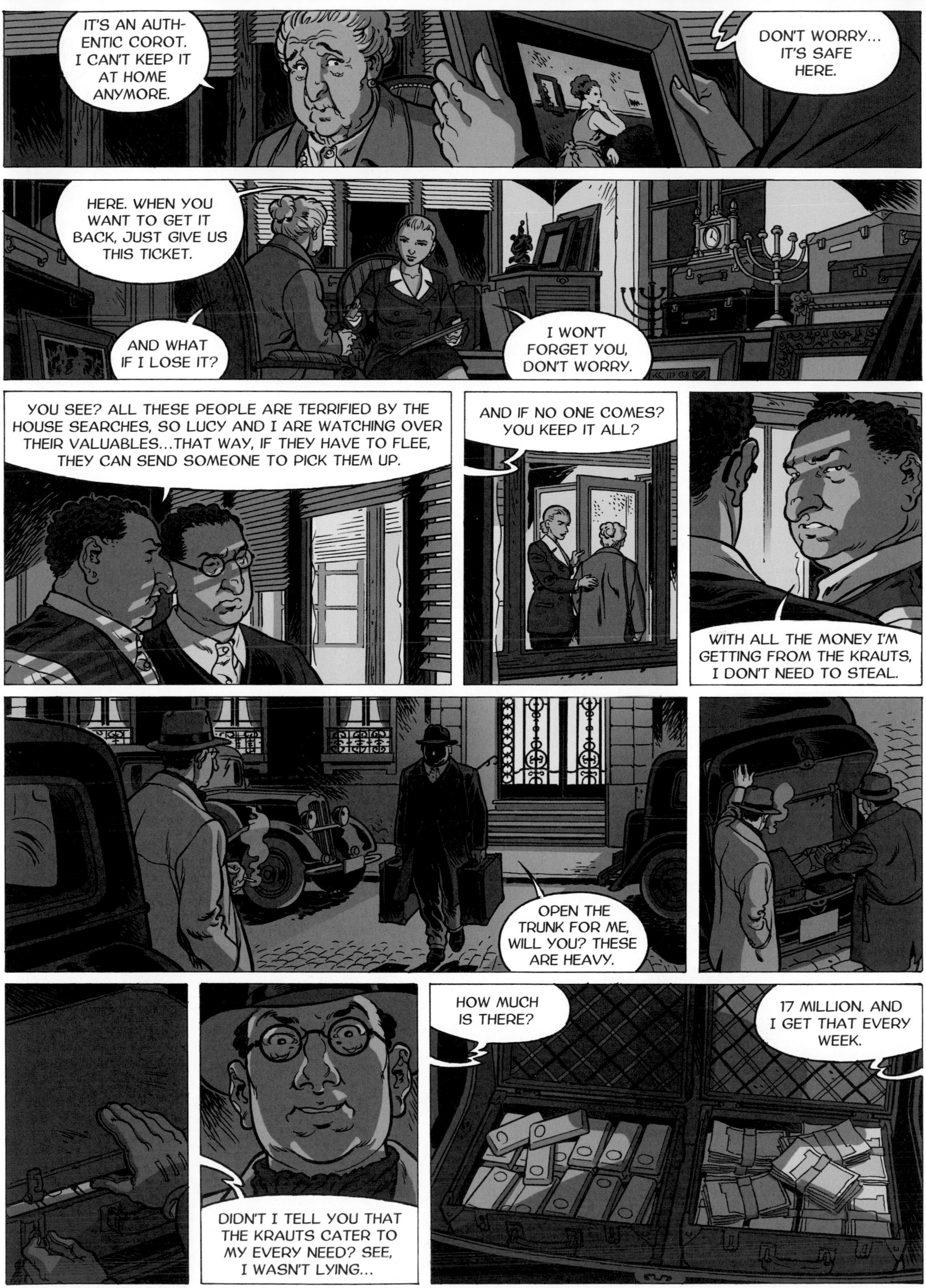
IT'S AN AUTHENTIC COROT. I CAN'T KEEP IT AT HOME ANYMORE.
DON'T WORRY... IT'S SAFE HERE.
HERE. WHEN YOU WANT TO GET IT BACK, JUST GIVE US THIS TICKET.
AND WHAT IF I LOSE IT?
I WON'T FORGET YOU, DON'T WORRY.
YOU SEE? ALL THESE PEOPLE ARE TERRIFIED BY THE HOUSE SEARCHES, SO LUCY AND I ARE WATCHING OVER THEIR VALUABLES...THAT WAY, IF THEY HAVE TO FLEE, THEY CAN SEND SOMEONE TO PICK THEM UP.
AND IF NO ONE COMES? YOU KEEP IT ALL?
WITH ALL THE MONEY I'M GETTING FROM THE KRAUTS, I DON'T NEED TO STEAL.
OPEN THE TRUNK FOR ME, WILL YOU? THESE ARE HEAVY.
DIDN'T I TELL YOU THAT THE KRAUTS CATER TO MY EVERY NEED? SEE, I WASN'T LYING...
HOW MUCH IS THERE?
17 MILLION. AND I GET THAT EVERY WEEK.
23

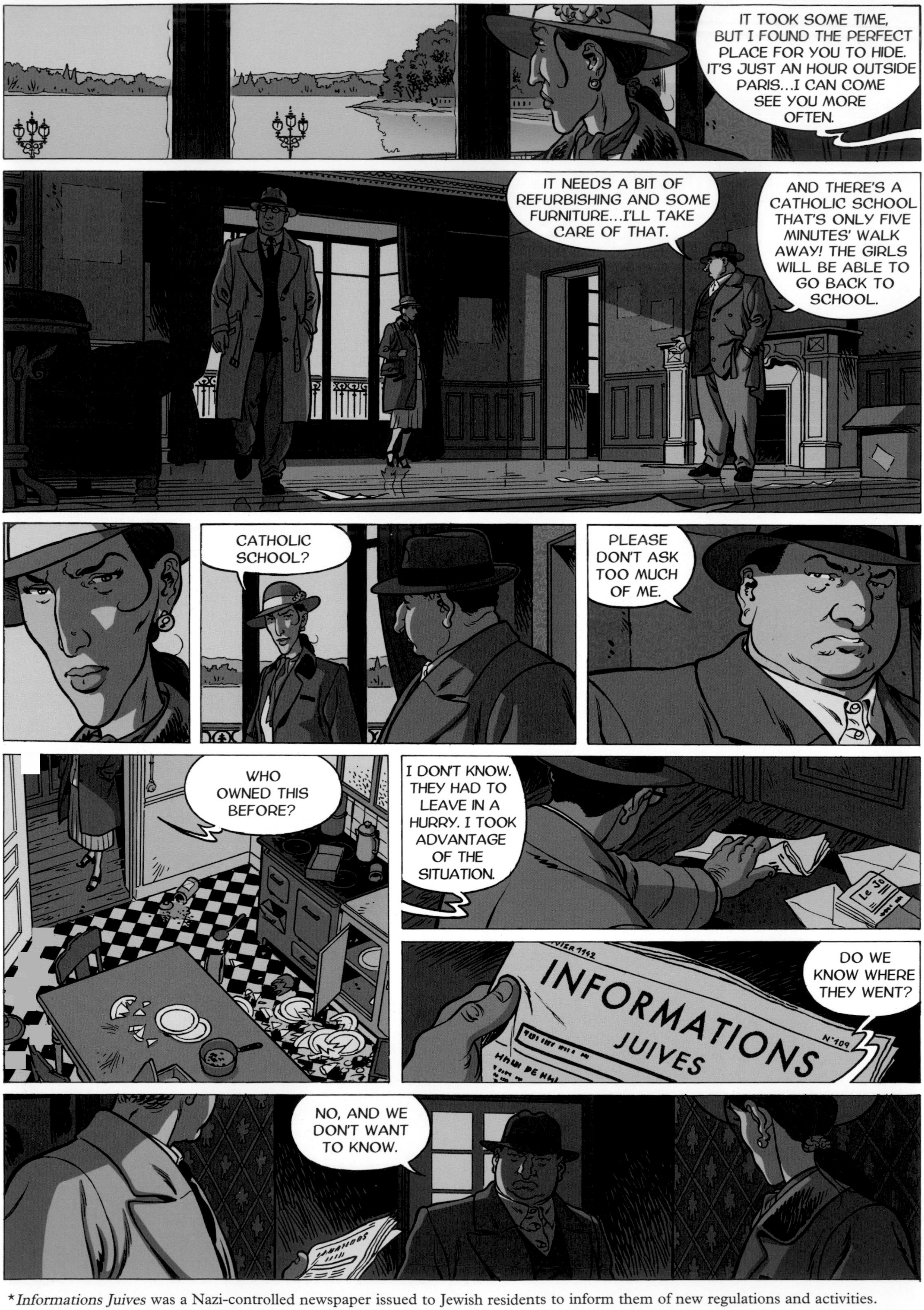
IT TOOK SOME TIME, BUT I FOUND THE PERFECT PLACE FOR YOU TO HIDE. IT'S JUST AN HOUR OUTSIDE PARIS...I CAN COME SEE YOU MORE OFTEN.
IT NEEDS A BIT OF REFURBISHING AND SOME FURNITURE...I'LL TAKE CARE OF THAT.
AND THERE'S A CATHOLIC SCHOOL THAT'S ONLY FIVE MINUTES' WALK AWAY! THE GIRLS WILL BE ABLE TO GO BACK TO SCHOOL.
CATHOLIC SCHOOL?
PLEASE DON'T ASK TOO MUCH OF ME.
WHO OWNED THIS BEFORE?
I DON'T KNOW. THEY HAD TO LEAVE IN A HURRY. I TOOK ADVANTAGE OF THE SITUATION.
INFORMATIONS JUIVES
DO WE KNOW WHERE THEY WENT?
NO, AND WE DON'T WANT TO KNOW.

Informations Juives was a Nazi-controlled newspaper issued to Jewish residents to inform them of new regulations and activities.

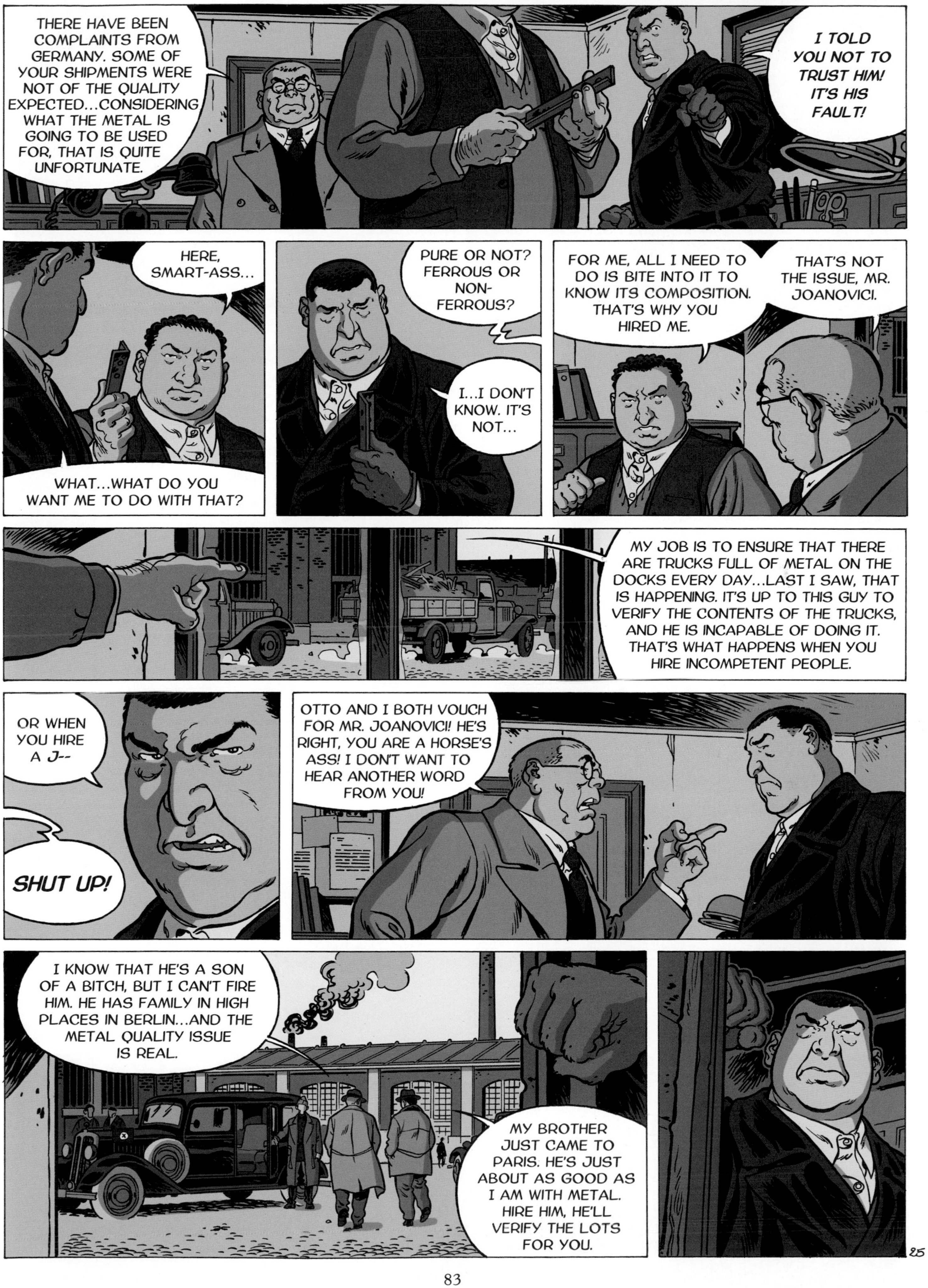
THERE HAVE BEEN COMPLAINTS FROM GERMANY. SOME OF YOUR SHIPMENTS WERE NOT OF THE QUALITY EXPECTED...CONSIDERING WHAT THE METAL IS GOING TO BE USED FOR, THAT IS QUITE UNFORTUNATE.
I TOLD YOU NOT TO TRUST HIM! IT'S HIS FAULT!
HERE, SMART-ASS...
WHAT...WHAT DO YOU WANT ME TO DO WITH THAT?
PURE OR NOT? FERROUS OR NON-FERROUS?
I...I DON'T KNOW. IT'S NOT...
FOR ME, ALL I NEED TO DO IS BITE INTO IT TO KNOW ITS COMPOSITION. THAT'S WHY YOU HIRED ME.
THAT'S NOT THE ISSUE, MR. JOANOVICI.
MY JOB IS TO ENSURE THAT THERE ARE TRUCKS FULL OF METAL ON THE DOCKS EVERY DAY...LAST I SAW, THAT IS HAPPENING. IT'S UP TO THIS GUY TO VERIFY THE CONTENTS OF THE TRUCKS, AND HE IS INCAPABLE OF DOING IT. THAT'S WHAT HAPPENS WHEN YOU HIRE INCOMPETENT PEOPLE.
OR WHEN YOU HIRE A J--
SHUT UP!
OTTO AND I BOTH VOUCH FOR MR. JOANOVICI! HE'S RIGHT, YOU ARE A HORSE'S ASS! I DON'T WANT TO HEAR ANOTHER WORD FROM YOU!
I KNOW THAT HE'S A SON OF A BITCH, BUT I CAN'T FIRE HIM. HE HAS FAMILY IN HIGH PLACES IN BERLIN...AND THE METAL QUALITY ISSUE IS REAL.
MY BROTHER JUST CAME TO PARIS. HE'S JUST ABOUT AS GOOD AS I AM WITH METAL. HIRE HIM, HE'LL VERIFY THE LOTS FOR YOU.
25

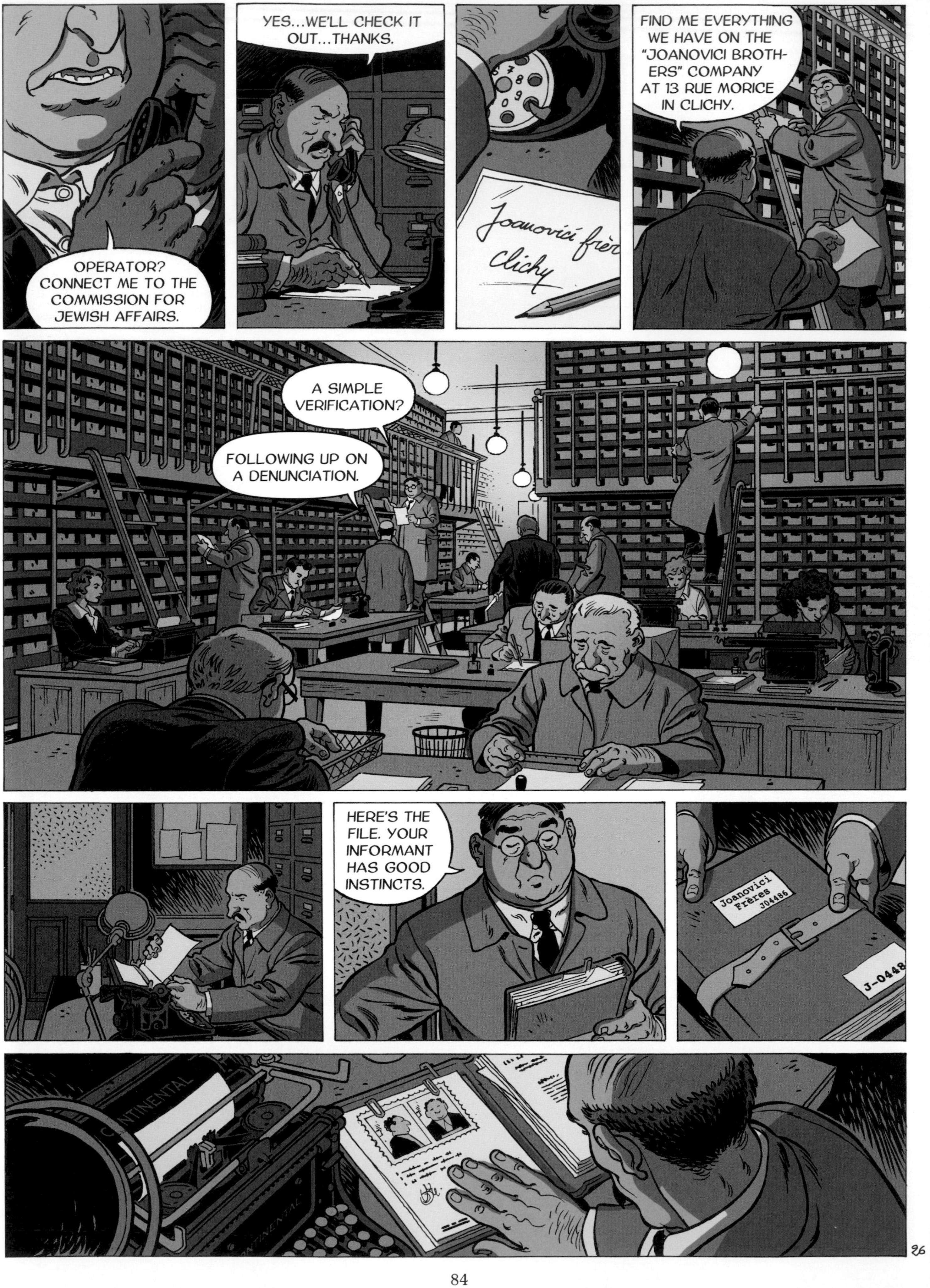
OPERATOR? CONNECT ME TO THE COMMISSION FOR JEWISH AFFAIRS.
YES...WE'LL CHECK IT OUT...THANKS.
Joanovici frèr
Clichy
FIND ME EVERYTHING WE HAVE ON THE "JOANOVICI BROTHERS" COMPANY AT 13 RUE MORICE IN CLICHY.
A SIMPLE VERIFICATION?
FOLLOWING UP ON A DENUNCIATION.
HERE'S THE FILE. YOUR INFORMANT HAS GOOD INSTINCTS.
Joanovici Frères
J04486
J-0448
CONTINENTAL
26

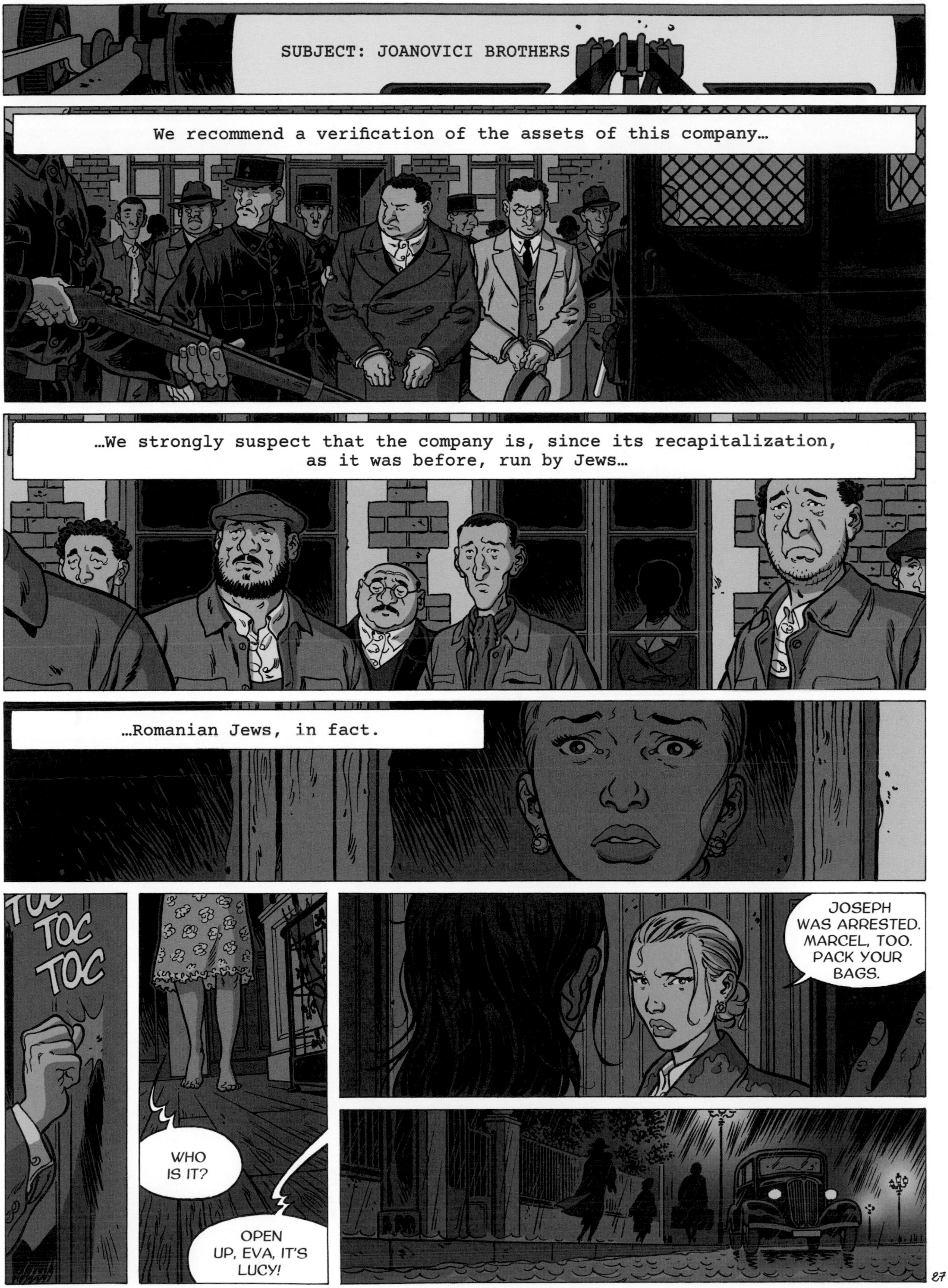
SUBJECT: JOANOVICI BROTHERS
We recommend a verification of the assets of this company…
…We strongly suspect that the company is, since its recapitalization, as it was before, run by Jews…
…Romanian Jews, in fact.
TOC TOC TOC
WHO IS IT?
OPEN UP, EVA, IT'S LUCY!
JOSEPH WAS ARRESTED. MARCEL, TOO. PACK YOUR BAGS.
27

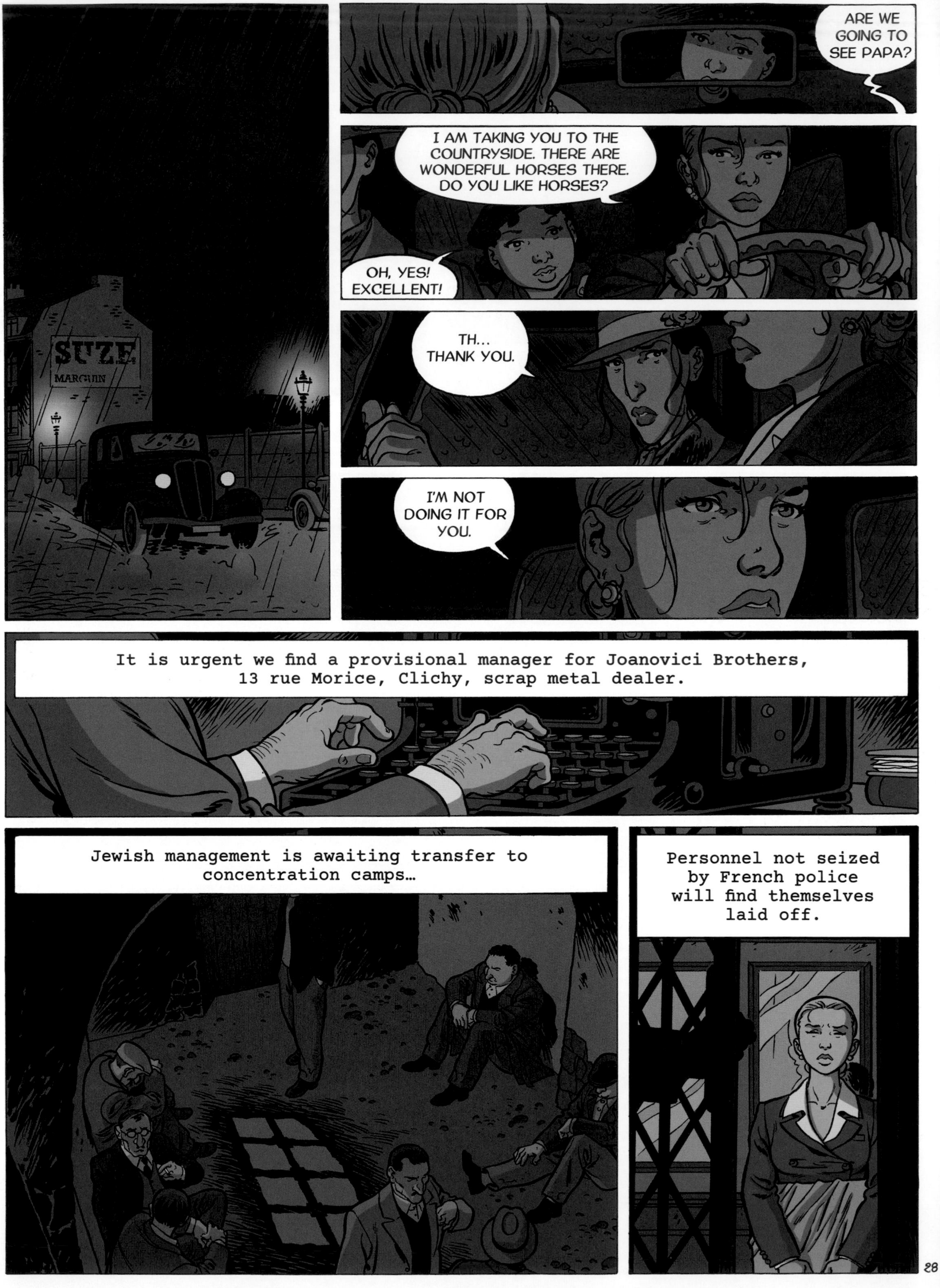
SUZE
MARGUIN
ARE WE GOING TO SEE PAPA?
I AM TAKING YOU TO THE COUNTRYSIDE. THERE ARE WONDERFUL HORSES THERE. DO YOU LIKE HORSES?
OH, YES! EXCELLENT!
TH... THANK YOU.
I'M NOT DOING IT FOR YOU.
It is urgent we find a provisional manager for Joanovici Brothers, 13 rue Morice, Clichy, scrap metal dealer.
Jewish management is awaiting transfer to concentration camps…
Personnel not seized by French police will find themselves laid off.
28

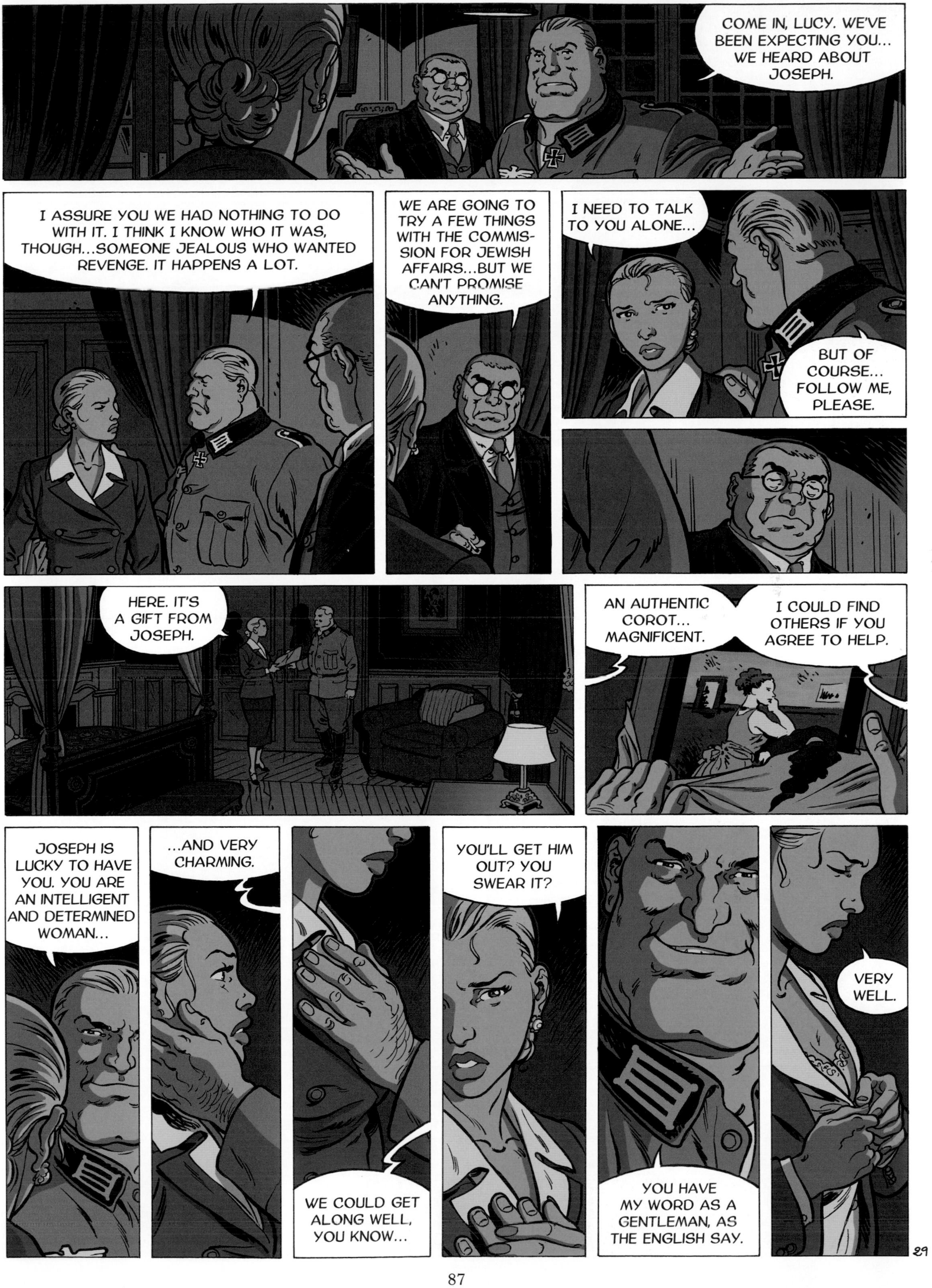
COME IN, LUCY. WE'VE BEEN EXPECTING YOU... WE HEARD ABOUT JOSEPH.
I ASSURE YOU WE HAD NOTHING TO DO WITH IT. I THINK I KNOW WHO IT WAS, THOUGH...SOMEONE JEALOUS WHO WANTED REVENGE. IT HAPPENS A LOT.
WE ARE GOING TO TRY A FEW THINGS WITH THE COMMISSION FOR JEWISH AFFAIRS...BUT WE CAN'T PROMISE ANYTHING.
I NEED TO TALK TO YOU ALONE...
BUT OF COURSE... FOLLOW ME, PLEASE.
HERE. IT'S A GIFT FROM JOSEPH.
AN AUTHENTIC COROT... MAGNIFICENT.
I COULD FIND OTHERS IF YOU AGREE TO HELP.
JOSEPH IS LUCKY TO HAVE YOU. YOU ARE AN INTELLIGENT AND DETERMINED WOMAN...
...AND VERY CHARMING.
WE COULD GET ALONG WELL, YOU KNOW...
YOU'LL GET HIM OUT? YOU SWEAR IT?
YOU HAVE MY WORD AS A GENTLEMAN, AS THE ENGLISH SAY.
VERY WELL.
29

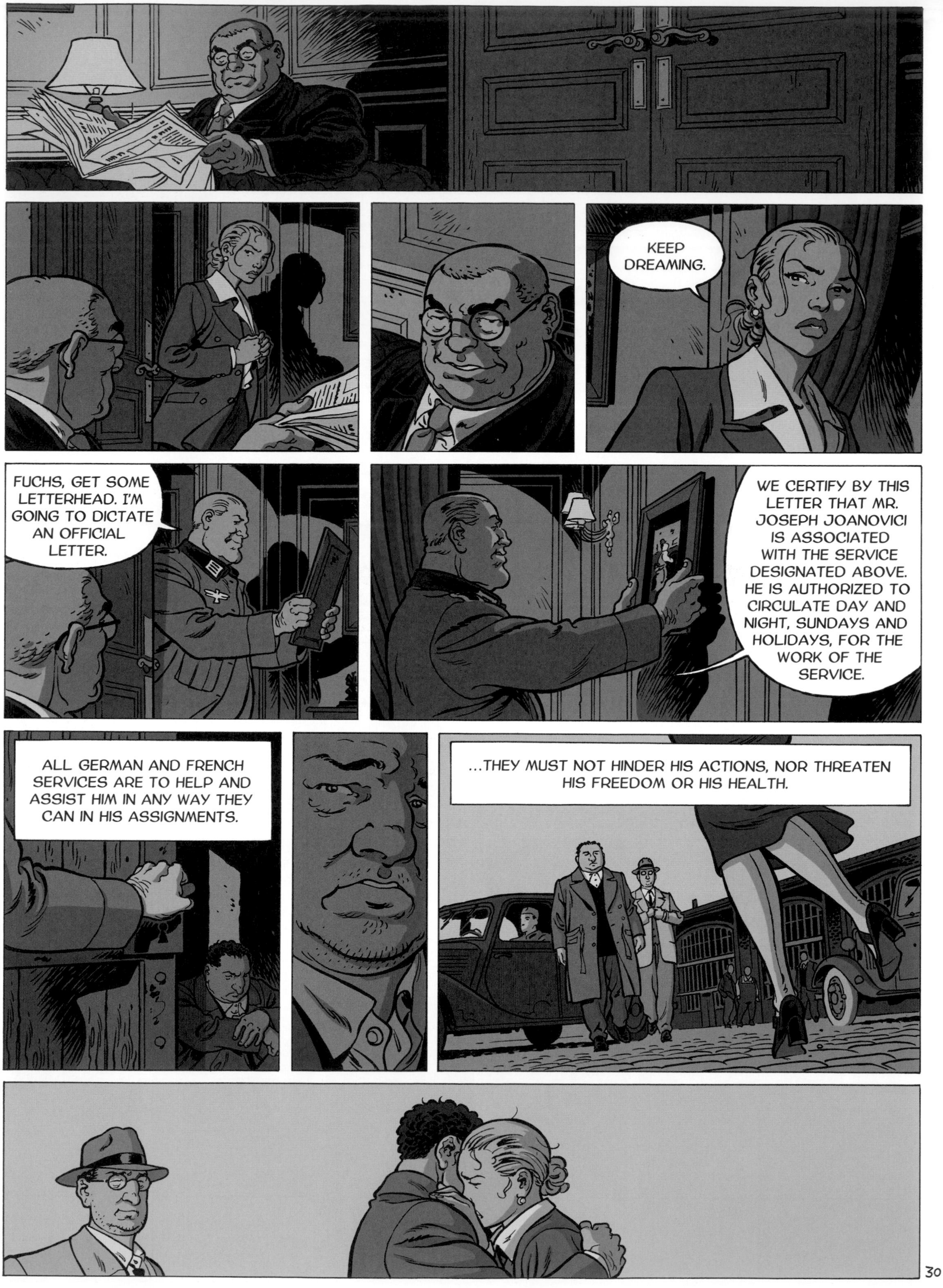
KEEP DREAMING.
FUCHS, GET SOME LETTERHEAD. I'M GOING TO DICTATE AN OFFICIAL LETTER.
WE CERTIFY BY THIS LETTER THAT MR. JOSEPH JOANOVICI IS ASSOCIATED WITH THE SERVICE DESIGNATED ABOVE. HE IS AUTHORIZED TO CIRCULATE DAY AND NIGHT, SUNDAYS AND HOLIDAYS, FOR THE WORK OF THE SERVICE.
ALL GERMAN AND FRENCH SERVICES ARE TO HELP AND ASSIST HIM IN ANY WAY THEY CAN IN HIS ASSIGNMENTS.
...THEY MUST NOT HINDER HIS ACTIONS, NOR THREATEN HIS FREEDOM OR HIS HEALTH.
30

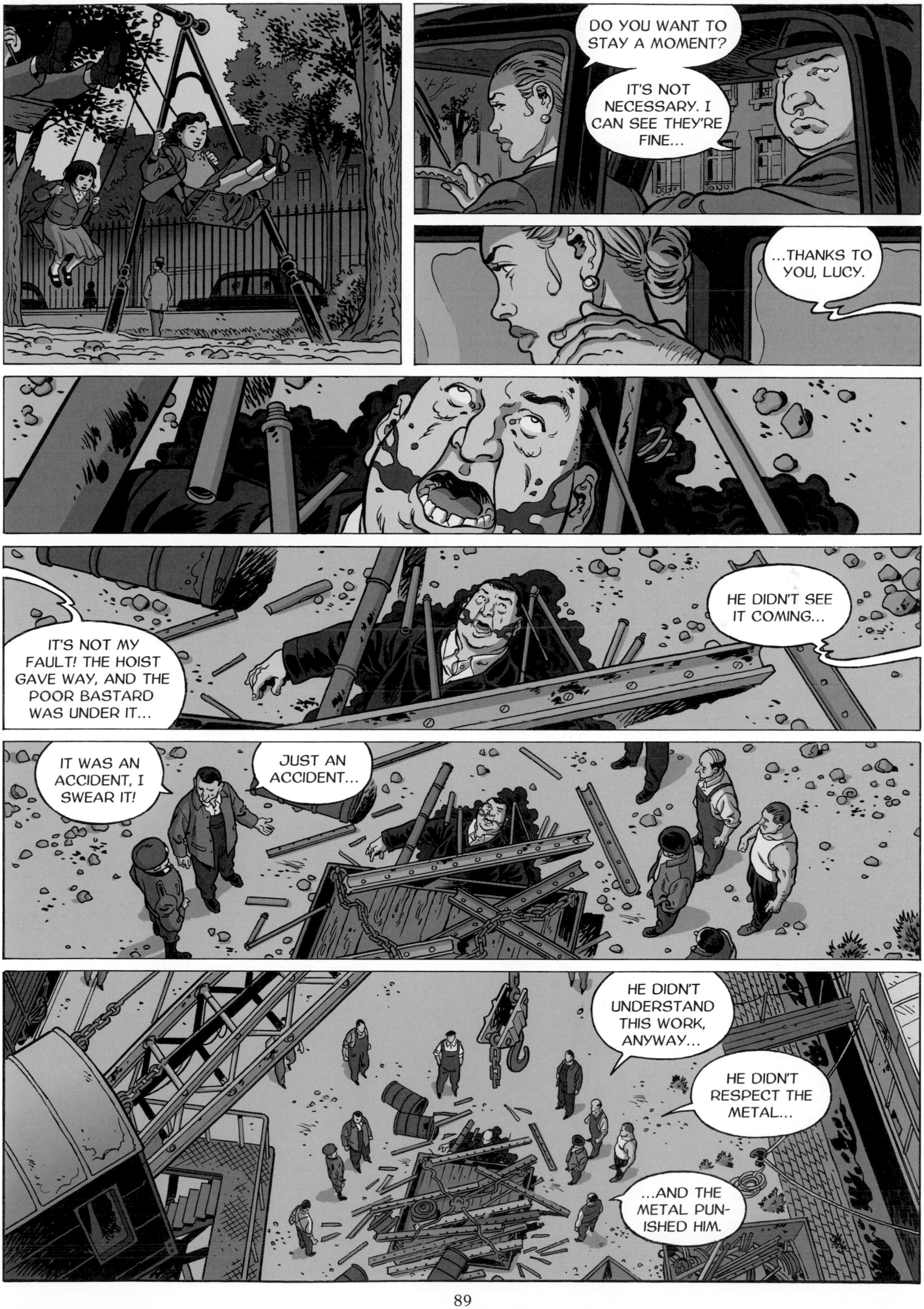
DO YOU WANT TO STAY A MOMENT?
IT'S NOT NECESSARY. I CAN SEE THEY'RE FINE...
...THANKS TO YOU, LUCY.
HE DIDN'T SEE IT COMING...
IT'S NOT MY FAULT! THE HOIST GAVE WAY, AND THE POOR BASTARD WAS UNDER IT...
IT WAS AN ACCIDENT, I SWEAR IT!
JUST AN ACCIDENT...
HE DIDN'T UNDERSTAND THIS WORK, ANYWAY...
HE DIDN'T RESPECT THE METAL...
...AND THE METAL PUN-ISHED HIM.
31

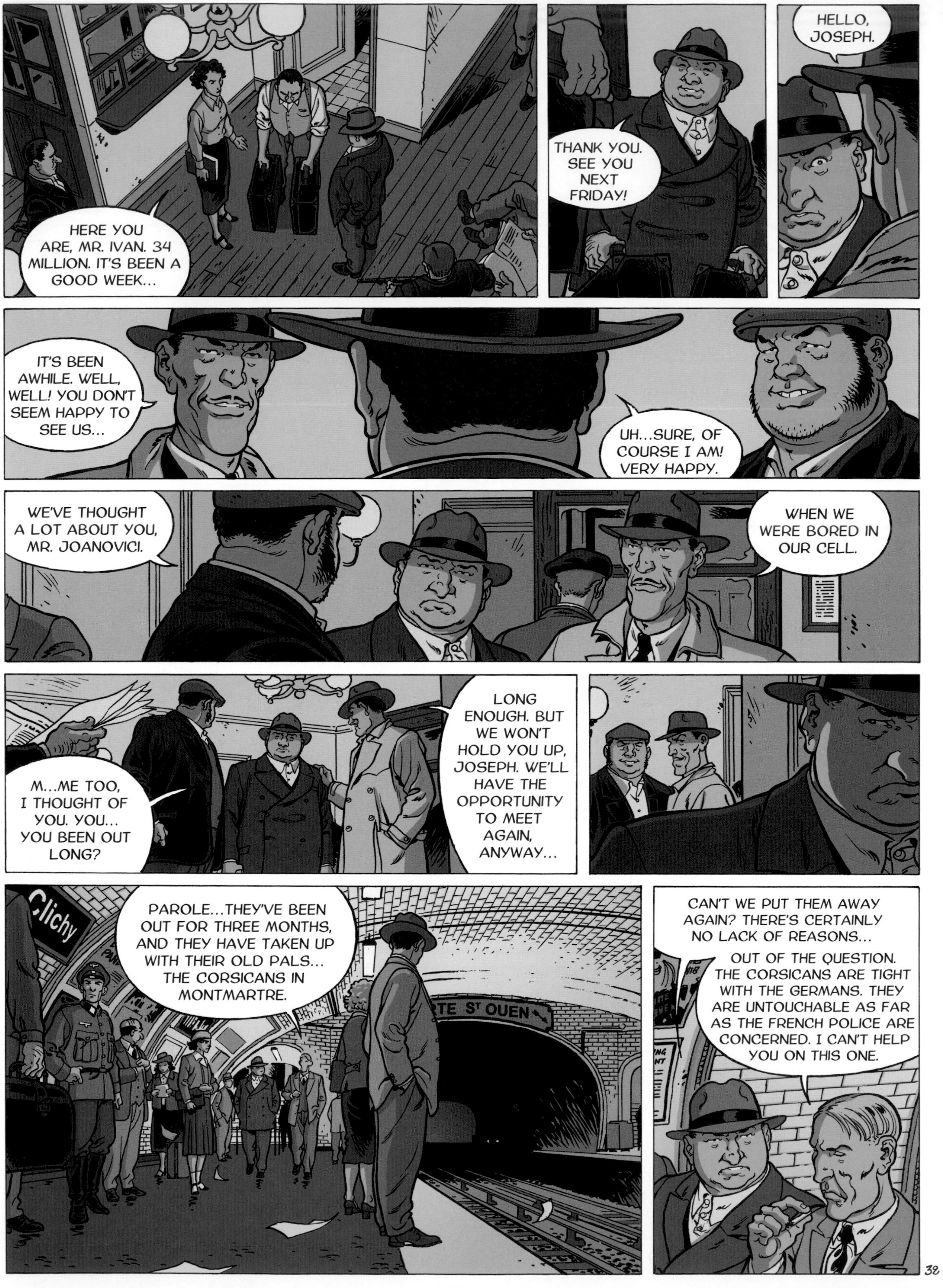
HERE YOU ARE, MR. IVAN. 34 MILLION. IT'S BEEN A GOOD WEEK...
THANK YOU. SEE YOU NEXT FRIDAY!
HELLO, JOSEPH.
IT'S BEEN AWHILE. WELL, WELL! YOU DON'T SEEM HAPPY TO SEE US...
UH...SURE, OF COURSE I AM! VERY HAPPY.
WE'VE THOUGHT A LOT ABOUT YOU, MR. JOANOVICI.
WHEN WE WERE BORED IN OUR CELL.
M...ME TOO, I THOUGHT OF YOU. YOU... YOU BEEN OUT LONG?
LONG ENOUGH. BUT WE WON'T HOLD YOU UP, JOSEPH. WE'LL HAVE THE OPPORTUNITY TO MEET AGAIN, ANYWAY...
Clichy
PAROLE...THEY'VE BEEN OUT FOR THREE MONTHS, AND THEY HAVE TAKEN UP WITH THEIR OLD PALS... THE CORSICANS IN MONTMARTRE.
TE St OUEN
CAN'T WE PUT THEM AWAY AGAIN? THERE'S CERTAINLY NO LACK OF REASONS...
OUT OF THE QUESTION. THE CORSICANS ARE TIGHT WITH THE GERMANS. THEY ARE UNTOUCHABLE AS FAR AS THE FRENCH POLICE ARE CONCERNED. I CAN'T HELP YOU ON THIS ONE.
32

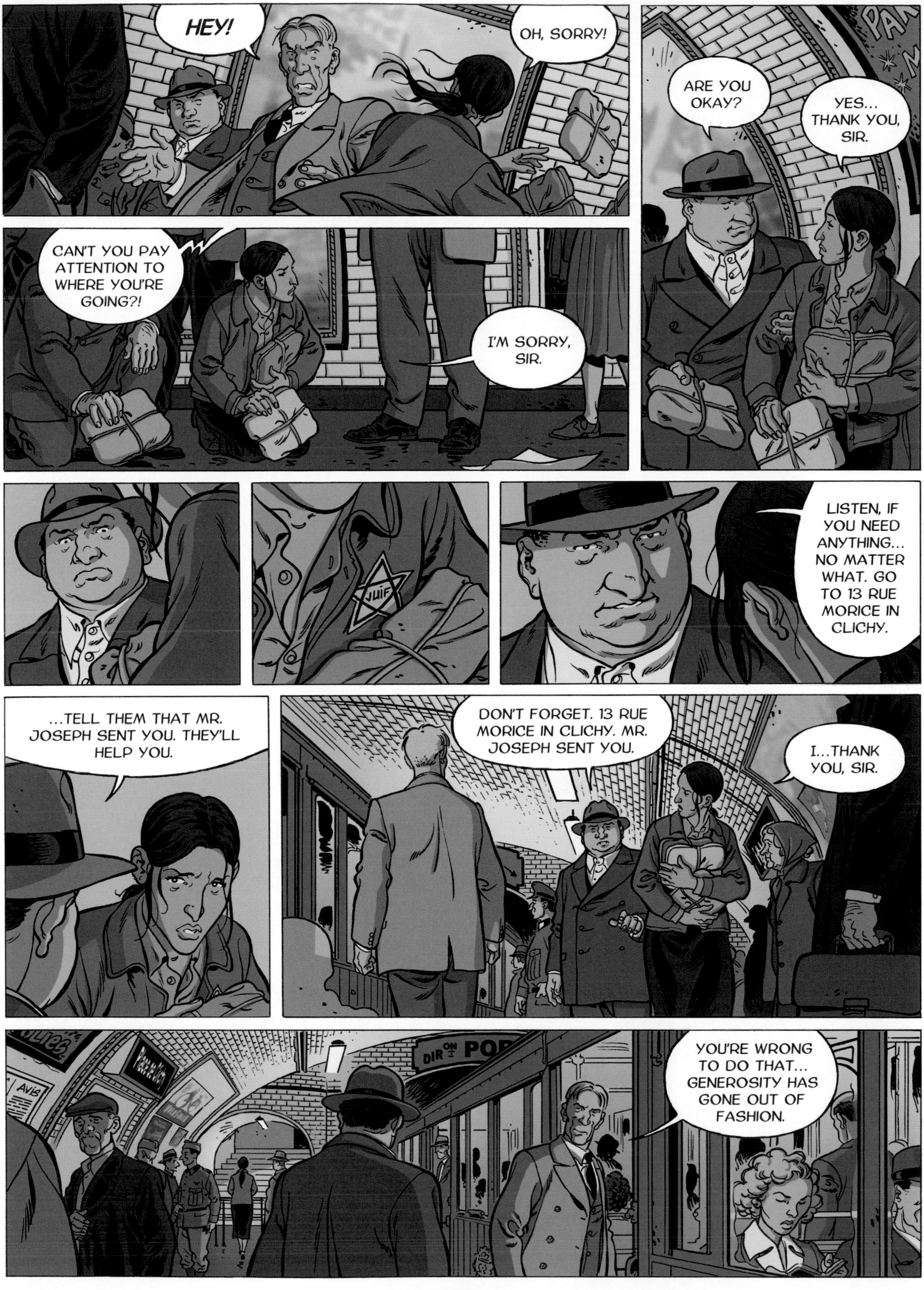
HEY!
OH, SORRY!
ARE YOU OKAY?
YES... THANK YOU, SIR.
CAN'T YOU PAY ATTENTION TO WHERE YOU'RE GOING?!
I'M SORRY, SIR.
JUIF
LISTEN, IF YOU NEED ANYTHING... NO MATTER WHAT. GO TO 13 RUE MORICE IN CLICHY.
...TELL THEM THAT MR. JOSEPH SENT YOU. THEY'LL HELP YOU.
DON'T FORGET. 13 RUE MORICE IN CLICHY. MR. JOSEPH SENT YOU.
I...THANK YOU, SIR.
AVIS
YOU'RE WRONG TO DO THAT... GENEROSITY HAS GONE OUT OF FASHION.
33

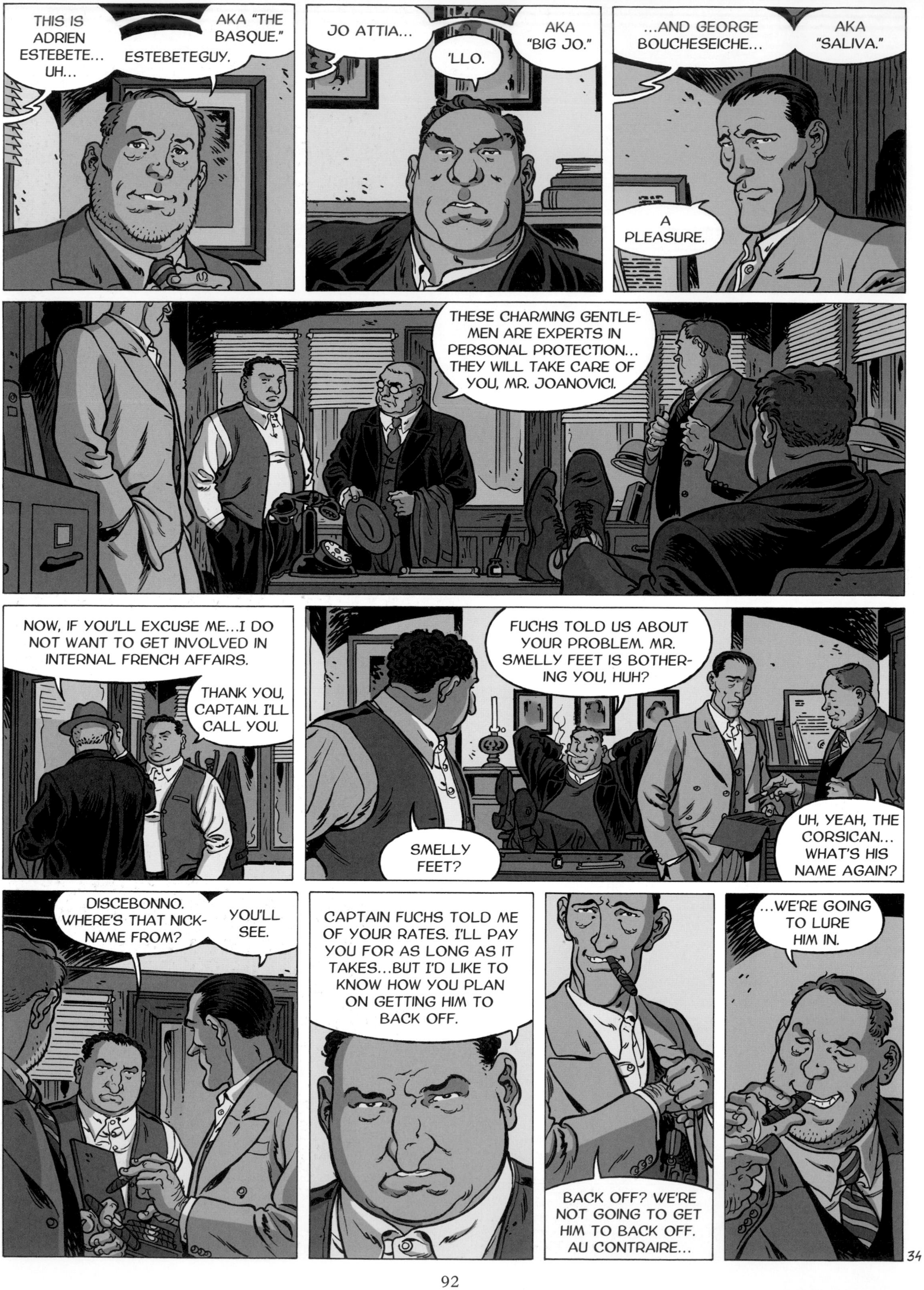
THIS IS ADRIEN ESTEBETE... UH...
AKA "THE BASQUE."
ESTEBETEGUY.
JO ATTIA...
'LLO.
AKA "BIG JO."
...AND GEORGE BOUCHESEICHE...
AKA "SALIVA."
A PLEASURE.
THESE CHARMING GENTLEMEN ARE EXPERTS IN PERSONAL PROTECTION... THEY WILL TAKE CARE OF YOU, MR. JOANOVICI.
NOW, IF YOU'LL EXCUSE ME...I DO NOT WANT TO GET INVOLVED IN INTERNAL FRENCH AFFAIRS.
THANK YOU, CAPTAIN. I'LL CALL YOU.
FUCHS TOLD US ABOUT YOUR PROBLEM. MR. SMELLY FEET IS BOTHERING YOU, HUH?
SMELLY FEET?
UH, YEAH, THE CORSICAN... WHAT'S HIS NAME AGAIN?
DISCEBONNO. WHERE'S THAT NICKNAME FROM?
YOU'LL SEE.
CAPTAIN FUCHS TOLD ME OF YOUR RATES. I'LL PAY YOU FOR AS LONG AS IT TAKES...BUT I'D LIKE TO KNOW HOW YOU PLAN ON GETTING HIM TO BACK OFF.
BACK OFF? WE'RE NOT GOING TO GET HIM TO BACK OFF. AU CONTRAIRE...
...WE'RE GOING TO LURE HIM IN.
34

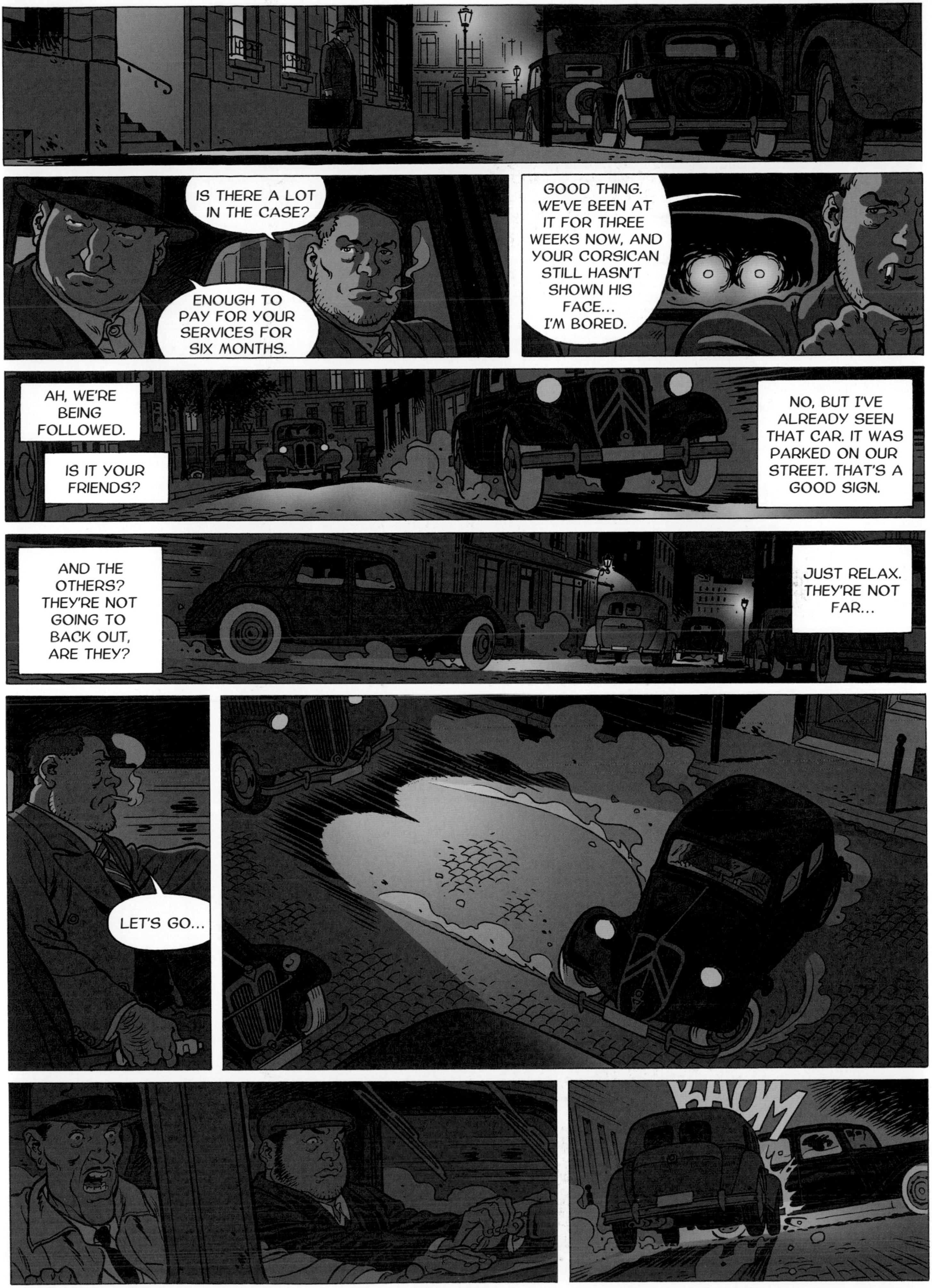
IS THERE A LOT IN THE CASE?
ENOUGH TO PAY FOR YOUR SERVICES FOR SIX MONTHS.
GOOD THING. WE'VE BEEN AT IT FOR THREE WEEKS NOW, AND YOUR CORSICAN STILL HASN'T SHOWN HIS FACE... I'M BORED.
AH, WE'RE BEING FOLLOWED.
IS IT YOUR FRIENDS?
NO, BUT I'VE ALREADY SEEN THAT CAR. IT WAS PARKED ON OUR STREET. THAT'S A GOOD SIGN.
AND THE OTHERS? THEY'RE NOT GOING TO BACK OUT, ARE THEY?
JUST RELAX. THEY'RE NOT FAR...
LET'S GO...
BAOM

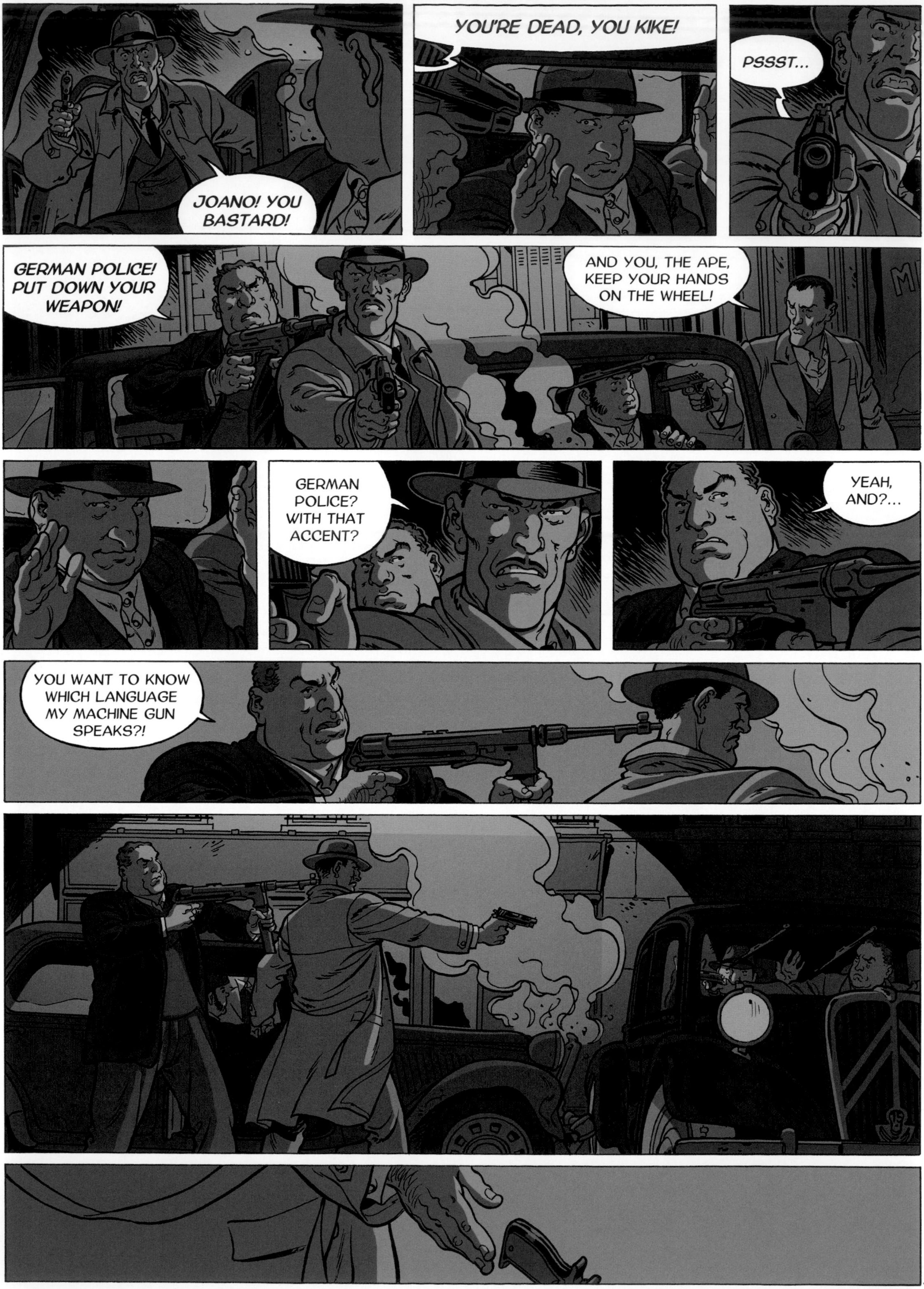
JOANO! YOU BASTARD!
YOU'RE DEAD, YOU KIKE!
PSSST...
GERMAN POLICE! PUT DOWN YOUR WEAPON!
AND YOU, THE APE, KEEP YOUR HANDS ON THE WHEEL!
GERMAN POLICE? WITH THAT ACCENT?
YEAH, AND?...
YOU WANT TO KNOW WHICH LANGUAGE MY MACHINE GUN SPEAKS?!

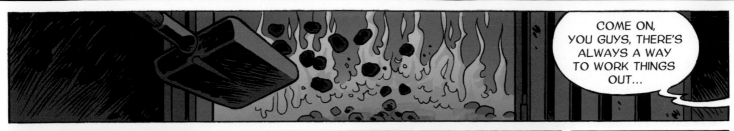

COME ON, YOU GUYS, THERE'S ALWAYS A WAY TO WORK THINGS OUT...

IT'S TRUE, JOSEPH AND I HAVE EXCHANGED WORDS, BUT I DIDN'T REALLY WANT TO HURT HIM.

COME ON, CUT US A BREAK...BETWEEN COLLEAGUES, WE NEED TO HELP EACH OTHER! IF IT'S MONEY YOU WANT, I HAVE LOTS OF IT... YOU'RE MAKING A BIG MISTAKE HERE!

I HAVE FRIENDS WHO ARE GOING TO COME LOOKING FOR ME...

WILL YOU SHUT YOUR TRAP?!

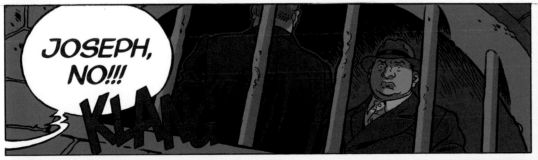

JOSEPH, NO!!!

KLANG

IT'S DONE.

37

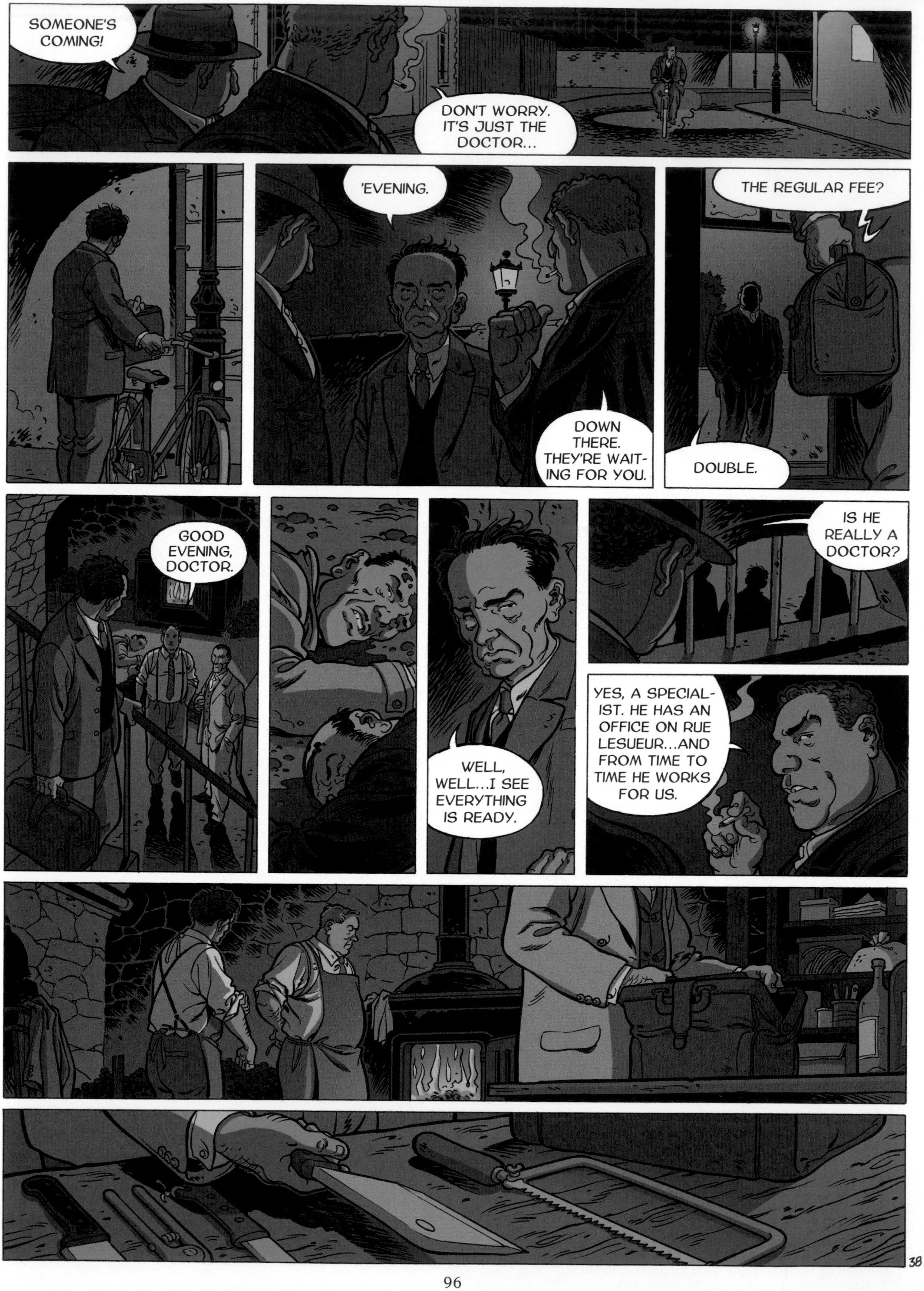
SOMEONE'S COMING!
DON'T WORRY. IT'S JUST THE DOCTOR...
'EVENING.
DOWN THERE. THEY'RE WAIT-ING FOR YOU.
THE REGULAR FEE?
DOUBLE.
GOOD EVENING, DOCTOR.
WELL, WELL...I SEE EVERYTHING IS READY.
IS HE REALLY A DOCTOR?
YES, A SPECIAL-IST. HE HAS AN OFFICE ON RUE LESUEUR...AND FROM TIME TO TIME HE WORKS FOR US.
38

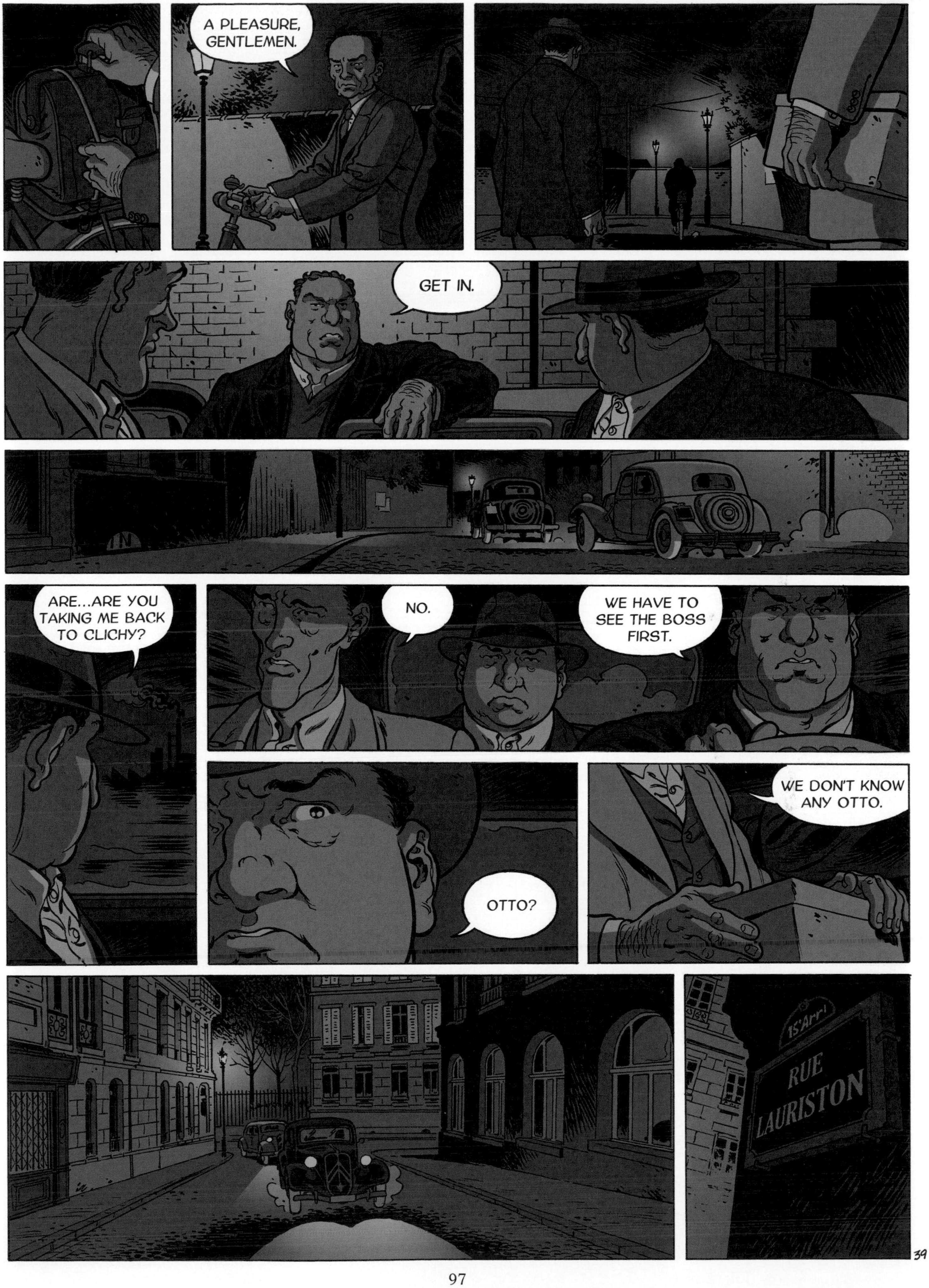

A PLEASURE, GENTLEMEN.
GET IN.
ARE...ARE YOU TAKING ME BACK TO CLICHY?
NO.
WE HAVE TO SEE THE BOSS FIRST.
OTTO?
WE DON'T KNOW ANY OTTO.
15e Arrt
RUE LAURISTON
39

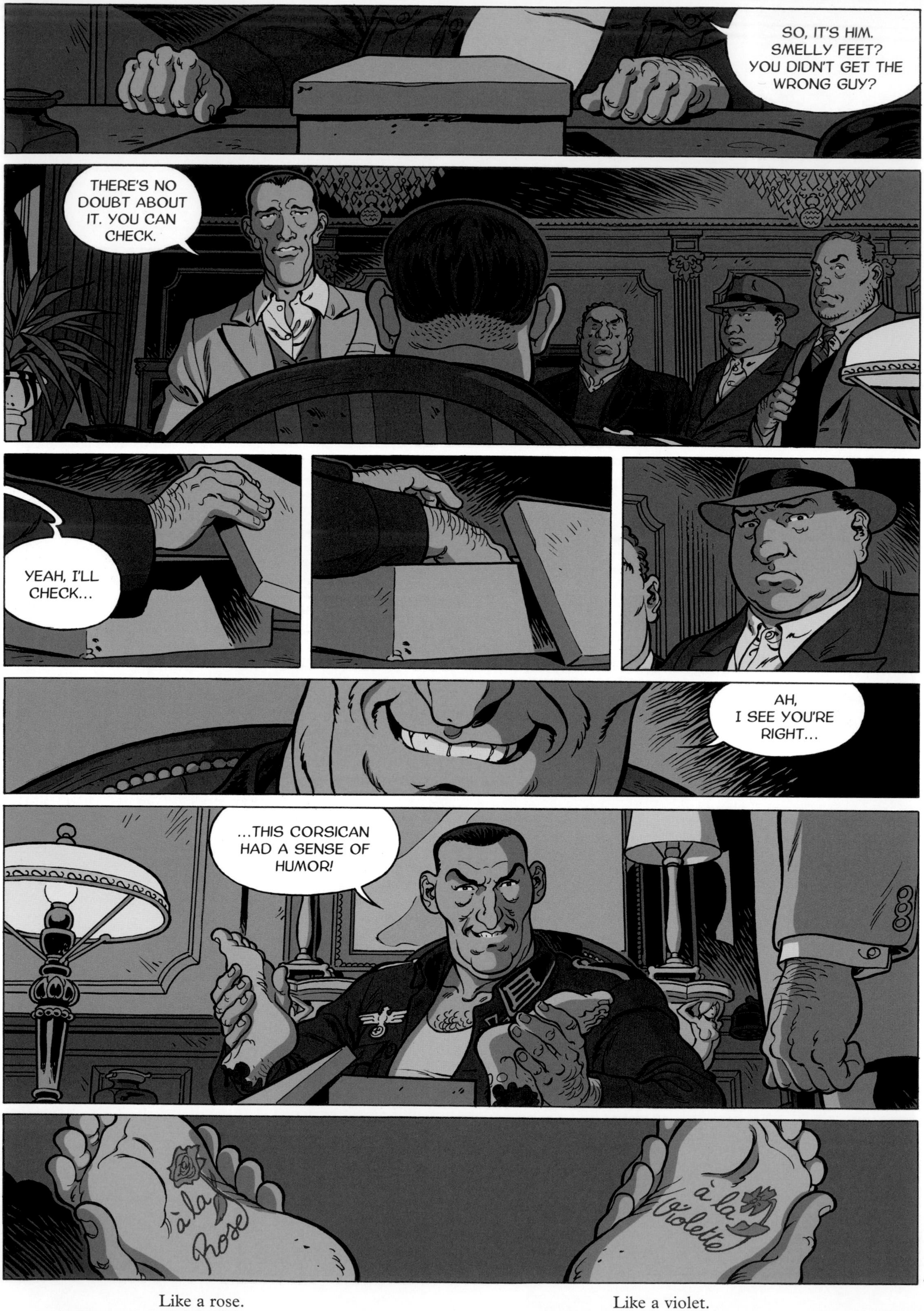
SO, IT'S HIM. SMELLY FEET? YOU DIDN'T GET THE WRONG GUY?
THERE'S NO DOUBT ABOUT IT. YOU CAN CHECK.
YEAH, I'LL CHECK...
AH, I SEE YOU'RE RIGHT...
...THIS CORSICAN HAD A SENSE OF HUMOR!
à la Rose
à la Violette

Like a rose. Like a violet.

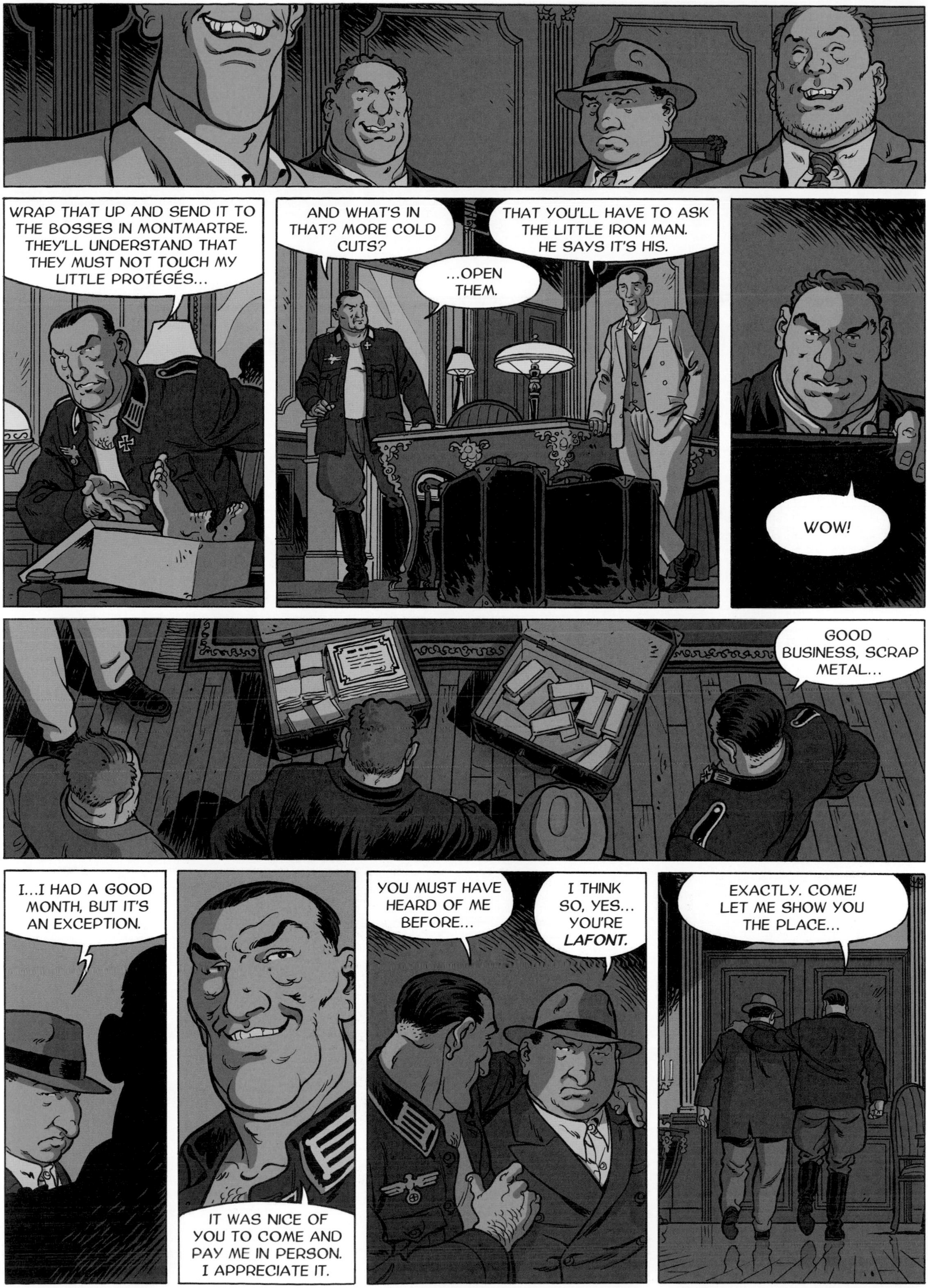
WRAP THAT UP AND SEND IT TO THE BOSSES IN MONTMARTRE. THEY'LL UNDERSTAND THAT THEY MUST NOT TOUCH MY LITTLE PROTÉGÉS...
AND WHAT'S IN THAT? MORE COLD CUTS?
THAT YOU'LL HAVE TO ASK THE LITTLE IRON MAN. HE SAYS IT'S HIS.
...OPEN THEM.
WOW!
GOOD BUSINESS, SCRAP METAL...
I...I HAD A GOOD MONTH, BUT IT'S AN EXCEPTION.
IT WAS NICE OF YOU TO COME AND PAY ME IN PERSON. I APPRECIATE IT.
YOU MUST HAVE HEARD OF ME BEFORE...
I THINK SO, YES... YOU'RE *LAFONT.*
EXACTLY. COME! LET ME SHOW YOU THE PLACE...

41

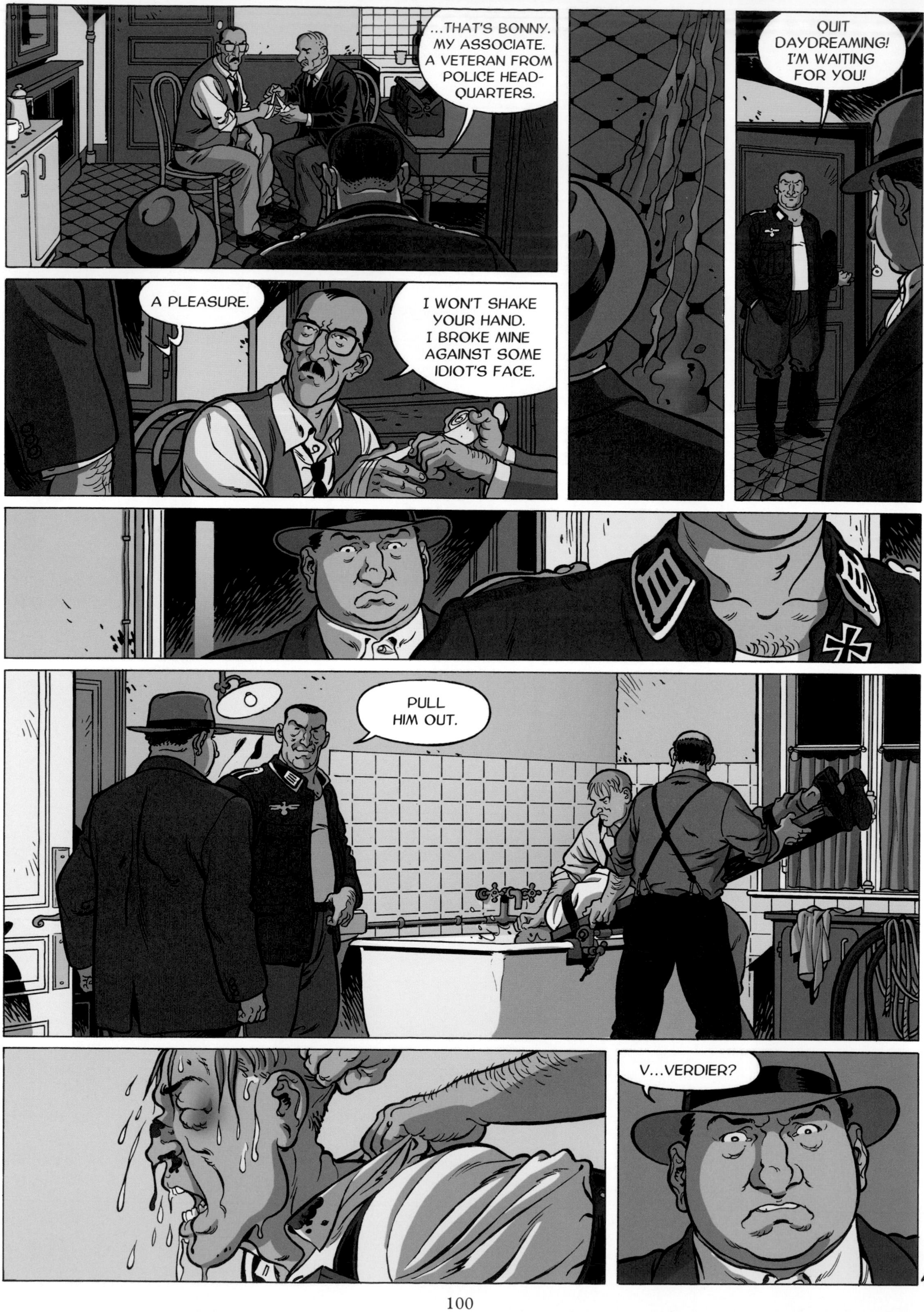

...THAT'S BONNY. MY ASSOCIATE. A VETERAN FROM POLICE HEAD-QUARTERS.
QUIT DAYDREAMING! I'M WAITING FOR YOU!
A PLEASURE.
I WON'T SHAKE YOUR HAND. I BROKE MINE AGAINST SOME IDIOT'S FACE.
PULL HIM OUT.
V...VERDIER?
42

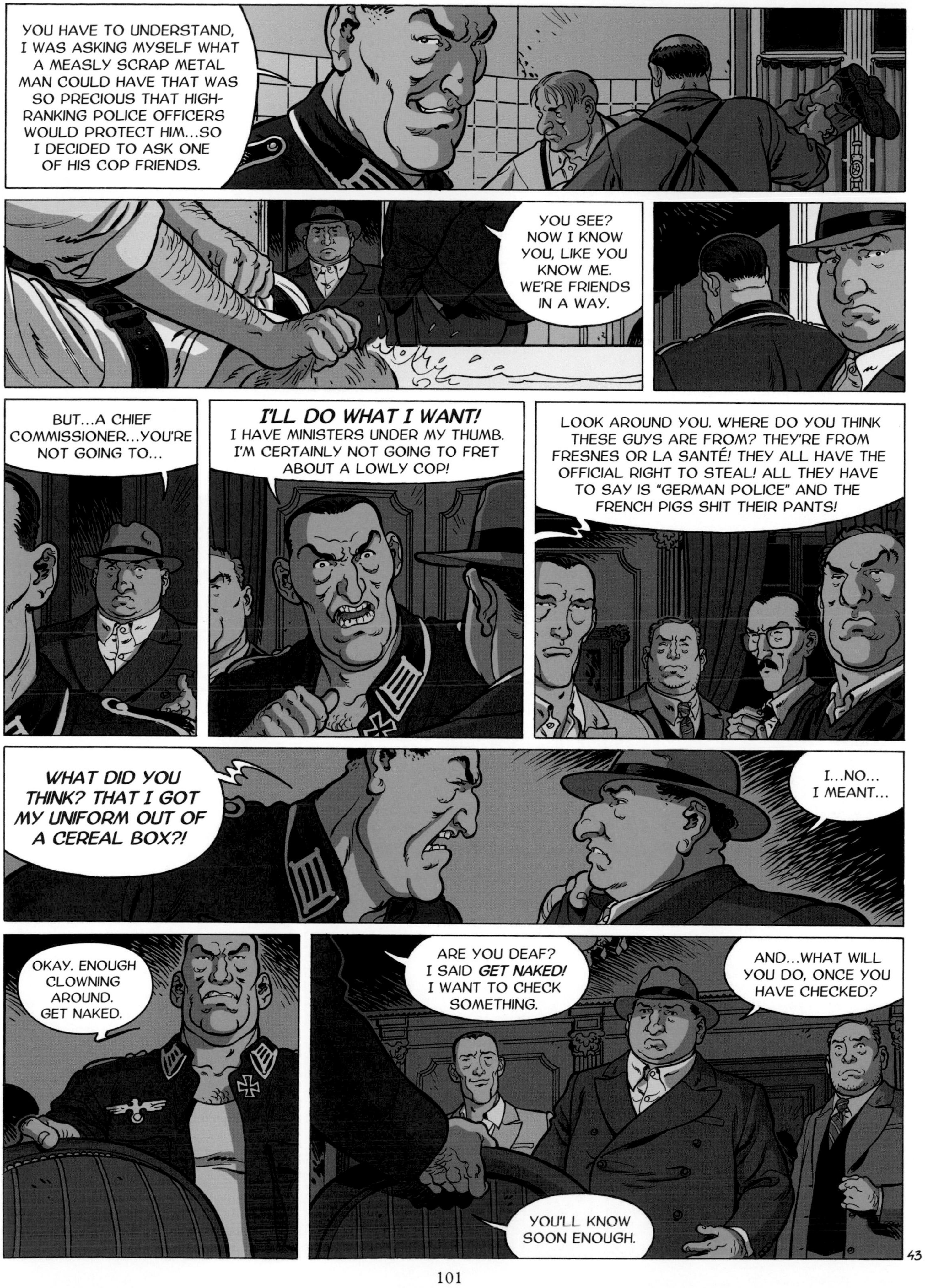
YOU HAVE TO UNDERSTAND, I WAS ASKING MYSELF WHAT A MEASLY SCRAP METAL MAN COULD HAVE THAT WAS SO PRECIOUS THAT HIGH-RANKING POLICE OFFICERS WOULD PROTECT HIM...SO I DECIDED TO ASK ONE OF HIS COP FRIENDS.
YOU SEE? NOW I KNOW YOU, LIKE YOU KNOW ME. WE'RE FRIENDS IN A WAY.
BUT...A CHIEF COMMISSIONER...YOU'RE NOT GOING TO...
I'LL DO WHAT I WANT! I HAVE MINISTERS UNDER MY THUMB. I'M CERTAINLY NOT GOING TO FRET ABOUT A LOWLY COP!
LOOK AROUND YOU. WHERE DO YOU THINK THESE GUYS ARE FROM? THEY'RE FROM FRESNES OR LA SANTÉ! THEY ALL HAVE THE OFFICIAL RIGHT TO STEAL! ALL THEY HAVE TO SAY IS "GERMAN POLICE" AND THE FRENCH PIGS SHIT THEIR PANTS!
WHAT DID YOU THINK? THAT I GOT MY UNIFORM OUT OF A CEREAL BOX?!
I...NO... I MEANT...
OKAY. ENOUGH CLOWNING AROUND. GET NAKED.
ARE YOU DEAF? I SAID GET NAKED! I WANT TO CHECK SOMETHING.
AND...WHAT WILL YOU DO, ONCE YOU HAVE CHECKED?
YOU'LL KNOW SOON ENOUGH.
43

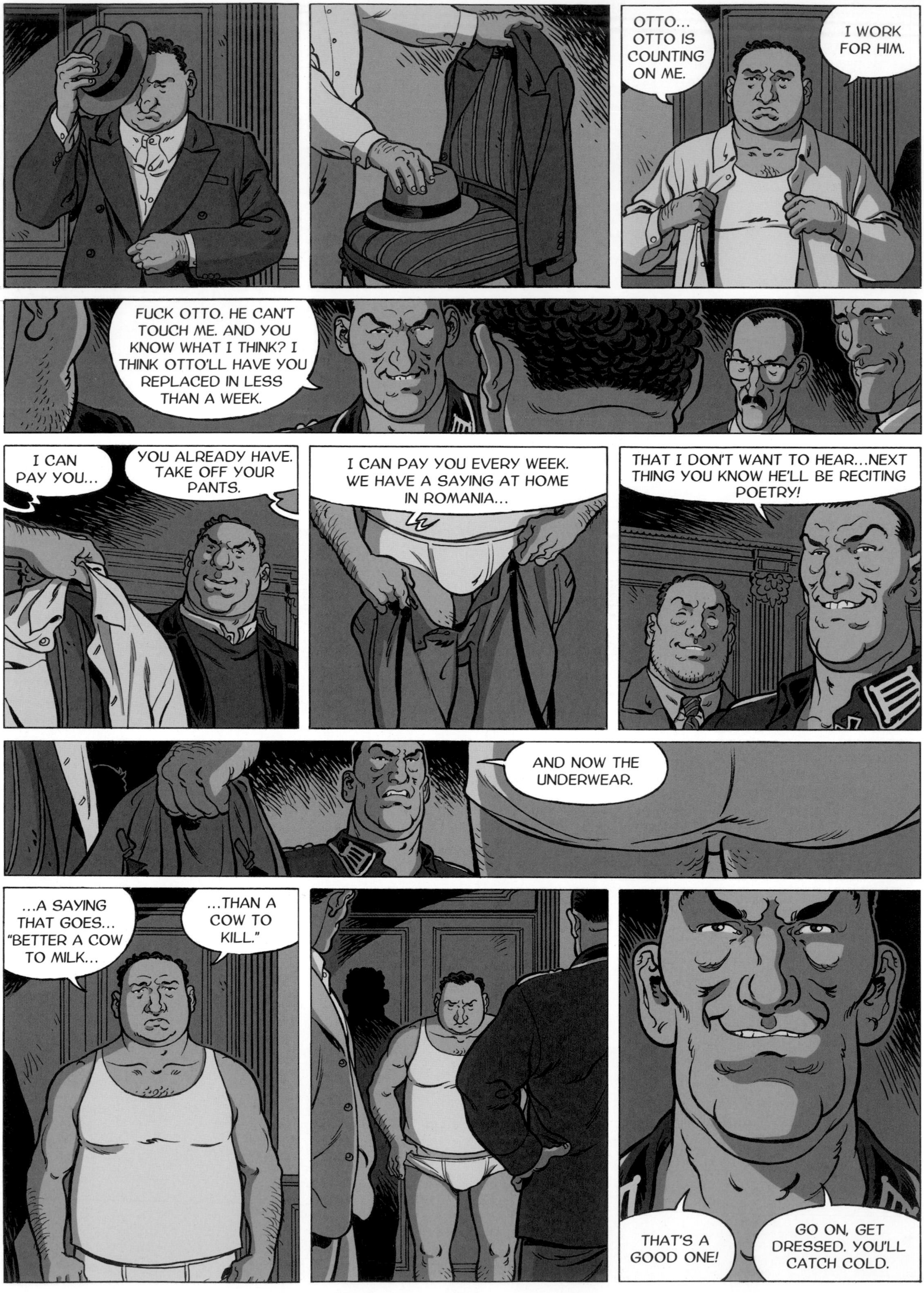
OTTO... OTTO IS COUNTING ON ME.
I WORK FOR HIM.
FUCK OTTO. HE CAN'T TOUCH ME. AND YOU KNOW WHAT I THINK? I THINK OTTO'LL HAVE YOU REPLACED IN LESS THAN A WEEK.
I CAN PAY YOU...
YOU ALREADY HAVE. TAKE OFF YOUR PANTS.
I CAN PAY YOU EVERY WEEK. WE HAVE A SAYING AT HOME IN ROMANIA...
THAT I DON'T WANT TO HEAR...NEXT THING YOU KNOW HE'LL BE RECITING POETRY!
AND NOW THE UNDERWEAR.
...A SAYING THAT GOES... "BETTER A COW TO MILK...
...THAN A COW TO KILL."
THAT'S A GOOD ONE!
GO ON, GET DRESSED. YOU'LL CATCH COLD.
44

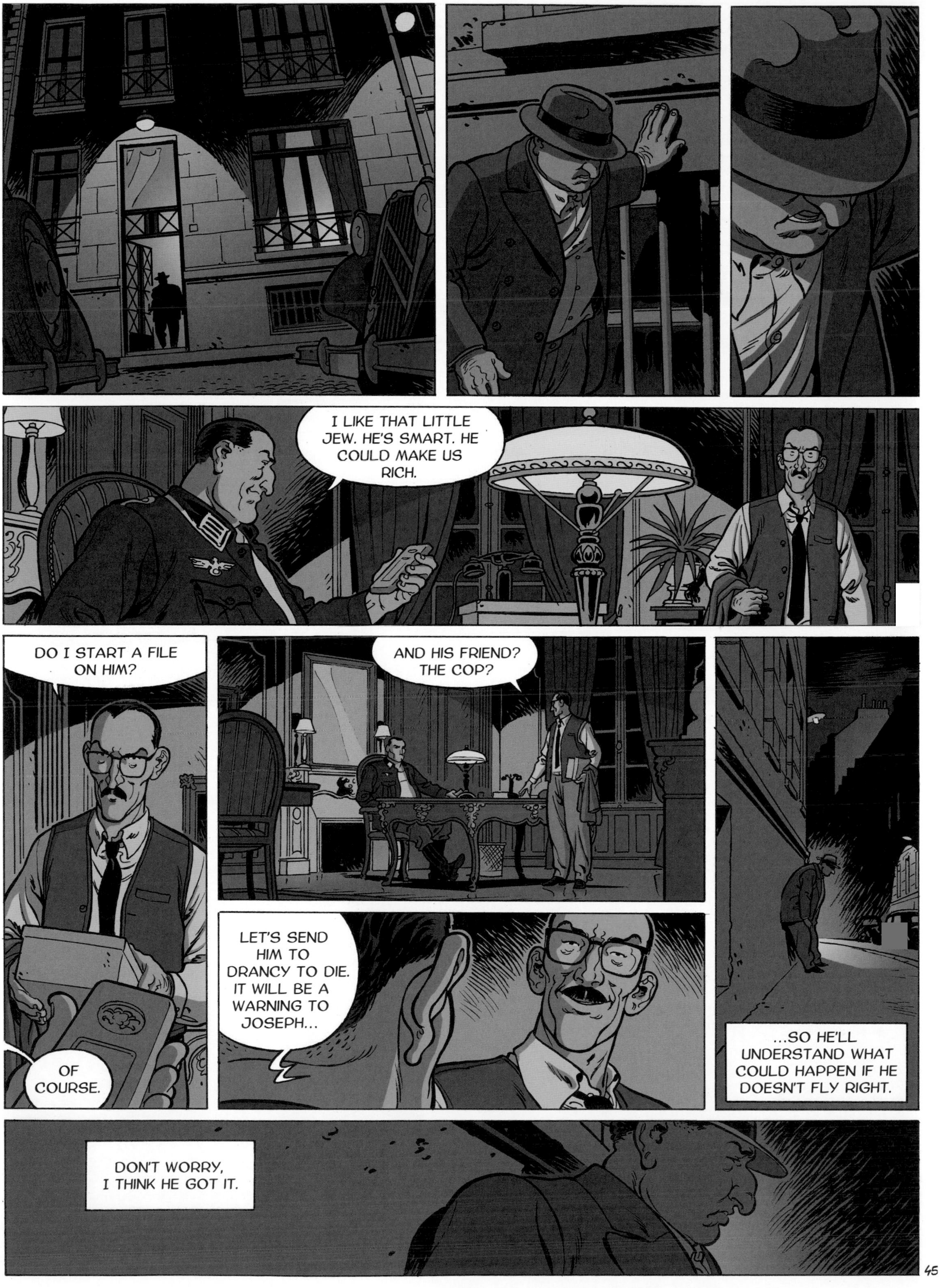

I LIKE THAT LITTLE JEW. HE'S SMART. HE COULD MAKE US RICH.
DO I START A FILE ON HIM?
OF COURSE.
AND HIS FRIEND? THE COP?
LET'S SEND HIM TO DRANCY TO DIE. IT WILL BE A WARNING TO JOSEPH...
...SO HE'LL UNDERSTAND WHAT COULD HAPPEN IF HE DOESN'T FLY RIGHT.
DON'T WORRY, I THINK HE GOT IT.
45

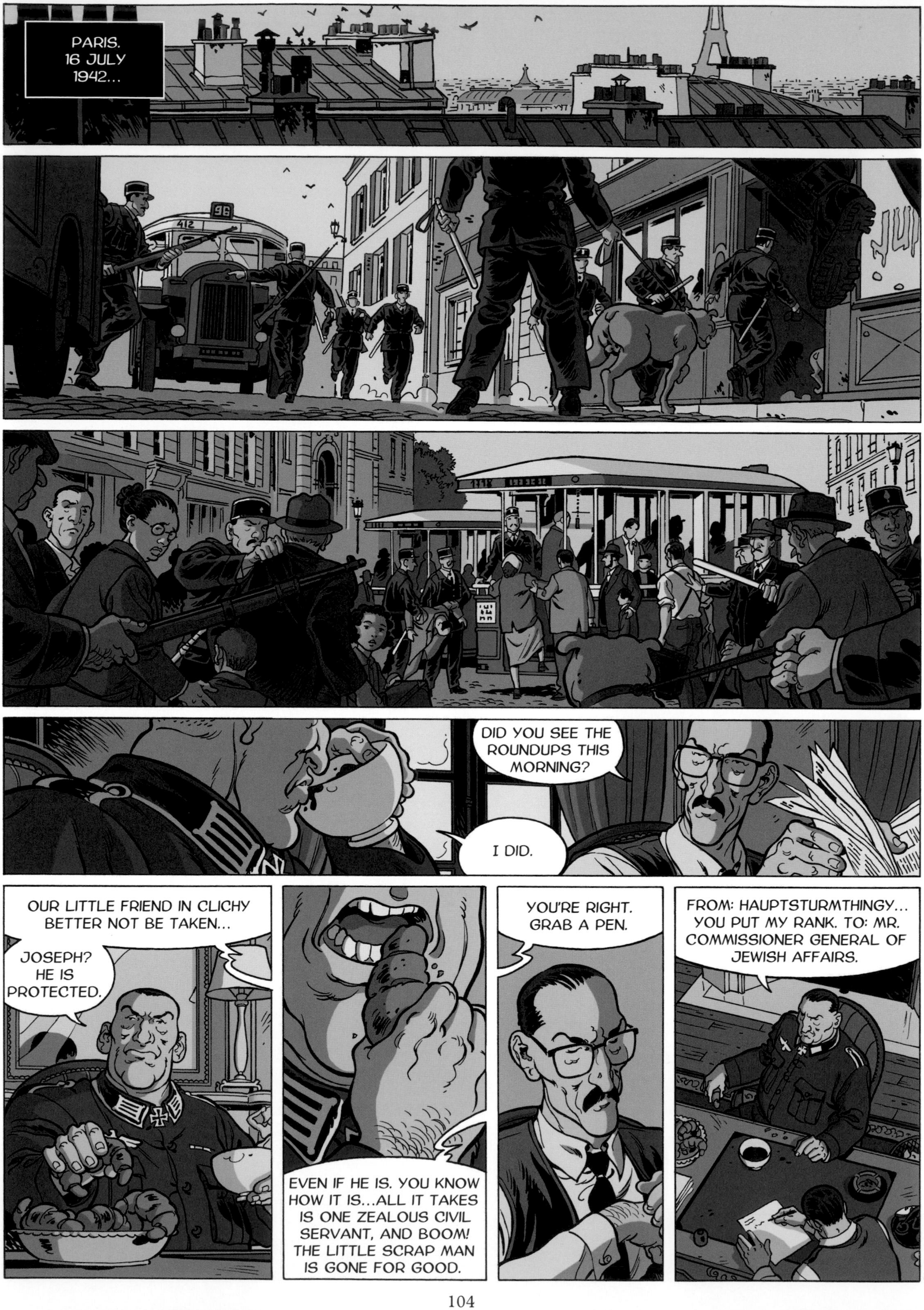
PARIS. 16 JULY 1942...
DID YOU SEE THE ROUNDUPS THIS MORNING?
I DID.
OUR LITTLE FRIEND IN CLICHY BETTER NOT BE TAKEN...
JOSEPH? HE IS PROTECTED.
EVEN IF HE IS. YOU KNOW HOW IT IS...ALL IT TAKES IS ONE ZEALOUS CIVIL SERVANT, AND BOOM! THE LITTLE SCRAP MAN IS GONE FOR GOOD.
YOU'RE RIGHT. GRAB A PEN.
FROM: HAUPTSTURMTHINGY... YOU PUT MY RANK. TO: MR. COMMISSIONER GENERAL OF JEWISH AFFAIRS.
46

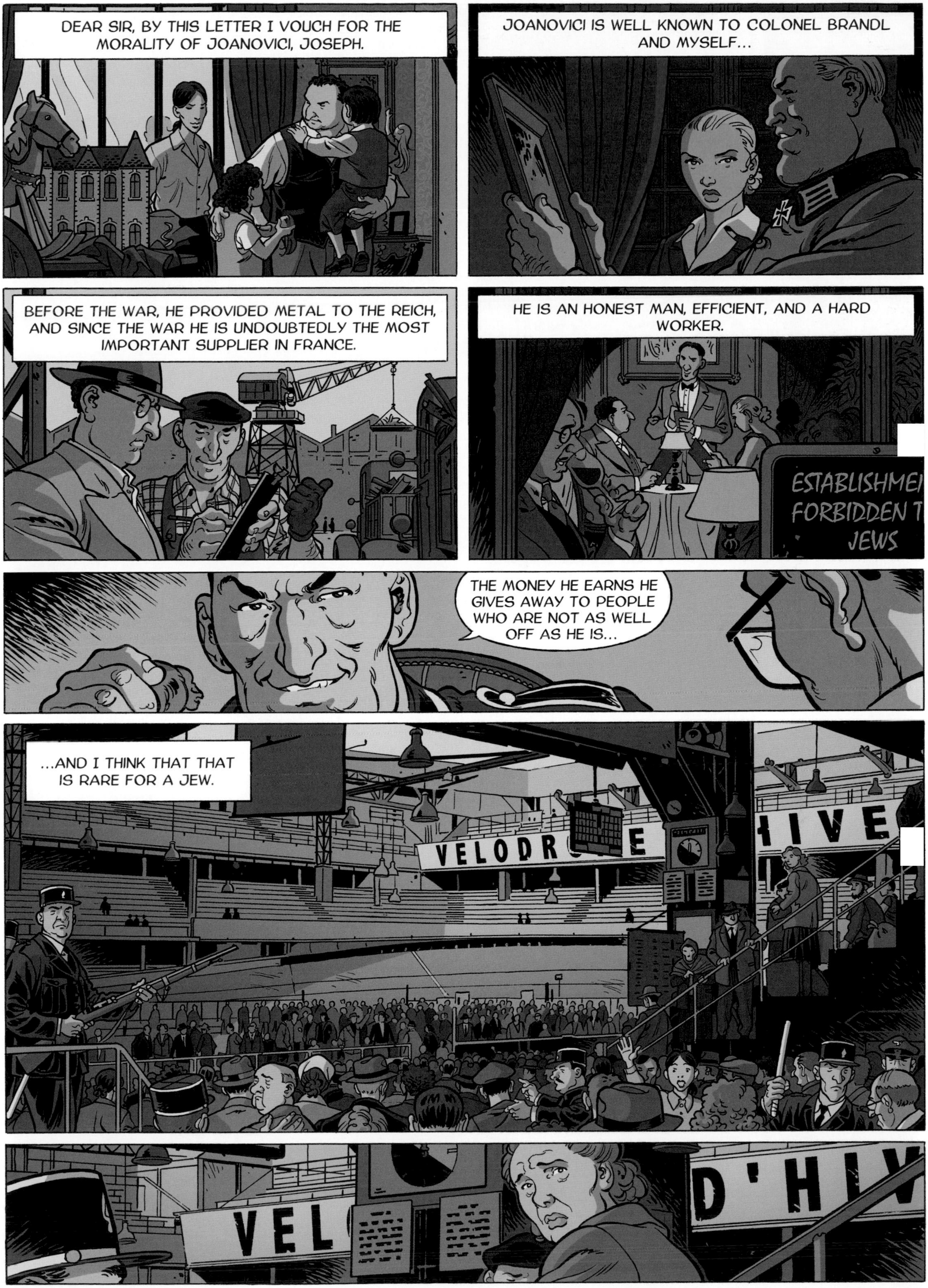
DEAR SIR, BY THIS LETTER I VOUCH FOR THE MORALITY OF JOANOVICI, JOSEPH.
JOANOVICI IS WELL KNOWN TO COLONEL BRANDL AND MYSELF...
BEFORE THE WAR, HE PROVIDED METAL TO THE REICH, AND SINCE THE WAR HE IS UNDOUBTEDLY THE MOST IMPORTANT SUPPLIER IN FRANCE.
HE IS AN HONEST MAN, EFFICIENT, AND A HARD WORKER.
ESTABLISHME
FORBIDDEN T
JEWS
THE MONEY HE EARNS HE GIVES AWAY TO PEOPLE WHO ARE NOT AS WELL OFF AS HE IS...
...AND I THINK THAT THAT IS RARE FOR A JEW.
VELODR E HIVE
VEL
D'HIV

47

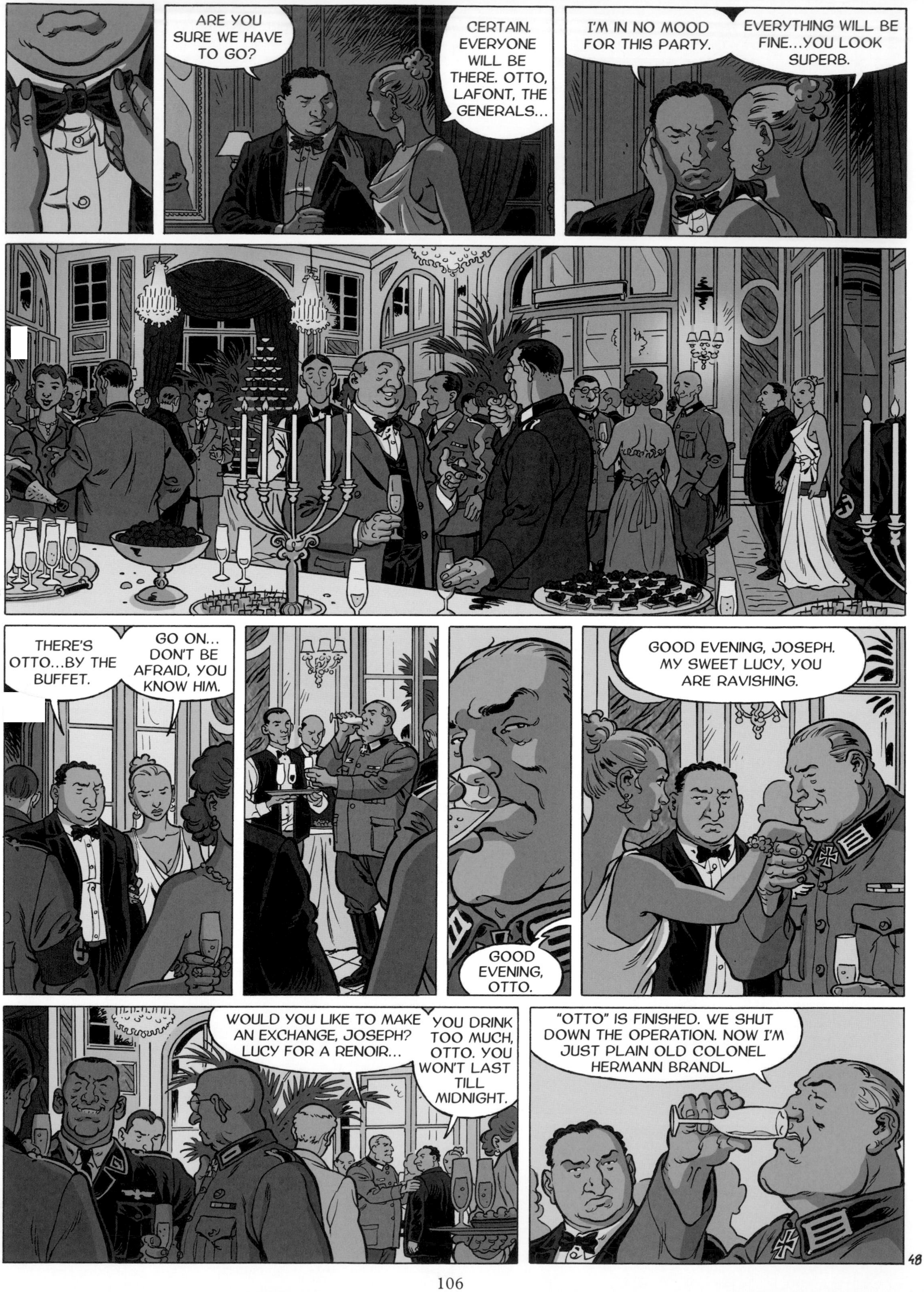
ARE YOU SURE WE HAVE TO GO?
CERTAIN. EVERYONE WILL BE THERE. OTTO, LAFONT, THE GENERALS...
I'M IN NO MOOD FOR THIS PARTY.
EVERYTHING WILL BE FINE...YOU LOOK SUPERB.
THERE'S OTTO...BY THE BUFFET.
GO ON... DON'T BE AFRAID, YOU KNOW HIM.
GOOD EVENING, OTTO.
GOOD EVENING, JOSEPH. MY SWEET LUCY, YOU ARE RAVISHING.
WOULD YOU LIKE TO MAKE AN EXCHANGE, JOSEPH? LUCY FOR A RENOIR...
YOU DRINK TOO MUCH, OTTO. YOU WON'T LAST TILL MIDNIGHT.
"OTTO" IS FINISHED. WE SHUT DOWN THE OPERATION. NOW I'M JUST PLAIN OLD COLONEL HERMANN BRANDL.
48

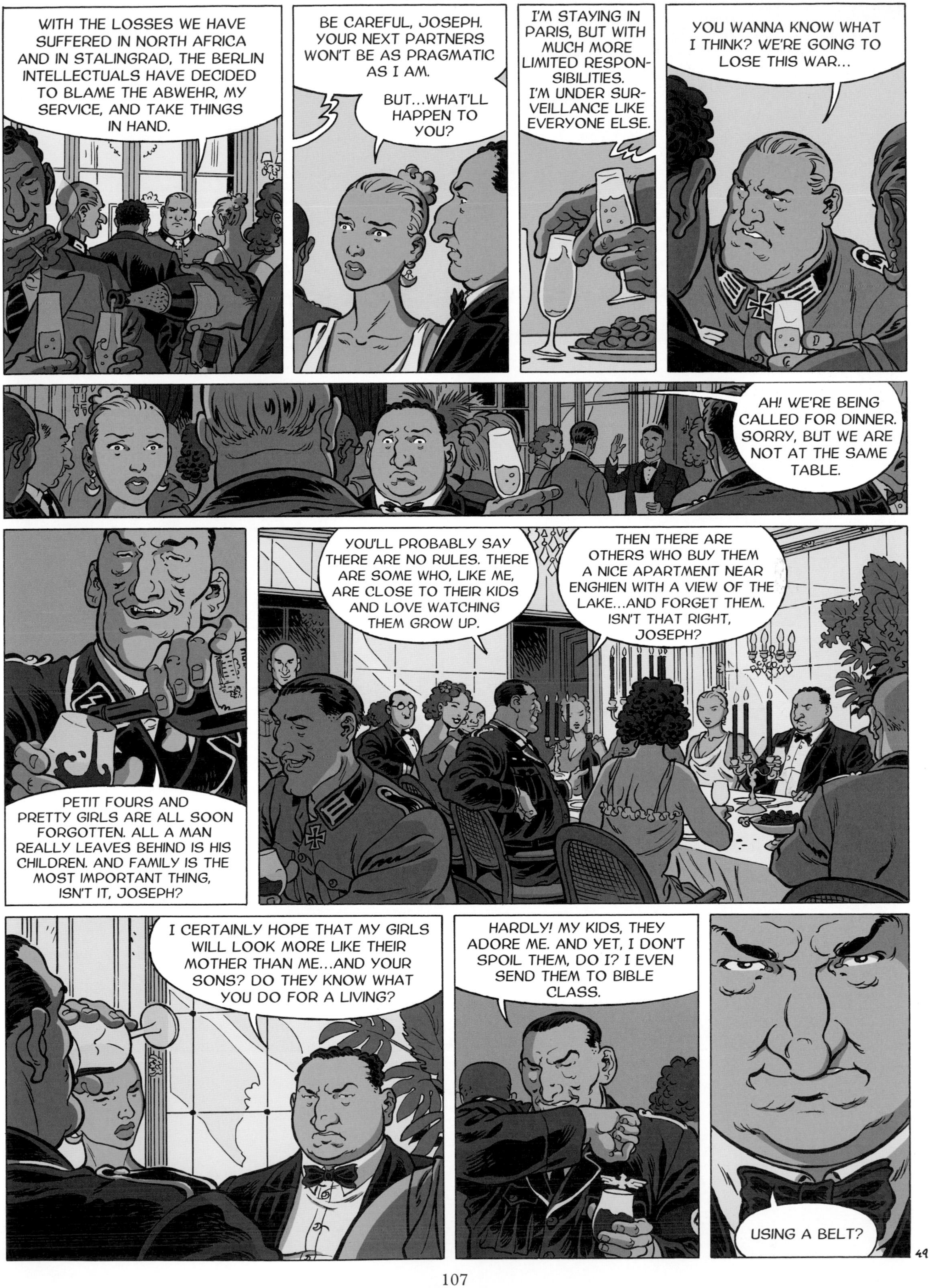

WITH THE LOSSES WE HAVE SUFFERED IN NORTH AFRICA AND IN STALINGRAD, THE BERLIN INTELLECTUALS HAVE DECIDED TO BLAME THE ABWEHR, MY SERVICE, AND TAKE THINGS IN HAND.
BE CAREFUL, JOSEPH. YOUR NEXT PARTNERS WON'T BE AS PRAGMATIC AS I AM.
BUT...WHAT'LL HAPPEN TO YOU?
I'M STAYING IN PARIS, BUT WITH MUCH MORE LIMITED RESPON-SIBILITIES. I'M UNDER SUR-VEILLANCE LIKE EVERYONE ELSE.
YOU WANNA KNOW WHAT I THINK? WE'RE GOING TO LOSE THIS WAR...
AH! WE'RE BEING CALLED FOR DINNER. SORRY, BUT WE ARE NOT AT THE SAME TABLE.
PETIT FOURS AND PRETTY GIRLS ARE ALL SOON FORGOTTEN. ALL A MAN REALLY LEAVES BEHIND IS HIS CHILDREN. AND FAMILY IS THE MOST IMPORTANT THING, ISN'T IT, JOSEPH?
YOU'LL PROBABLY SAY THERE ARE NO RULES. THERE ARE SOME WHO, LIKE ME, ARE CLOSE TO THEIR KIDS AND LOVE WATCHING THEM GROW UP.
THEN THERE ARE OTHERS WHO BUY THEM A NICE APARTMENT NEAR ENGHIEN WITH A VIEW OF THE LAKE...AND FORGET THEM. ISN'T THAT RIGHT, JOSEPH?
I CERTAINLY HOPE THAT MY GIRLS WILL LOOK MORE LIKE THEIR MOTHER THAN ME...AND YOUR SONS? DO THEY KNOW WHAT YOU DO FOR A LIVING?
HARDLY! MY KIDS, THEY ADORE ME. AND YET, I DON'T SPOIL THEM, DO I? I EVEN SEND THEM TO BIBLE CLASS.
USING A BELT?

49

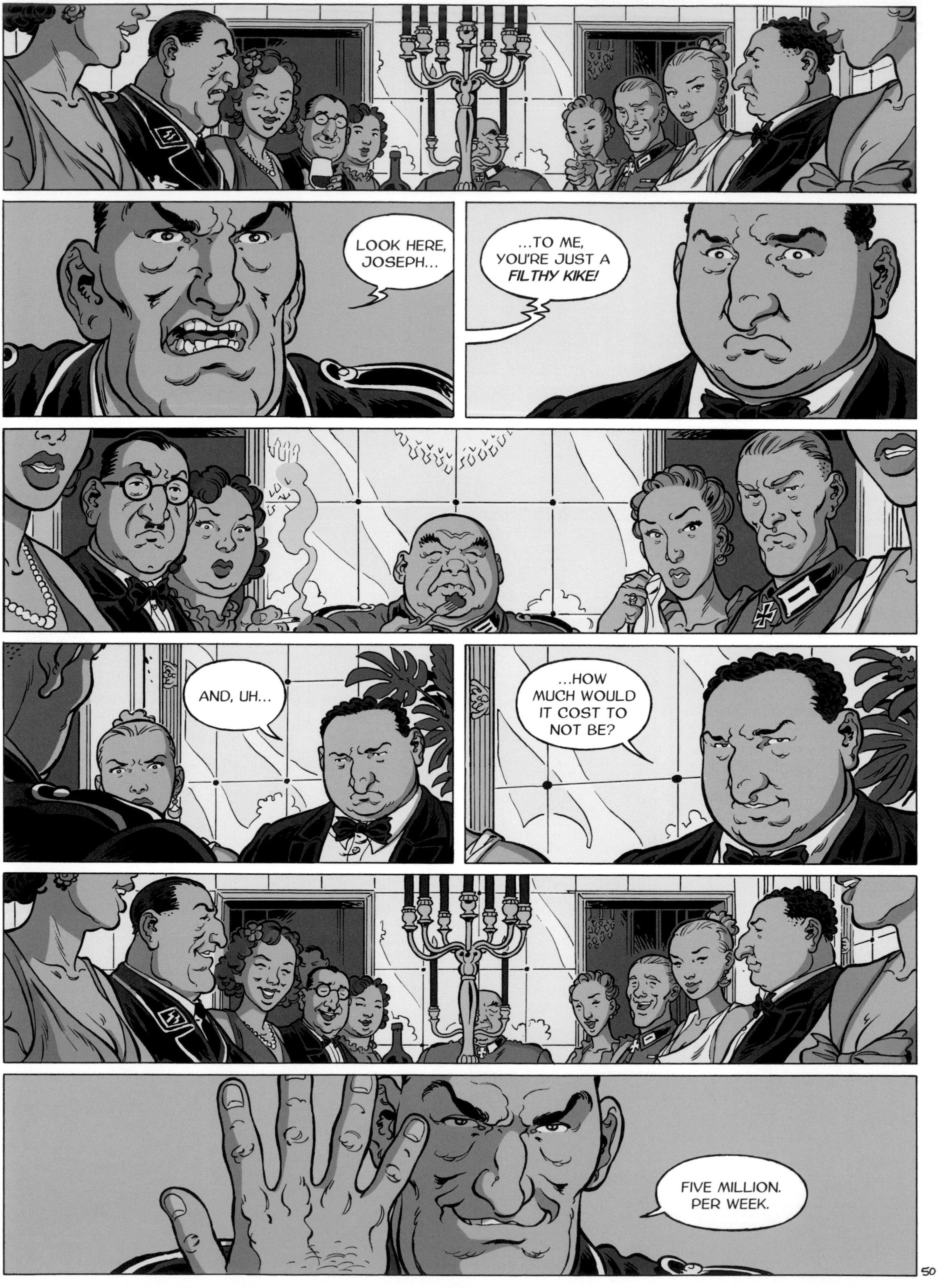
LOOK HERE, JOSEPH...
...TO ME, YOU'RE JUST A *FILTHY KIKE!*
AND, UH...
...HOW MUCH WOULD IT COST TO NOT BE?
FIVE MILLION. PER WEEK.
50

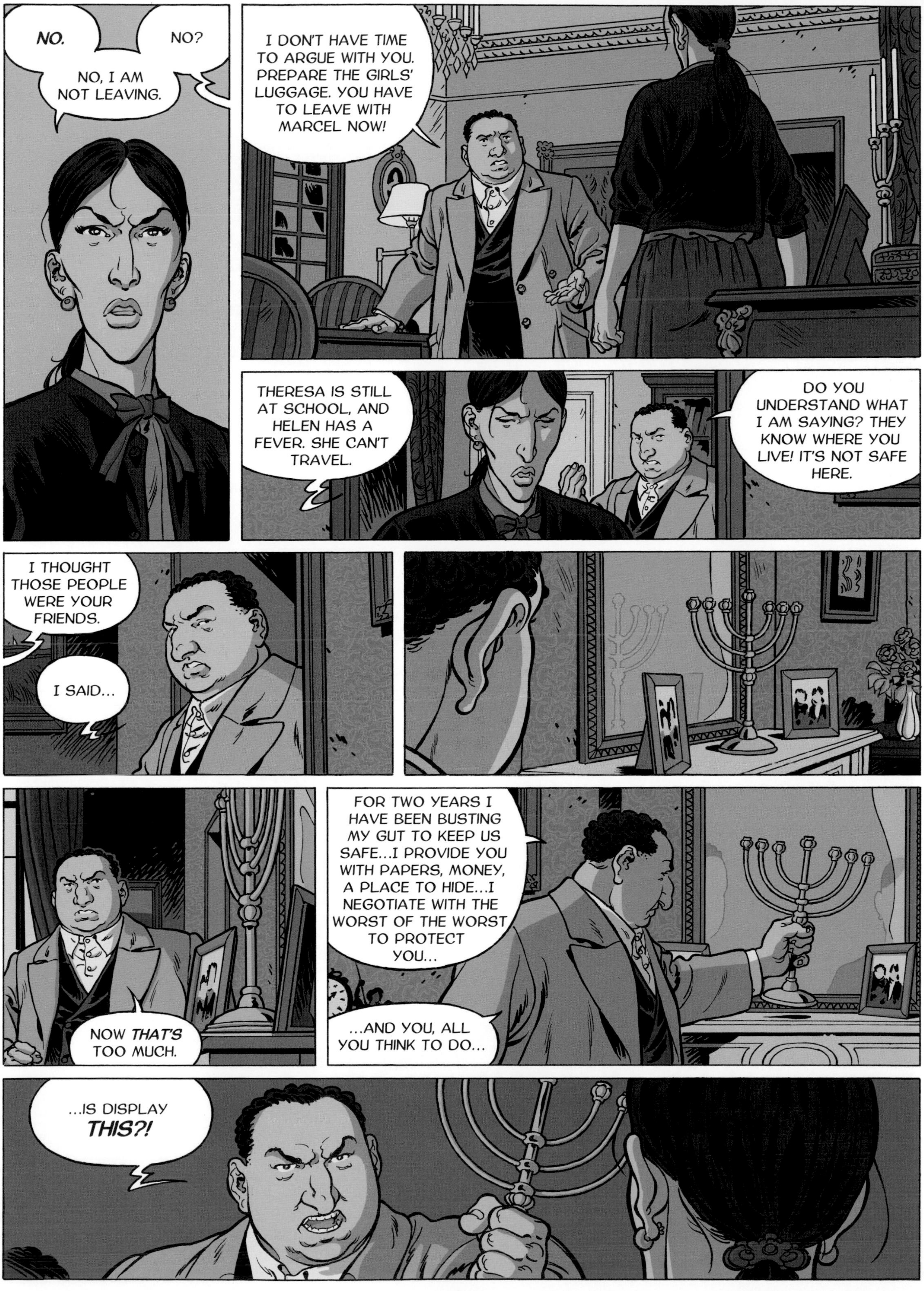
NO.
NO?
NO, I AM NOT LEAVING.
I DON'T HAVE TIME TO ARGUE WITH YOU. PREPARE THE GIRLS' LUGGAGE. YOU HAVE TO LEAVE WITH MARCEL NOW!
THERESA IS STILL AT SCHOOL, AND HELEN HAS A FEVER. SHE CAN'T TRAVEL.
DO YOU UNDERSTAND WHAT I AM SAYING? THEY KNOW WHERE YOU LIVE! IT'S NOT SAFE HERE.
I THOUGHT THOSE PEOPLE WERE YOUR FRIENDS.
I SAID...
NOW THAT'S TOO MUCH.
FOR TWO YEARS I HAVE BEEN BUSTING MY GUT TO KEEP US SAFE...I PROVIDE YOU WITH PAPERS, MONEY, A PLACE TO HIDE...I NEGOTIATE WITH THE WORST OF THE WORST TO PROTECT YOU...
...AND YOU, ALL YOU THINK TO DO...
...IS DISPLAY THIS?!
51

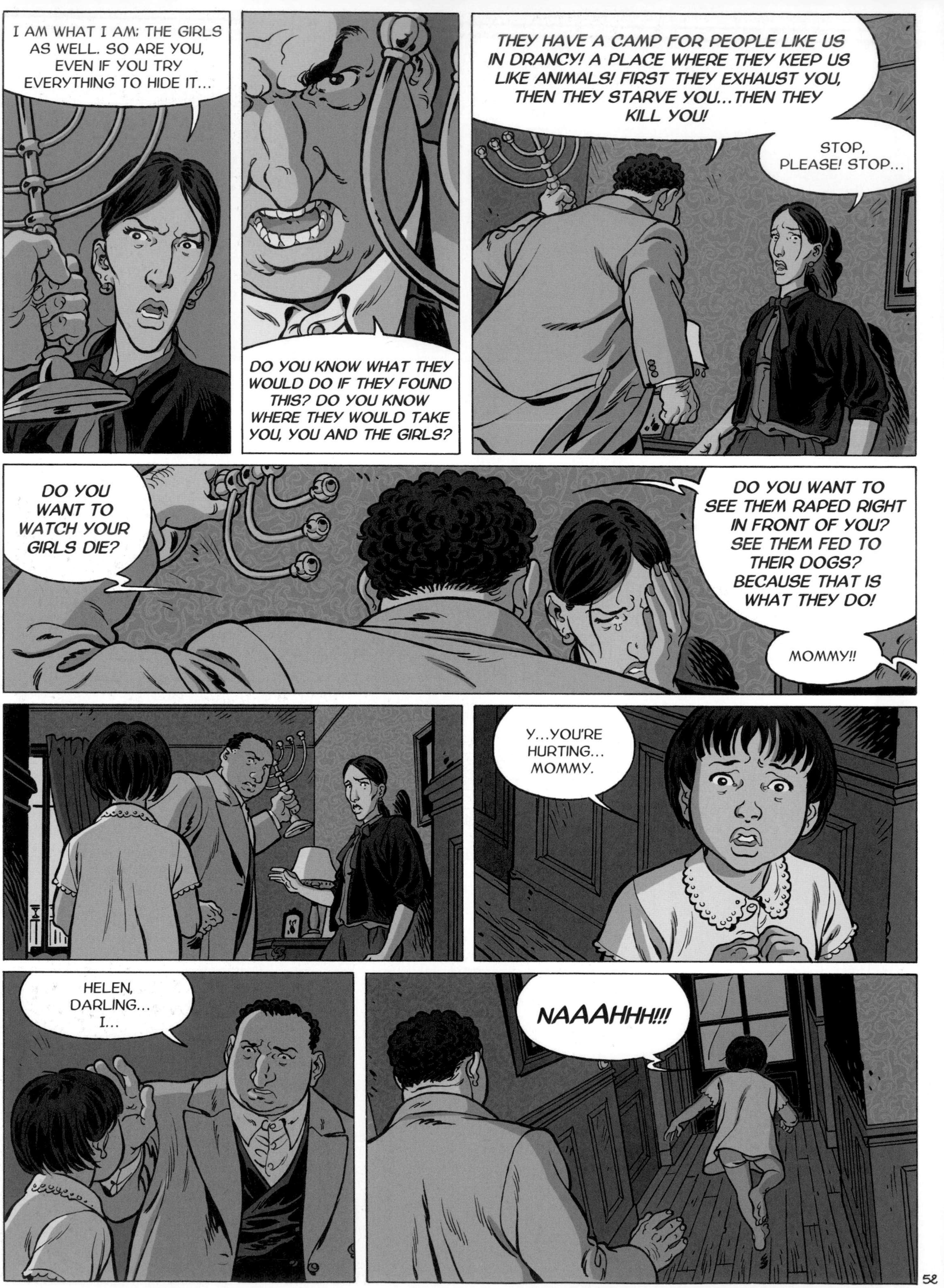
I AM WHAT I AM; THE GIRLS AS WELL. SO ARE YOU, EVEN IF YOU TRY EVERYTHING TO HIDE IT...
DO YOU KNOW WHAT THEY WOULD DO IF THEY FOUND THIS? DO YOU KNOW WHERE THEY WOULD TAKE YOU, YOU AND THE GIRLS?
THEY HAVE A CAMP FOR PEOPLE LIKE US IN DRANCY! A PLACE WHERE THEY KEEP US LIKE ANIMALS! FIRST THEY EXHAUST YOU, THEN THEY STARVE YOU...THEN THEY KILL YOU!
STOP, PLEASE! STOP...
DO YOU WANT TO WATCH YOUR GIRLS DIE?
DO YOU WANT TO SEE THEM RAPED RIGHT IN FRONT OF YOU? SEE THEM FED TO THEIR DOGS? BECAUSE THAT IS WHAT THEY DO!
MOMMY!!
Y...YOU'RE HURTING... MOMMY.
HELEN, DARLING... I...
NAAAHHH!!!
52

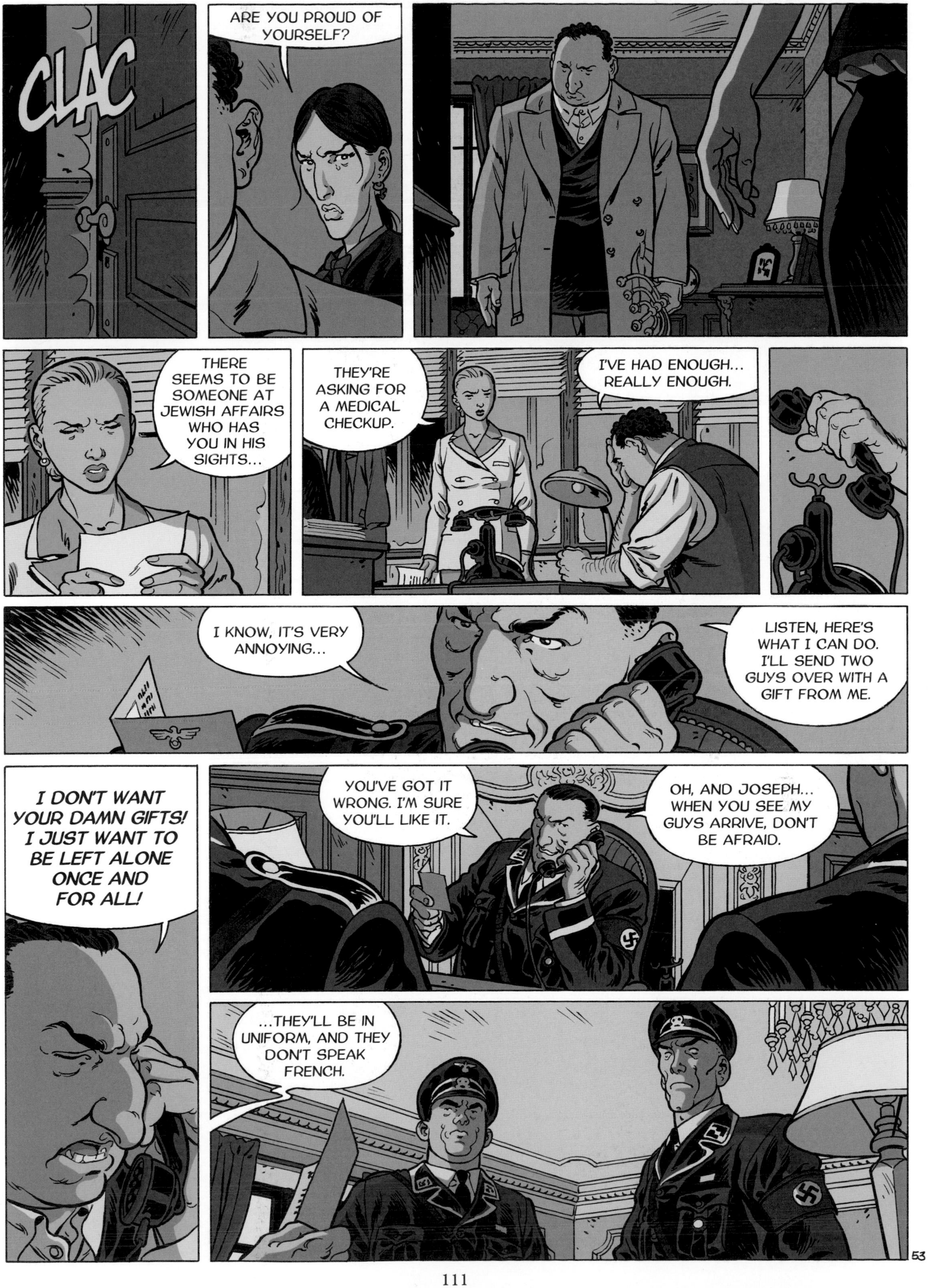
CLAC
ARE YOU PROUD OF YOURSELF?
THERE SEEMS TO BE SOMEONE AT JEWISH AFFAIRS WHO HAS YOU IN HIS SIGHTS...
THEY'RE ASKING FOR A MEDICAL CHECKUP.
I'VE HAD ENOUGH... REALLY ENOUGH.
I KNOW, IT'S VERY ANNOYING...
LISTEN, HERE'S WHAT I CAN DO. I'LL SEND TWO GUYS OVER WITH A GIFT FROM ME.
I DON'T WANT YOUR DAMN GIFTS! I JUST WANT TO BE LEFT ALONE ONCE AND FOR ALL!
YOU'VE GOT IT WRONG. I'M SURE YOU'LL LIKE IT.
OH, AND JOSEPH... WHEN YOU SEE MY GUYS ARRIVE, DON'T BE AFRAID.
...THEY'LL BE IN UNIFORM, AND THEY DON'T SPEAK FRENCH.
53

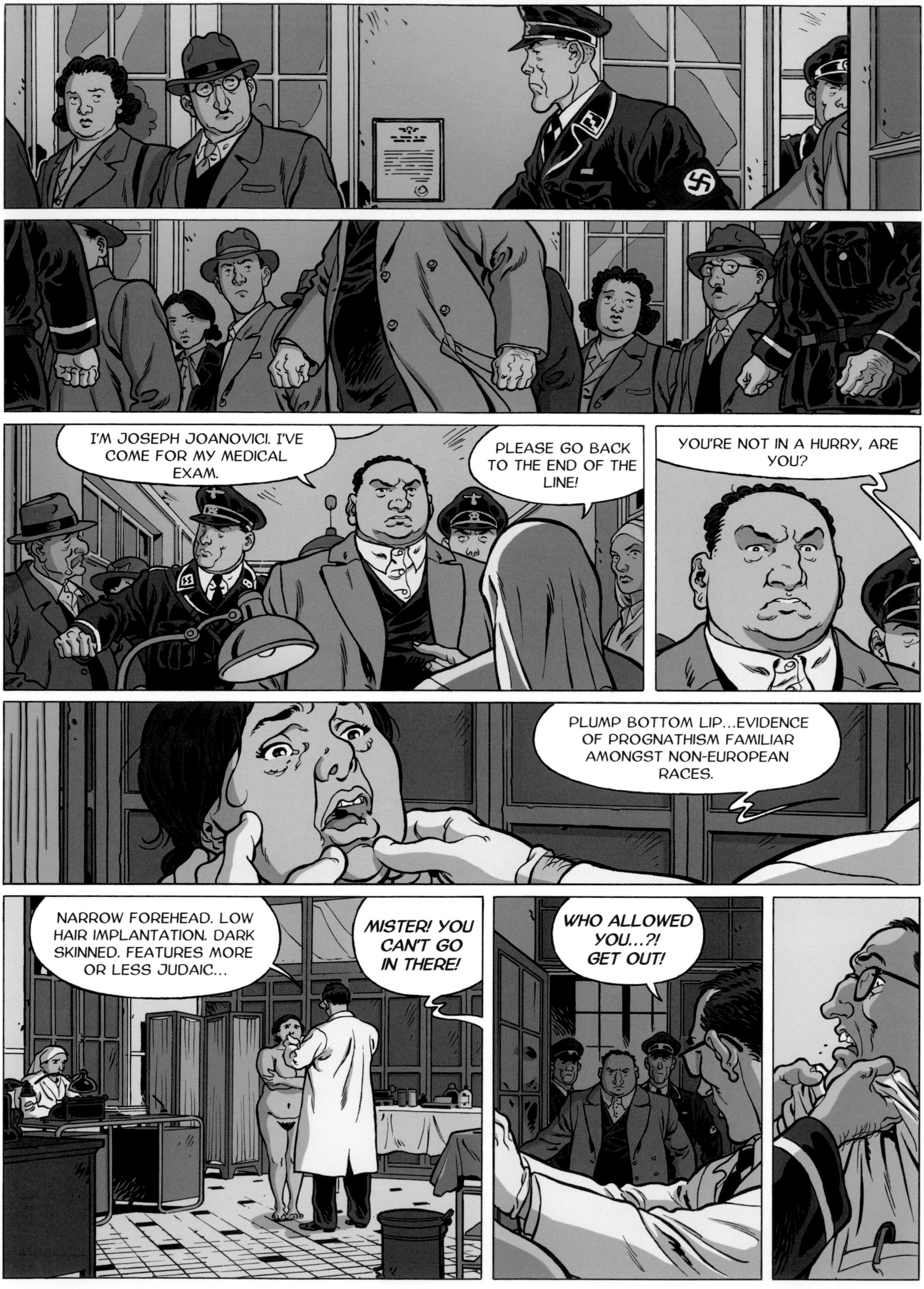

I'M JOSEPH JOANOVICI. I'VE COME FOR MY MEDICAL EXAM.
PLEASE GO BACK TO THE END OF THE LINE!
YOU'RE NOT IN A HURRY, ARE YOU?
PLUMP BOTTOM LIP...EVIDENCE OF PROGNATHISM FAMILIAR AMONGST NON-EUROPEAN RACES.
NARROW FOREHEAD. LOW HAIR IMPLANTATION. DARK SKINNED. FEATURES MORE OR LESS JUDAIC...
MISTER! YOU CAN'T GO IN THERE!
WHO ALLOWED YOU...?! GET OUT!
54

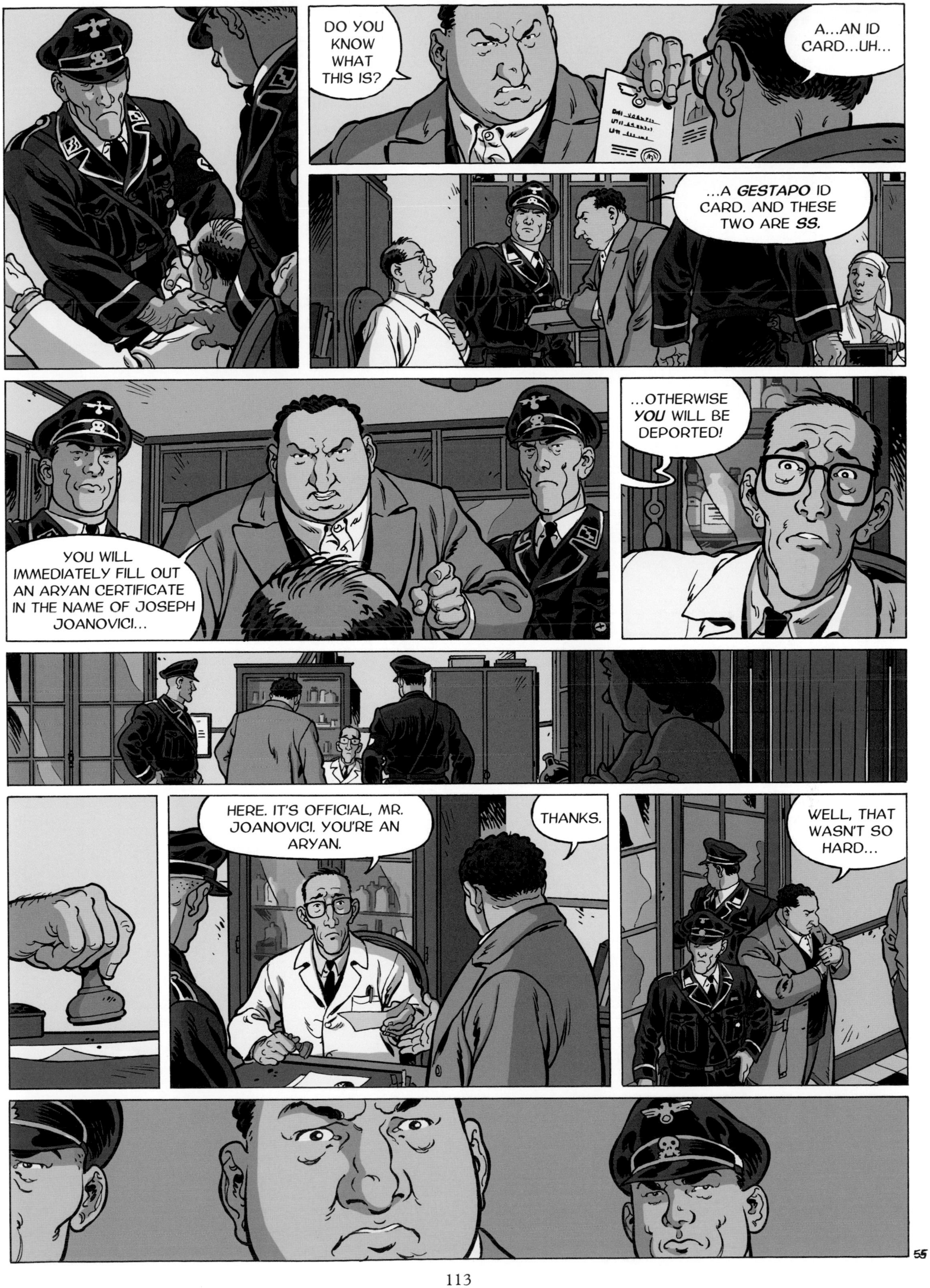
DO YOU KNOW WHAT THIS IS?
A...AN ID CARD...UH...
...A GESTAPO ID CARD. AND THESE TWO ARE SS.
YOU WILL IMMEDIATELY FILL OUT AN ARYAN CERTIFICATE IN THE NAME OF JOSEPH JOANOVICI...
...OTHERWISE YOU WILL BE DEPORTED!
HERE. IT'S OFFICIAL, MR. JOANOVICI. YOU'RE AN ARYAN.
THANKS.
WELL, THAT WASN'T SO HARD...
55

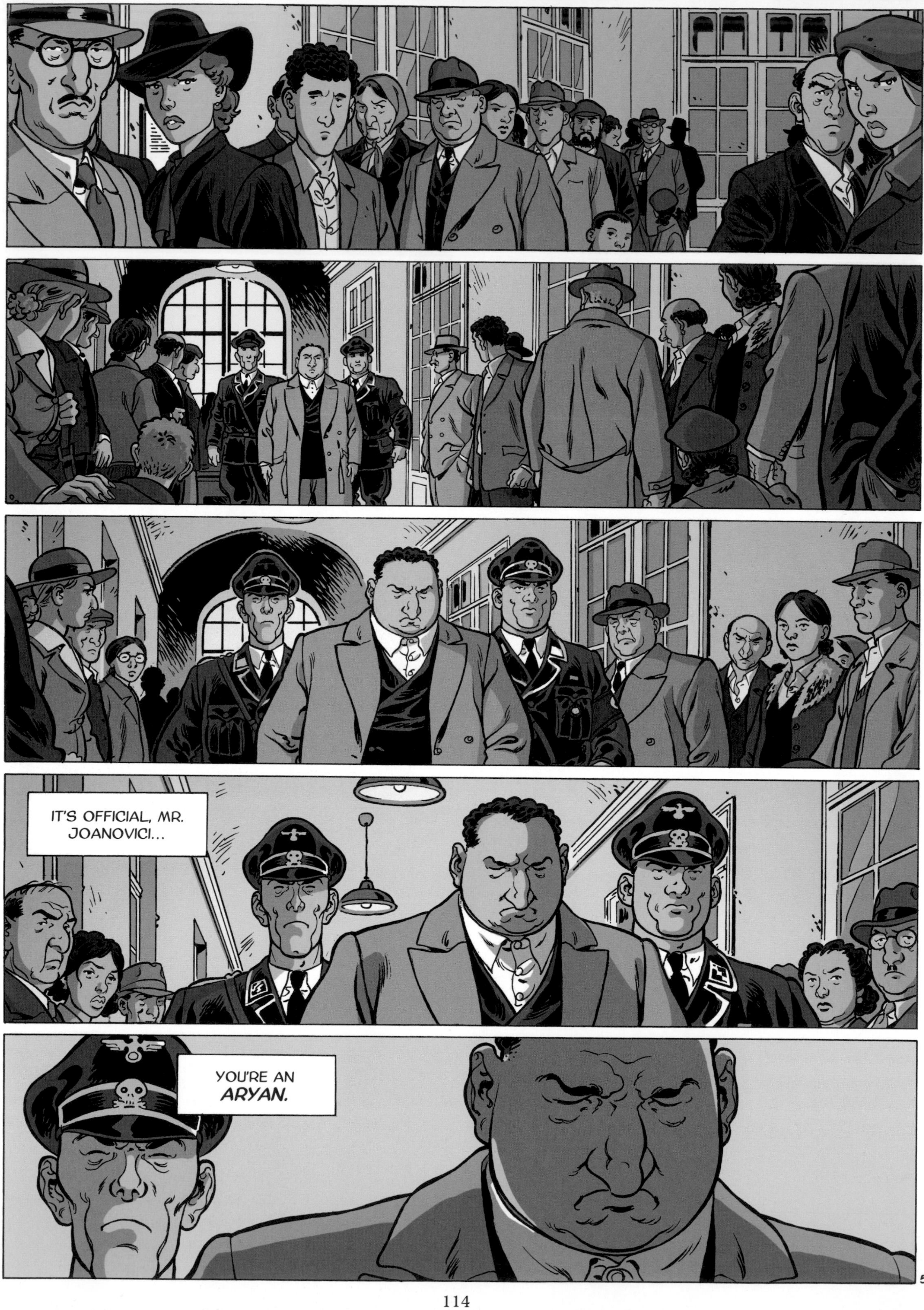
IT'S OFFICIAL, MR. JOANOVICI...
YOU'RE AN ARYAN.
56

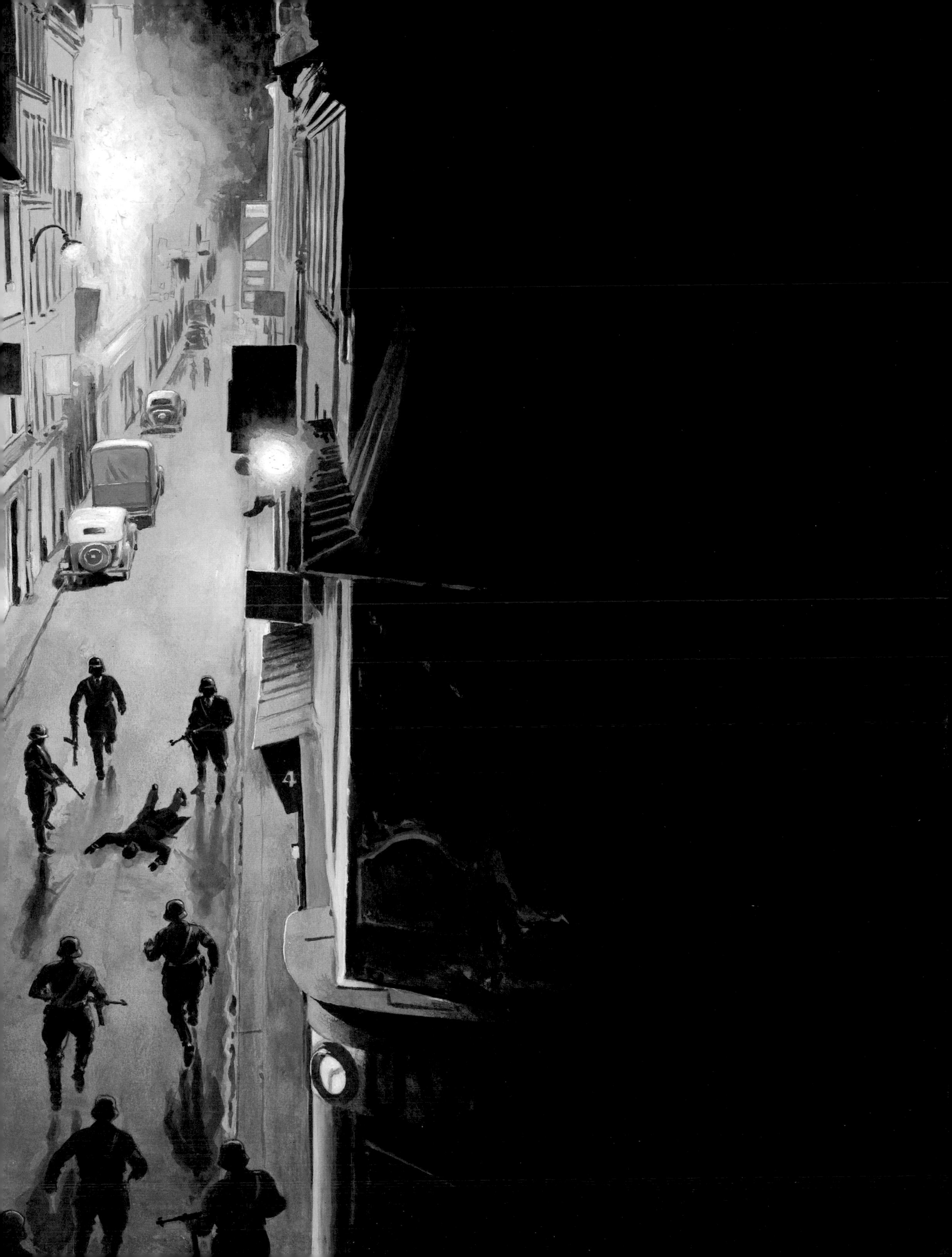

"What we are showing you is known everywhere:
the gangster drama that everyone has lived."

BERTOLT BRECHT

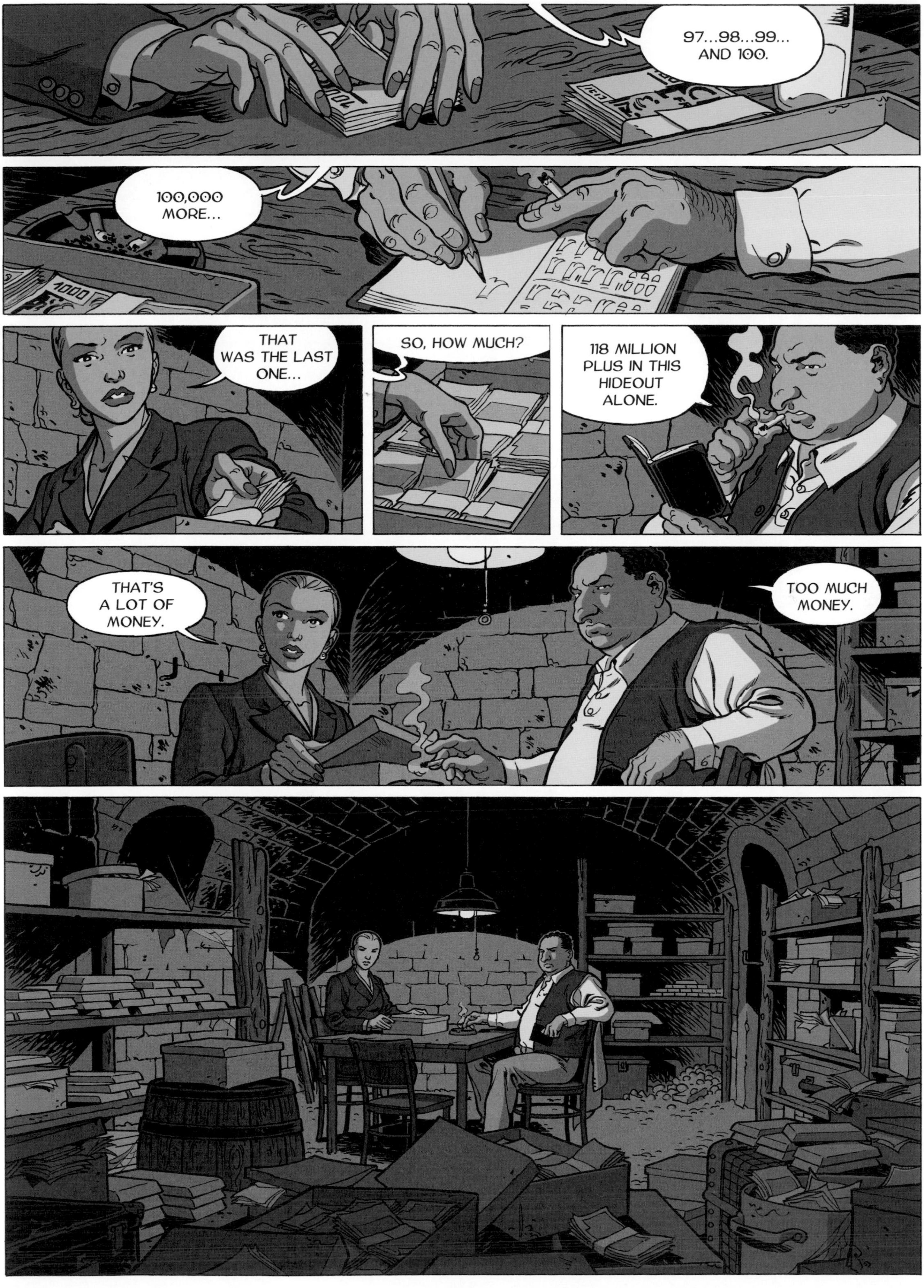
97...98...99...
AND 100.
100,000
MORE...
THAT
WAS THE LAST
ONE...
SO, HOW MUCH?
118 MILLION
PLUS IN THIS
HIDEOUT
ALONE.
THAT'S
A LOT OF
MONEY.
TOO MUCH
MONEY.

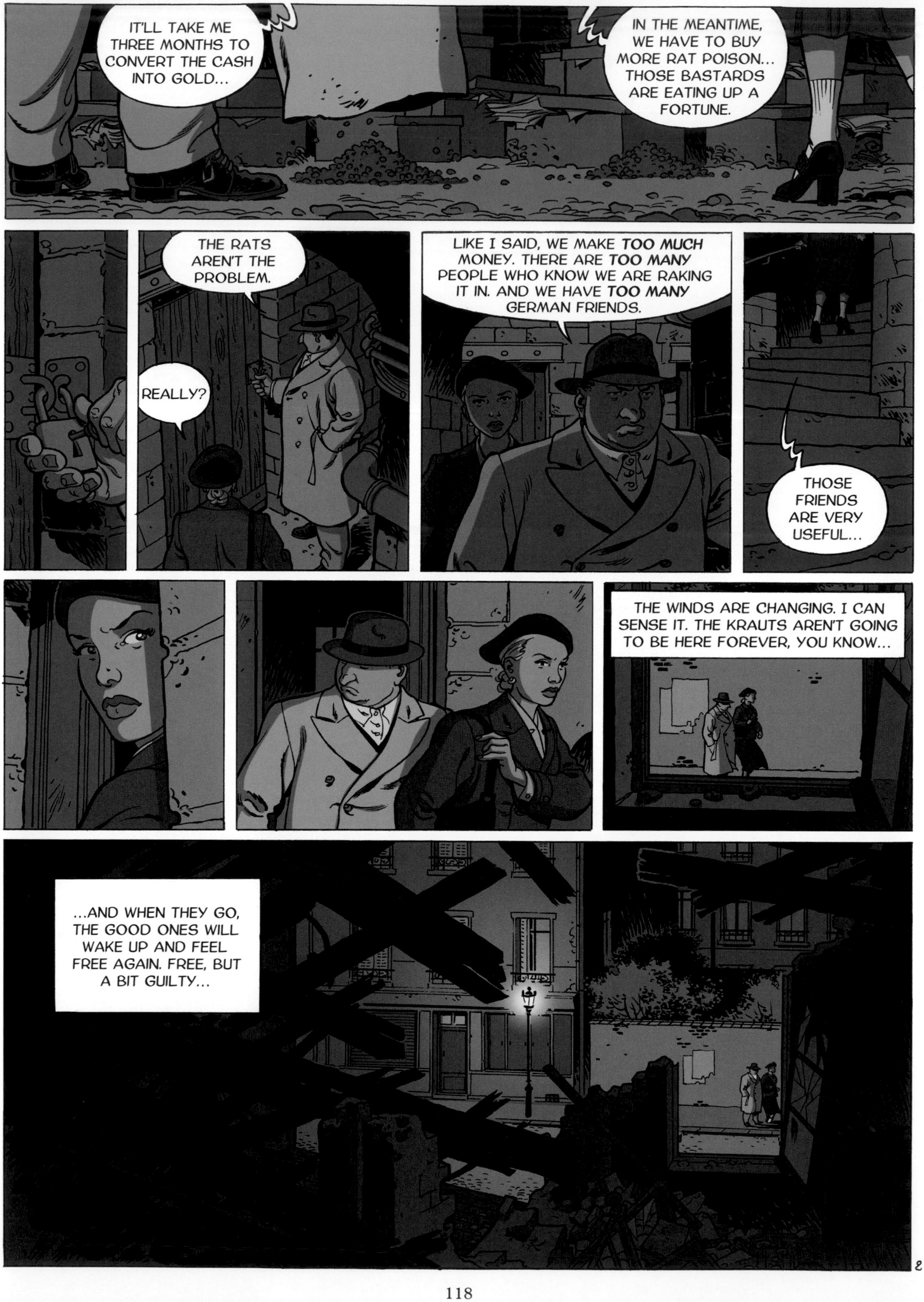
IT'LL TAKE ME THREE MONTHS TO CONVERT THE CASH INTO GOLD...
IN THE MEANTIME, WE HAVE TO BUY MORE RAT POISON... THOSE BASTARDS ARE EATING UP A FORTUNE.
THE RATS AREN'T THE PROBLEM.
REALLY?
LIKE I SAID, WE MAKE **TOO MUCH** MONEY. THERE ARE **TOO MANY** PEOPLE WHO KNOW WE ARE RAKING IT IN. AND WE HAVE **TOO MANY** GERMAN FRIENDS.
THOSE FRIENDS ARE VERY USEFUL...
THE WINDS ARE CHANGING. I CAN SENSE IT. THE KRAUTS AREN'T GOING TO BE HERE FOREVER, YOU KNOW...
...AND WHEN THEY GO, THE GOOD ONES WILL WAKE UP AND FEEL FREE AGAIN. FREE, BUT A BIT GUILTY...

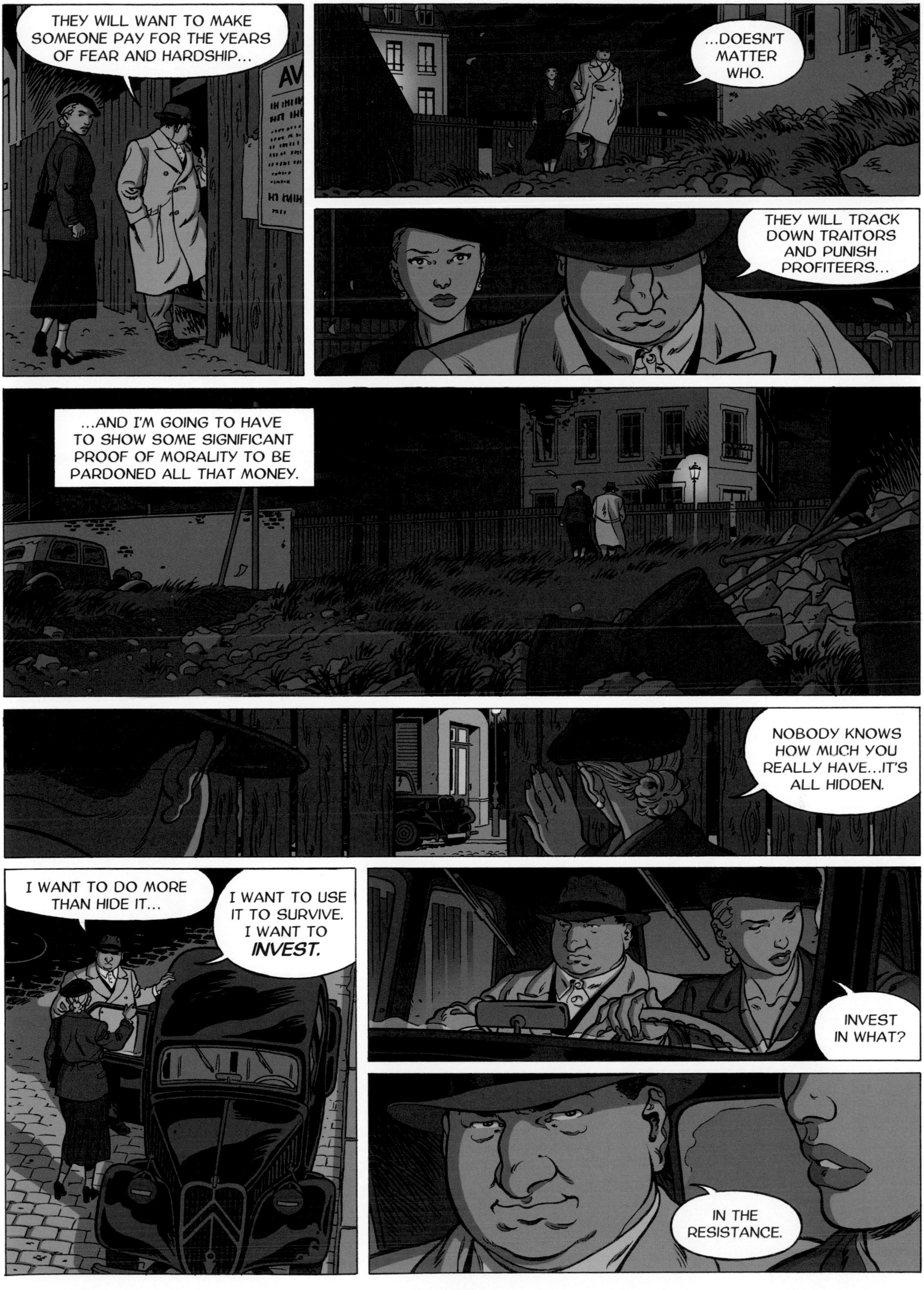
THEY WILL WANT TO MAKE SOMEONE PAY FOR THE YEARS OF FEAR AND HARDSHIP...
...DOESN'T MATTER WHO.
THEY WILL TRACK DOWN TRAITORS AND PUNISH PROFITEERS...
...AND I'M GOING TO HAVE TO SHOW SOME SIGNIFICANT PROOF OF MORALITY TO BE PARDONED ALL THAT MONEY.
NOBODY KNOWS HOW MUCH YOU REALLY HAVE...IT'S ALL HIDDEN.
I WANT TO DO MORE THAN HIDE IT...
I WANT TO USE IT TO SURVIVE. I WANT TO ***INVEST.***
INVEST IN WHAT?
IN THE RESISTANCE.

3

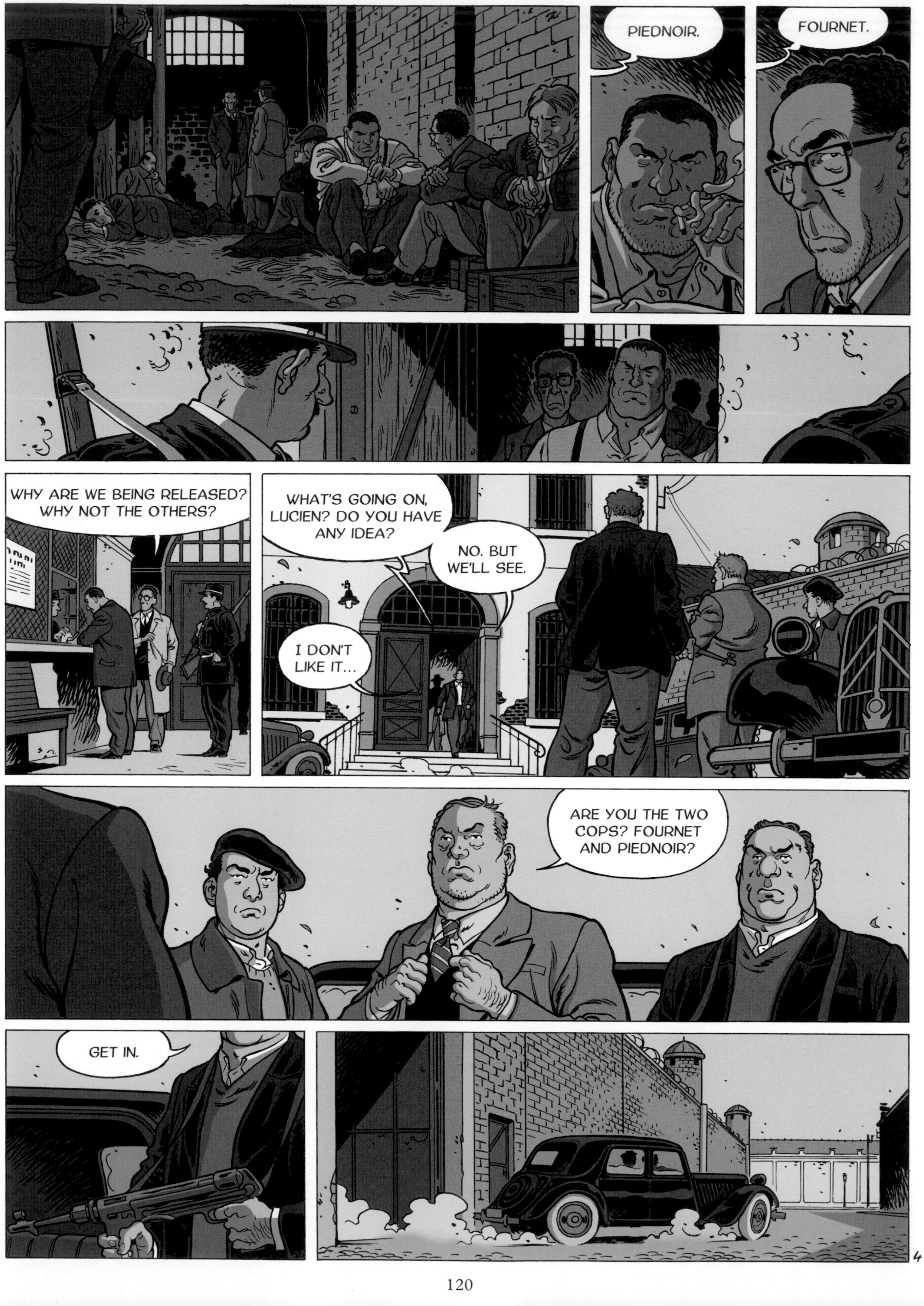
PIEDNOIR.
FOURNET.
WHY ARE WE BEING RELEASED? WHY NOT THE OTHERS?
WHAT'S GOING ON, LUCIEN? DO YOU HAVE ANY IDEA?
NO. BUT WE'LL SEE.
I DON'T LIKE IT...
ARE YOU THE TWO COPS? FOURNET AND PIEDNOIR?
GET IN.
4

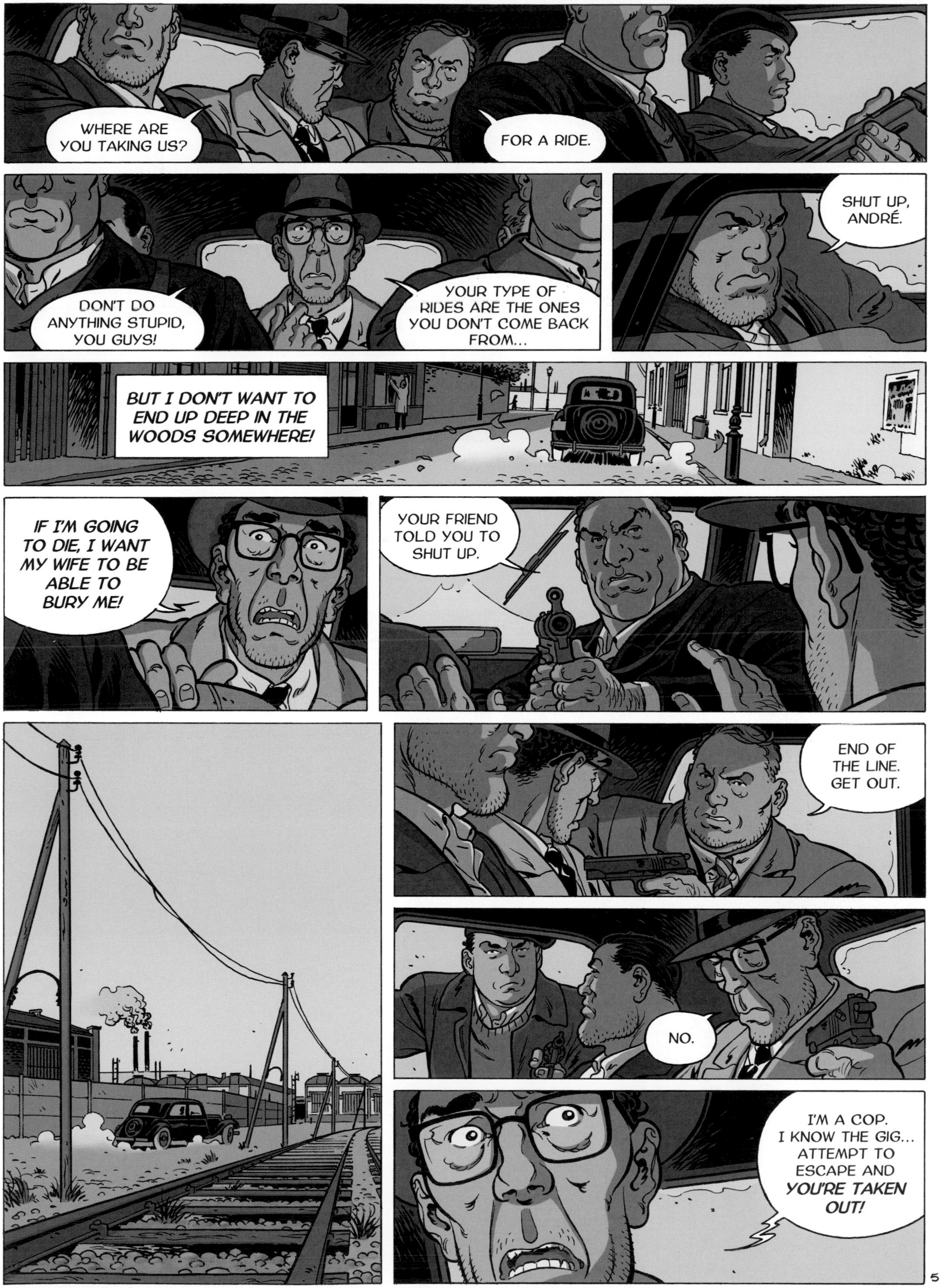

WHERE ARE YOU TAKING US?
FOR A RIDE.
DON'T DO ANYTHING STUPID, YOU GUYS!
YOUR TYPE OF RIDES ARE THE ONES YOU DON'T COME BACK FROM...
SHUT UP, ANDRÉ.
BUT I DON'T WANT TO END UP DEEP IN THE WOODS SOMEWHERE!
IF I'M GOING TO DIE, I WANT MY WIFE TO BE ABLE TO BURY ME!
YOUR FRIEND TOLD YOU TO SHUT UP.
END OF THE LINE. GET OUT.
NO.
I'M A COP. I KNOW THE GIG... ATTEMPT TO ESCAPE AND YOU'RE TAKEN OUT!
5

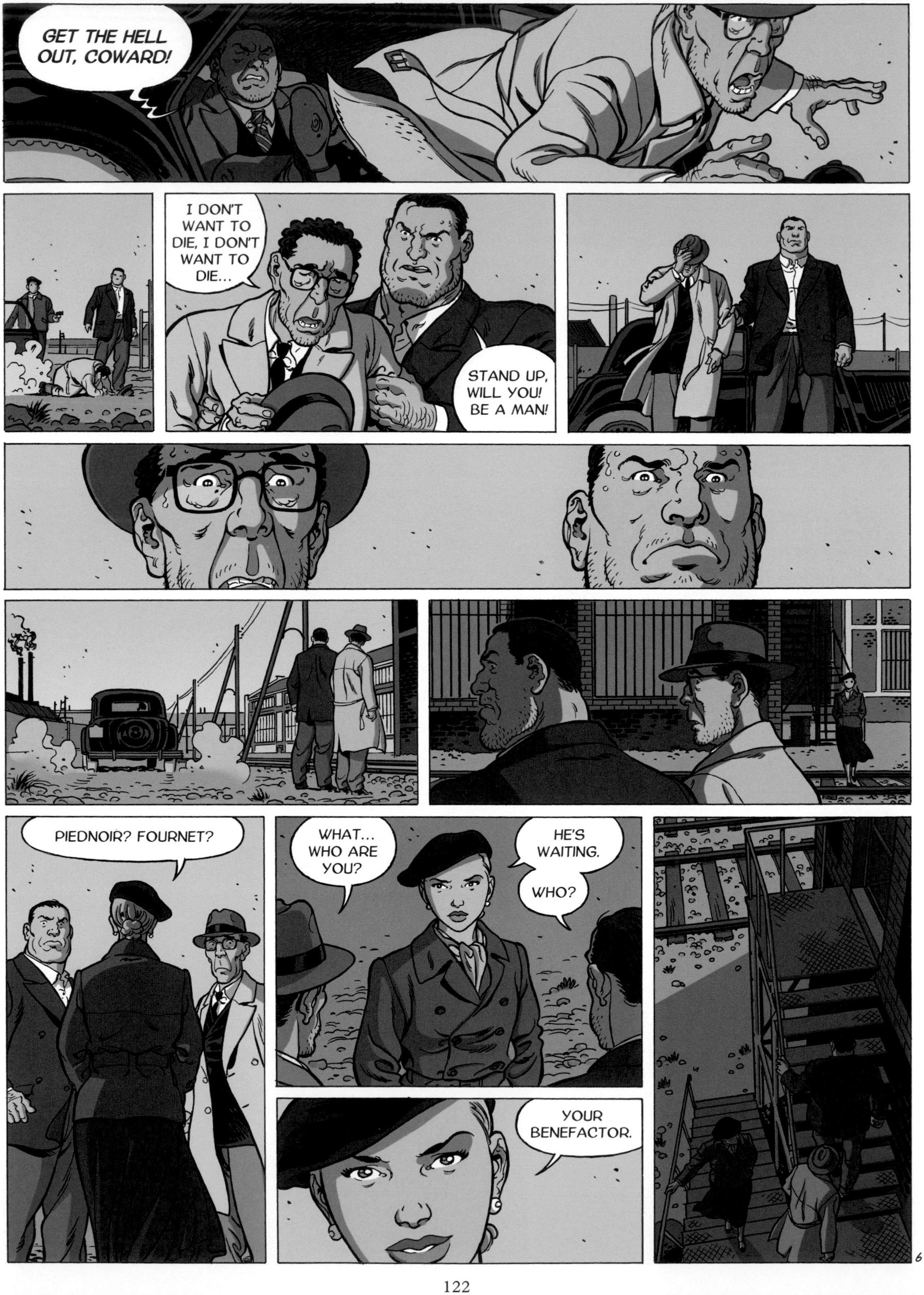
GET THE HELL OUT, COWARD!
I DON'T WANT TO DIE, I DON'T WANT TO DIE...
STAND UP, WILL YOU! BE A MAN!
PIEDNOIR? FOURNET?
WHAT... WHO ARE YOU?
HE'S WAITING.
WHO?
YOUR BENEFACTOR.
6

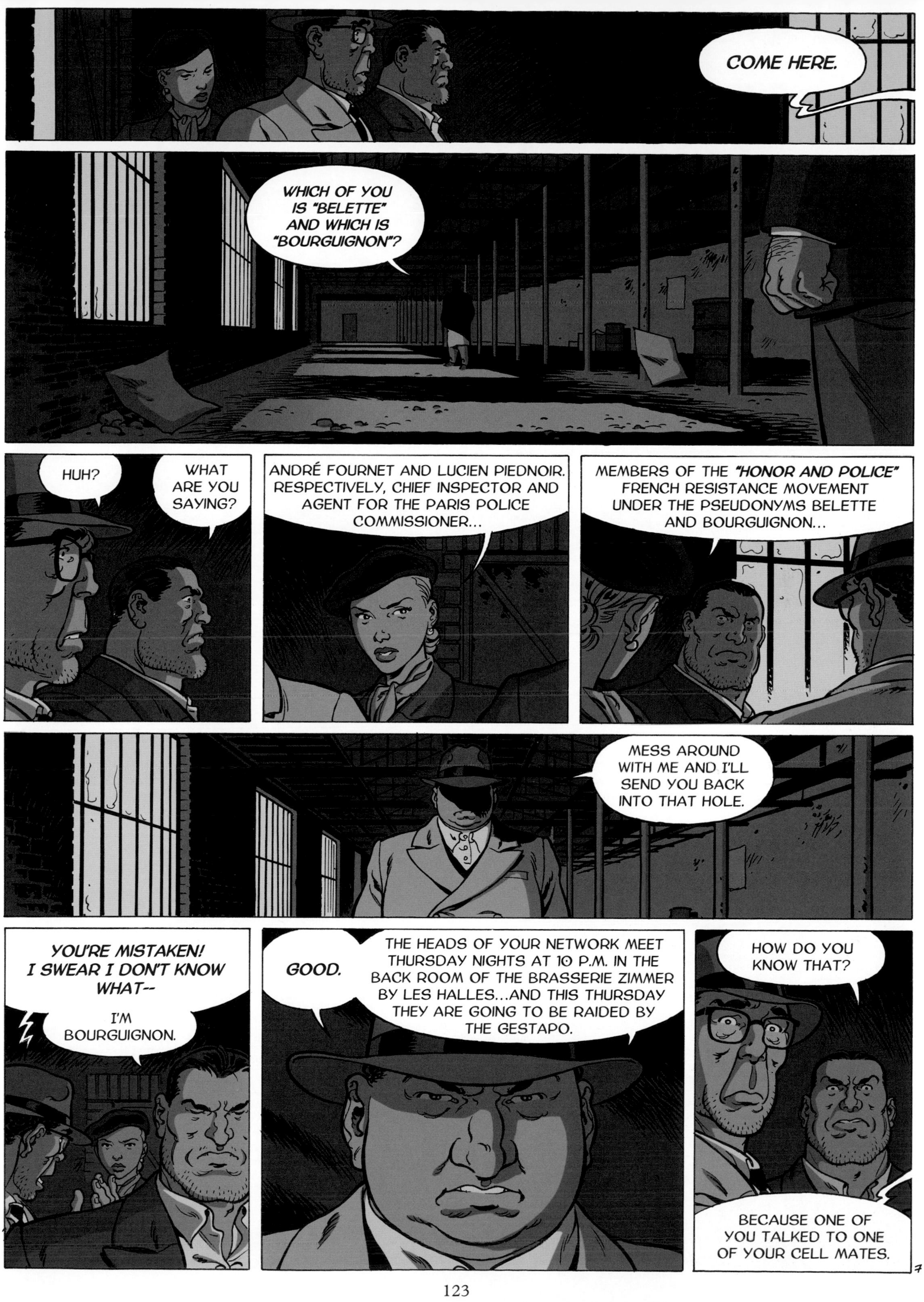
COME HERE.
WHICH OF YOU IS "BELETTE" AND WHICH IS "BOURGUIGNON"?
HUH?
WHAT ARE YOU SAYING?
ANDRÉ FOURNET AND LUCIEN PIEDNOIR. RESPECTIVELY, CHIEF INSPECTOR AND AGENT FOR THE PARIS POLICE COMMISSIONER...
MEMBERS OF THE "HONOR AND POLICE" FRENCH RESISTANCE MOVEMENT UNDER THE PSEUDONYMS BELETTE AND BOURGUIGNON...
MESS AROUND WITH ME AND I'LL SEND YOU BACK INTO THAT HOLE.
YOU'RE MISTAKEN! I SWEAR I DON'T KNOW WHAT--
I'M BOURGUIGNON.
GOOD.
THE HEADS OF YOUR NETWORK MEET THURSDAY NIGHTS AT 10 P.M. IN THE BACK ROOM OF THE BRASSERIE ZIMMER BY LES HALLES...AND THIS THURSDAY THEY ARE GOING TO BE RAIDED BY THE GESTAPO.
HOW DO YOU KNOW THAT?
BECAUSE ONE OF YOU TALKED TO ONE OF YOUR CELL MATES.
7

LUCIEN, I SWEAR...

YOU FUCKING RAT!!!

BASTARD!!! I'M GOING TO SHUT YOU UP FOR GOOD!!!

GLLL... RRRH...

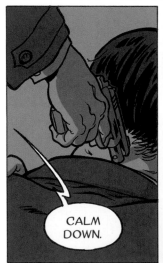

CALM DOWN.

HE SHOULD DIE A THOUSAND DEATHS, THE SHIT!

DON'T BE SO HARD ON HIM, HE'S THE ONLY FRIEND YOU HAVE LEFT...

HUH? WHAT DO YOU MEAN BY THAT? WE HAVE TO WARN THE NETWORK! CANCEL THE MEETING...

CANCEL IT? WHY? WE'LL JUST MOVE IT UP A DAY, THAT'S ALL.

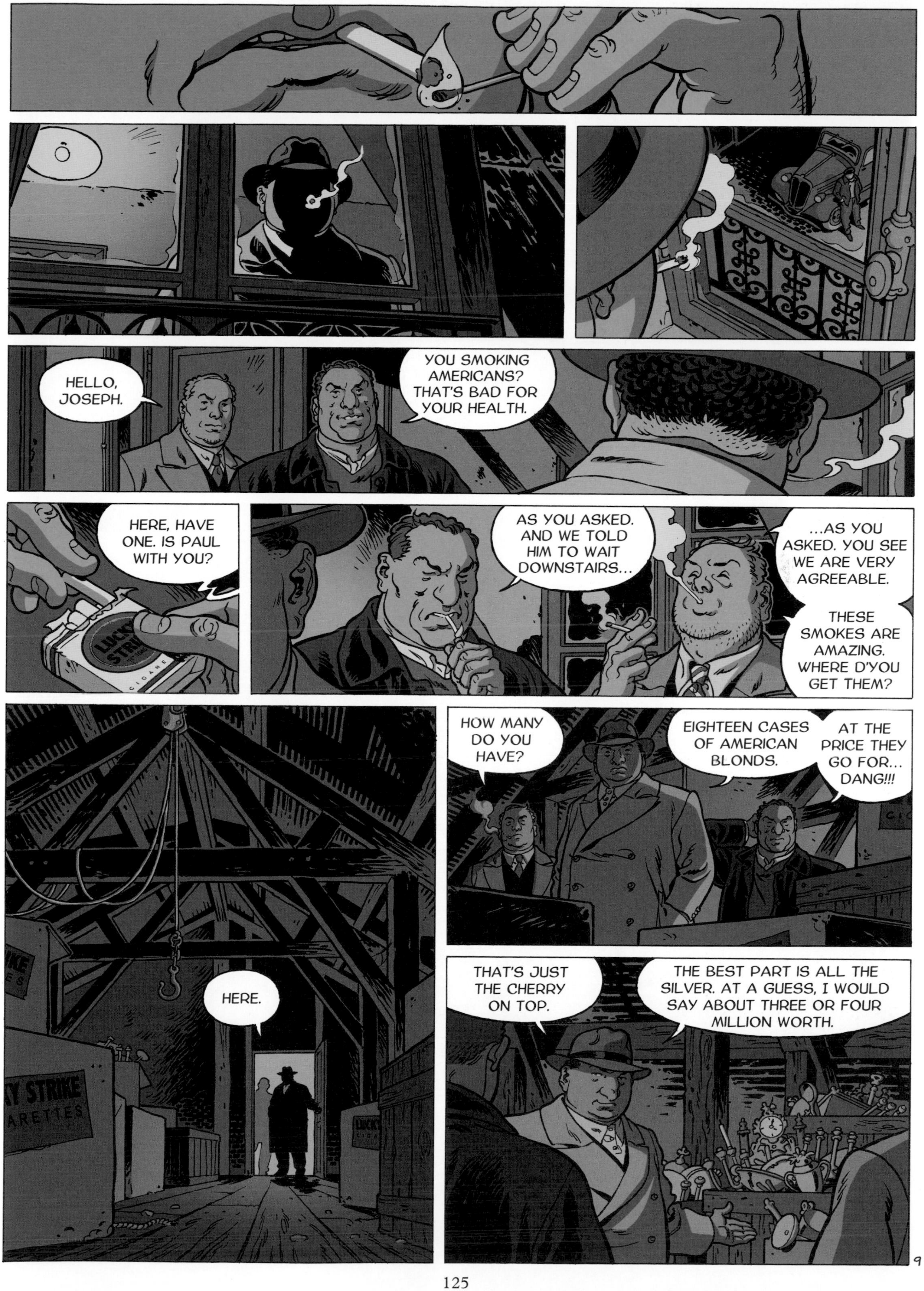
HELLO, JOSEPH.
YOU SMOKING AMERICANS? THAT'S BAD FOR YOUR HEALTH.
HERE, HAVE ONE. IS PAUL WITH YOU?
AS YOU ASKED. AND WE TOLD HIM TO WAIT DOWNSTAIRS...
...AS YOU ASKED. YOU SEE WE ARE VERY AGREEABLE.
THESE SMOKES ARE AMAZING. WHERE D'YOU GET THEM?
HERE.
HOW MANY DO YOU HAVE?
EIGHTEEN CASES OF AMERICAN BLONDS.
AT THE PRICE THEY GO FOR... DANG!!!
THAT'S JUST THE CHERRY ON TOP.
THE BEST PART IS ALL THE SILVER. AT A GUESS, I WOULD SAY ABOUT THREE OR FOUR MILLION WORTH.
9

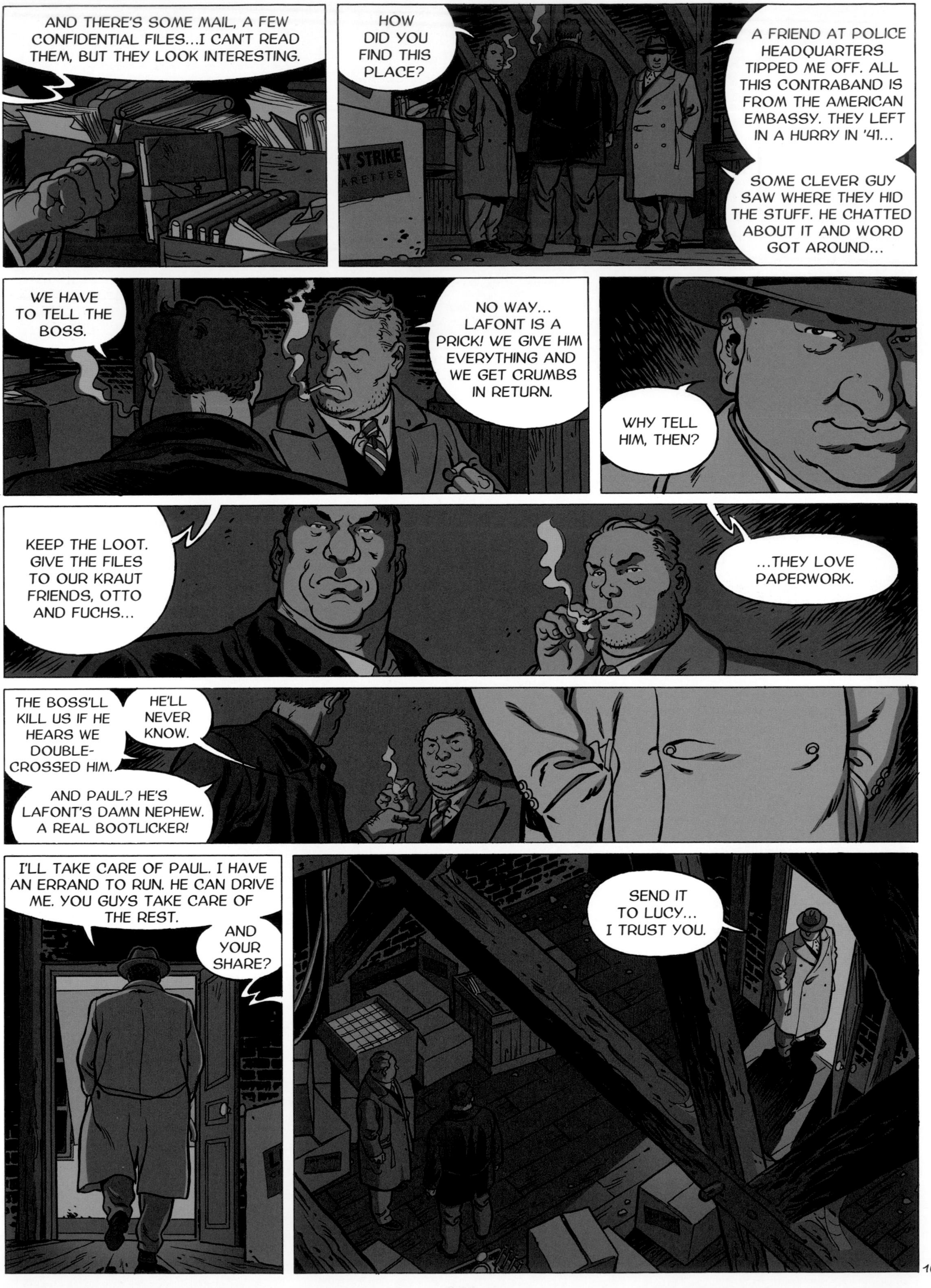
AND THERE'S SOME MAIL, A FEW CONFIDENTIAL FILES...I CAN'T READ THEM, BUT THEY LOOK INTERESTING.
HOW DID YOU FIND THIS PLACE?
A FRIEND AT POLICE HEADQUARTERS TIPPED ME OFF. ALL THIS CONTRABAND IS FROM THE AMERICAN EMBASSY. THEY LEFT IN A HURRY IN '41...
SOME CLEVER GUY SAW WHERE THEY HID THE STUFF. HE CHATTED ABOUT IT AND WORD GOT AROUND...
WE HAVE TO TELL THE BOSS.
NO WAY... LAFONT IS A PRICK! WE GIVE HIM EVERYTHING AND WE GET CRUMBS IN RETURN.
WHY TELL HIM, THEN?
KEEP THE LOOT. GIVE THE FILES TO OUR KRAUT FRIENDS, OTTO AND FUCHS...
...THEY LOVE PAPERWORK.
THE BOSS'LL KILL US IF HE HEARS WE DOUBLE-CROSSED HIM.
HE'LL NEVER KNOW.
AND PAUL? HE'S LAFONT'S DAMN NEPHEW. A REAL BOOTLICKER!
I'LL TAKE CARE OF PAUL. I HAVE AN ERRAND TO RUN. HE CAN DRIVE ME. YOU GUYS TAKE CARE OF THE REST.
AND YOUR SHARE?
SEND IT TO LUCY... I TRUST YOU.
10

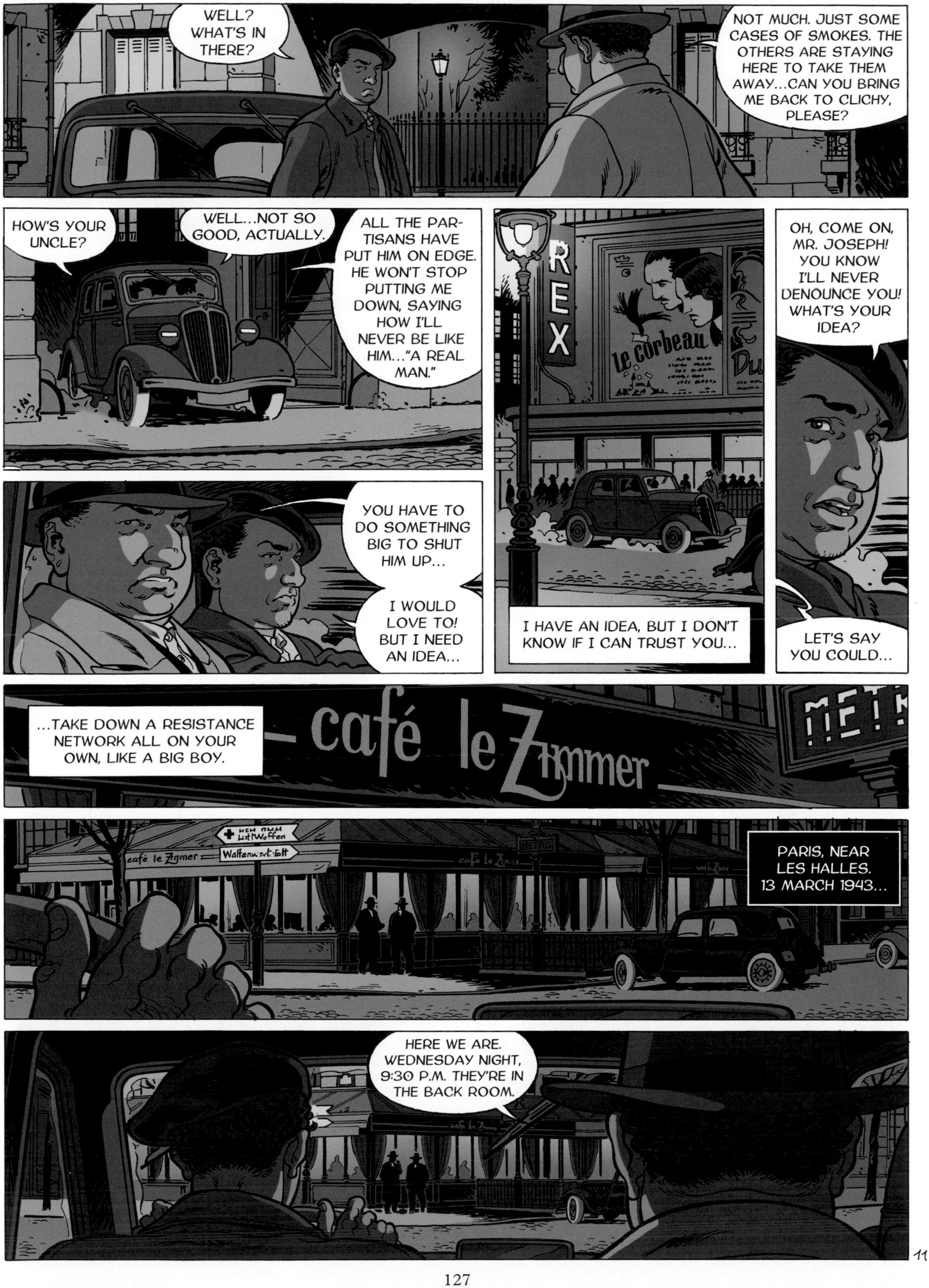
WELL? WHAT'S IN THERE?
NOT MUCH. JUST SOME CASES OF SMOKES. THE OTHERS ARE STAYING HERE TO TAKE THEM AWAY...CAN YOU BRING ME BACK TO CLICHY, PLEASE?
HOW'S YOUR UNCLE?
WELL...NOT SO GOOD, ACTUALLY.
ALL THE PARTISANS HAVE PUT HIM ON EDGE. HE WON'T STOP PUTTING ME DOWN, SAYING HOW I'LL NEVER BE LIKE HIM..."A REAL MAN."
YOU HAVE TO DO SOMETHING BIG TO SHUT HIM UP...
I WOULD LOVE TO! BUT I NEED AN IDEA...
REX
Le corbeau
I HAVE AN IDEA, BUT I DON'T KNOW IF I CAN TRUST YOU...
OH, COME ON, MR. JOSEPH! YOU KNOW I'LL NEVER DENOUNCE YOU! WHAT'S YOUR IDEA?
LET'S SAY YOU COULD...
...TAKE DOWN A RESISTANCE NETWORK ALL ON YOUR OWN, LIKE A BIG BOY.
café le Zimmer
café le Zimmer
PARIS, NEAR LES HALLES. 13 MARCH 1943...
HERE WE ARE. WEDNESDAY NIGHT, 9:30 P.M. THEY'RE IN THE BACK ROOM.
11

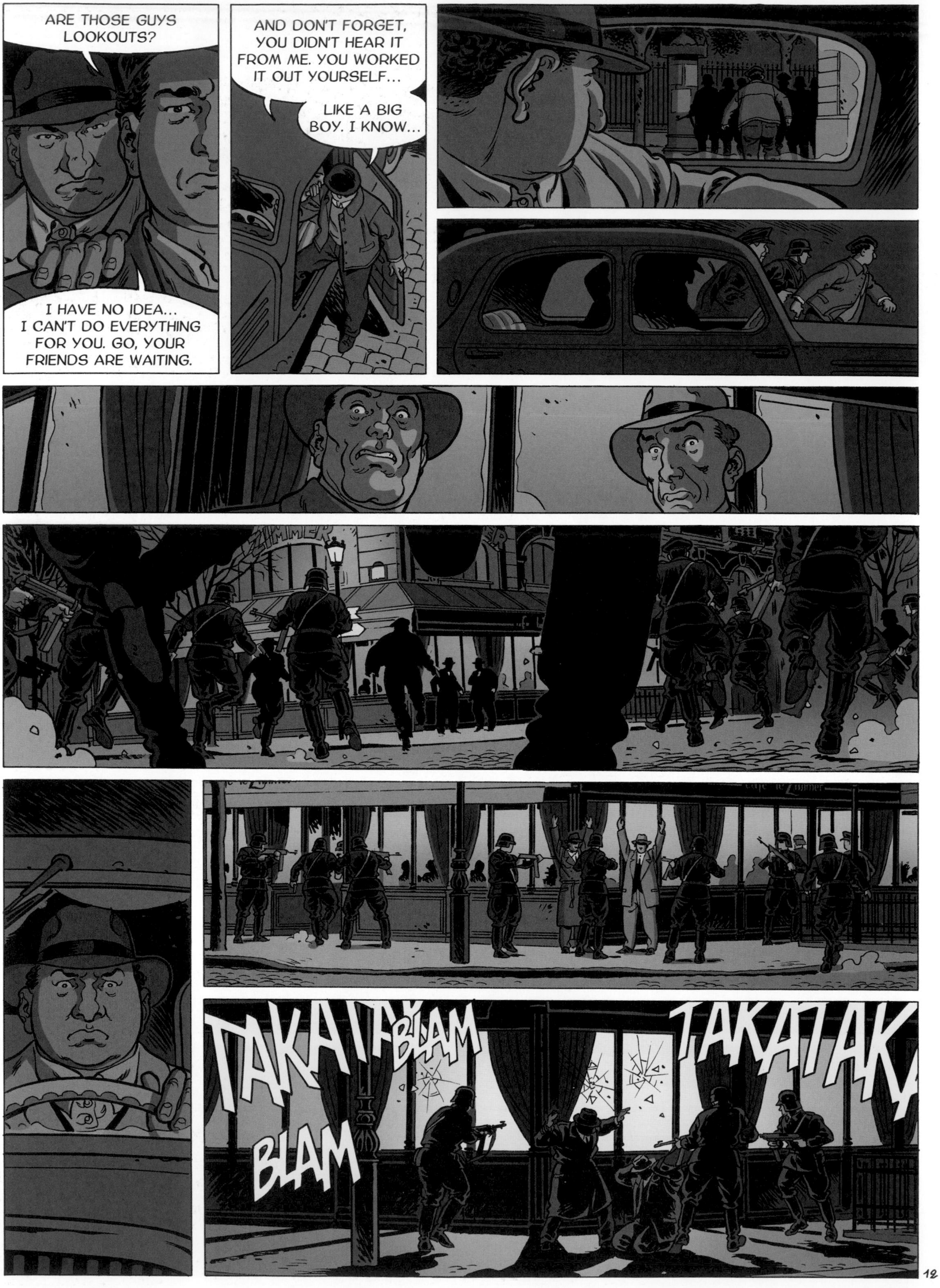

ARE THOSE GUYS LOOKOUTS?
I HAVE NO IDEA... I CAN'T DO EVERYTHING FOR YOU. GO, YOUR FRIENDS ARE WAITING.
AND DON'T FORGET, YOU DIDN'T HEAR IT FROM ME. YOU WORKED IT OUT YOURSELF...
LIKE A BIG BOY. I KNOW...
TAKAT
BLAM
BLAM
TAKATAKA
12

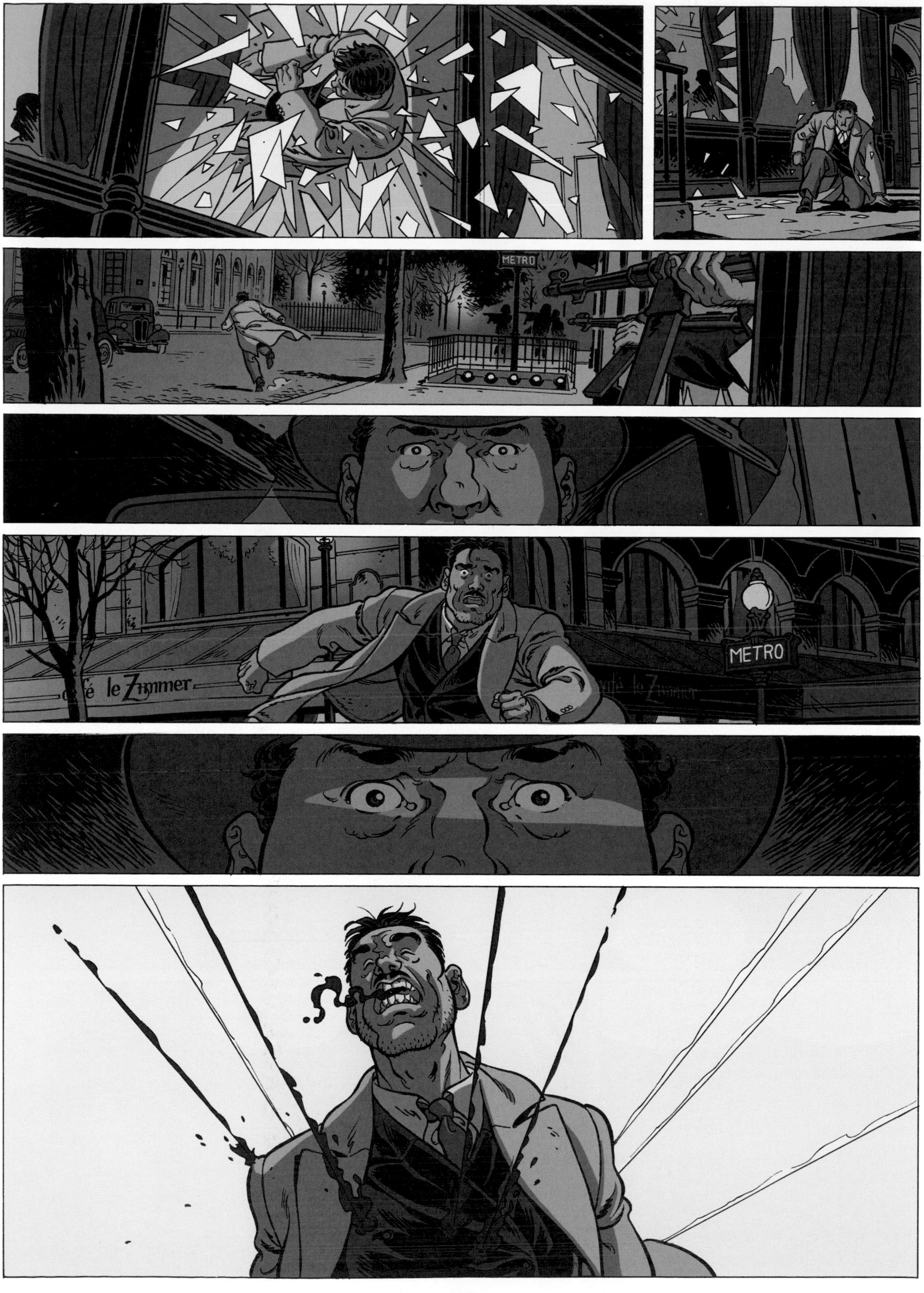
METRO
Café le Zimmer
METRO
13

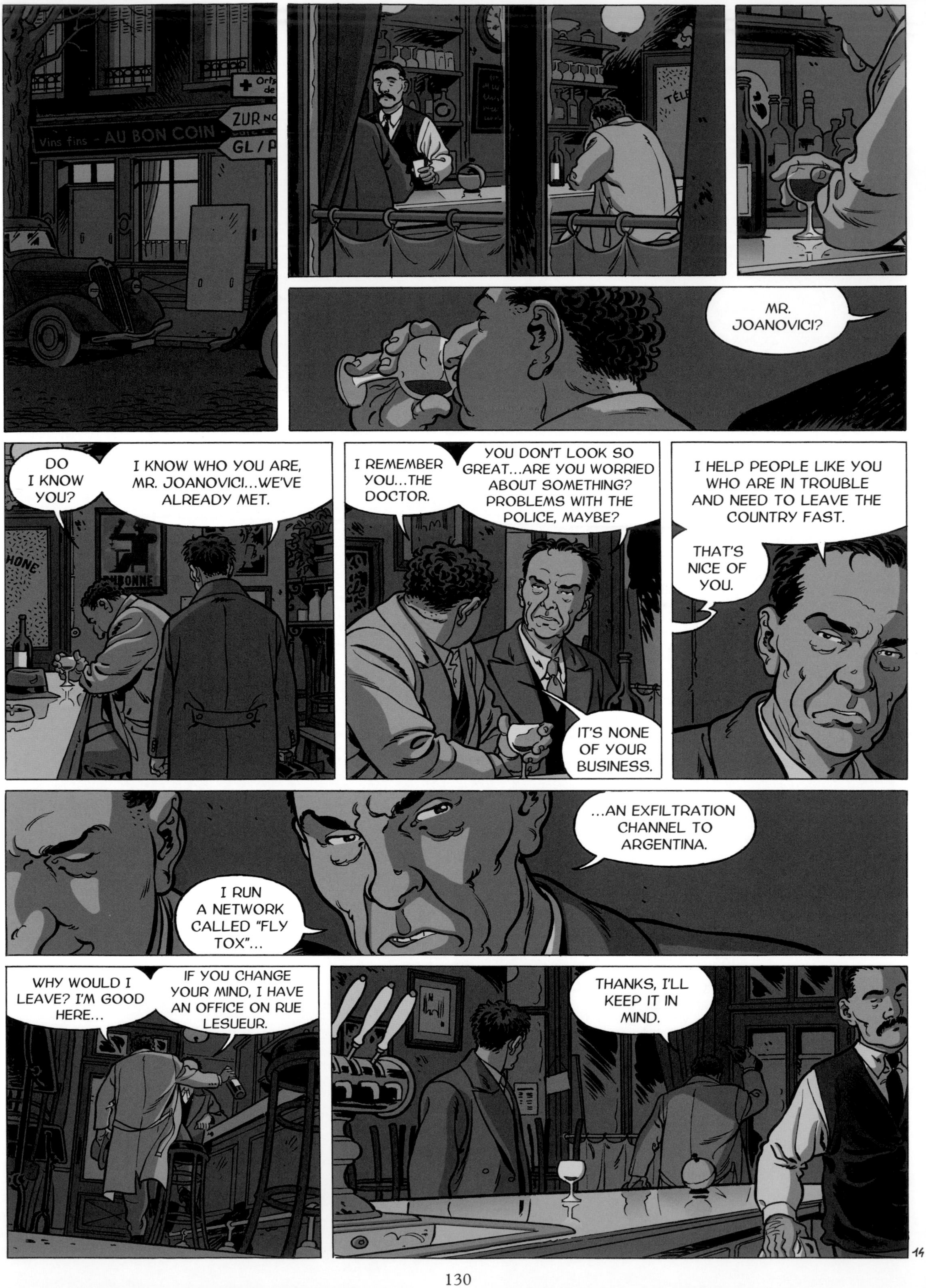
Vins fins - AU BON COIN
ZUR
GL / P
MR. JOANOVICI?
DO I KNOW YOU?
I KNOW WHO YOU ARE, MR. JOANOVICI...WE'VE ALREADY MET.
I REMEMBER YOU...THE DOCTOR.
YOU DON'T LOOK SO GREAT...ARE YOU WORRIED ABOUT SOMETHING? PROBLEMS WITH THE POLICE, MAYBE?
IT'S NONE OF YOUR BUSINESS.
I HELP PEOPLE LIKE YOU WHO ARE IN TROUBLE AND NEED TO LEAVE THE COUNTRY FAST.
THAT'S NICE OF YOU.
I RUN A NETWORK CALLED "FLY TOX"...
...AN EXFILTRATION CHANNEL TO ARGENTINA.
WHY WOULD I LEAVE? I'M GOOD HERE...
IF YOU CHANGE YOUR MIND, I HAVE AN OFFICE ON RUE LESUEUR.
THANKS, I'LL KEEP IT IN MIND.
14

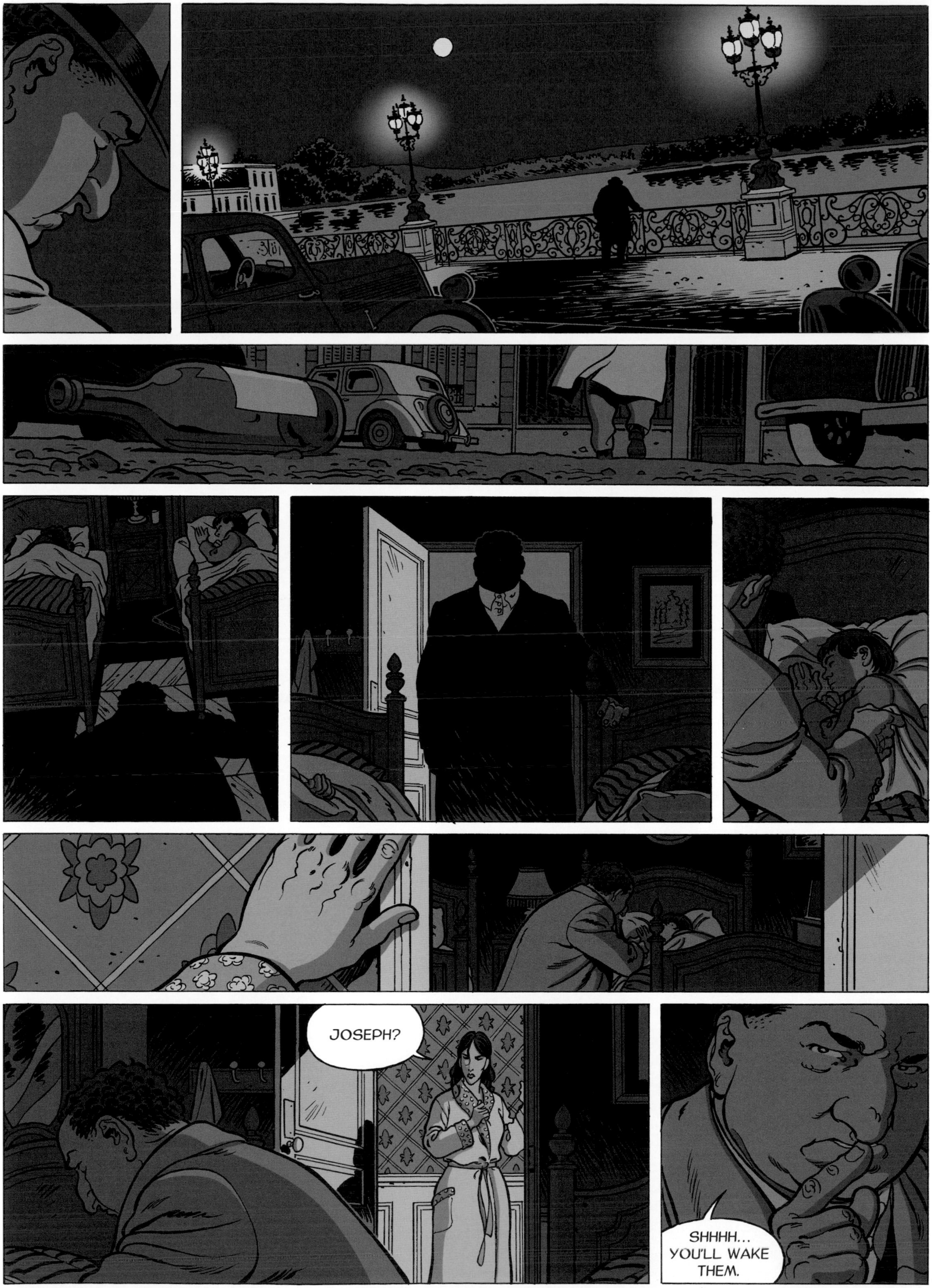
JOSEPH?
SHHHH...
YOU'LL WAKE
THEM.

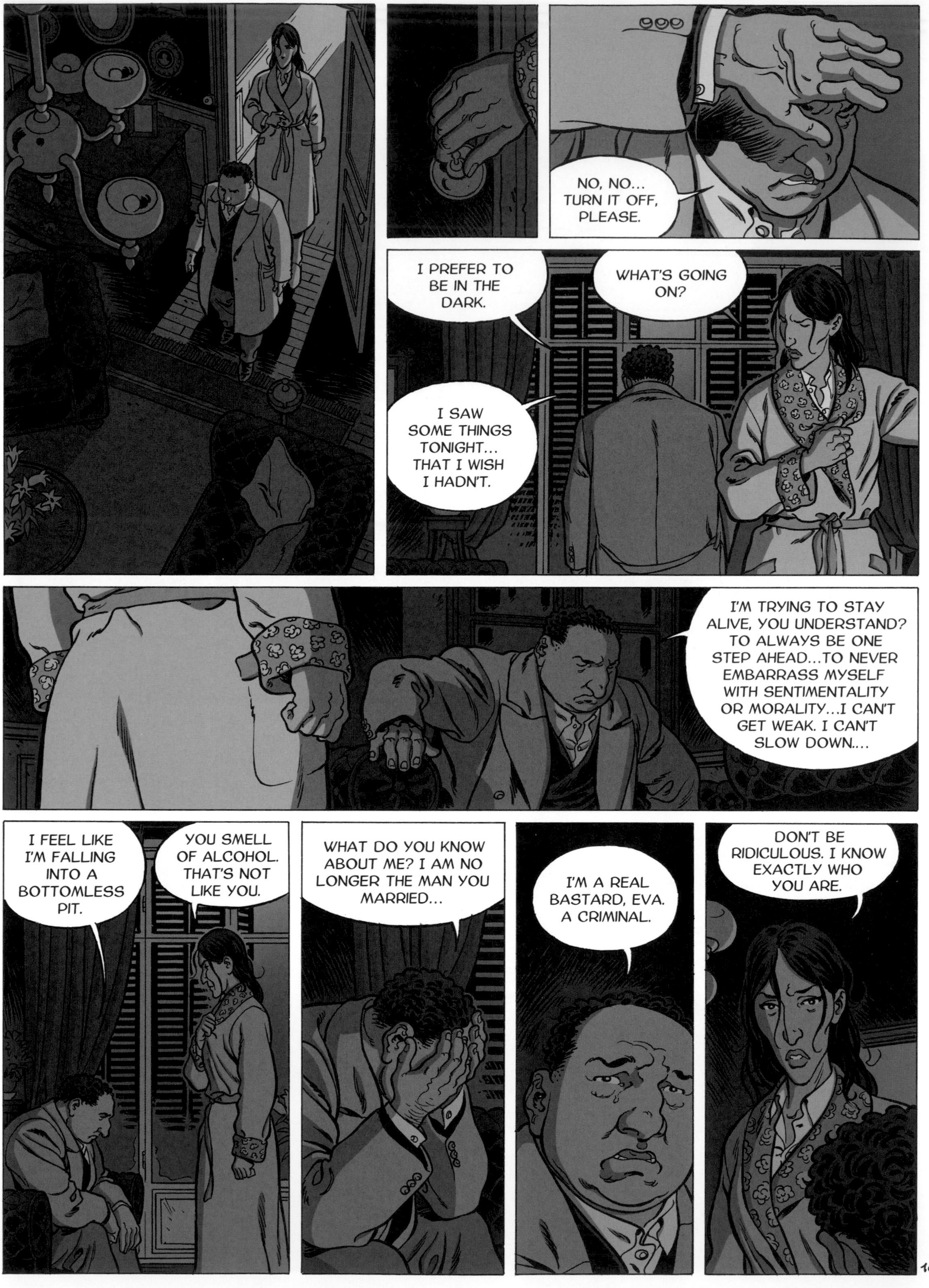
NO, NO... TURN IT OFF, PLEASE.
I PREFER TO BE IN THE DARK.
WHAT'S GOING ON?
I SAW SOME THINGS TONIGHT... THAT I WISH I HADN'T.
I'M TRYING TO STAY ALIVE, YOU UNDERSTAND? TO ALWAYS BE ONE STEP AHEAD...TO NEVER EMBARRASS MYSELF WITH SENTIMENTALITY OR MORALITY...I CAN'T GET WEAK. I CAN'T SLOW DOWN....
I FEEL LIKE I'M FALLING INTO A BOTTOMLESS PIT.
YOU SMELL OF ALCOHOL. THAT'S NOT LIKE YOU.
WHAT DO YOU KNOW ABOUT ME? I AM NO LONGER THE MAN YOU MARRIED...
I'M A REAL BASTARD, EVA. A CRIMINAL.
DON'T BE RIDICULOUS. I KNOW EXACTLY WHO YOU ARE.
16

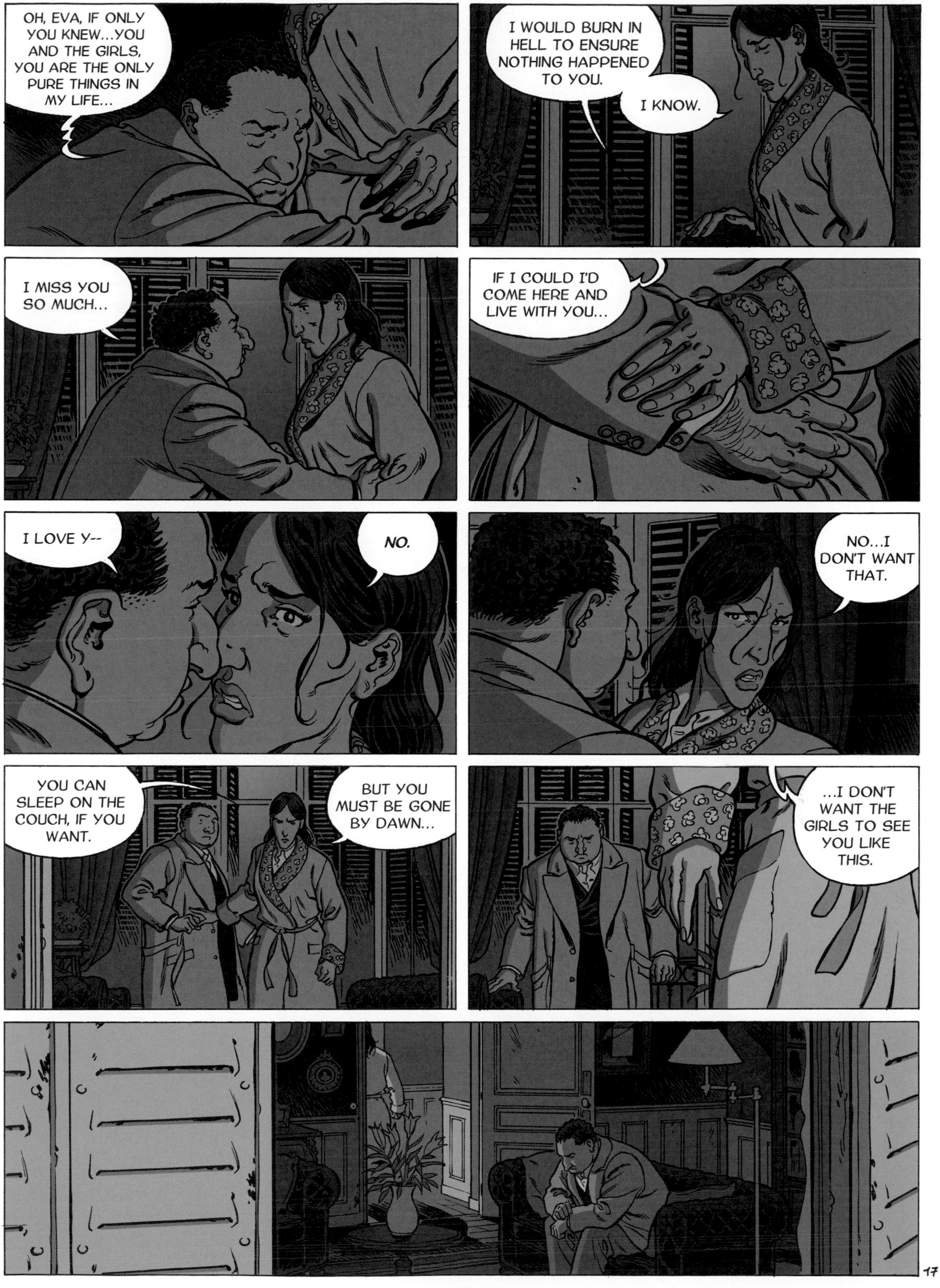
OH, EVA, IF ONLY YOU KNEW...YOU AND THE GIRLS, YOU ARE THE ONLY PURE THINGS IN MY LIFE...
I WOULD BURN IN HELL TO ENSURE NOTHING HAPPENED TO YOU.
I KNOW.
I MISS YOU SO MUCH...
IF I COULD I'D COME HERE AND LIVE WITH YOU...
I LOVE Y--
NO.
NO...I DON'T WANT THAT.
YOU CAN SLEEP ON THE COUCH, IF YOU WANT.
BUT YOU MUST BE GONE BY DAWN...
...I DON'T WANT THE GIRLS TO SEE YOU LIKE THIS.
17

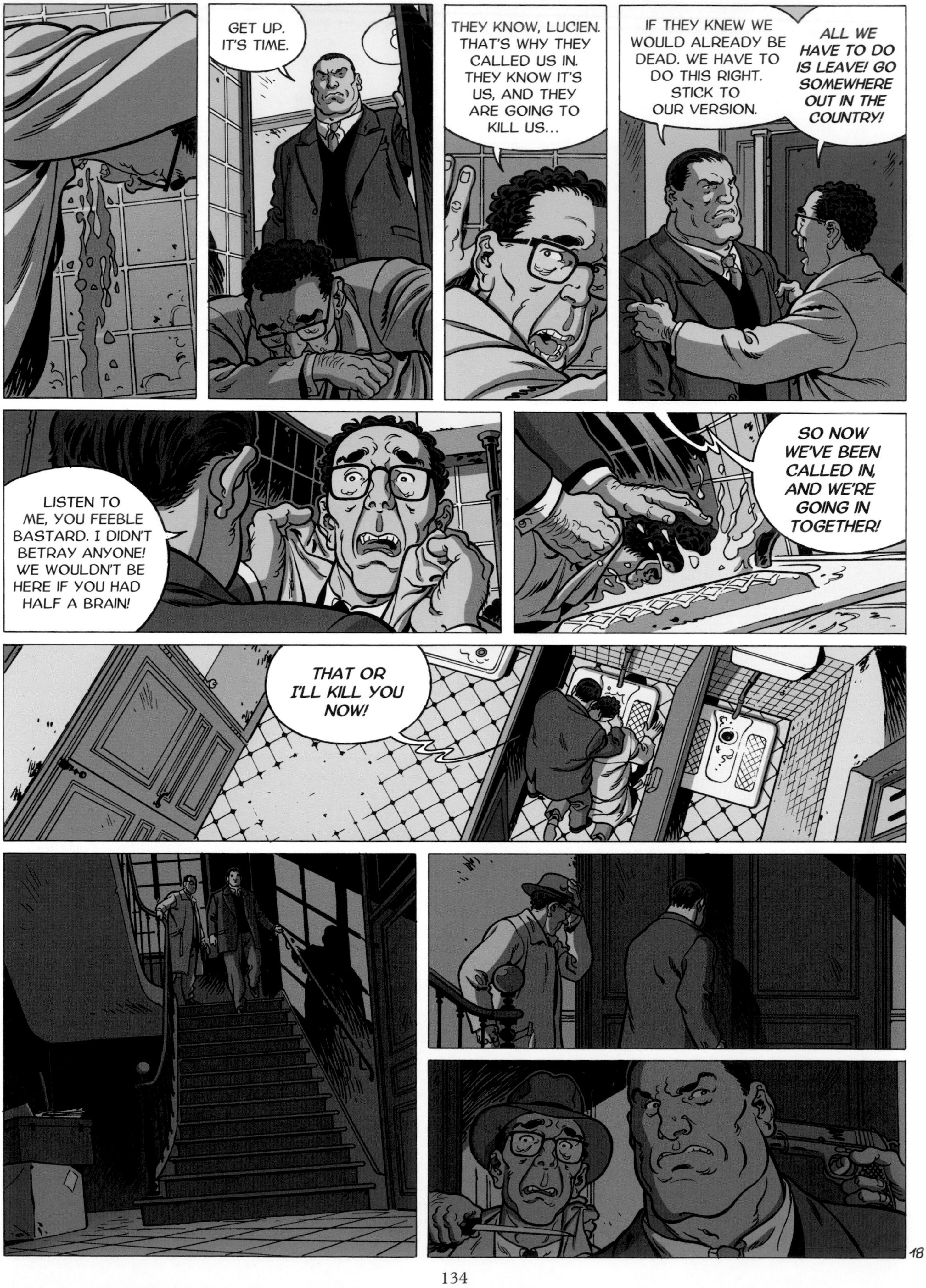

GET UP. IT'S TIME.
THEY KNOW, LUCIEN. THAT'S WHY THEY CALLED US IN. THEY KNOW IT'S US, AND THEY ARE GOING TO KILL US...
IF THEY KNEW WE WOULD ALREADY BE DEAD. WE HAVE TO DO THIS RIGHT. STICK TO OUR VERSION.
ALL WE HAVE TO DO IS LEAVE! GO SOMEWHERE OUT IN THE COUNTRY!
LISTEN TO ME, YOU FEEBLE BASTARD. I DIDN'T BETRAY ANYONE! WE WOULDN'T BE HERE IF YOU HAD HALF A BRAIN!
SO NOW WE'VE BEEN CALLED IN, AND WE'RE GOING IN TOGETHER!
THAT OR I'LL KILL YOU NOW!
18

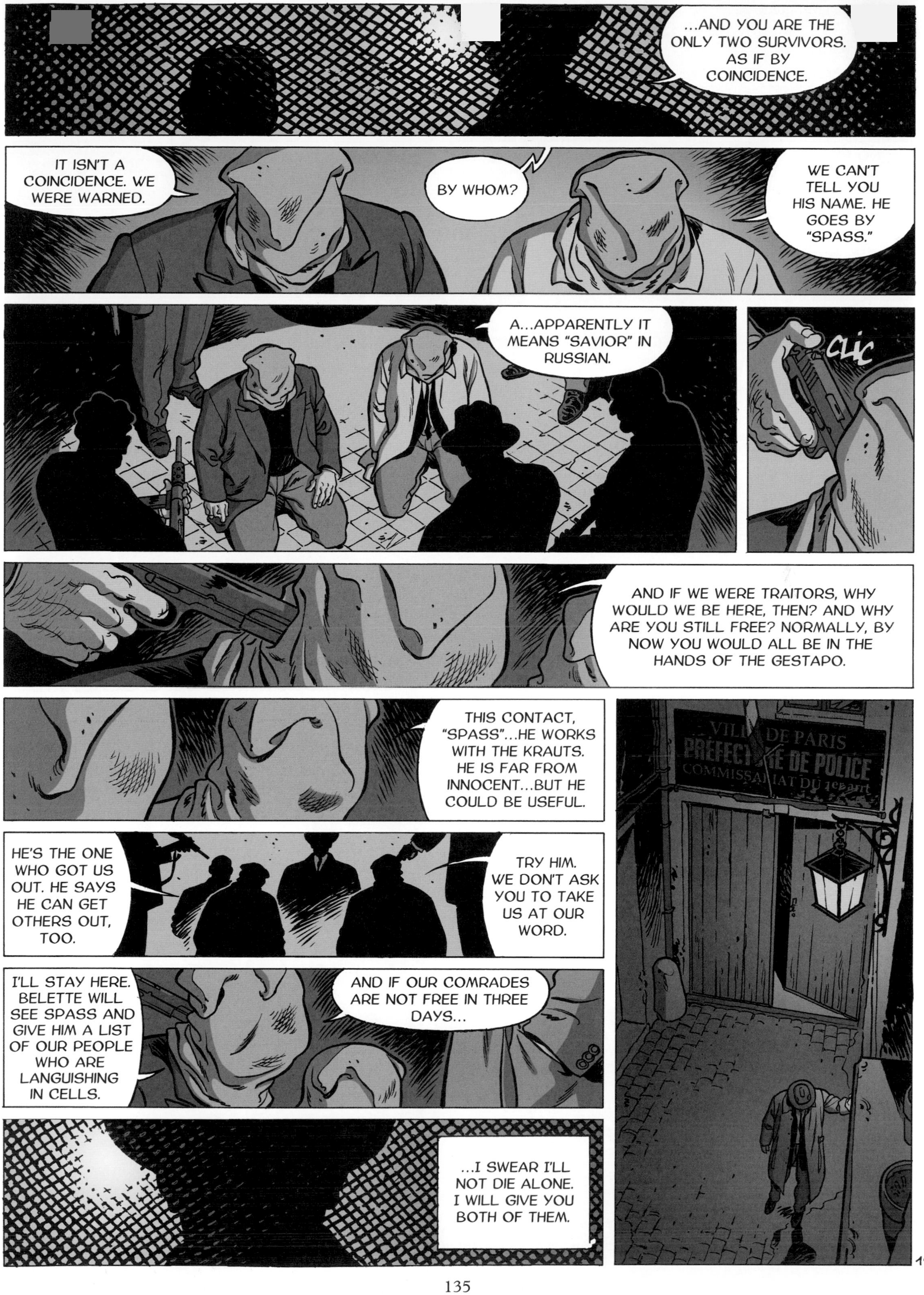
...AND YOU ARE THE ONLY TWO SURVIVORS. AS IF BY COINCIDENCE.
IT ISN'T A COINCIDENCE. WE WERE WARNED.
BY WHOM?
WE CAN'T TELL YOU HIS NAME. HE GOES BY "SPASS."
A...APPARENTLY IT MEANS "SAVIOR" IN RUSSIAN.
CLIC
AND IF WE WERE TRAITORS, WHY WOULD WE BE HERE, THEN? AND WHY ARE YOU STILL FREE? NORMALLY, BY NOW YOU WOULD ALL BE IN THE HANDS OF THE GESTAPO.
THIS CONTACT, "SPASS"...HE WORKS WITH THE KRAUTS. HE IS FAR FROM INNOCENT...BUT HE COULD BE USEFUL.
HE'S THE ONE WHO GOT US OUT. HE SAYS HE CAN GET OTHERS OUT, TOO.
TRY HIM. WE DON'T ASK YOU TO TAKE US AT OUR WORD.
I'LL STAY HERE. BELETTE WILL SEE SPASS AND GIVE HIM A LIST OF OUR PEOPLE WHO ARE LANGUISHING IN CELLS.
AND IF OUR COMRADES ARE NOT FREE IN THREE DAYS...
...I SWEAR I'LL NOT DIE ALONE. I WILL GIVE YOU BOTH OF THEM.
19

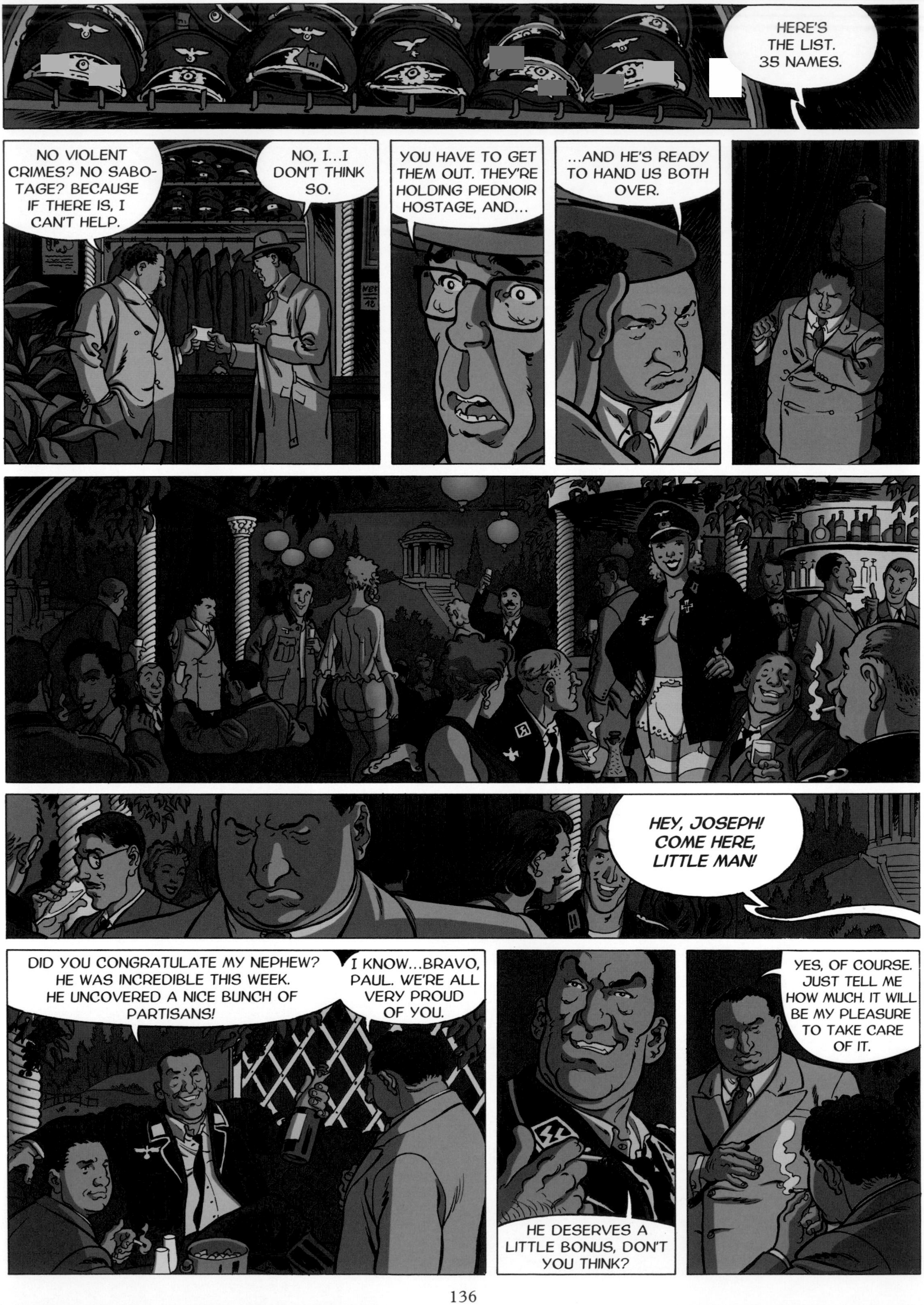
HERE'S THE LIST. 35 NAMES.
NO VIOLENT CRIMES? NO SABO-TAGE? BECAUSE IF THERE IS, I CAN'T HELP.
NO, I...I DON'T THINK SO.
YOU HAVE TO GET THEM OUT. THEY'RE HOLDING PIEDNOIR HOSTAGE, AND...
...AND HE'S READY TO HAND US BOTH OVER.
HEY, JOSEPH! COME HERE, LITTLE MAN!
DID YOU CONGRATULATE MY NEPHEW? HE WAS INCREDIBLE THIS WEEK. HE UNCOVERED A NICE BUNCH OF PARTISANS!
I KNOW...BRAVO, PAUL. WE'RE ALL VERY PROUD OF YOU.
HE DESERVES A LITTLE BONUS, DON'T YOU THINK?
YES, OF COURSE. JUST TELL ME HOW MUCH. IT WILL BE MY PLEASURE TO TAKE CARE OF IT.

20

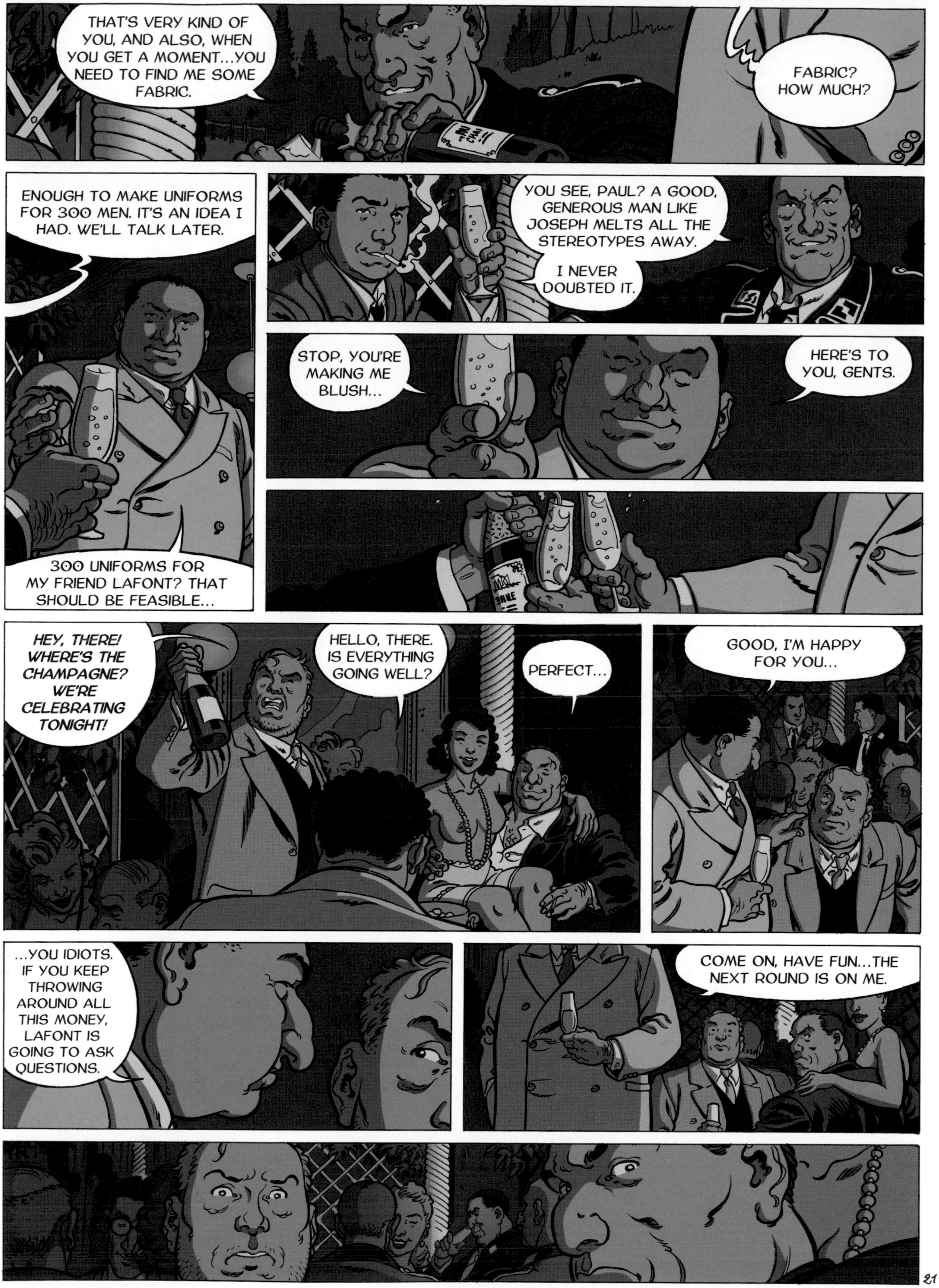
THAT'S VERY KIND OF YOU, AND ALSO, WHEN YOU GET A MOMENT...YOU NEED TO FIND ME SOME FABRIC.
FABRIC? HOW MUCH?
ENOUGH TO MAKE UNIFORMS FOR 300 MEN. IT'S AN IDEA I HAD. WE'LL TALK LATER.
YOU SEE, PAUL? A GOOD, GENEROUS MAN LIKE JOSEPH MELTS ALL THE STEREOTYPES AWAY.
I NEVER DOUBTED IT.
300 UNIFORMS FOR MY FRIEND LAFONT? THAT SHOULD BE FEASIBLE...
STOP, YOU'RE MAKING ME BLUSH...
HERE'S TO YOU, GENTS.
HEY, THERE! WHERE'S THE CHAMPAGNE? WE'RE CELEBRATING TONIGHT!
HELLO, THERE. IS EVERYTHING GOING WELL?
PERFECT...
GOOD, I'M HAPPY FOR YOU...
...YOU IDIOTS. IF YOU KEEP THROWING AROUND ALL THIS MONEY, LAFONT IS GOING TO ASK QUESTIONS.
COME ON, HAVE FUN...THE NEXT ROUND IS ON ME.
21

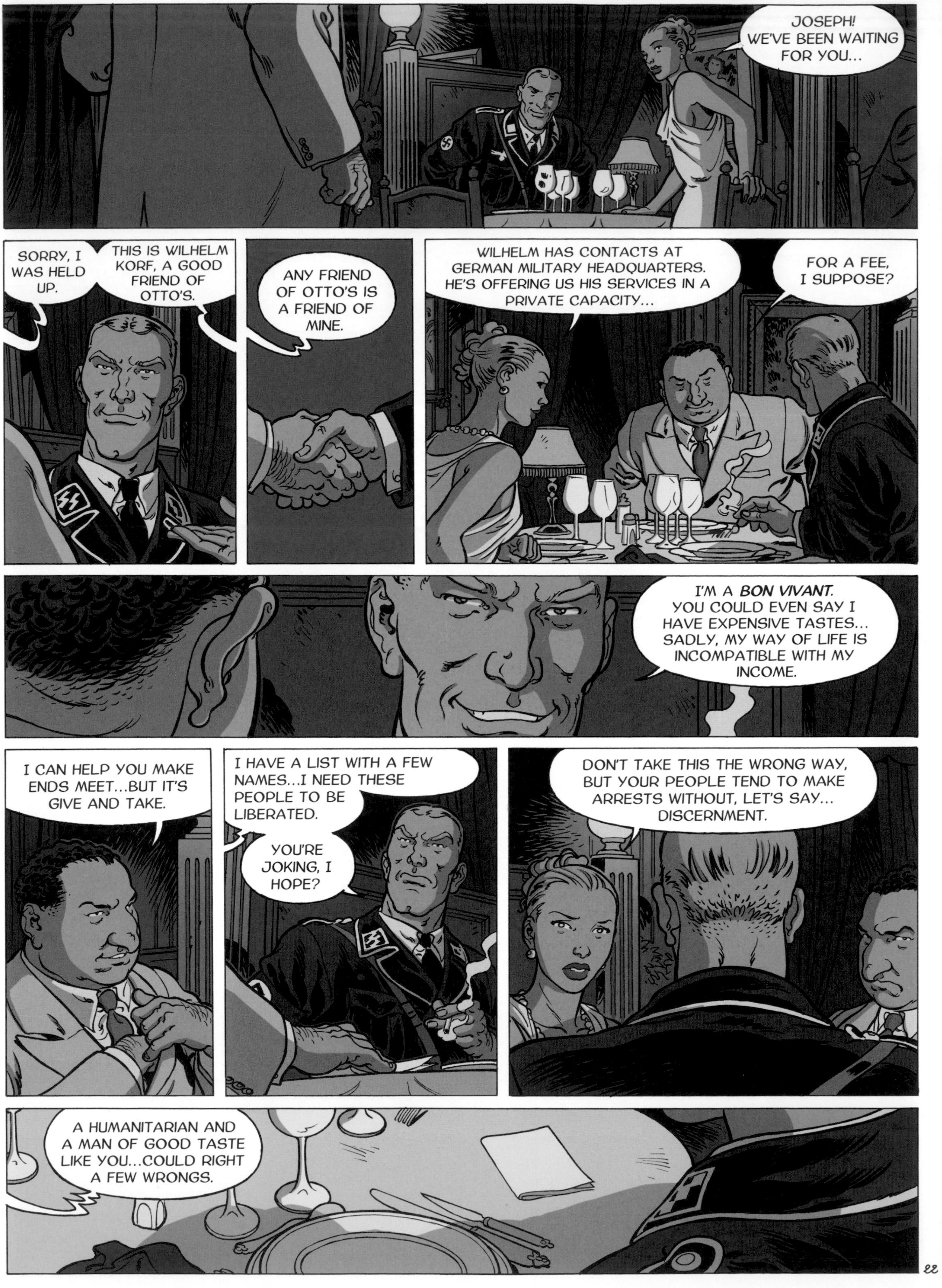
JOSEPH! WE'VE BEEN WAITING FOR YOU...
SORRY, I WAS HELD UP.
THIS IS WILHELM KORF, A GOOD FRIEND OF OTTO'S.
ANY FRIEND OF OTTO'S IS A FRIEND OF MINE.
WILHELM HAS CONTACTS AT GERMAN MILITARY HEADQUARTERS. HE'S OFFERING US HIS SERVICES IN A PRIVATE CAPACITY...
FOR A FEE, I SUPPOSE?
I'M A BON VIVANT. YOU COULD EVEN SAY I HAVE EXPENSIVE TASTES... SADLY, MY WAY OF LIFE IS INCOMPATIBLE WITH MY INCOME.
I CAN HELP YOU MAKE ENDS MEET...BUT IT'S GIVE AND TAKE.
I HAVE A LIST WITH A FEW NAMES...I NEED THESE PEOPLE TO BE LIBERATED.
YOU'RE JOKING, I HOPE?
DON'T TAKE THIS THE WRONG WAY, BUT YOUR PEOPLE TEND TO MAKE ARRESTS WITHOUT, LET'S SAY... DISCERNMENT.
A HUMANITARIAN AND A MAN OF GOOD TASTE LIKE YOU...COULD RIGHT A FEW WRONGS.
22

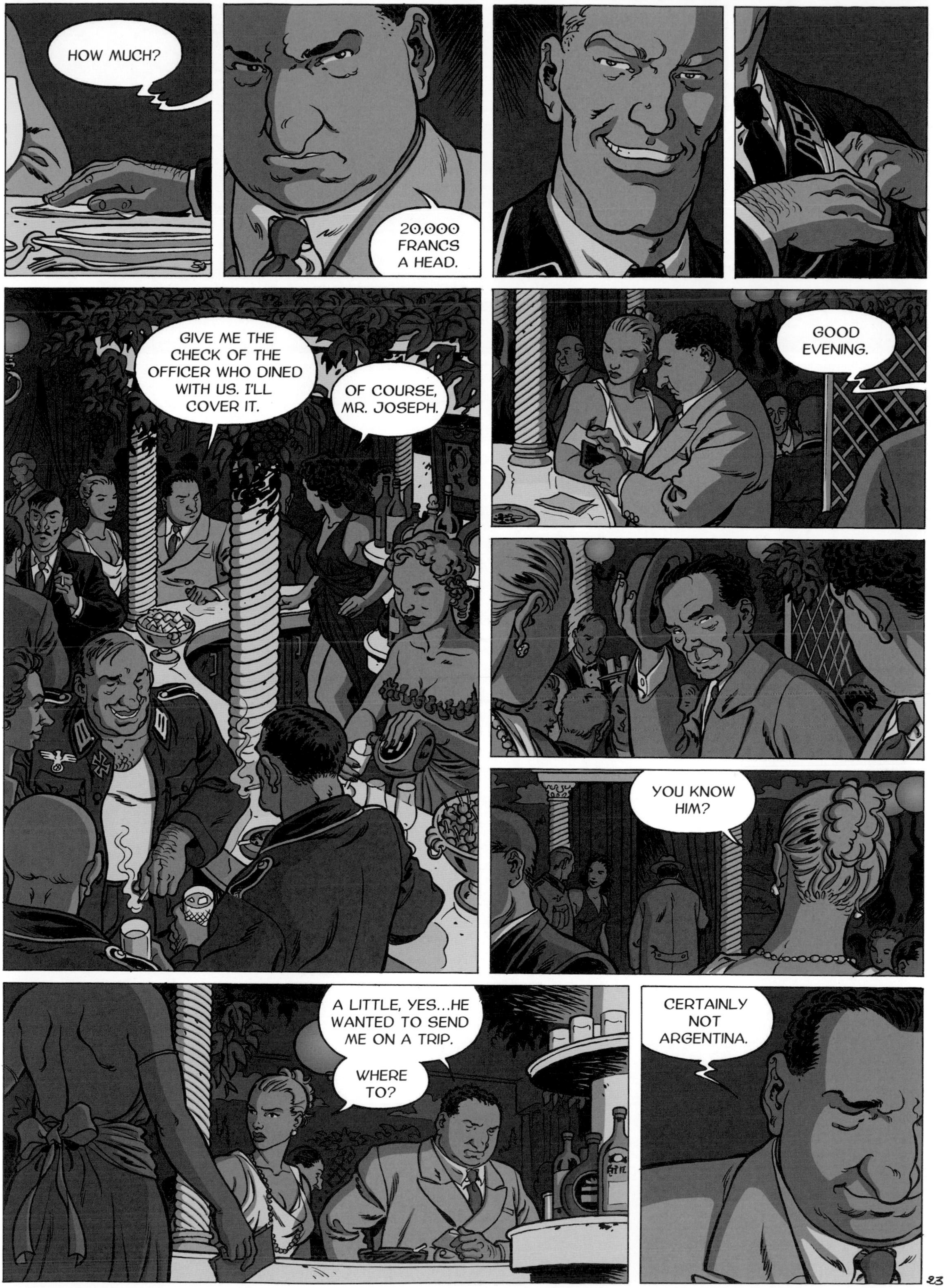
HOW MUCH?
20,000 FRANCS A HEAD.
GIVE ME THE CHECK OF THE OFFICER WHO DINED WITH US. I'LL COVER IT.
OF COURSE, MR. JOSEPH.
GOOD EVENING.
YOU KNOW HIM?
A LITTLE, YES...HE WANTED TO SEND ME ON A TRIP.
WHERE TO?
CERTAINLY NOT ARGENTINA.
23

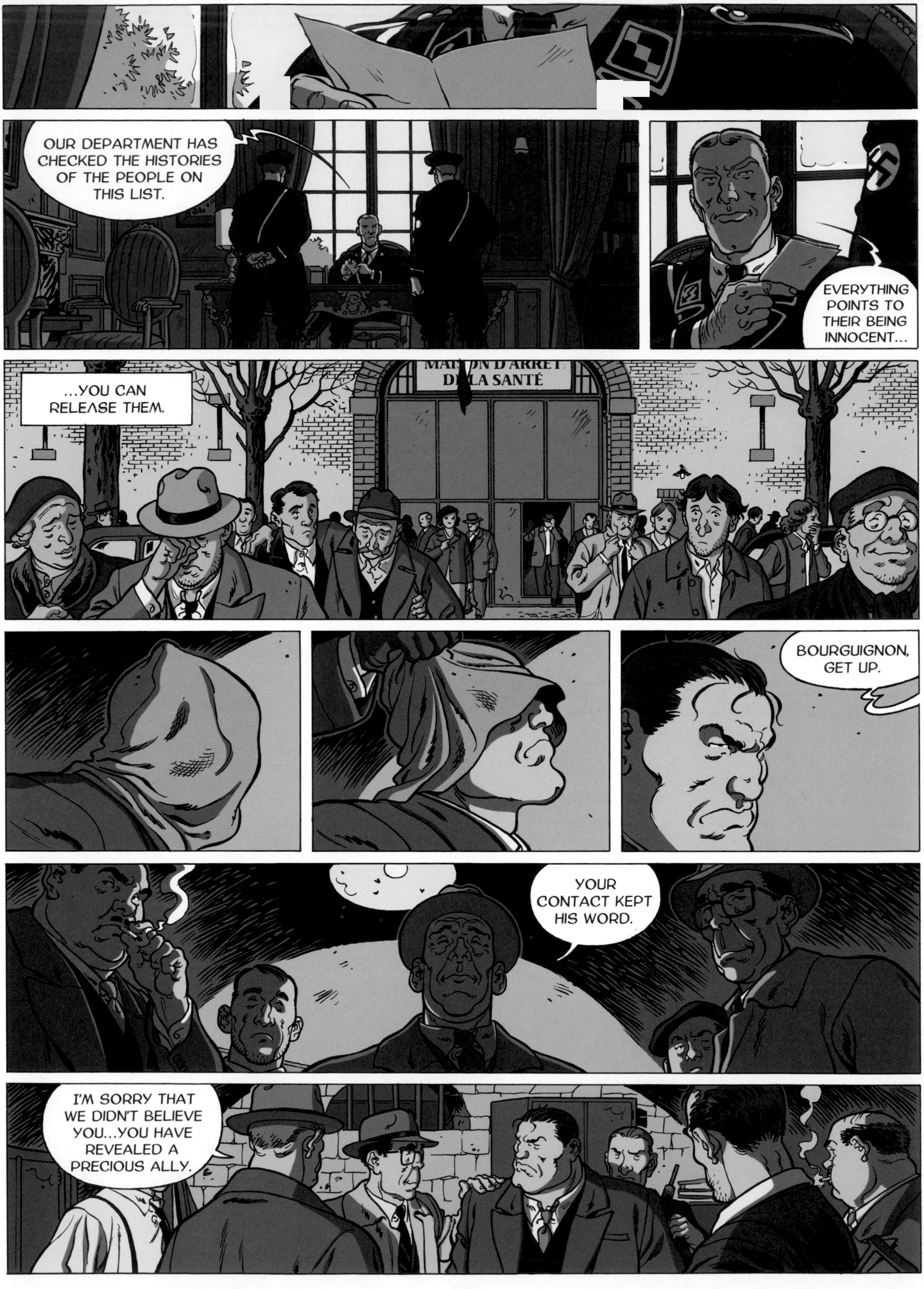
OUR DEPARTMENT HAS CHECKED THE HISTORIES OF THE PEOPLE ON THIS LIST.
EVERYTHING POINTS TO THEIR BEING INNOCENT...
...YOU CAN RELEASE THEM.
MAISON D'ARRET DE LA SANTÉ
BOURGUIGNON, GET UP.
YOUR CONTACT KEPT HIS WORD.
I'M SORRY THAT WE DIDN'T BELIEVE YOU...YOU HAVE REVEALED A PRECIOUS ALLY.
24

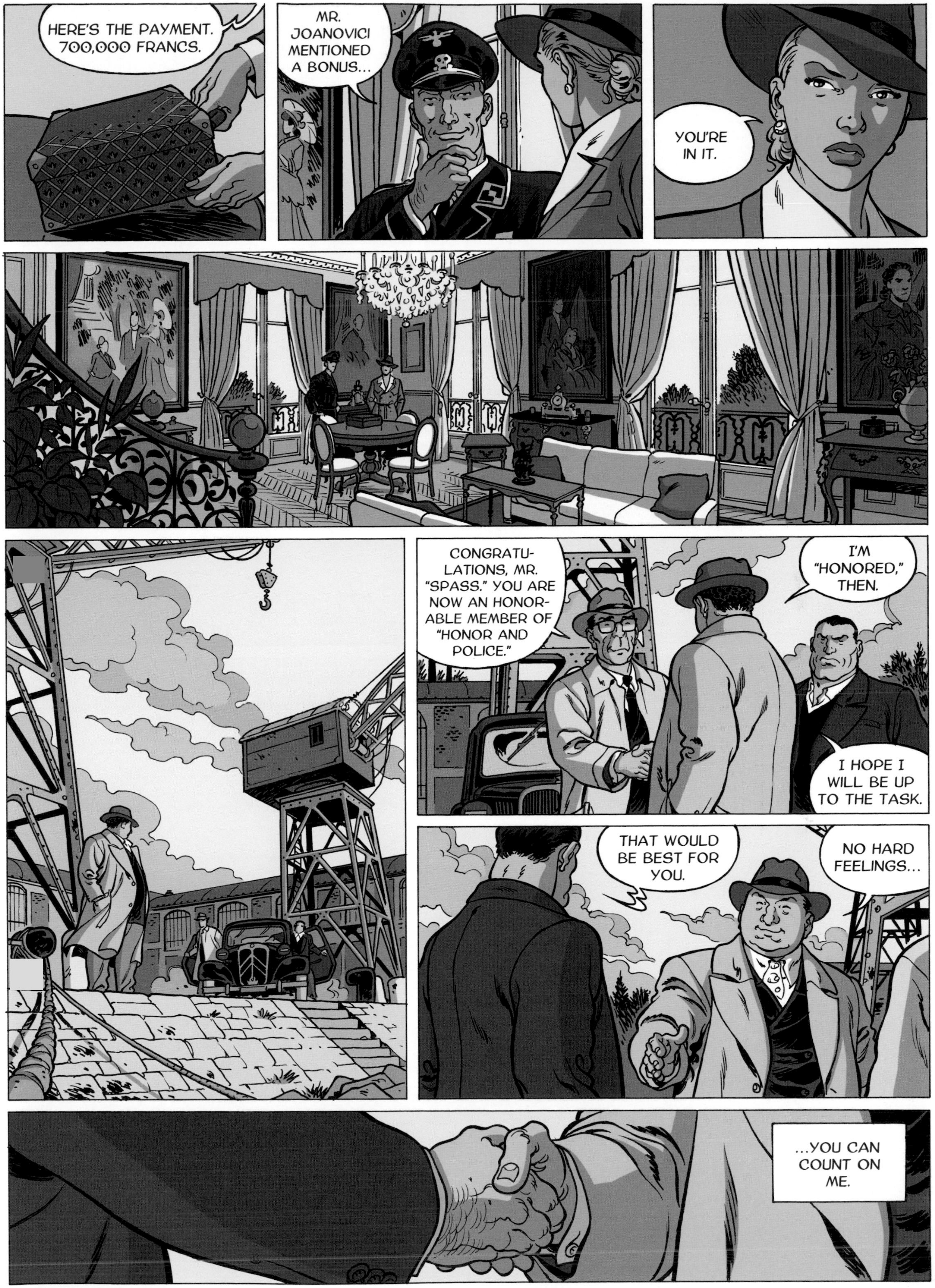
HERE'S THE PAYMENT. 700,000 FRANCS.
MR. JOANOVICI MENTIONED A BONUS...
YOU'RE IN IT.
CONGRATULATIONS, MR. "SPASS." YOU ARE NOW AN HONORABLE MEMBER OF "HONOR AND POLICE."
I'M "HONORED," THEN.
I HOPE I WILL BE UP TO THE TASK.
THAT WOULD BE BEST FOR YOU.
NO HARD FEELINGS...
...YOU CAN COUNT ON ME.
25

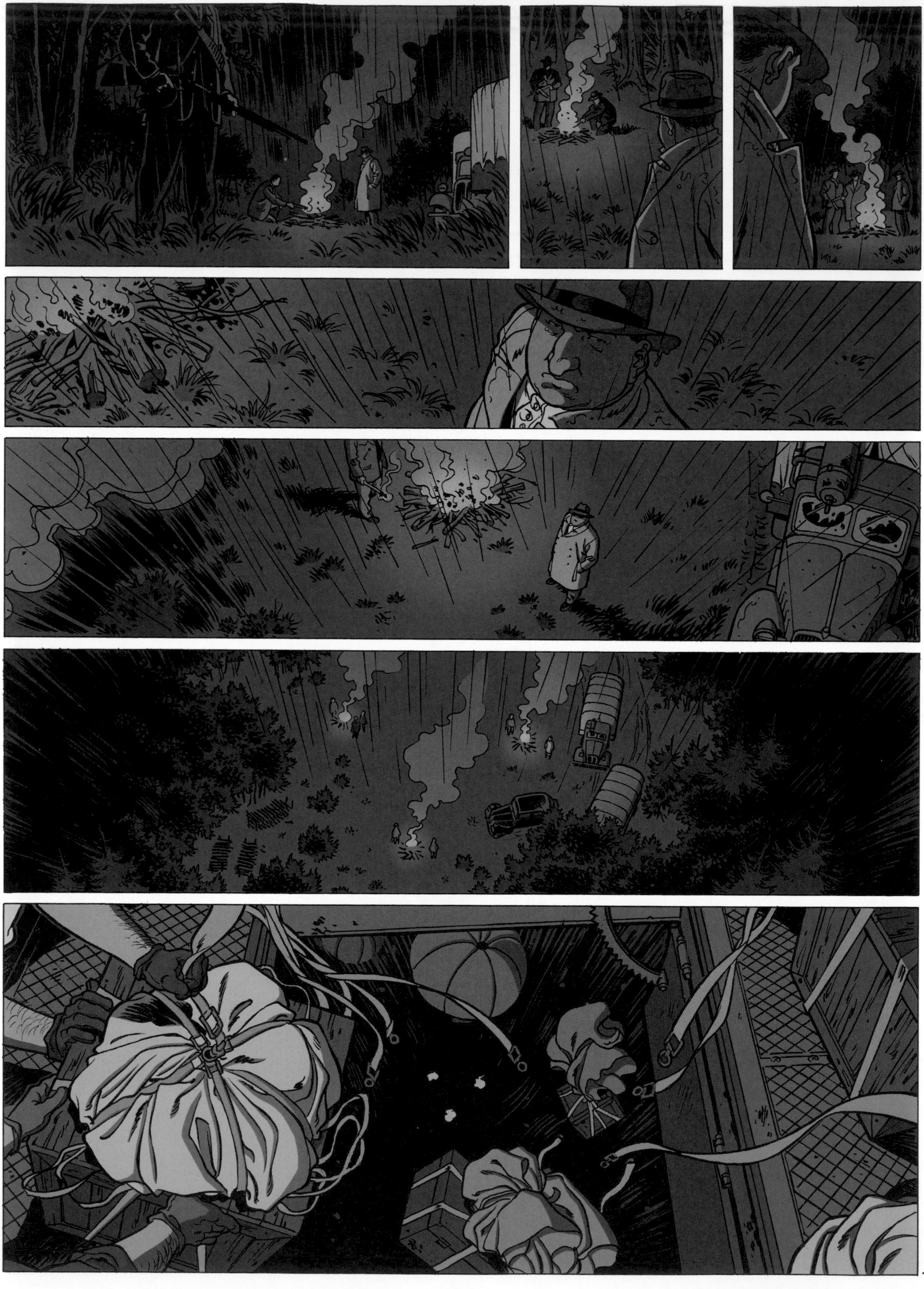
26

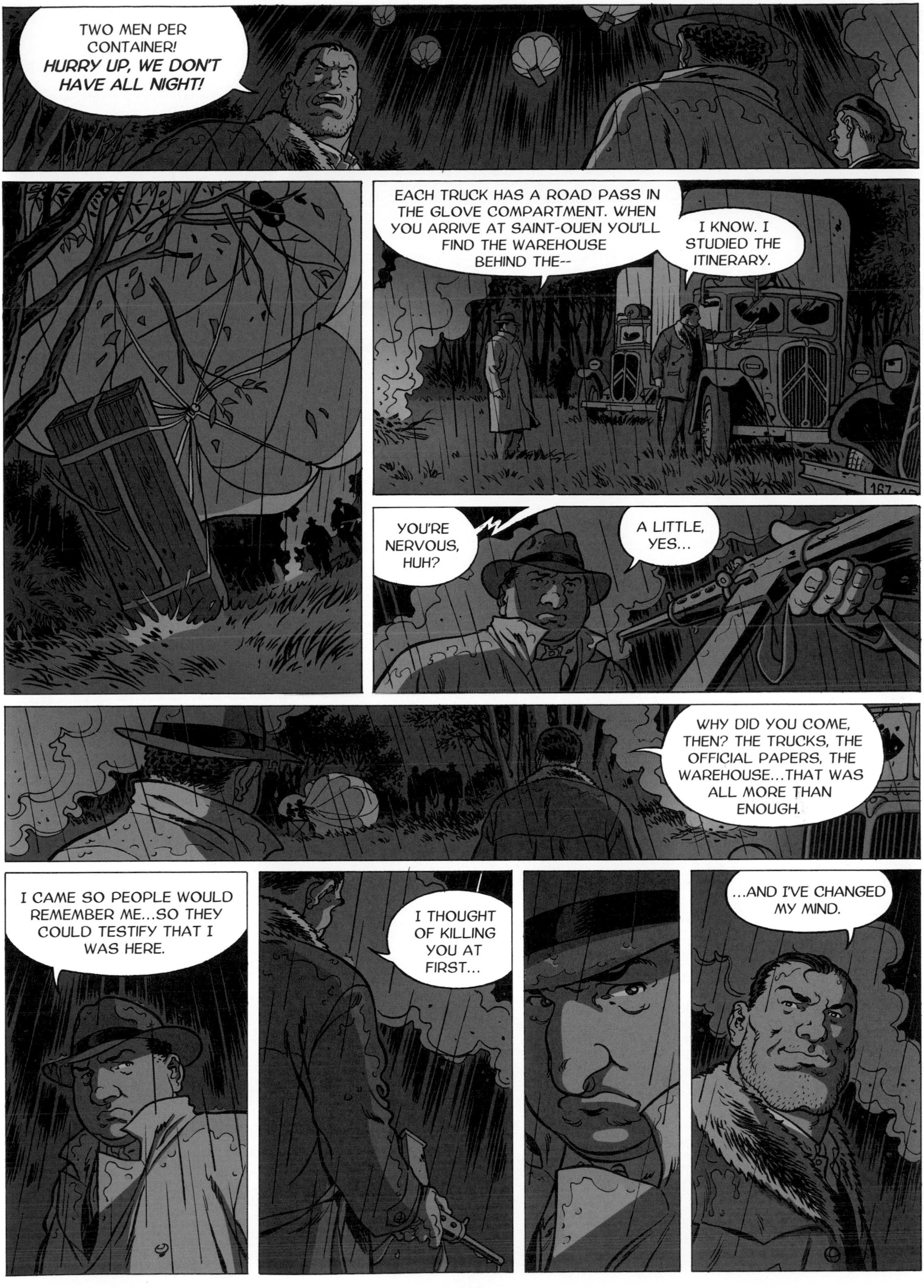
TWO MEN PER CONTAINER! HURRY UP, WE DON'T HAVE ALL NIGHT!
EACH TRUCK HAS A ROAD PASS IN THE GLOVE COMPARTMENT. WHEN YOU ARRIVE AT SAINT-OUEN YOU'LL FIND THE WAREHOUSE BEHIND THE--
I KNOW. I STUDIED THE ITINERARY.
YOU'RE NERVOUS, HUH?
A LITTLE, YES...
WHY DID YOU COME, THEN? THE TRUCKS, THE OFFICIAL PAPERS, THE WAREHOUSE...THAT WAS ALL MORE THAN ENOUGH.
I CAME SO PEOPLE WOULD REMEMBER ME...SO THEY COULD TESTIFY THAT I WAS HERE.
I THOUGHT OF KILLING YOU AT FIRST...
...AND I'VE CHANGED MY MIND.
27

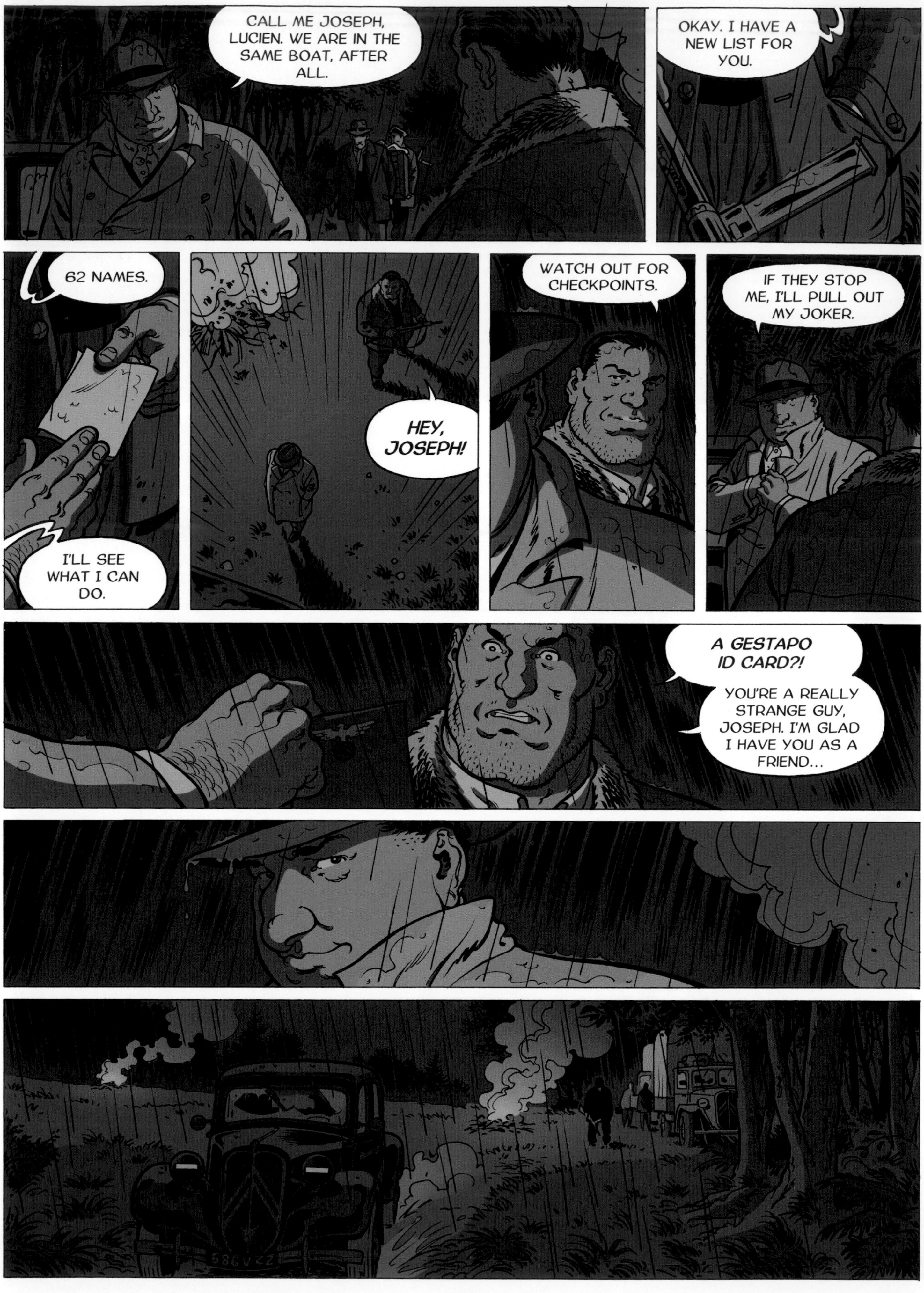
CALL ME JOSEPH, LUCIEN. WE ARE IN THE SAME BOAT, AFTER ALL.
OKAY. I HAVE A NEW LIST FOR YOU.
62 NAMES.
I'LL SEE WHAT I CAN DO.
HEY, JOSEPH!
WATCH OUT FOR CHECKPOINTS.
IF THEY STOP ME, I'LL PULL OUT MY JOKER.
A GESTAPO ID CARD?!
YOU'RE A REALLY STRANGE GUY, JOSEPH. I'M GLAD I HAVE YOU AS A FRIEND...
28

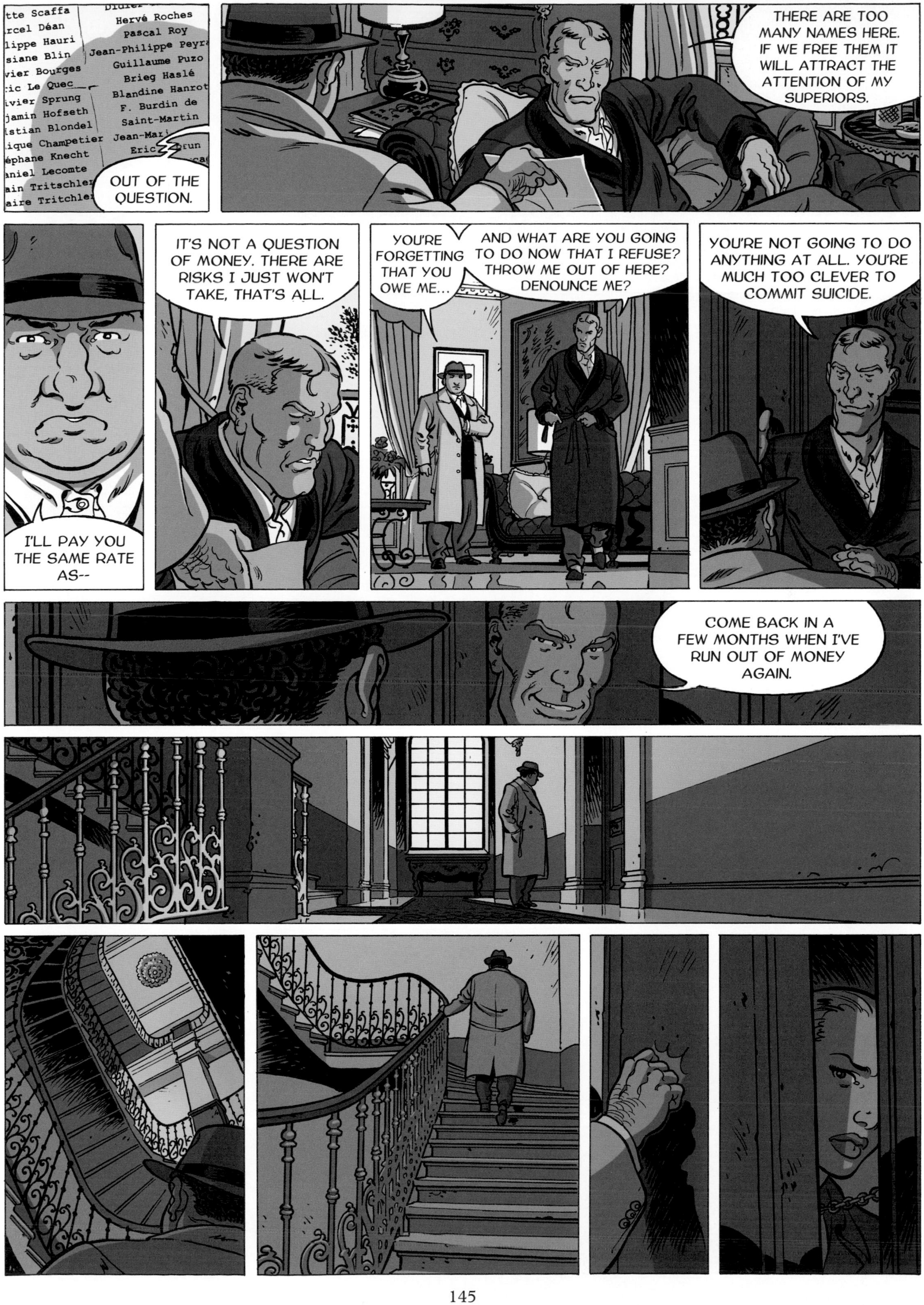
Hervé Roches
Pascal Roy
Guillaume Puzo
Brieg Haslé
Blandine Hanrot
F. Burdin de
Saint-Martin
OUT OF THE QUESTION.
THERE ARE TOO MANY NAMES HERE. IF WE FREE THEM IT WILL ATTRACT THE ATTENTION OF MY SUPERIORS.
I'LL PAY YOU THE SAME RATE AS--
IT'S NOT A QUESTION OF MONEY. THERE ARE RISKS I JUST WON'T TAKE, THAT'S ALL.
YOU'RE FORGETTING THAT YOU OWE ME...
AND WHAT ARE YOU GOING TO DO NOW THAT I REFUSE? THROW ME OUT OF HERE? DENOUNCE ME?
YOU'RE NOT GOING TO DO ANYTHING AT ALL. YOU'RE MUCH TOO CLEVER TO COMMIT SUICIDE.
COME BACK IN A FEW MONTHS WHEN I'VE RUN OUT OF MONEY AGAIN.

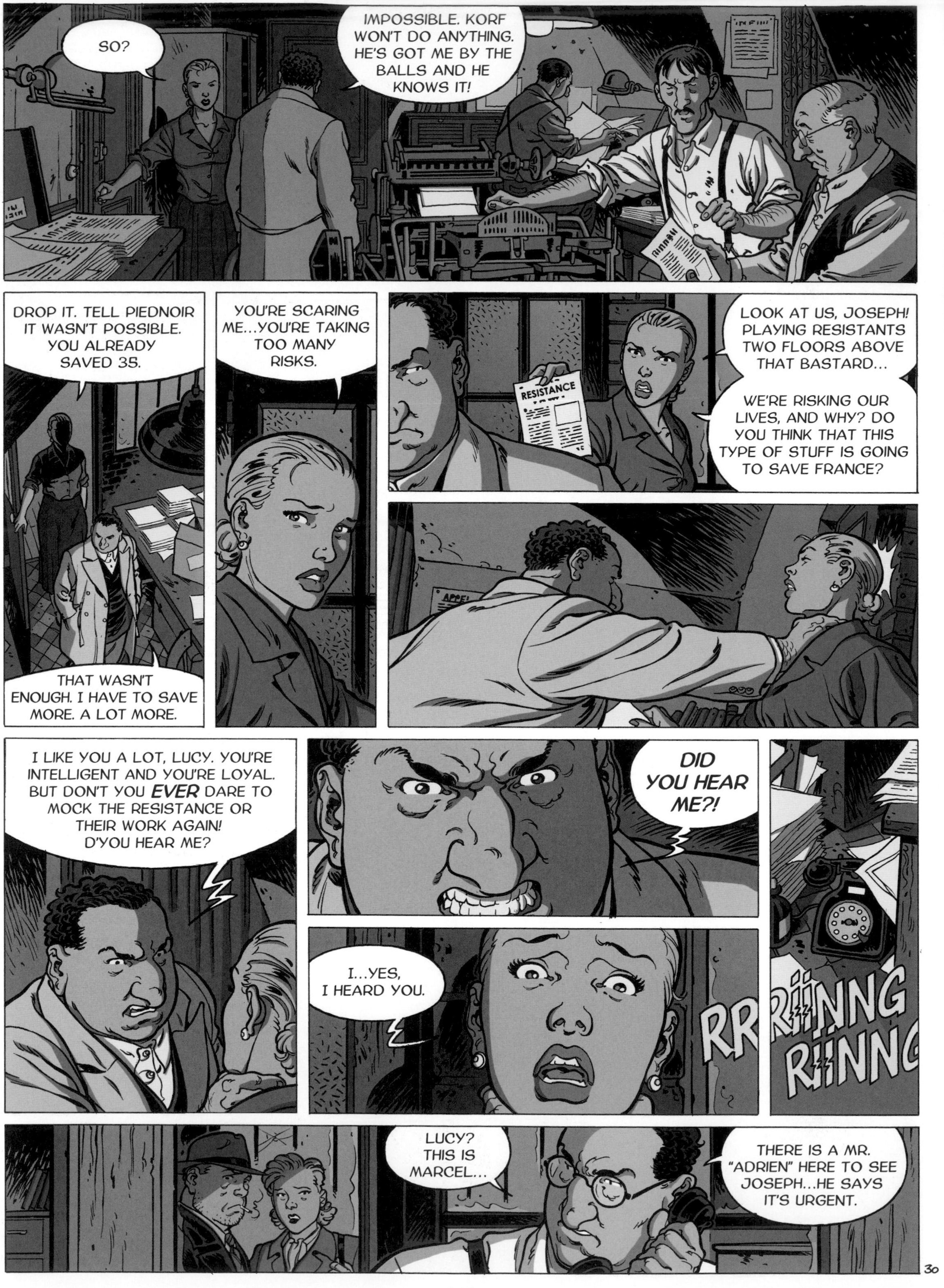

SO?
IMPOSSIBLE. KORF WON'T DO ANYTHING. HE'S GOT ME BY THE BALLS AND HE KNOWS IT!
DROP IT. TELL PIEDNOIR IT WASN'T POSSIBLE. YOU ALREADY SAVED 35.
THAT WASN'T ENOUGH. I HAVE TO SAVE MORE. A LOT MORE.
YOU'RE SCARING ME...YOU'RE TAKING TOO MANY RISKS.
LOOK AT US, JOSEPH! PLAYING RESISTANTS TWO FLOORS ABOVE THAT BASTARD...
WE'RE RISKING OUR LIVES, AND WHY? DO YOU THINK THAT THIS TYPE OF STUFF IS GOING TO SAVE FRANCE?
RESISTANCE
I LIKE YOU A LOT, LUCY. YOU'RE INTELLIGENT AND YOU'RE LOYAL. BUT DON'T YOU EVER DARE TO MOCK THE RESISTANCE OR THEIR WORK AGAIN! D'YOU HEAR ME?
DID YOU HEAR ME?!
I...YES, I HEARD YOU.
RRRIINNG RIINNG
LUCY? THIS IS MARCEL...
THERE IS A MR. "ADRIEN" HERE TO SEE JOSEPH...HE SAYS IT'S URGENT.
30

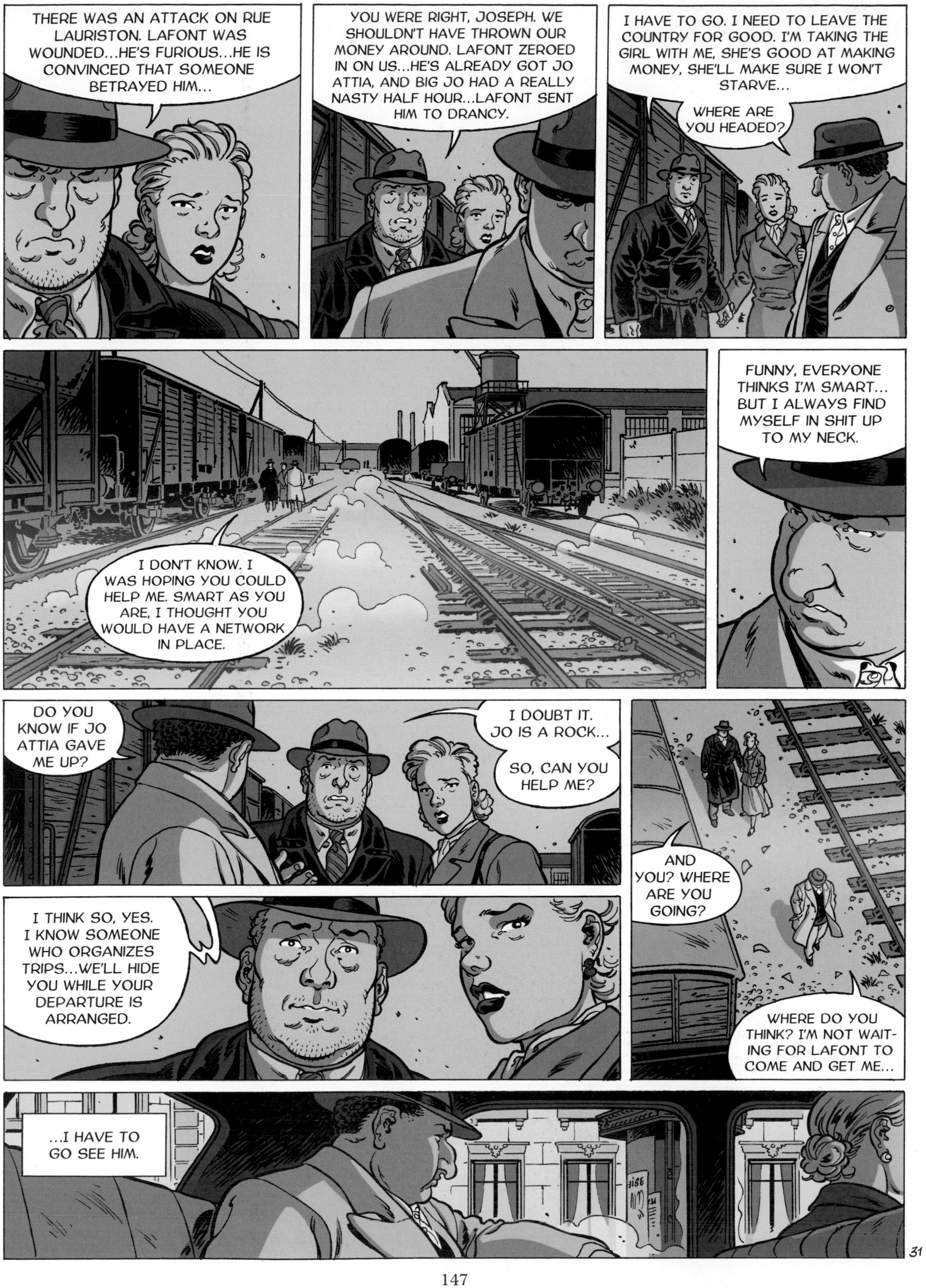
THERE WAS AN ATTACK ON RUE LAURISTON. LAFONT WAS WOUNDED...HE'S FURIOUS...HE IS CONVINCED THAT SOMEONE BETRAYED HIM...
YOU WERE RIGHT, JOSEPH. WE SHOULDN'T HAVE THROWN OUR MONEY AROUND. LAFONT ZEROED IN ON US...HE'S ALREADY GOT JO ATTIA, AND BIG JO HAD A REALLY NASTY HALF HOUR...LAFONT SENT HIM TO DRANCY.
I HAVE TO GO. I NEED TO LEAVE THE COUNTRY FOR GOOD. I'M TAKING THE GIRL WITH ME, SHE'S GOOD AT MAKING MONEY, SHE'LL MAKE SURE I WON'T STARVE...
WHERE ARE YOU HEADED?
I DON'T KNOW. I WAS HOPING YOU COULD HELP ME. SMART AS YOU ARE, I THOUGHT YOU WOULD HAVE A NETWORK IN PLACE.
FUNNY, EVERYONE THINKS I'M SMART... BUT I ALWAYS FIND MYSELF IN SHIT UP TO MY NECK.
DO YOU KNOW IF JO ATTIA GAVE ME UP?
I DOUBT IT. JO IS A ROCK...
SO, CAN YOU HELP ME?
I THINK SO, YES. I KNOW SOMEONE WHO ORGANIZES TRIPS...WE'LL HIDE YOU WHILE YOUR DEPARTURE IS ARRANGED.
AND YOU? WHERE ARE YOU GOING?
WHERE DO YOU THINK? I'M NOT WAITING FOR LAFONT TO COME AND GET ME...
...I HAVE TO GO SEE HIM.
31

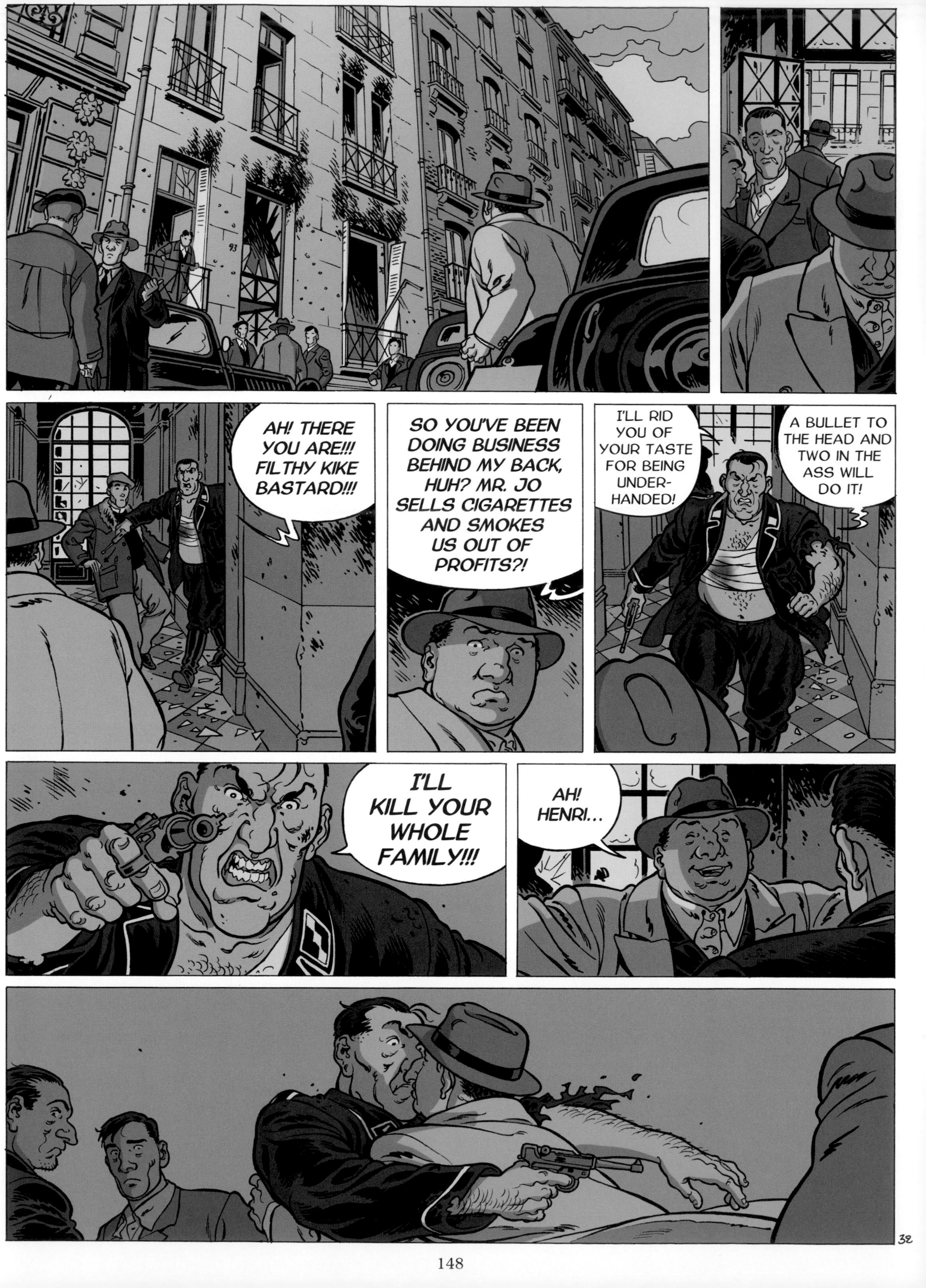
AH! THERE YOU ARE!!! FILTHY KIKE BASTARD!!!
SO YOU'VE BEEN DOING BUSINESS BEHIND MY BACK, HUH? MR. JO SELLS CIGARETTES AND SMOKES US OUT OF PROFITS?!
I'LL RID YOU OF YOUR TASTE FOR BEING UNDER-HANDED!
A BULLET TO THE HEAD AND TWO IN THE ASS WILL DO IT!
I'LL KILL YOUR WHOLE FAMILY!!!
AH! HENRI...
32

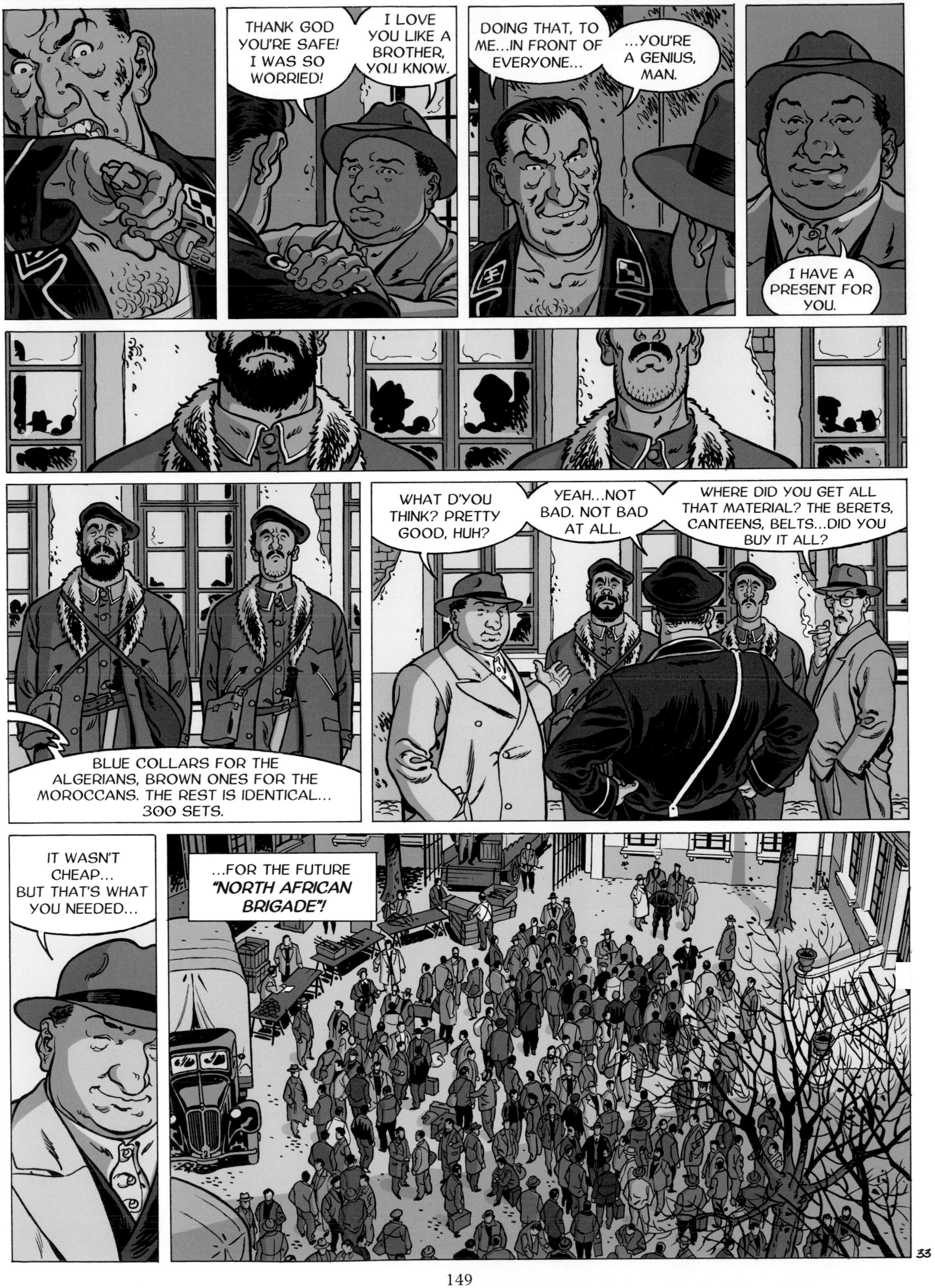

THANK GOD YOU'RE SAFE! I WAS SO WORRIED!
I LOVE YOU LIKE A BROTHER, YOU KNOW.
DOING THAT, TO ME...IN FRONT OF EVERYONE...
...YOU'RE A GENIUS, MAN.
I HAVE A PRESENT FOR YOU.
WHAT D'YOU THINK? PRETTY GOOD, HUH?
YEAH...NOT BAD. NOT BAD AT ALL.
WHERE DID YOU GET ALL THAT MATERIAL? THE BERETS, CANTEENS, BELTS...DID YOU BUY IT ALL?
BLUE COLLARS FOR THE ALGERIANS, BROWN ONES FOR THE MOROCCANS. THE REST IS IDENTICAL... 300 SETS.
IT WASN'T CHEAP... BUT THAT'S WHAT YOU NEEDED...
...FOR THE FUTURE "NORTH AFRICAN BRIGADE"!
33

YOU'RE RIGHT. THEY'RE GOOD. WAIT TILL THEY SEE US ARRIVE IN THEIR FUCKING MAQUIS SHRUBLAND... THEY'LL SHIT THEIR PANTS!

ARE YOU GOING ON AN OPERATION SOON?

NEXT WEEK. THIS WINTER, ME AND MY LITTLE WOGS ARE GOING TO HUNT DOWN RESISTANTS!

I OWE YOU, JOSEPH. WITH THE BUDGET THE KRAUTS GAVE ME I DIDN'T EVEN HAVE ENOUGH TO BUY THE SOCKS!

BAH, IT'S A PLEA-SURE...

...UH, ACTUALLY, I DO HAVE A LITTLE FAVOR, BUT I HESITATE TO ASK.

DON'T BE COY! YOU CAN ASK ME ANYTHING!

WELL, YOU KNOW, I HAVE A LOT OF EMPLOYEES, AND THEY HAVE FAMILIES...AND SOMETIMES, SOME GET ARRESTED FOR BULLSHIT, SO THEIR PARENTS COME TO SEE ME...

...AND THEY, WELL, GAVE ME A SHORT LIST, AND I WAS WONDERING...

NO PROBLEM. BONNY WILL TAKE CARE OF IT.

HEY, BY THE WAY...

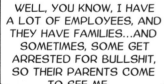

YOU'LL HAVE TO GREASE SOME PALMS TO GET THEM OUT...ARE THERE A LOT OF THEM?

62. I'LL PAY.

WHAT A PHILANTHROPIST!

YOU HAVEN'T SEEN ADRIEN BY ANY CHANCE? WE'VE LOOKED FOR HIM EVERY-WHERE, THAT SHIT!

ADRIEN? NO... I HAVEN'T SEEN HIM...WHY? DO YOU HAVE A MESSAGE FOR HIM?

34

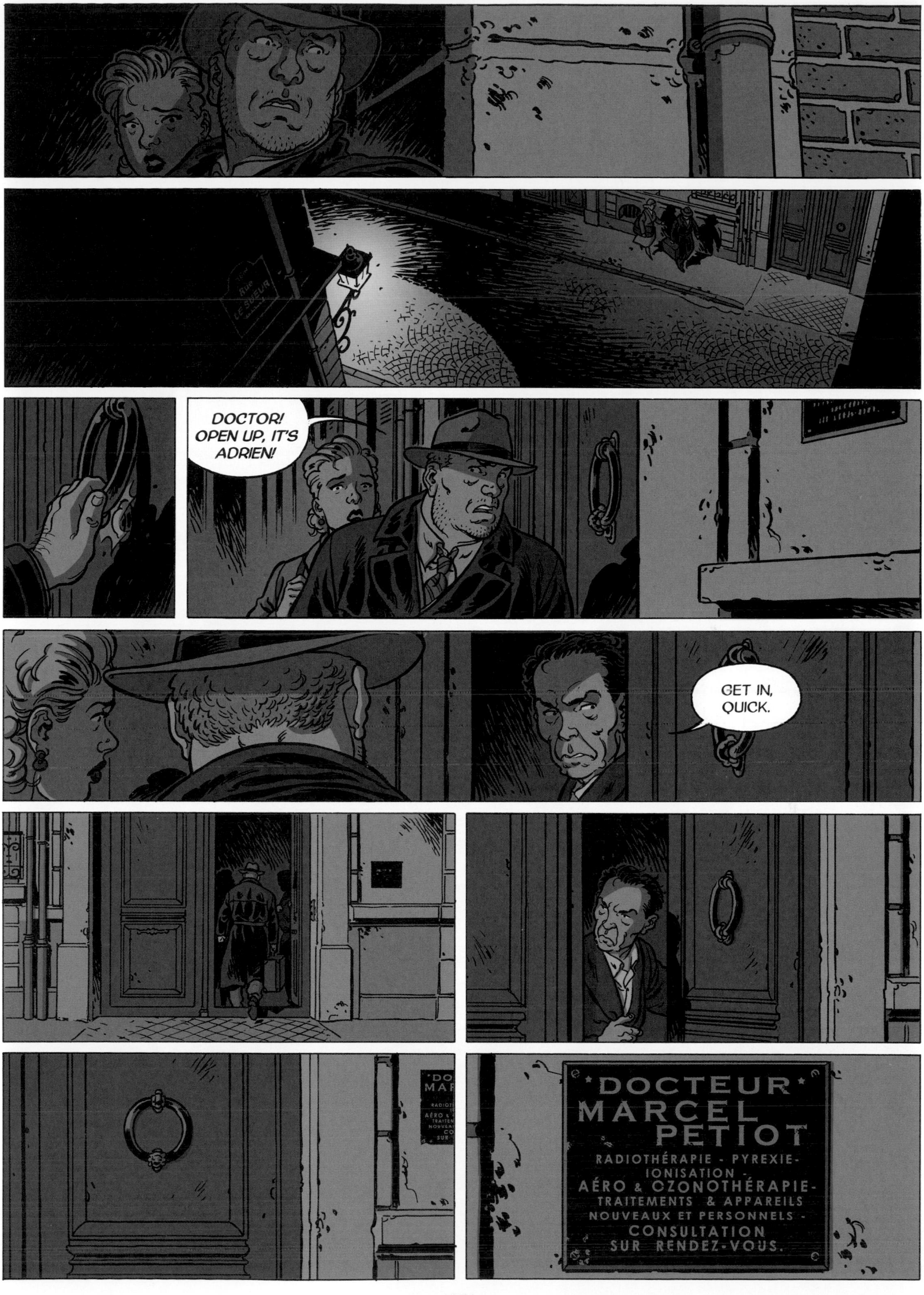

Rue LESUEUR
DOCTOR! OPEN UP, IT'S ADRIEN!
GET IN, QUICK.
DOCTEUR MARCEL PETIOT
RADIOTHÉRAPIE - PYREXIE-
IONISATION -
AÉRO & CZONOTHÉRAPIE-
TRAITEMENTS & APPAREILS
NOUVEAUX ET PERSONNELS -
CONSULTATION
SUR RENDEZ-VOUS.
35

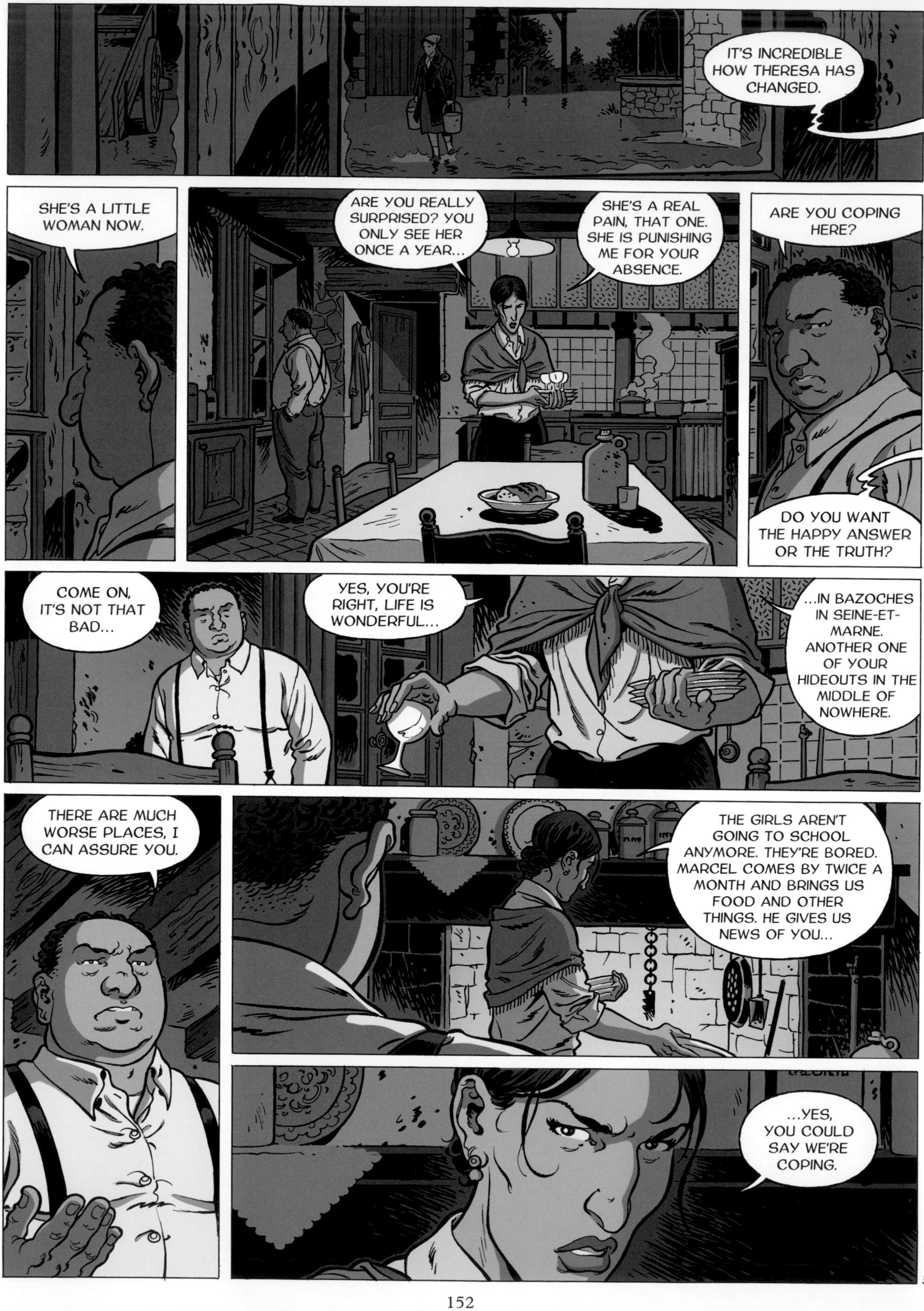
IT'S INCREDIBLE HOW THERESA HAS CHANGED.
SHE'S A LITTLE WOMAN NOW.
ARE YOU REALLY SURPRISED? YOU ONLY SEE HER ONCE A YEAR...
SHE'S A REAL PAIN, THAT ONE. SHE IS PUNISHING ME FOR YOUR ABSENCE.
ARE YOU COPING HERE?
DO YOU WANT THE HAPPY ANSWER OR THE TRUTH?
COME ON, IT'S NOT THAT BAD...
YES, YOU'RE RIGHT, LIFE IS WONDERFUL...
...IN BAZOCHES IN SEINE-ET-MARNE. ANOTHER ONE OF YOUR HIDEOUTS IN THE MIDDLE OF NOWHERE.
THERE ARE MUCH WORSE PLACES, I CAN ASSURE YOU.
THE GIRLS AREN'T GOING TO SCHOOL ANYMORE. THEY'RE BORED. MARCEL COMES BY TWICE A MONTH AND BRINGS US FOOD AND OTHER THINGS. HE GIVES US NEWS OF YOU...
...YES, YOU COULD SAY WE'RE COPING.
36

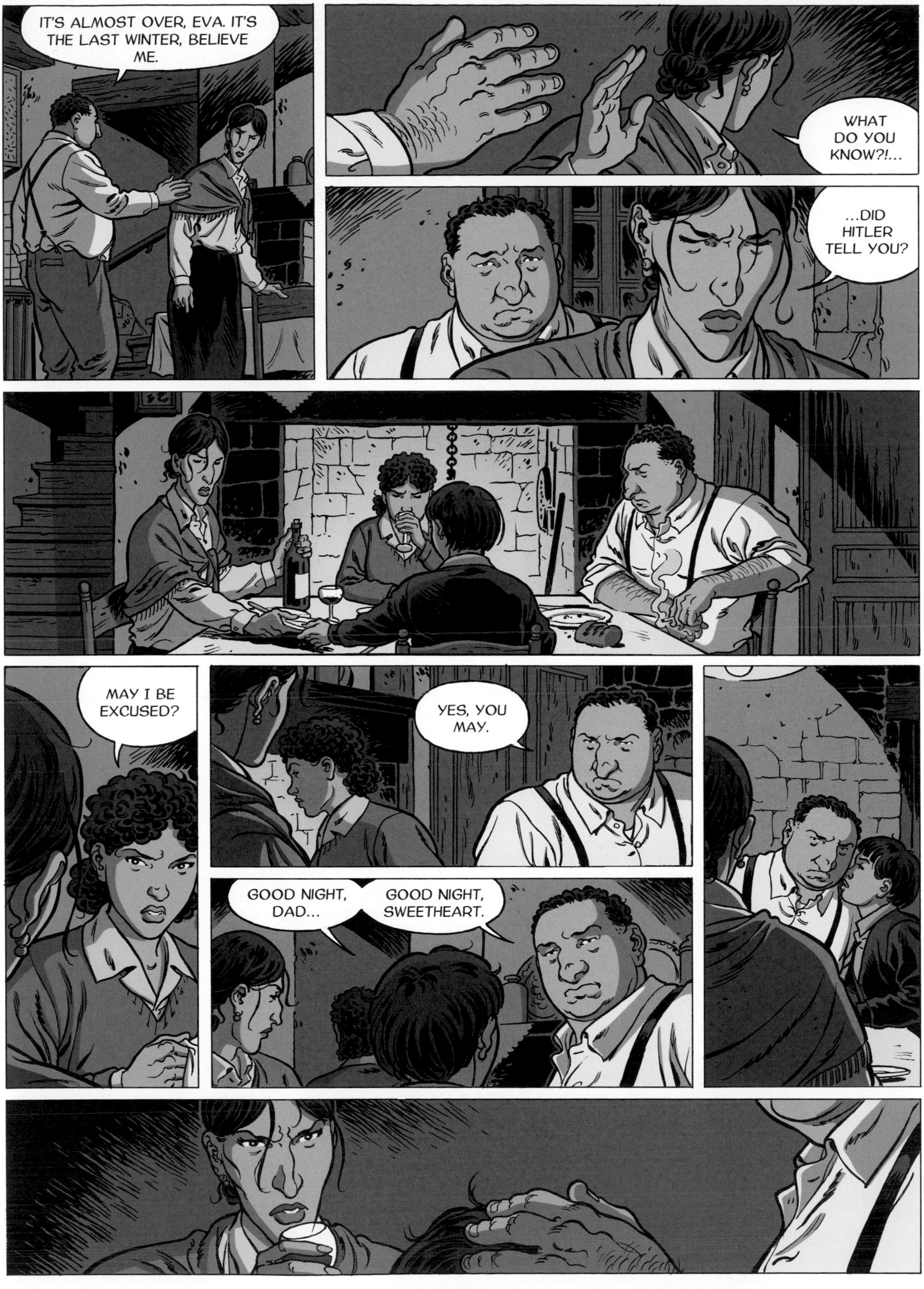
IT'S ALMOST OVER, EVA. IT'S THE LAST WINTER, BELIEVE ME.
WHAT DO YOU KNOW?!...
...DID HITLER TELL YOU?
MAY I BE EXCUSED?
YES, YOU MAY.
GOOD NIGHT, DAD...
GOOD NIGHT, SWEETHEART.
37

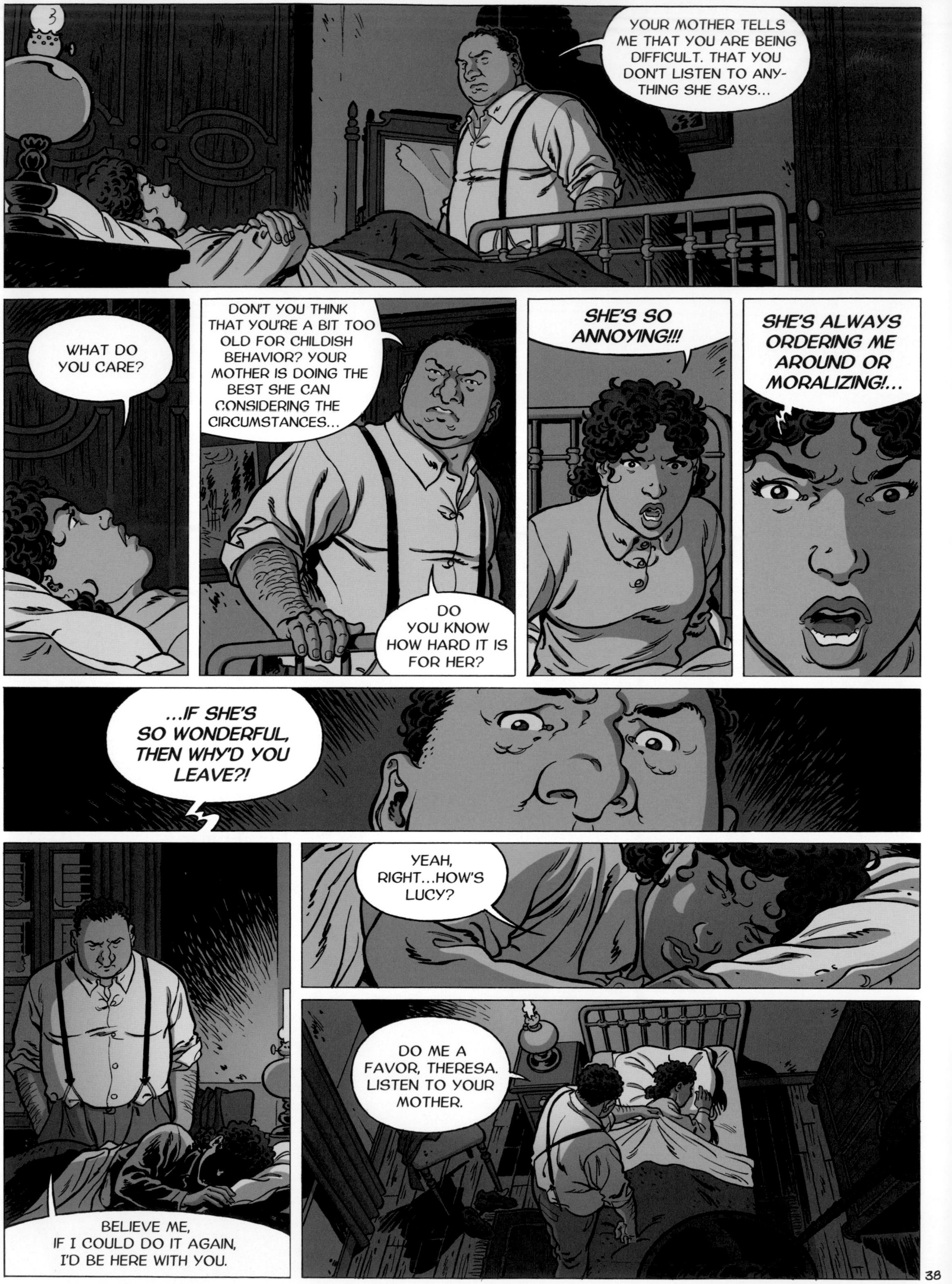

YOUR MOTHER TELLS ME THAT YOU ARE BEING DIFFICULT. THAT YOU DON'T LISTEN TO ANYTHING SHE SAYS...
WHAT DO YOU CARE?
DON'T YOU THINK THAT YOU'RE A BIT TOO OLD FOR CHILDISH BEHAVIOR? YOUR MOTHER IS DOING THE BEST SHE CAN CONSIDERING THE CIRCUMSTANCES...
DO YOU KNOW HOW HARD IT IS FOR HER?
SHE'S SO ANNOYING!!!
SHE'S ALWAYS ORDERING ME AROUND OR MORALIZING!...
...IF SHE'S SO WONDERFUL, THEN WHY'D YOU LEAVE?!
YEAH, RIGHT...HOW'S LUCY?
BELIEVE ME, IF I COULD DO IT AGAIN, I'D BE HERE WITH YOU.
DO ME A FAVOR, THERESA. LISTEN TO YOUR MOTHER.
38

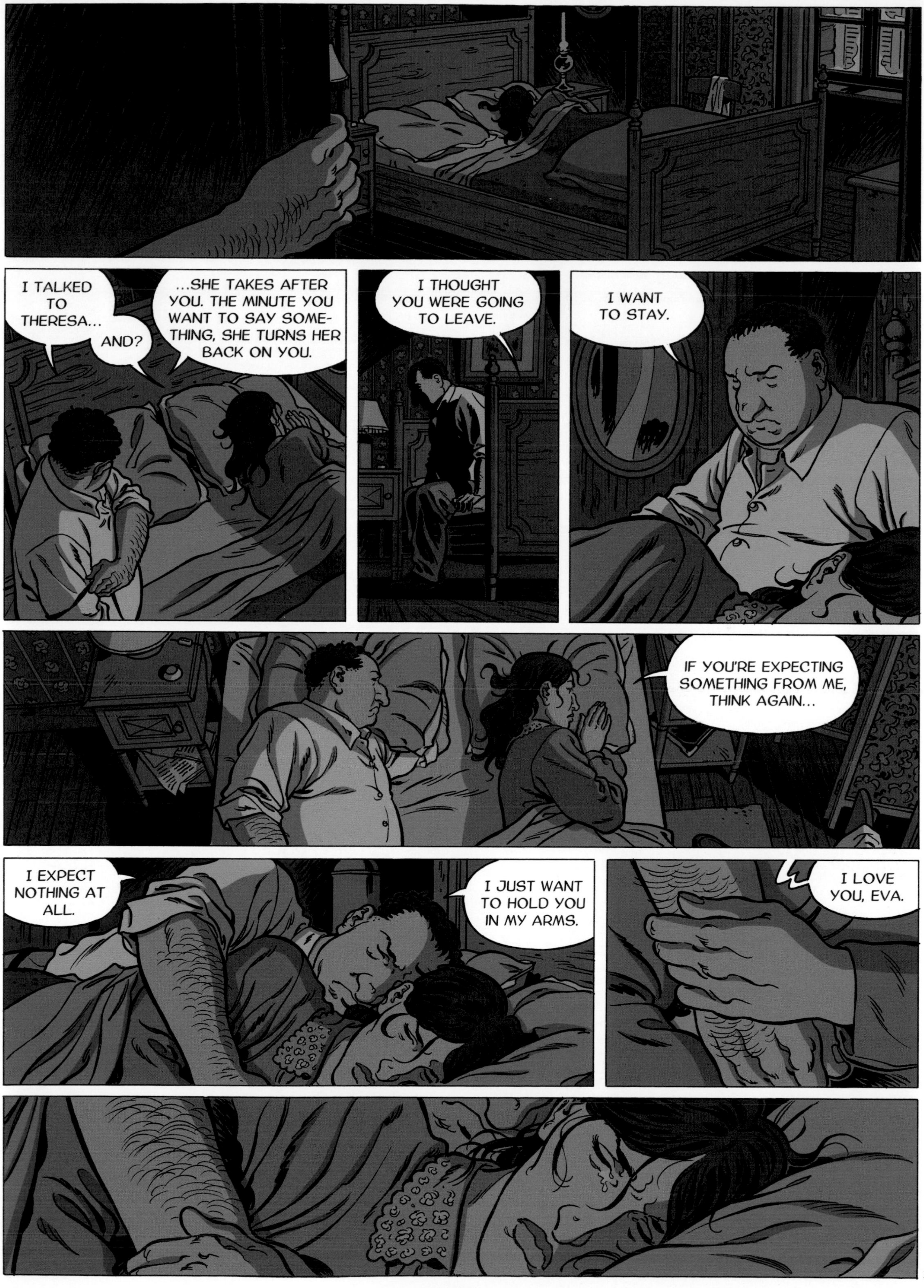
I TALKED TO THERESA...
AND?
...SHE TAKES AFTER YOU. THE MINUTE YOU WANT TO SAY SOME-THING, SHE TURNS HER BACK ON YOU.
I THOUGHT YOU WERE GOING TO LEAVE.
I WANT TO STAY.
IF YOU'RE EXPECTING SOMETHING FROM ME, THINK AGAIN...
I EXPECT NOTHING AT ALL.
I JUST WANT TO HOLD YOU IN MY ARMS.
I LOVE YOU, EVA.

39

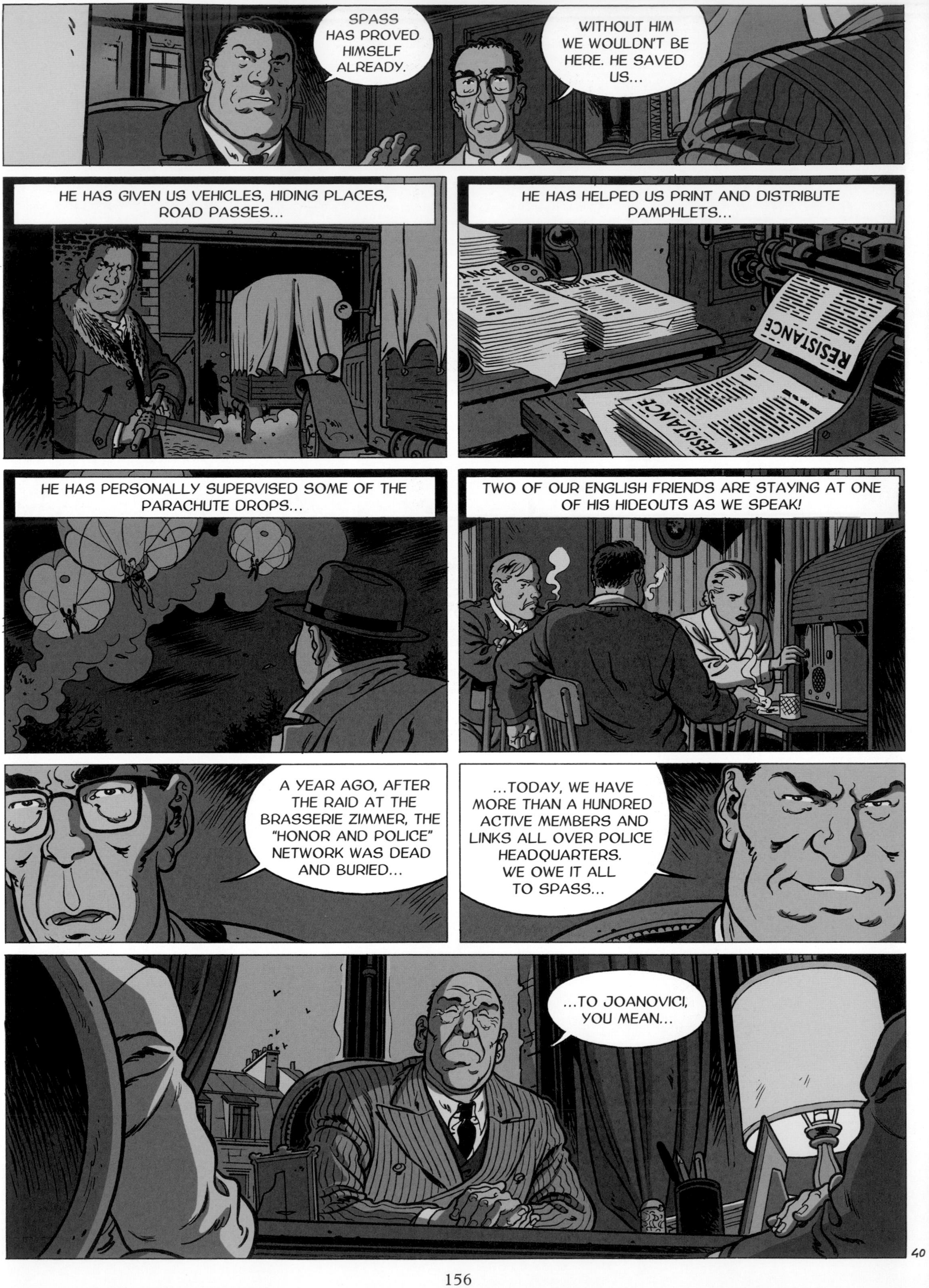
SPASS HAS PROVED HIMSELF ALREADY.
WITHOUT HIM WE WOULDN'T BE HERE. HE SAVED US...
HE HAS GIVEN US VEHICLES, HIDING PLACES, ROAD PASSES...
HE HAS HELPED US PRINT AND DISTRIBUTE PAMPHLETS...
RESISTANCE
RESISTANCE
HE HAS PERSONALLY SUPERVISED SOME OF THE PARACHUTE DROPS...
TWO OF OUR ENGLISH FRIENDS ARE STAYING AT ONE OF HIS HIDEOUTS AS WE SPEAK!
A YEAR AGO, AFTER THE RAID AT THE BRASSERIE ZIMMER, THE "HONOR AND POLICE" NETWORK WAS DEAD AND BURIED...
...TODAY, WE HAVE MORE THAN A HUNDRED ACTIVE MEMBERS AND LINKS ALL OVER POLICE HEADQUARTERS. WE OWE IT ALL TO SPASS...
...TO JOANOVICI, YOU MEAN...
40

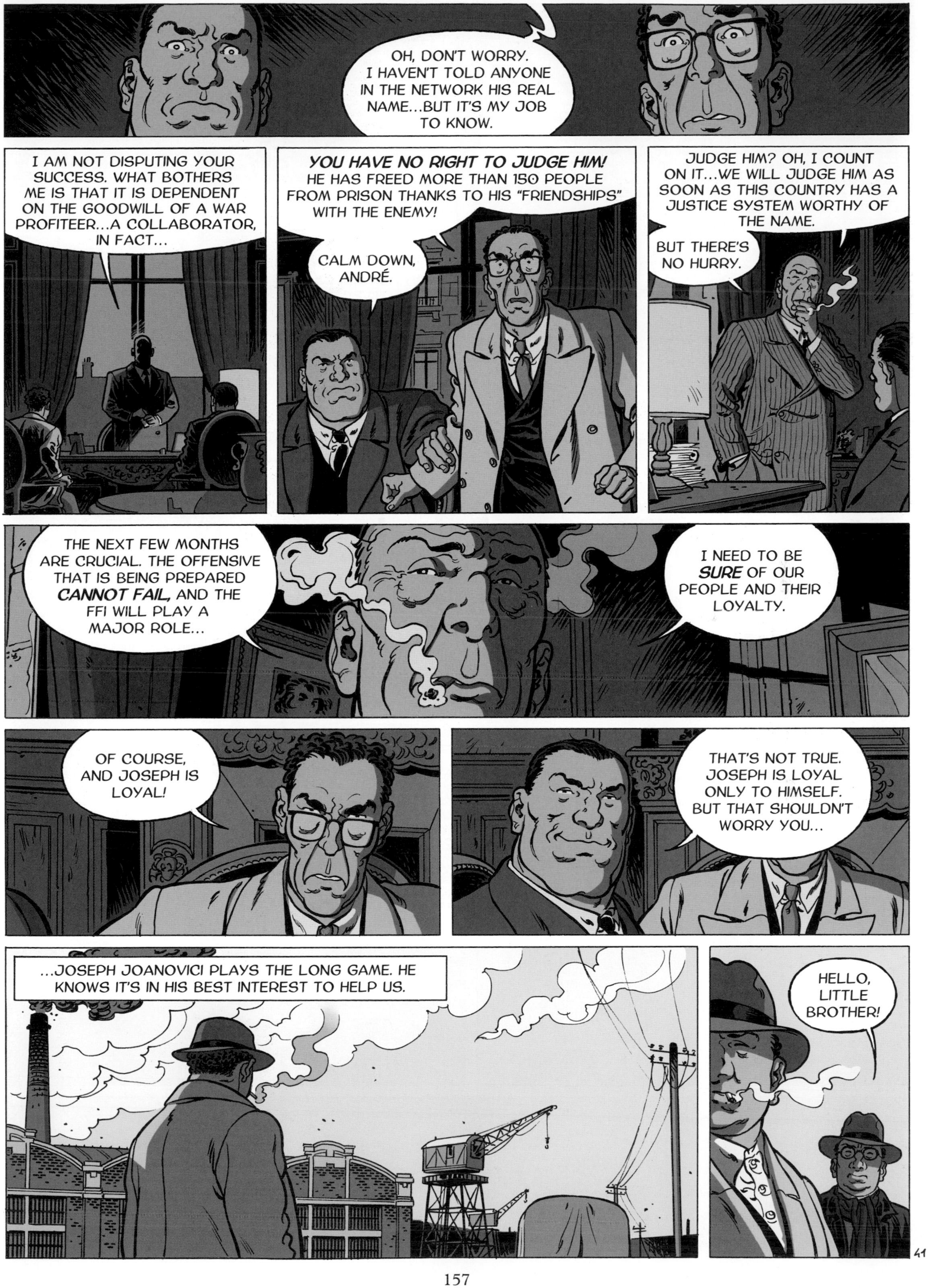
OH, DON'T WORRY. I HAVEN'T TOLD ANYONE IN THE NETWORK HIS REAL NAME...BUT IT'S MY JOB TO KNOW.
I AM NOT DISPUTING YOUR SUCCESS. WHAT BOTHERS ME IS THAT IT IS DEPENDENT ON THE GOODWILL OF A WAR PROFITEER...A COLLABORATOR, IN FACT...
YOU HAVE NO RIGHT TO JUDGE HIM! HE HAS FREED MORE THAN 150 PEOPLE FROM PRISON THANKS TO HIS "FRIENDSHIPS" WITH THE ENEMY!
CALM DOWN, ANDRÉ.
JUDGE HIM? OH, I COUNT ON IT...WE WILL JUDGE HIM AS SOON AS THIS COUNTRY HAS A JUSTICE SYSTEM WORTHY OF THE NAME.
BUT THERE'S NO HURRY.
THE NEXT FEW MONTHS ARE CRUCIAL. THE OFFENSIVE THAT IS BEING PREPARED CANNOT FAIL, AND THE FFI WILL PLAY A MAJOR ROLE...
I NEED TO BE SURE OF OUR PEOPLE AND THEIR LOYALTY.
OF COURSE, AND JOSEPH IS LOYAL!
THAT'S NOT TRUE. JOSEPH IS LOYAL ONLY TO HIMSELF. BUT THAT SHOULDN'T WORRY YOU...
...JOSEPH JOANOVICI PLAYS THE LONG GAME. HE KNOWS IT'S IN HIS BEST INTEREST TO HELP US.
HELLO, LITTLE BROTHER!
41

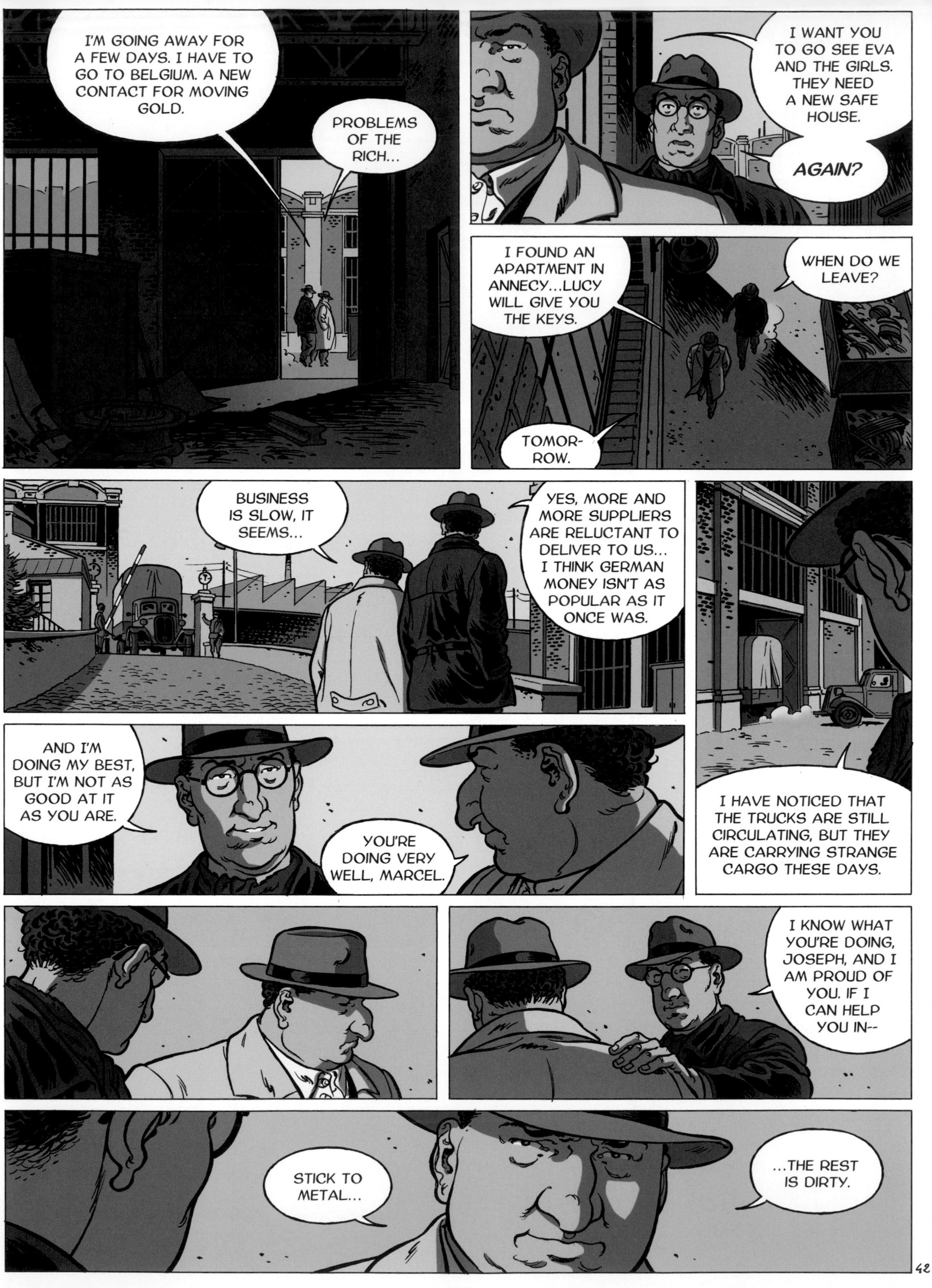
I'M GOING AWAY FOR A FEW DAYS. I HAVE TO GO TO BELGIUM. A NEW CONTACT FOR MOVING GOLD.
PROBLEMS OF THE RICH...
I WANT YOU TO GO SEE EVA AND THE GIRLS. THEY NEED A NEW SAFE HOUSE.
AGAIN?
I FOUND AN APARTMENT IN ANNECY...LUCY WILL GIVE YOU THE KEYS.
WHEN DO WE LEAVE?
TOMOR-ROW.
BUSINESS IS SLOW, IT SEEMS...
YES, MORE AND MORE SUPPLIERS ARE RELUCTANT TO DELIVER TO US... I THINK GERMAN MONEY ISN'T AS POPULAR AS IT ONCE WAS.
AND I'M DOING MY BEST, BUT I'M NOT AS GOOD AT IT AS YOU ARE.
YOU'RE DOING VERY WELL, MARCEL.
I HAVE NOTICED THAT THE TRUCKS ARE STILL CIRCULATING, BUT THEY ARE CARRYING STRANGE CARGO THESE DAYS.
I KNOW WHAT YOU'RE DOING, JOSEPH, AND I AM PROUD OF YOU. IF I CAN HELP YOU IN--
STICK TO METAL...
...THE REST IS DIRTY.
42

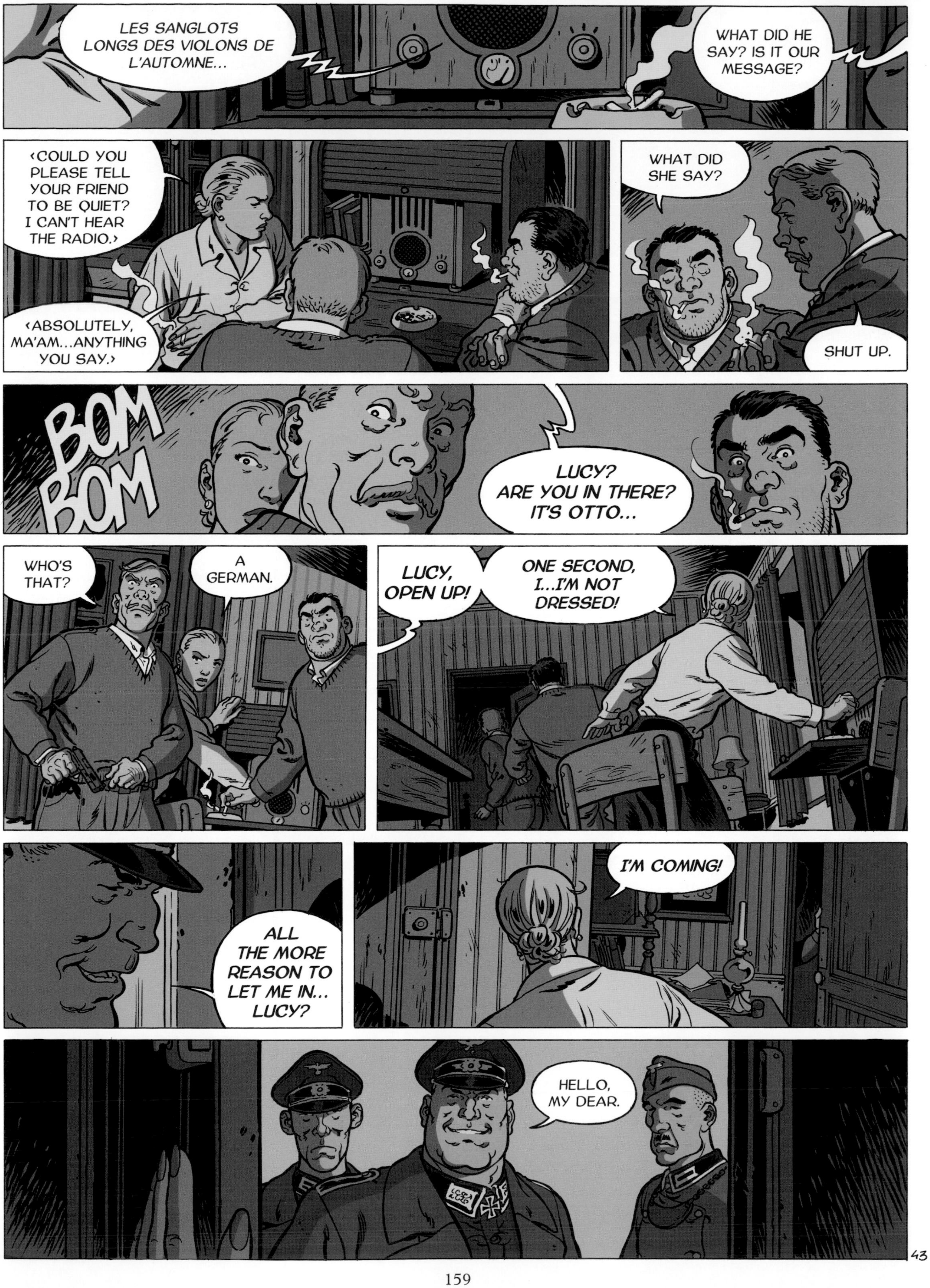
LES SANGLOTS LONGS DES VIOLONS DE L'AUTOMNE...
WHAT DID HE SAY? IS IT OUR MESSAGE?
‹COULD YOU PLEASE TELL YOUR FRIEND TO BE QUIET? I CAN'T HEAR THE RADIO.›
‹ABSOLUTELY, MA'AM...ANYTHING YOU SAY.›
WHAT DID SHE SAY?
SHUT UP.
BOM BOM
LUCY? ARE YOU IN THERE? IT'S OTTO...
WHO'S THAT?
A GERMAN.
LUCY, OPEN UP!
ONE SECOND, I...I'M NOT DRESSED!
ALL THE MORE REASON TO LET ME IN... LUCY?
I'M COMING!
HELLO, MY DEAR.
43

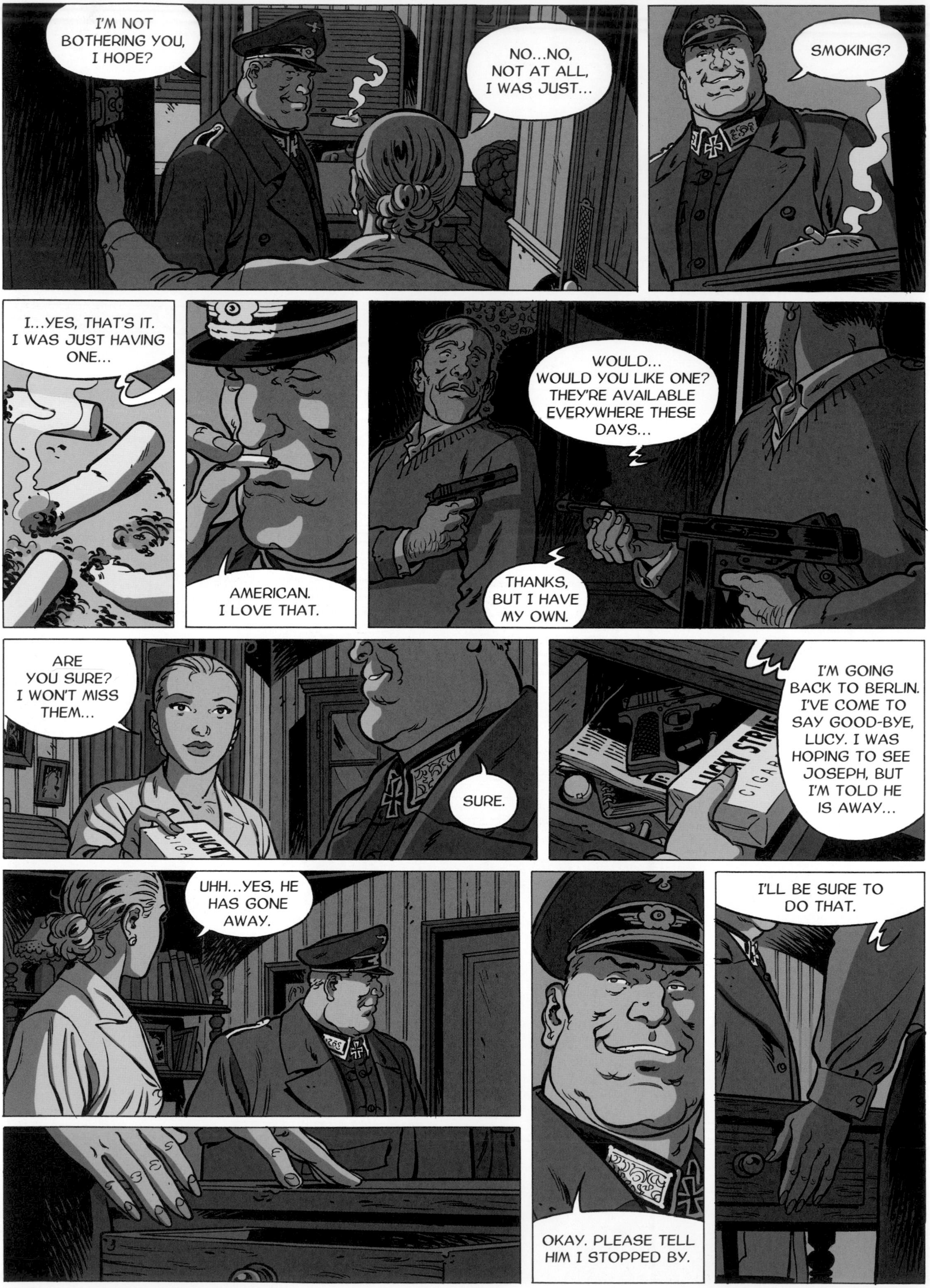
I'M NOT BOTHERING YOU, I HOPE?
NO...NO, NOT AT ALL, I WAS JUST...
SMOKING?
I...YES, THAT'S IT. I WAS JUST HAVING ONE...
AMERICAN. I LOVE THAT.
WOULD... WOULD YOU LIKE ONE? THEY'RE AVAILABLE EVERYWHERE THESE DAYS...
THANKS, BUT I HAVE MY OWN.
ARE YOU SURE? I WON'T MISS THEM...
SURE.
LUCKY STRIKE CIGAR
I'M GOING BACK TO BERLIN. I'VE COME TO SAY GOOD-BYE, LUCY. I WAS HOPING TO SEE JOSEPH, BUT I'M TOLD HE IS AWAY...
UHH...YES, HE HAS GONE AWAY.
OKAY. PLEASE TELL HIM I STOPPED BY.
I'LL BE SURE TO DO THAT.

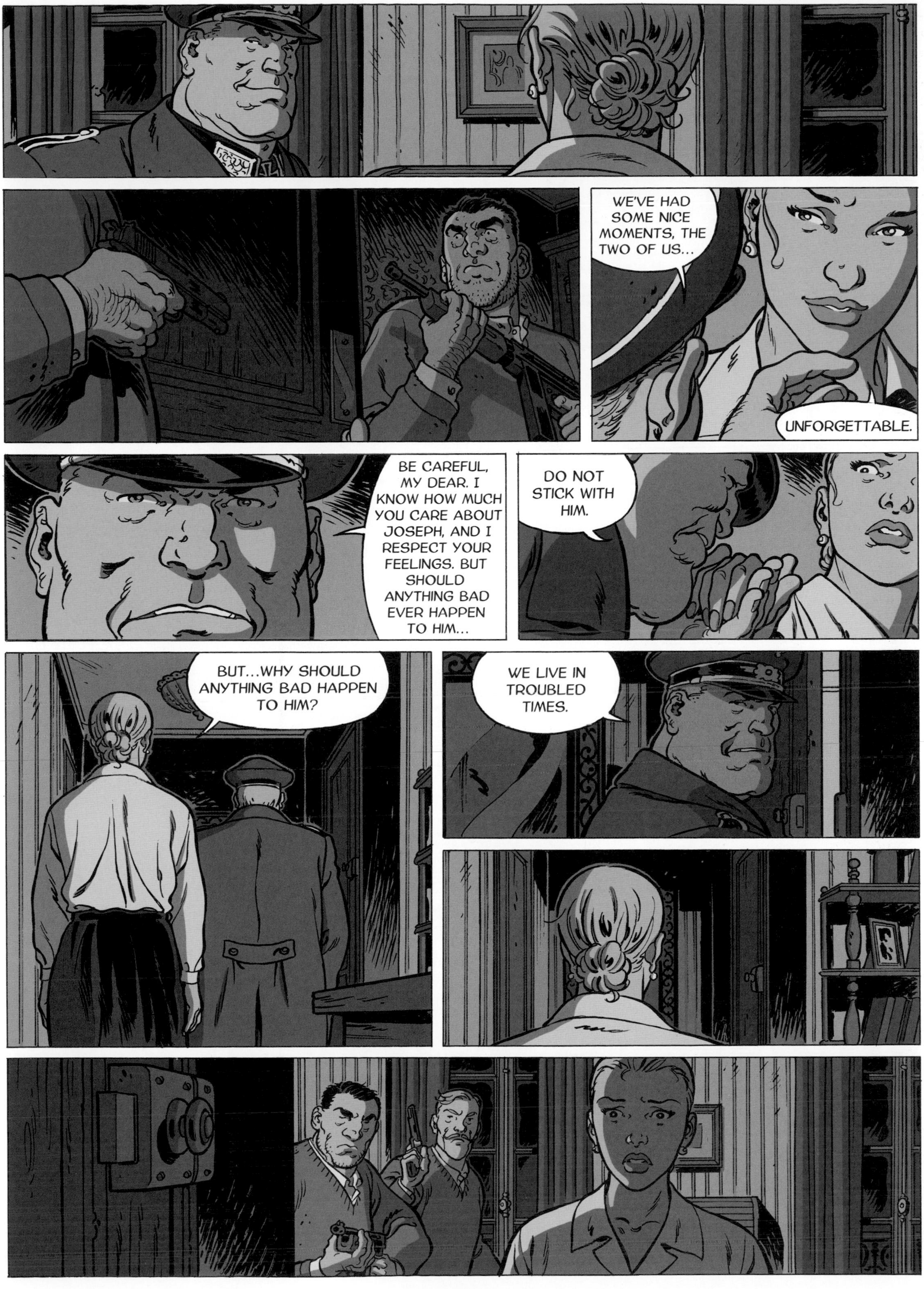
WE'VE HAD SOME NICE MOMENTS, THE TWO OF US...
UNFORGETTABLE.
BE CAREFUL, MY DEAR. I KNOW HOW MUCH YOU CARE ABOUT JOSEPH, AND I RESPECT YOUR FEELINGS. BUT SHOULD ANYTHING BAD EVER HAPPEN TO HIM...
DO NOT STICK WITH HIM.
BUT...WHY SHOULD ANYTHING BAD HAPPEN TO HIM?
WE LIVE IN TROUBLED TIMES.
45

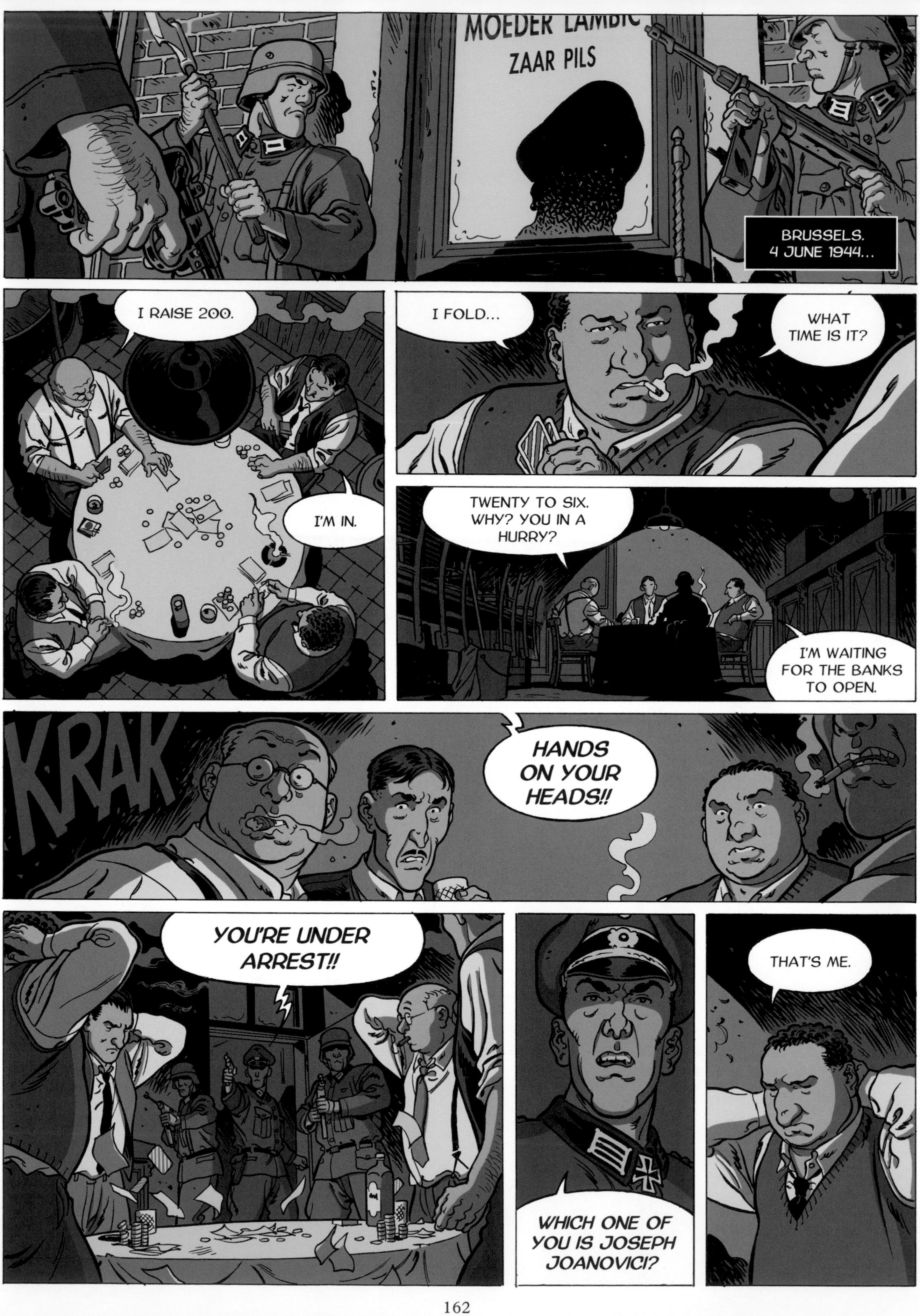
MOEDER LAMBIC
ZAAR PILS
BRUSSELS.
4 JUNE 1944...
I RAISE 200.
I'M IN.
I FOLD...
WHAT TIME IS IT?
TWENTY TO SIX. WHY? YOU IN A HURRY?
I'M WAITING FOR THE BANKS TO OPEN.
KRAK
HANDS ON YOUR HEADS!!
YOU'RE UNDER ARREST!!
WHICH ONE OF YOU IS JOSEPH JOANOVICI?
THAT'S ME.
46

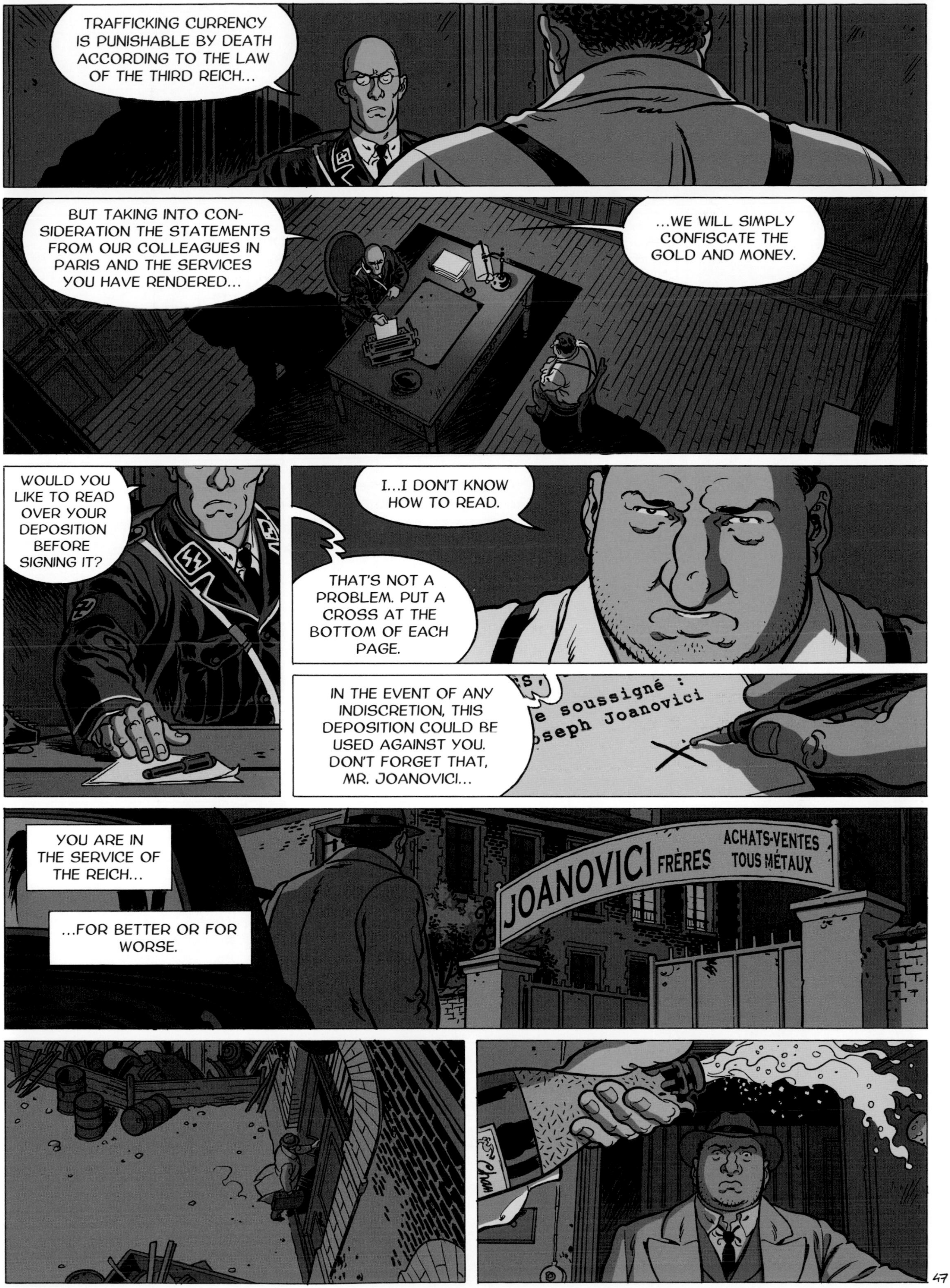
TRAFFICKING CURRENCY IS PUNISHABLE BY DEATH ACCORDING TO THE LAW OF THE THIRD REICH...
BUT TAKING INTO CONSIDERATION THE STATEMENTS FROM OUR COLLEAGUES IN PARIS AND THE SERVICES YOU HAVE RENDERED...
...WE WILL SIMPLY CONFISCATE THE GOLD AND MONEY.
WOULD YOU LIKE TO READ OVER YOUR DEPOSITION BEFORE SIGNING IT?
I...I DON'T KNOW HOW TO READ.
THAT'S NOT A PROBLEM. PUT A CROSS AT THE BOTTOM OF EACH PAGE.
IN THE EVENT OF ANY INDISCRETION, THIS DEPOSITION COULD BE USED AGAINST YOU. DON'T FORGET THAT, MR. JOANOVICI...
e soussigné :
oseph Joanovici
YOU ARE IN THE SERVICE OF THE REICH...
...FOR BETTER OR FOR WORSE.
JOANOVICI FRÈRES
ACHATS-VENTES TOUS MÉTAUX
47

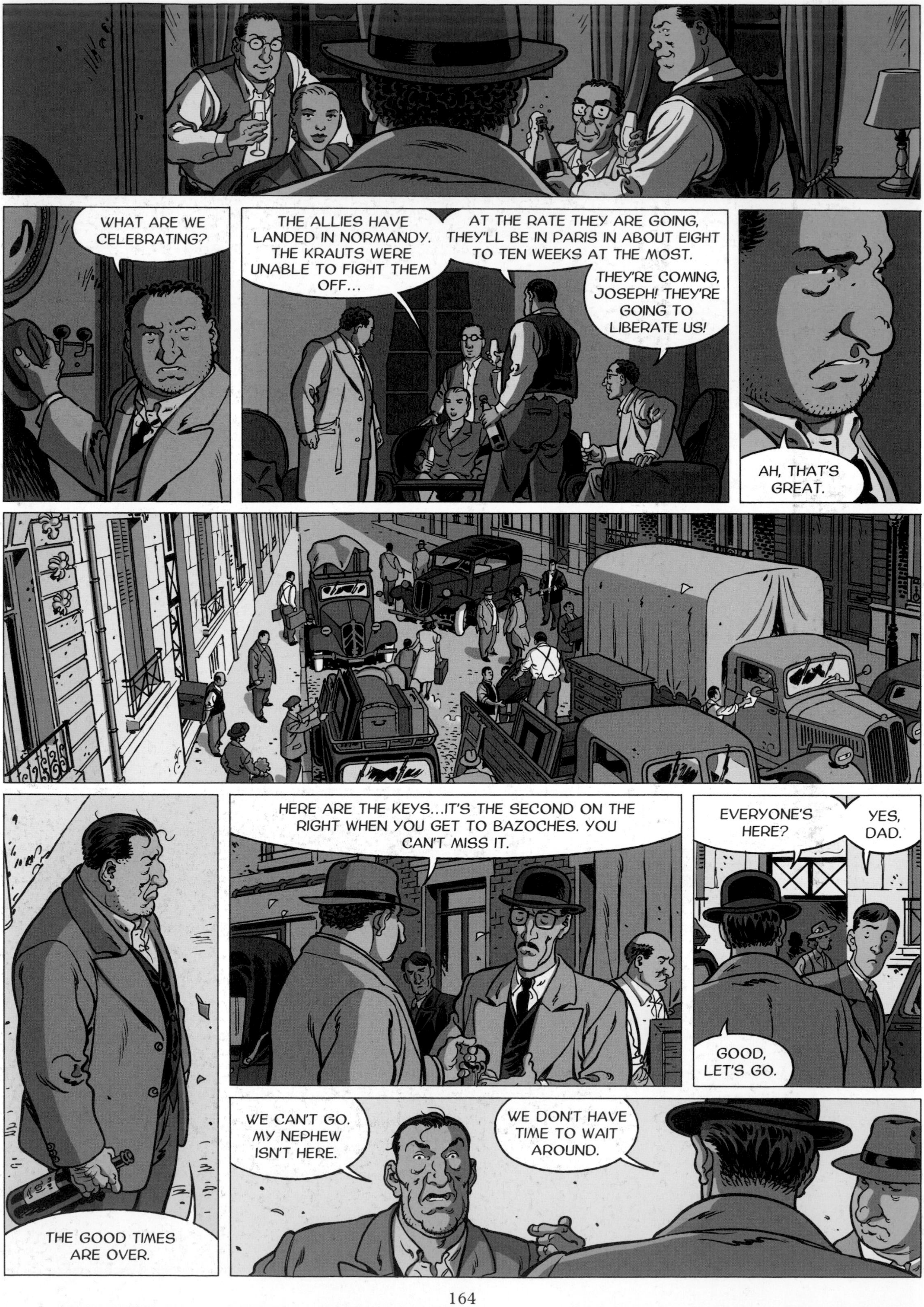
WHAT ARE WE CELEBRATING?
THE ALLIES HAVE LANDED IN NORMANDY. THE KRAUTS WERE UNABLE TO FIGHT THEM OFF...
AT THE RATE THEY ARE GOING, THEY'LL BE IN PARIS IN ABOUT EIGHT TO TEN WEEKS AT THE MOST.
THEY'RE COMING, JOSEPH! THEY'RE GOING TO LIBERATE US!
AH, THAT'S GREAT.
THE GOOD TIMES ARE OVER.
HERE ARE THE KEYS...IT'S THE SECOND ON THE RIGHT WHEN YOU GET TO BAZOCHES. YOU CAN'T MISS IT.
EVERYONE'S HERE?
YES, DAD.
GOOD, LET'S GO.
WE CAN'T GO. MY NEPHEW ISN'T HERE.
WE DON'T HAVE TIME TO WAIT AROUND.
48

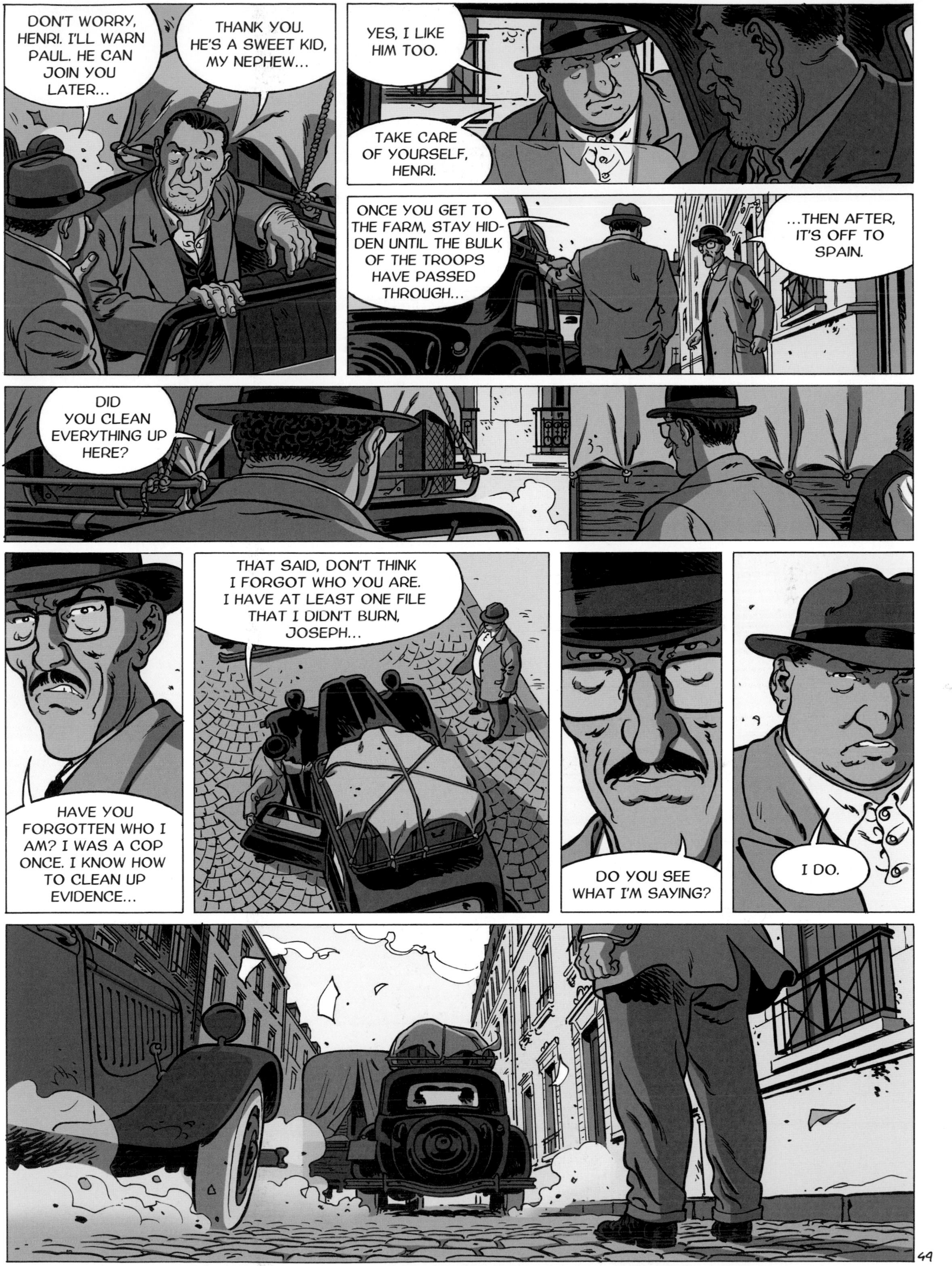
DON'T WORRY, HENRI. I'LL WARN PAUL. HE CAN JOIN YOU LATER...
THANK YOU. HE'S A SWEET KID, MY NEPHEW...
YES, I LIKE HIM TOO.
TAKE CARE OF YOURSELF, HENRI.
ONCE YOU GET TO THE FARM, STAY HIDDEN UNTIL THE BULK OF THE TROOPS HAVE PASSED THROUGH...
...THEN AFTER, IT'S OFF TO SPAIN.
DID YOU CLEAN EVERYTHING UP HERE?
HAVE YOU FORGOTTEN WHO I AM? I WAS A COP ONCE. I KNOW HOW TO CLEAN UP EVIDENCE...
THAT SAID, DON'T THINK I FORGOT WHO YOU ARE. I HAVE AT LEAST ONE FILE THAT I DIDN'T BURN, JOSEPH...
DO YOU SEE WHAT I'M SAYING?
I DO.
44

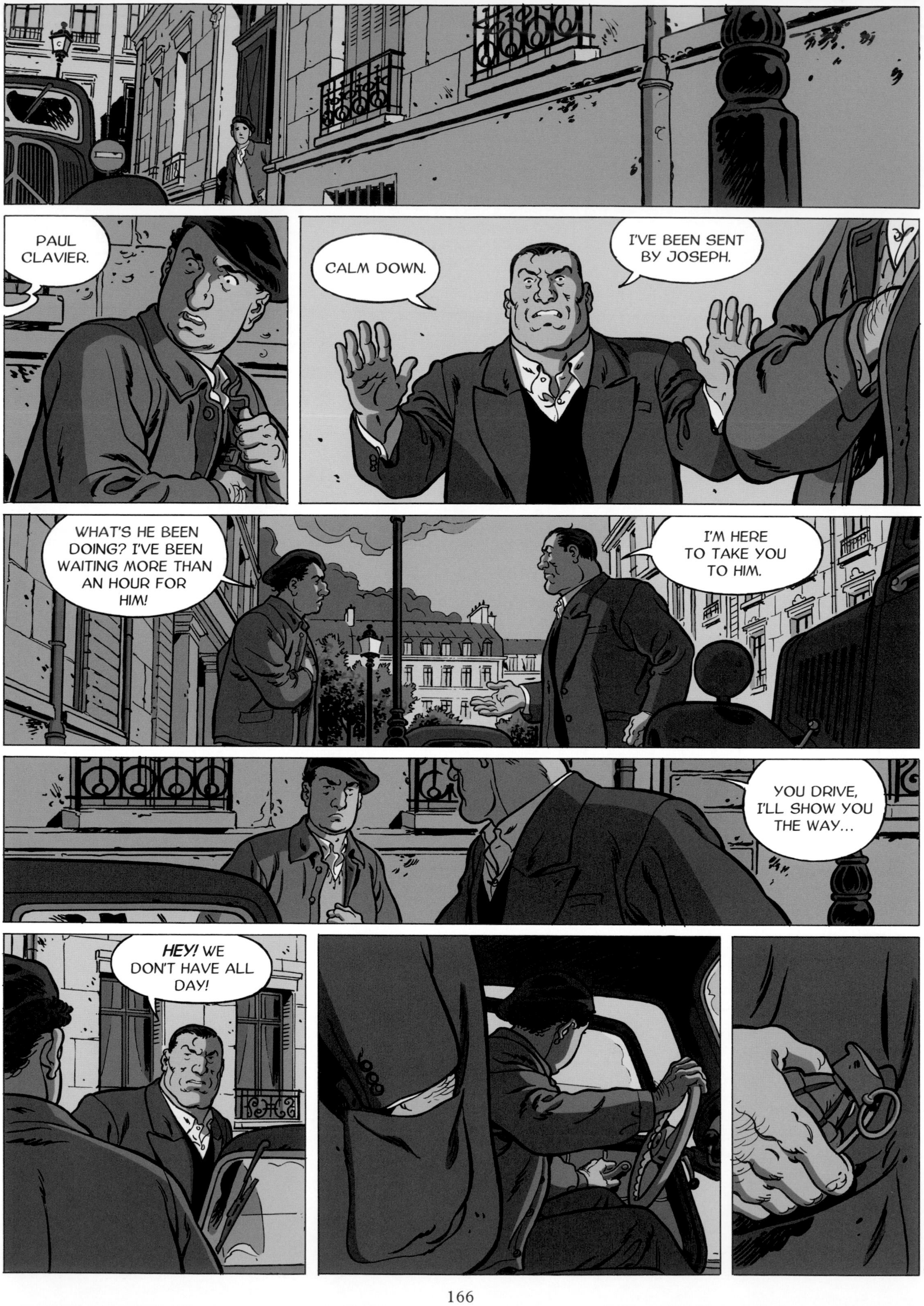
PAUL CLAVIER.
CALM DOWN.
I'VE BEEN SENT BY JOSEPH.
WHAT'S HE BEEN DOING? I'VE BEEN WAITING MORE THAN AN HOUR FOR HIM!
I'M HERE TO TAKE YOU TO HIM.
YOU DRIVE, I'LL SHOW YOU THE WAY...
HEY! WE DON'T HAVE ALL DAY!

50

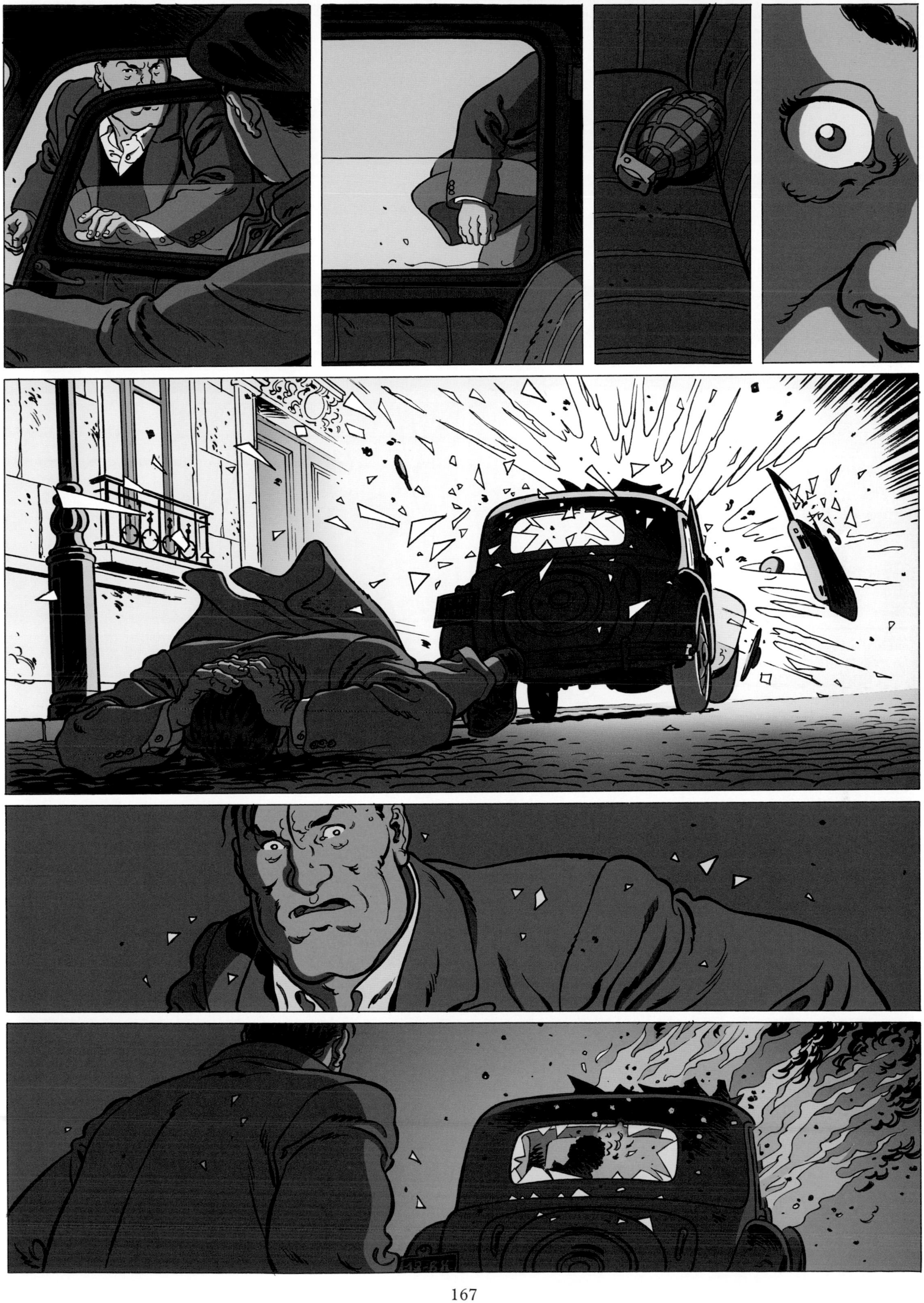

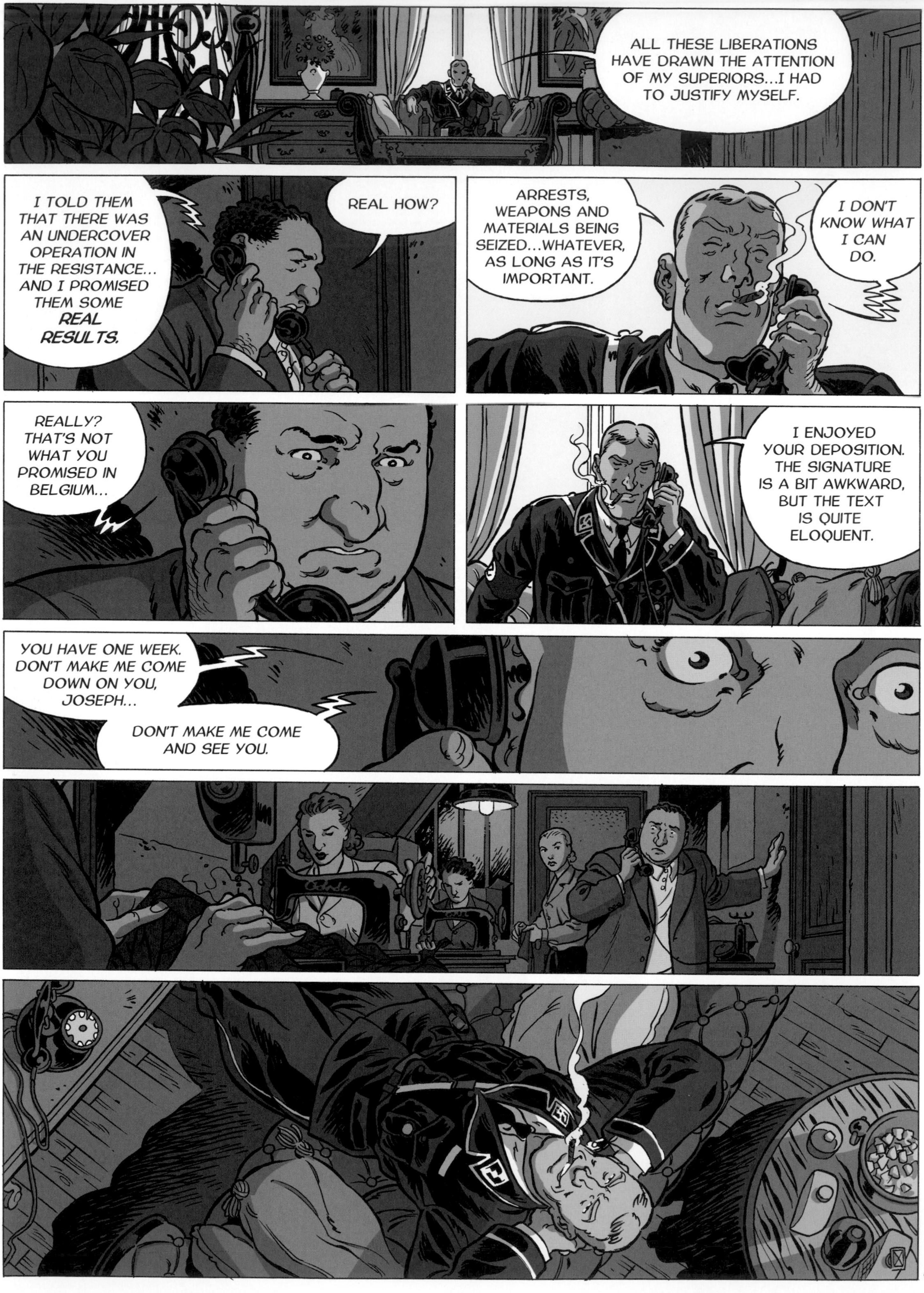
ALL THESE LIBERATIONS HAVE DRAWN THE ATTENTION OF MY SUPERIORS...I HAD TO JUSTIFY MYSELF.
I TOLD THEM THAT THERE WAS AN UNDERCOVER OPERATION IN THE RESISTANCE... AND I PROMISED THEM SOME REAL RESULTS.
REAL HOW?
ARRESTS, WEAPONS AND MATERIALS BEING SEIZED...WHATEVER, AS LONG AS IT'S IMPORTANT.
I DON'T KNOW WHAT I CAN DO.
REALLY? THAT'S NOT WHAT YOU PROMISED IN BELGIUM...
I ENJOYED YOUR DEPOSITION. THE SIGNATURE IS A BIT AWKWARD, BUT THE TEXT IS QUITE ELOQUENT.
YOU HAVE ONE WEEK. DON'T MAKE ME COME DOWN ON YOU, JOSEPH...
DON'T MAKE ME COME AND SEE YOU.
58

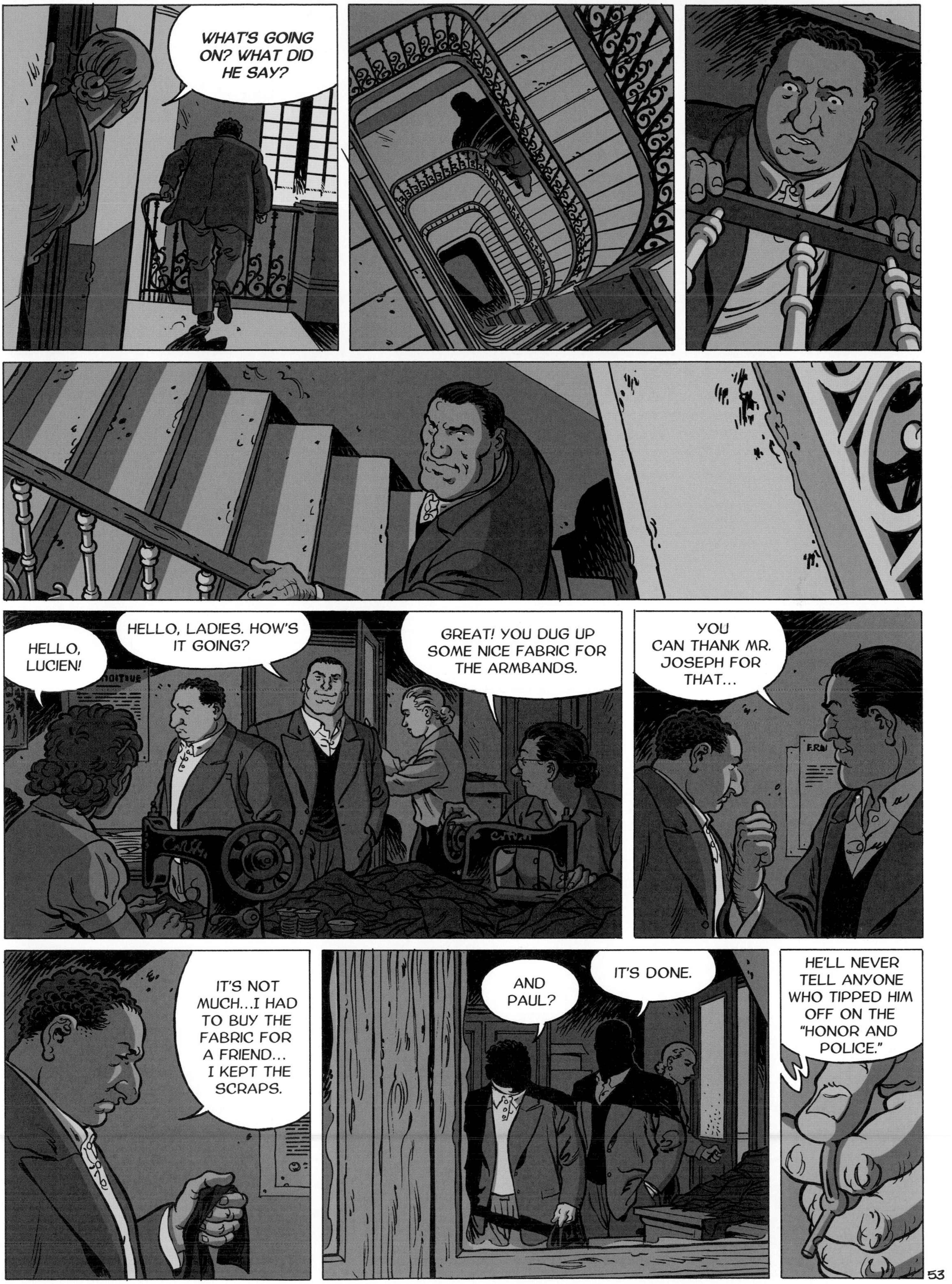
WHAT'S GOING ON? WHAT DID HE SAY?
HELLO, LUCIEN!
HELLO, LADIES. HOW'S IT GOING?
GREAT! YOU DUG UP SOME NICE FABRIC FOR THE ARMBANDS.
YOU CAN THANK MR. JOSEPH FOR THAT...
IT'S NOT MUCH...I HAD TO BUY THE FABRIC FOR A FRIEND... I KEPT THE SCRAPS.
AND PAUL?
IT'S DONE.
HE'LL NEVER TELL ANYONE WHO TIPPED HIM OFF ON THE "HONOR AND POLICE."
53

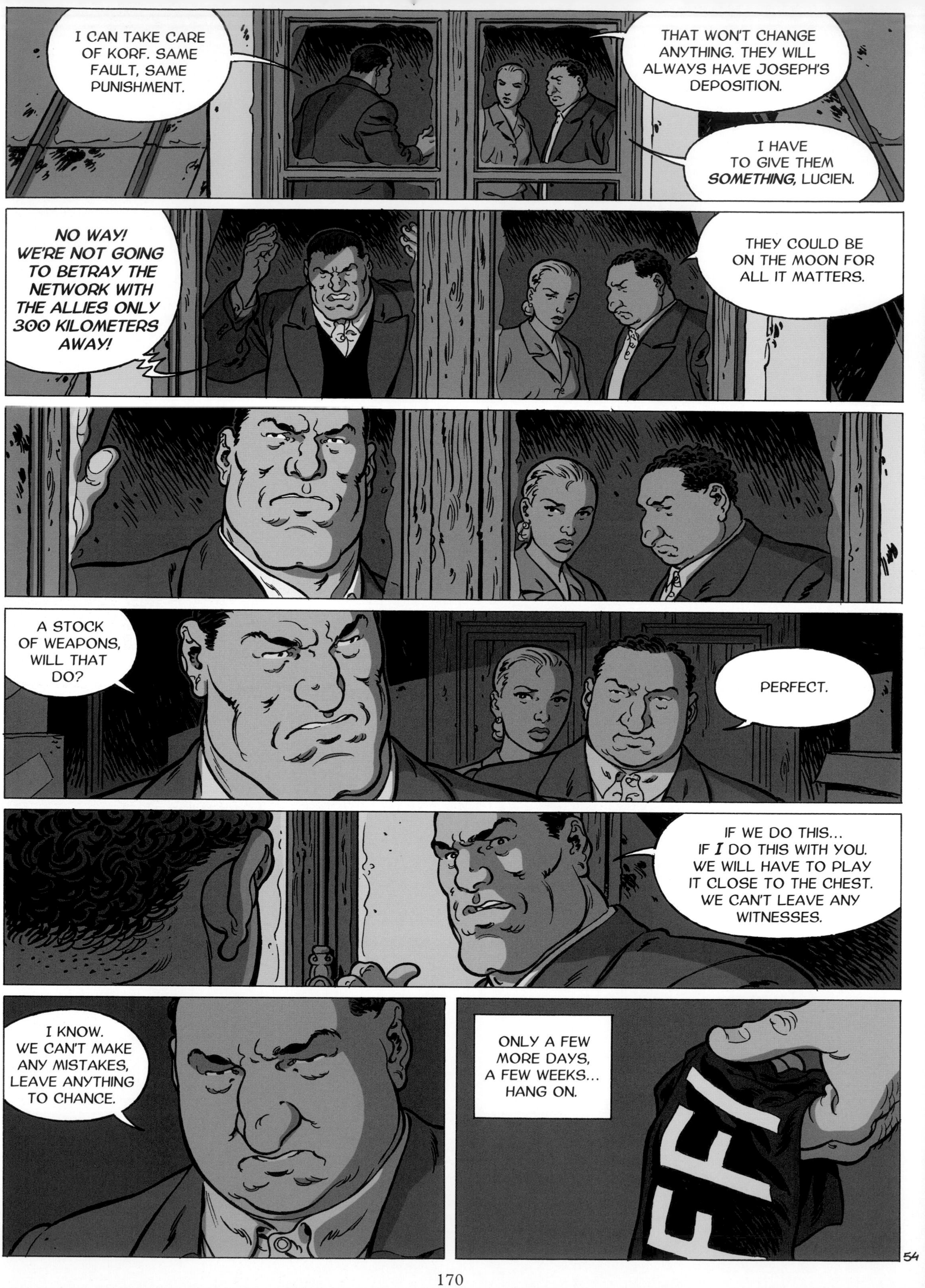
I CAN TAKE CARE OF KORF. SAME FAULT, SAME PUNISHMENT.
THAT WON'T CHANGE ANYTHING. THEY WILL ALWAYS HAVE JOSEPH'S DEPOSITION.
I HAVE TO GIVE THEM SOMETHING, LUCIEN.
NO WAY! WE'RE NOT GOING TO BETRAY THE NETWORK WITH THE ALLIES ONLY 300 KILOMETERS AWAY!
THEY COULD BE ON THE MOON FOR ALL IT MATTERS.
A STOCK OF WEAPONS, WILL THAT DO?
PERFECT.
IF WE DO THIS... IF I DO THIS WITH YOU. WE WILL HAVE TO PLAY IT CLOSE TO THE CHEST. WE CAN'T LEAVE ANY WITNESSES.
I KNOW. WE CAN'T MAKE ANY MISTAKES, LEAVE ANYTHING TO CHANCE.
ONLY A FEW MORE DAYS, A FEW WEEKS... HANG ON.
FFI
54

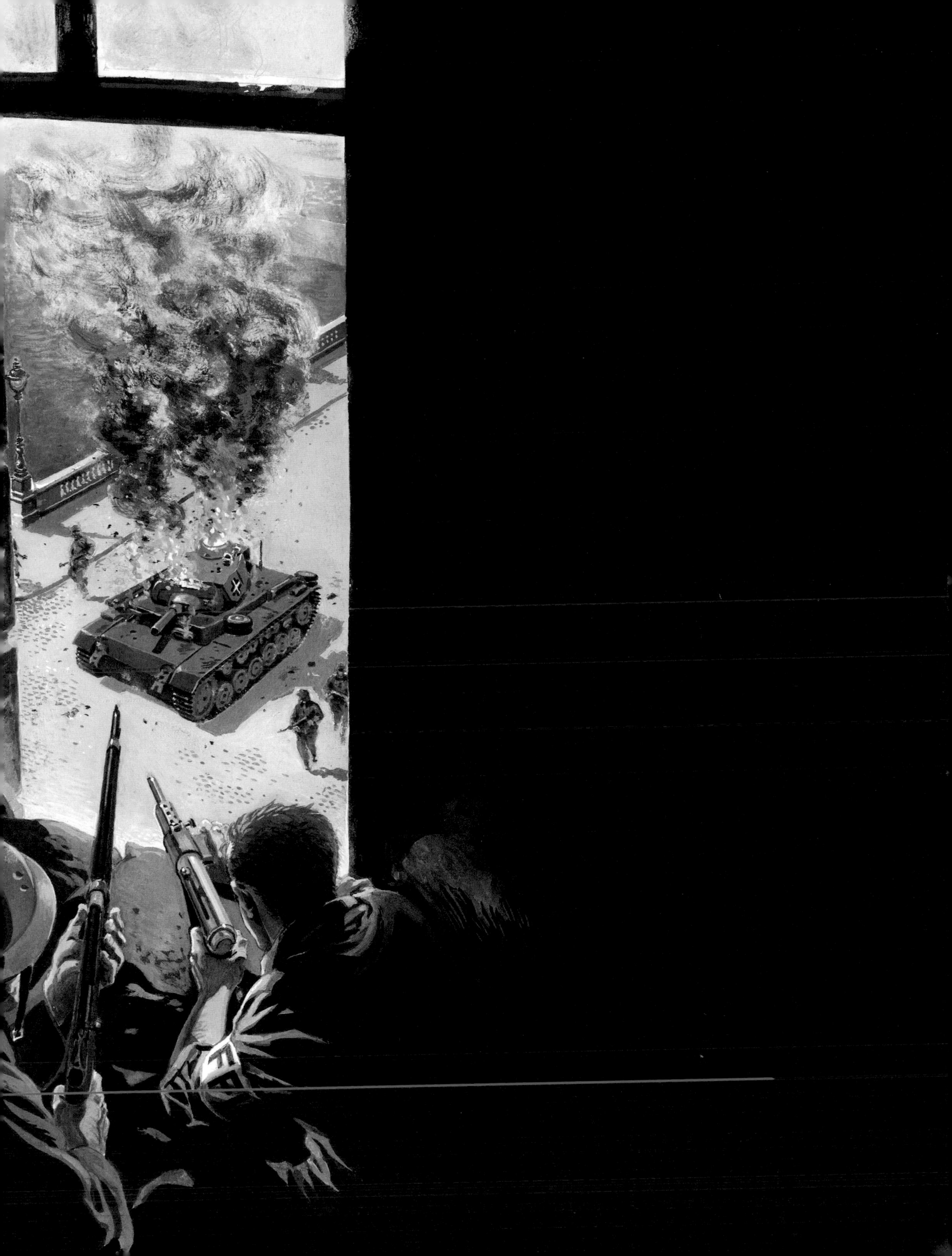

"You can't imagine what a man is capable of,
what heroism, what horrors to save his own skin."

CURZIO MALAPARTE

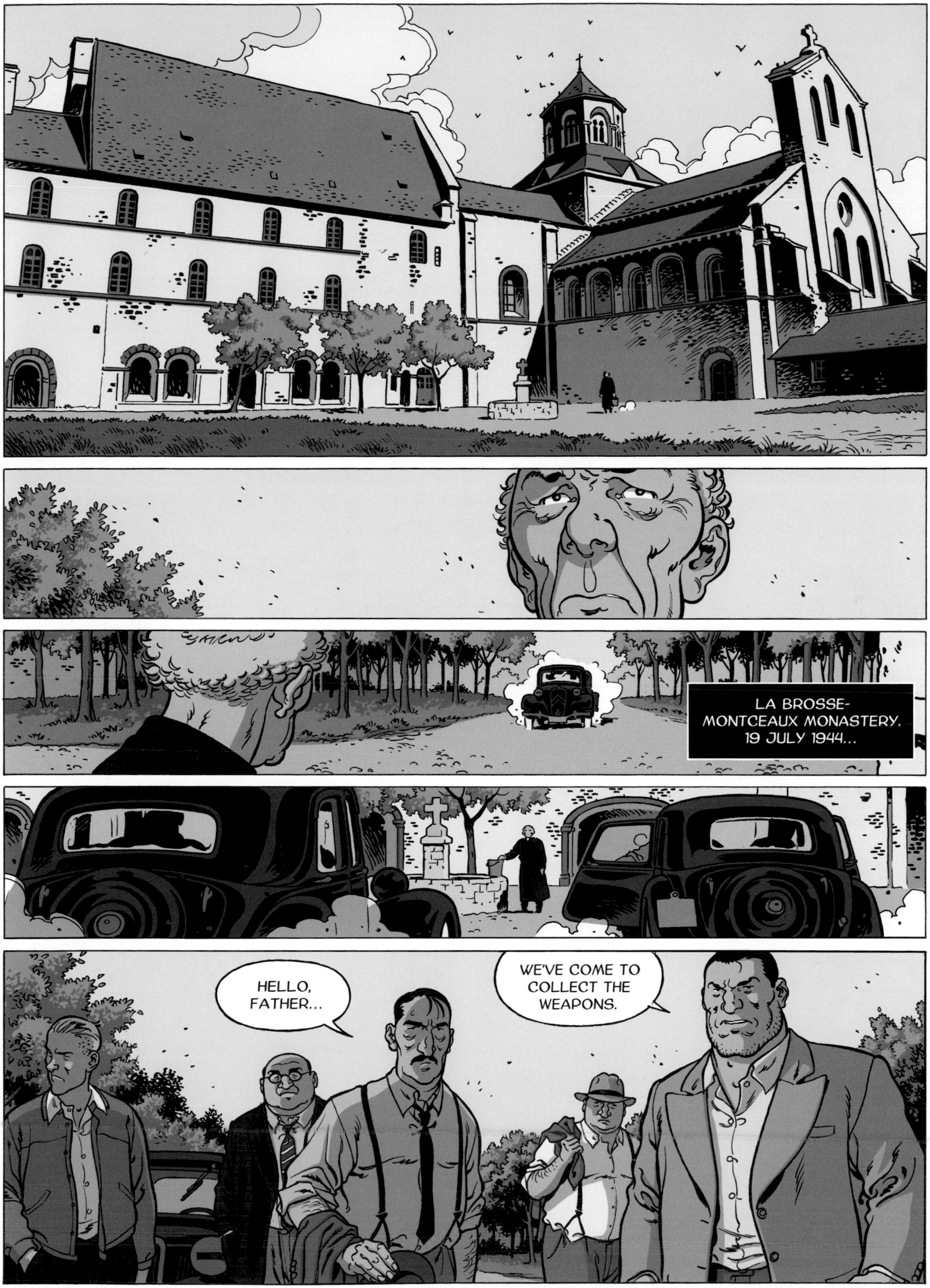
LA BROSSE-MONTCEAUX MONASTERY. 19 JULY 1944...
HELLO, FATHER...
WE'VE COME TO COLLECT THE WEAPONS.

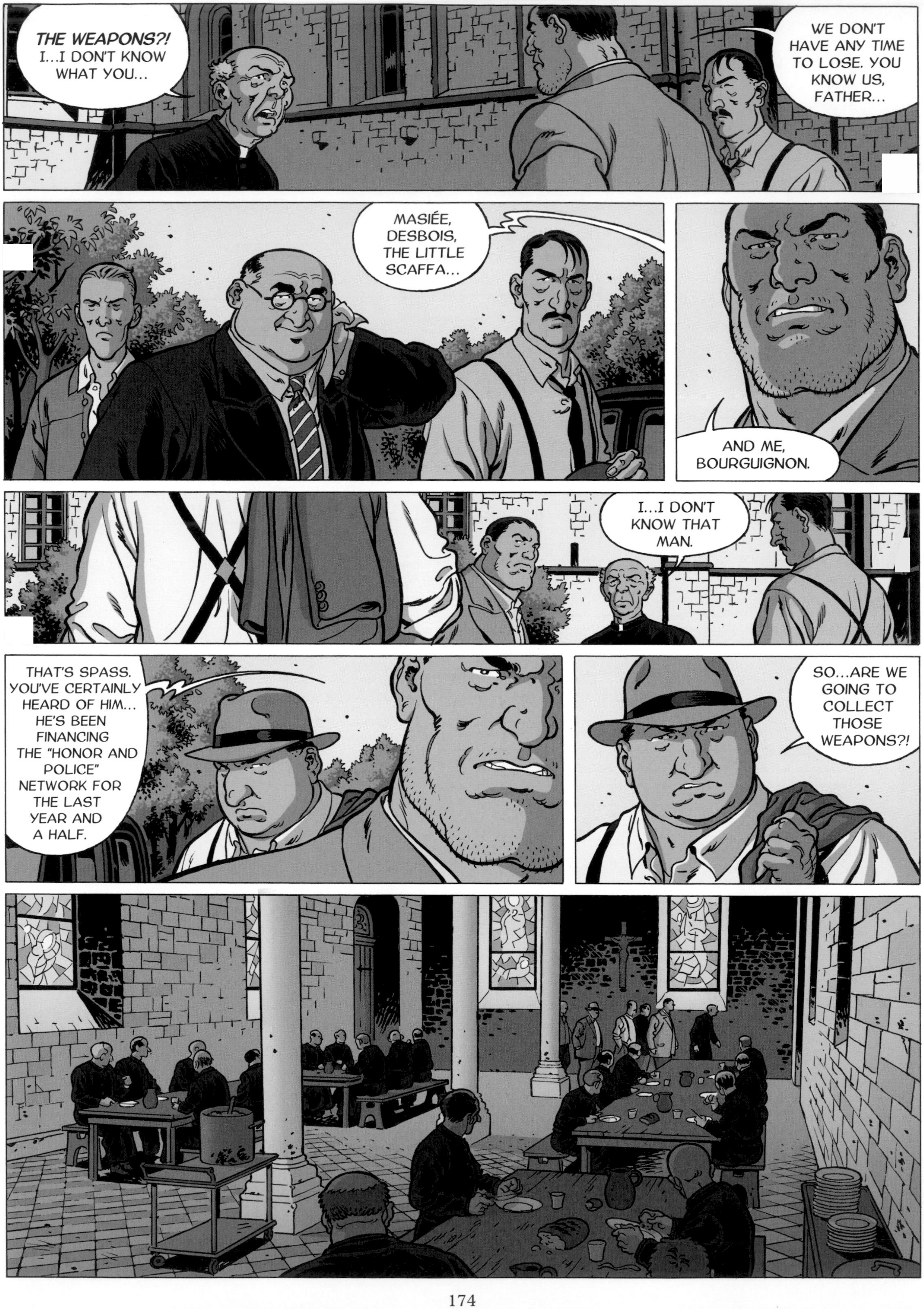
THE WEAPONS?! I...I DON'T KNOW WHAT YOU...
WE DON'T HAVE ANY TIME TO LOSE. YOU KNOW US, FATHER...
MASIÉE, DESBOIS, THE LITTLE SCAFFA...
AND ME, BOURGUIGNON.
I...I DON'T KNOW THAT MAN.
THAT'S SPASS. YOU'VE CERTAINLY HEARD OF HIM... HE'S BEEN FINANCING THE "HONOR AND POLICE" NETWORK FOR THE LAST YEAR AND A HALF.
SO...ARE WE GOING TO COLLECT THOSE WEAPONS?!

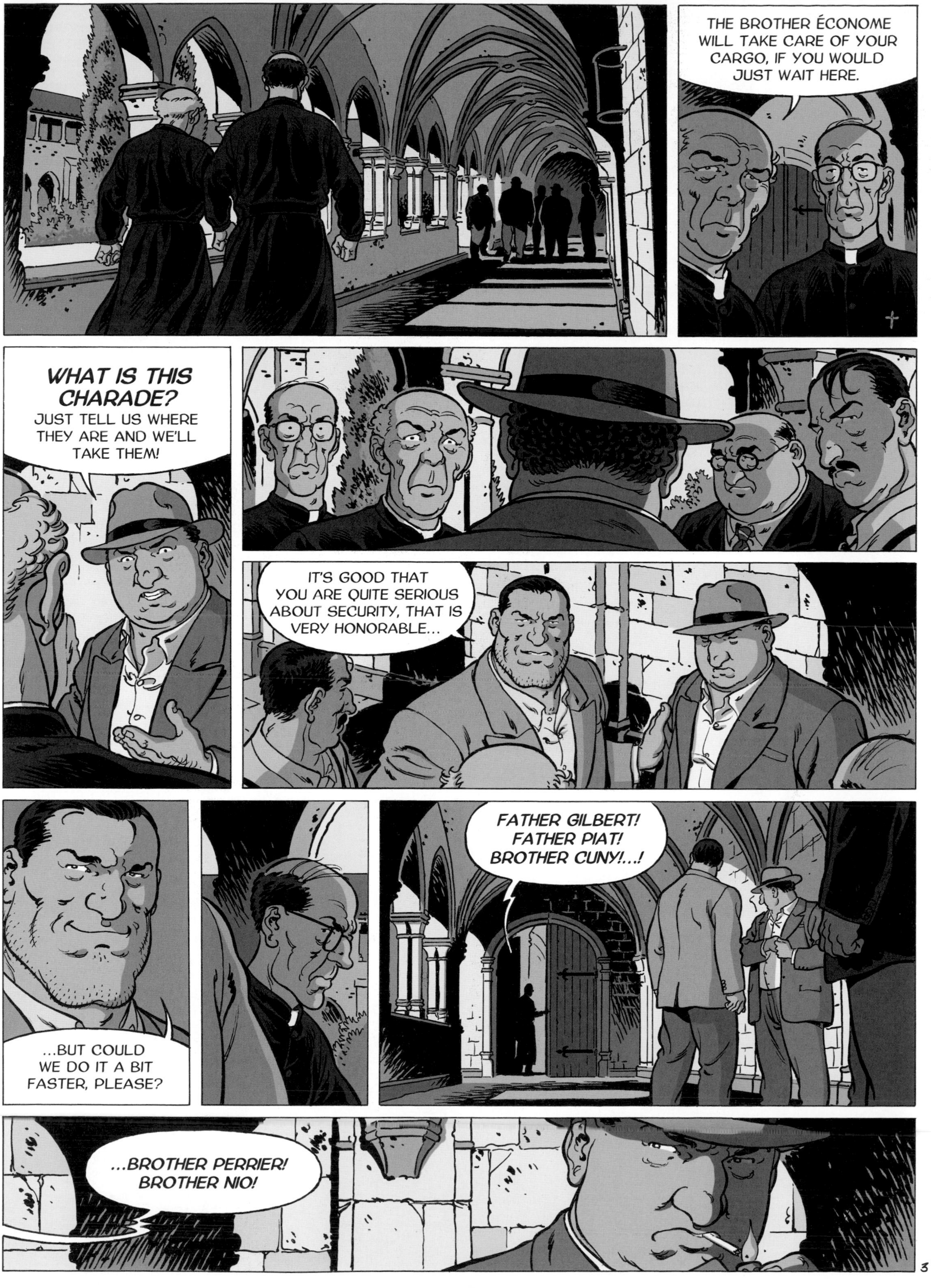
THE BROTHER ÉCONOME WILL TAKE CARE OF YOUR CARGO, IF YOU WOULD JUST WAIT HERE.
WHAT IS THIS CHARADE? JUST TELL US WHERE THEY ARE AND WE'LL TAKE THEM!
IT'S GOOD THAT YOU ARE QUITE SERIOUS ABOUT SECURITY, THAT IS VERY HONORABLE...
...BUT COULD WE DO IT A BIT FASTER, PLEASE?
FATHER GILBERT! FATHER PIAT! BROTHER CUNY!...!
...BROTHER PERRIER! BROTHER NIO!
3

DID YOU GET THEIR NAMES?

SOME, YES!

MR. SPASS?...

...MAY I HAVE A CIGARETTE, PLEASE?

LUCKY STRIKES. SMOKING THOSE RIGHT UNDER THE KRAUTS' NOSES IS PRETTY GOOD!

IS IT TRUE THAT YOU HAVE A GESTAPO ID, TOO?...

ROBERT IS OUR LIAISON WITH THE OTHER GROUPS. HE'S A GOOD MAN...BUT HE NEEDS TO LEARN TO SHUT IT EVERY ONCE IN A WHILE.

IT'S OKAY. WE WERE ALL YOUNG ONCE.

I...I KNOW THAT IT'S NOT REALLY DONE... BUT I'D LIKE TO THANK YOU, SIR.

FOR WHAT?

MY MOTHER WAS ARRESTED BY THE KRAUTS IN NOVEMBER '43 WITH A TSF POST.* HER NAME WAS ON ONE OF YOUR FAMOUS LISTS.

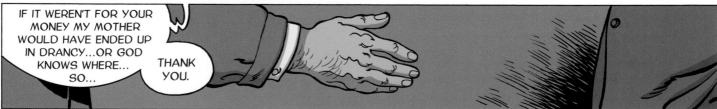

IF IT WEREN'T FOR YOUR MONEY MY MOTHER WOULD HAVE ENDED UP IN DRANCY...OR GOD KNOWS WHERE... SO...

THANK YOU.

YOU'RE WELCOME... IT'S THE LEAST I COULD DO.

4

*A radio setup for intercepting German transmissions.

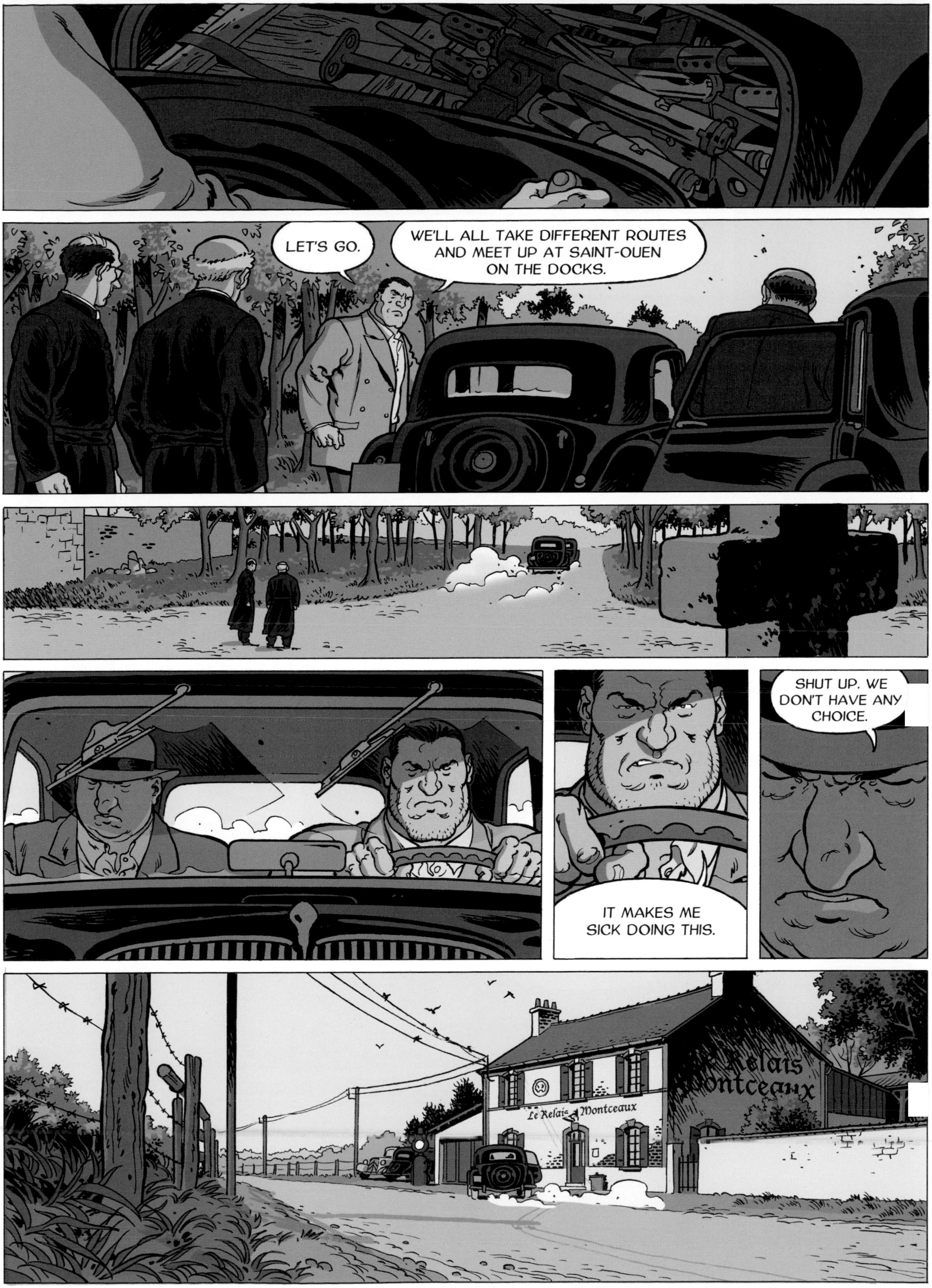
LET'S GO.
WE'LL ALL TAKE DIFFERENT ROUTES AND MEET UP AT SAINT-OUEN ON THE DOCKS.
IT MAKES ME SICK DOING THIS.
SHUT UP. WE DON'T HAVE ANY CHOICE.
Le Relais Montceaux
Le Relais Montceaux
5

SHOULD I WAIT?

WITH WHAT WE HAVE IN THE TRUNK? DON'T BE STUPID! GO MEET UP WITH THE OTHERS IN SAINT-OUEN AND HELP THEM STORE THE STUFF.

MR. JOANOVICI!

WE WERE WAITING FOR YOU TO PLACE OUR ORDER...

I RECOMMEND THE PORK FILLET. IT'S EXCELLENT.

Plat du jour
let mignon
ot au feu
Truite
mages

OH, I FORGOT... YOU DON'T EAT PORK, RIGHT?

I'M NOT HUNGRY.

WELL THEN, I'LL EAT FOR TWO WHILE YOU TELL ME ABOUT YOUR MORNING...

...IN GREAT DETAIL.

6

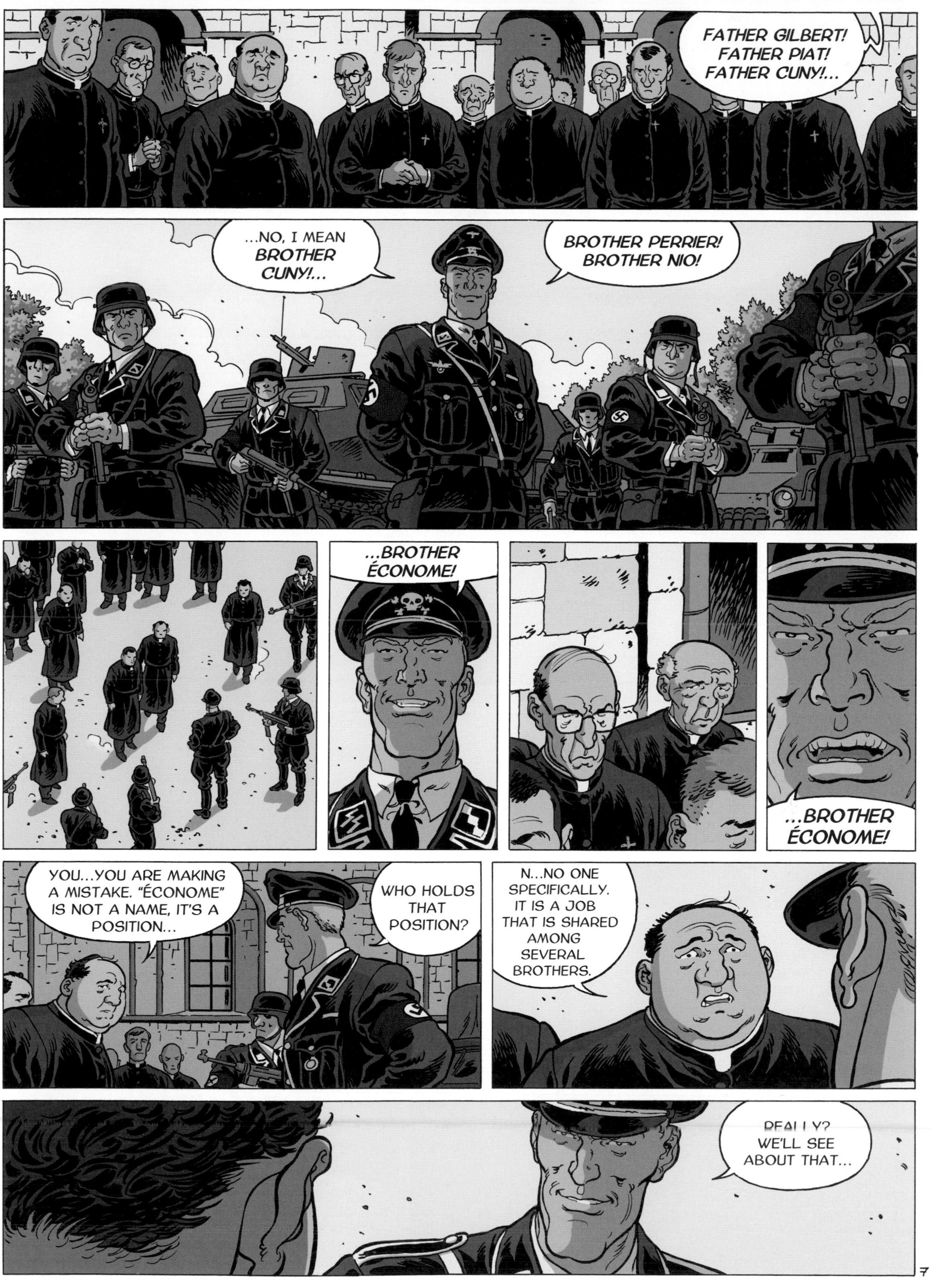
FATHER GILBERT! FATHER PIAT! FATHER CUNY!...
...NO, I MEAN BROTHER CUNY!...
BROTHER PERRIER! BROTHER NIO!
...BROTHER ÉCONOME!
...BROTHER ÉCONOME!
YOU...YOU ARE MAKING A MISTAKE. "ÉCONOME" IS NOT A NAME, IT'S A POSITION...
WHO HOLDS THAT POSITION?
N...NO ONE SPECIFICALLY. IT IS A JOB THAT IS SHARED AMONG SEVERAL BROTHERS.
REALLY? WE'LL SEE ABOUT THAT...
7

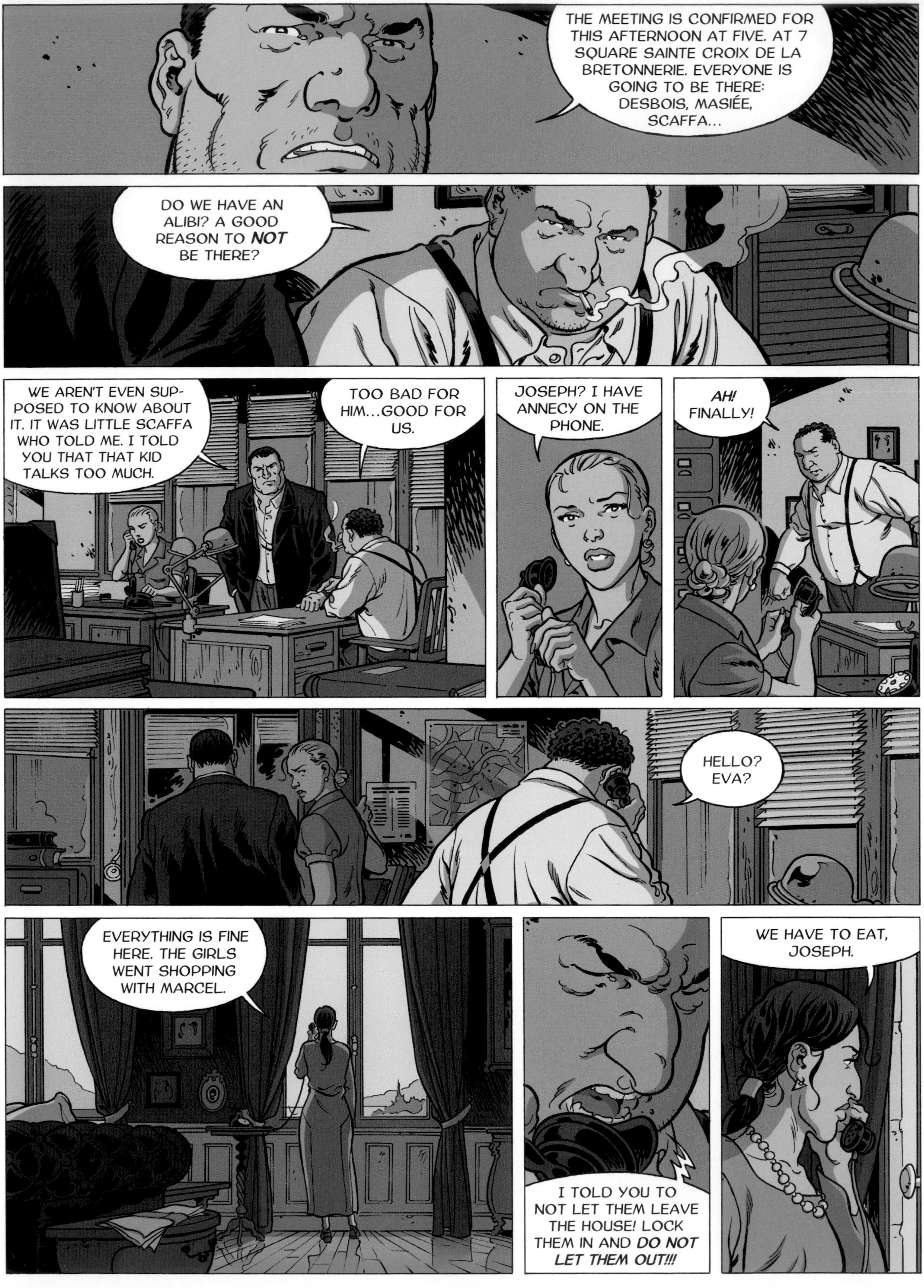
THE MEETING IS CONFIRMED FOR THIS AFTERNOON AT FIVE. AT 7 SQUARE SAINTE CROIX DE LA BRETONNERIE. EVERYONE IS GOING TO BE THERE: DESBOIS, MASIÉE, SCAFFA...
DO WE HAVE AN ALIBI? A GOOD REASON TO NOT BE THERE?
WE AREN'T EVEN SUPPOSED TO KNOW ABOUT IT. IT WAS LITTLE SCAFFA WHO TOLD ME. I TOLD YOU THAT THAT KID TALKS TOO MUCH.
TOO BAD FOR HIM...GOOD FOR US.
JOSEPH? I HAVE ANNECY ON THE PHONE.
AH! FINALLY!
HELLO? EVA?
EVERYTHING IS FINE HERE. THE GIRLS WENT SHOPPING WITH MARCEL.
I TOLD YOU TO NOT LET THEM LEAVE THE HOUSE! LOCK THEM IN AND DO NOT LET THEM OUT!!!
WE HAVE TO EAT, JOSEPH.
8

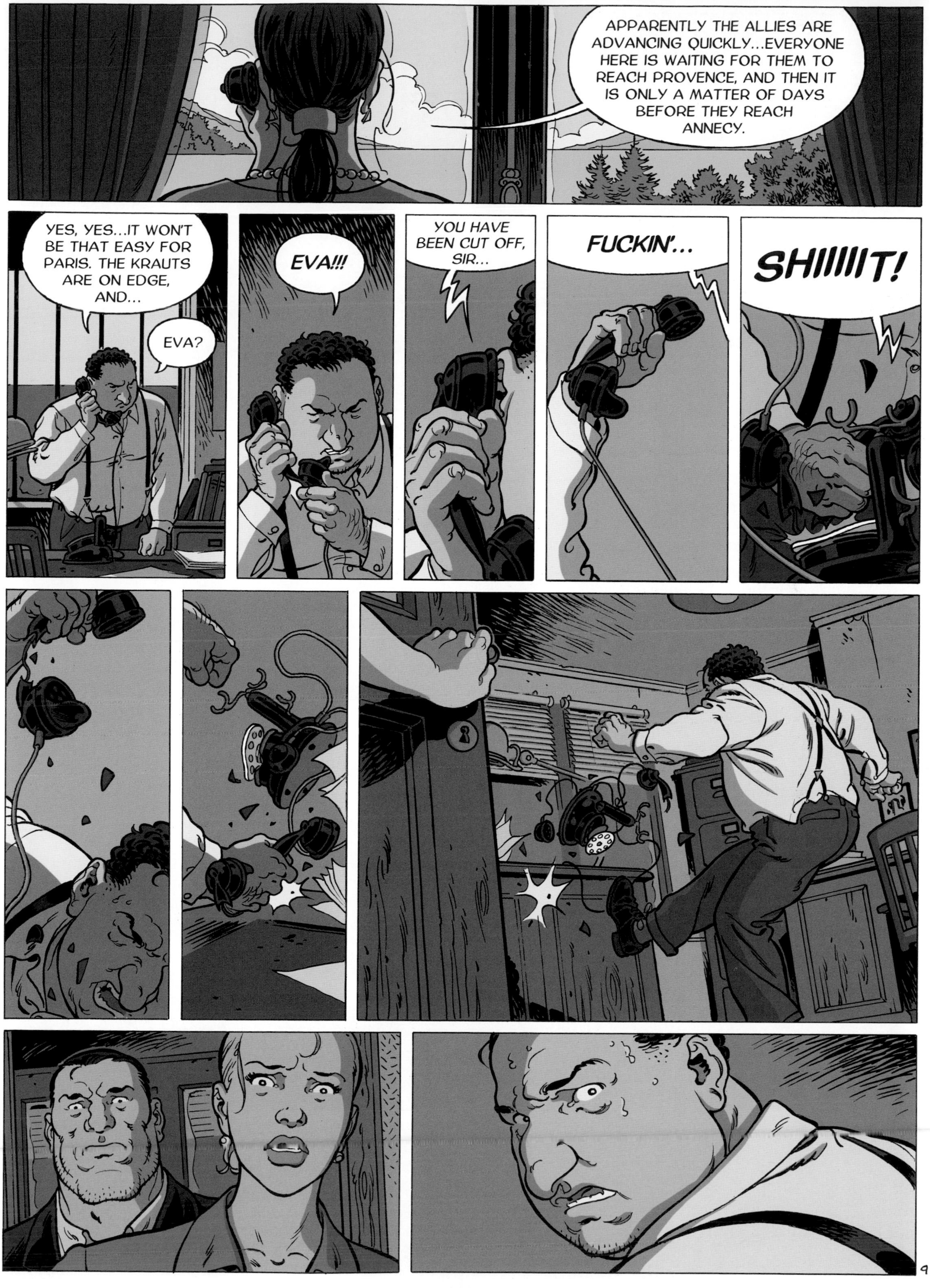

APPARENTLY THE ALLIES ARE ADVANCING QUICKLY...EVERYONE HERE IS WAITING FOR THEM TO REACH PROVENCE, AND THEN IT IS ONLY A MATTER OF DAYS BEFORE THEY REACH ANNECY.
YES, YES...IT WON'T BE THAT EASY FOR PARIS. THE KRAUTS ARE ON EDGE, AND...
EVA?
EVA!!!
YOU HAVE BEEN CUT OFF, SIR...
FUCKIN'...
SHIIIIIT!
9

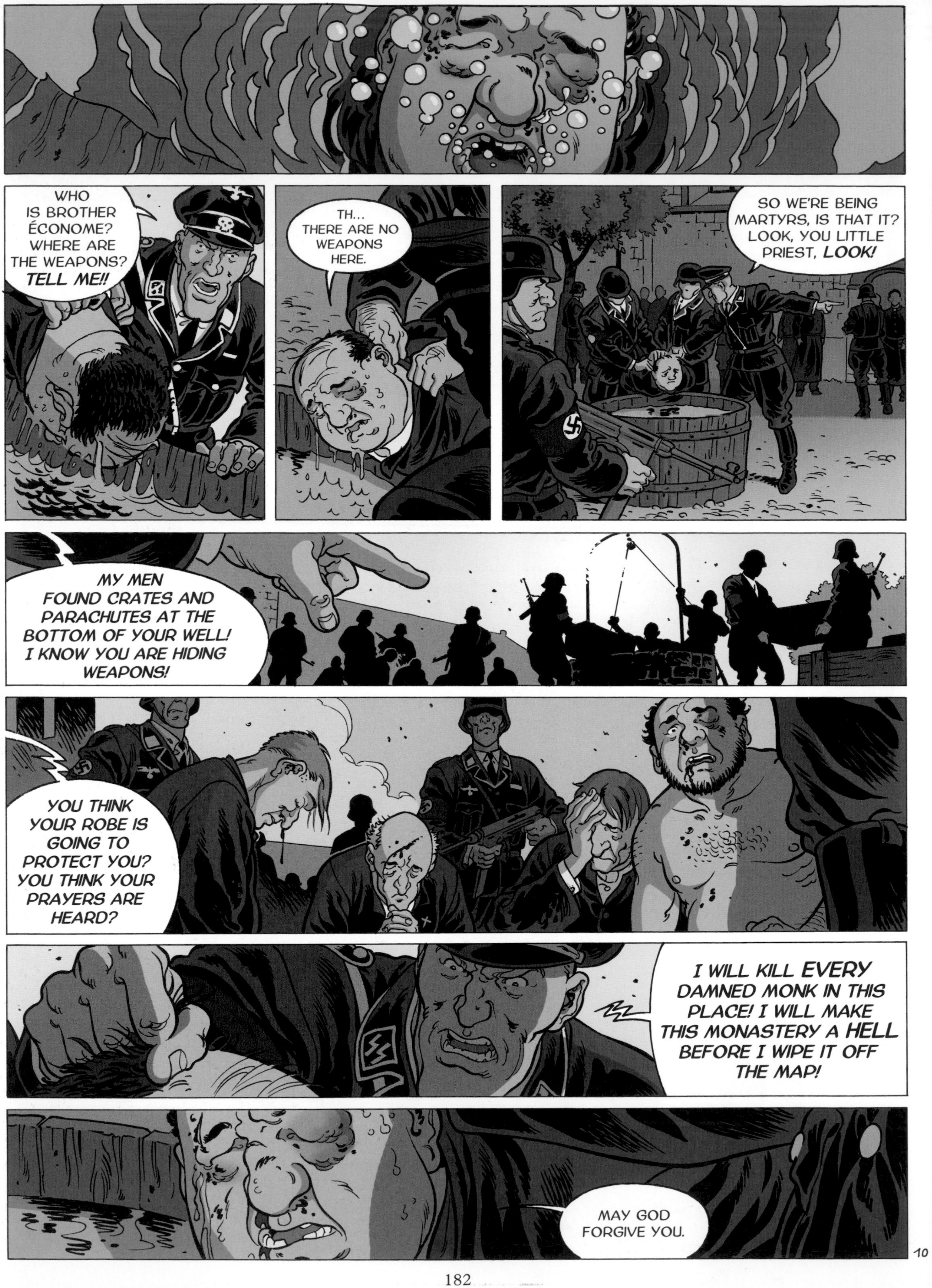
WHO IS BROTHER ÉCONOME? WHERE ARE THE WEAPONS? TELL ME!!
TH... THERE ARE NO WEAPONS HERE.
SO WE'RE BEING MARTYRS, IS THAT IT? LOOK, YOU LITTLE PRIEST, LOOK!
MY MEN FOUND CRATES AND PARACHUTES AT THE BOTTOM OF YOUR WELL! I KNOW YOU ARE HIDING WEAPONS!
YOU THINK YOUR ROBE IS GOING TO PROTECT YOU? YOU THINK YOUR PRAYERS ARE HEARD?
I WILL KILL EVERY DAMNED MONK IN THIS PLACE! I WILL MAKE THIS MONASTERY A HELL BEFORE I WIPE IT OFF THE MAP!
MAY GOD FORGIVE YOU.
10

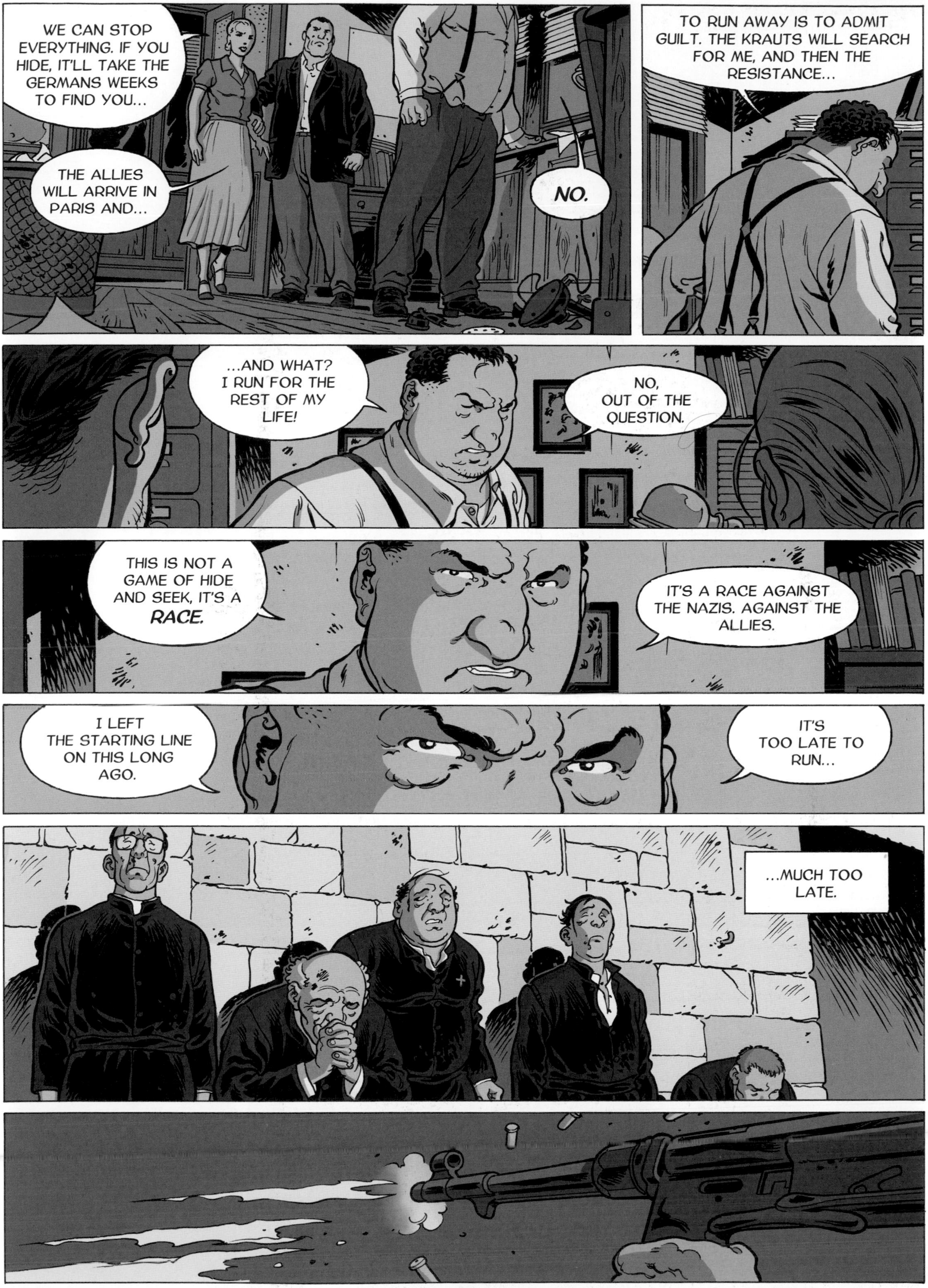
WE CAN STOP EVERYTHING. IF YOU HIDE, IT'LL TAKE THE GERMANS WEEKS TO FIND YOU...
THE ALLIES WILL ARRIVE IN PARIS AND...
NO.
TO RUN AWAY IS TO ADMIT GUILT. THE KRAUTS WILL SEARCH FOR ME, AND THEN THE RESISTANCE...
...AND WHAT? I RUN FOR THE REST OF MY LIFE!
NO, OUT OF THE QUESTION.
THIS IS NOT A GAME OF HIDE AND SEEK, IT'S A RACE.
IT'S A RACE AGAINST THE NAZIS. AGAINST THE ALLIES.
I LEFT THE STARTING LINE ON THIS LONG AGO.
IT'S TOO LATE TO RUN...
...MUCH TOO LATE.

11

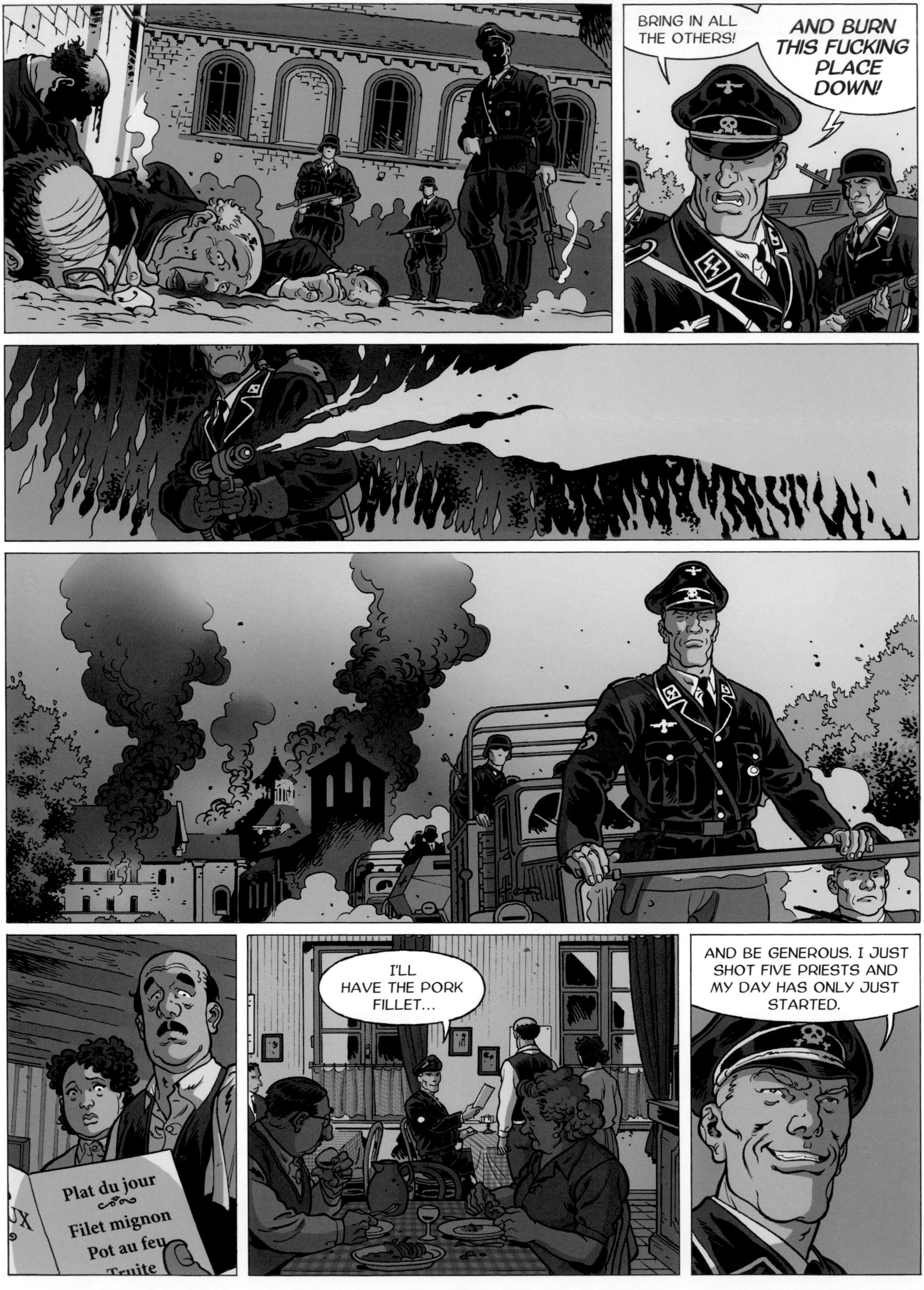
BRING IN ALL THE OTHERS!
AND BURN THIS FUCKING PLACE DOWN!
Plat du jour
Filet mignon
Pot au feu
Truite
I'LL HAVE THE PORK FILLET...
AND BE GENEROUS. I JUST SHOT FIVE PRIESTS AND MY DAY HAS ONLY JUST STARTED.
12

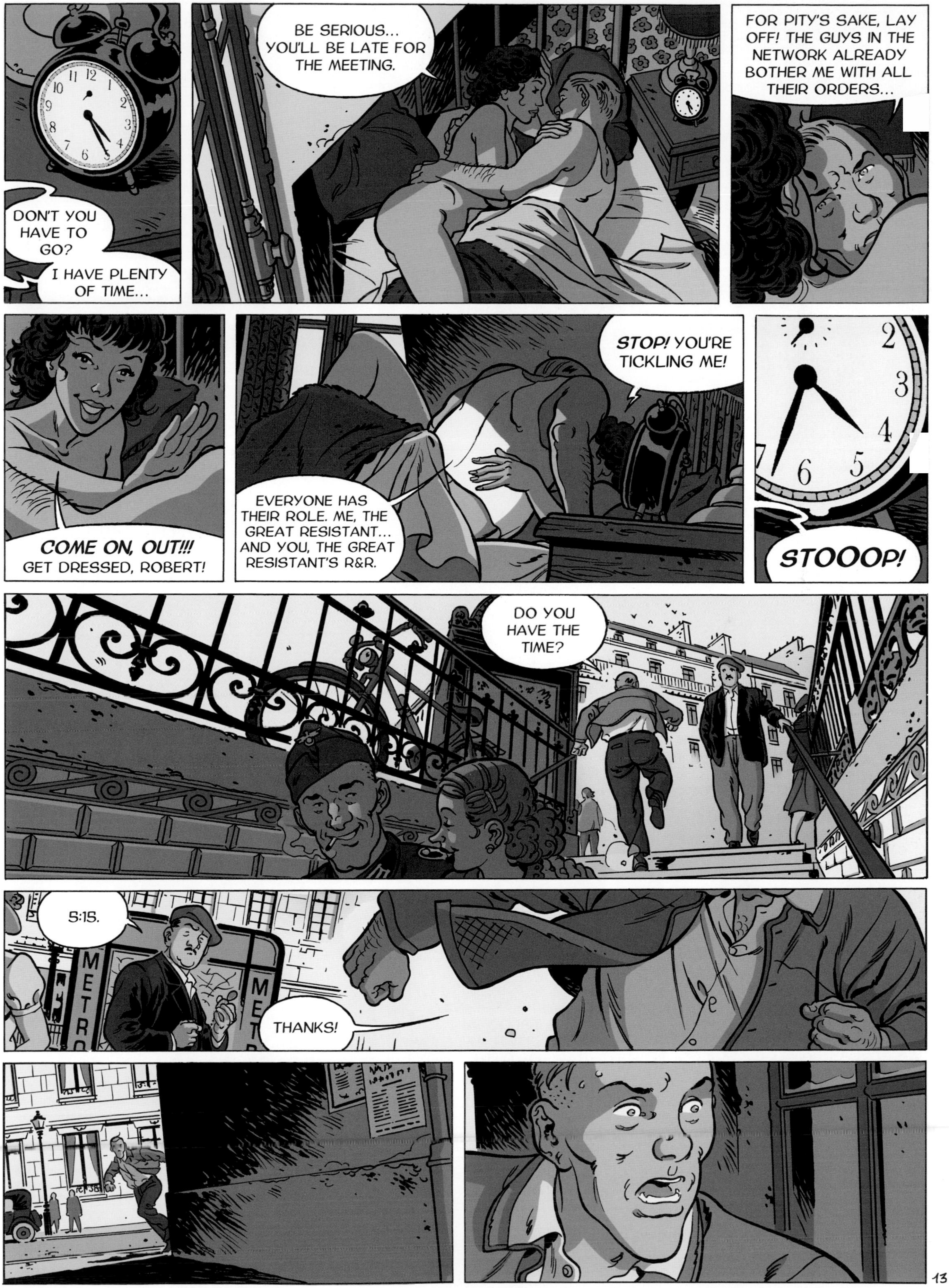
DON'T YOU HAVE TO GO?
I HAVE PLENTY OF TIME...
BE SERIOUS... YOU'LL BE LATE FOR THE MEETING.
FOR PITY'S SAKE, LAY OFF! THE GUYS IN THE NETWORK ALREADY BOTHER ME WITH ALL THEIR ORDERS...
COME ON, OUT!!!
GET DRESSED, ROBERT!
EVERYONE HAS THEIR ROLE. ME, THE GREAT RESISTANT... AND YOU, THE GREAT RESISTANT'S R&R.
STOP! YOU'RE TICKLING ME!
STOOOP!
DO YOU HAVE THE TIME?
5:15.
METRO
THANKS!
13

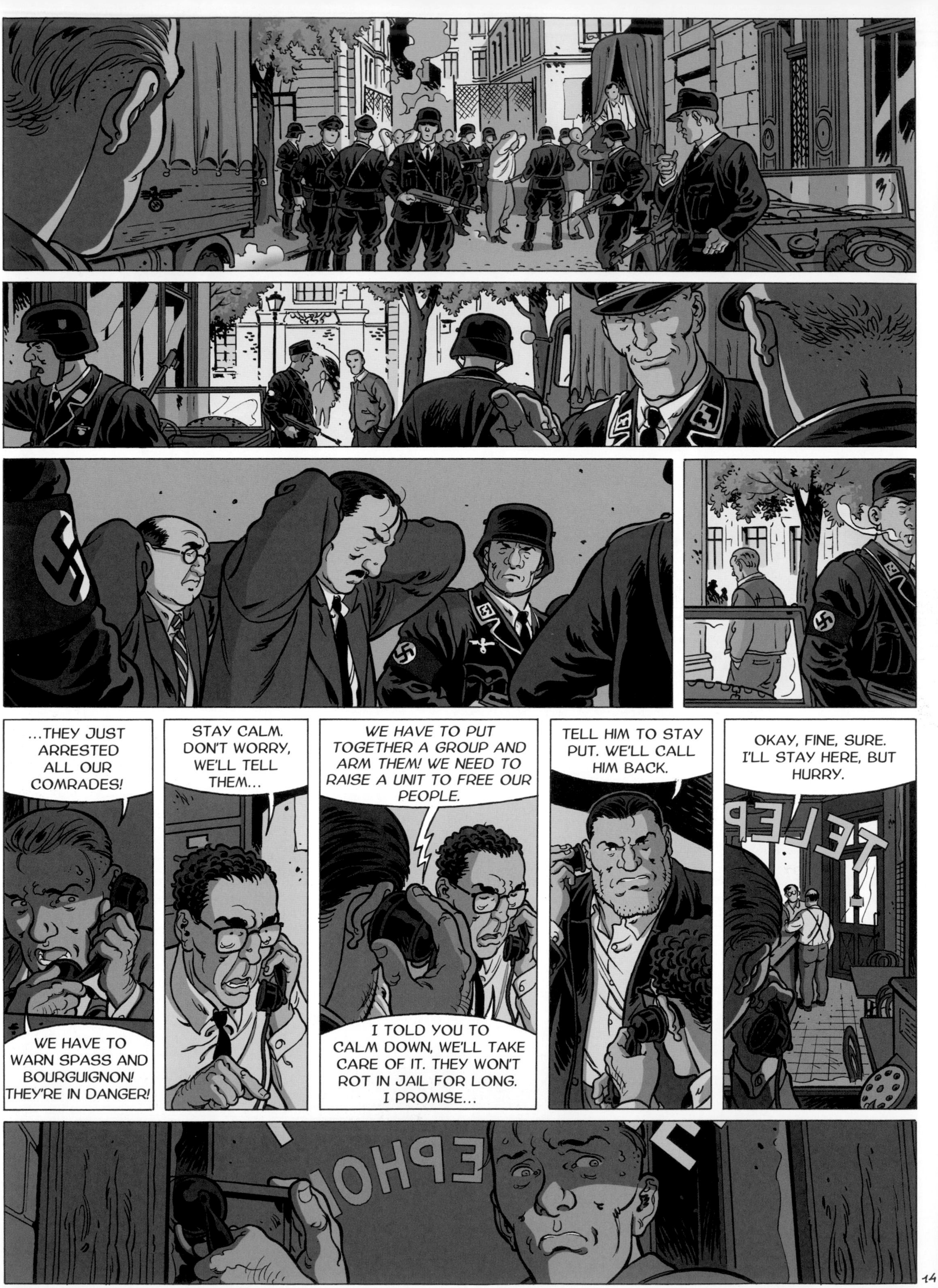
...THEY JUST ARRESTED ALL OUR COMRADES!
WE HAVE TO WARN SPASS AND BOURGUIGNON! THEY'RE IN DANGER!
STAY CALM. DON'T WORRY, WE'LL TELL THEM...
WE HAVE TO PUT TOGETHER A GROUP AND ARM THEM! WE NEED TO RAISE A UNIT TO FREE OUR PEOPLE.
I TOLD YOU TO CALM DOWN, WE'LL TAKE CARE OF IT. THEY WON'T ROT IN JAIL FOR LONG. I PROMISE...
TELL HIM TO STAY PUT. WE'LL CALL HIM BACK.
OKAY, FINE, SURE. I'LL STAY HERE, BUT HURRY.
TELEP
EPHO
14

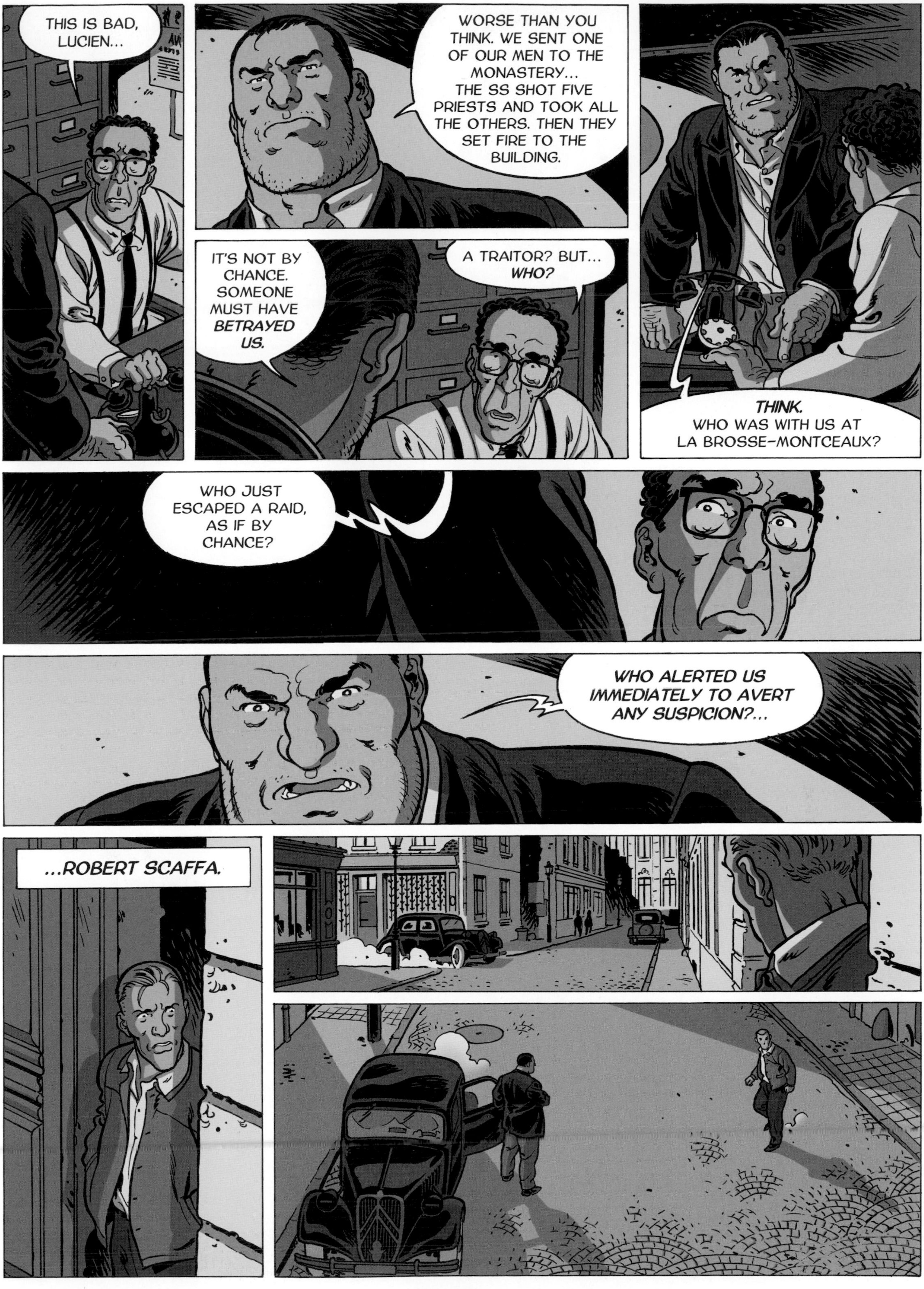
THIS IS BAD, LUCIEN...
WORSE THAN YOU THINK. WE SENT ONE OF OUR MEN TO THE MONASTERY... THE SS SHOT FIVE PRIESTS AND TOOK ALL THE OTHERS. THEN THEY SET FIRE TO THE BUILDING.
IT'S NOT BY CHANCE. SOMEONE MUST HAVE *BETRAYED* US.
A TRAITOR? BUT... *WHO?*
THINK. WHO WAS WITH US AT LA BROSSE-MONTCEAUX?
WHO JUST ESCAPED A RAID, AS IF BY CHANCE?
WHO ALERTED US IMMEDIATELY TO AVERT ANY SUSPICION?...
...ROBERT SCAFFA.
15

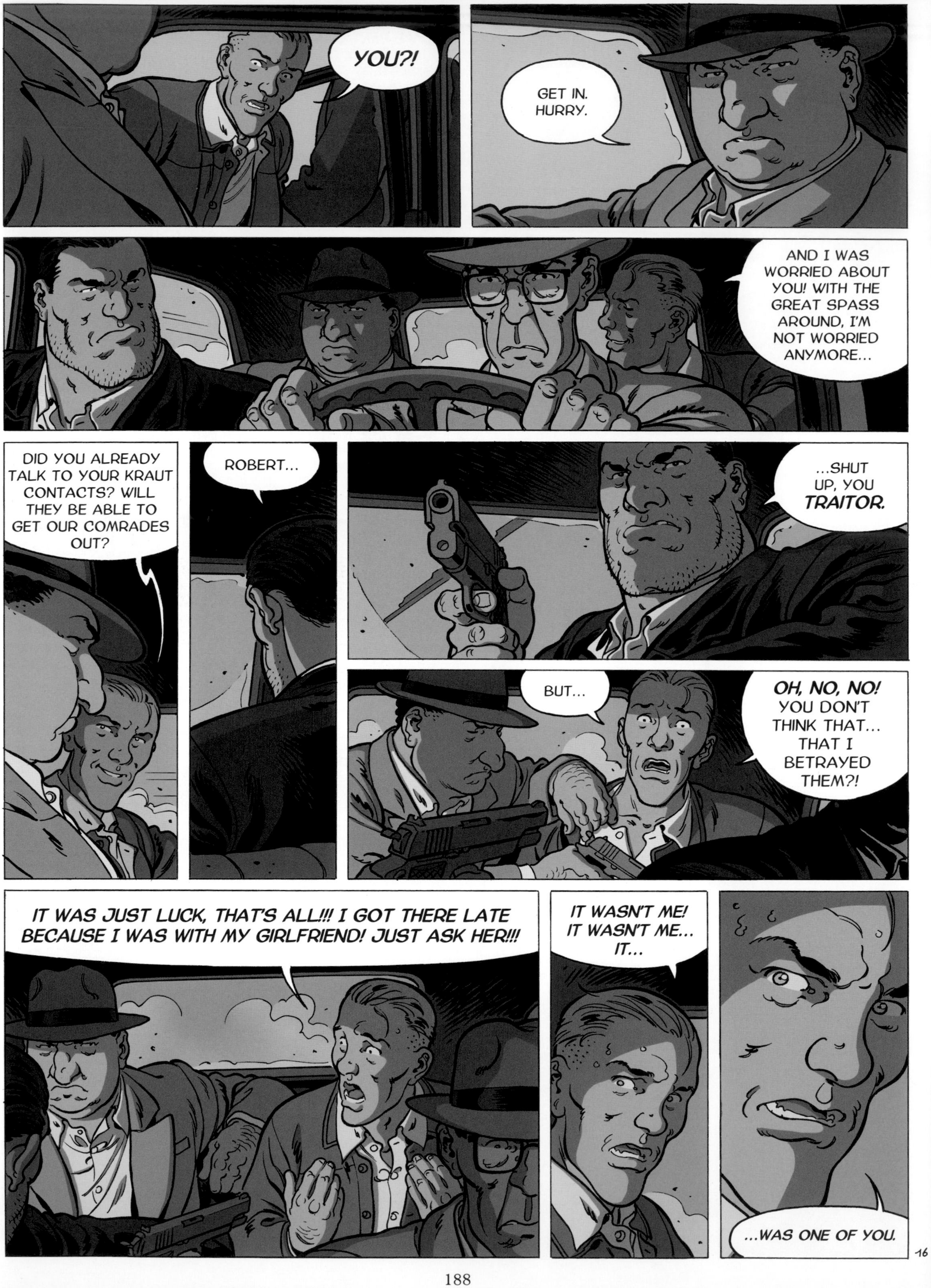
YOU?!
GET IN. HURRY.
AND I WAS WORRIED ABOUT YOU! WITH THE GREAT SPASS AROUND, I'M NOT WORRIED ANYMORE...
DID YOU ALREADY TALK TO YOUR KRAUT CONTACTS? WILL THEY BE ABLE TO GET OUR COMRADES OUT?
ROBERT...
...SHUT UP, YOU TRAITOR.
BUT...
OH, NO, NO! YOU DON'T THINK THAT... THAT I BETRAYED THEM?!
IT WAS JUST LUCK, THAT'S ALL!!! I GOT THERE LATE BECAUSE I WAS WITH MY GIRLFRIEND! JUST ASK HER!!!
IT WASN'T ME! IT WASN'T ME... IT...
...WAS ONE OF YOU.
16

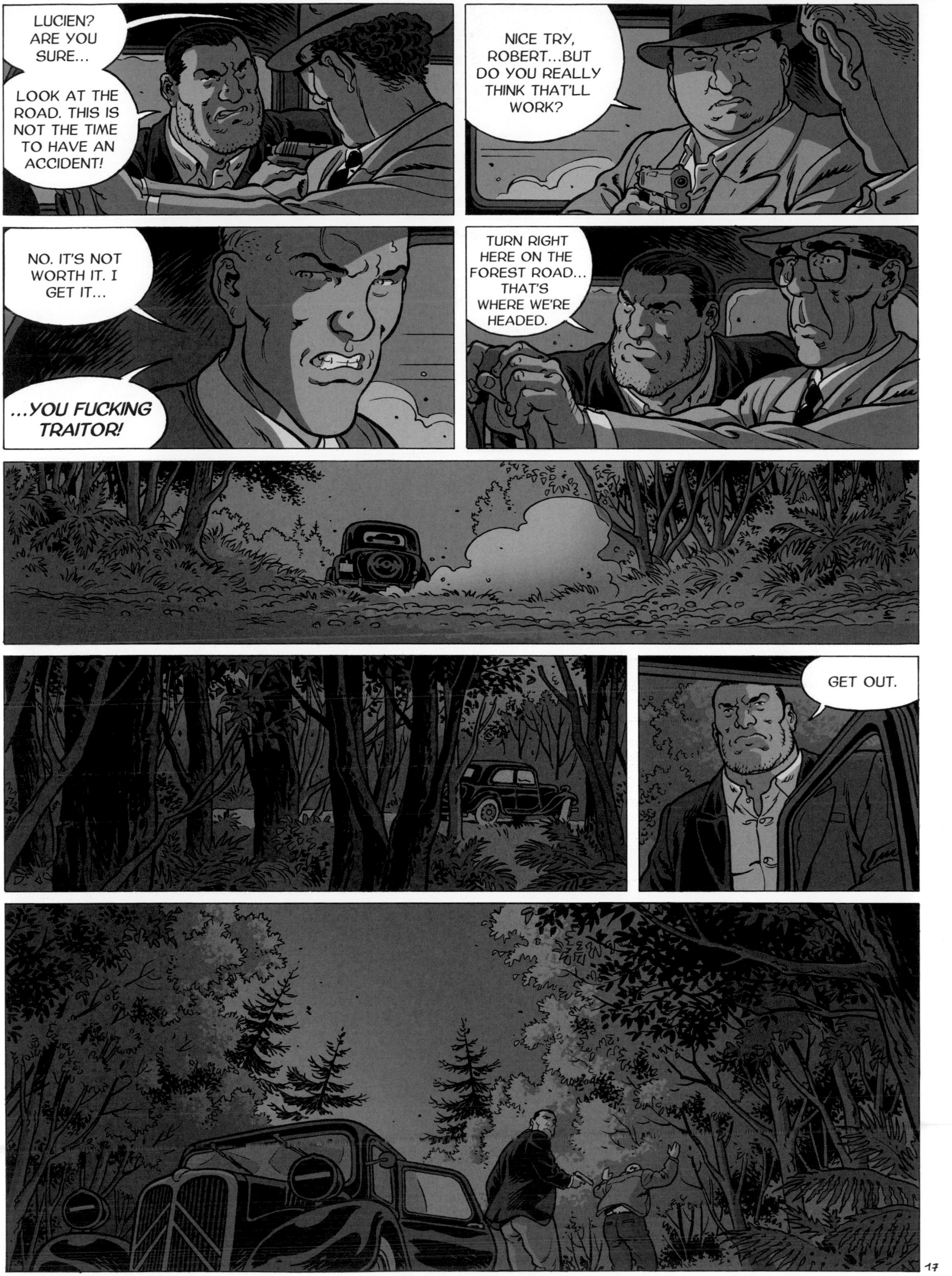
LUCIEN? ARE YOU SURE...
LOOK AT THE ROAD. THIS IS NOT THE TIME TO HAVE AN ACCIDENT!
NICE TRY, ROBERT...BUT DO YOU REALLY THINK THAT'LL WORK?
NO. IT'S NOT WORTH IT. I GET IT...
...YOU FUCKING TRAITOR!
TURN RIGHT HERE ON THE FOREST ROAD... THAT'S WHERE WE'RE HEADED.
GET OUT.
17

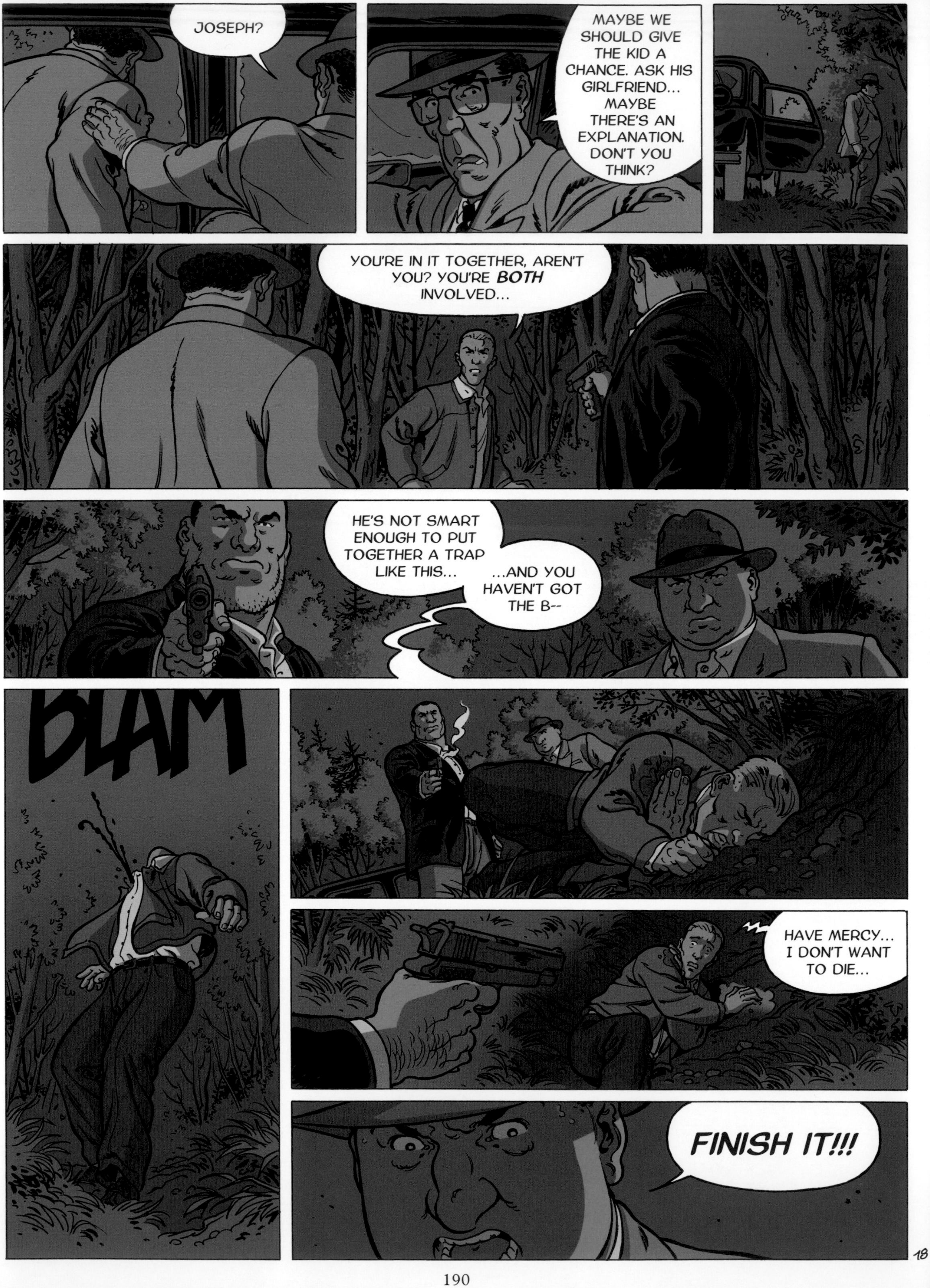

JOSEPH?
MAYBE WE SHOULD GIVE THE KID A CHANCE. ASK HIS GIRLFRIEND... MAYBE THERE'S AN EXPLANATION. DON'T YOU THINK?
YOU'RE IN IT TOGETHER, AREN'T YOU? YOU'RE BOTH INVOLVED...
HE'S NOT SMART ENOUGH TO PUT TOGETHER A TRAP LIKE THIS...
...AND YOU HAVEN'T GOT THE B--
BLAM
HAVE MERCY... I DON'T WANT TO DIE...
FINISH IT!!!
18

NO.
YOU FINISH IT.
OH, NO...NO, NOT ME...
NO MORE OF YOUR ORDERS! NO MORE OF YOUR DIRTY WORK! YOU WANT THIS KID DEAD?! THEN KILL HIM YOURSELF!!!
HOLY MARY, MOTHER OF GOD, PRAY FOR US SINNERS...
NO, DON'T DO IT! I'M BEGGING YOU...
...DON'T KILL ME!
...NOW AND AT THE HOUR OF OUR DEATH...
19

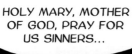

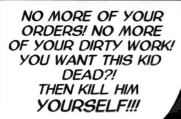

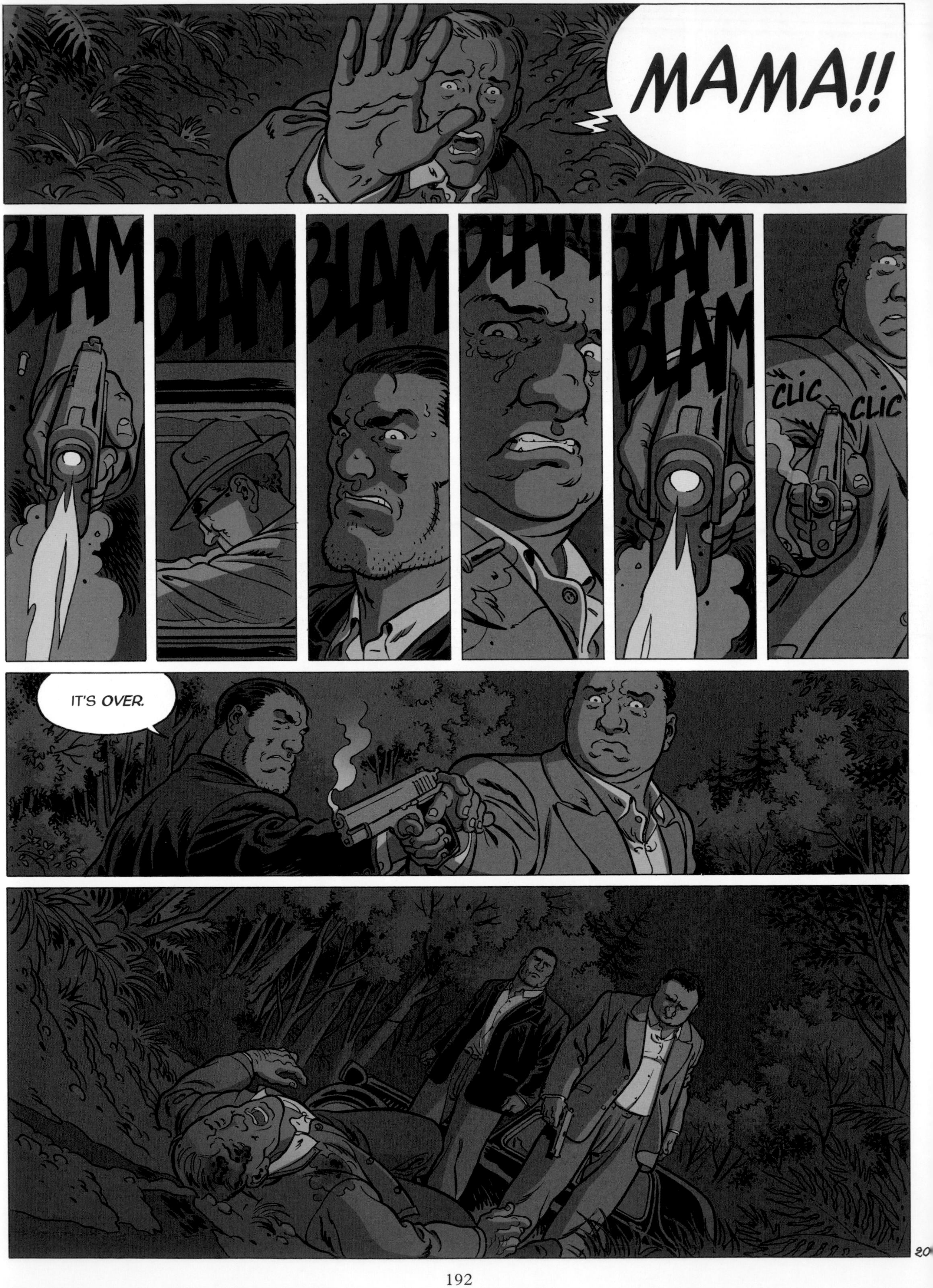
MAMA!!
BLAM
BLAM
BLAM
BLAM
BLAM
BLAM
CLIC
CLIC
IT'S OVER.
20

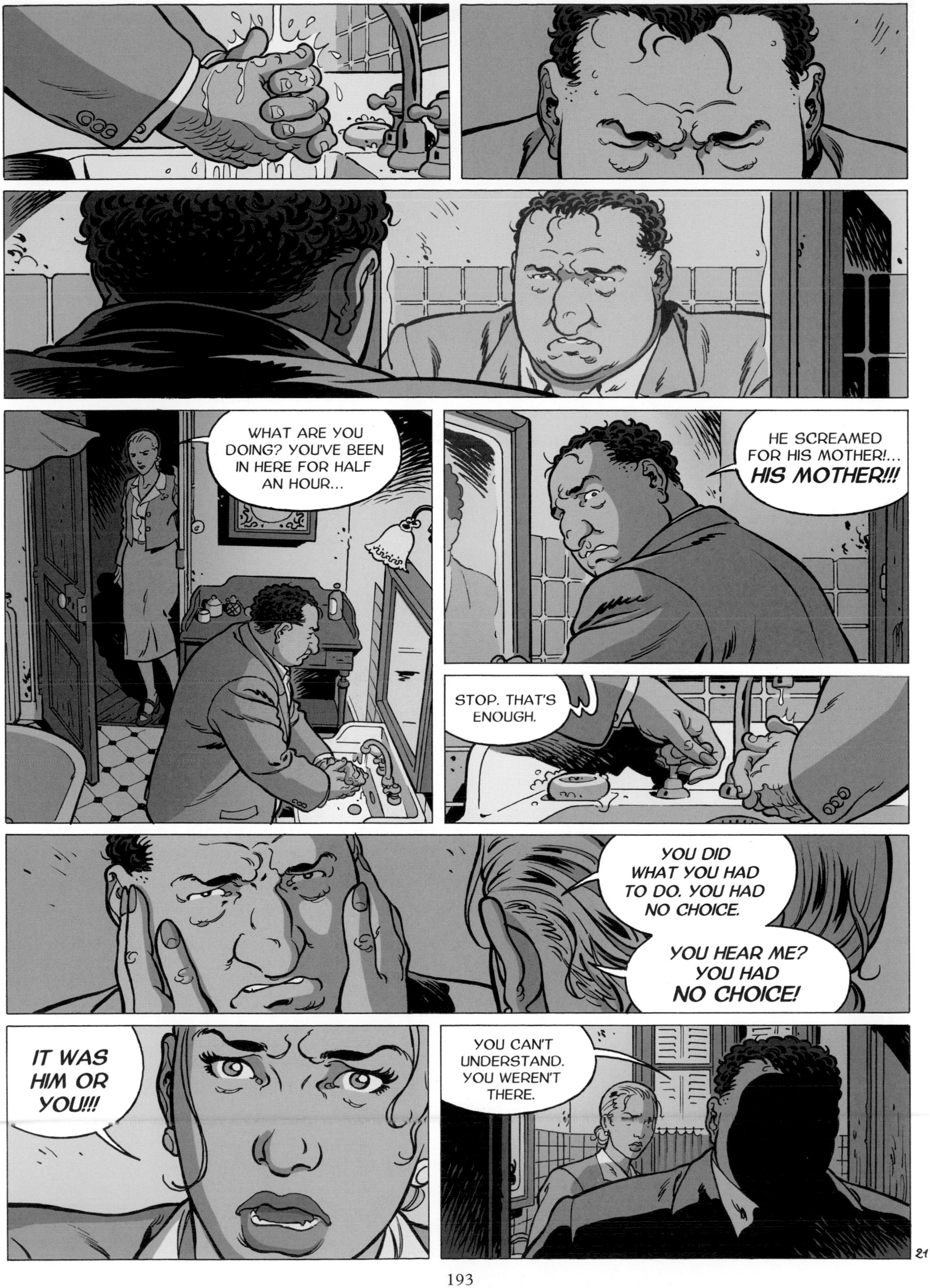

WHAT ARE YOU DOING? YOU'VE BEEN IN HERE FOR HALF AN HOUR...
HE SCREAMED FOR HIS MOTHER!... HIS MOTHER!!!
STOP. THAT'S ENOUGH.
YOU DID WHAT YOU HAD TO DO. YOU HAD NO CHOICE.
YOU HEAR ME? YOU HAD NO CHOICE!
IT WAS HIM OR YOU!!!
YOU CAN'T UNDERSTAND. YOU WEREN'T THERE.
21

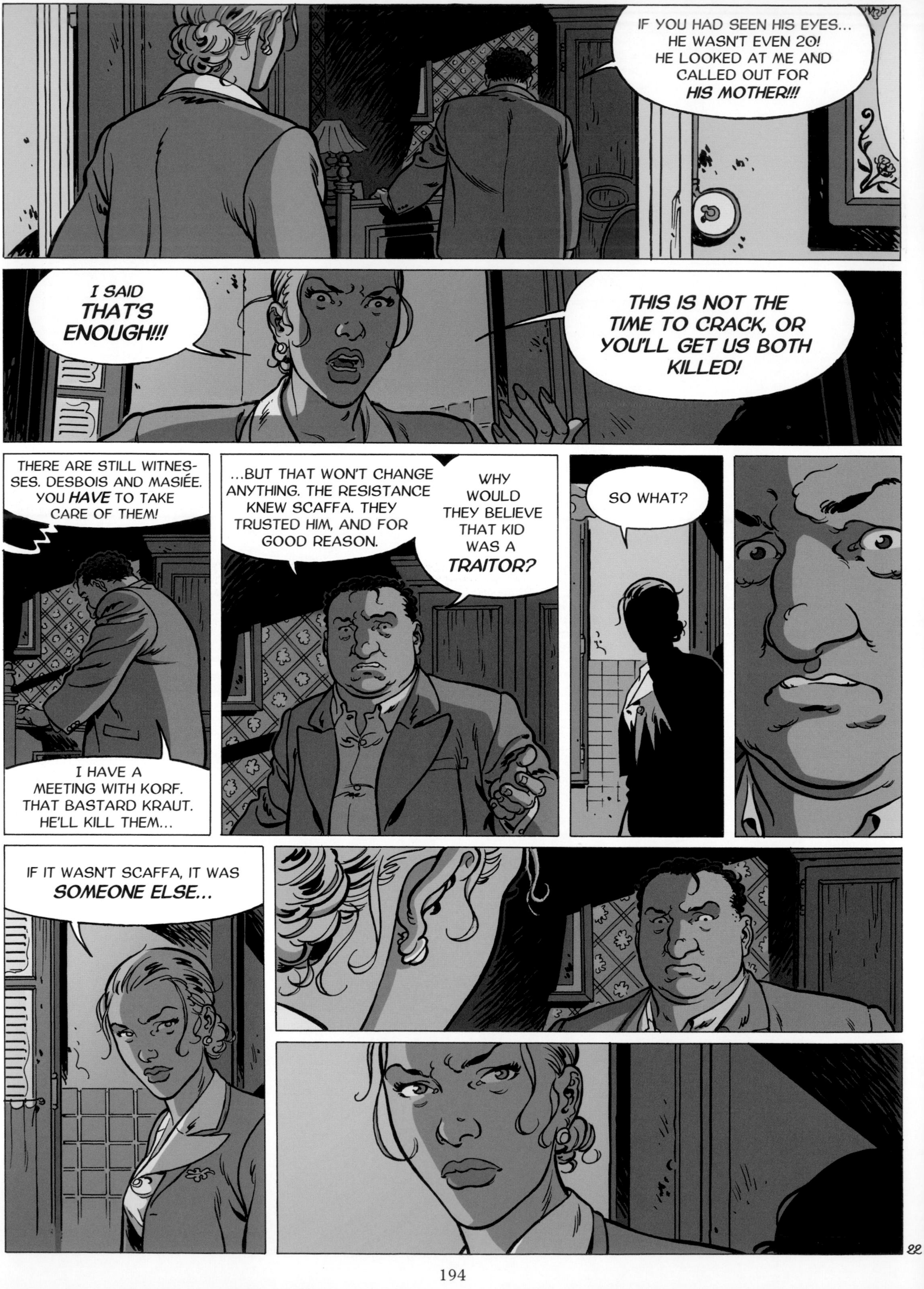
IF YOU HAD SEEN HIS EYES... HE WASN'T EVEN 20! HE LOOKED AT ME AND CALLED OUT FOR HIS MOTHER!!!
I SAID THAT'S ENOUGH!!!
THIS IS NOT THE TIME TO CRACK, OR YOU'LL GET US BOTH KILLED!
THERE ARE STILL WITNES-SES. DESBOIS AND MASIÉE. YOU HAVE TO TAKE CARE OF THEM!
I HAVE A MEETING WITH KORF. THAT BASTARD KRAUT. HE'LL KILL THEM...
...BUT THAT WON'T CHANGE ANYTHING. THE RESISTANCE KNEW SCAFFA. THEY TRUSTED HIM, AND FOR GOOD REASON.
WHY WOULD THEY BELIEVE THAT KID WAS A TRAITOR?
SO WHAT?
IF IT WASN'T SCAFFA, IT WAS SOMEONE ELSE...
22

PIEDNOIR?

YOU AND I BOTH SAW THAT KID. DID HE SEEM LIKE A COLLABORATOR TO YOU?

NO, I...I DON'T KNOW. YOU'RE THE ONE WHO TOLD ME...

IT WAS *PIEDNOIR* WHO TOLD YOU...AND I HOPE IT'S TRUE. I HOPE THAT WE EXECUTED A LITTLE SHIT.

BUT *IF* LITTLE SCAFFA WAS INNOCENT...

...THEN IT MUST HAVE BEEN MR. JOSEPH.

STOP! IT WAS SCAFFA. OBVIOUSLY SCAFFA.

THEY WANT TO QUESTION JOSEPH. YOU AND I ARE SUPPOSED TO GO GET HIM TOGETHER.

IT'S AN *ORDER*, LUCIEN. WE DON'T HAVE A CHOICE.

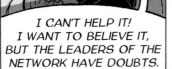
I CAN'T HELP IT! I WANT TO BELIEVE IT, BUT THE LEADERS OF THE NETWORK HAVE DOUBTS.

IT WORKED. I HAVE A MEETING WITH HIM IN TWO HOURS.

23

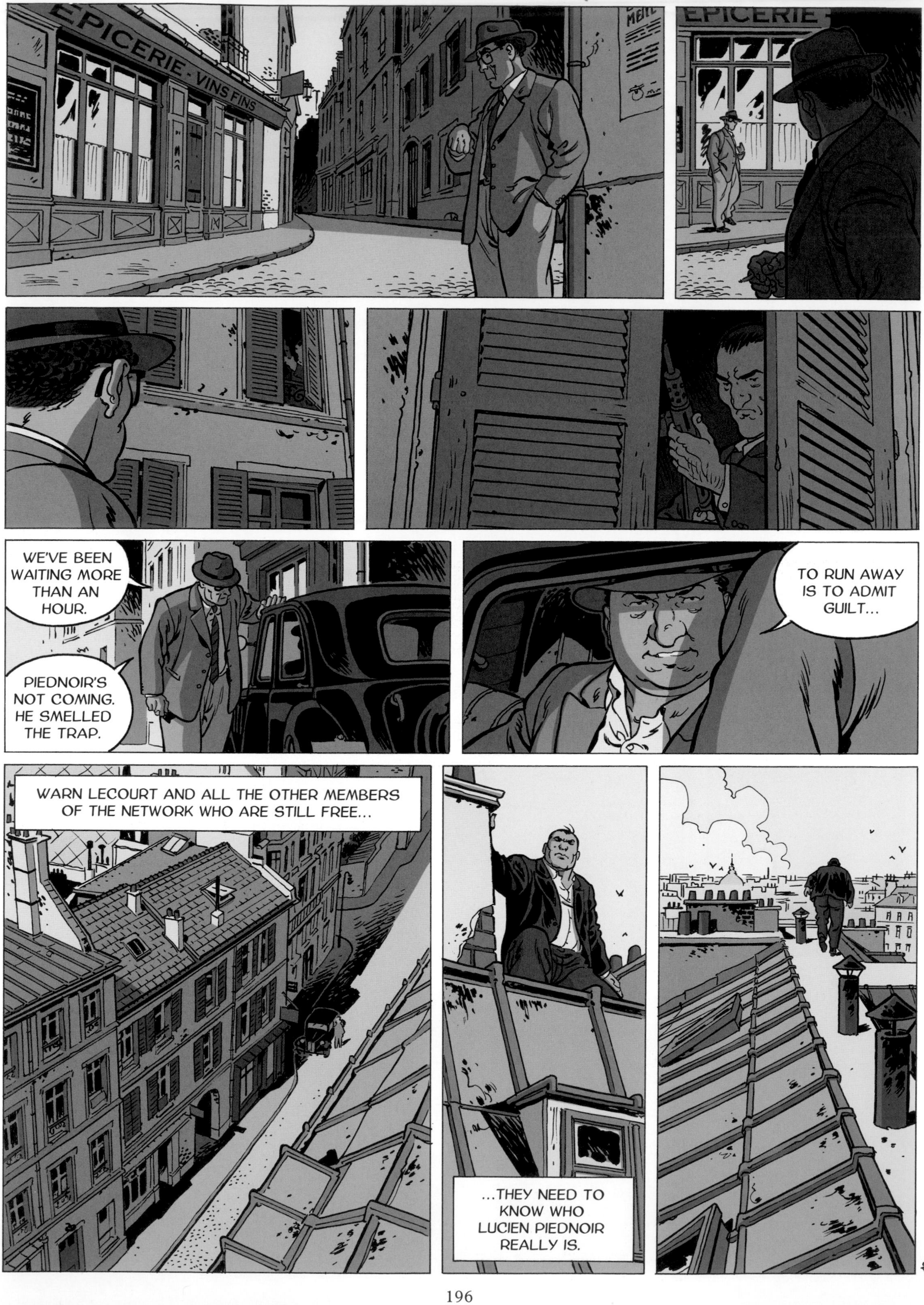

EPICERIE - VINS FINS
EPICERIE
WE'VE BEEN WAITING MORE THAN AN HOUR.
PIEDNOIR'S NOT COMING. HE SMELLED THE TRAP.
TO RUN AWAY IS TO ADMIT GUILT...
WARN LECOURT AND ALL THE OTHER MEMBERS OF THE NETWORK WHO ARE STILL FREE...
...THEY NEED TO KNOW WHO LUCIEN PIEDNOIR REALLY IS.

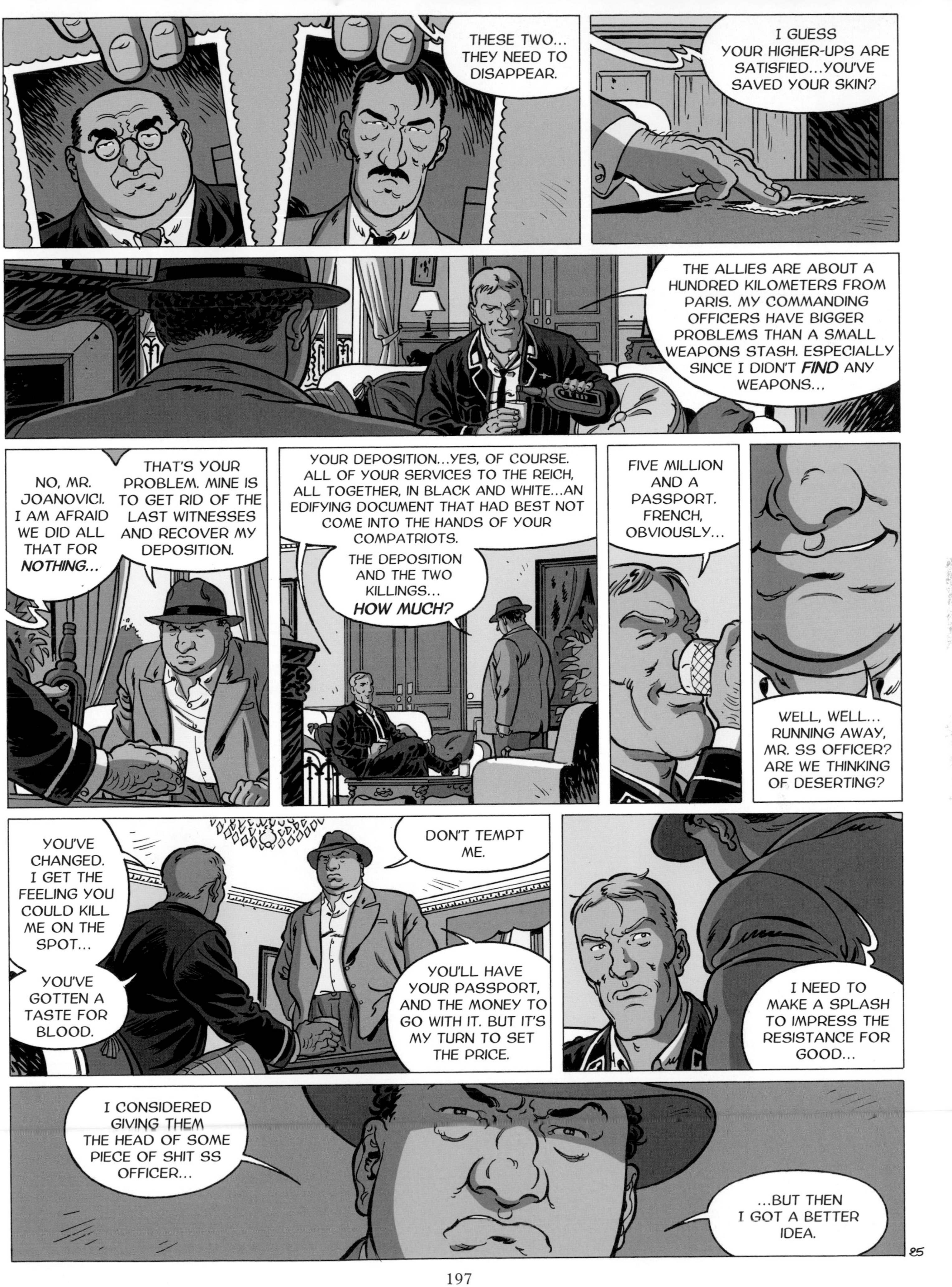
THESE TWO... THEY NEED TO DISAPPEAR.
I GUESS YOUR HIGHER-UPS ARE SATISFIED...YOU'VE SAVED YOUR SKIN?
THE ALLIES ARE ABOUT A HUNDRED KILOMETERS FROM PARIS. MY COMMANDING OFFICERS HAVE BIGGER PROBLEMS THAN A SMALL WEAPONS STASH. ESPECIALLY SINCE I DIDN'T *FIND* ANY WEAPONS...
NO, MR. JOANOVICI. I AM AFRAID WE DID ALL THAT FOR *NOTHING...*
THAT'S YOUR PROBLEM. MINE IS TO GET RID OF THE LAST WITNESSES AND RECOVER MY DEPOSITION.
YOUR DEPOSITION...YES, OF COURSE. ALL OF YOUR SERVICES TO THE REICH, ALL TOGETHER, IN BLACK AND WHITE...AN EDIFYING DOCUMENT THAT HAD BEST NOT COME INTO THE HANDS OF YOUR COMPATRIOTS.
THE DEPOSITION AND THE TWO KILLINGS... *HOW MUCH?*
FIVE MILLION AND A PASSPORT. FRENCH, OBVIOUSLY...
WELL, WELL... RUNNING AWAY, MR. SS OFFICER? ARE WE THINKING OF DESERTING?
YOU'VE CHANGED. I GET THE FEELING YOU COULD KILL ME ON THE SPOT...
DON'T TEMPT ME.
YOU'VE GOTTEN A TASTE FOR BLOOD.
YOU'LL HAVE YOUR PASSPORT, AND THE MONEY TO GO WITH IT. BUT IT'S MY TURN TO SET THE PRICE.
I NEED TO MAKE A SPLASH TO IMPRESS THE RESISTANCE FOR GOOD...
I CONSIDERED GIVING THEM THE HEAD OF SOME PIECE OF SHIT SS OFFICER...
...BUT THEN I GOT A BETTER IDEA.
25

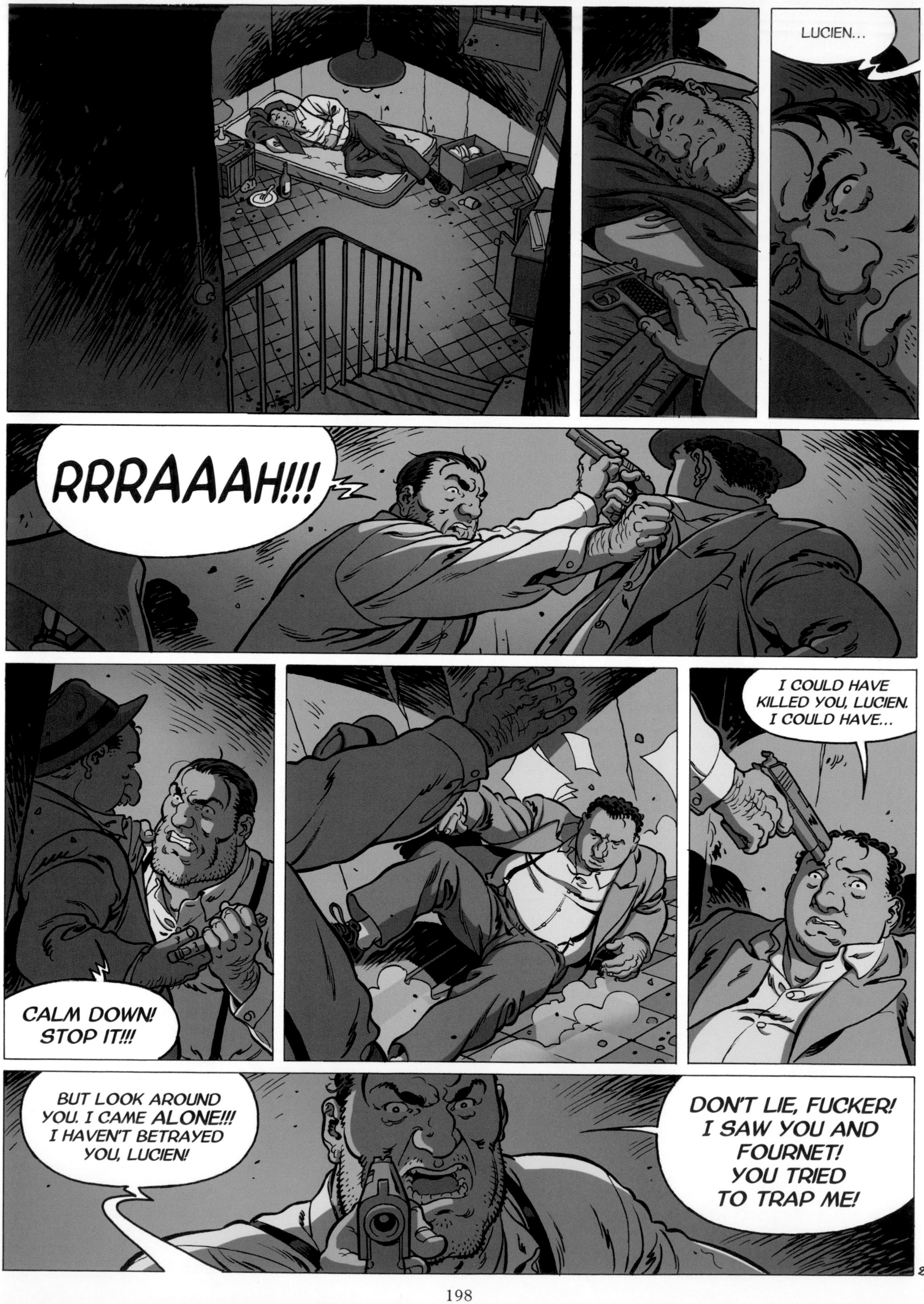
LUCIEN...
RRRAAAH!!!
CALM DOWN! STOP IT!!!
I COULD HAVE KILLED YOU, LUCIEN. I COULD HAVE...
BUT LOOK AROUND YOU. I CAME ALONE!!! I HAVEN'T BETRAYED YOU, LUCIEN!
DON'T LIE, FUCKER! I SAW YOU AND FOURNET! YOU TRIED TO TRAP ME!
26

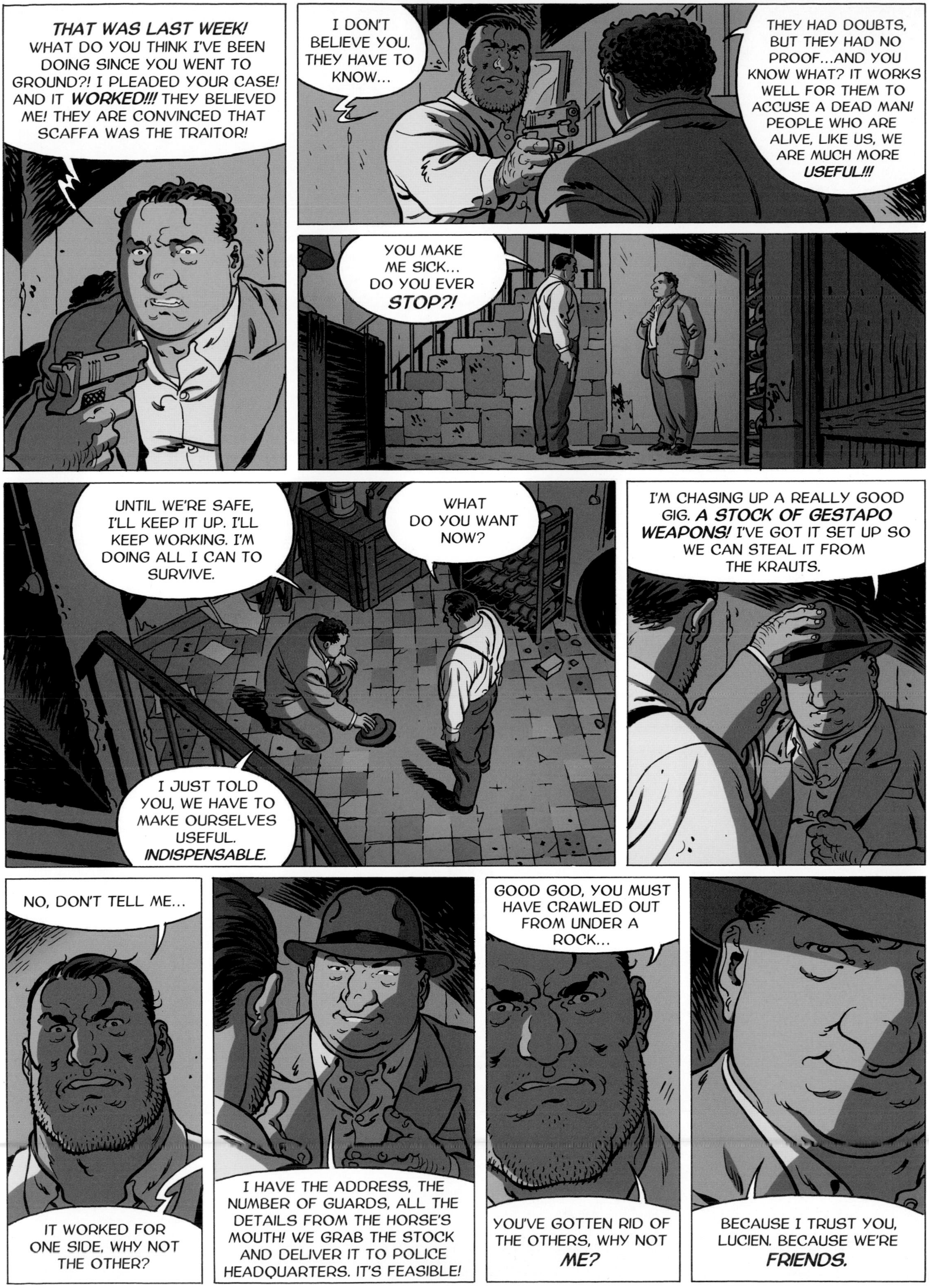
THAT WAS LAST WEEK! WHAT DO YOU THINK I'VE BEEN DOING SINCE YOU WENT TO GROUND?! I PLEADED YOUR CASE! AND IT WORKED!!! THEY BELIEVED ME! THEY ARE CONVINCED THAT SCAFFA WAS THE TRAITOR!
I DON'T BELIEVE YOU. THEY HAVE TO KNOW...
THEY HAD DOUBTS, BUT THEY HAD NO PROOF...AND YOU KNOW WHAT? IT WORKS WELL FOR THEM TO ACCUSE A DEAD MAN! PEOPLE WHO ARE ALIVE, LIKE US, WE ARE MUCH MORE USEFUL!!!
YOU MAKE ME SICK... DO YOU EVER STOP?!
UNTIL WE'RE SAFE, I'LL KEEP IT UP. I'LL KEEP WORKING. I'M DOING ALL I CAN TO SURVIVE.
WHAT DO YOU WANT NOW?
I JUST TOLD YOU, WE HAVE TO MAKE OURSELVES USEFUL. INDISPENSABLE.
I'M CHASING UP A REALLY GOOD GIG. A STOCK OF GESTAPO WEAPONS! I'VE GOT IT SET UP SO WE CAN STEAL IT FROM THE KRAUTS.
NO, DON'T TELL ME...
IT WORKED FOR ONE SIDE, WHY NOT THE OTHER?
I HAVE THE ADDRESS, THE NUMBER OF GUARDS, ALL THE DETAILS FROM THE HORSE'S MOUTH! WE GRAB THE STOCK AND DELIVER IT TO POLICE HEADQUARTERS. IT'S FEASIBLE!
GOOD GOD, YOU MUST HAVE CRAWLED OUT FROM UNDER A ROCK...
YOU'VE GOTTEN RID OF THE OTHERS, WHY NOT ME?
BECAUSE I TRUST YOU, LUCIEN. BECAUSE WE'RE FRIENDS.
27

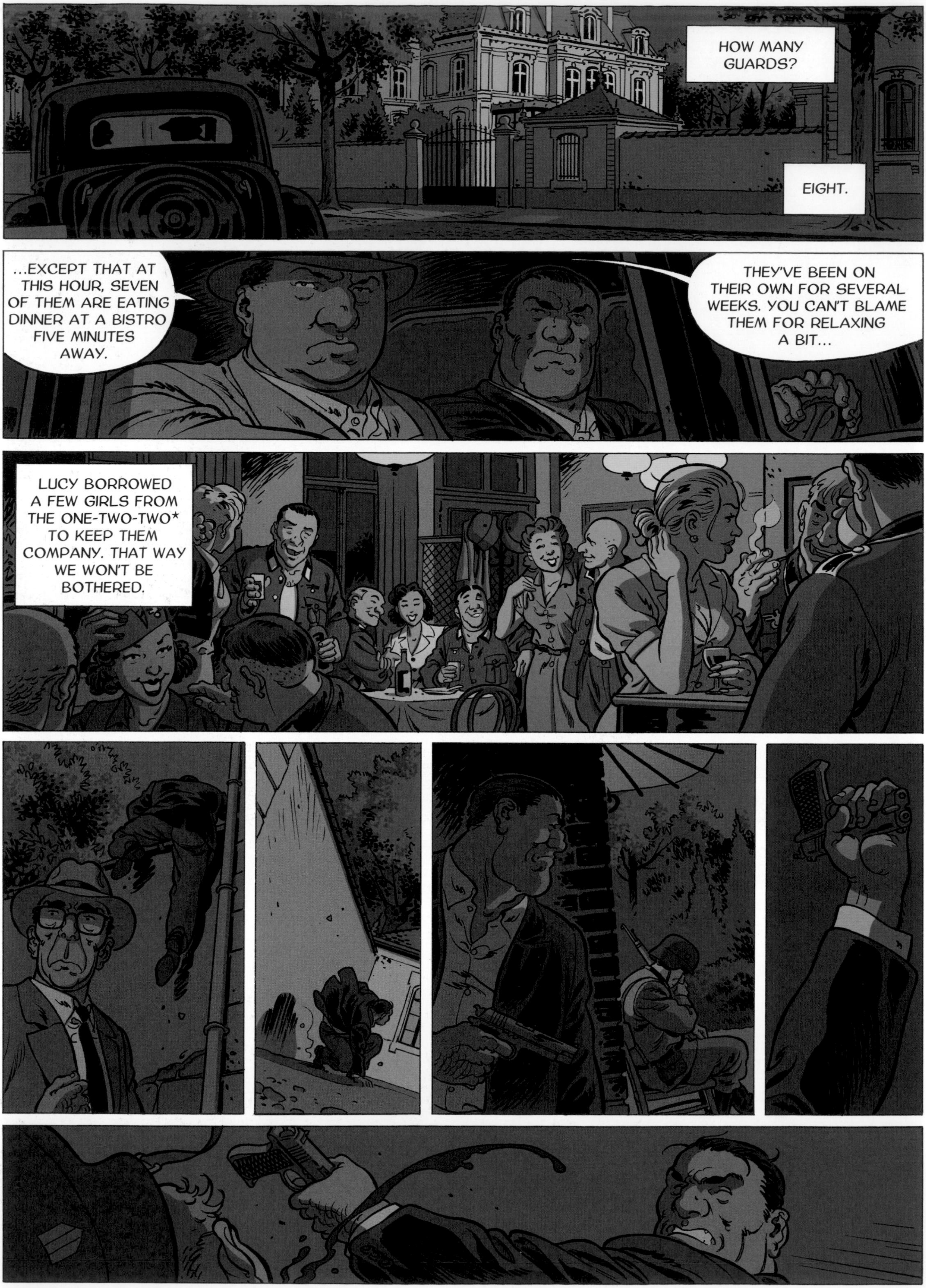
HOW MANY GUARDS?
EIGHT.
...EXCEPT THAT AT THIS HOUR, SEVEN OF THEM ARE EATING DINNER AT A BISTRO FIVE MINUTES AWAY.
THEY'VE BEEN ON THEIR OWN FOR SEVERAL WEEKS. YOU CAN'T BLAME THEM FOR RELAXING A BIT...
LUCY BORROWED A FEW GIRLS FROM THE ONE-TWO-TWO* TO KEEP THEM COMPANY. THAT WAY WE WON'T BE BOTHERED.

*A famous brothel for members of high society.

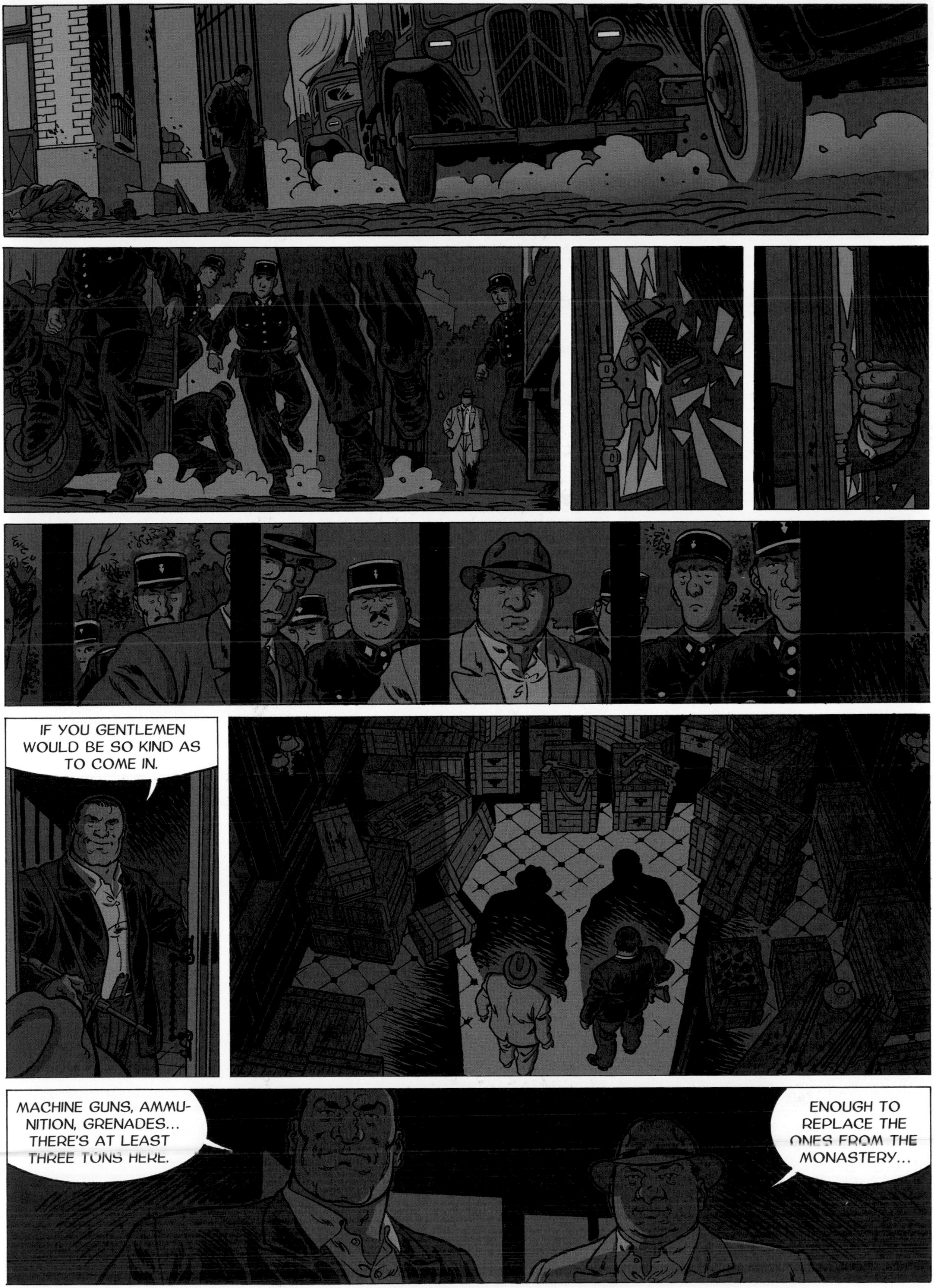

IF YOU GENTLEMEN WOULD BE SO KIND AS TO COME IN.
MACHINE GUNS, AMMUNITION, GRENADES... THERE'S AT LEAST THREE TONS HERE.
ENOUGH TO REPLACE THE ONES FROM THE MONASTERY...
29

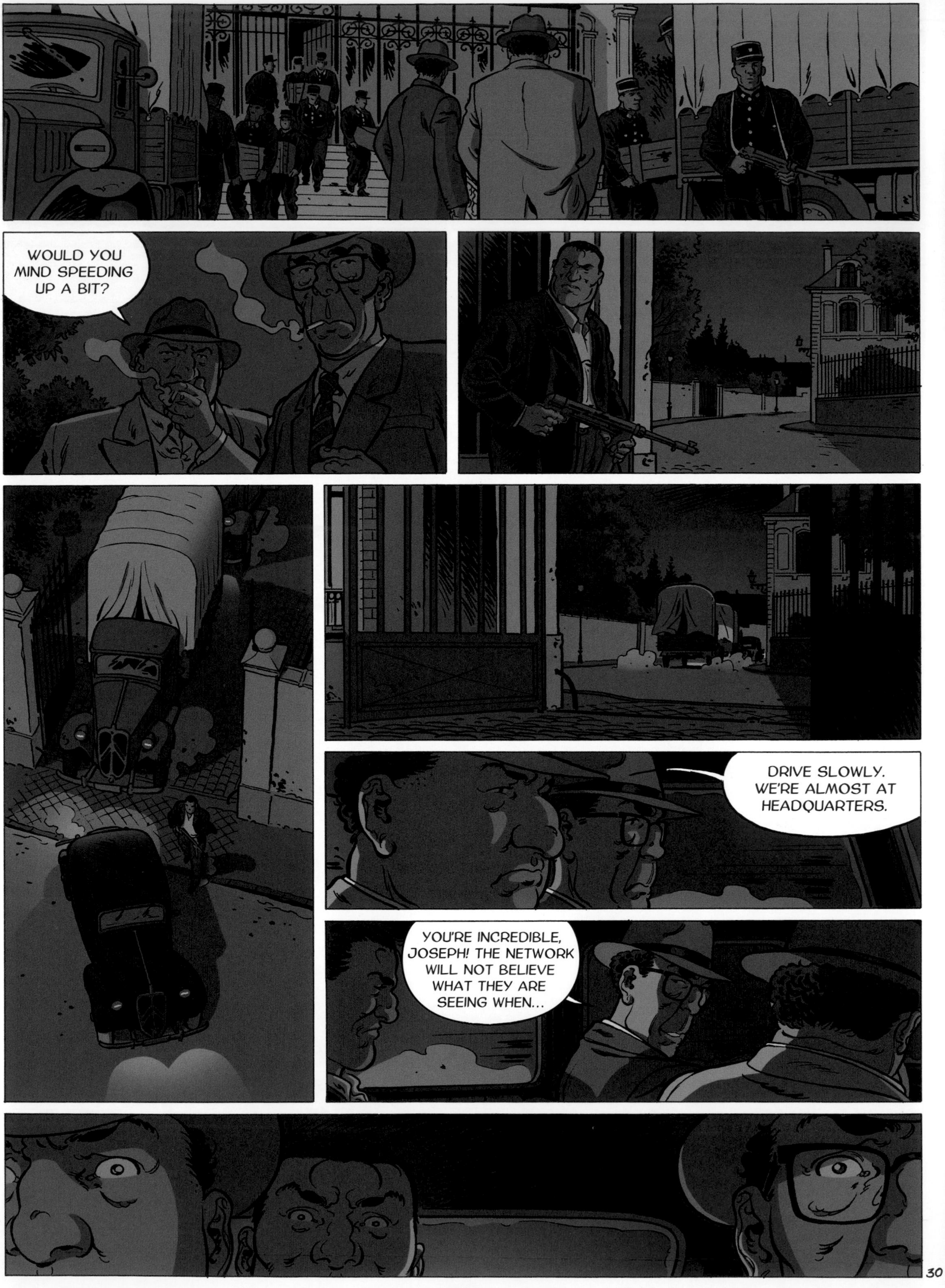
WOULD YOU MIND SPEEDING UP A BIT?
DRIVE SLOWLY. WE'RE ALMOST AT HEADQUARTERS.
YOU'RE INCREDIBLE, JOSEPH! THE NETWORK WILL NOT BELIEVE WHAT THEY ARE SEEING WHEN...
30

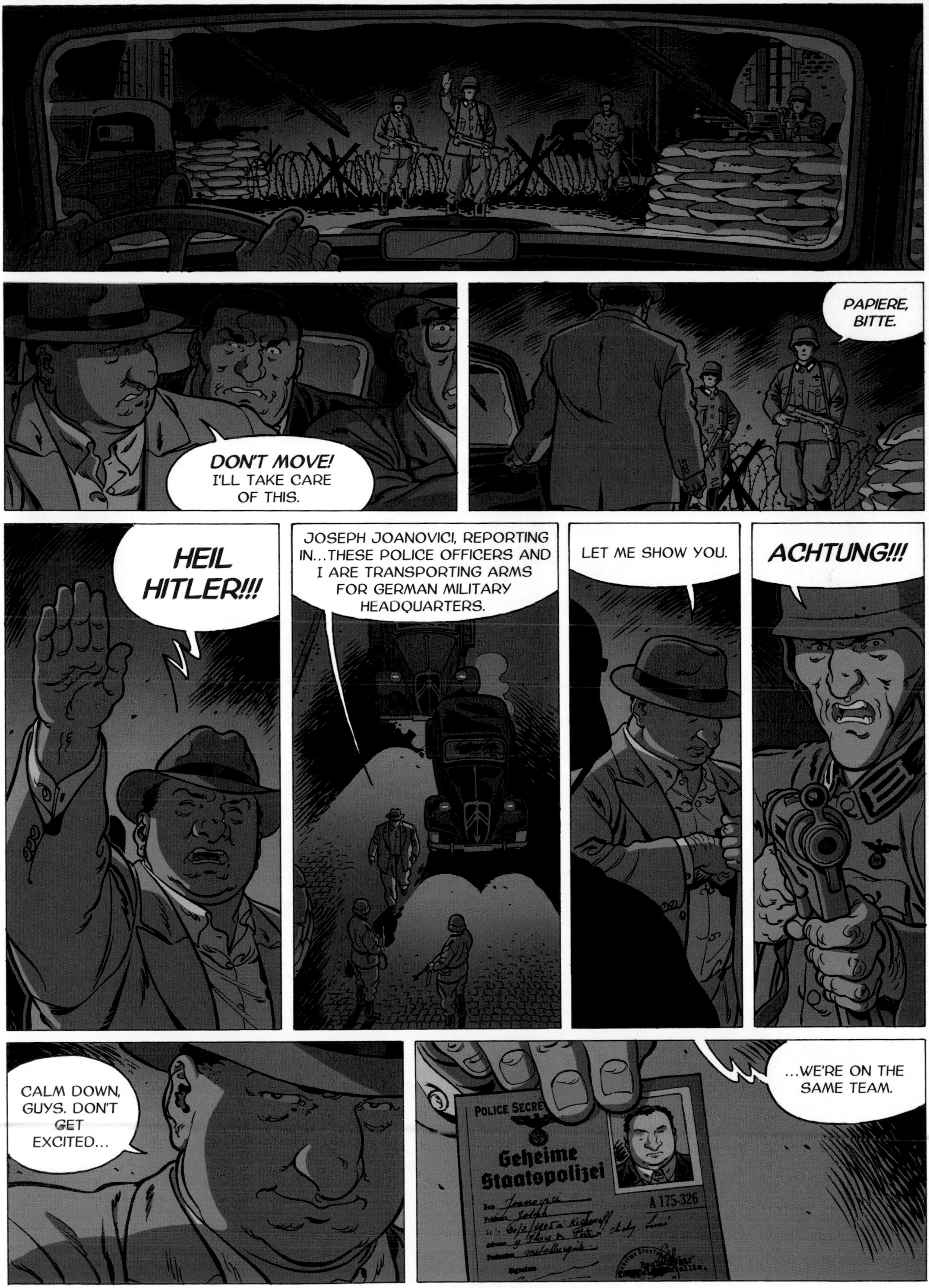
DON'T MOVE! I'LL TAKE CARE OF THIS.
PAPIERE, BITTE.
HEIL HITLER!!!
JOSEPH JOANOVICI, REPORTING IN...THESE POLICE OFFICERS AND I ARE TRANSPORTING ARMS FOR GERMAN MILITARY HEADQUARTERS.
LET ME SHOW YOU.
ACHTUNG!!!
CALM DOWN, GUYS. DON'T GET EXCITED...
...WE'RE ON THE SAME TEAM.
POLICE SECRE
Geheime Staatspolizei
A 175-326

31

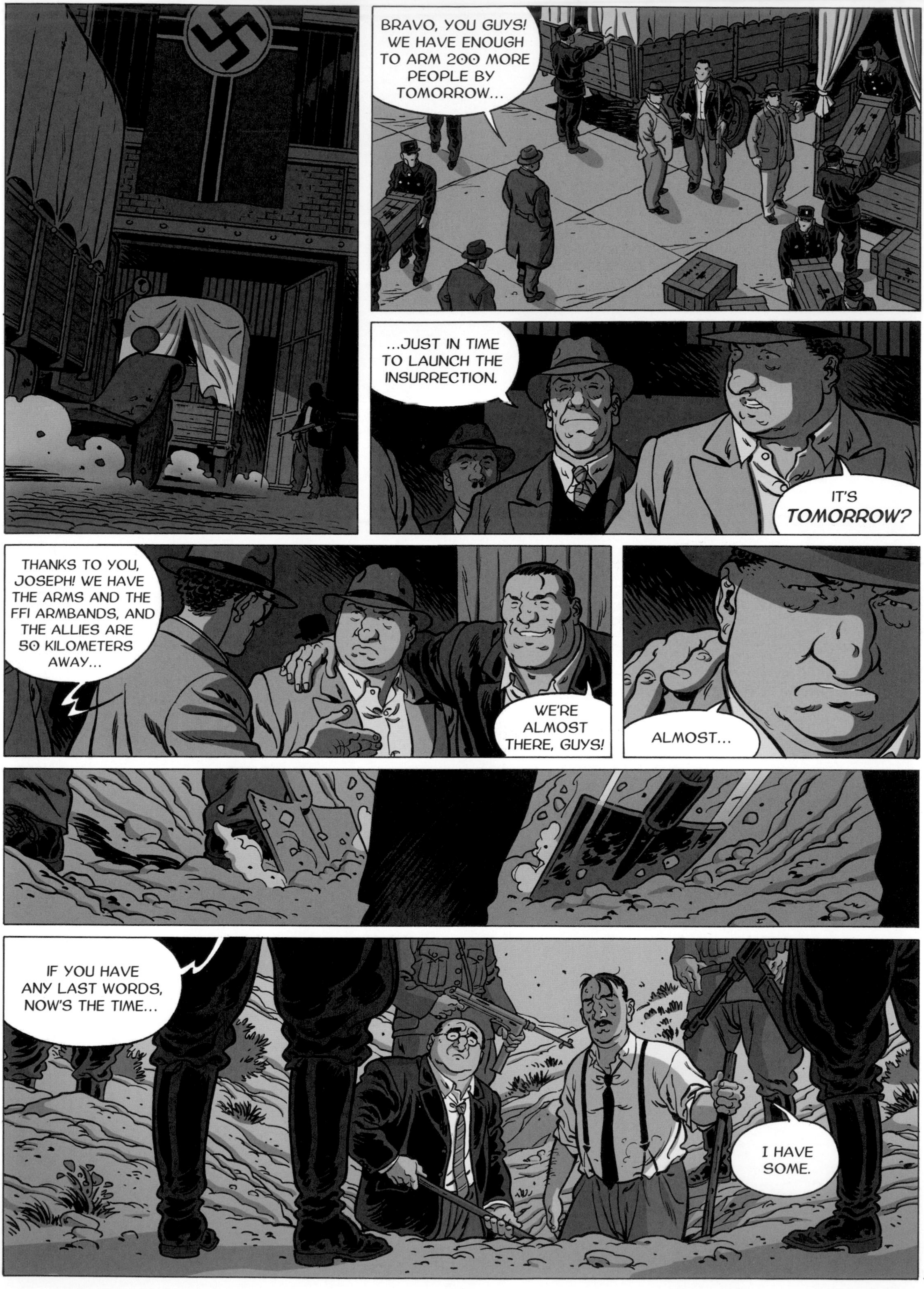
BRAVO, YOU GUYS! WE HAVE ENOUGH TO ARM 200 MORE PEOPLE BY TOMORROW...
...JUST IN TIME TO LAUNCH THE INSURRECTION.
IT'S *TOMORROW?*
THANKS TO YOU, JOSEPH! WE HAVE THE ARMS AND THE FFI ARMBANDS, AND THE ALLIES ARE 50 KILOMETERS AWAY...
WE'RE ALMOST THERE, GUYS!
ALMOST...
IF YOU HAVE ANY LAST WORDS, NOW'S THE TIME...
I HAVE SOME.
32

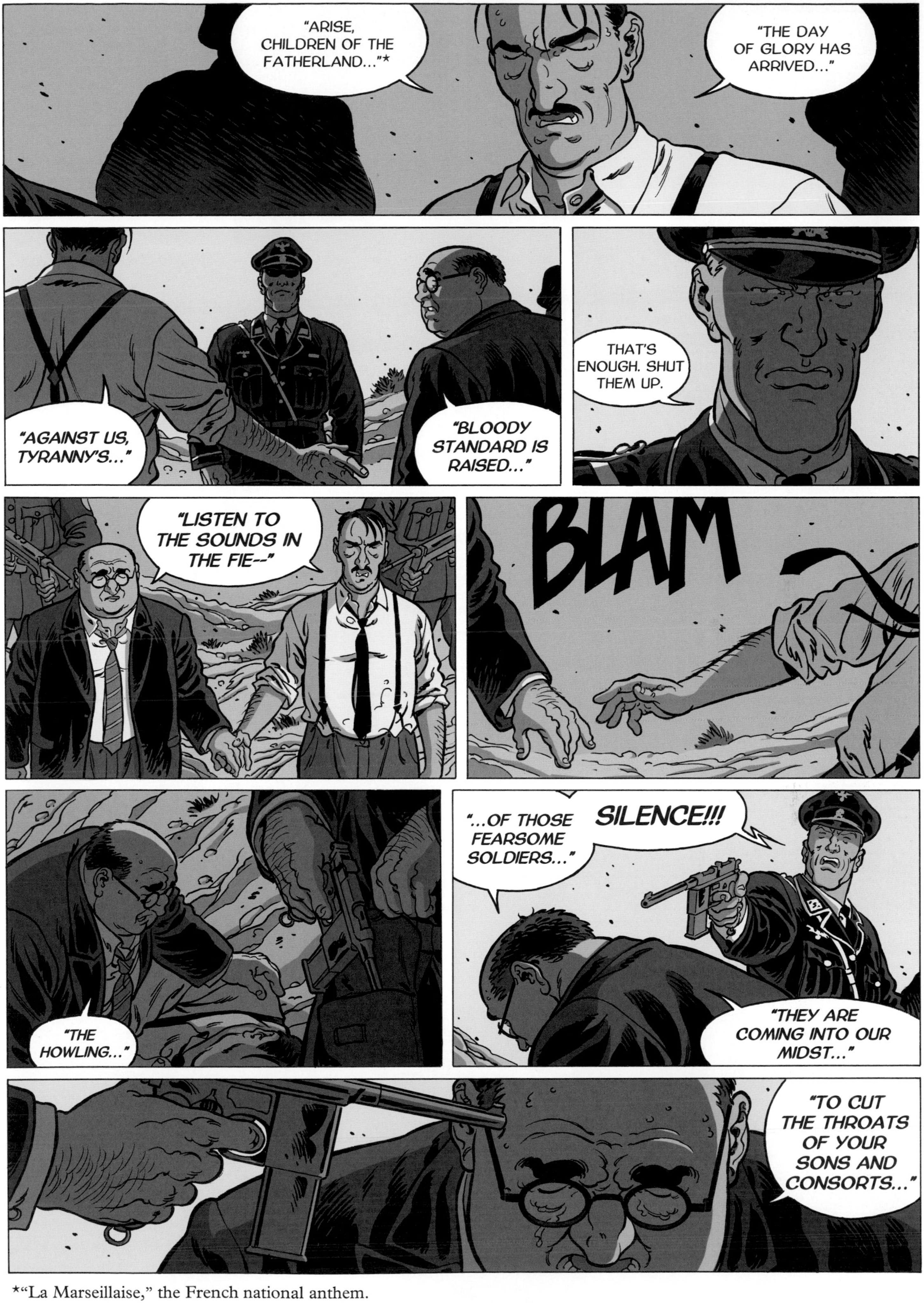
"ARISE, CHILDREN OF THE FATHERLAND..."*
"THE DAY OF GLORY HAS ARRIVED..."
"AGAINST US, TYRANNY'S..."
"BLOODY STANDARD IS RAISED..."
THAT'S ENOUGH. SHUT THEM UP.
"LISTEN TO THE SOUNDS IN THE FIE--"
BLAM
"THE HOWLING..."
"...OF THOSE FEARSOME SOLDIERS..."
SILENCE!!!
"THEY ARE COMING INTO OUR MIDST..."
"TO CUT THE THROATS OF YOUR SONS AND CONSORTS..."

*"La Marseillaise," the French national anthem.

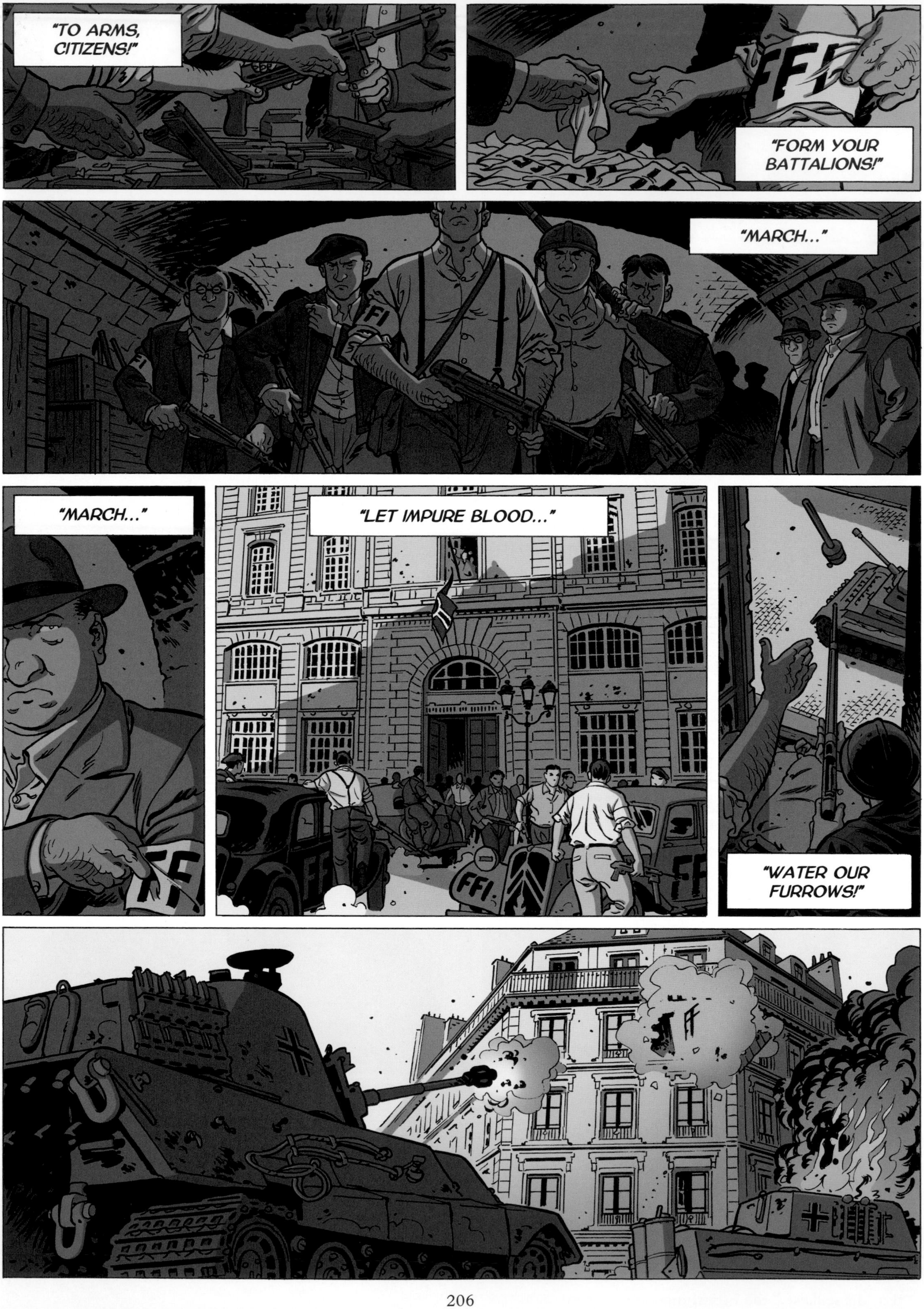
"TO ARMS, CITIZENS!"
"FORM YOUR BATTALIONS!"
FFI
"MARCH..."
FFI
"MARCH..."
FF
"LET IMPURE BLOOD..."
FFI
FF
"WATER OUR FURROWS!"
34

THE ROLE OF THE FFI IS TO OPEN THE ROAD TO PARIS FOR THE ALLIED TROOPS AND LEAD THE INSURRECTION THROUGHOUT THE CAPITAL...

THE ALLIES ARE BLOCKED AT CHARTRES. FROM WHAT I HAVE HEARD, THEY PLAN ON GOING AROUND PARIS.

WE HAVE TO HOLD ON! MULTIPLY THE SKIRMISHES IN EVERY QUARTER!

TOO SOON. WE STARTED TOO SOON!

HOLD ON WITH WHAT?! WE HAVE SHORTAGES OF EVERYTHING! WE WON'T HOLD TWO DAYS WITH THE AMMUNITION WE HAVE...THE KRAUTS HAVE MACHINE GUNS...AND OUR MEN ARE *ON FOOT!*

MAYBE WE CAN FIX THAT.

COME ON, GUYS! TWO DRIVERS PER TRUCK!

HEAD STRAIGHT FOR POLICE HEADQUARTERS AND ROUND UP ALL THE VOLUNTEERS YOU CAN FIND...

...THEN HEAD FOR LA CHAPELLE, LES BATIGNOLLES, LES GOBELINS... EVERYWHERE THERE'S FIGHTING!

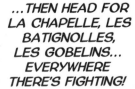

WELL DONE, JOSEPH. THIS WAY WE CAN BRING REINFORCEMENTS WHEREVER THEY'RE NEEDED.

WHAT'S THE POINT IF ALL THEY HAVE IS THEIR BALLS AND A KNIFE?

35

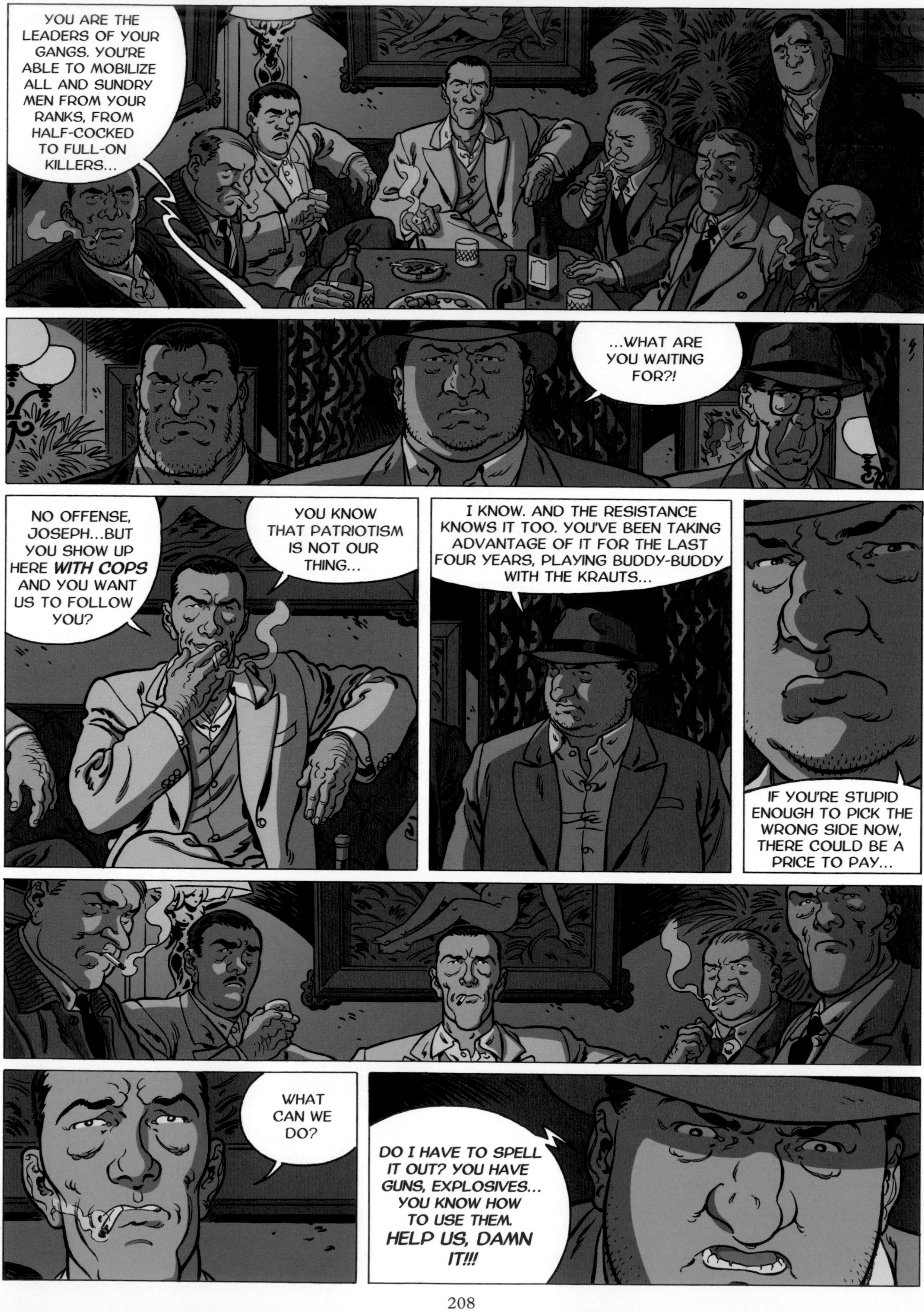
YOU ARE THE LEADERS OF YOUR GANGS. YOU'RE ABLE TO MOBILIZE ALL AND SUNDRY MEN FROM YOUR RANKS, FROM HALF-COCKED TO FULL-ON KILLERS...
...WHAT ARE YOU WAITING FOR?!
NO OFFENSE, JOSEPH...BUT YOU SHOW UP HERE WITH COPS AND YOU WANT US TO FOLLOW YOU?
YOU KNOW THAT PATRIOTISM IS NOT OUR THING...
I KNOW. AND THE RESISTANCE KNOWS IT TOO. YOU'VE BEEN TAKING ADVANTAGE OF IT FOR THE LAST FOUR YEARS, PLAYING BUDDY-BUDDY WITH THE KRAUTS...
IF YOU'RE STUPID ENOUGH TO PICK THE WRONG SIDE NOW, THERE COULD BE A PRICE TO PAY...
WHAT CAN WE DO?
DO I HAVE TO SPELL IT OUT? YOU HAVE GUNS, EXPLOSIVES... YOU KNOW HOW TO USE THEM. HELP US, DAMN IT!!!
36

THIS WAY, GENTS! I'LL GIVE YOU YOUR ASSIGNMENTS...

TALK ABOUT AN ELITE GROUP...

IT'S BETTER THAN NOTHING.

BOUCHESEICHE. COME HERE.

I HAVE A JOB FOR YOU. A *PAYING* JOB.

APPEAL

To the Paris police, the Republican Guard, the Gendarmerie, the Mobile Guard, the GMR, and the prison guards.

The hour of liberation has come.

APPEAL

To the Paris police, the Republican Guard, the Gendarmerie, the GMR, and the prison guards.

The hour of liberation has come.

YOU KNOW LUCY, MY SECRETARY.

SHE HAS A MEETING TONIGHT WITH A GUY NAMED KORF...YOU'VE COME ACROSS HIM TOO, I'M SURE.

KORF, FROM THE SS? YES, WE'VE HAD A COUPLE OF MEALS TOGETHER...

GREAT. I WANT YOU TO FOLLOW LUCY TO THE MEETING POINT. SHE'LL GIVE YOU THE DETAILS. YOU LET HER DO HER BUSINESS WITH KORF...

...AND THEN YOU DO YOUR PATRIOTIC DUTY...

KILL THE BASTARD FOR ME.

37

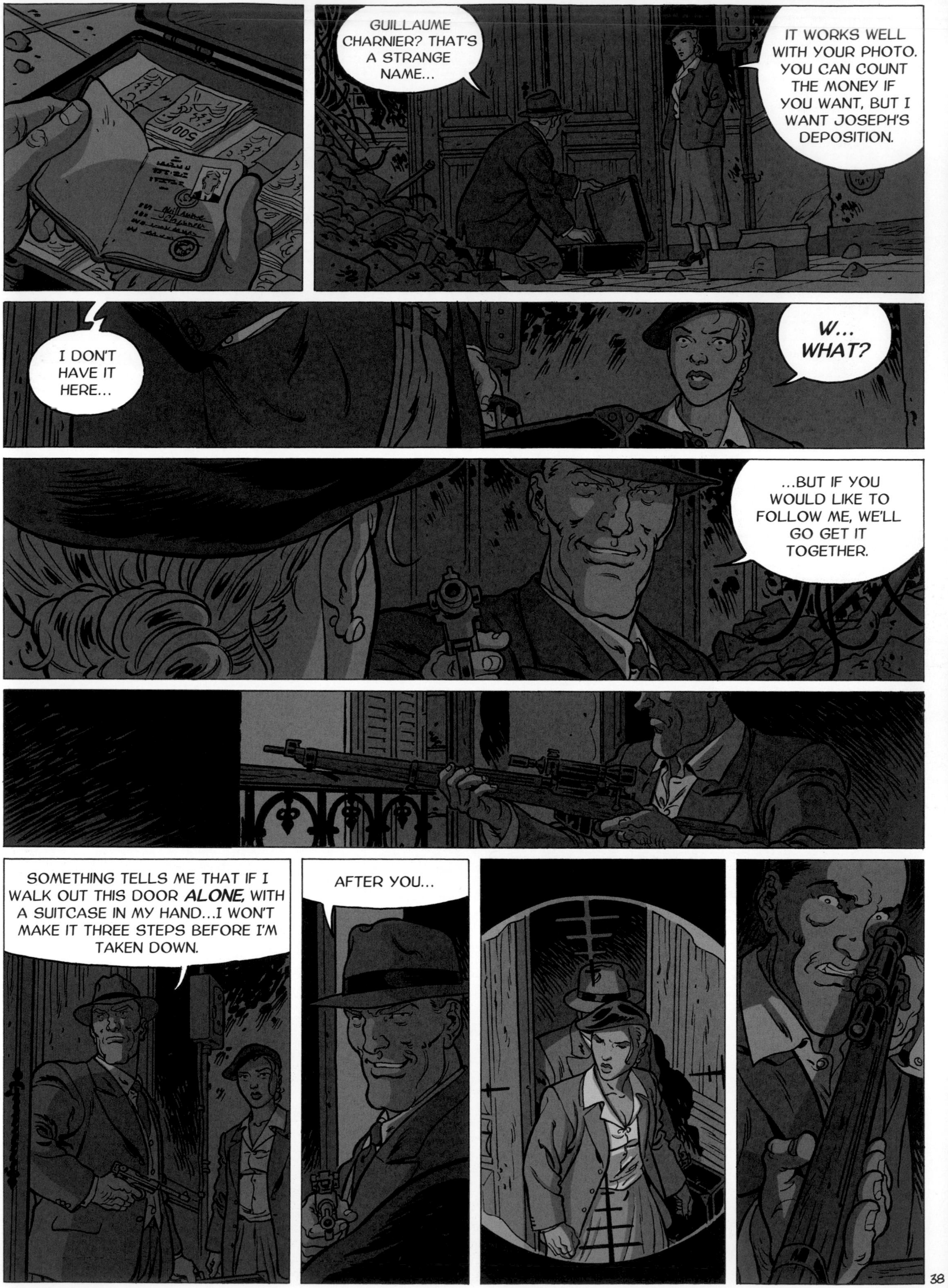
GUILLAUME CHARNIER? THAT'S A STRANGE NAME...
IT WORKS WELL WITH YOUR PHOTO. YOU CAN COUNT THE MONEY IF YOU WANT, BUT I WANT JOSEPH'S DEPOSITION.
I DON'T HAVE IT HERE...
W... WHAT?
...BUT IF YOU WOULD LIKE TO FOLLOW ME, WE'LL GO GET IT TOGETHER.
SOMETHING TELLS ME THAT IF I WALK OUT THIS DOOR ALONE, WITH A SUITCASE IN MY HAND...I WON'T MAKE IT THREE STEPS BEFORE I'M TAKEN DOWN.
AFTER YOU...
38

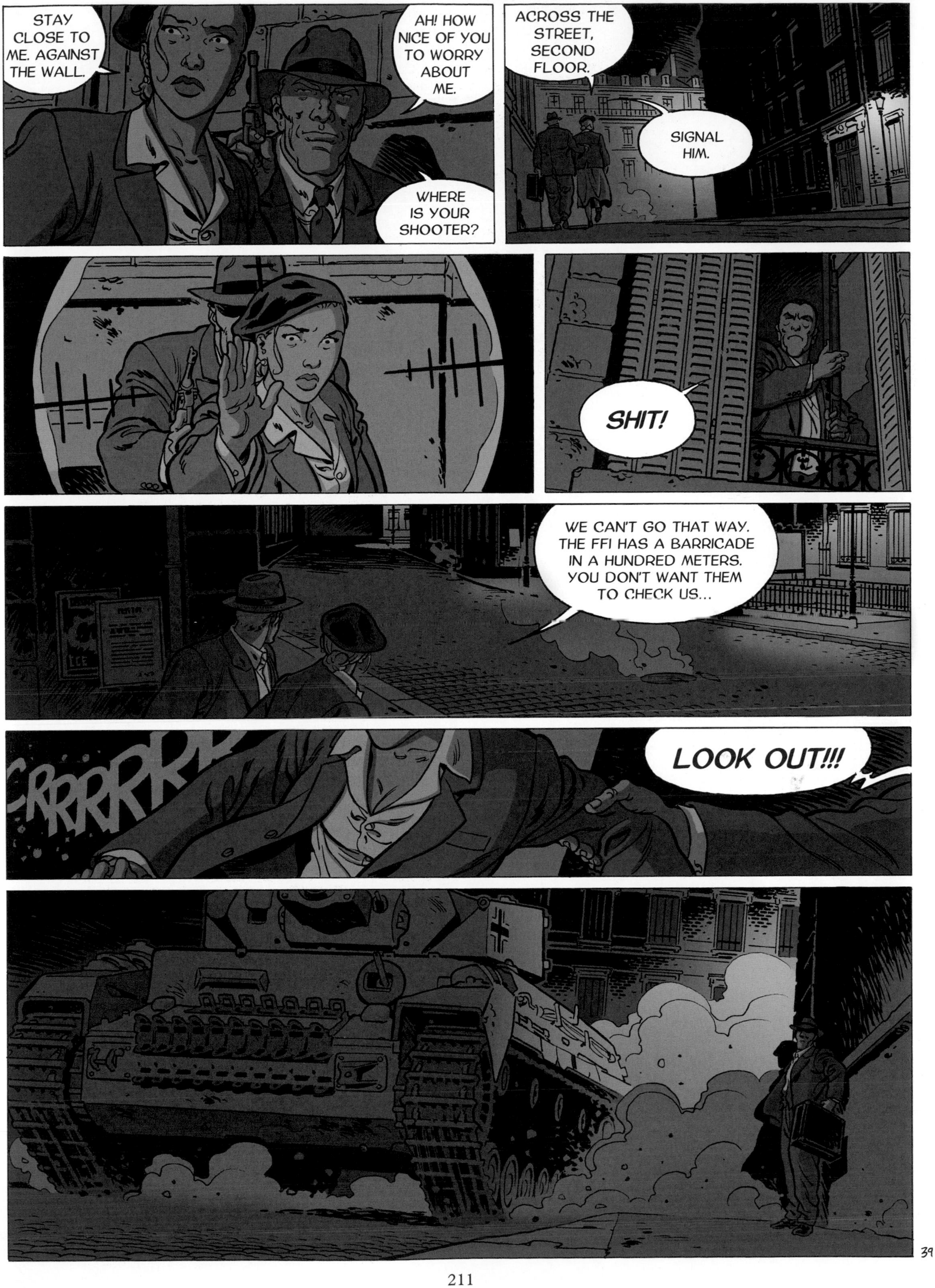
STAY CLOSE TO ME. AGAINST THE WALL.
AH! HOW NICE OF YOU TO WORRY ABOUT ME.
WHERE IS YOUR SHOOTER?
ACROSS THE STREET, SECOND FLOOR.
SIGNAL HIM.
SHIT!
WE CAN'T GO THAT WAY. THE FFI HAS A BARRICADE IN A HUNDRED METERS. YOU DON'T WANT THEM TO CHECK US...
CRRRRR
LOOK OUT!!!
39

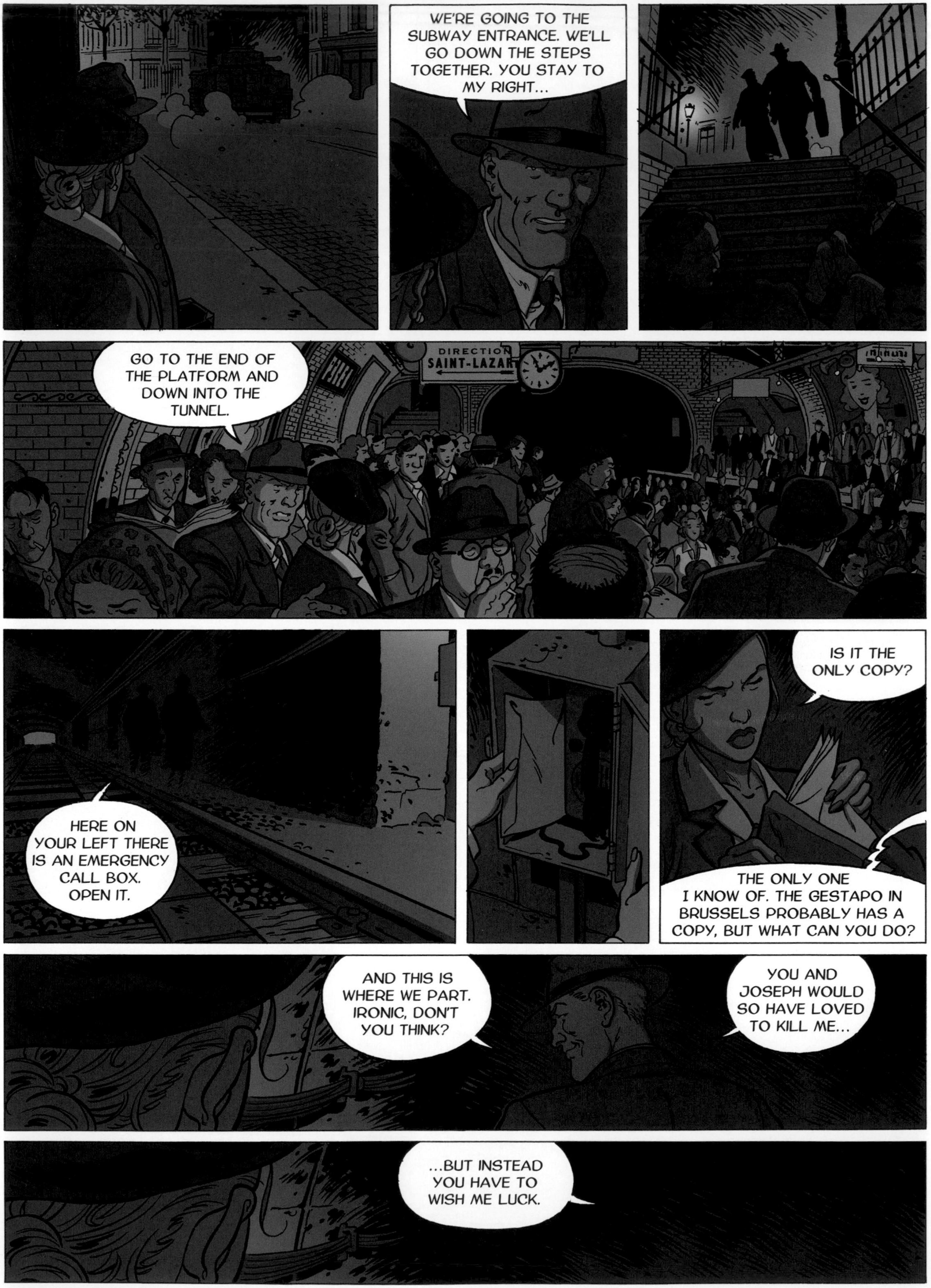
WE'RE GOING TO THE SUBWAY ENTRANCE. WE'LL GO DOWN THE STEPS TOGETHER. YOU STAY TO MY RIGHT...
GO TO THE END OF THE PLATFORM AND DOWN INTO THE TUNNEL.
DIRECTION SAINT-LAZAR
HERE ON YOUR LEFT THERE IS AN EMERGENCY CALL BOX. OPEN IT.
IS IT THE ONLY COPY?
THE ONLY ONE I KNOW OF. THE GESTAPO IN BRUSSELS PROBABLY HAS A COPY, BUT WHAT CAN YOU DO?
AND THIS IS WHERE WE PART. IRONIC, DON'T YOU THINK?
YOU AND JOSEPH WOULD SO HAVE LOVED TO KILL ME...
...BUT INSTEAD YOU HAVE TO WISH ME LUCK.
40

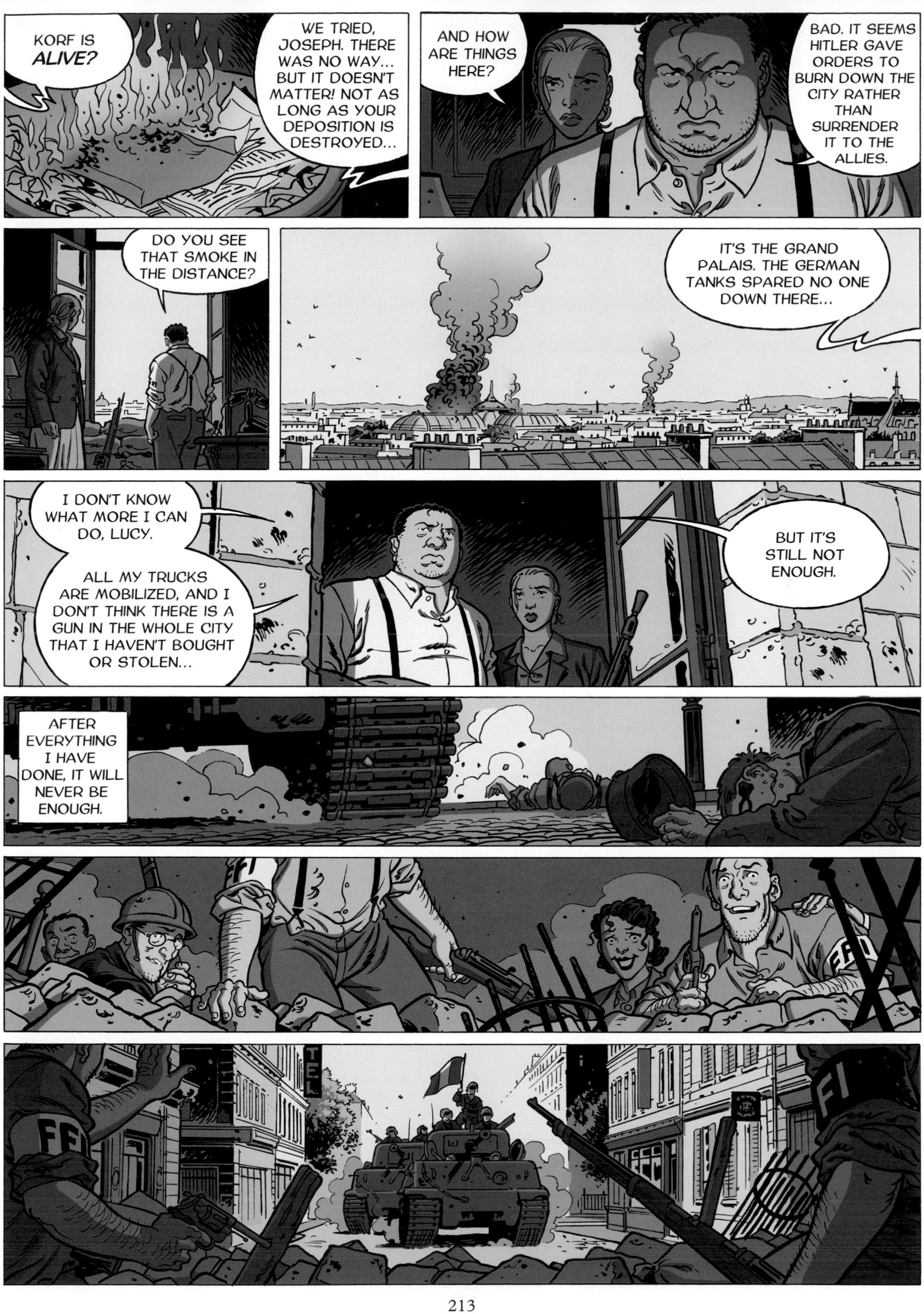
KORF IS *ALIVE?*
WE TRIED, JOSEPH. THERE WAS NO WAY... BUT IT DOESN'T MATTER! NOT AS LONG AS YOUR DEPOSITION IS DESTROYED...
AND HOW ARE THINGS HERE?
BAD. IT SEEMS HITLER GAVE ORDERS TO BURN DOWN THE CITY RATHER THAN SURRENDER IT TO THE ALLIES.
DO YOU SEE THAT SMOKE IN THE DISTANCE?
IT'S THE GRAND PALAIS. THE GERMAN TANKS SPARED NO ONE DOWN THERE...
I DON'T KNOW WHAT MORE I CAN DO, LUCY.
ALL MY TRUCKS ARE MOBILIZED, AND I DON'T THINK THERE IS A GUN IN THE WHOLE CITY THAT I HAVEN'T BOUGHT OR STOLEN...
BUT IT'S STILL NOT ENOUGH.
AFTER EVERYTHING I HAVE DONE, IT WILL NEVER BE ENOUGH.
FFI
TEL
FFI
FI
41

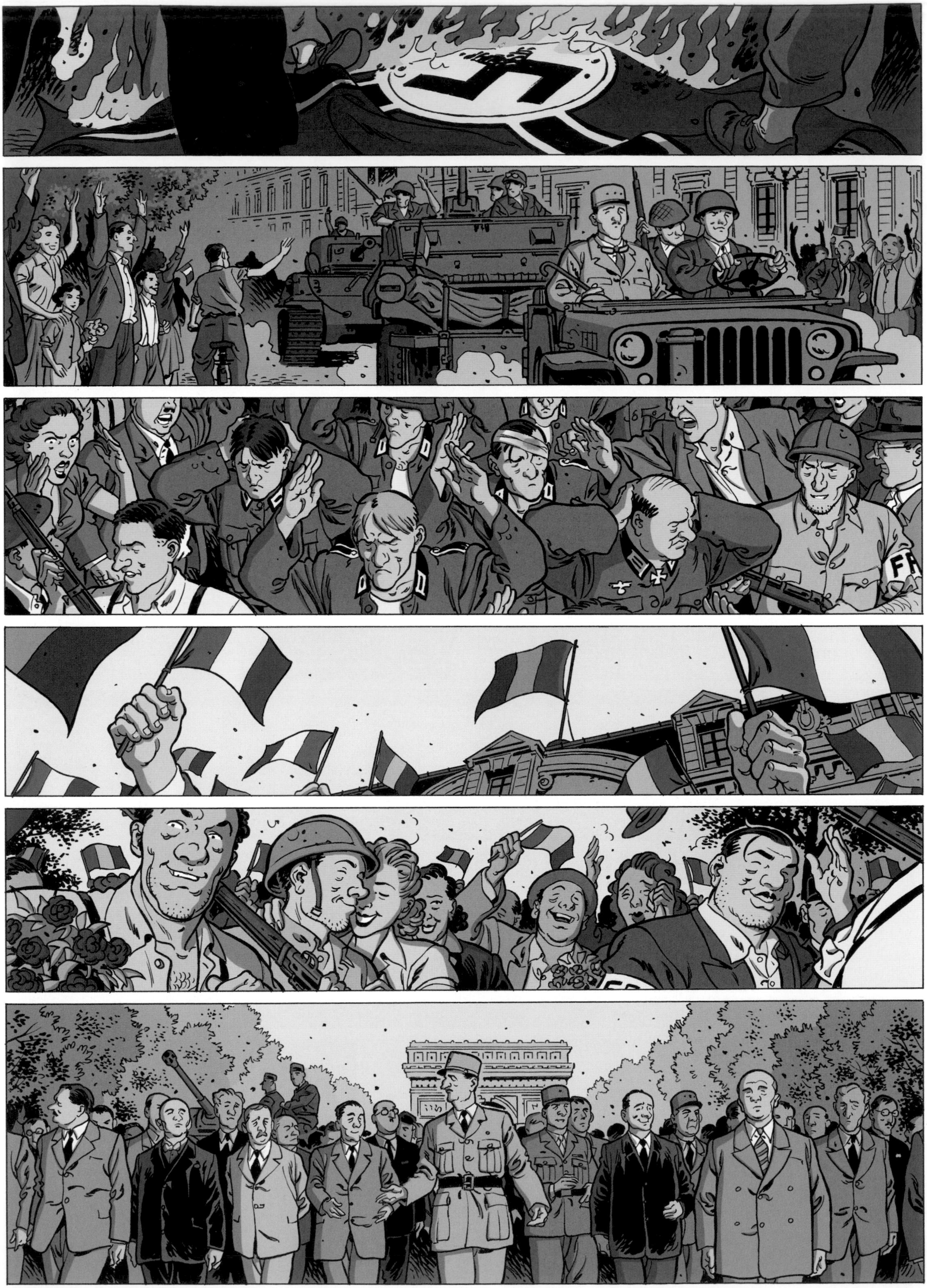

42

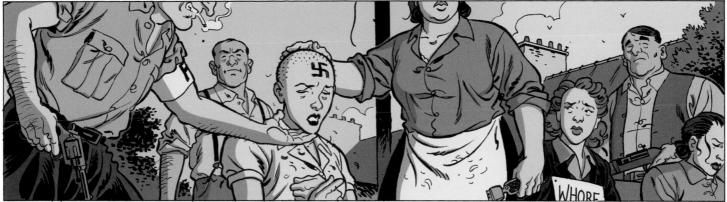

WHORE

LOOK AT THEM, LUCY. LOOK AT WHAT THESE GOOD PEOPLE ARE DOING TO THEM.

AND ALL THEY'RE ACCUSING THEM OF IS SPREADING THEIR LEGS...

...WHAT DO YOU THINK THEY'LL DO *TO US?*

43

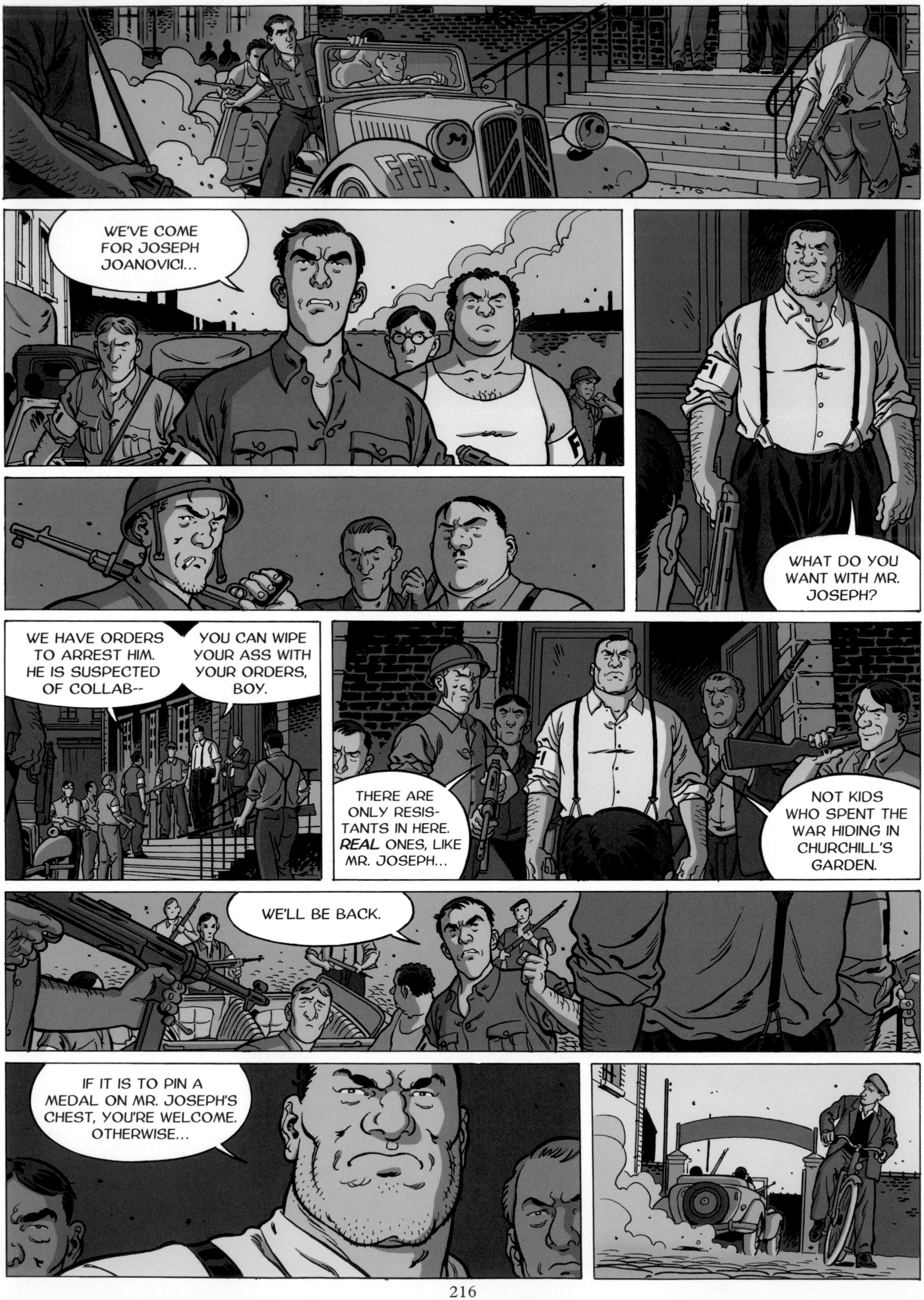
WE'VE COME FOR JOSEPH JOANOVICI...
FFI
WHAT DO YOU WANT WITH MR. JOSEPH?
WE HAVE ORDERS TO ARREST HIM. HE IS SUSPECTED OF COLLAB--
YOU CAN WIPE YOUR ASS WITH YOUR ORDERS, BOY.
THERE ARE ONLY RESISTANTS IN HERE. ***REAL*** ONES, LIKE MR. JOSEPH...
NOT KIDS WHO SPENT THE WAR HIDING IN CHURCHILL'S GARDEN.
WE'LL BE BACK.
IF IT IS TO PIN A MEDAL ON MR. JOSEPH'S CHEST, YOU'RE WELCOME. OTHERWISE...
44

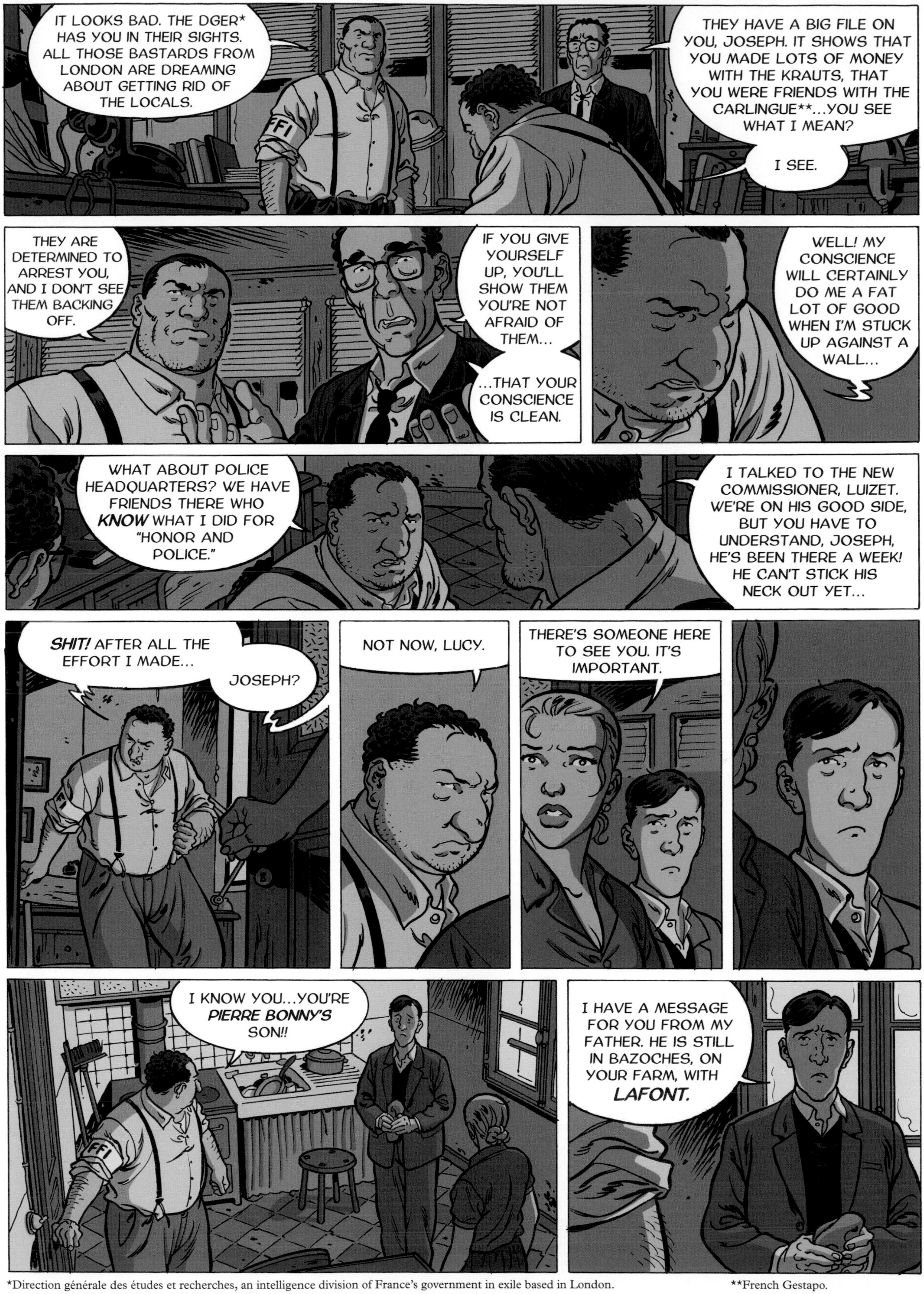

IT LOOKS BAD. THE DGER* HAS YOU IN THEIR SIGHTS. ALL THOSE BASTARDS FROM LONDON ARE DREAMING ABOUT GETTING RID OF THE LOCALS.
FFI
THEY HAVE A BIG FILE ON YOU, JOSEPH. IT SHOWS THAT YOU MADE LOTS OF MONEY WITH THE KRAUTS, THAT YOU WERE FRIENDS WITH THE CARLINGUE**...YOU SEE WHAT I MEAN?
I SEE.
THEY ARE DETERMINED TO ARREST YOU, AND I DON'T SEE THEM BACKING OFF.
IF YOU GIVE YOURSELF UP, YOU'LL SHOW THEM YOU'RE NOT AFRAID OF THEM...
...THAT YOUR CONSCIENCE IS CLEAN.
WELL! MY CONSCIENCE WILL CERTAINLY DO ME A FAT LOT OF GOOD WHEN I'M STUCK UP AGAINST A WALL...
WHAT ABOUT POLICE HEADQUARTERS? WE HAVE FRIENDS THERE WHO KNOW WHAT I DID FOR "HONOR AND POLICE."
I TALKED TO THE NEW COMMISSIONER, LUIZET. WE'RE ON HIS GOOD SIDE, BUT YOU HAVE TO UNDERSTAND, JOSEPH, HE'S BEEN THERE A WEEK! HE CAN'T STICK HIS NECK OUT YET...
SHIT! AFTER ALL THE EFFORT I MADE...
JOSEPH?
NOT NOW, LUCY.
THERE'S SOMEONE HERE TO SEE YOU. IT'S IMPORTANT.
I KNOW YOU...YOU'RE PIERRE BONNY'S SON!!
FFI
I HAVE A MESSAGE FOR YOU FROM MY FATHER. HE IS STILL IN BAZOCHES, ON YOUR FARM, WITH LAFONT.

*Direction générale des études et recherches, an intelligence division of France's government in exile based in London.

**French Gestapo.

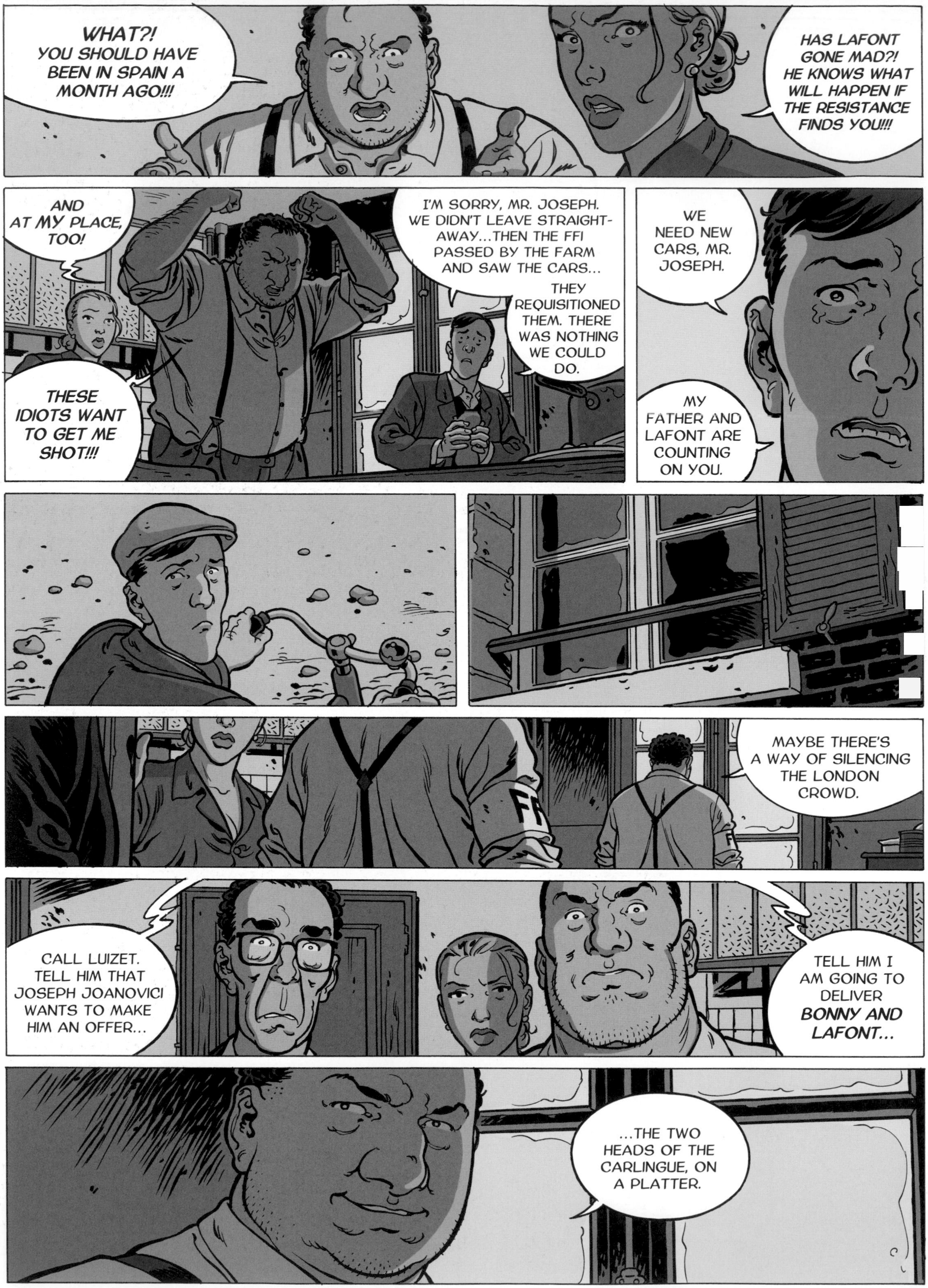
WHAT?! YOU SHOULD HAVE BEEN IN SPAIN A MONTH AGO!!!
HAS LAFONT GONE MAD?! HE KNOWS WHAT WILL HAPPEN IF THE RESISTANCE FINDS YOU!!!
AND AT MY PLACE, TOO!
THESE IDIOTS WANT TO GET ME SHOT!!!
I'M SORRY, MR. JOSEPH. WE DIDN'T LEAVE STRAIGHT-AWAY...THEN THE FFI PASSED BY THE FARM AND SAW THE CARS...
THEY REQUISITIONED THEM. THERE WAS NOTHING WE COULD DO.
WE NEED NEW CARS, MR. JOSEPH.
MY FATHER AND LAFONT ARE COUNTING ON YOU.
FFI
MAYBE THERE'S A WAY OF SILENCING THE LONDON CROWD.
CALL LUIZET. TELL HIM THAT JOSEPH JOANOVICI WANTS TO MAKE HIM AN OFFER...
TELL HIM I AM GOING TO DELIVER BONNY AND LAFONT...
...THE TWO HEADS OF THE CARLINGUE, ON A PLATTER.
46

THEY'RE STILL THERE. I JUST SAW BONNY.

WHAT DO WE DO? DO WE ALL GO IN AT ONCE?

NO. I'LL GO IN *ALONE* AND CONVINCE THEM TO SURRENDER.

ARE YOU *CRAZY?*

WHAT'S IT TO YOU? IF THEY SHOOT ME YOU CAN ALWAYS SOUND THE ALARM, COMMISSIONER...

...BUT IF YOU TAKE THEM ALIVE, THE PLEASURE WILL LAST FOR WEEKS OR MONTHS...THEY ARE ENTITLED TO A VERY *PUBLIC TRIAL...*

...SO ALL OF FRANCE WILL KNOW JUSTICE HAS BEEN SERVED.

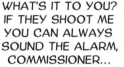

47

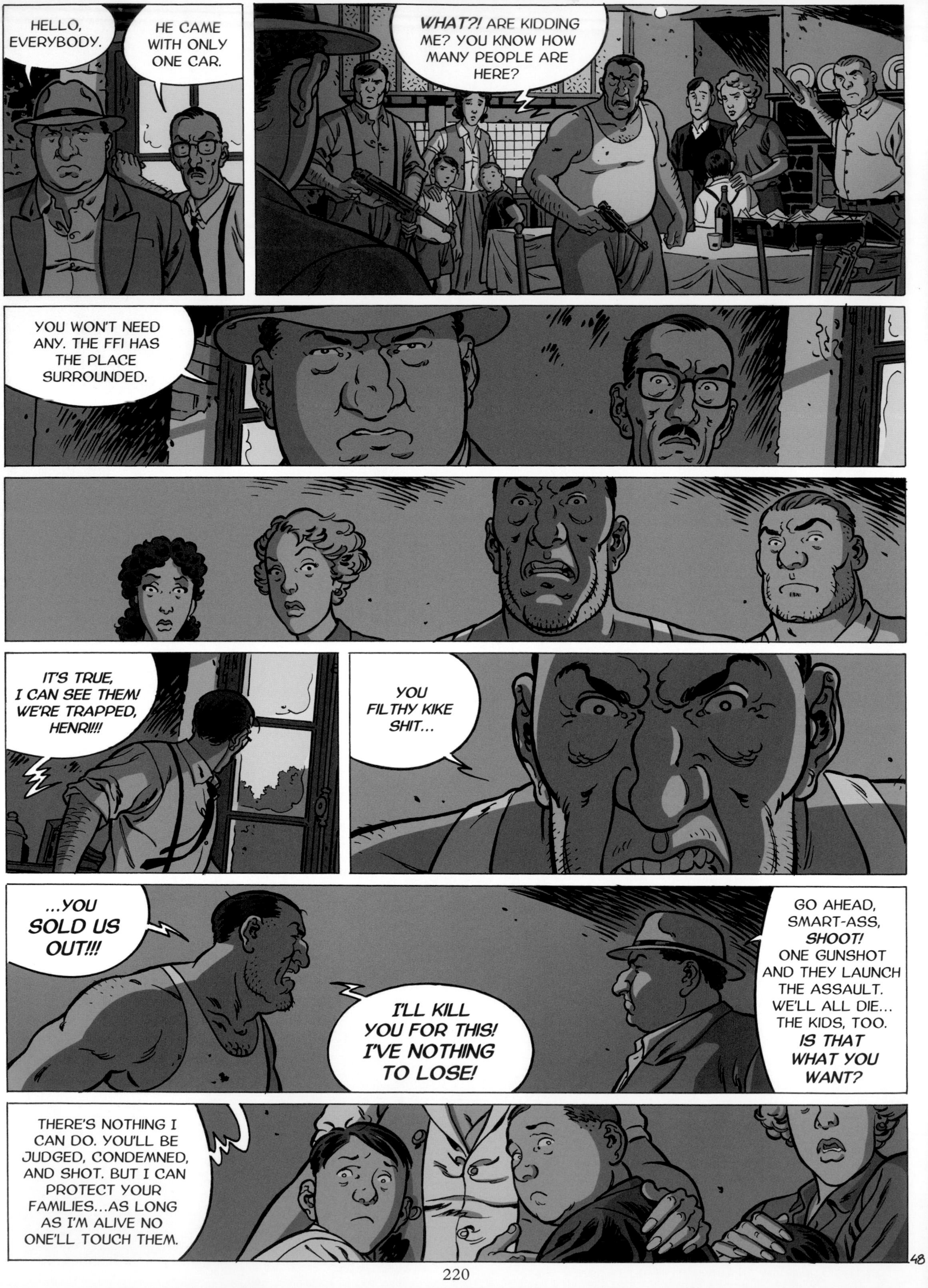
HELLO, EVERYBODY.
HE CAME WITH ONLY ONE CAR.
WHAT?! ARE KIDDING ME? YOU KNOW HOW MANY PEOPLE ARE HERE?
YOU WON'T NEED ANY. THE FFI HAS THE PLACE SURROUNDED.
IT'S TRUE, I CAN SEE THEM! WE'RE TRAPPED, HENRI!!!
YOU FILTHY KIKE SHIT...
...YOU SOLD US OUT!!!
I'LL KILL YOU FOR THIS! I'VE NOTHING TO LOSE!
GO AHEAD, SMART-ASS, SHOOT! ONE GUNSHOT AND THEY LAUNCH THE ASSAULT. WE'LL ALL DIE... THE KIDS, TOO. IS THAT WHAT YOU WANT?
THERE'S NOTHING I CAN DO. YOU'LL BE JUDGED, CONDEMNED, AND SHOT. BUT I CAN PROTECT YOUR FAMILIES...AS LONG AS I'M ALIVE NO ONE'LL TOUCH THEM.
48

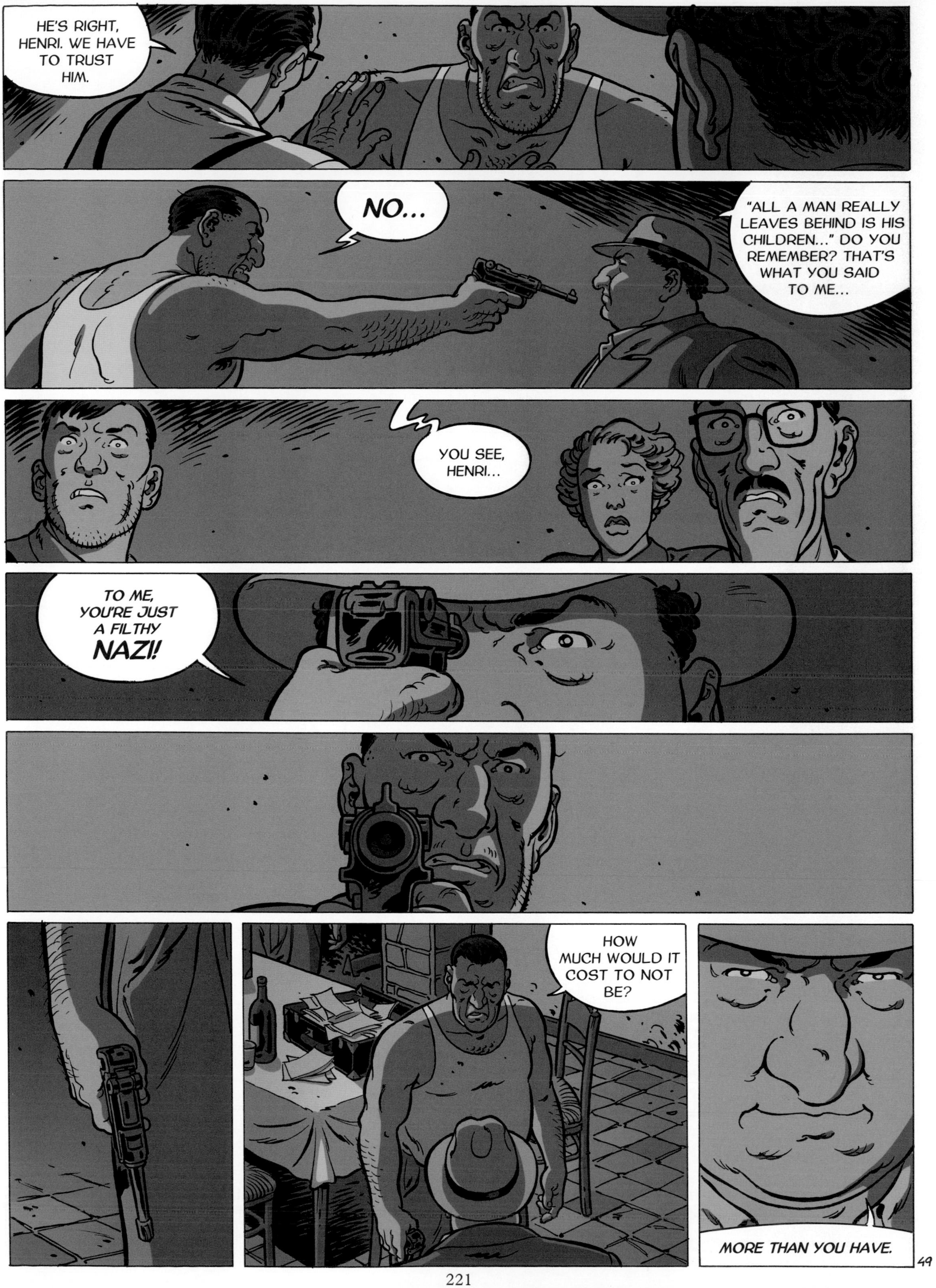
HE'S RIGHT, HENRI. WE HAVE TO TRUST HIM.
NO...
"ALL A MAN REALLY LEAVES BEHIND IS HIS CHILDREN..." DO YOU REMEMBER? THAT'S WHAT YOU SAID TO ME...
YOU SEE, HENRI...
TO ME, YOU'RE JUST A FILTHY NAZI!
HOW MUCH WOULD IT COST TO NOT BE?
MORE THAN YOU HAVE.
49

BONNY, WAIT.

YOU SAID THAT YOU HAVE *A FILE* ON ME. IF YOU WANT THIS ARRANGEMENT TO HOLD, I NEED TO HAVE THAT.

WE BURNED IT. WE TRUSTED YOU, JOSEPH.

CONGRATU-LATIONS... COMMISSIONER.

a Liberté

Edition du 5 septembre 1

BONNY AND LAFONT BEHIND BARS

Two "Bosses" of the Parisian Gestapo Arrested Yesterday Morning.

C'est dans une modeste ferme de Bazoches-sur-le-Betz que les sinistres Henri Chamberlain, dit "Lafont" et l'ancien inspecteur de police Pierre Bonny se terraient, avec femmes et enfants, depuis la libération de la capitale. Hier à l'aube

...AND COMMISSIONER LUIZET SAID: "THE ARREST WAS MOSTLY THANKS TO THE COURAGE AND THE SELFLESSNESS OF MR. JOSEPH."

50

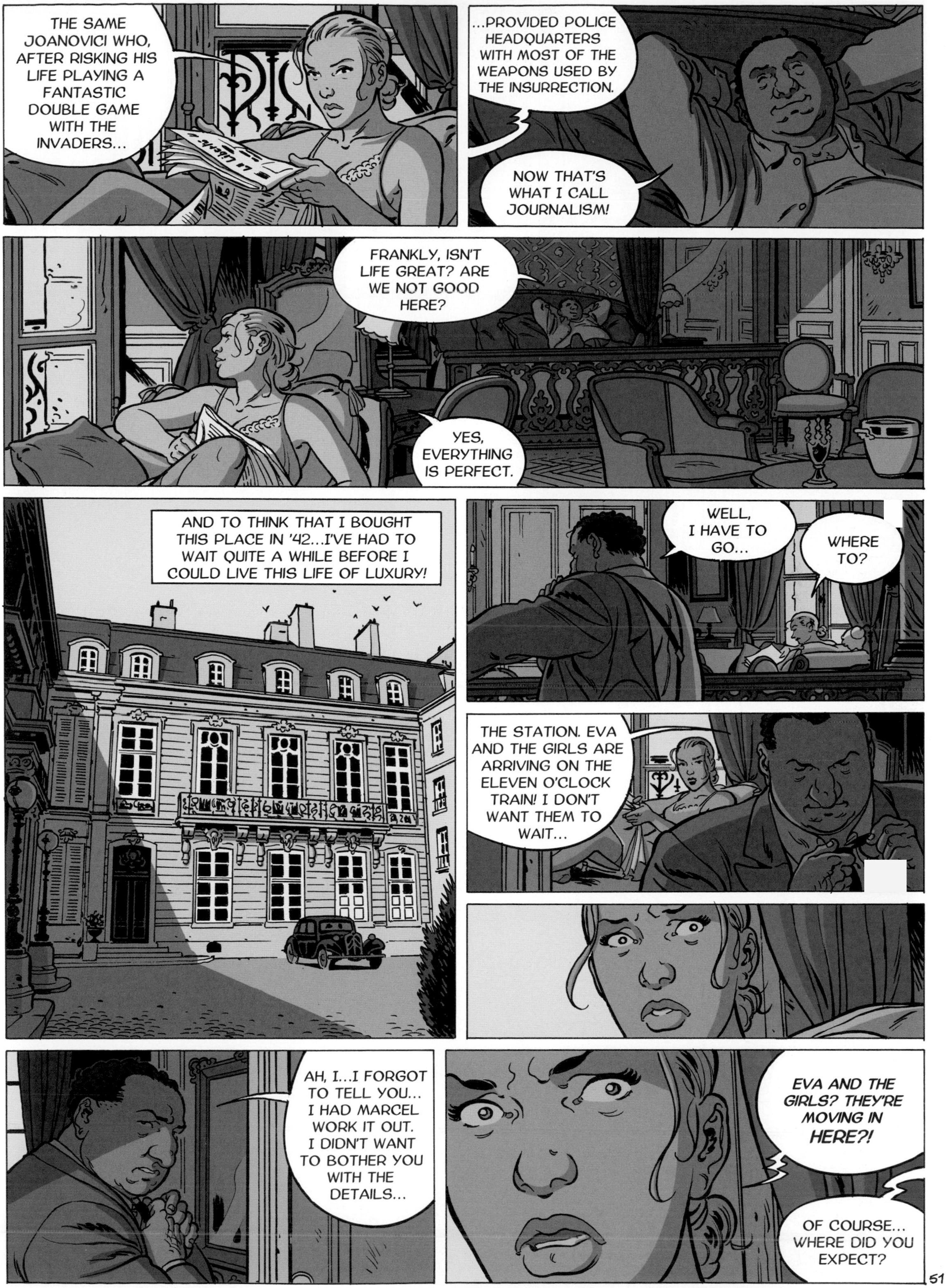
THE SAME JOANOVICI WHO, AFTER RISKING HIS LIFE PLAYING A FANTASTIC DOUBLE GAME WITH THE INVADERS...
...PROVIDED POLICE HEADQUARTERS WITH MOST OF THE WEAPONS USED BY THE INSURRECTION.
NOW THAT'S WHAT I CALL JOURNALISM!
FRANKLY, ISN'T LIFE GREAT? ARE WE NOT GOOD HERE?
YES, EVERYTHING IS PERFECT.
AND TO THINK THAT I BOUGHT THIS PLACE IN '42...I'VE HAD TO WAIT QUITE A WHILE BEFORE I COULD LIVE THIS LIFE OF LUXURY!
WELL, I HAVE TO GO...
WHERE TO?
THE STATION. EVA AND THE GIRLS ARE ARRIVING ON THE ELEVEN O'CLOCK TRAIN! I DON'T WANT THEM TO WAIT...
AH, I...I FORGOT TO TELL YOU... I HAD MARCEL WORK IT OUT. I DIDN'T WANT TO BOTHER YOU WITH THE DETAILS...
EVA AND THE GIRLS? THEY'RE MOVING IN HERE?!
OF COURSE... WHERE DID YOU EXPECT?
51

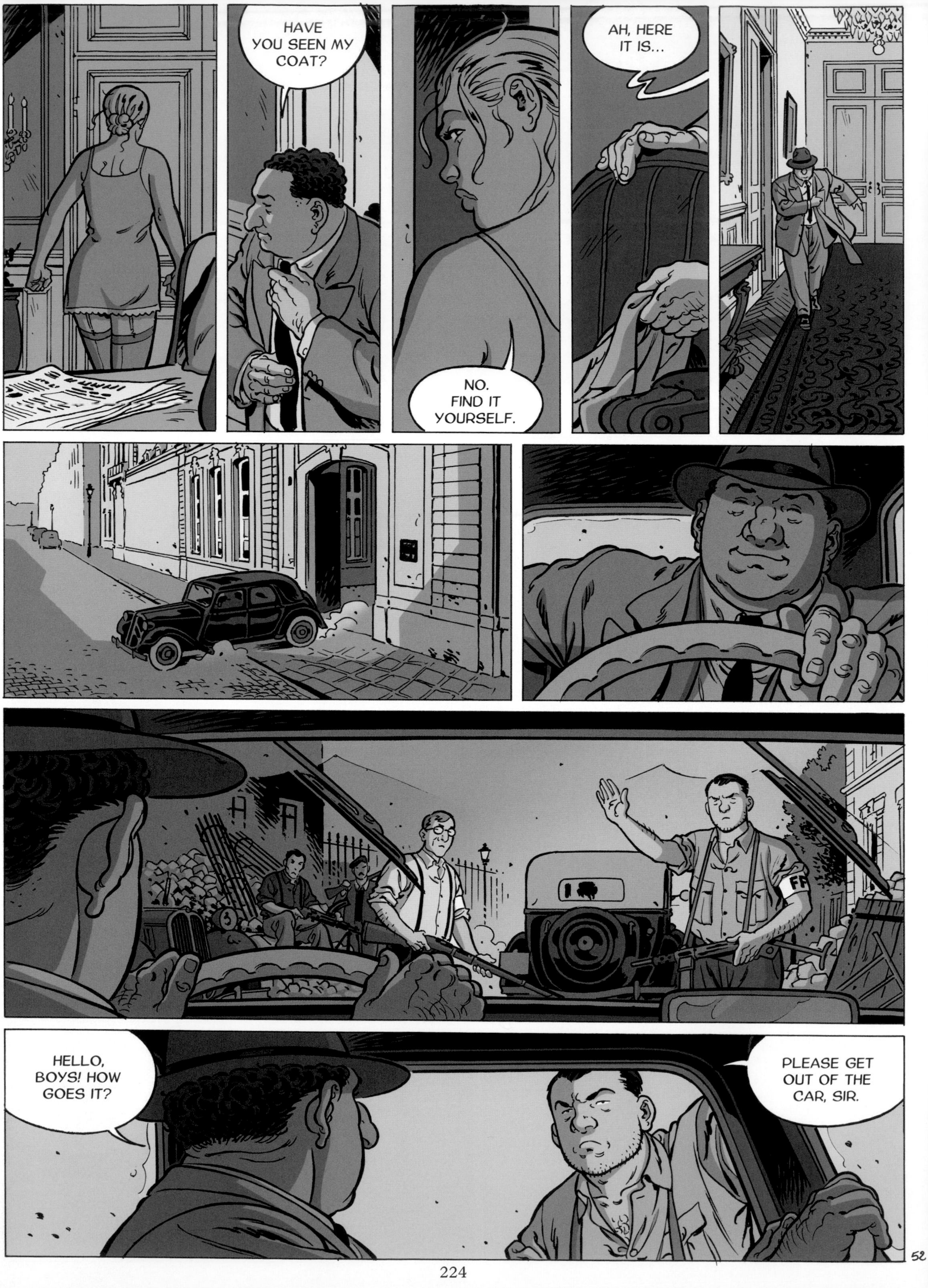
HAVE YOU SEEN MY COAT?
NO. FIND IT YOURSELF.
AH, HERE IT IS...
FFI
HELLO, BOYS! HOW GOES IT?
PLEASE GET OUT OF THE CAR, SIR.
52

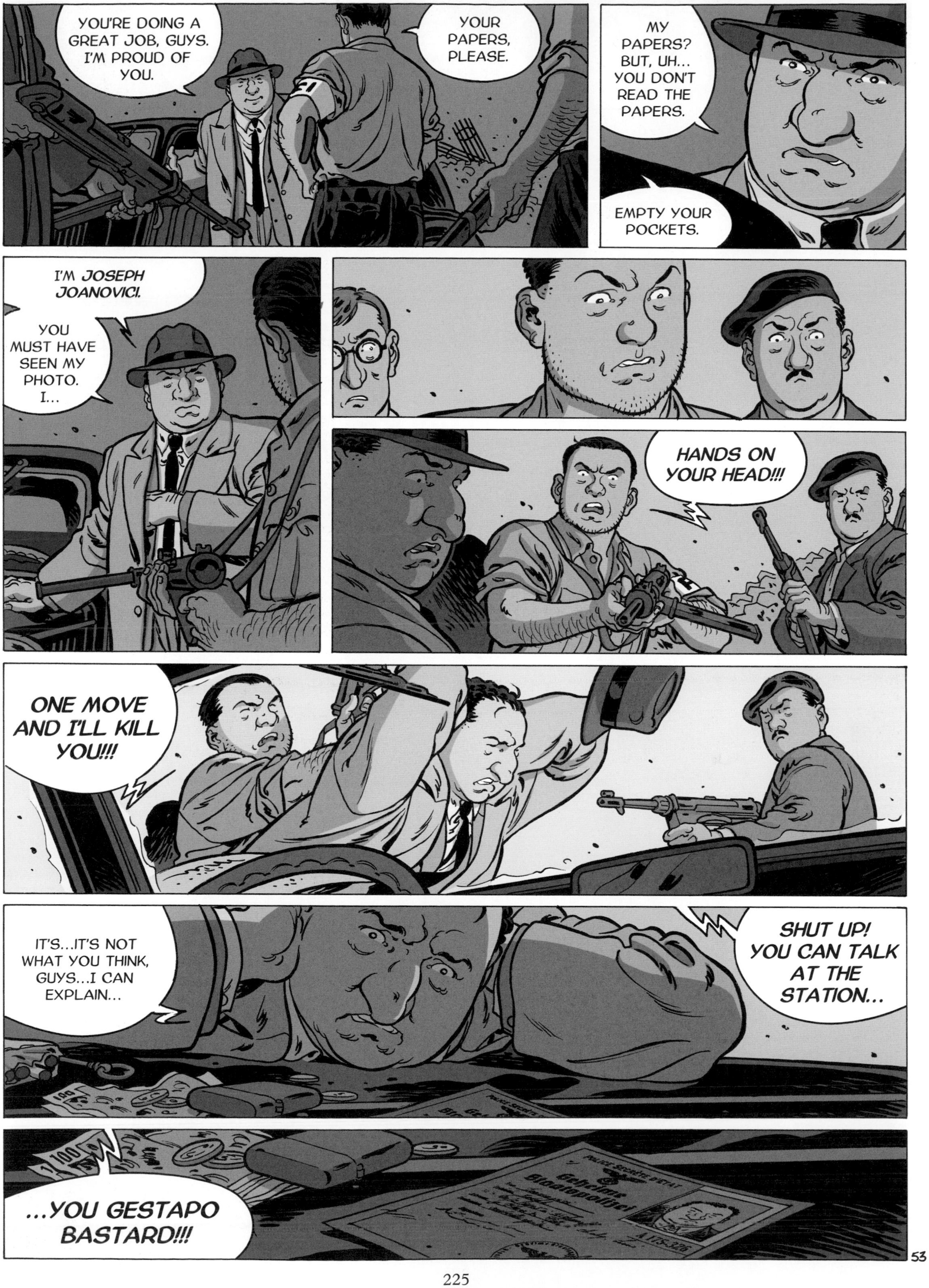
YOU'RE DOING A GREAT JOB, GUYS. I'M PROUD OF YOU.
YOUR PAPERS, PLEASE.
MY PAPERS? BUT, UH... YOU DON'T READ THE PAPERS.
EMPTY YOUR POCKETS.
I'M *JOSEPH JOANOVICI.*
YOU MUST HAVE SEEN MY PHOTO. I...
HANDS ON YOUR HEAD!!!
ONE MOVE AND I'LL KILL YOU!!!
IT'S...IT'S NOT WHAT YOU THINK, GUYS...I CAN EXPLAIN...
SHUT UP! YOU CAN TALK AT THE STATION...
...YOU GESTAPO BASTARD!!!
53

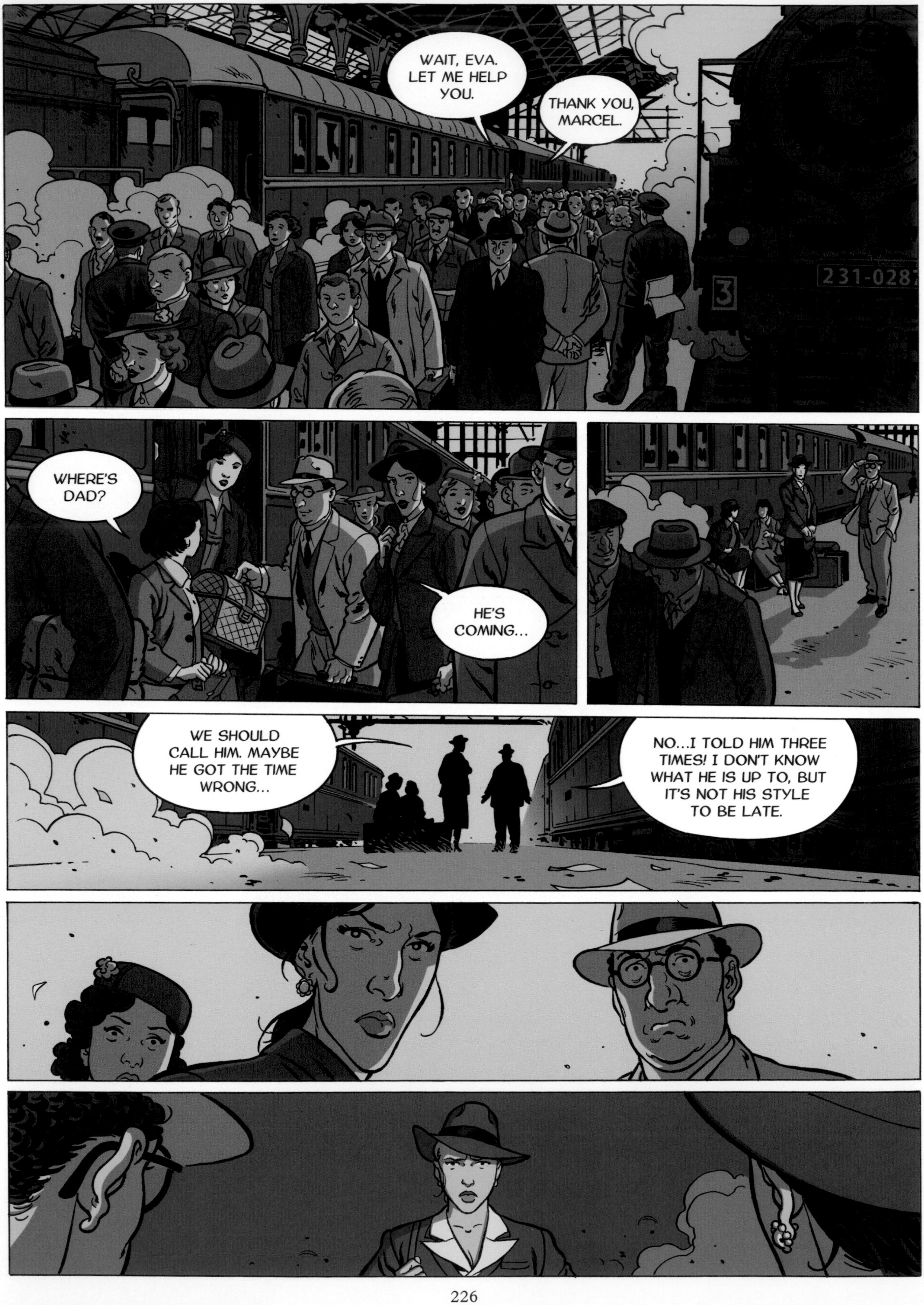
WAIT, EVA. LET ME HELP YOU.
THANK YOU, MARCEL.
231-0287
3
WHERE'S DAD?
HE'S COMING...
WE SHOULD CALL HIM. MAYBE HE GOT THE TIME WRONG...
NO...I TOLD HIM THREE TIMES! I DON'T KNOW WHAT HE IS UP TO, BUT IT'S NOT HIS STYLE TO BE LATE.

54

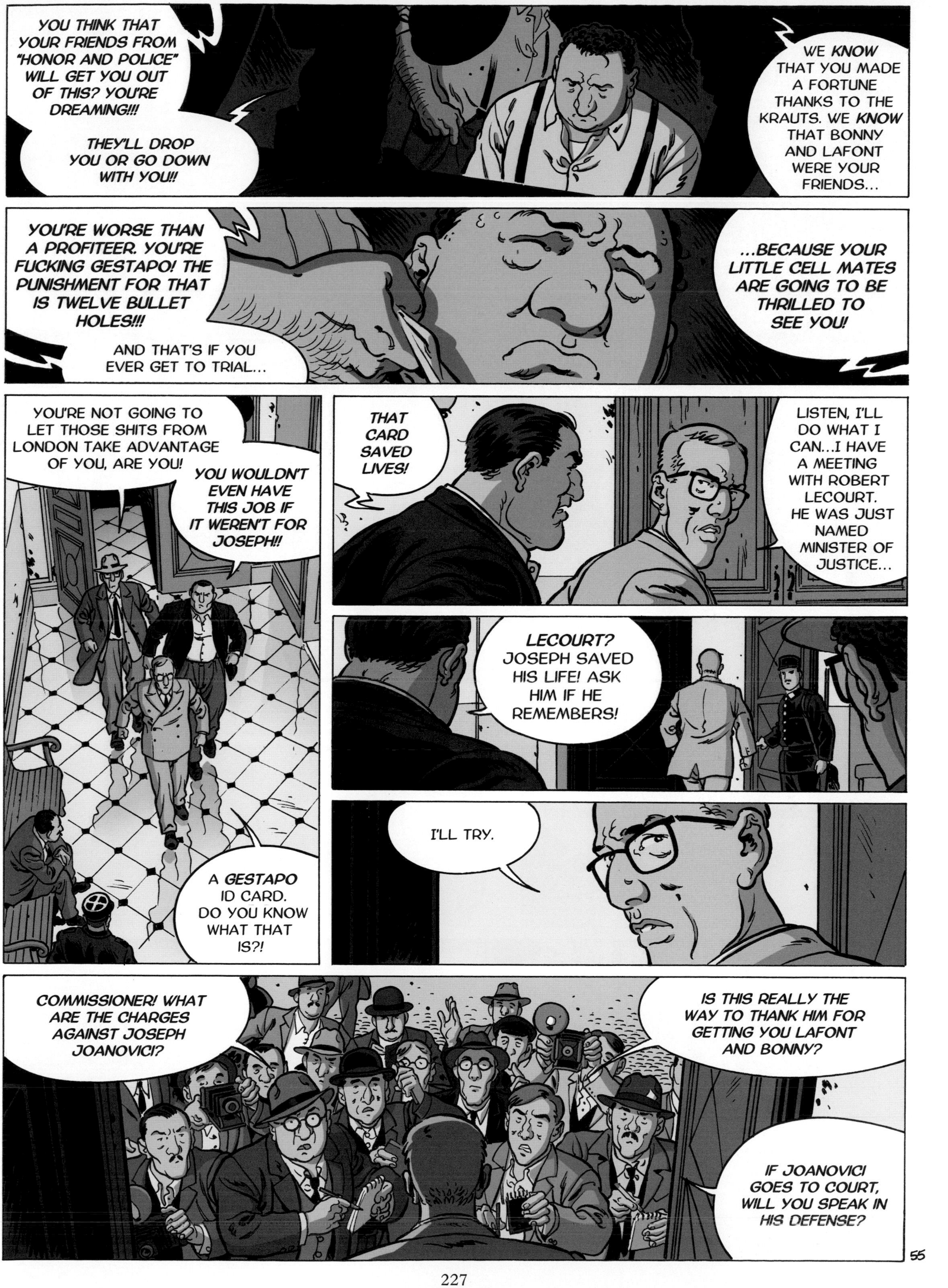
YOU THINK THAT YOUR FRIENDS FROM "HONOR AND POLICE" WILL GET YOU OUT OF THIS? YOU'RE DREAMING!!!
THEY'LL DROP YOU OR GO DOWN WITH YOU!!
WE KNOW THAT YOU MADE A FORTUNE THANKS TO THE KRAUTS. WE KNOW THAT BONNY AND LAFONT WERE YOUR FRIENDS...
YOU'RE WORSE THAN A PROFITEER. YOU'RE FUCKING GESTAPO! THE PUNISHMENT FOR THAT IS TWELVE BULLET HOLES!!!
AND THAT'S IF YOU EVER GET TO TRIAL...
...BECAUSE YOUR LITTLE CELL MATES ARE GOING TO BE THRILLED TO SEE YOU!
YOU'RE NOT GOING TO LET THOSE SHITS FROM LONDON TAKE ADVANTAGE OF YOU, ARE YOU!
YOU WOULDN'T EVEN HAVE THIS JOB IF IT WEREN'T FOR JOSEPH!!
A GESTAPO ID CARD. DO YOU KNOW WHAT THAT IS?!
THAT CARD SAVED LIVES!
LISTEN, I'LL DO WHAT I CAN...I HAVE A MEETING WITH ROBERT LECOURT. HE WAS JUST NAMED MINISTER OF JUSTICE...
LECOURT? JOSEPH SAVED HIS LIFE! ASK HIM IF HE REMEMBERS!
I'LL TRY.
COMMISSIONER! WHAT ARE THE CHARGES AGAINST JOSEPH JOANOVICI?
IS THIS REALLY THE WAY TO THANK HIM FOR GETTING YOU LAFONT AND BONNY?
IF JOANOVICI GOES TO COURT, WILL YOU SPEAK IN HIS DEFENSE?
55

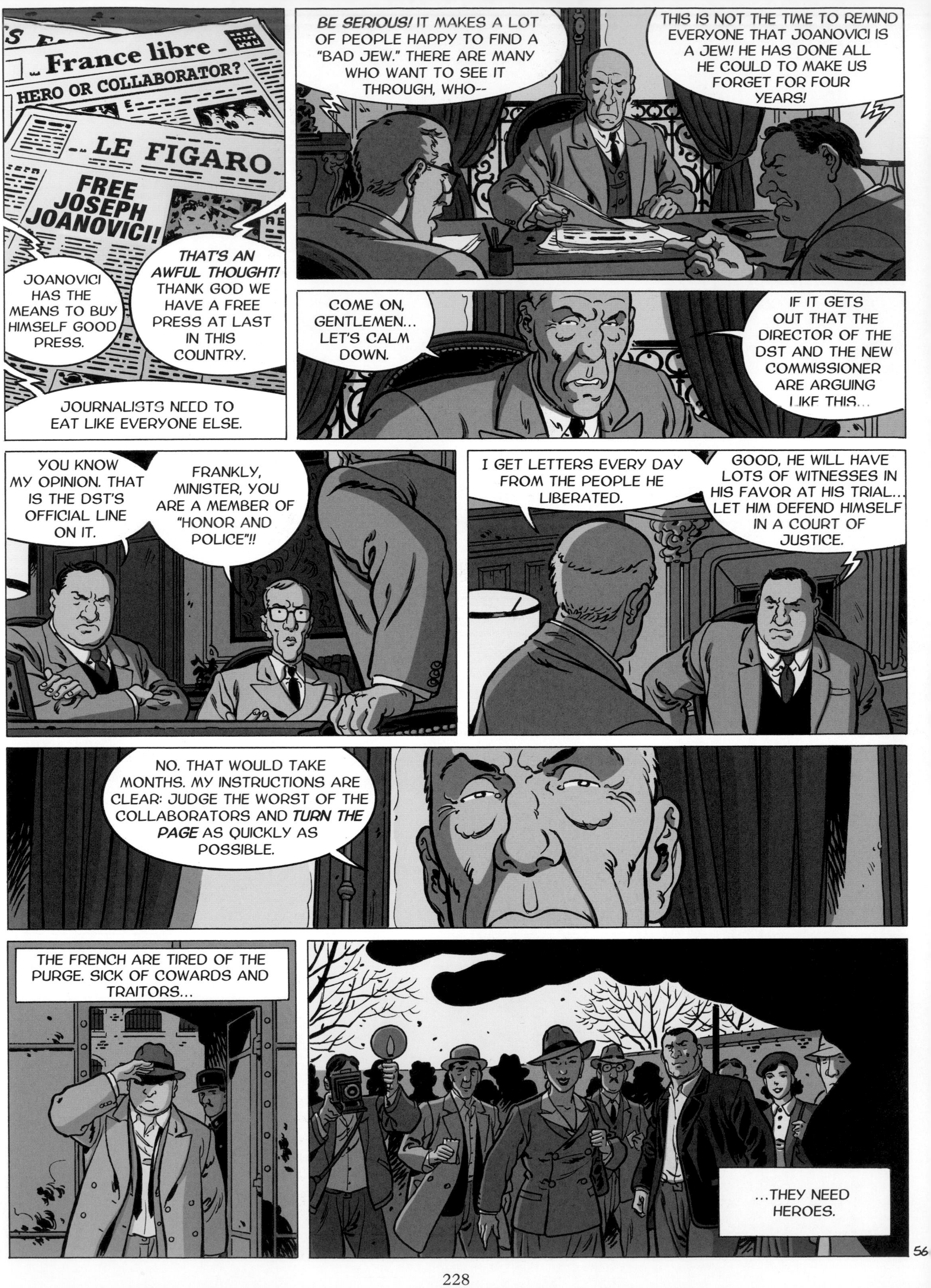
France libre
HERO OR COLLABORATOR?
LE FIGARO
FREE JOSEPH JOANOVICI!
JOANOVICI HAS THE MEANS TO BUY HIMSELF GOOD PRESS.
THAT'S AN AWFUL THOUGHT! THANK GOD WE HAVE A FREE PRESS AT LAST IN THIS COUNTRY.
JOURNALISTS NEED TO EAT LIKE EVERYONE ELSE.
BE SERIOUS! IT MAKES A LOT OF PEOPLE HAPPY TO FIND A "BAD JEW." THERE ARE MANY WHO WANT TO SEE IT THROUGH, WHO--
THIS IS NOT THE TIME TO REMIND EVERYONE THAT JOANOVICI IS A JEW! HE HAS DONE ALL HE COULD TO MAKE US FORGET FOR FOUR YEARS!
COME ON, GENTLEMEN... LET'S CALM DOWN.
IF IT GETS OUT THAT THE DIRECTOR OF THE DST AND THE NEW COMMISSIONER ARE ARGUING LIKE THIS...
YOU KNOW MY OPINION. THAT IS THE DST'S OFFICIAL LINE ON IT.
FRANKLY, MINISTER, YOU ARE A MEMBER OF "HONOR AND POLICE"!!
I GET LETTERS EVERY DAY FROM THE PEOPLE HE LIBERATED.
GOOD, HE WILL HAVE LOTS OF WITNESSES IN HIS FAVOR AT HIS TRIAL... LET HIM DEFEND HIMSELF IN A COURT OF JUSTICE.
NO. THAT WOULD TAKE MONTHS. MY INSTRUCTIONS ARE CLEAR: JUDGE THE WORST OF THE COLLABORATORS AND TURN THE PAGE AS QUICKLY AS POSSIBLE.
THE FRENCH ARE TIRED OF THE PURGE. SICK OF COWARDS AND TRAITORS...
...THEY NEED HEROES.
56

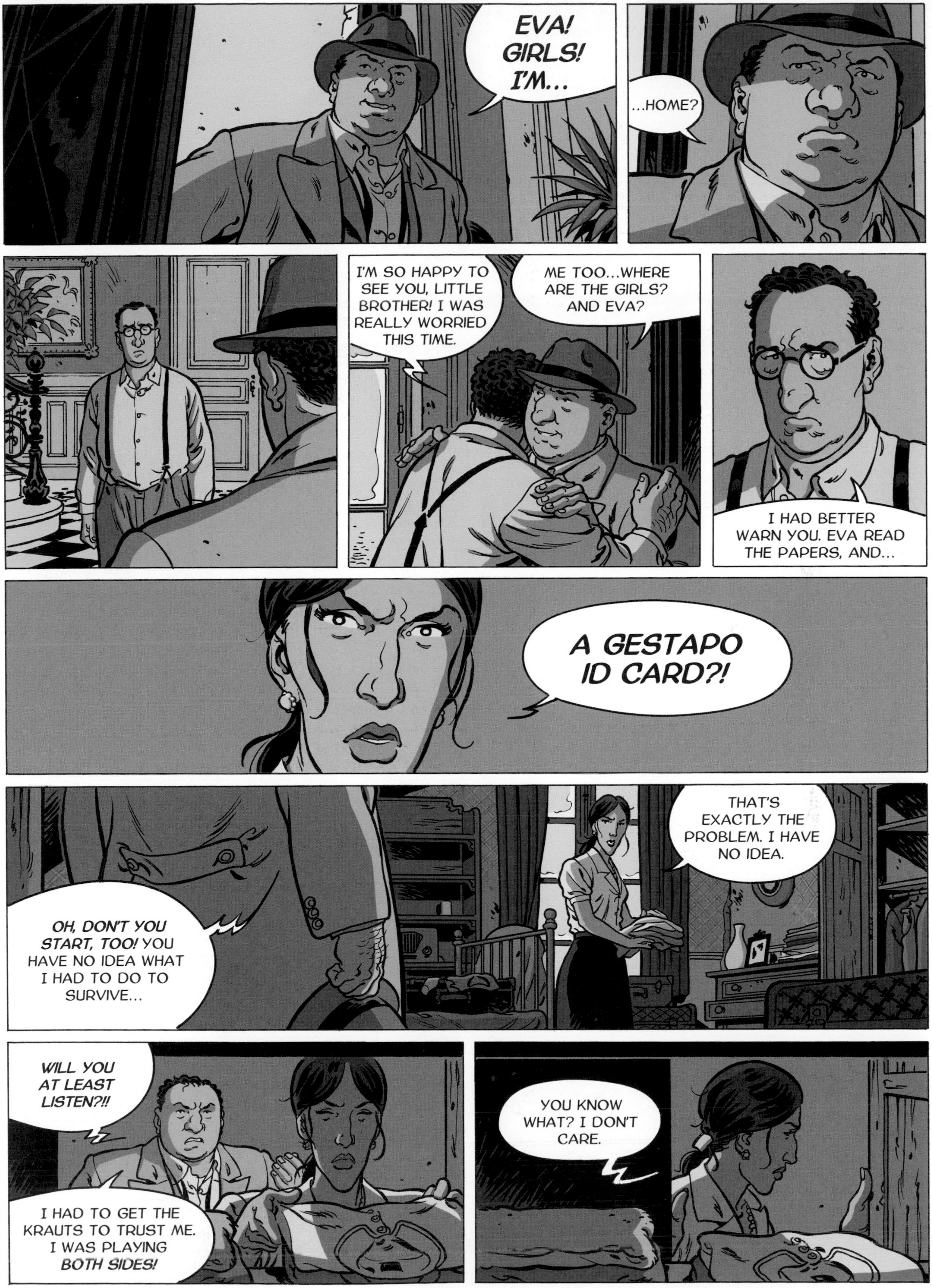
EVA! GIRLS! I'M...
...HOME?
I'M SO HAPPY TO SEE YOU, LITTLE BROTHER! I WAS REALLY WORRIED THIS TIME.
ME TOO...WHERE ARE THE GIRLS? AND EVA?
I HAD BETTER WARN YOU. EVA READ THE PAPERS, AND...
A GESTAPO ID CARD?!
THAT'S EXACTLY THE PROBLEM. I HAVE NO IDEA.
OH, DON'T YOU START, TOO! YOU HAVE NO IDEA WHAT I HAD TO DO TO SURVIVE...
WILL YOU AT LEAST LISTEN?!!
I HAD TO GET THE KRAUTS TO TRUST ME. I WAS PLAYING BOTH SIDES!
YOU KNOW WHAT? I DON'T CARE.
57

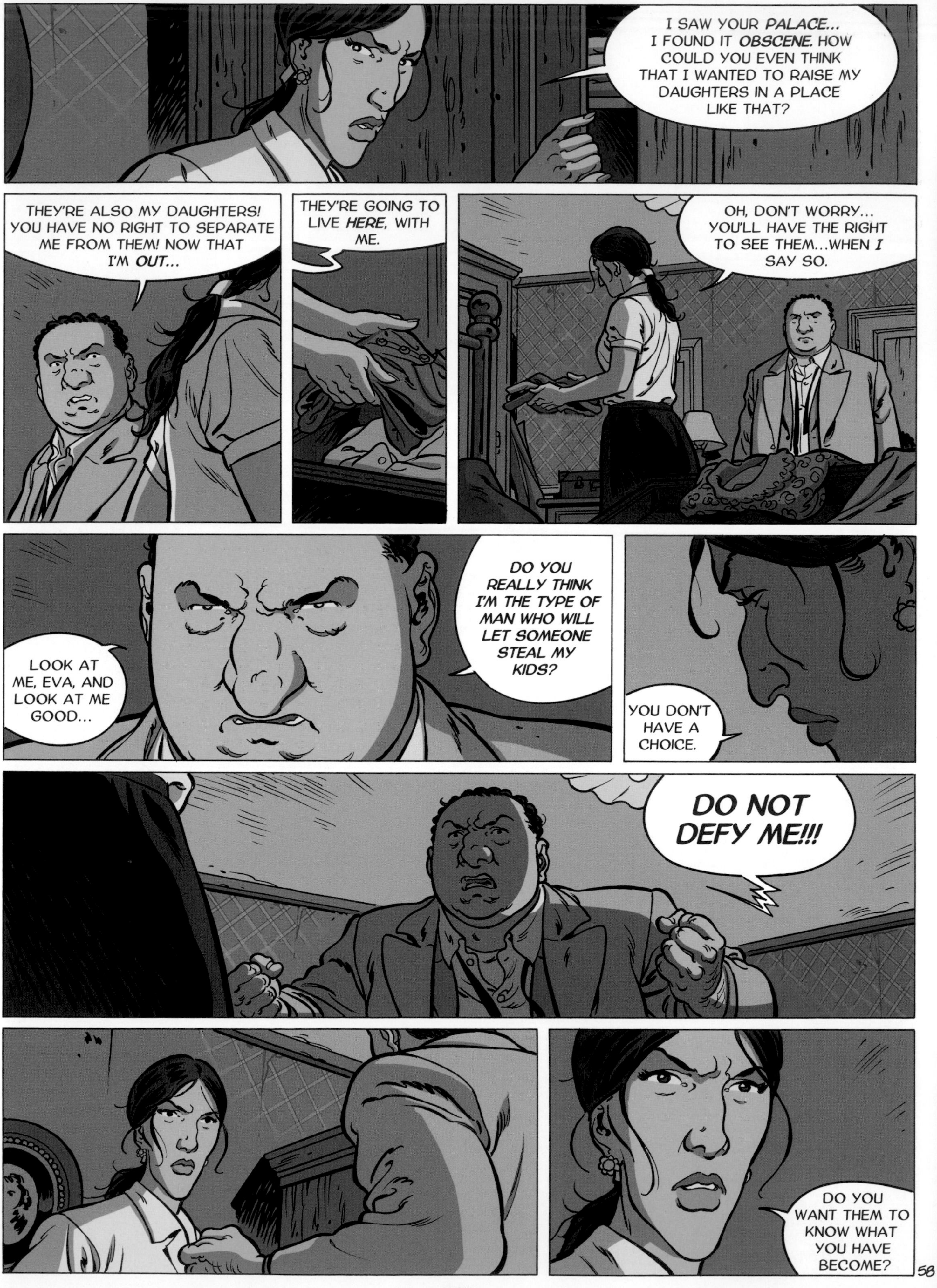
I SAW YOUR PALACE... I FOUND IT OBSCENE. HOW COULD YOU EVEN THINK THAT I WANTED TO RAISE MY DAUGHTERS IN A PLACE LIKE THAT?
THEY'RE ALSO MY DAUGHTERS! YOU HAVE NO RIGHT TO SEPARATE ME FROM THEM! NOW THAT I'M OUT...
THEY'RE GOING TO LIVE HERE, WITH ME.
OH, DON'T WORRY... YOU'LL HAVE THE RIGHT TO SEE THEM...WHEN I SAY SO.
LOOK AT ME, EVA, AND LOOK AT ME GOOD...
DO YOU REALLY THINK I'M THE TYPE OF MAN WHO WILL LET SOMEONE STEAL MY KIDS?
YOU DON'T HAVE A CHOICE.
DO NOT DEFY ME!!!
DO YOU WANT THEM TO KNOW WHAT YOU HAVE BECOME?
58

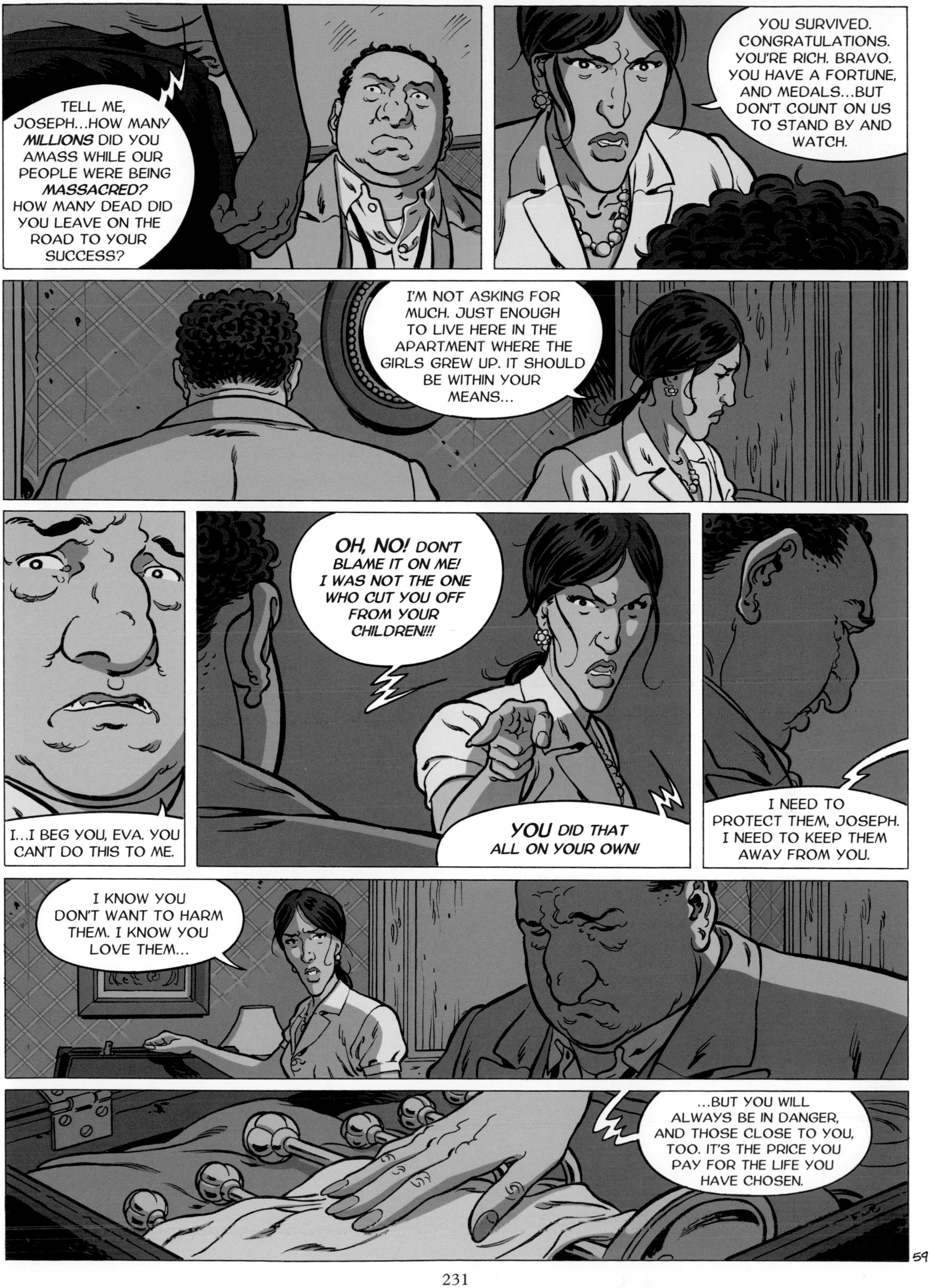
TELL ME, JOSEPH...HOW MANY MILLIONS DID YOU AMASS WHILE OUR PEOPLE WERE BEING MASSACRED? HOW MANY DEAD DID YOU LEAVE ON THE ROAD TO YOUR SUCCESS?
YOU SURVIVED. CONGRATULATIONS. YOU'RE RICH. BRAVO. YOU HAVE A FORTUNE, AND MEDALS...BUT DON'T COUNT ON US TO STAND BY AND WATCH.
I'M NOT ASKING FOR MUCH. JUST ENOUGH TO LIVE HERE IN THE APARTMENT WHERE THE GIRLS GREW UP. IT SHOULD BE WITHIN YOUR MEANS...
I...I BEG YOU, EVA. YOU CAN'T DO THIS TO ME.
OH, NO! DON'T BLAME IT ON ME! I WAS NOT THE ONE WHO CUT YOU OFF FROM YOUR CHILDREN!!!
YOU DID THAT ALL ON YOUR OWN!
I NEED TO PROTECT THEM, JOSEPH. I NEED TO KEEP THEM AWAY FROM YOU.
I KNOW YOU DON'T WANT TO HARM THEM. I KNOW YOU LOVE THEM...
...BUT YOU WILL ALWAYS BE IN DANGER, AND THOSE CLOSE TO YOU, TOO. IT'S THE PRICE YOU PAY FOR THE LIFE YOU HAVE CHOSEN.
59

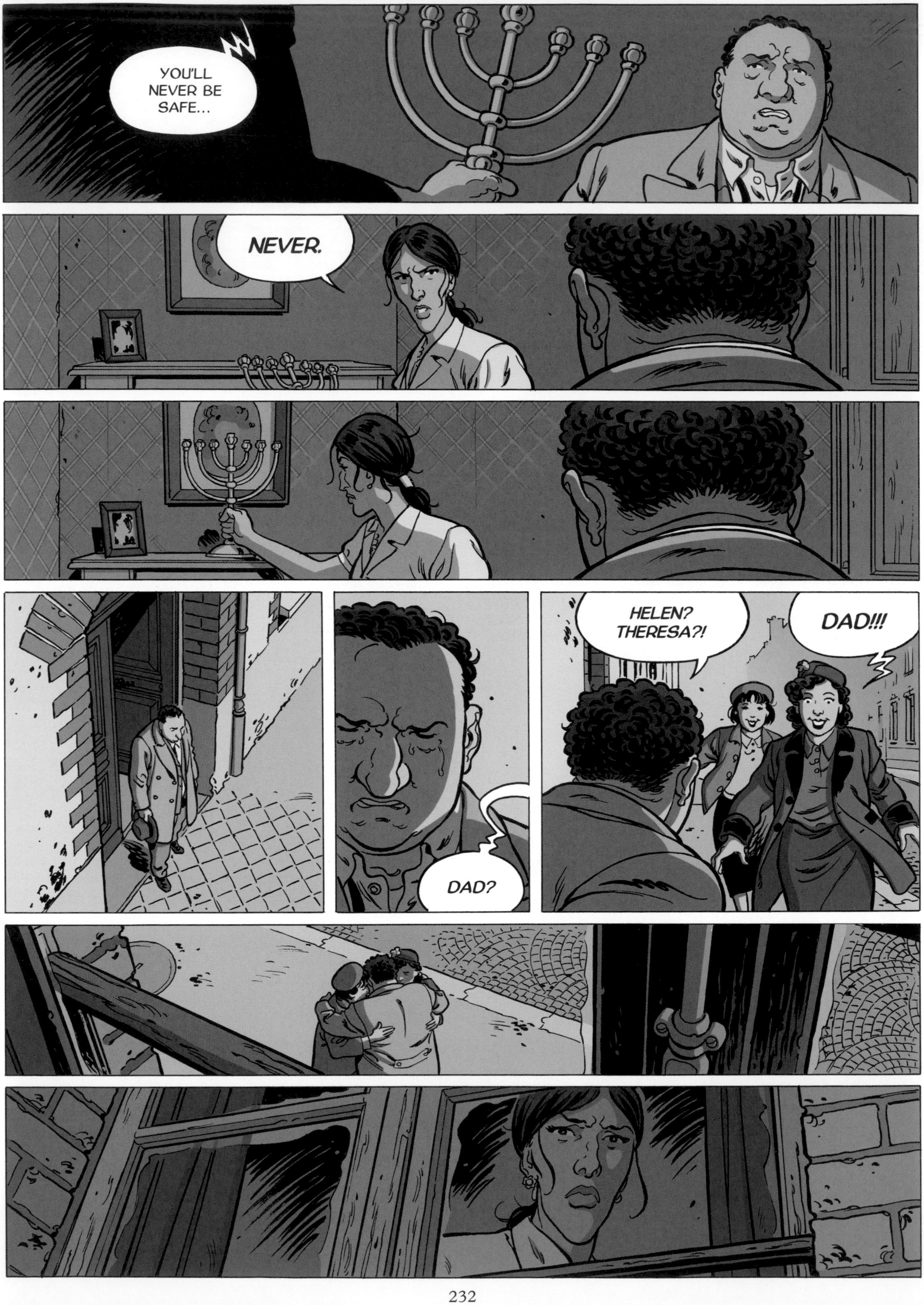
YOU'LL NEVER BE SAFE...
NEVER.
HELEN? THERESA?!
DAD!!!
DAD?

60

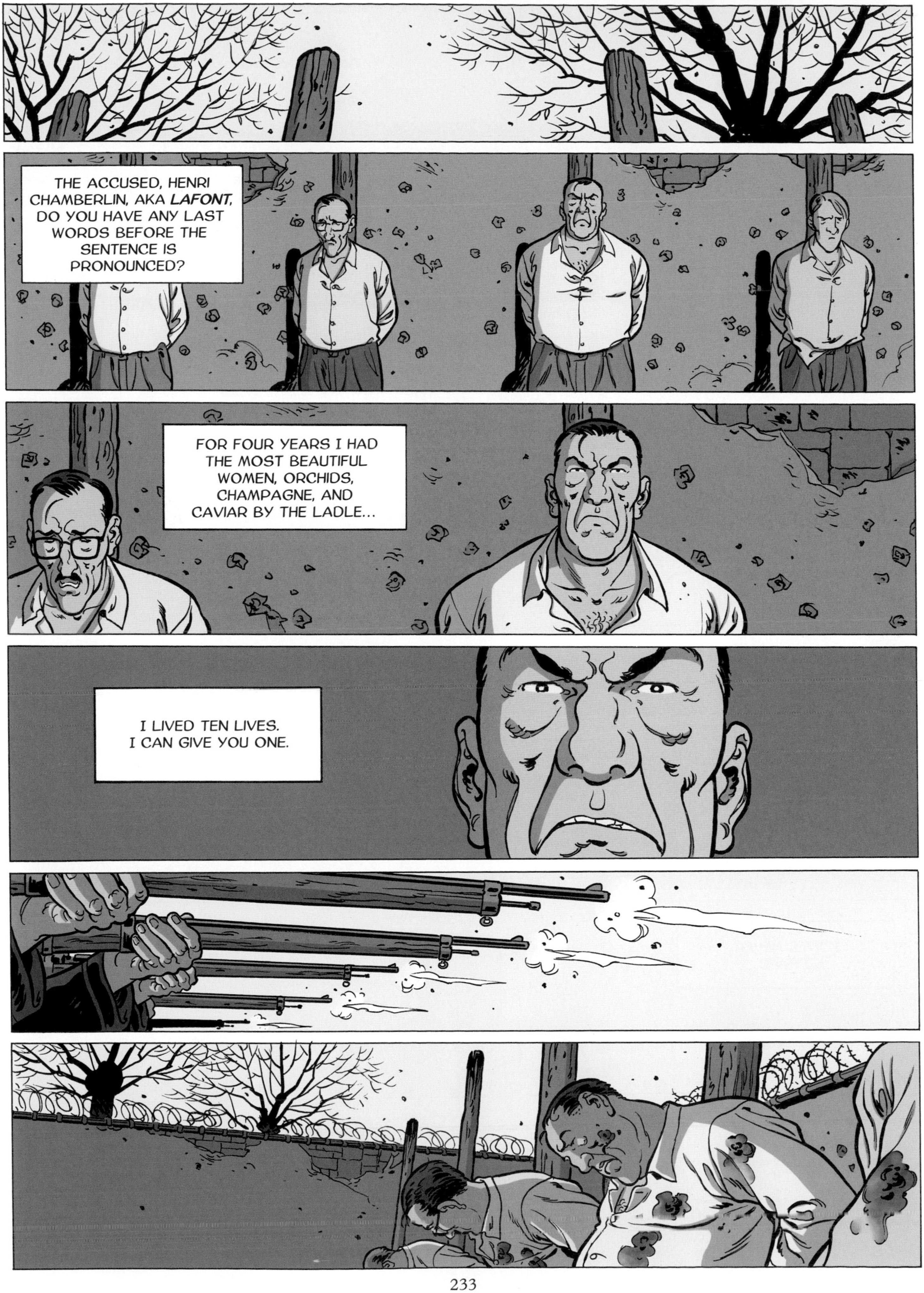
THE ACCUSED, HENRI CHAMBERLIN, AKA *LAFONT*, DO YOU HAVE ANY LAST WORDS BEFORE THE SENTENCE IS PRONOUNCED?
FOR FOUR YEARS I HAD THE MOST BEAUTIFUL WOMEN, ORCHIDS, CHAMPAGNE, AND CAVIAR BY THE LADLE...
I LIVED TEN LIVES. I CAN GIVE YOU ONE.

61

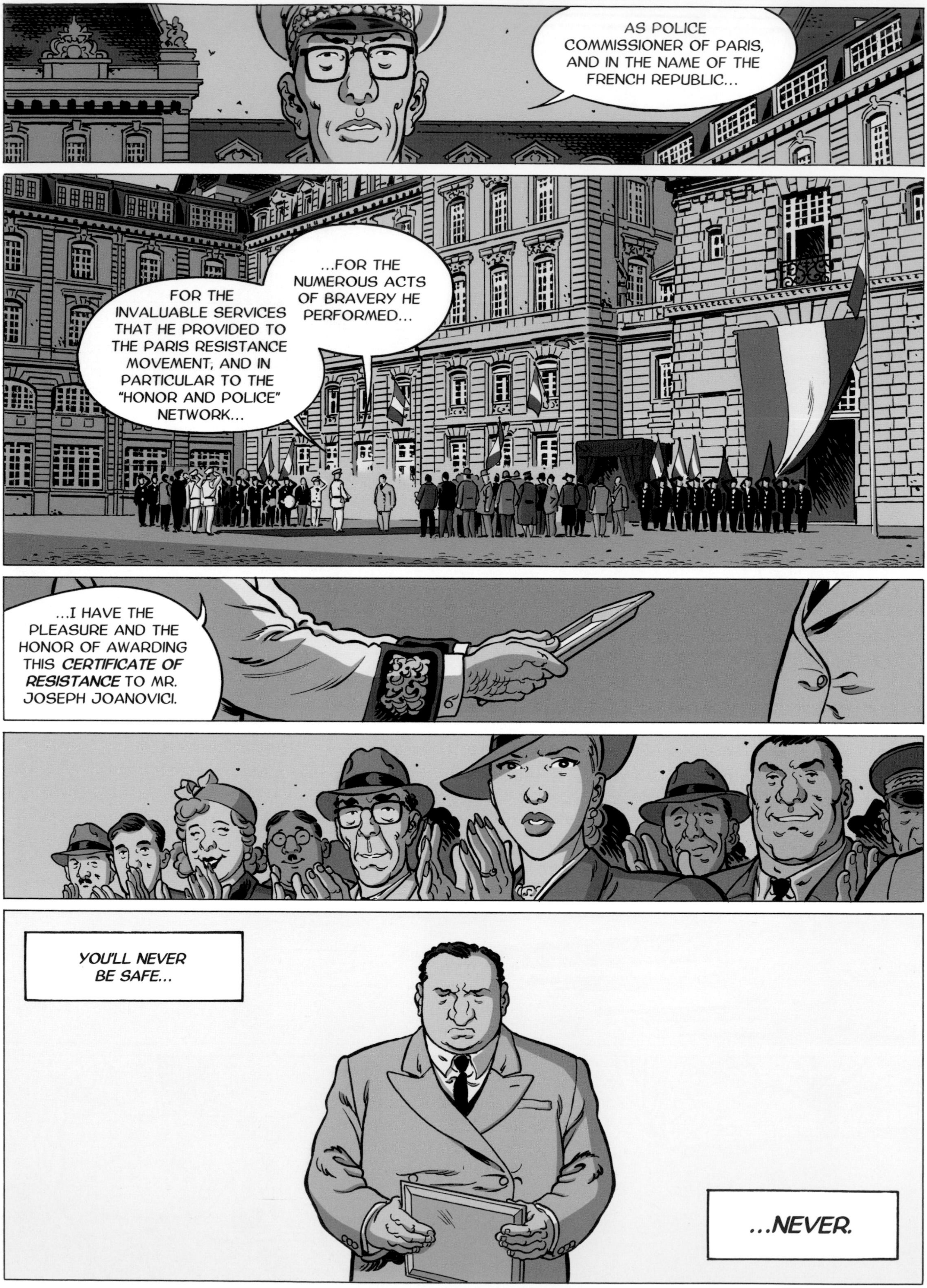
AS POLICE COMMISSIONER OF PARIS, AND IN THE NAME OF THE FRENCH REPUBLIC...
FOR THE INVALUABLE SERVICES THAT HE PROVIDED TO THE PARIS RESISTANCE MOVEMENT; AND IN PARTICULAR TO THE "HONOR AND POLICE" NETWORK...
...FOR THE NUMEROUS ACTS OF BRAVERY HE PERFORMED...
...I HAVE THE PLEASURE AND THE HONOR OF AWARDING THIS ***CERTIFICATE OF RESISTANCE*** TO MR. JOSEPH JOANOVICI.
YOU'LL NEVER BE SAFE...
...NEVER.
68

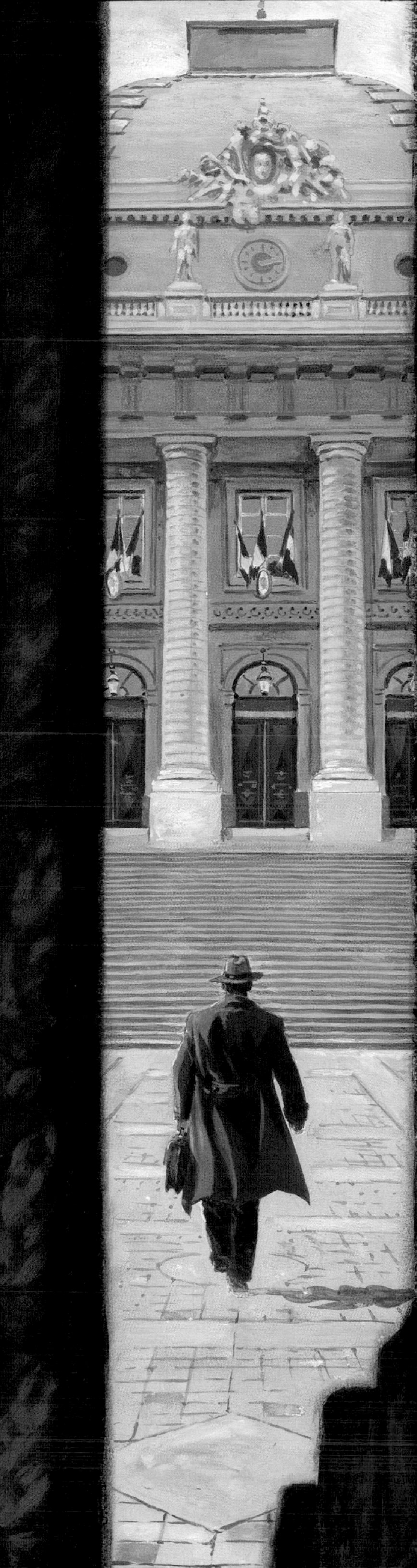

"Whoever fights monsters should see to it
that in the process he does not become a monster."
FRIEDRICH NIETZSCHE

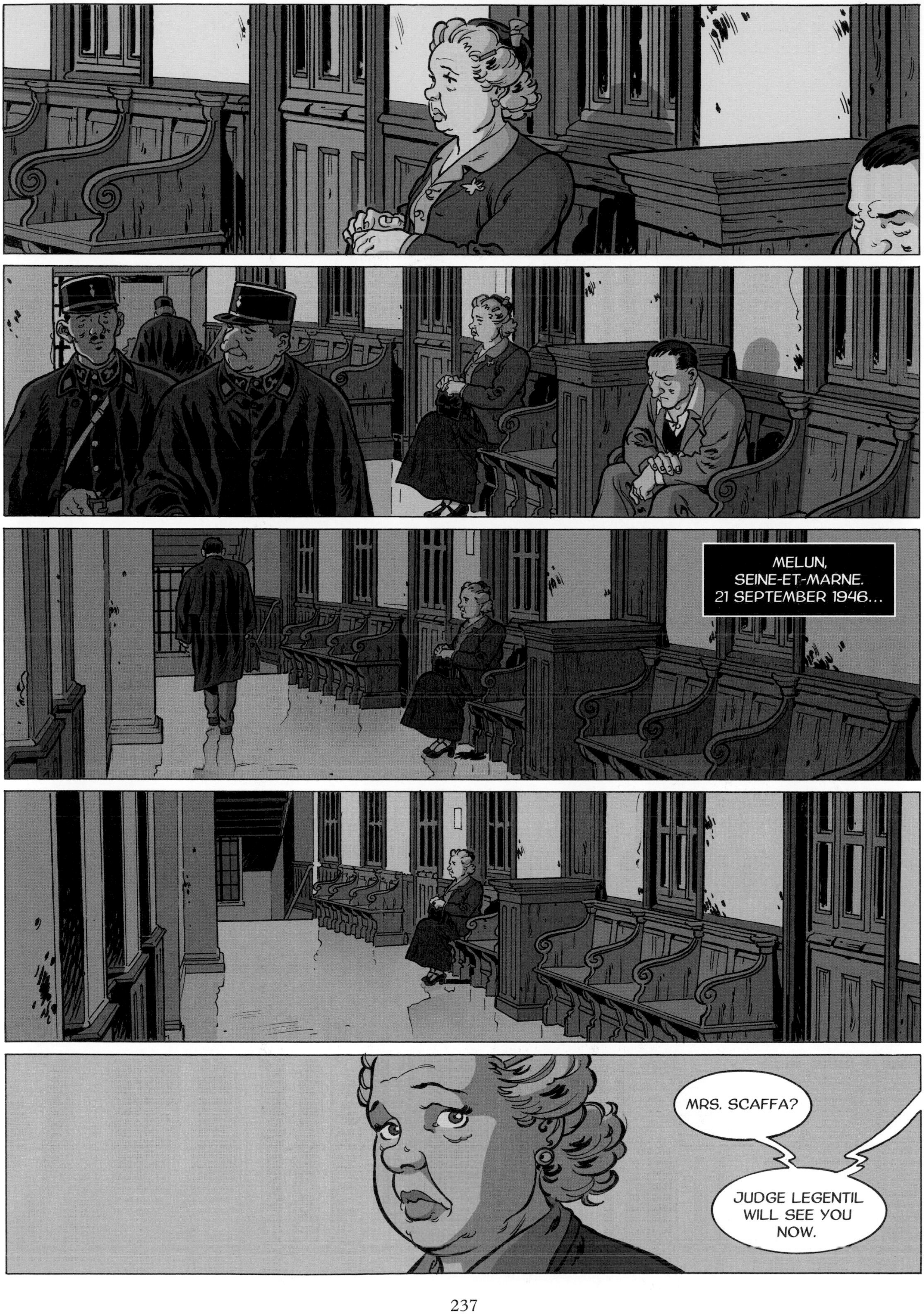
MELUN, SEINE-ET-MARNE. 21 SEPTEMBER 1946...
MRS. SCAFFA?
JUDGE LEGENTIL WILL SEE YOU NOW.

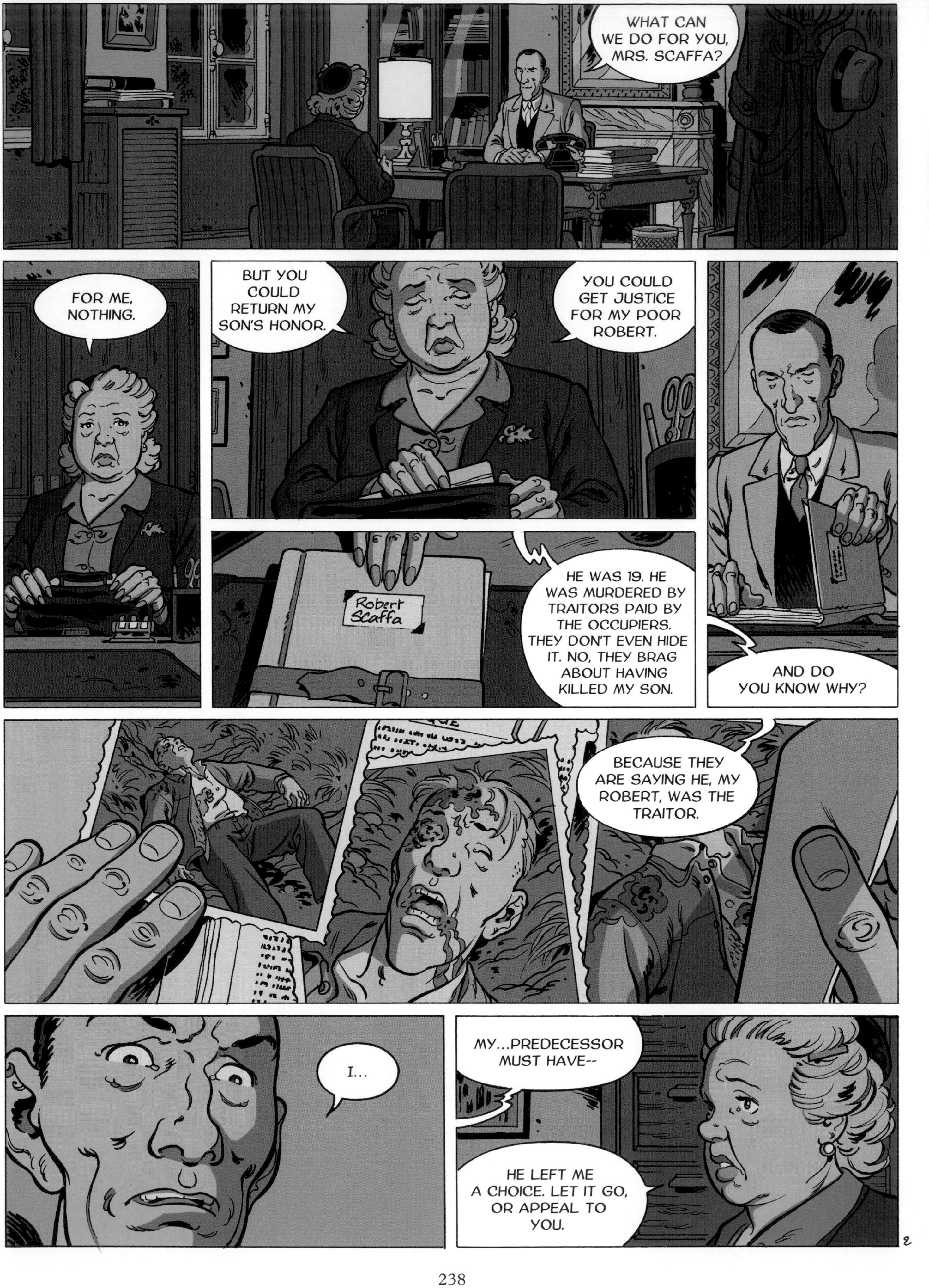
WHAT CAN WE DO FOR YOU, MRS. SCAFFA?
FOR ME, NOTHING.
BUT YOU COULD RETURN MY SON'S HONOR.
YOU COULD GET JUSTICE FOR MY POOR ROBERT.
Robert Scaffa
HE WAS 19. HE WAS MURDERED BY TRAITORS PAID BY THE OCCUPIERS. THEY DON'T EVEN HIDE IT. NO, THEY BRAG ABOUT HAVING KILLED MY SON.
AND DO YOU KNOW WHY?
BECAUSE THEY ARE SAYING HE, MY ROBERT, WAS THE TRAITOR.
I...
MY...PREDECESSOR MUST HAVE--
HE LEFT ME A CHOICE. LET IT GO, OR APPEAL TO YOU.
2

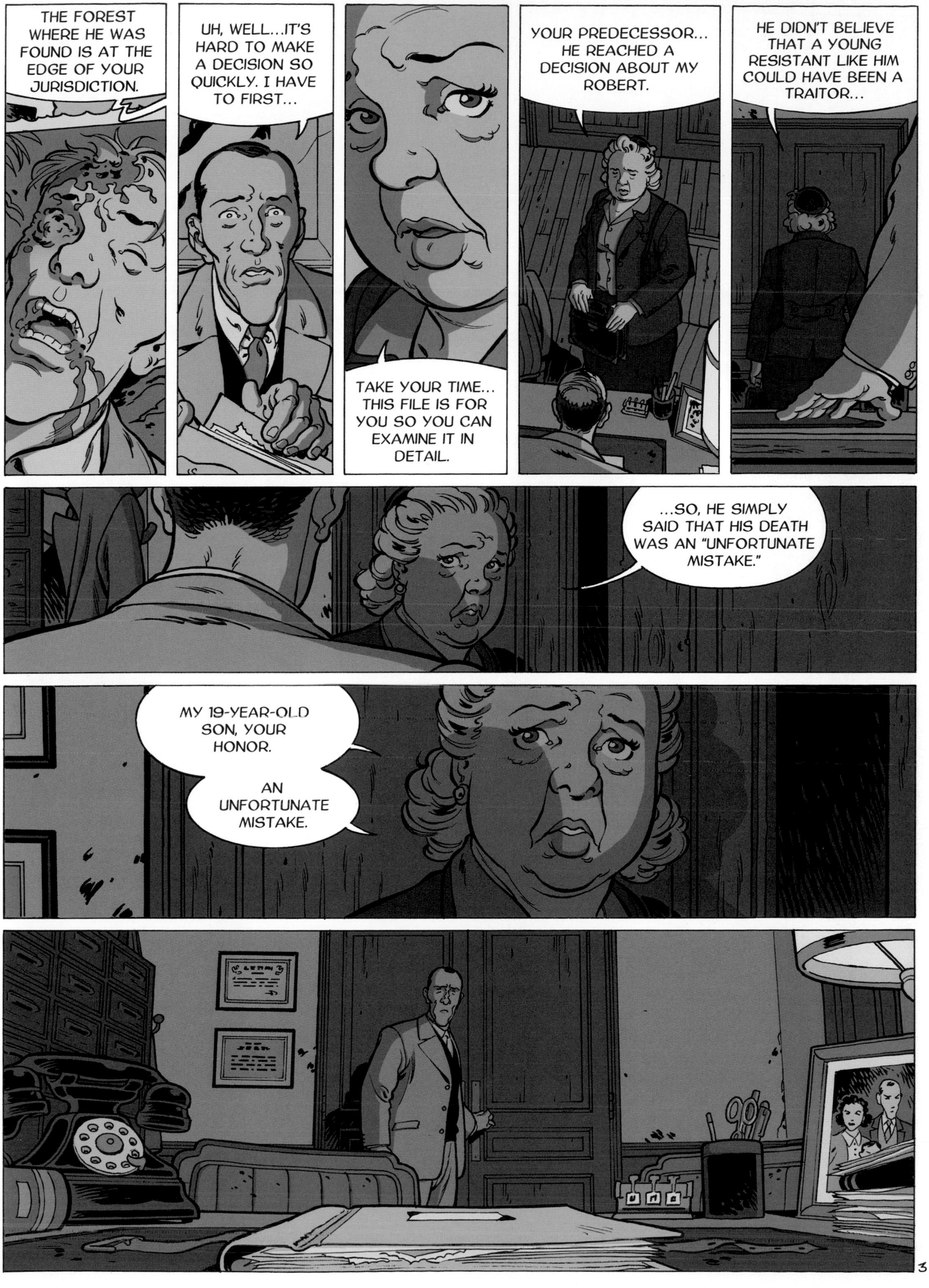
THE FOREST WHERE HE WAS FOUND IS AT THE EDGE OF YOUR JURISDICTION.
UH, WELL...IT'S HARD TO MAKE A DECISION SO QUICKLY. I HAVE TO FIRST...
TAKE YOUR TIME... THIS FILE IS FOR YOU SO YOU CAN EXAMINE IT IN DETAIL.
YOUR PREDECESSOR... HE REACHED A DECISION ABOUT MY ROBERT.
HE DIDN'T BELIEVE THAT A YOUNG RESISTANT LIKE HIM COULD HAVE BEEN A TRAITOR...
...SO, HE SIMPLY SAID THAT HIS DEATH WAS AN "UNFORTUNATE MISTAKE."
MY 19-YEAR-OLD SON, YOUR HONOR.
AN UNFORTUNATE MISTAKE.
3

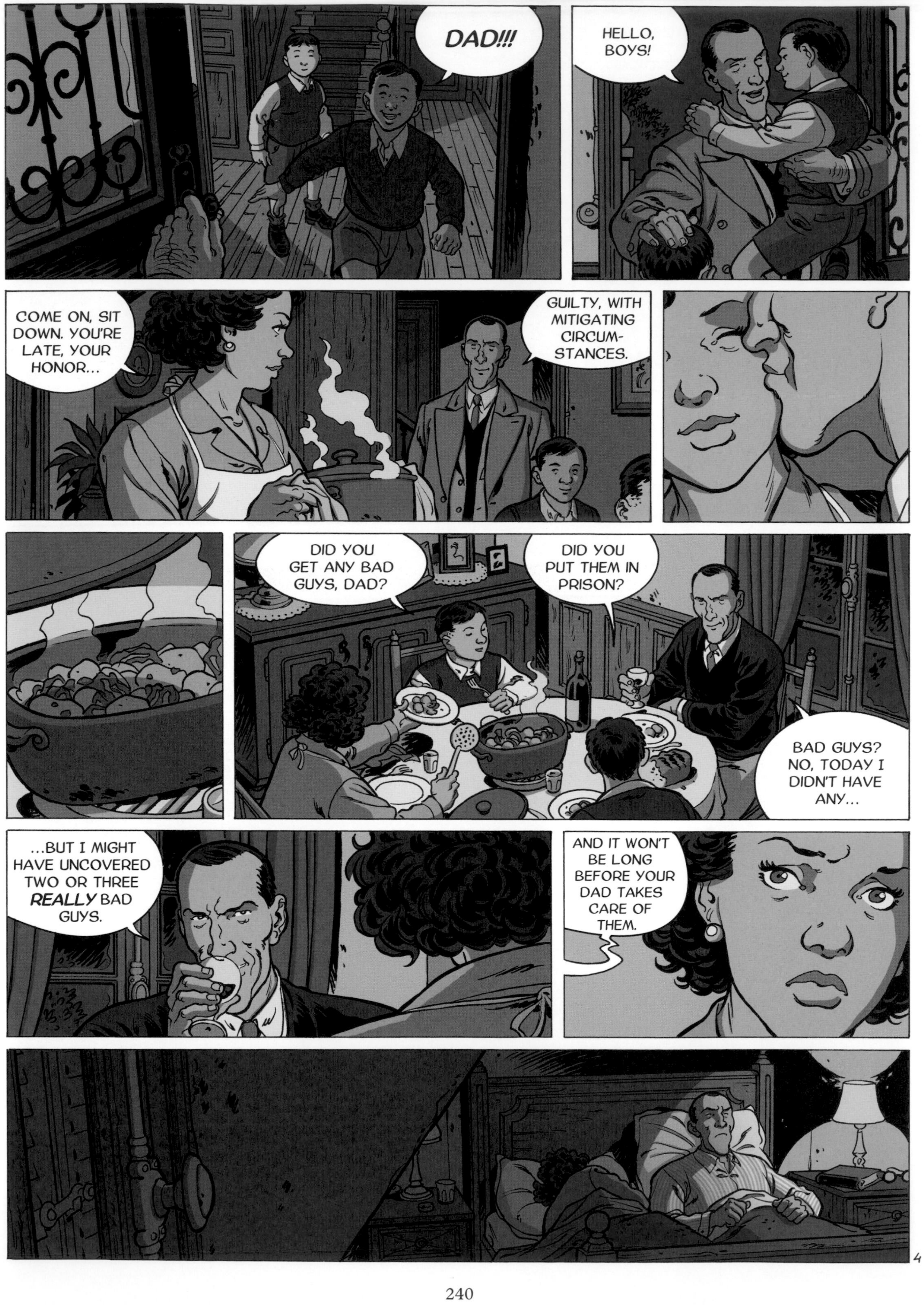
DAD!!!
HELLO, BOYS!
COME ON, SIT DOWN. YOU'RE LATE, YOUR HONOR...
GUILTY, WITH MITIGATING CIRCUM-STANCES.
DID YOU GET ANY BAD GUYS, DAD?
DID YOU PUT THEM IN PRISON?
BAD GUYS? NO, TODAY I DIDN'T HAVE ANY...
...BUT I MIGHT HAVE UNCOVERED TWO OR THREE REALLY BAD GUYS.
AND IT WON'T BE LONG BEFORE YOUR DAD TAKES CARE OF THEM.
4

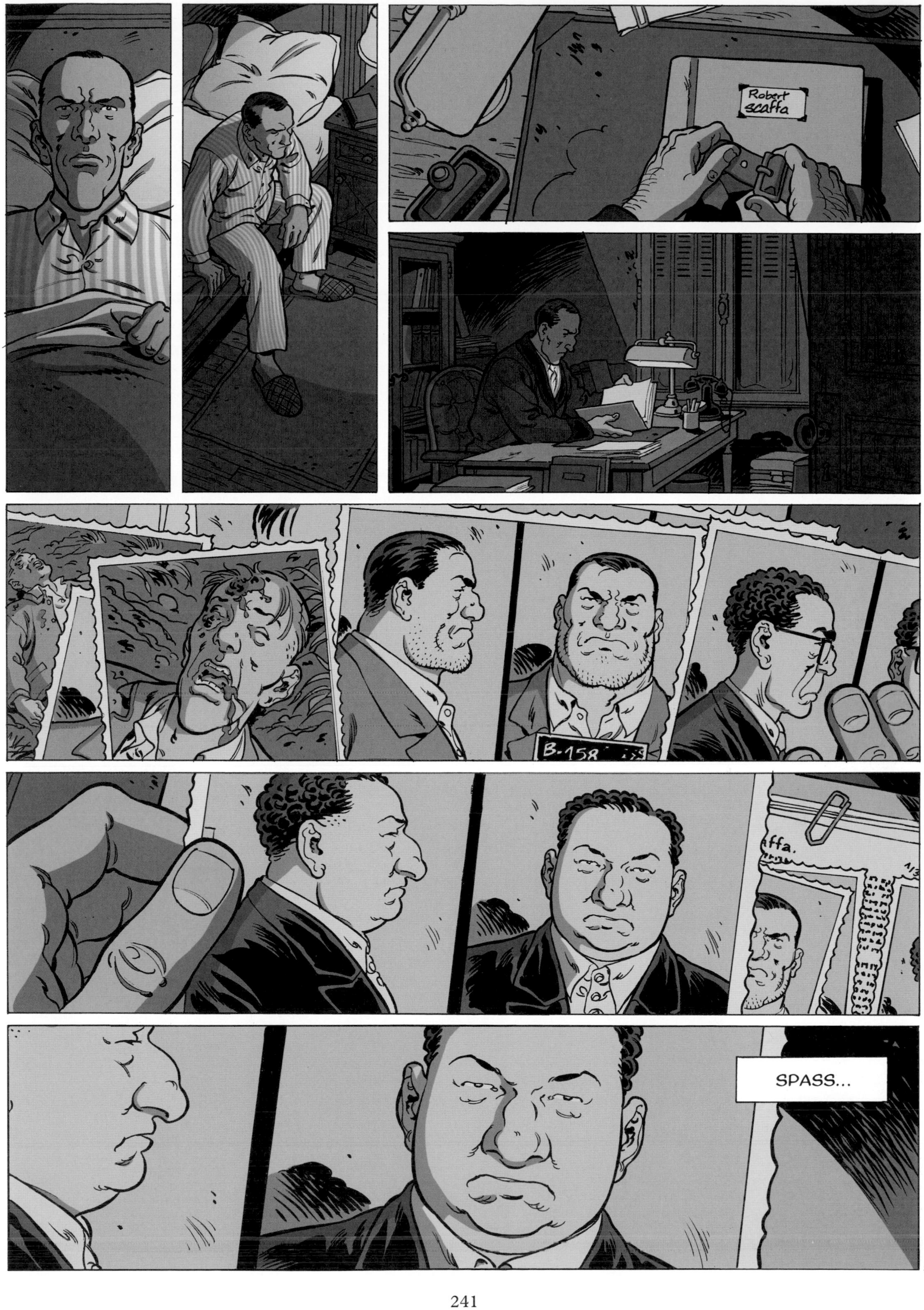
Robert
scaffa
B-158
SPASS...
5

THE DAY HE DIED, ROBERT HAD JUST MISSED A RAID.

THEY CLAIMED THAT HE WAS THE ONE WHO DENOUNCED HIS COMRADES TO THE KRAUTS. BUT IT'S NOT TRUE. I KNOW WHY HE WAS LATE.

ROBERT WAS WITH ME. WE...WE WERE HAVING A ROMP...

ROBERT WENT TO THE MEETING WITHOUT THE SLIGHTEST IDEA OF WHAT WAS GOING ON. AND IF IT WASN'T HIM, WHO WAS IT? IT COULD ONLY BE *BOURGUIGNON OR SPASS.*

WOULD YOU BE WILLING TO TESTIFY IN COURT? AGAINST DECORATED VETERANS OF THE RESISTANCE?

HE ADMIRED THEM, YOU KNOW. HE WAS PROUD TO KNOW THEM.

YOU HAVEN'T ANSWERED MY QUESTION.

I'LL DO WHAT IT TAKES TO HELP MRS. SCAFFA. HE WAS HER ONLY CHILD.

IT WON'T COME OFF...

I SCRUBBED HARD, BUT IT WON'T COME OFF.

ROBERT SCAFFA
11 FÉVRIER 1921 - JUILLET 1944
TRAITRE

TRAITOR

6

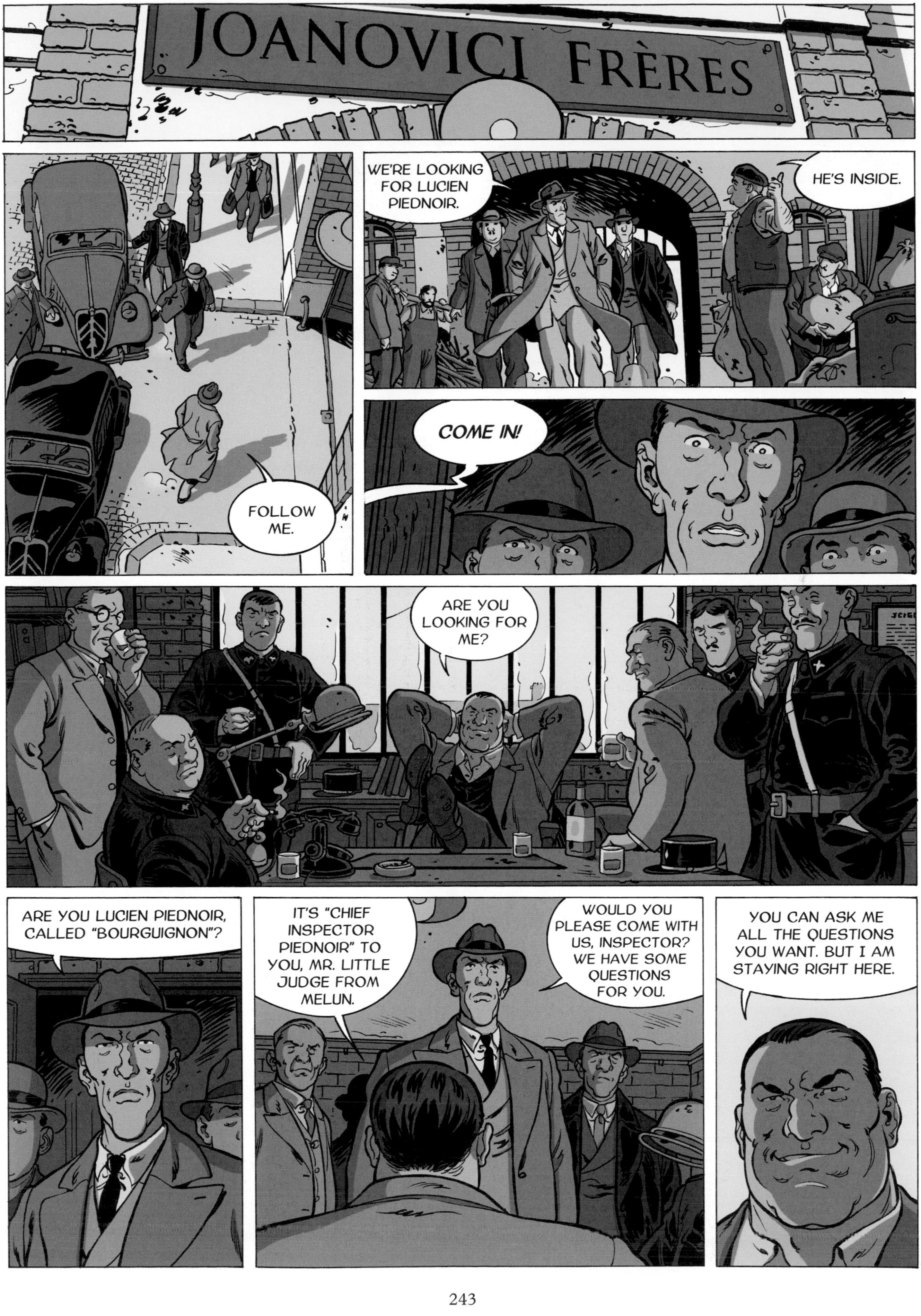
JOANOVICI FRÈRES
FOLLOW ME.
WE'RE LOOKING FOR LUCIEN PIEDNOIR.
HE'S INSIDE.
COME IN!
ARE YOU LOOKING FOR ME?
ARE YOU LUCIEN PIEDNOIR, CALLED "BOURGUIGNON"?
IT'S "CHIEF INSPECTOR PIEDNOIR" TO YOU, MR. LITTLE JUDGE FROM MELUN.
WOULD YOU PLEASE COME WITH US, INSPECTOR? WE HAVE SOME QUESTIONS FOR YOU.
YOU CAN ASK ME ALL THE QUESTIONS YOU WANT. BUT I AM STAYING RIGHT HERE.
7

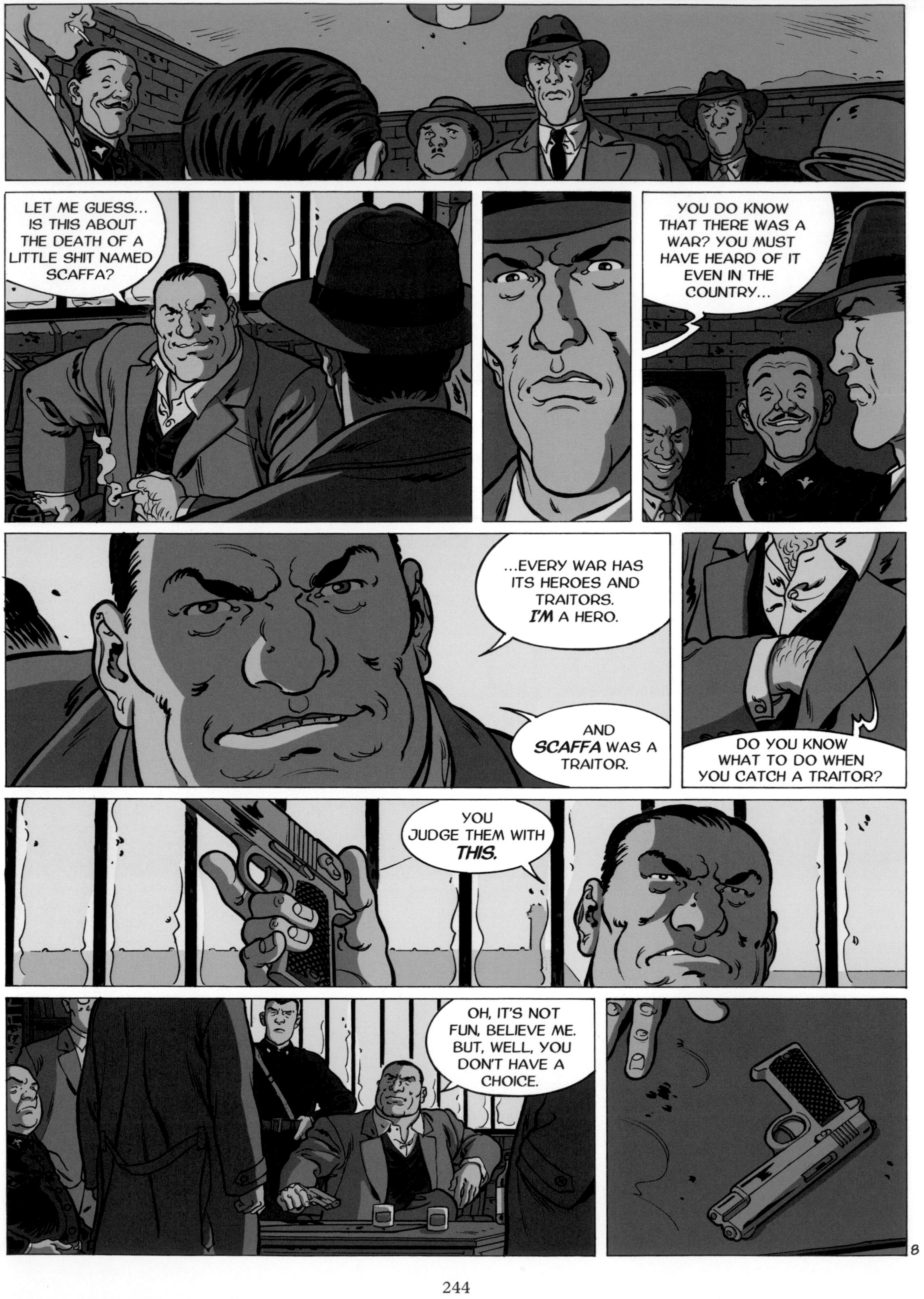
LET ME GUESS... IS THIS ABOUT THE DEATH OF A LITTLE SHIT NAMED SCAFFA?
YOU DO KNOW THAT THERE WAS A WAR? YOU MUST HAVE HEARD OF IT EVEN IN THE COUNTRY...
...EVERY WAR HAS ITS HEROES AND TRAITORS. I'M A HERO.
AND SCAFFA WAS A TRAITOR.
DO YOU KNOW WHAT TO DO WHEN YOU CATCH A TRAITOR?
YOU JUDGE THEM WITH THIS.
OH, IT'S NOT FUN, BELIEVE ME. BUT, WELL, YOU DON'T HAVE A CHOICE.
8

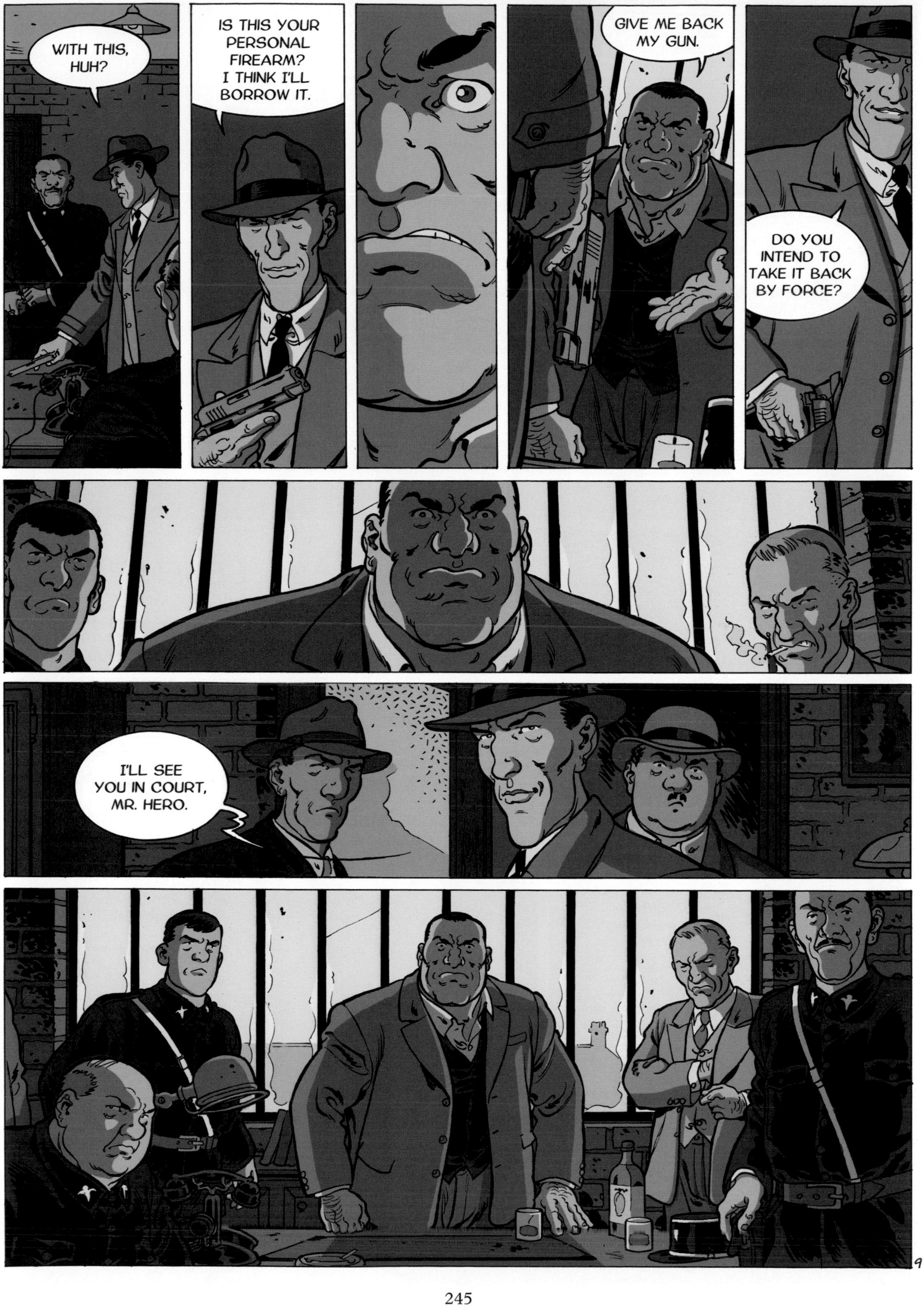
WITH THIS, HUH?
IS THIS YOUR PERSONAL FIREARM? I THINK I'LL BORROW IT.
GIVE ME BACK MY GUN.
DO YOU INTEND TO TAKE IT BACK BY FORCE?
I'LL SEE YOU IN COURT, MR. HERO.
9

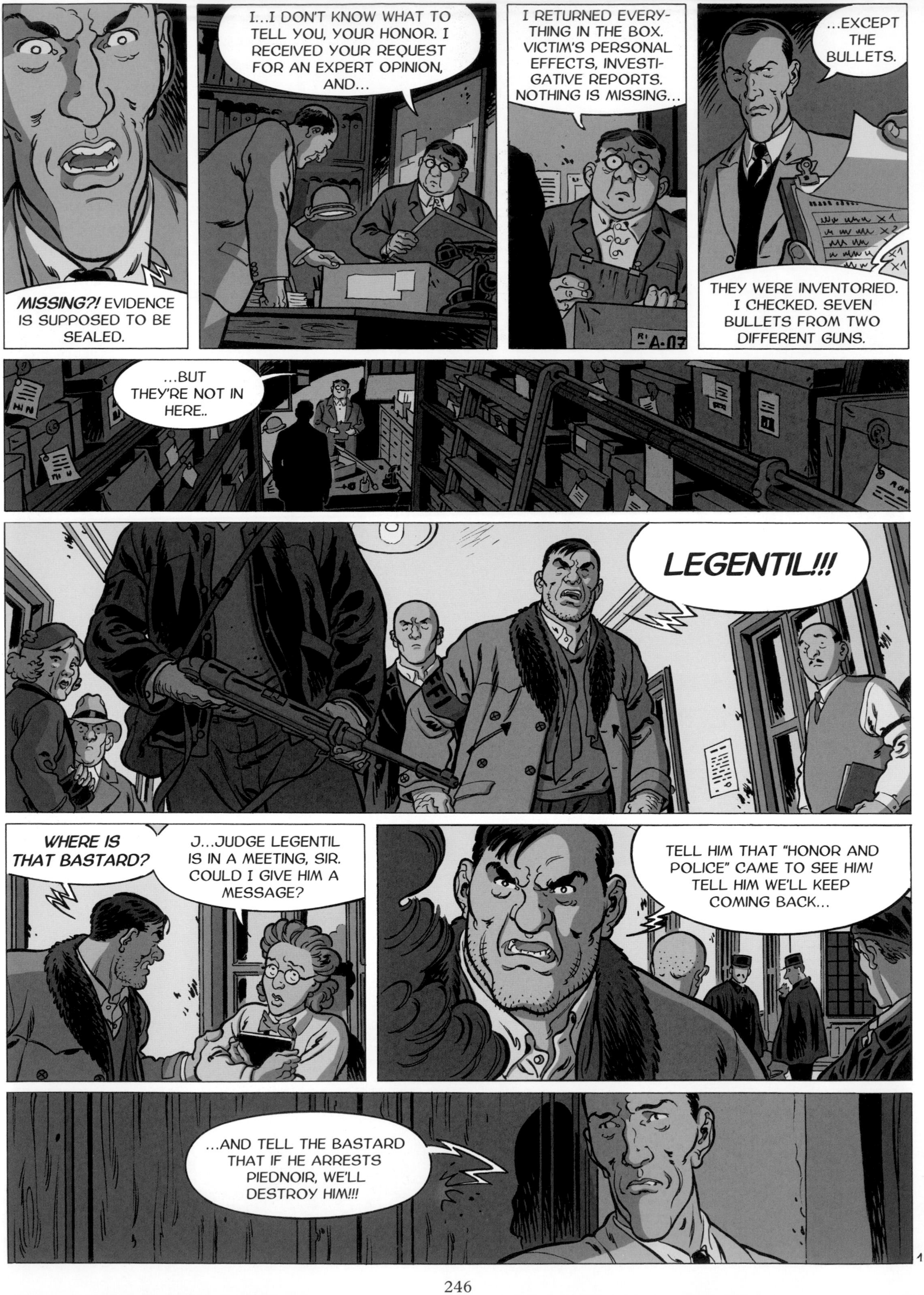
MISSING?! EVIDENCE IS SUPPOSED TO BE SEALED.
I...I DON'T KNOW WHAT TO TELL YOU, YOUR HONOR. I RECEIVED YOUR REQUEST FOR AN EXPERT OPINION, AND...
I RETURNED EVERYTHING IN THE BOX. VICTIM'S PERSONAL EFFECTS, INVESTIGATIVE REPORTS. NOTHING IS MISSING...
...EXCEPT THE BULLETS.
THEY WERE INVENTORIED. I CHECKED. SEVEN BULLETS FROM TWO DIFFERENT GUNS.
...BUT THEY'RE NOT IN HERE..
LEGENTIL!!!
WHERE IS THAT BASTARD?
J...JUDGE LEGENTIL IS IN A MEETING, SIR. COULD I GIVE HIM A MESSAGE?
TELL HIM THAT "HONOR AND POLICE" CAME TO SEE HIM! TELL HIM WE'LL KEEP COMING BACK...
...AND TELL THE BASTARD THAT IF HE ARRESTS PIEDNOIR, WE'LL DESTROY HIM!!!
10

JACQUES, YOU HAVE A VISITOR.

GOOD EVENING, YOUR HONOR...

I'M MR. MARCHAT. AN ATTORNEY AND ADVISER TO THE MINISTER OF JUSTICE.

THIS MAN SAYS...HE SAID YOU'VE BEEN THREATENED?

DON'T BE AFRAID, MRS. LEGENTIL, I AM HERE TO CLEAR UP THIS MISUNDERSTANDING...

...WE ALL KNOW THAT YOUR HUSBAND IS JUST DOING HIS JOB. WE ARE NOT BLAMING HIM FOR THAT.

INSPECTOR PIEDNOIR SAYS HE IS SORRY, YOUR HONOR, AND HE IS NOT RESPONSIBLE FOR THE BEHAVIOR OF HIS OLD RESISTANCE COMRADES...

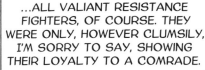

...ALL VALIANT RESISTANCE FIGHTERS, OF COURSE. THEY WERE ONLY, HOWEVER CLUMSILY, I'M SORRY TO SAY, SHOWING THEIR LOYALTY TO A COMRADE.

I UNDERSTAND THEM.

AH, PERFECT! ALL IS IN ORDER IN THAT CASE.

WOULD YOU GIVE INSPECTOR PIEDNOIR BACK HIS GUN? HE'S QUITE ATTACHED TO IT. A WAR SOUVENIR, YOU UNDERSTAND...

GOOD NIGHT, COUNSELOR.

ONE MORE THING, YOUR HONOR.

11

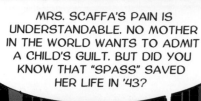

MRS. SCAFFA'S PAIN IS UNDERSTANDABLE. NO MOTHER IN THE WORLD WANTS TO ADMIT A CHILD'S GUILT. BUT DID YOU KNOW THAT "SPASS" SAVED HER LIFE IN '43?

I...PARDON?

MRS. SCAFFA WAS ARRESTED BY THE GESTAPO FOR HAVING A TSF POST. LUCKILY, SOMEONE WROTE HER NAME DOWN ON A LIST.

YOU KNOW WHAT KIND OF LIST I MEAN?

THOSE SPASS REDEEMED FROM THE GESTAPO.

EXACTLY.

IT'S TRUE THAT WE COULD CRITICIZE HIS METHODS... BUYING SOMEONE'S LIFE IS NOT AS HEROIC AS FREEING THEM WITH A WEAPON.

BUT I AM WELL PLACED TO KNOW THAT IT WORKS...

MY NAME WAS ALSO ON THAT LIST.

WHAT'S GOING ON, JACQUES?

WHAT DID YOU DO?

NOTHING, A MINOR MISUNDERSTANDING AT WORK, THAT'S ALL.

12

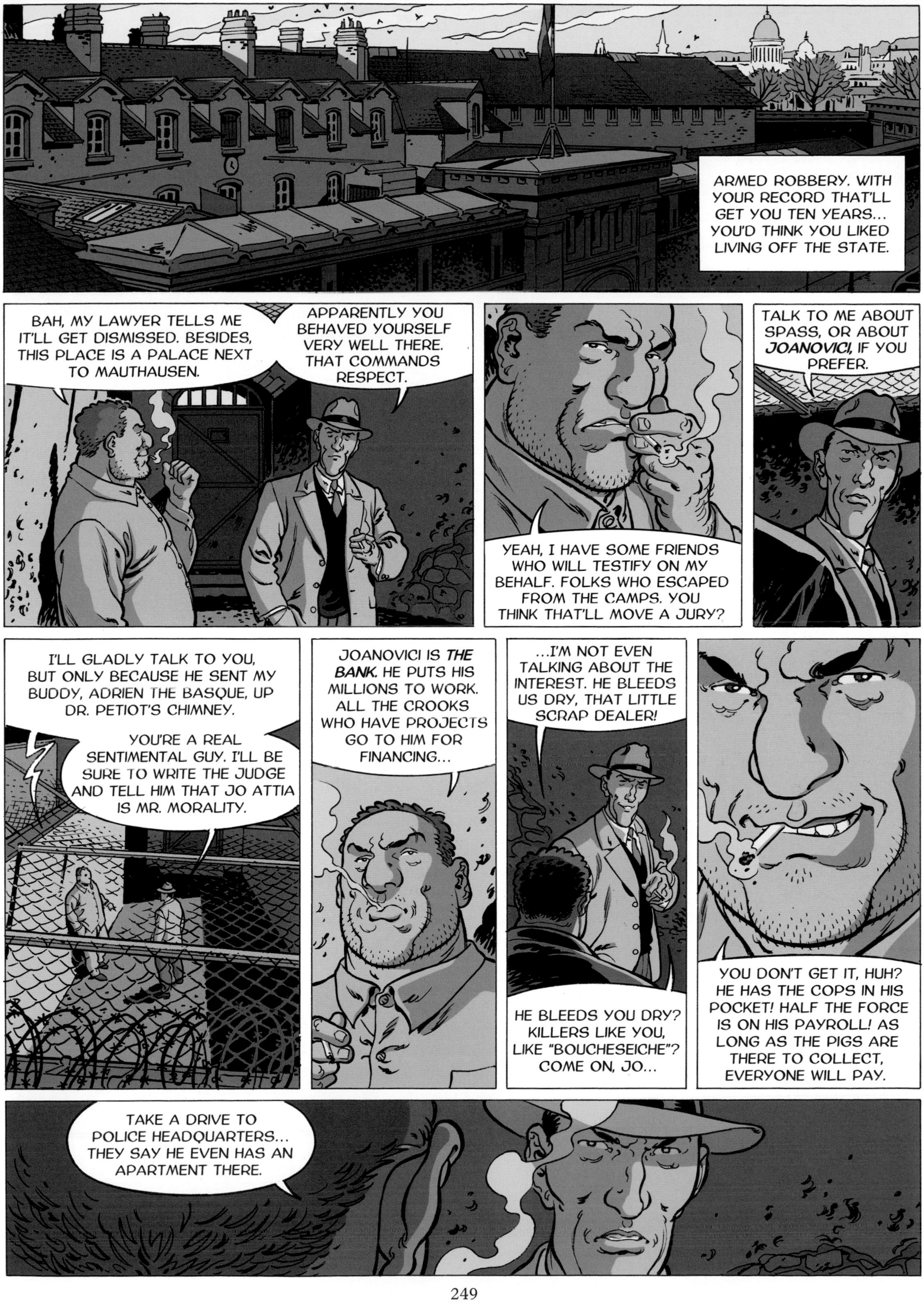
ARMED ROBBERY. WITH YOUR RECORD THAT'LL GET YOU TEN YEARS... YOU'D THINK YOU LIKED LIVING OFF THE STATE.
BAH, MY LAWYER TELLS ME IT'LL GET DISMISSED. BESIDES, THIS PLACE IS A PALACE NEXT TO MAUTHAUSEN.
APPARENTLY YOU BEHAVED YOURSELF VERY WELL THERE. THAT COMMANDS RESPECT.
YEAH, I HAVE SOME FRIENDS WHO WILL TESTIFY ON MY BEHALF. FOLKS WHO ESCAPED FROM THE CAMPS. YOU THINK THAT'LL MOVE A JURY?
TALK TO ME ABOUT SPASS, OR ABOUT JOANOVICI, IF YOU PREFER.
I'LL GLADLY TALK TO YOU, BUT ONLY BECAUSE HE SENT MY BUDDY, ADRIEN THE BASQUE, UP DR. PETIOT'S CHIMNEY.
YOU'RE A REAL SENTIMENTAL GUY. I'LL BE SURE TO WRITE THE JUDGE AND TELL HIM THAT JO ATTIA IS MR. MORALITY.
JOANOVICI IS THE BANK. HE PUTS HIS MILLIONS TO WORK. ALL THE CROOKS WHO HAVE PROJECTS GO TO HIM FOR FINANCING...
...I'M NOT EVEN TALKING ABOUT THE INTEREST. HE BLEEDS US DRY, THAT LITTLE SCRAP DEALER!
HE BLEEDS YOU DRY? KILLERS LIKE YOU, LIKE "BOUCHESEICHE"? COME ON, JO...
YOU DON'T GET IT, HUH? HE HAS THE COPS IN HIS POCKET! HALF THE FORCE IS ON HIS PAYROLL! AS LONG AS THE PIGS ARE THERE TO COLLECT, EVERYONE WILL PAY.
TAKE A DRIVE TO POLICE HEADQUARTERS... THEY SAY HE EVEN HAS AN APARTMENT THERE.
13

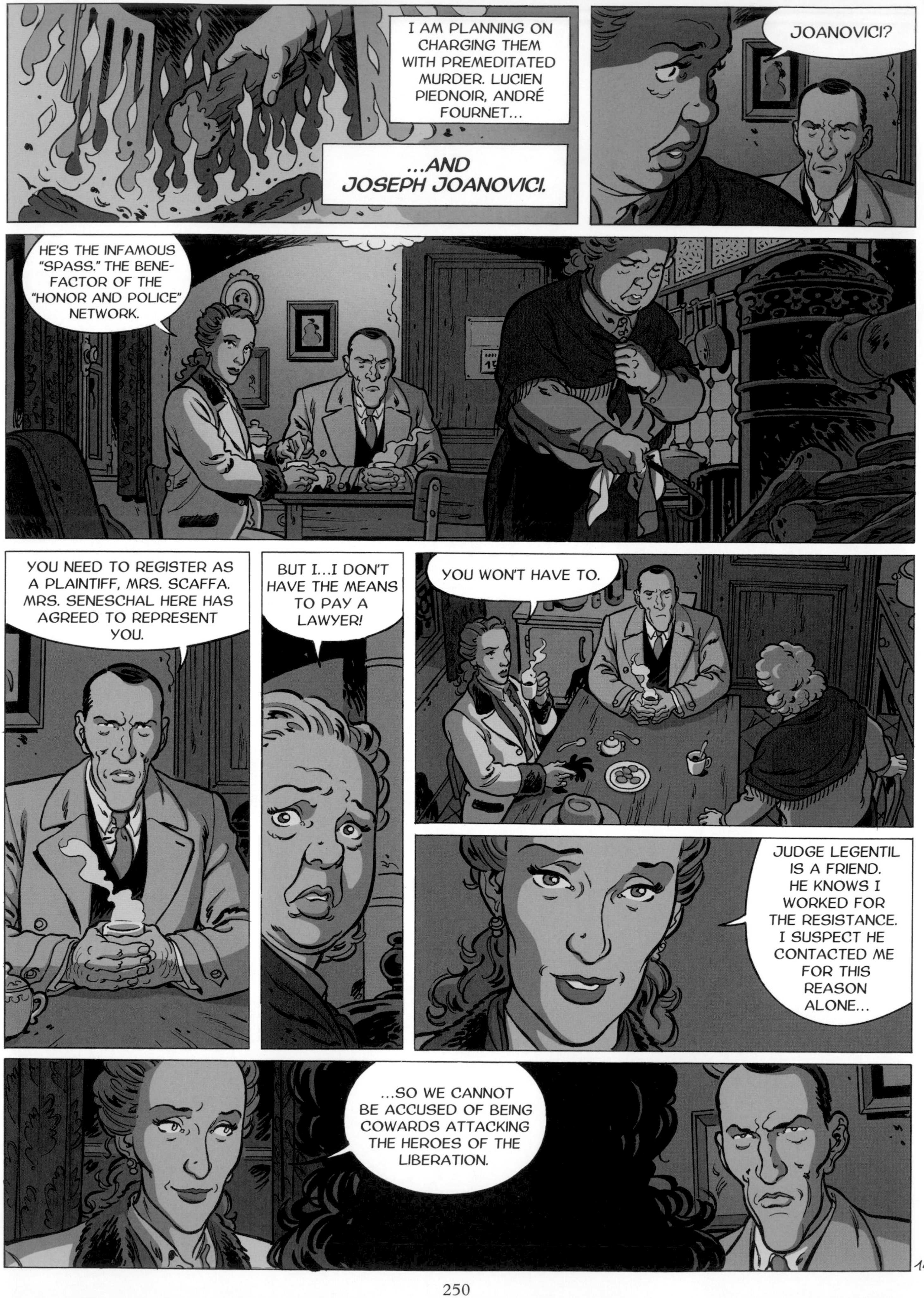
I AM PLANNING ON CHARGING THEM WITH PREMEDITATED MURDER. LUCIEN PIEDNOIR, ANDRÉ FOURNET...
...AND JOSEPH JOANOVICI.
JOANOVICI?
HE'S THE INFAMOUS "SPASS." THE BENEFACTOR OF THE "HONOR AND POLICE" NETWORK.
YOU NEED TO REGISTER AS A PLAINTIFF, MRS. SCAFFA. MRS. SENESCHAL HERE HAS AGREED TO REPRESENT YOU.
BUT I...I DON'T HAVE THE MEANS TO PAY A LAWYER!
YOU WON'T HAVE TO.
JUDGE LEGENTIL IS A FRIEND. HE KNOWS I WORKED FOR THE RESISTANCE. I SUSPECT HE CONTACTED ME FOR THIS REASON ALONE...
...SO WE CANNOT BE ACCUSED OF BEING COWARDS ATTACKING THE HEROES OF THE LIBERATION.
14

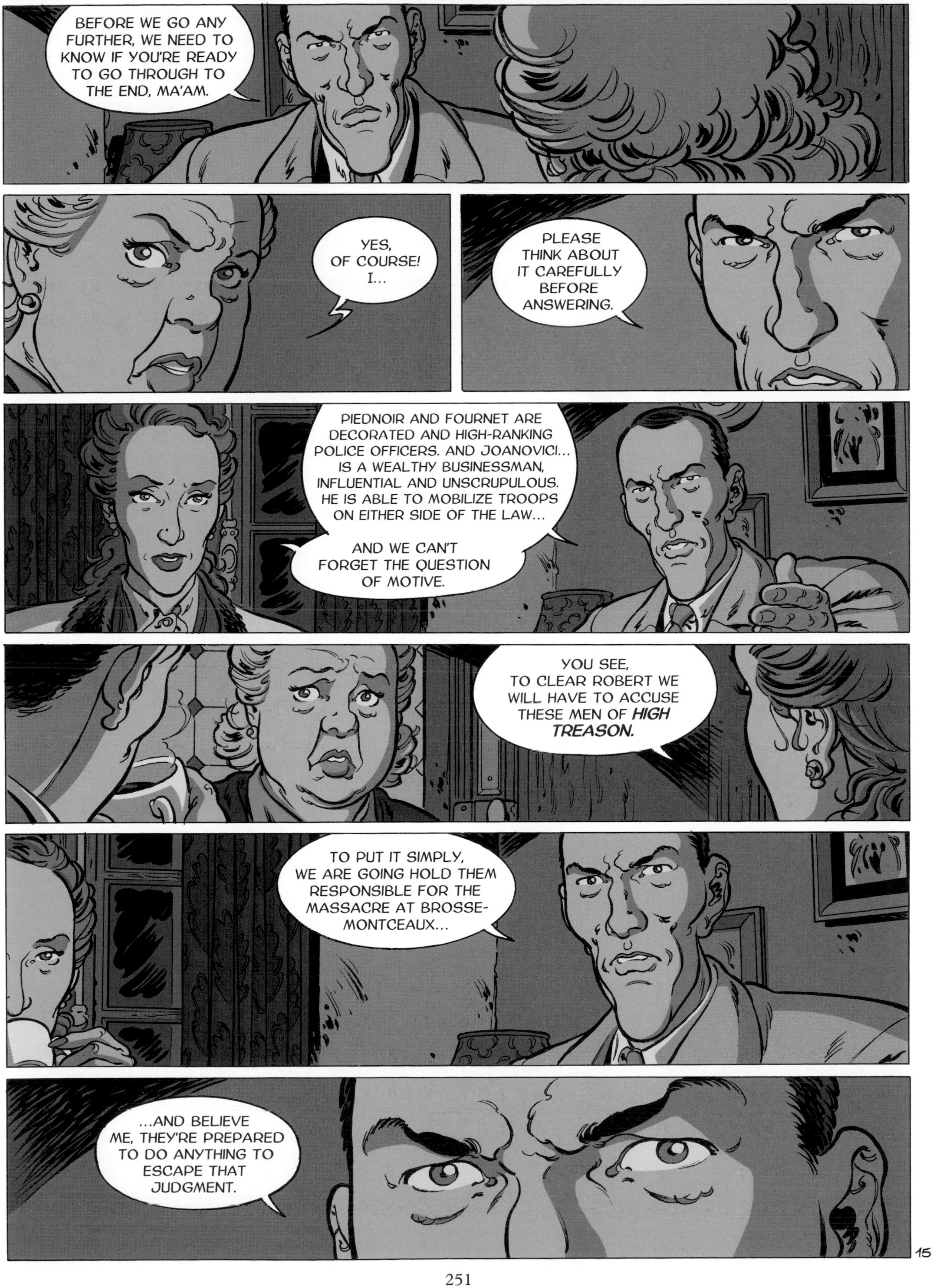
BEFORE WE GO ANY FURTHER, WE NEED TO KNOW IF YOU'RE READY TO GO THROUGH TO THE END, MA'AM.
YES, OF COURSE! I...
PLEASE THINK ABOUT IT CAREFULLY BEFORE ANSWERING.
PIEDNOIR AND FOURNET ARE DECORATED AND HIGH-RANKING POLICE OFFICERS. AND JOANOVICI... IS A WEALTHY BUSINESSMAN, INFLUENTIAL AND UNSCRUPULOUS. HE IS ABLE TO MOBILIZE TROOPS ON EITHER SIDE OF THE LAW...
AND WE CAN'T FORGET THE QUESTION OF MOTIVE.
YOU SEE, TO CLEAR ROBERT WE WILL HAVE TO ACCUSE THESE MEN OF ***HIGH TREASON.***
TO PUT IT SIMPLY, WE ARE GOING HOLD THEM RESPONSIBLE FOR THE MASSACRE AT BROSSE-MONTCEAUX...
...AND BELIEVE ME, THEY'RE PREPARED TO DO ANYTHING TO ESCAPE THAT JUDGMENT.
15

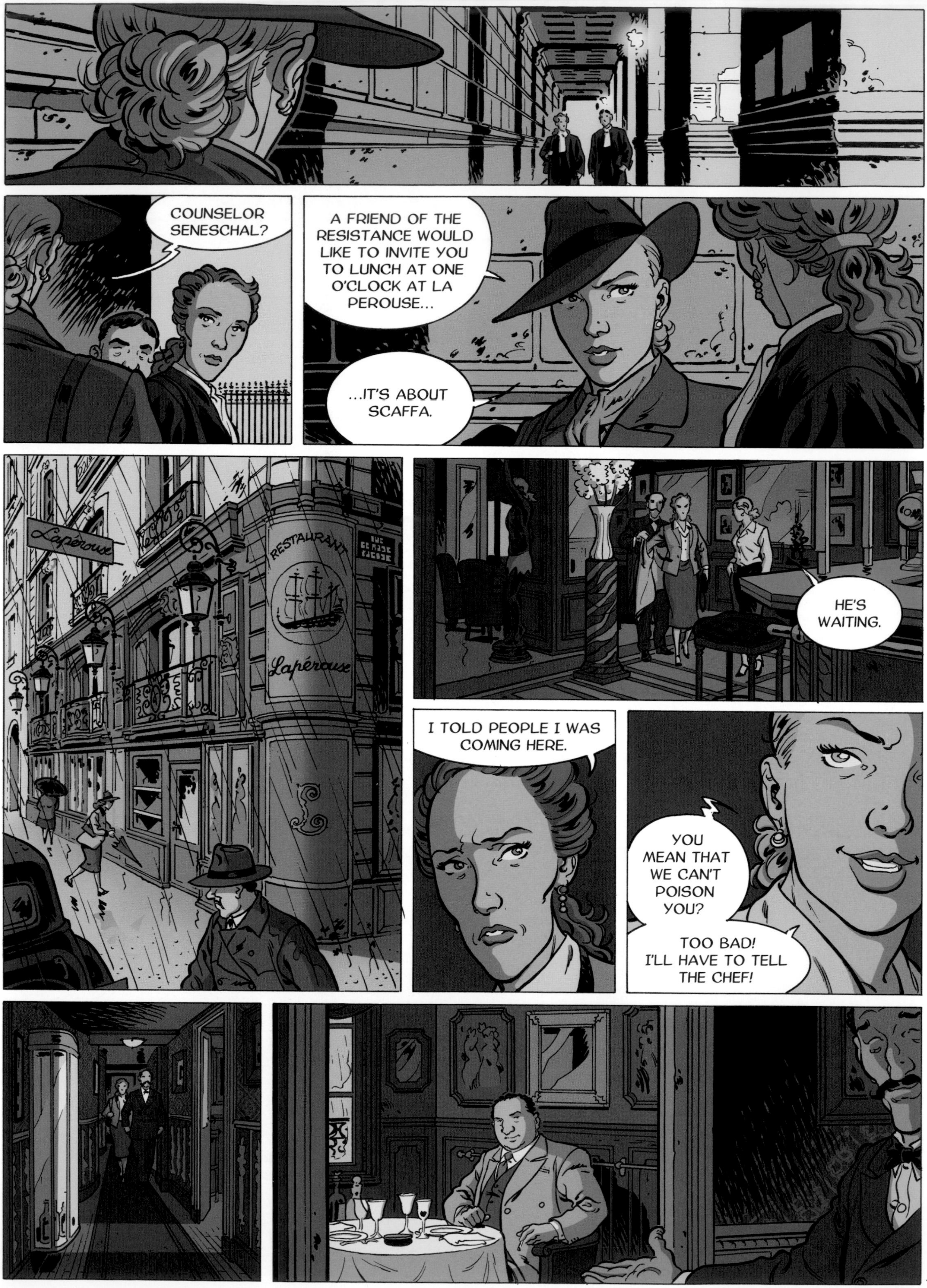
COUNSELOR SENESCHAL?
A FRIEND OF THE RESISTANCE WOULD LIKE TO INVITE YOU TO LUNCH AT ONE O'CLOCK AT LA PEROUSE...
...IT'S ABOUT SCAFFA.
Lapérouse
RESTAURANT
Lapérouse
HE'S WAITING.
I TOLD PEOPLE I WAS COMING HERE.
YOU MEAN THAT WE CAN'T POISON YOU?
TOO BAD! I'LL HAVE TO TELL THE CHEF!

16

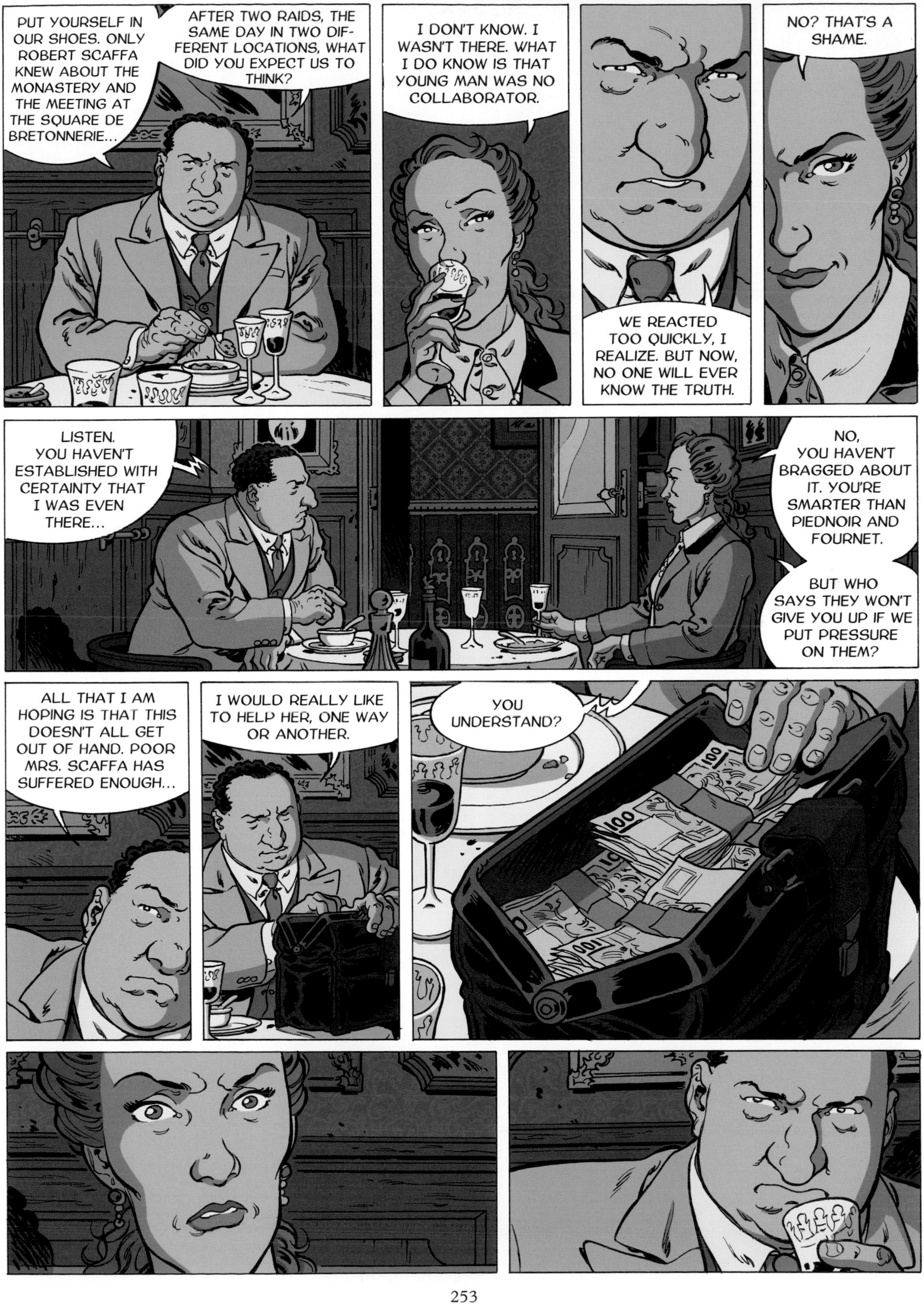
PUT YOURSELF IN OUR SHOES. ONLY ROBERT SCAFFA KNEW ABOUT THE MONASTERY AND THE MEETING AT THE SQUARE DE BRETONNERIE...
AFTER TWO RAIDS, THE SAME DAY IN TWO DIFFERENT LOCATIONS, WHAT DID YOU EXPECT US TO THINK?
I DON'T KNOW. I WASN'T THERE. WHAT I DO KNOW IS THAT YOUNG MAN WAS NO COLLABORATOR.
WE REACTED TOO QUICKLY, I REALIZE. BUT NOW, NO ONE WILL EVER KNOW THE TRUTH.
NO? THAT'S A SHAME.
LISTEN. YOU HAVEN'T ESTABLISHED WITH CERTAINTY THAT I WAS EVEN THERE...
NO, YOU HAVEN'T BRAGGED ABOUT IT. YOU'RE SMARTER THAN PIEDNOIR AND FOURNET.
BUT WHO SAYS THEY WON'T GIVE YOU UP IF WE PUT PRESSURE ON THEM?
ALL THAT I AM HOPING IS THAT THIS DOESN'T ALL GET OUT OF HAND. POOR MRS. SCAFFA HAS SUFFERED ENOUGH...
I WOULD REALLY LIKE TO HELP HER, ONE WAY OR ANOTHER.
YOU UNDERSTAND?
17

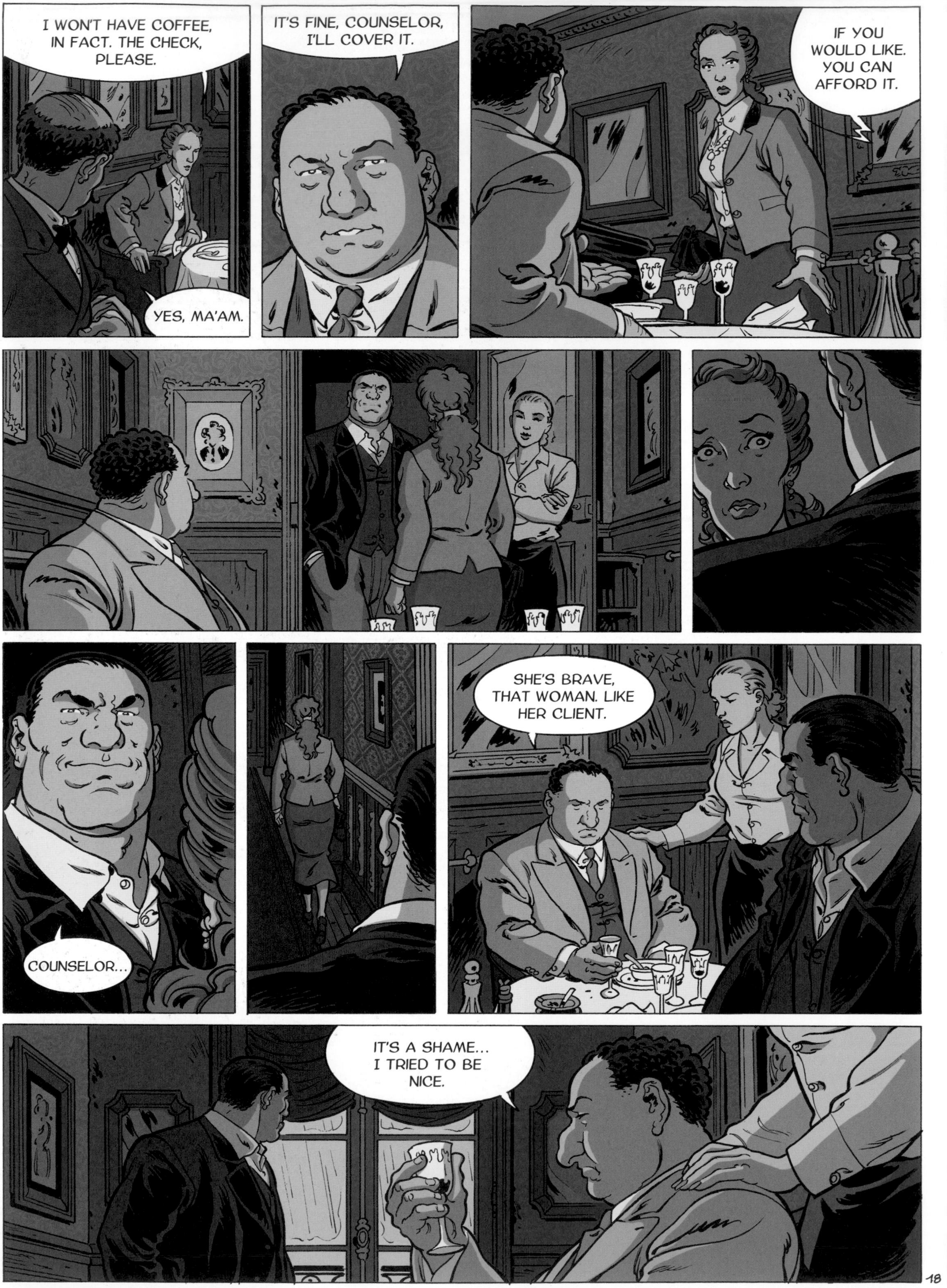

I WON'T HAVE COFFEE, IN FACT. THE CHECK, PLEASE.
YES, MA'AM.
IT'S FINE, COUNSELOR, I'LL COVER IT.
IF YOU WOULD LIKE. YOU CAN AFFORD IT.
COUNSELOR...
SHE'S BRAVE, THAT WOMAN. LIKE HER CLIENT.
IT'S A SHAME... I TRIED TO BE NICE.
18

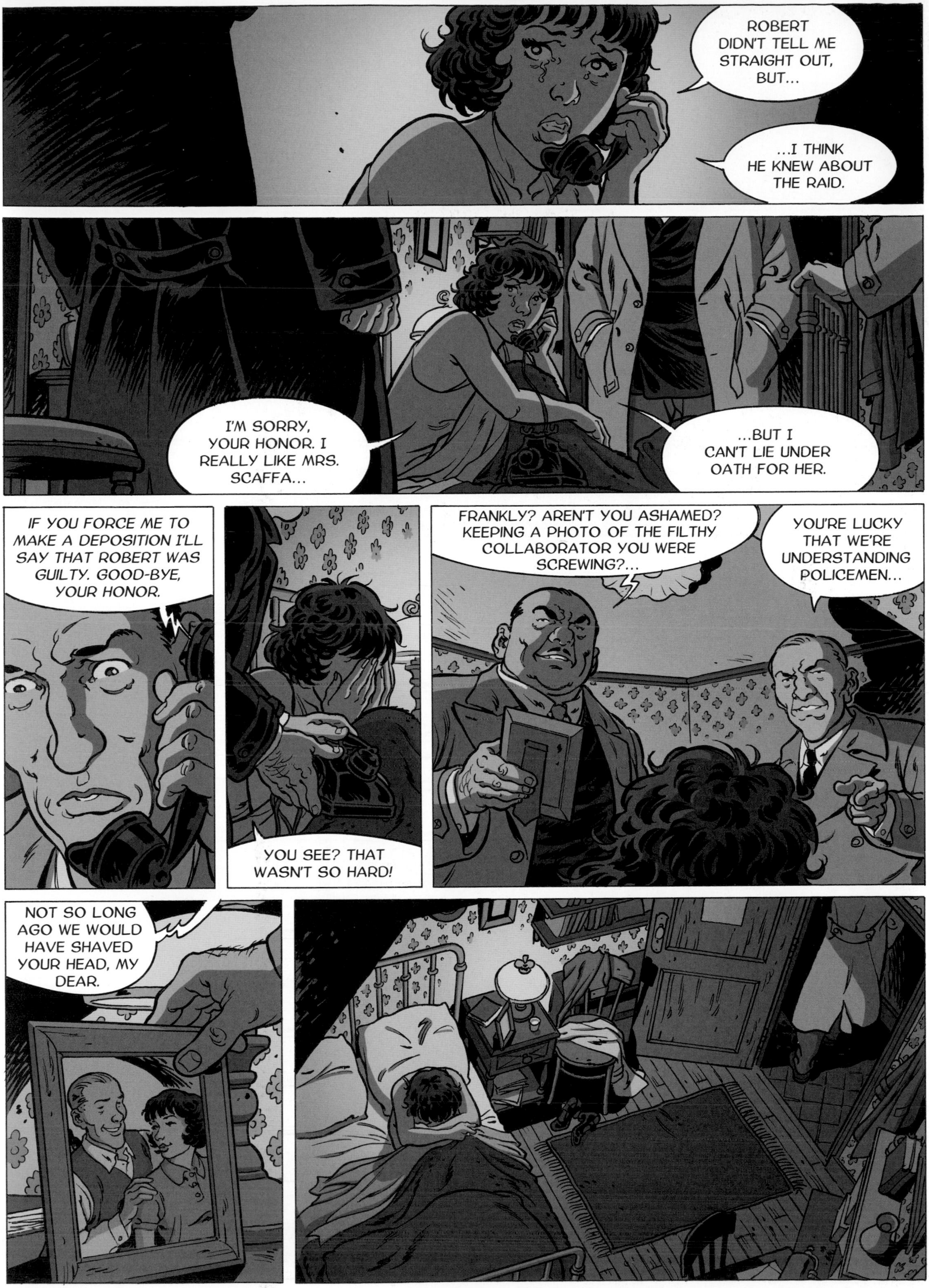
ROBERT DIDN'T TELL ME STRAIGHT OUT, BUT...
...I THINK HE KNEW ABOUT THE RAID.
I'M SORRY, YOUR HONOR. I REALLY LIKE MRS. SCAFFA...
...BUT I CAN'T LIE UNDER OATH FOR HER.
IF YOU FORCE ME TO MAKE A DEPOSITION I'LL SAY THAT ROBERT WAS GUILTY. GOOD-BYE, YOUR HONOR.
YOU SEE? THAT WASN'T SO HARD!
FRANKLY? AREN'T YOU ASHAMED? KEEPING A PHOTO OF THE FILTHY COLLABORATOR YOU WERE SCREWING?...
YOU'RE LUCKY THAT WE'RE UNDERSTANDING POLICEMEN...
NOT SO LONG AGO WE WOULD HAVE SHAVED YOUR HEAD, MY DEAR.

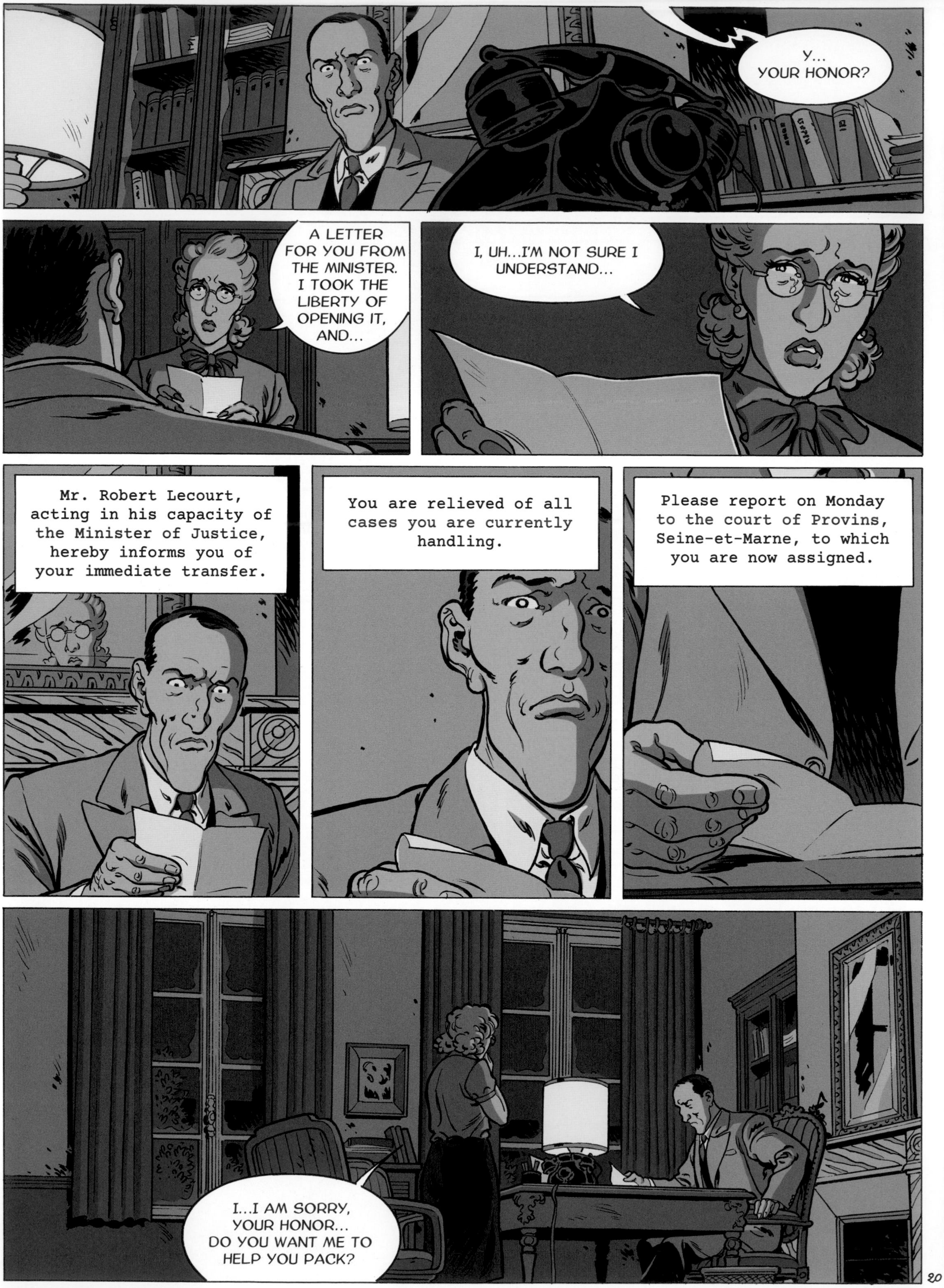
Y... YOUR HONOR?
A LETTER FOR YOU FROM THE MINISTER. I TOOK THE LIBERTY OF OPENING IT, AND...
I, UH...I'M NOT SURE I UNDERSTAND...
Mr. Robert Lecourt, acting in his capacity of the Minister of Justice, hereby informs you of your immediate transfer.
You are relieved of all cases you are currently handling.
Please report on Monday to the court of Provins, Seine-et-Marne, to which you are now assigned.
I...I AM SORRY, YOUR HONOR... DO YOU WANT ME TO HELP YOU PACK?
20

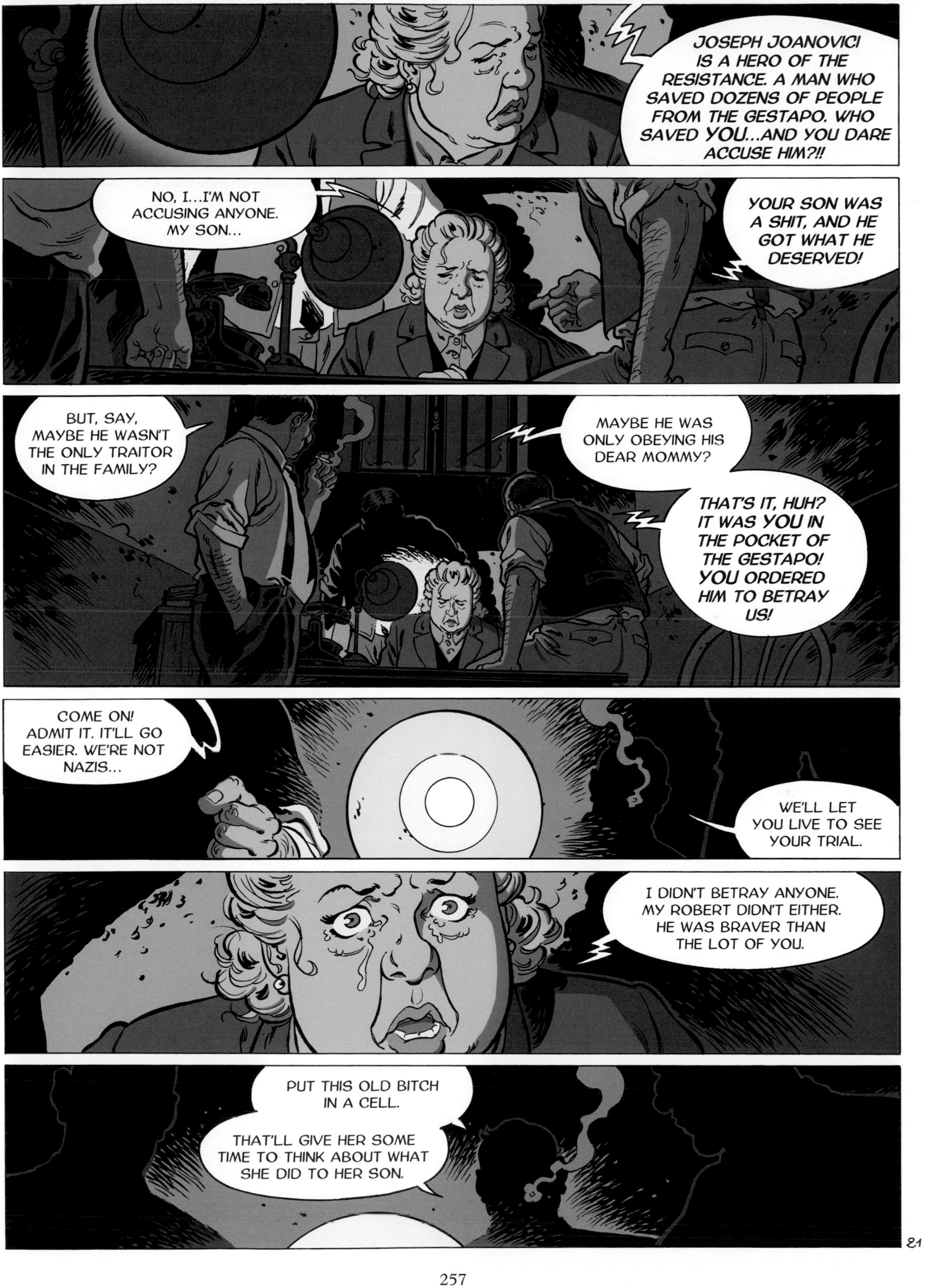
JOSEPH JOANOVICI IS A HERO OF THE RESISTANCE. A MAN WHO SAVED DOZENS OF PEOPLE FROM THE GESTAPO. WHO SAVED YOU...AND YOU DARE ACCUSE HIM?!!
NO, I...I'M NOT ACCUSING ANYONE. MY SON...
YOUR SON WAS A SHIT, AND HE GOT WHAT HE DESERVED!
BUT, SAY, MAYBE HE WASN'T THE ONLY TRAITOR IN THE FAMILY?
MAYBE HE WAS ONLY OBEYING HIS DEAR MOMMY?
THAT'S IT, HUH? IT WAS YOU IN THE POCKET OF THE GESTAPO! YOU ORDERED HIM TO BETRAY US!
COME ON! ADMIT IT. IT'LL GO EASIER. WE'RE NOT NAZIS...
WE'LL LET YOU LIVE TO SEE YOUR TRIAL.
I DIDN'T BETRAY ANYONE. MY ROBERT DIDN'T EITHER. HE WAS BRAVER THAN THE LOT OF YOU.
PUT THIS OLD BITCH IN A CELL.
THAT'LL GIVE HER SOME TIME TO THINK ABOUT WHAT SHE DID TO HER SON.
21

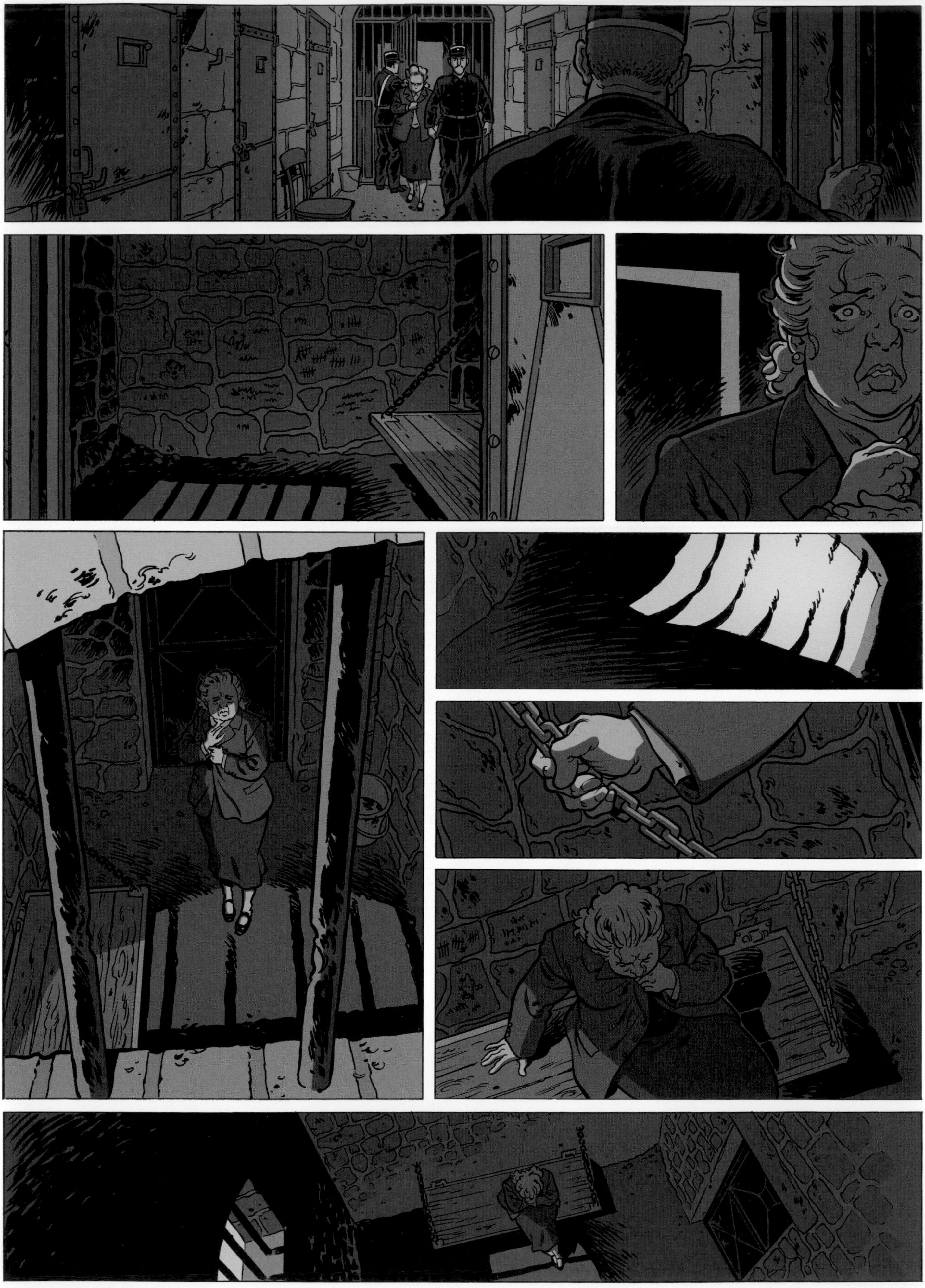

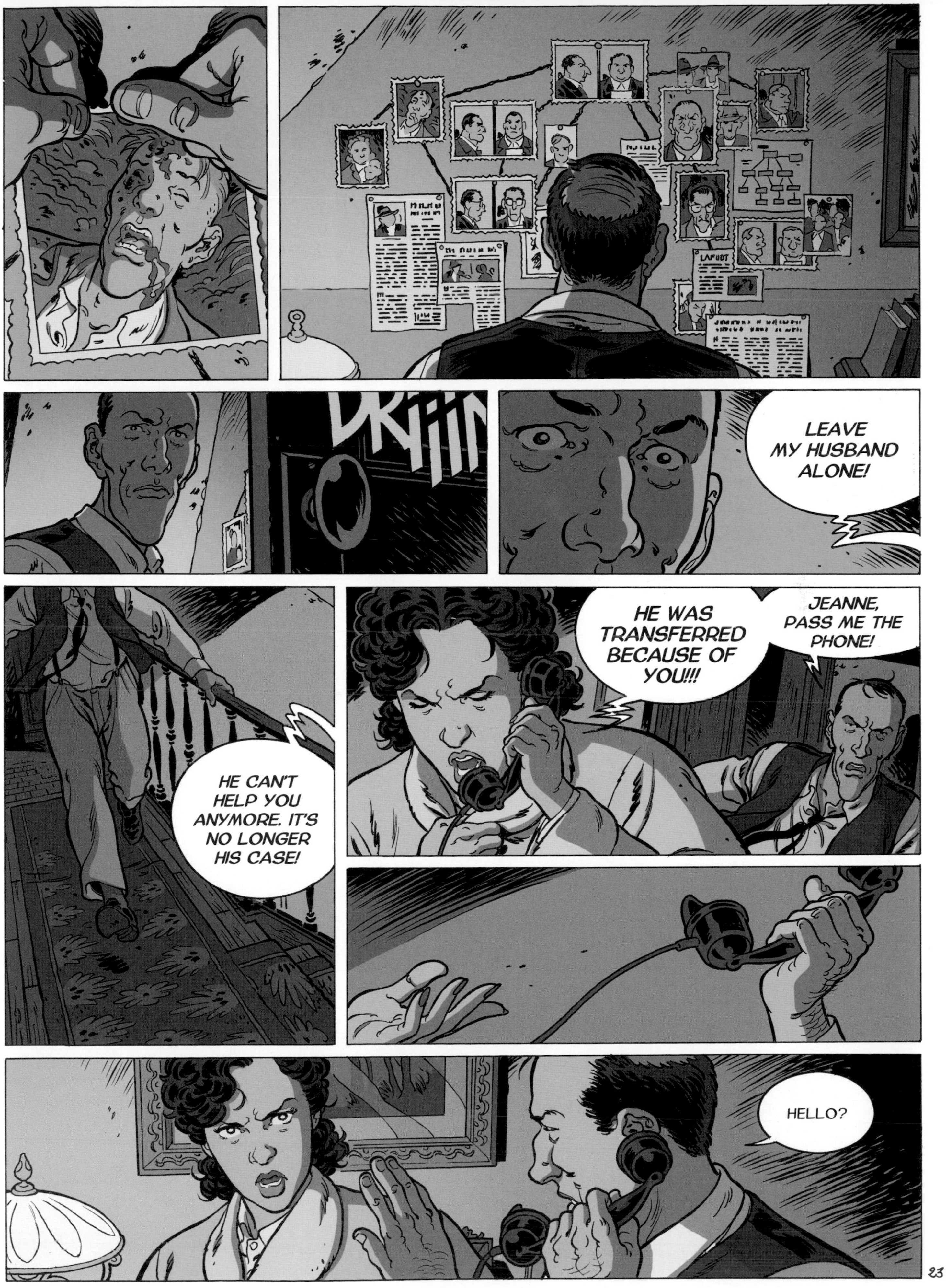
LEAVE MY HUSBAND ALONE!
HE WAS TRANSFERRED BECAUSE OF YOU!!!
JEANNE, PASS ME THE PHONE!
HE CAN'T HELP YOU ANYMORE. IT'S NO LONGER HIS CASE!
HELLO?
23

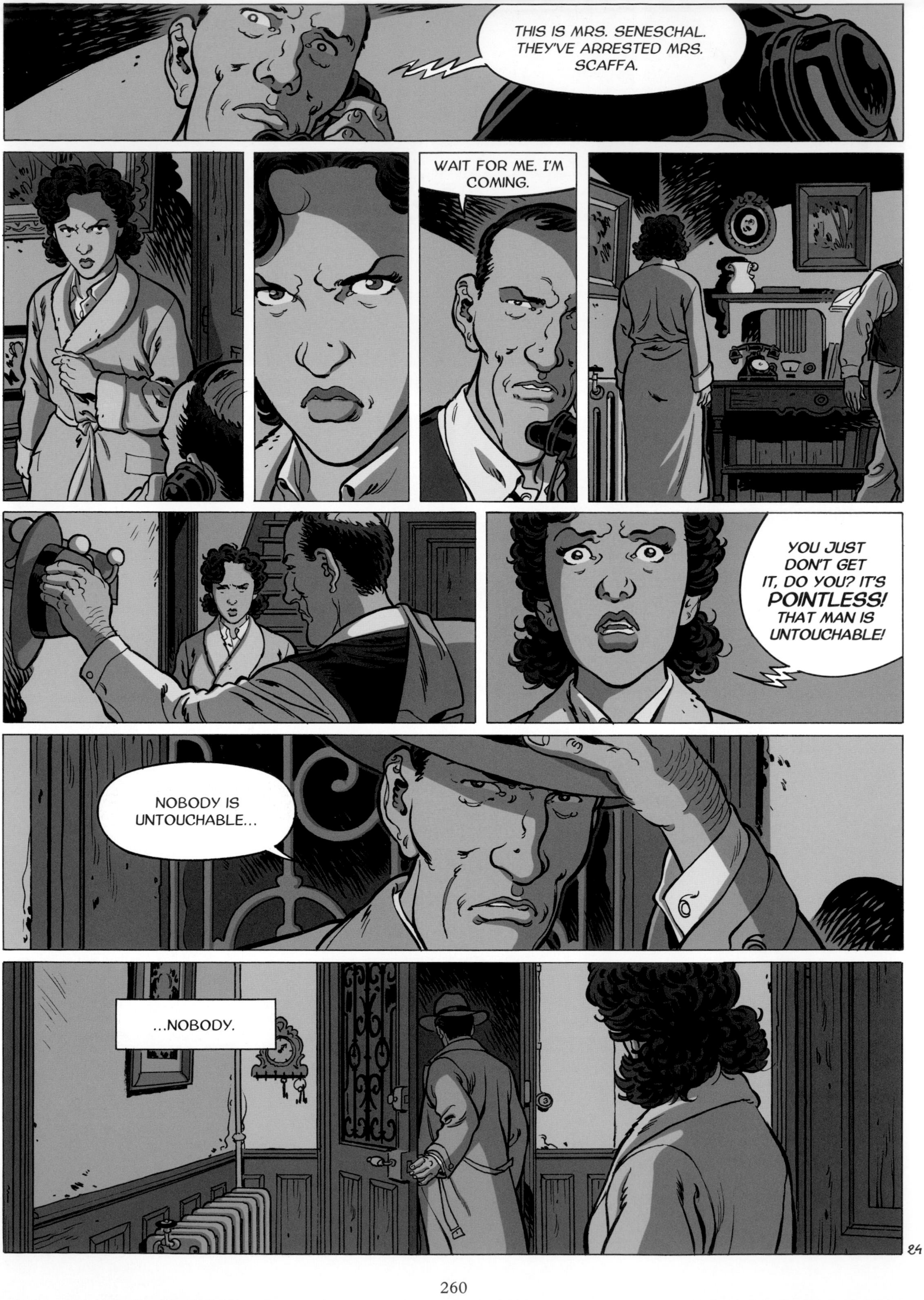
THIS IS MRS. SENESCHAL. THEY'VE ARRESTED MRS. SCAFFA.
WAIT FOR ME. I'M COMING.
YOU JUST DON'T GET IT, DO YOU? IT'S POINTLESS! THAT MAN IS UNTOUCHABLE!
NOBODY IS UNTOUCHABLE...
...NOBODY.
24

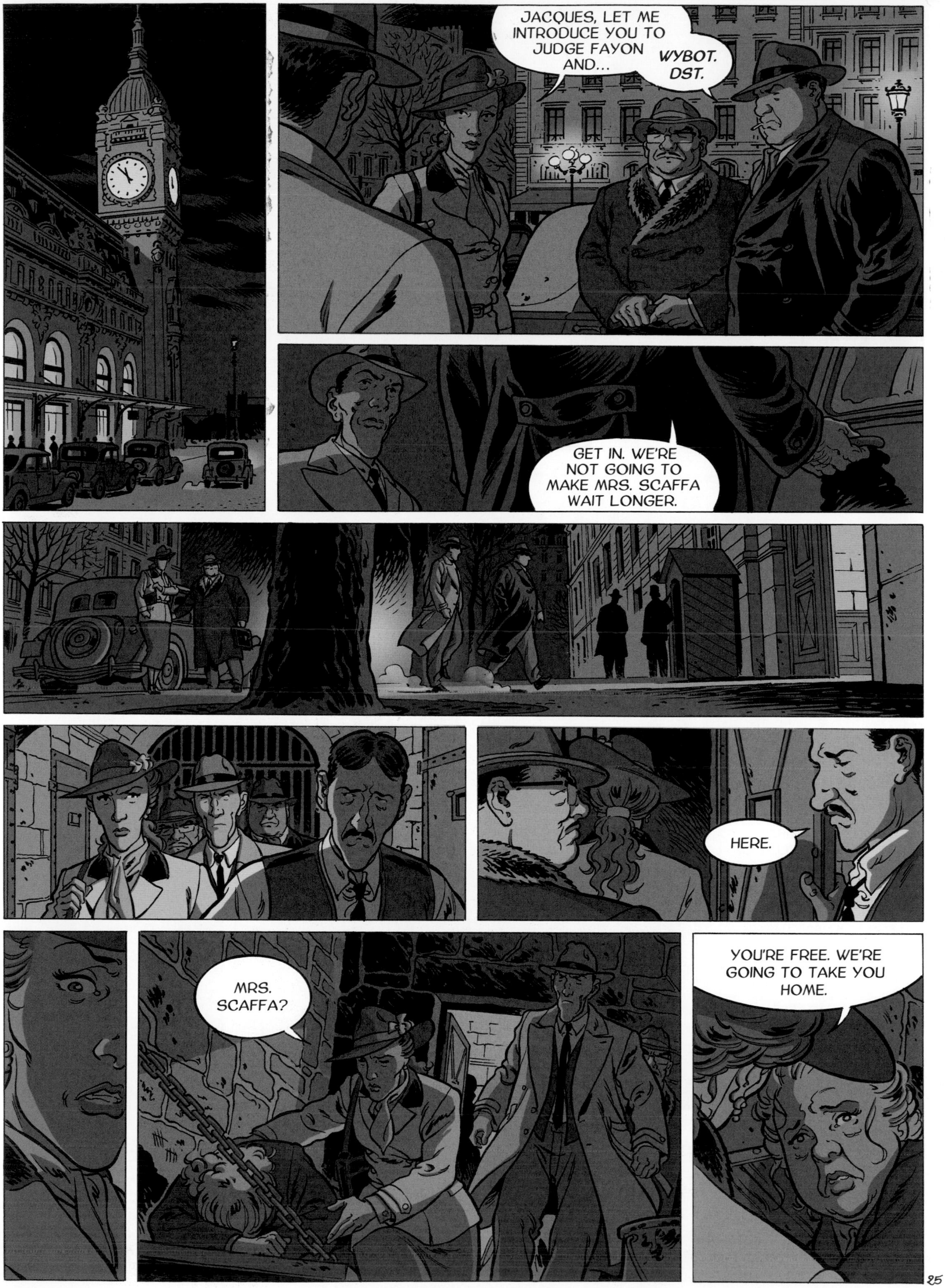
JACQUES, LET ME INTRODUCE YOU TO JUDGE FAYON AND...
WYBOT. DST.
GET IN. WE'RE NOT GOING TO MAKE MRS. SCAFFA WAIT LONGER.
HERE.
MRS. SCAFFA?
YOU'RE FREE. WE'RE GOING TO TAKE YOU HOME.
25

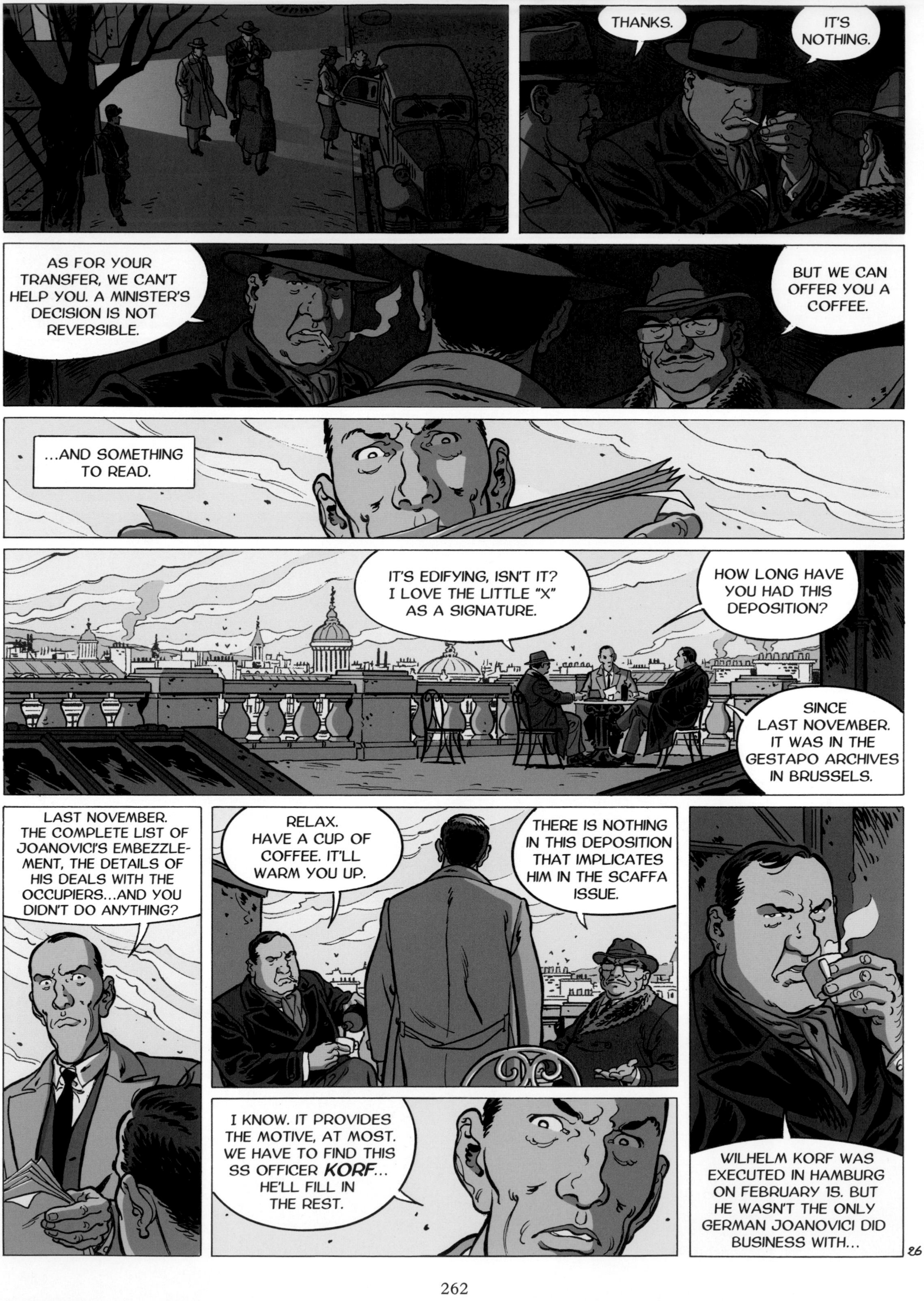
THANKS.
IT'S NOTHING.
AS FOR YOUR TRANSFER, WE CAN'T HELP YOU. A MINISTER'S DECISION IS NOT REVERSIBLE.
BUT WE CAN OFFER YOU A COFFEE.
...AND SOMETHING TO READ.
IT'S EDIFYING, ISN'T IT? I LOVE THE LITTLE "X" AS A SIGNATURE.
HOW LONG HAVE YOU HAD THIS DEPOSITION?
SINCE LAST NOVEMBER. IT WAS IN THE GESTAPO ARCHIVES IN BRUSSELS.
LAST NOVEMBER. THE COMPLETE LIST OF JOANOVICI'S EMBEZZLE-MENT, THE DETAILS OF HIS DEALS WITH THE OCCUPIERS...AND YOU DIDN'T DO ANYTHING?
RELAX. HAVE A CUP OF COFFEE. IT'LL WARM YOU UP.
THERE IS NOTHING IN THIS DEPOSITION THAT IMPLICATES HIM IN THE SCAFFA ISSUE.
I KNOW. IT PROVIDES THE MOTIVE, AT MOST. WE HAVE TO FIND THIS SS OFFICER KORF... HE'LL FILL IN THE REST.
WILHELM KORF WAS EXECUTED IN HAMBURG ON FEBRUARY 15. BUT HE WASN'T THE ONLY GERMAN JOANOVICI DID BUSINESS WITH...
26

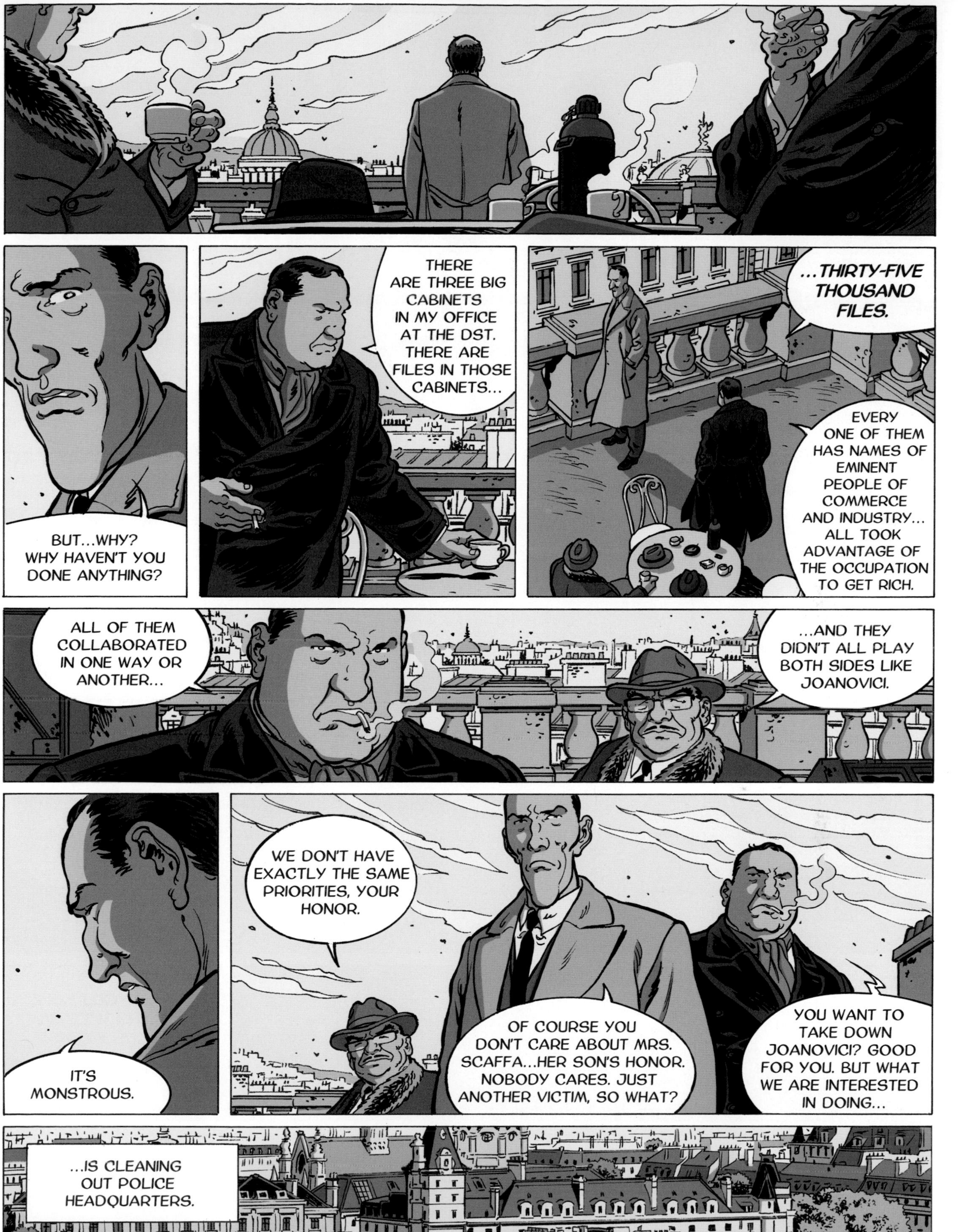

BUT...WHY? WHY HAVEN'T YOU DONE ANYTHING?
THERE ARE THREE BIG CABINETS IN MY OFFICE AT THE DST. THERE ARE FILES IN THOSE CABINETS...
...THIRTY-FIVE THOUSAND FILES.
EVERY ONE OF THEM HAS NAMES OF EMINENT PEOPLE OF COMMERCE AND INDUSTRY... ALL TOOK ADVANTAGE OF THE OCCUPATION TO GET RICH.
ALL OF THEM COLLABORATED IN ONE WAY OR ANOTHER...
...AND THEY DIDN'T ALL PLAY BOTH SIDES LIKE JOANOVICI.
IT'S MONSTROUS.
WE DON'T HAVE EXACTLY THE SAME PRIORITIES, YOUR HONOR.
OF COURSE YOU DON'T CARE ABOUT MRS. SCAFFA...HER SON'S HONOR. NOBODY CARES. JUST ANOTHER VICTIM, SO WHAT?
YOU WANT TO TAKE DOWN JOANOVICI? GOOD FOR YOU. BUT WHAT WE ARE INTERESTED IN DOING...
...IS CLEANING OUT POLICE HEADQUARTERS.
27

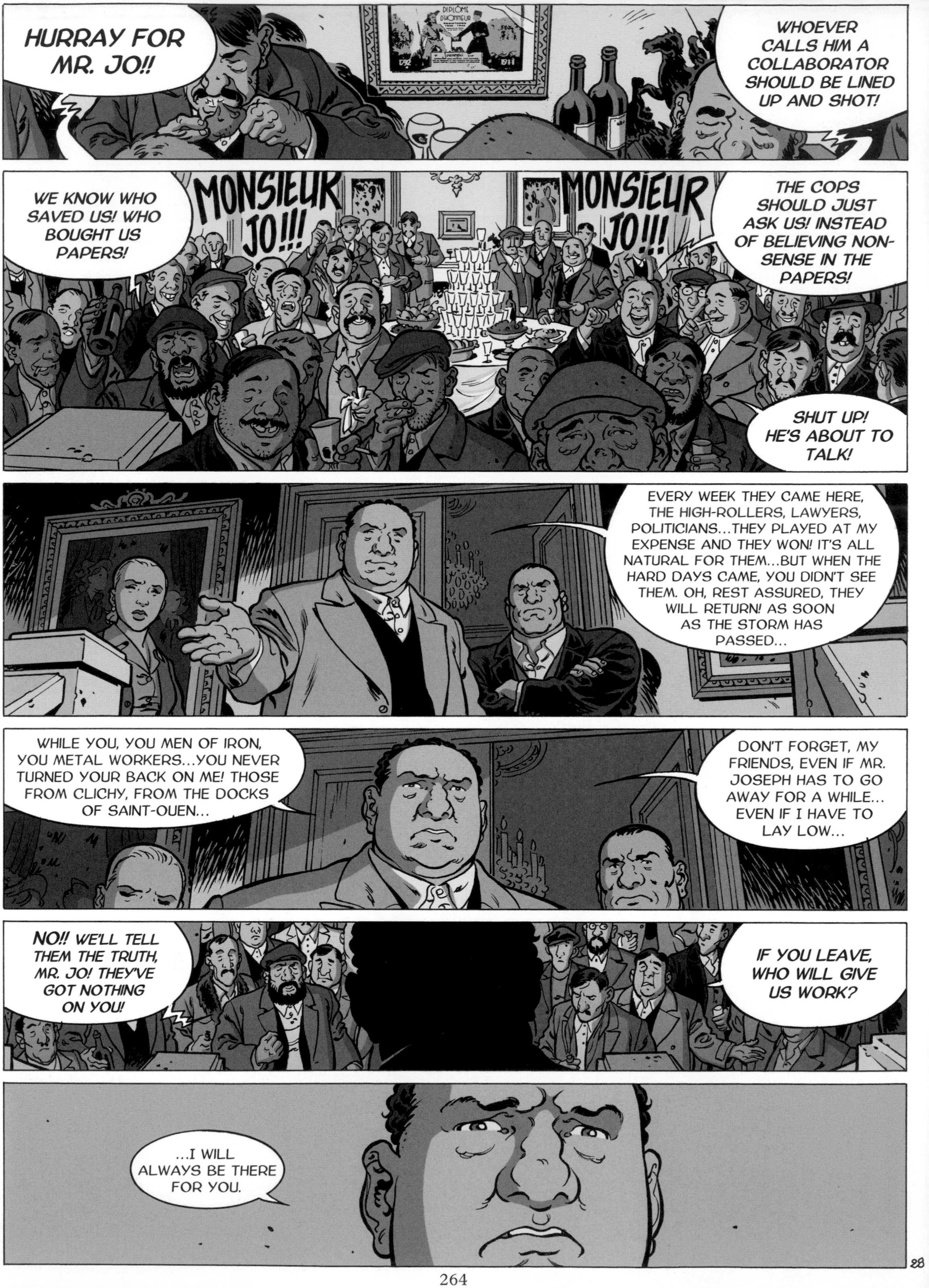
HURRAY FOR MR. JO!!
WHOEVER CALLS HIM A COLLABORATOR SHOULD BE LINED UP AND SHOT!
WE KNOW WHO SAVED US! WHO BOUGHT US PAPERS!
MONSIEUR JO!!!
MONSIEUR JO!!!
THE COPS SHOULD JUST ASK US! INSTEAD OF BELIEVING NON-SENSE IN THE PAPERS!
SHUT UP! HE'S ABOUT TO TALK!
EVERY WEEK THEY CAME HERE, THE HIGH-ROLLERS, LAWYERS, POLITICIANS...THEY PLAYED AT MY EXPENSE AND THEY WON! IT'S ALL NATURAL FOR THEM...BUT WHEN THE HARD DAYS CAME, YOU DIDN'T SEE THEM. OH, REST ASSURED, THEY WILL RETURN! AS SOON AS THE STORM HAS PASSED...
WHILE YOU, YOU MEN OF IRON, YOU METAL WORKERS...YOU NEVER TURNED YOUR BACK ON ME! THOSE FROM CLICHY, FROM THE DOCKS OF SAINT-OUEN...
DON'T FORGET, MY FRIENDS, EVEN IF MR. JOSEPH HAS TO GO AWAY FOR A WHILE... EVEN IF I HAVE TO LAY LOW...
NO!! WE'LL TELL THEM THE TRUTH, MR. JO! THEY'VE GOT NOTHING ON YOU!
IF YOU LEAVE, WHO WILL GIVE US WORK?
...I WILL ALWAYS BE THERE FOR YOU.
28

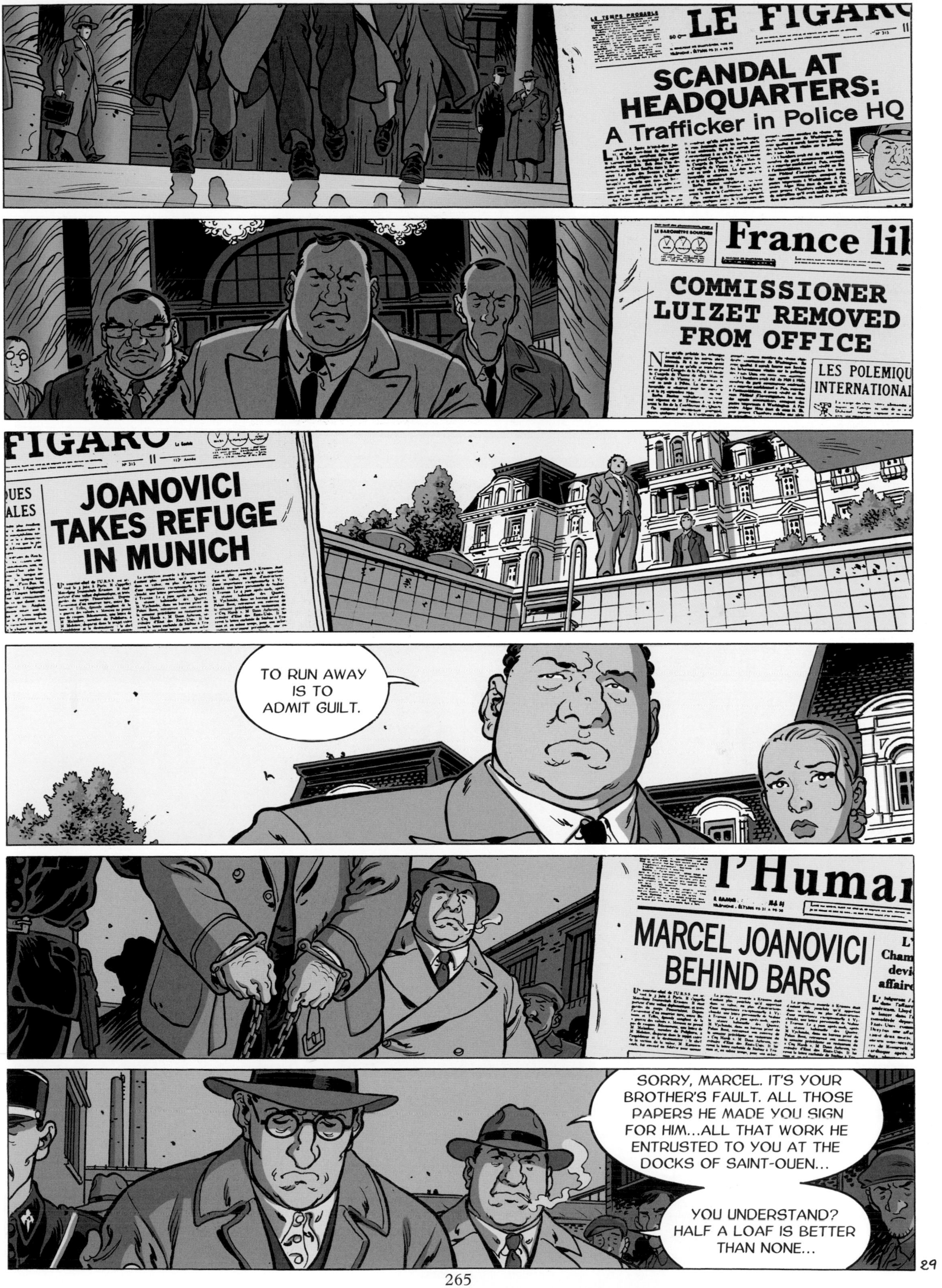
LE FIGARO
SCANDAL AT HEADQUARTERS: A Trafficker in Police HQ
France li
COMMISSIONER LUIZET REMOVED FROM OFFICE
LES POLEMIQU INTERNATIONAL
FIGARO
JOANOVICI TAKES REFUGE IN MUNICH
TO RUN AWAY IS TO ADMIT GUILT.
l'Human
MARCEL JOANOVICI BEHIND BARS
SORRY, MARCEL. IT'S YOUR BROTHER'S FAULT. ALL THOSE PAPERS HE MADE YOU SIGN FOR HIM...ALL THAT WORK HE ENTRUSTED TO YOU AT THE DOCKS OF SAINT-OUEN...
YOU UNDERSTAND? HALF A LOAF IS BETTER THAN NONE...
29

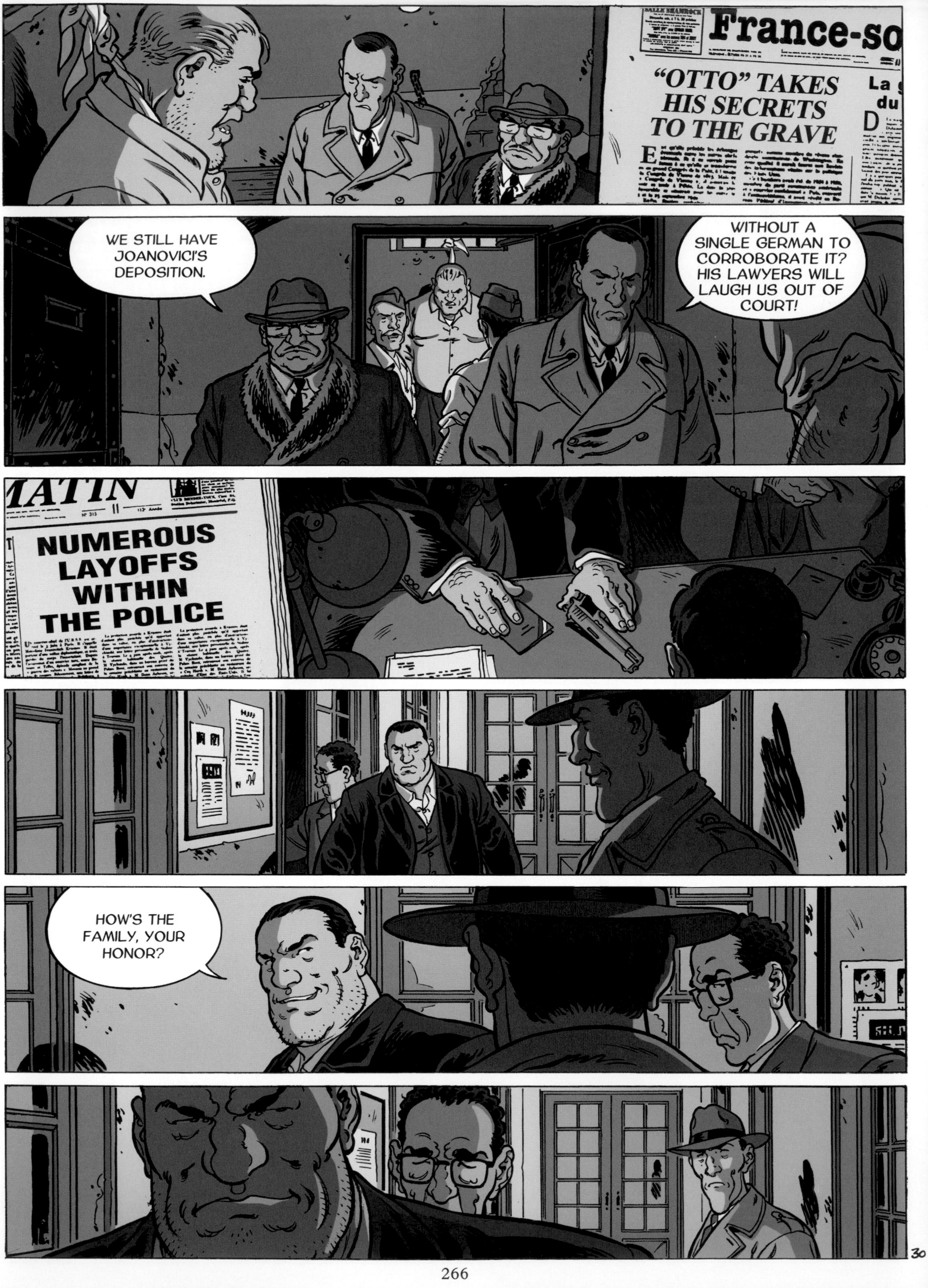
France-so
"OTTO" TAKES HIS SECRETS TO THE GRAVE
WE STILL HAVE JOANOVICI'S DEPOSITION.
WITHOUT A SINGLE GERMAN TO CORROBORATE IT? HIS LAWYERS WILL LAUGH US OUT OF COURT!
MATIN
NUMEROUS LAYOFFS WITHIN THE POLICE
HOW'S THE FAMILY, YOUR HONOR?
30

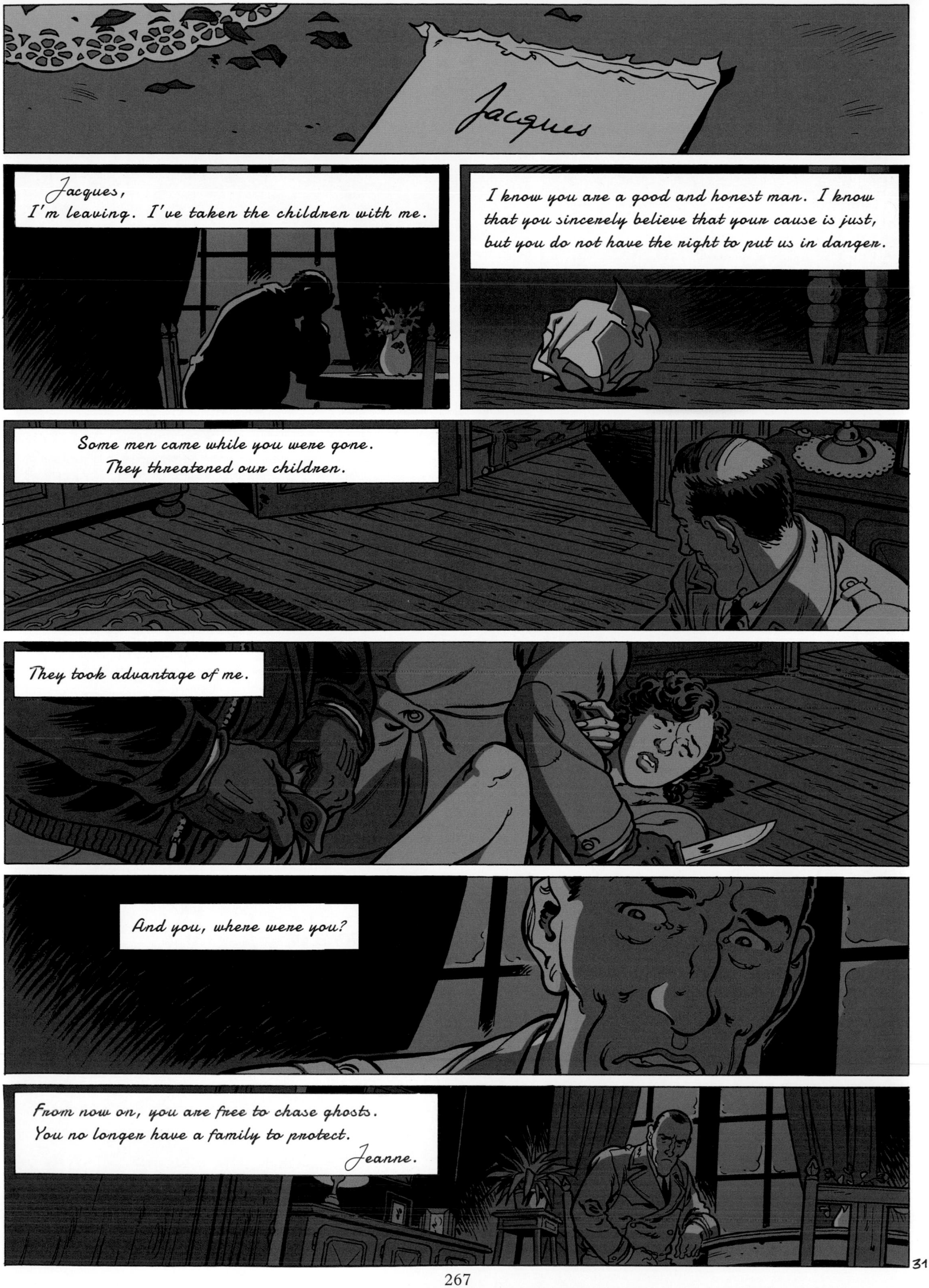
Jacques
Jacques,
I'm leaving. I've taken the children with me.
I know you are a good and honest man. I know that you sincerely believe that your cause is just, but you do not have the right to put us in danger.
Some men came while you were gone. They threatened our children.
They took advantage of me.
And you, where were you?
From now on, you are free to chase ghosts. You no longer have a family to protect.
Jeanne.
31

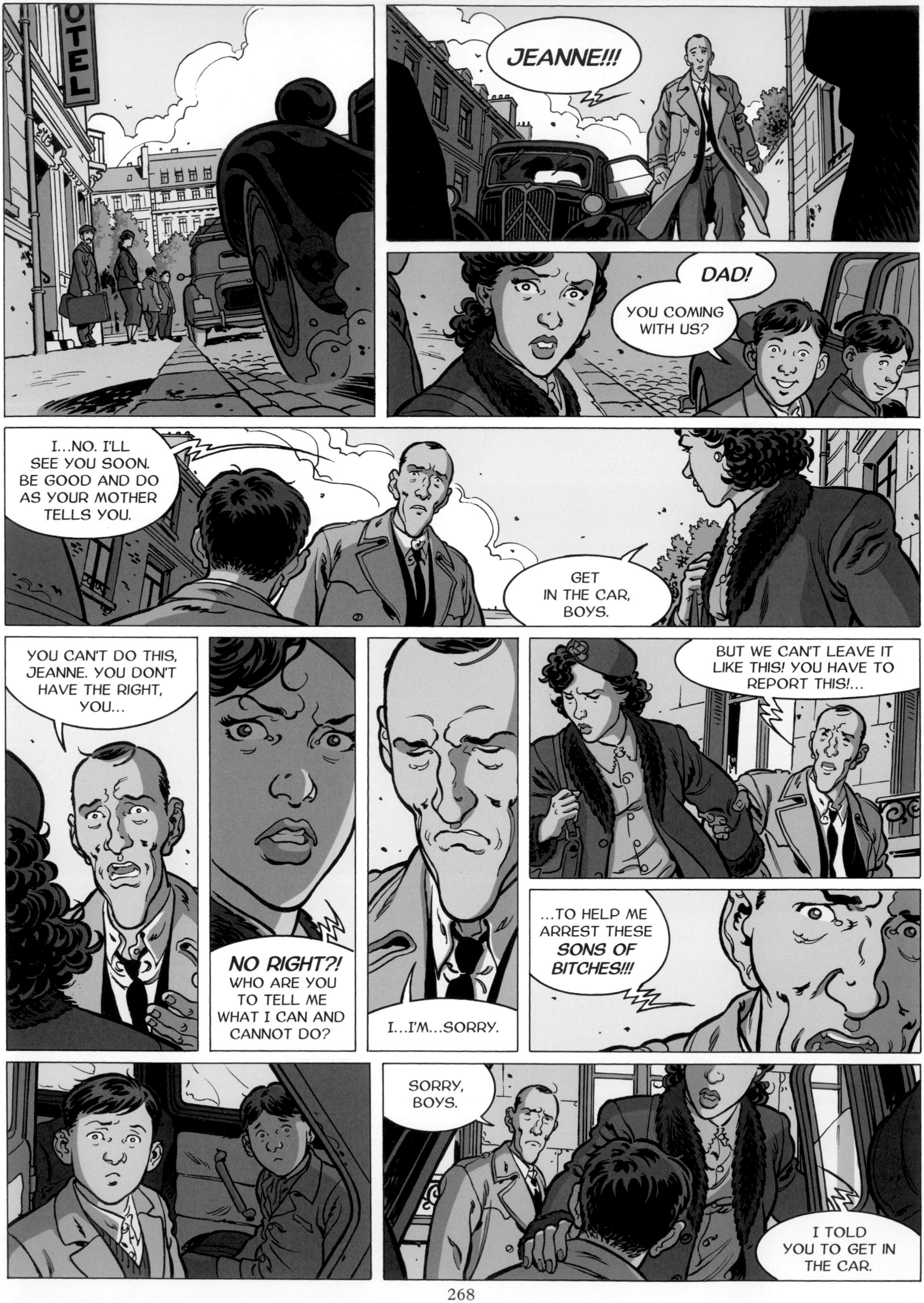
OTEL
JEANNE!!!
DAD!
YOU COMING WITH US?
I...NO. I'LL SEE YOU SOON. BE GOOD AND DO AS YOUR MOTHER TELLS YOU.
GET IN THE CAR, BOYS.
YOU CAN'T DO THIS, JEANNE. YOU DON'T HAVE THE RIGHT, YOU...
NO RIGHT?! WHO ARE YOU TO TELL ME WHAT I CAN AND CANNOT DO?
I...I'M...SORRY.
BUT WE CAN'T LEAVE IT LIKE THIS! YOU HAVE TO REPORT THIS!...
...TO HELP ME ARREST THESE SONS OF BITCHES!!!
SORRY, BOYS.
I TOLD YOU TO GET IN THE CAR.
32

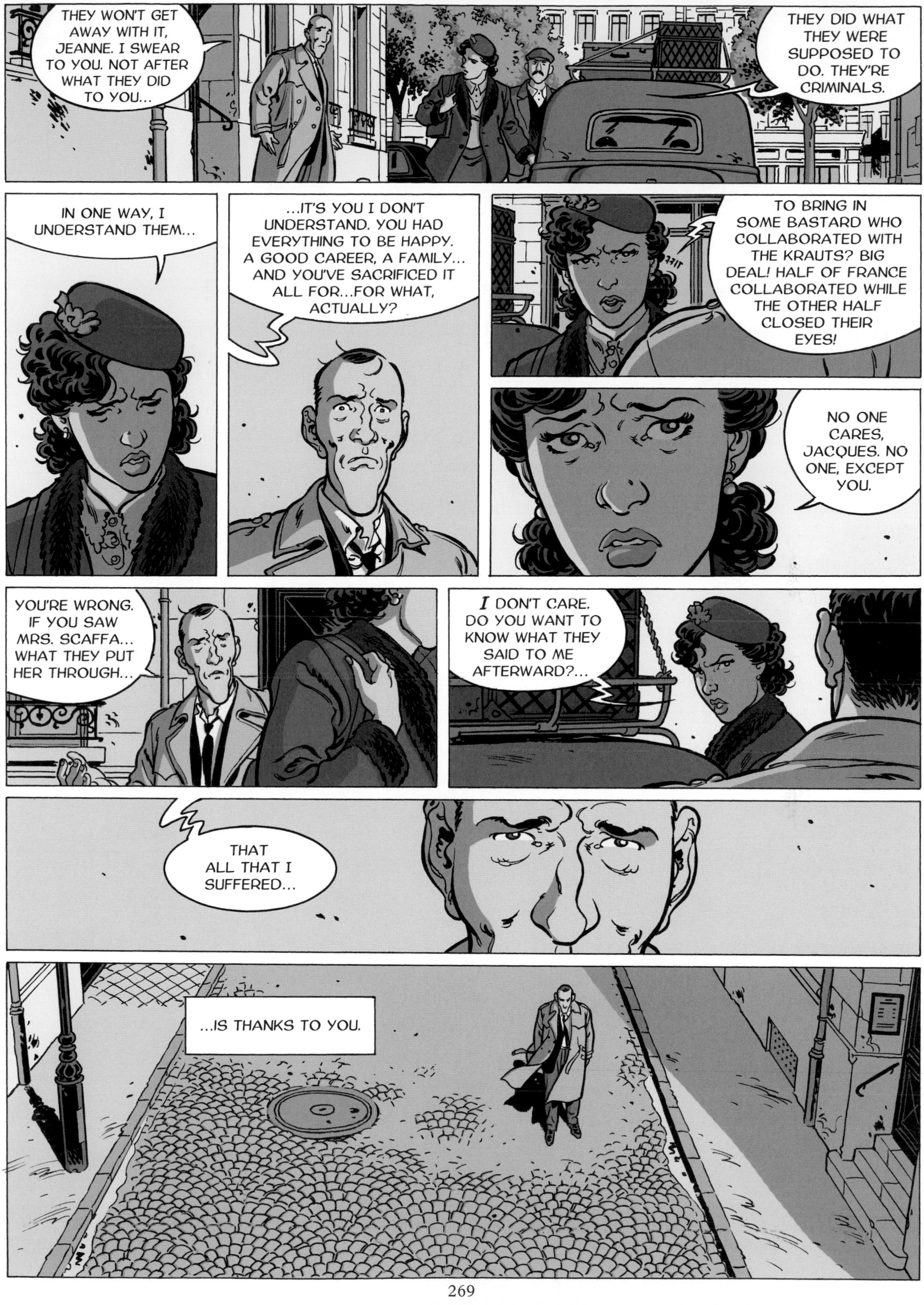
THEY WON'T GET AWAY WITH IT, JEANNE. I SWEAR TO YOU. NOT AFTER WHAT THEY DID TO YOU...
THEY DID WHAT THEY WERE SUPPOSED TO DO. THEY'RE CRIMINALS.
IN ONE WAY, I UNDERSTAND THEM...
...IT'S YOU I DON'T UNDERSTAND. YOU HAD EVERYTHING TO BE HAPPY. A GOOD CAREER, A FAMILY... AND YOU'VE SACRIFICED IT ALL FOR...FOR WHAT, ACTUALLY?
TO BRING IN SOME BASTARD WHO COLLABORATED WITH THE KRAUTS? BIG DEAL! HALF OF FRANCE COLLABORATED WHILE THE OTHER HALF CLOSED THEIR EYES!
NO ONE CARES, JACQUES. NO ONE, EXCEPT YOU.
YOU'RE WRONG. IF YOU SAW MRS. SCAFFA... WHAT THEY PUT HER THROUGH...
I DON'T CARE. DO YOU WANT TO KNOW WHAT THEY SAID TO ME AFTERWARD?...
THAT ALL THAT I SUFFERED...
...IS THANKS TO YOU.

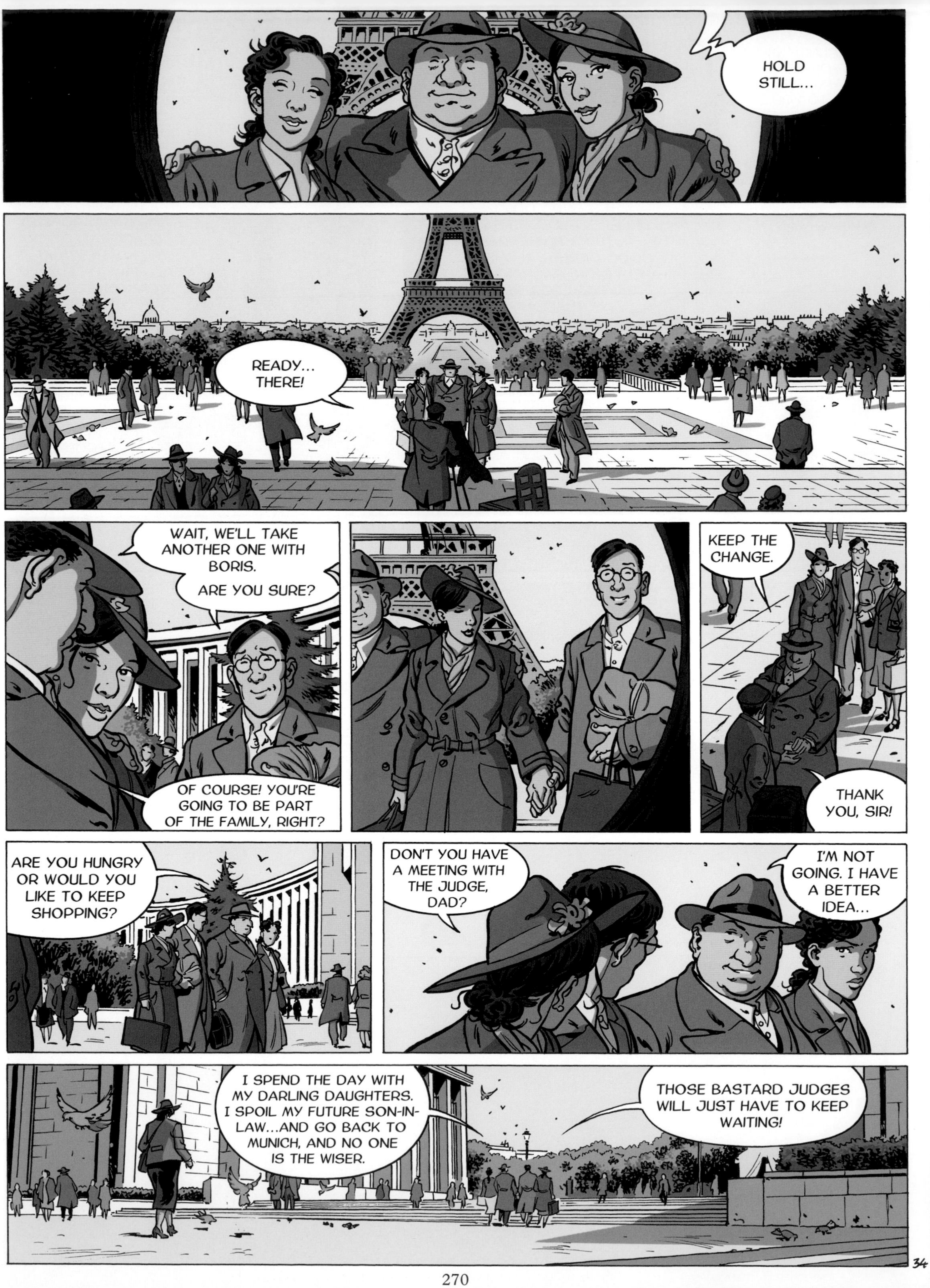
HOLD STILL...
READY... THERE!
WAIT, WE'LL TAKE ANOTHER ONE WITH BORIS.
ARE YOU SURE?
OF COURSE! YOU'RE GOING TO BE PART OF THE FAMILY, RIGHT?
KEEP THE CHANGE.
THANK YOU, SIR!
ARE YOU HUNGRY OR WOULD YOU LIKE TO KEEP SHOPPING?
DON'T YOU HAVE A MEETING WITH THE JUDGE, DAD?
I'M NOT GOING. I HAVE A BETTER IDEA...
I SPEND THE DAY WITH MY DARLING DAUGHTERS. I SPOIL MY FUTURE SON-IN-LAW...AND GO BACK TO MUNICH, AND NO ONE IS THE WISER.
THOSE BASTARD JUDGES WILL JUST HAVE TO KEEP WAITING!
34

YOU'VE ALREADY DROPPED THE ESSENTIAL ACCUSATION. A CHARGE FOR "ECONOMIC COLLABORATION"? I MUST BE DREAMING...

LIVE WITH IT, LEGENTIL. FOR NOW, WE CAN'T PROVE *ANYTHING.*

IF WE CAN BRING JOANOVICI TO COURT UNDER PROFITEERING CHARGES...IF HE ACTUALLY SHOWS UP FOR THE HEARING...IF WE FIND A MOTIVE FOR THE MURDER...

HE'S NOT COMING. HE'S MESSING WITH US.

IF...IF...IF... AND IF I WERE ARLETTY* YOU'D MARRY ME?

AND IN THE MEANTIME, THAT LITTLE SCRAP DEALER IS LAUGHING AT US!

ARE YOU OKAY, JACQUES?

I'VE HAD ENOUGH. I CAN'T TAKE ANY MORE.

I CAN'T TAKE ANY MORE OF THIS SHIT FROM...

...THAT FILTHY *JEW.*

WE'RE GOING TO HAVE TO PASS ON GETTING FURTHER HELP FROM YOU, MR. LEGENTIL.

I SUGGEST THAT YOU GO HOME AND THINK SERIOUSLY ABOUT WHAT YOU JUST SAID.

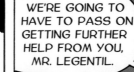

35

*A famous French actress who was found guilty of treason for her "horizontal collaboration" with a German officer.

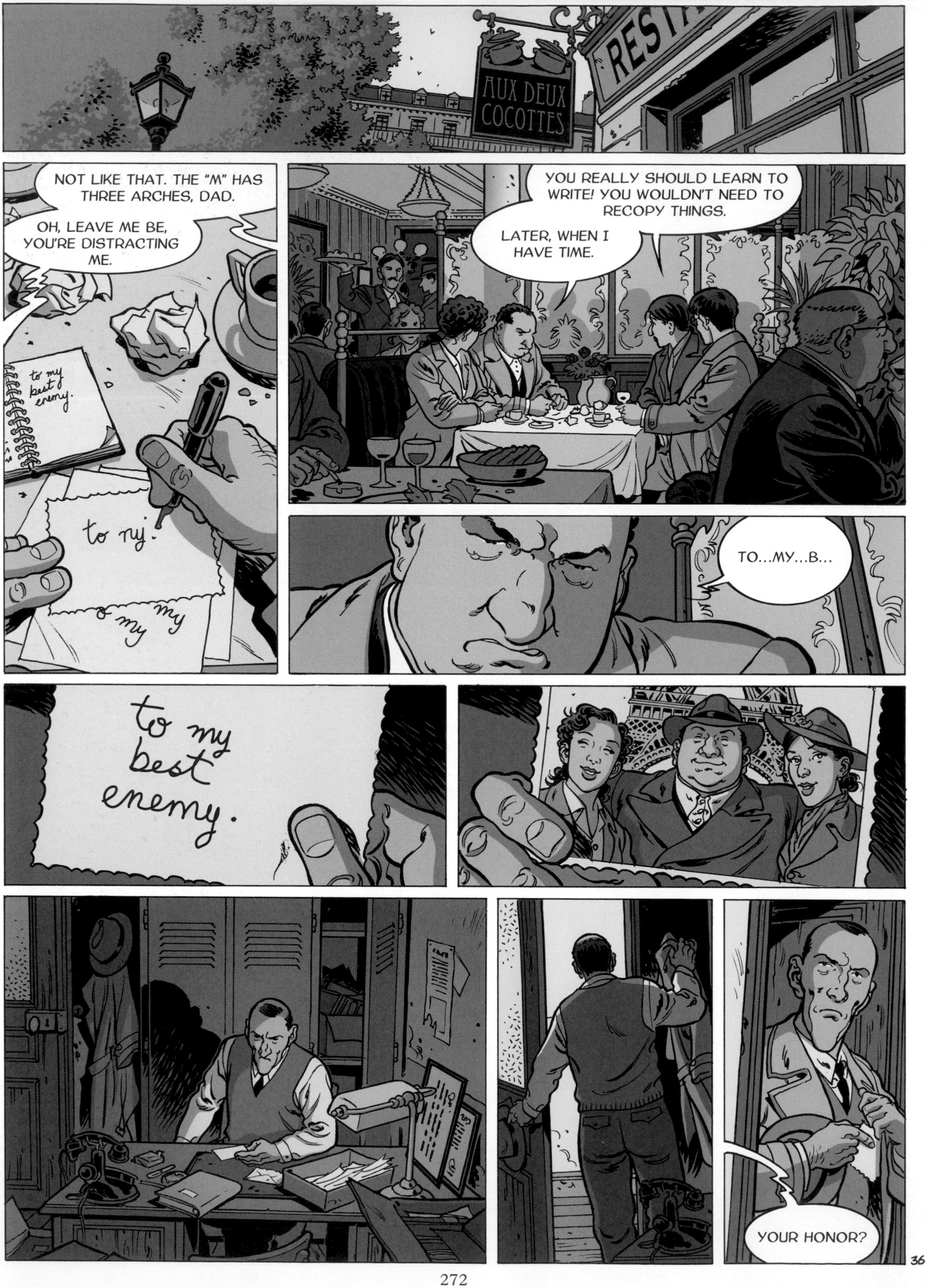

AUX DEUX COCOTTES
RESTA
NOT LIKE THAT. THE "M" HAS THREE ARCHES, DAD.
OH, LEAVE ME BE, YOU'RE DISTRACTING ME.
to my best enemy.
to my
my
my
YOU REALLY SHOULD LEARN TO WRITE! YOU WOULDN'T NEED TO RECOPY THINGS.
LATER, WHEN I HAVE TIME.
TO...MY...B...
to my best enemy.
YOUR HONOR?
36

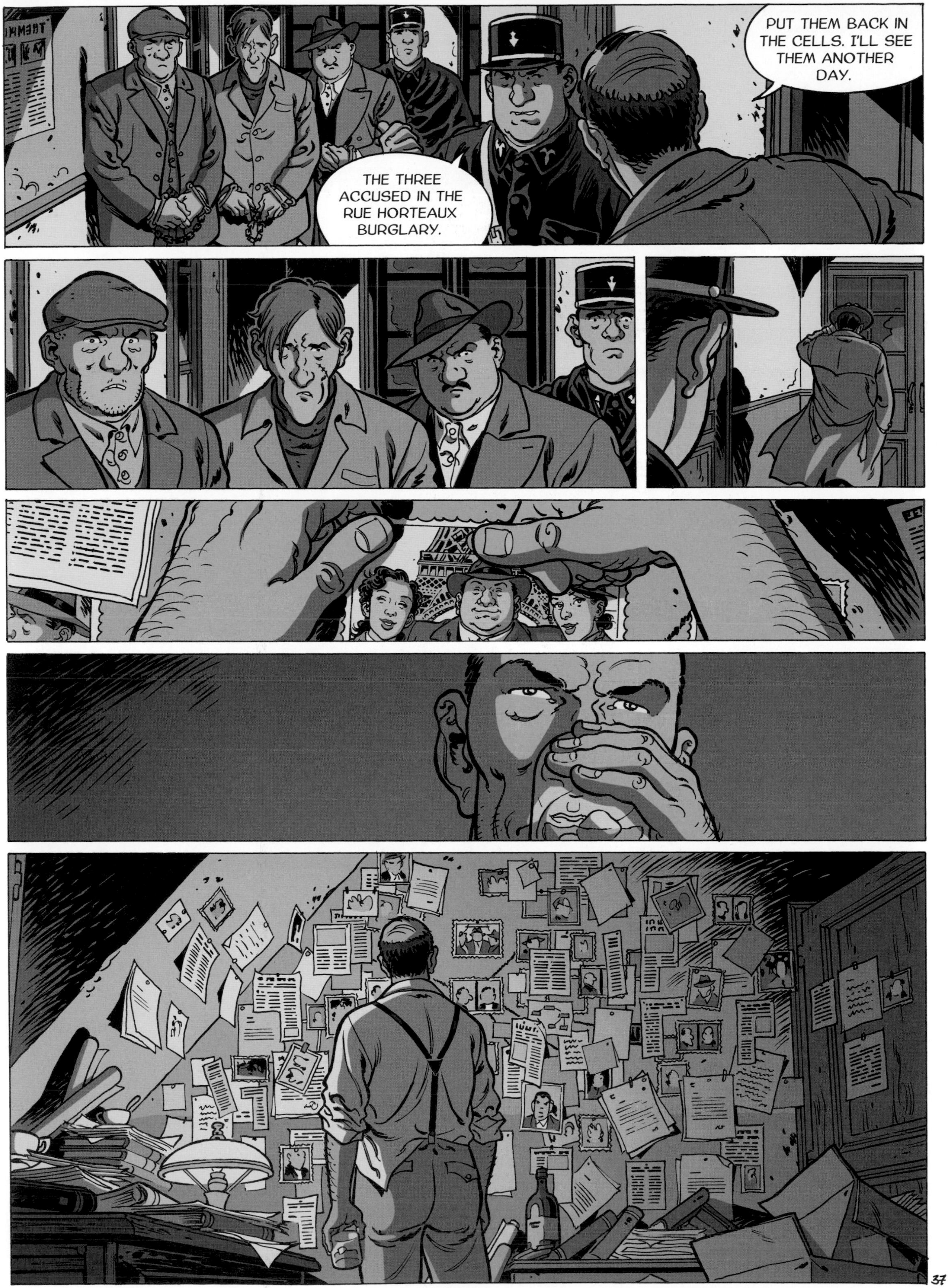
THE THREE ACCUSED IN THE RUE HORTEAUX BURGLARY.
PUT THEM BACK IN THE CELLS. I'LL SEE THEM ANOTHER DAY.
37

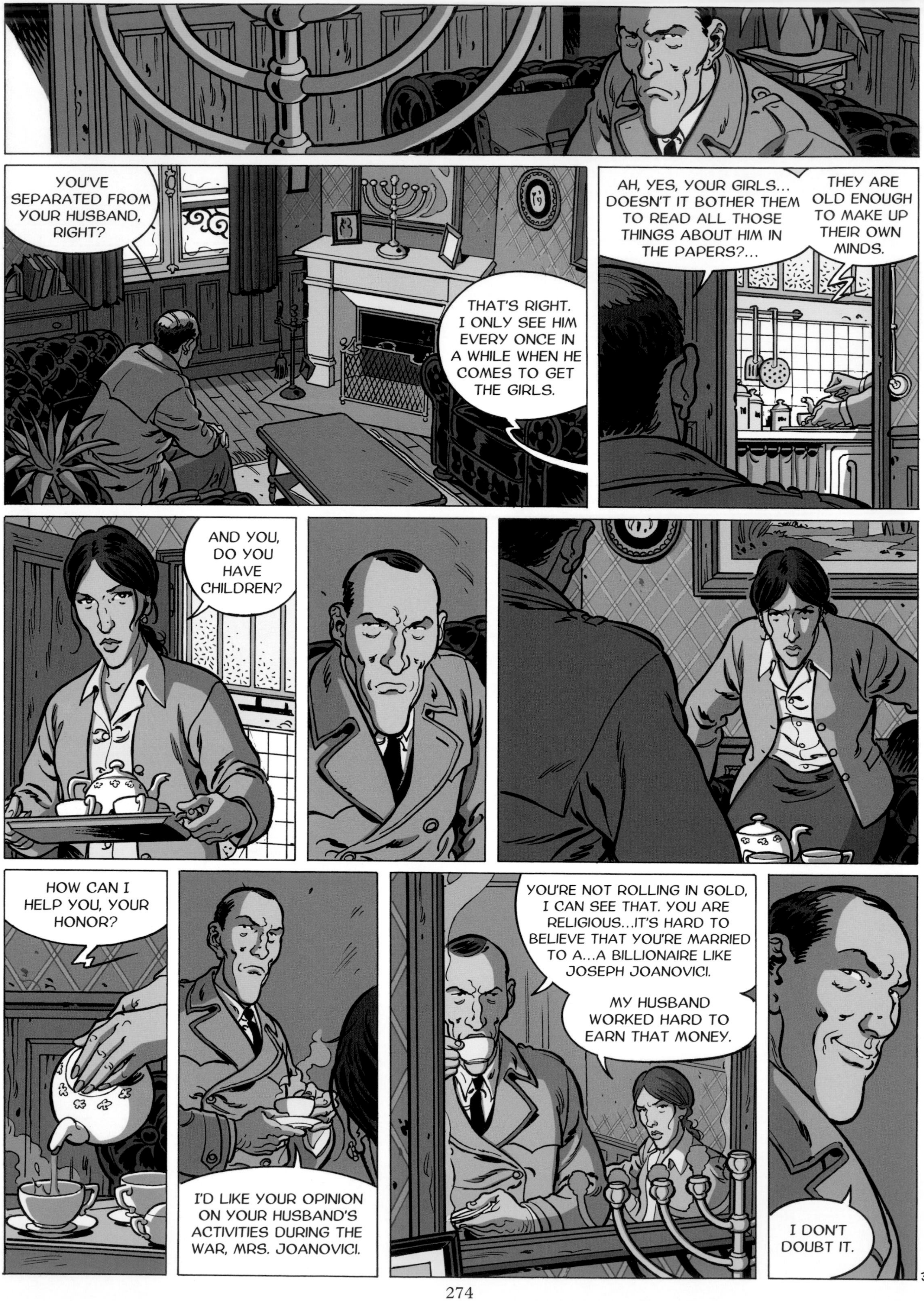
YOU'VE SEPARATED FROM YOUR HUSBAND, RIGHT?
THAT'S RIGHT. I ONLY SEE HIM EVERY ONCE IN A WHILE WHEN HE COMES TO GET THE GIRLS.
AH, YES, YOUR GIRLS... DOESN'T IT BOTHER THEM TO READ ALL THOSE THINGS ABOUT HIM IN THE PAPERS?...
THEY ARE OLD ENOUGH TO MAKE UP THEIR OWN MINDS.
AND YOU, DO YOU HAVE CHILDREN?
HOW CAN I HELP YOU, YOUR HONOR?
I'D LIKE YOUR OPINION ON YOUR HUSBAND'S ACTIVITIES DURING THE WAR, MRS. JOANOVICI.
YOU'RE NOT ROLLING IN GOLD, I CAN SEE THAT. YOU ARE RELIGIOUS...IT'S HARD TO BELIEVE THAT YOU'RE MARRIED TO A...A BILLIONAIRE LIKE JOSEPH JOANOVICI.
MY HUSBAND WORKED HARD TO EARN THAT MONEY.
I DON'T DOUBT IT.
38

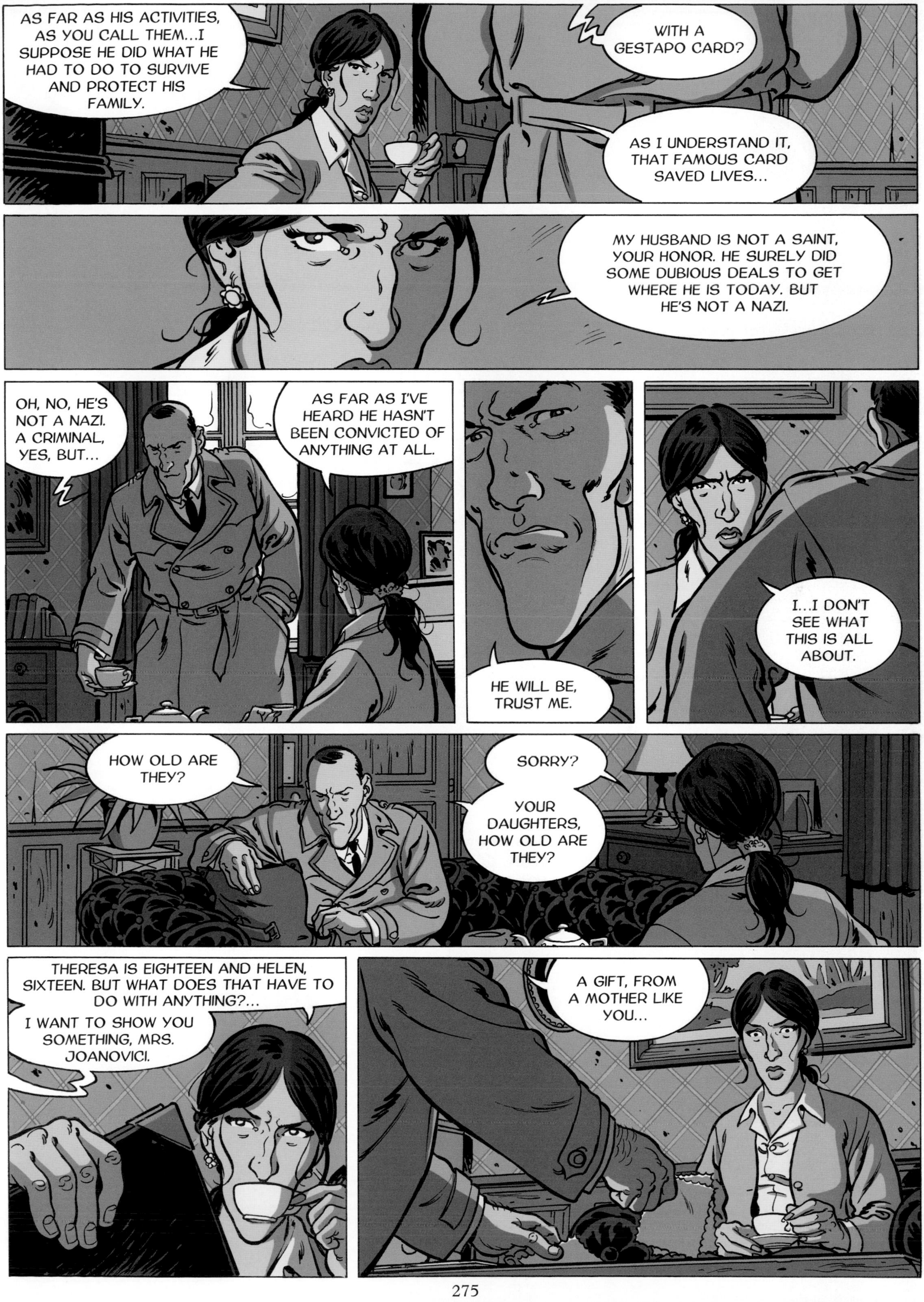
AS FAR AS HIS ACTIVITIES, AS YOU CALL THEM...I SUPPOSE HE DID WHAT HE HAD TO DO TO SURVIVE AND PROTECT HIS FAMILY.
WITH A GESTAPO CARD?
AS I UNDERSTAND IT, THAT FAMOUS CARD SAVED LIVES...
MY HUSBAND IS NOT A SAINT, YOUR HONOR. HE SURELY DID SOME DUBIOUS DEALS TO GET WHERE HE IS TODAY. BUT HE'S NOT A NAZI.
OH, NO, HE'S NOT A NAZI. A CRIMINAL, YES, BUT...
AS FAR AS I'VE HEARD HE HASN'T BEEN CONVICTED OF ANYTHING AT ALL.
HE WILL BE, TRUST ME.
I...I DON'T SEE WHAT THIS IS ALL ABOUT.
HOW OLD ARE THEY?
SORRY?
YOUR DAUGHTERS, HOW OLD ARE THEY?
THERESA IS EIGHTEEN AND HELEN, SIXTEEN. BUT WHAT DOES THAT HAVE TO DO WITH ANYTHING?...
I WANT TO SHOW YOU SOMETHING, MRS. JOANOVICI.
A GIFT, FROM A MOTHER LIKE YOU...

39

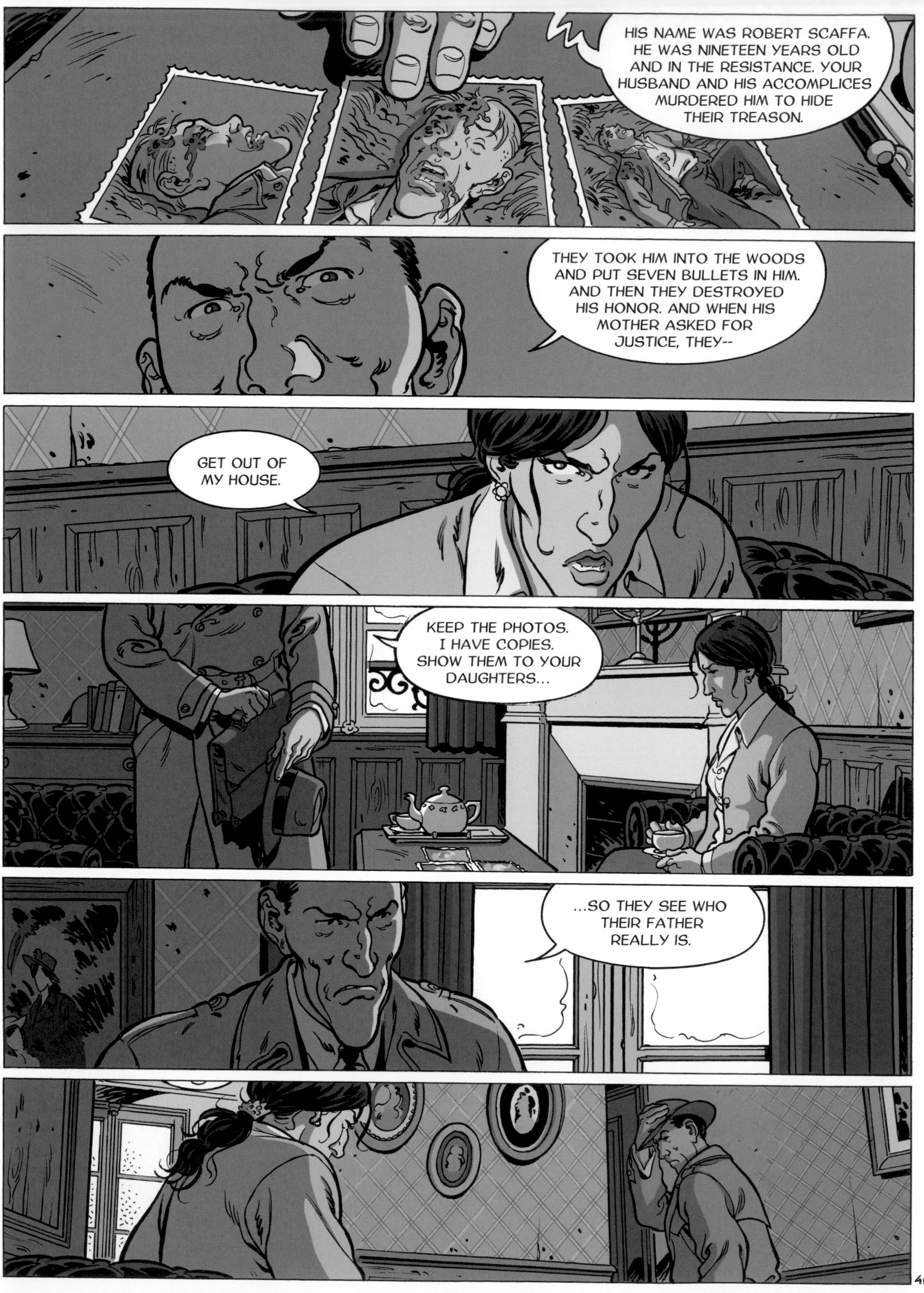
HIS NAME WAS ROBERT SCAFFA. HE WAS NINETEEN YEARS OLD AND IN THE RESISTANCE. YOUR HUSBAND AND HIS ACCOMPLICES MURDERED HIM TO HIDE THEIR TREASON.
THEY TOOK HIM INTO THE WOODS AND PUT SEVEN BULLETS IN HIM. AND THEN THEY DESTROYED HIS HONOR. AND WHEN HIS MOTHER ASKED FOR JUSTICE, THEY--
GET OUT OF MY HOUSE.
KEEP THE PHOTOS. I HAVE COPIES. SHOW THEM TO YOUR DAUGHTERS...
...SO THEY SEE WHO THEIR FATHER REALLY IS.

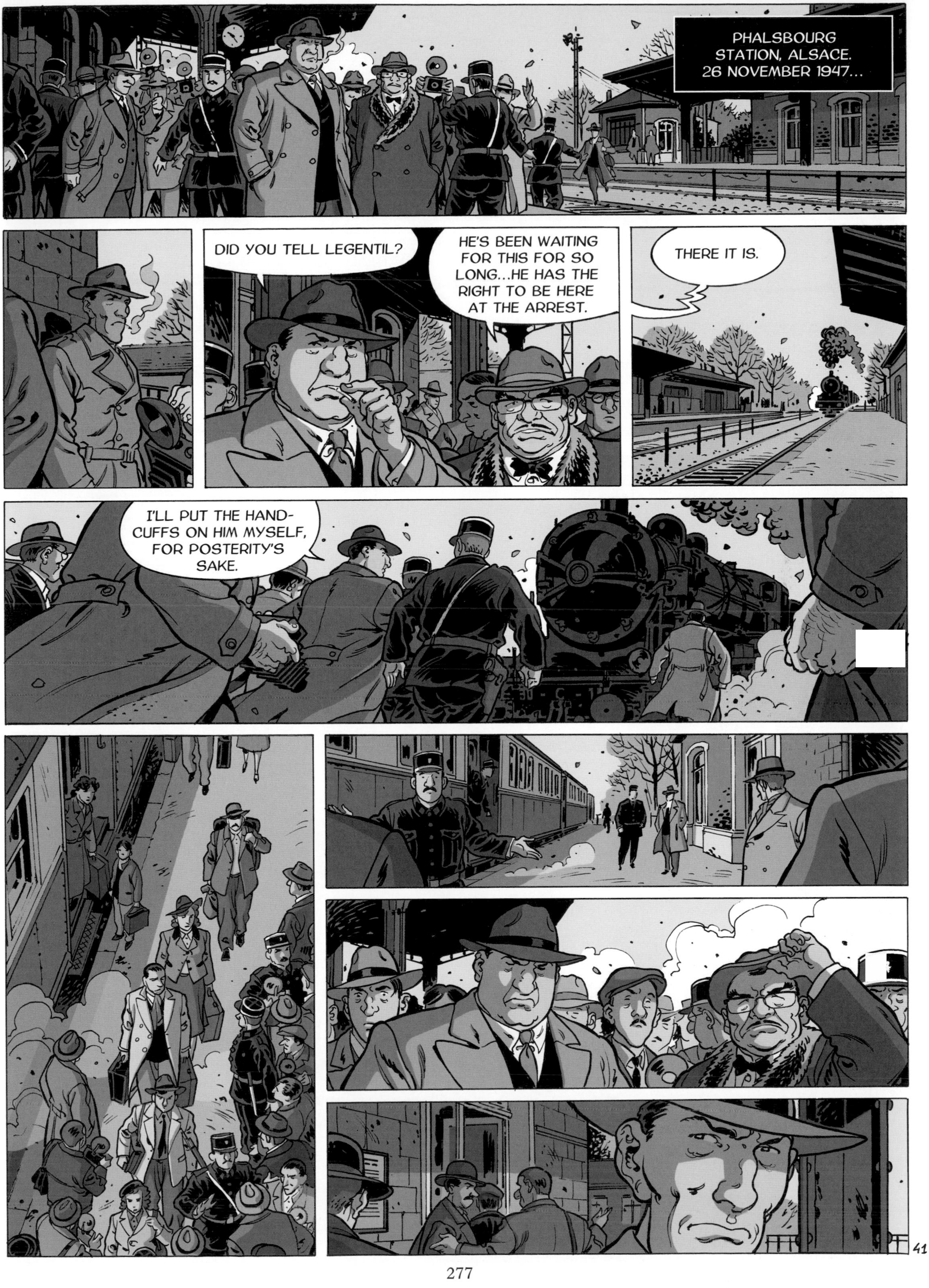
PHALSBOURG STATION, ALSACE. 26 NOVEMBER 1947...
DID YOU TELL LEGENTIL?
HE'S BEEN WAITING FOR THIS FOR SO LONG...HE HAS THE RIGHT TO BE HERE AT THE ARREST.
THERE IT IS.
I'LL PUT THE HAND-CUFFS ON HIM MYSELF, FOR POSTERITY'S SAKE.
41

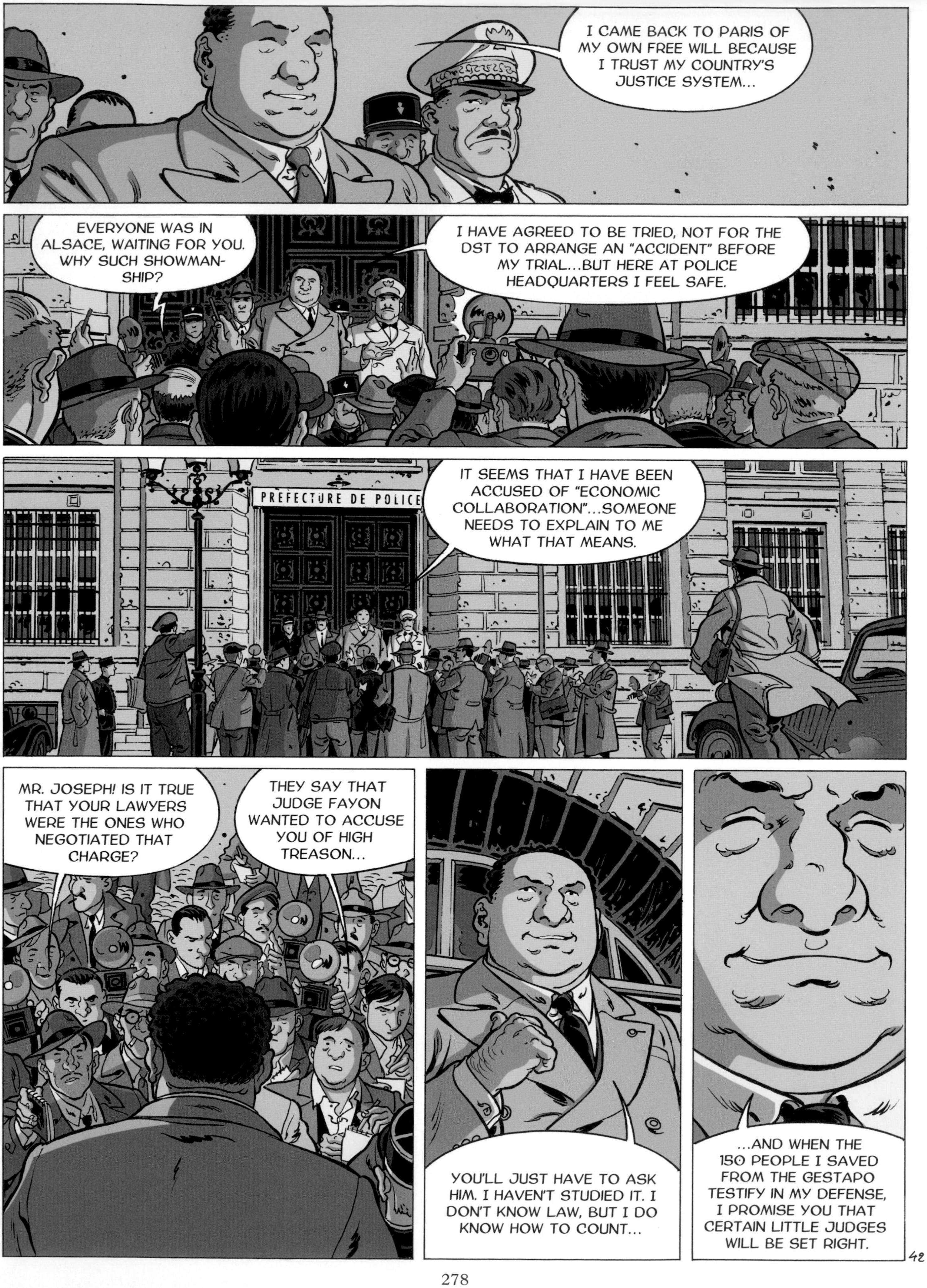
I CAME BACK TO PARIS OF MY OWN FREE WILL BECAUSE I TRUST MY COUNTRY'S JUSTICE SYSTEM...
EVERYONE WAS IN ALSACE, WAITING FOR YOU. WHY SUCH SHOWMAN-SHIP?
I HAVE AGREED TO BE TRIED, NOT FOR THE DST TO ARRANGE AN "ACCIDENT" BEFORE MY TRIAL...BUT HERE AT POLICE HEADQUARTERS I FEEL SAFE.
PREFECTURE DE POLICE
IT SEEMS THAT I HAVE BEEN ACCUSED OF "ECONOMIC COLLABORATION"...SOMEONE NEEDS TO EXPLAIN TO ME WHAT THAT MEANS.
MR. JOSEPH! IS IT TRUE THAT YOUR LAWYERS WERE THE ONES WHO NEGOTIATED THAT CHARGE?
THEY SAY THAT JUDGE FAYON WANTED TO ACCUSE YOU OF HIGH TREASON...
YOU'LL JUST HAVE TO ASK HIM. I HAVEN'T STUDIED IT. I DON'T KNOW LAW, BUT I DO KNOW HOW TO COUNT...
...AND WHEN THE 150 PEOPLE I SAVED FROM THE GESTAPO TESTIFY IN MY DEFENSE, I PROMISE YOU THAT CERTAIN LITTLE JUDGES WILL BE SET RIGHT.
42

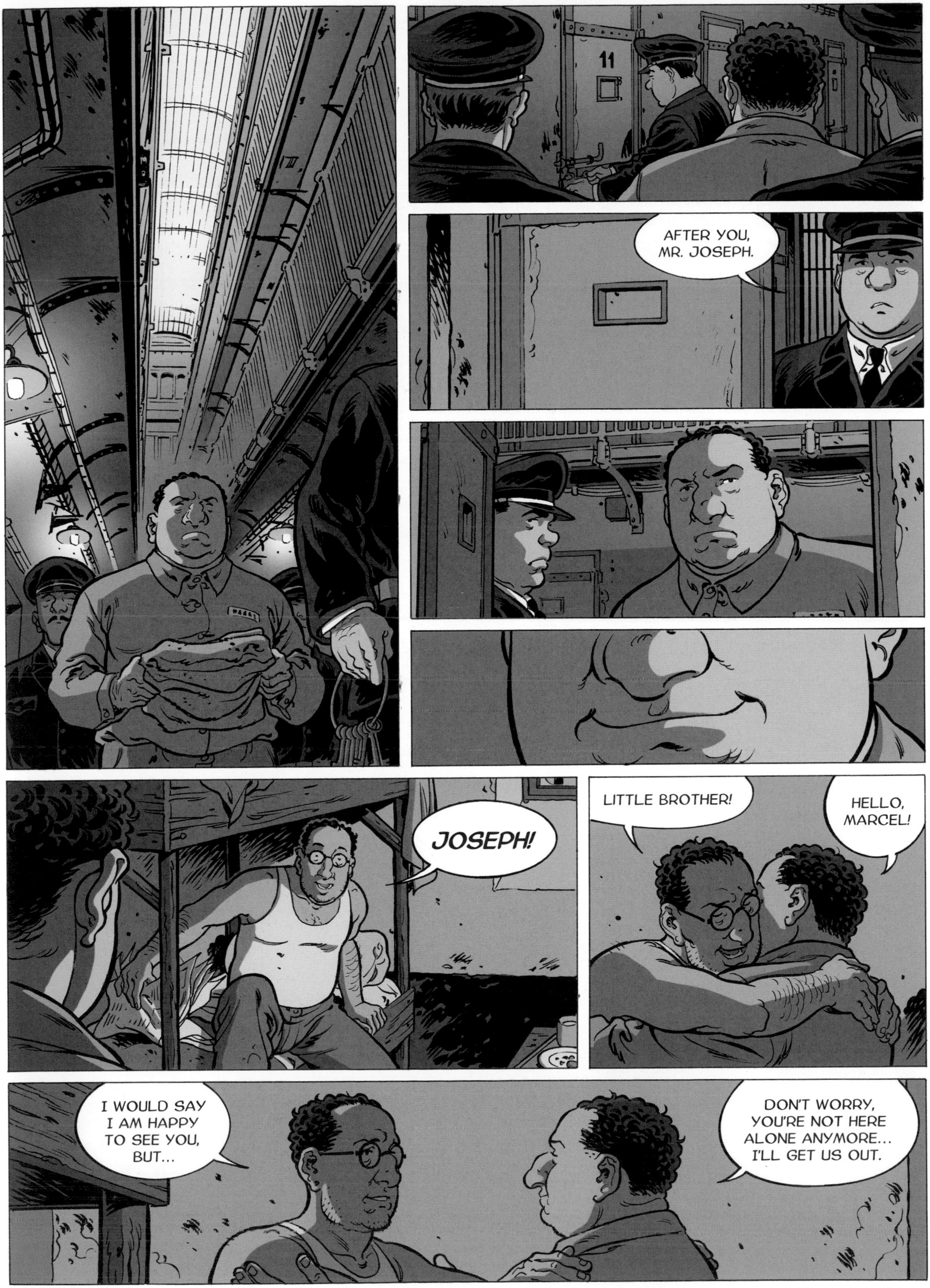
AFTER YOU, MR. JOSEPH.
JOSEPH!
LITTLE BROTHER!
HELLO, MARCEL!
I WOULD SAY I AM HAPPY TO SEE YOU, BUT...
DON'T WORRY, YOU'RE NOT HERE ALONE ANYMORE... I'LL GET US OUT.

43

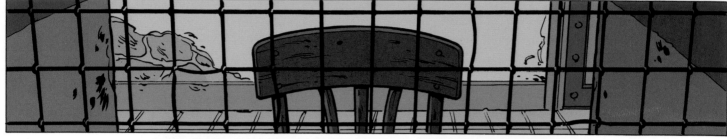

WHERE IS HE? WHAT ARE YOU WAITING FOR?

THERE IS NO RULE THAT OBLIGES PRISONERS TO SEE THEIR VISITORS. I'M SORRY, YOUR HONOR...

YOU'LL JUST HAVE TO SUMMON HIM TO APPEAR IN COURT. THEN HE'LL BE OBLIGATED TO COME. IF HE IS IMPLICATED IN THE CASE, OF COURSE.

90 SPADES.

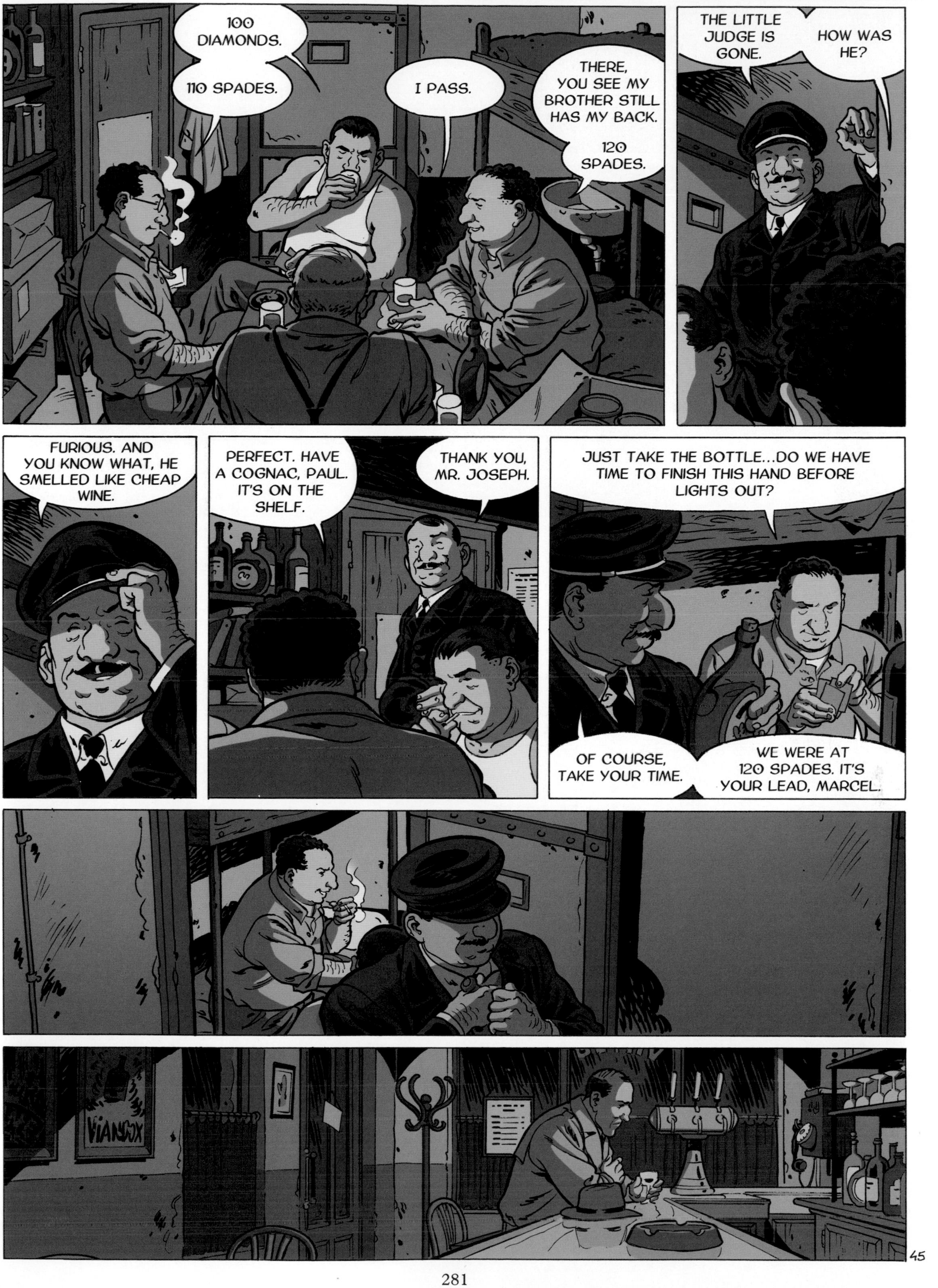
100 DIAMONDS.
110 SPADES.
I PASS.
THERE, YOU SEE MY BROTHER STILL HAS MY BACK.
120 SPADES.
THE LITTLE JUDGE IS GONE.
HOW WAS HE?
FURIOUS. AND YOU KNOW WHAT, HE SMELLED LIKE CHEAP WINE.
PERFECT. HAVE A COGNAC, PAUL. IT'S ON THE SHELF.
THANK YOU, MR. JOSEPH.
JUST TAKE THE BOTTLE...DO WE HAVE TIME TO FINISH THIS HAND BEFORE LIGHTS OUT?
OF COURSE, TAKE YOUR TIME.
WE WERE AT 120 SPADES. IT'S YOUR LEAD, MARCEL.

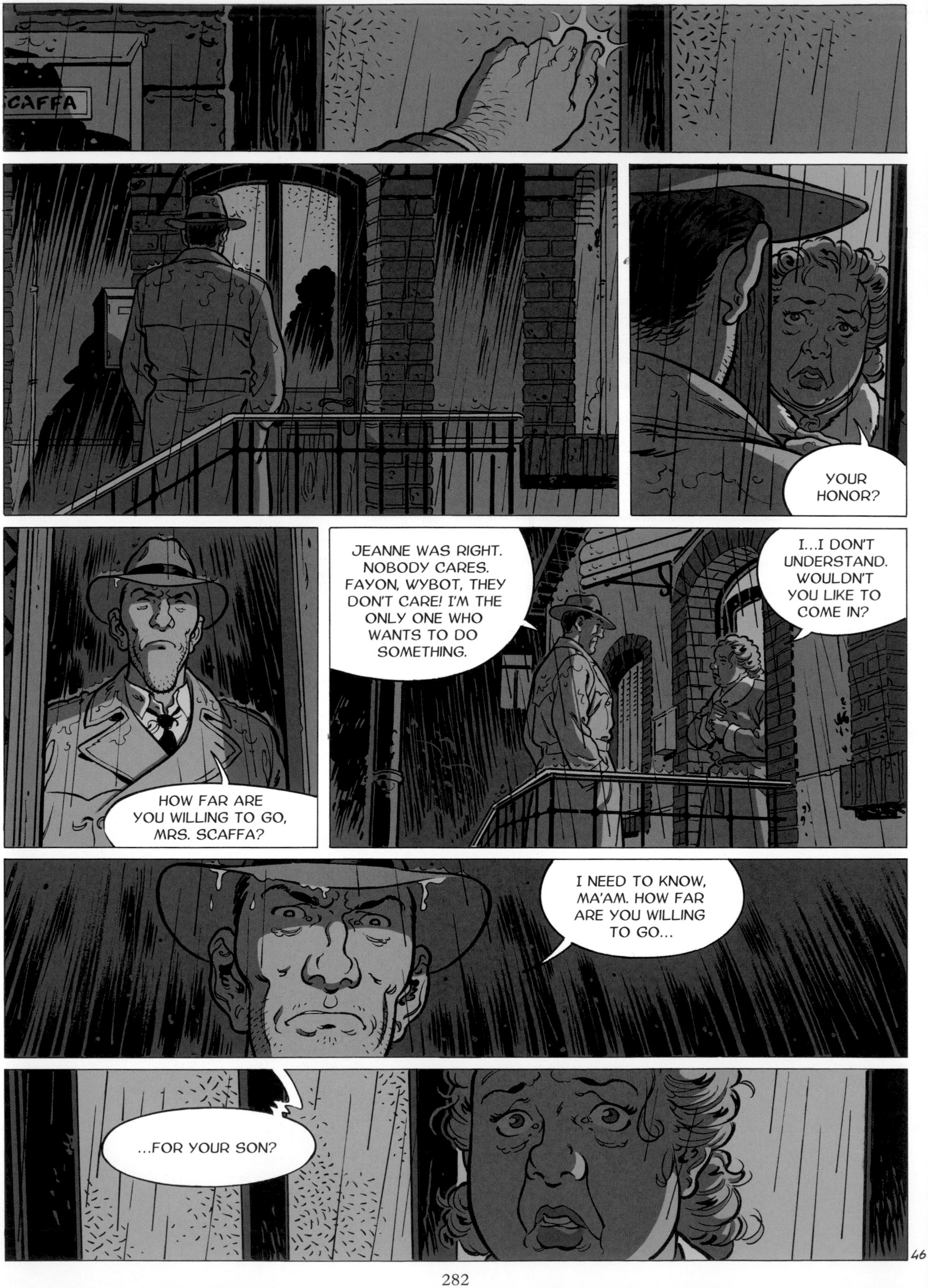
SCAFFA
YOUR HONOR?
HOW FAR ARE YOU WILLING TO GO, MRS. SCAFFA?
JEANNE WAS RIGHT. NOBODY CARES. FAYON, WYBOT, THEY DON'T CARE! I'M THE ONLY ONE WHO WANTS TO DO SOMETHING.
I...I DON'T UNDERSTAND. WOULDN'T YOU LIKE TO COME IN?
I NEED TO KNOW, MA'AM. HOW FAR ARE YOU WILLING TO GO...
...FOR YOUR SON?
46

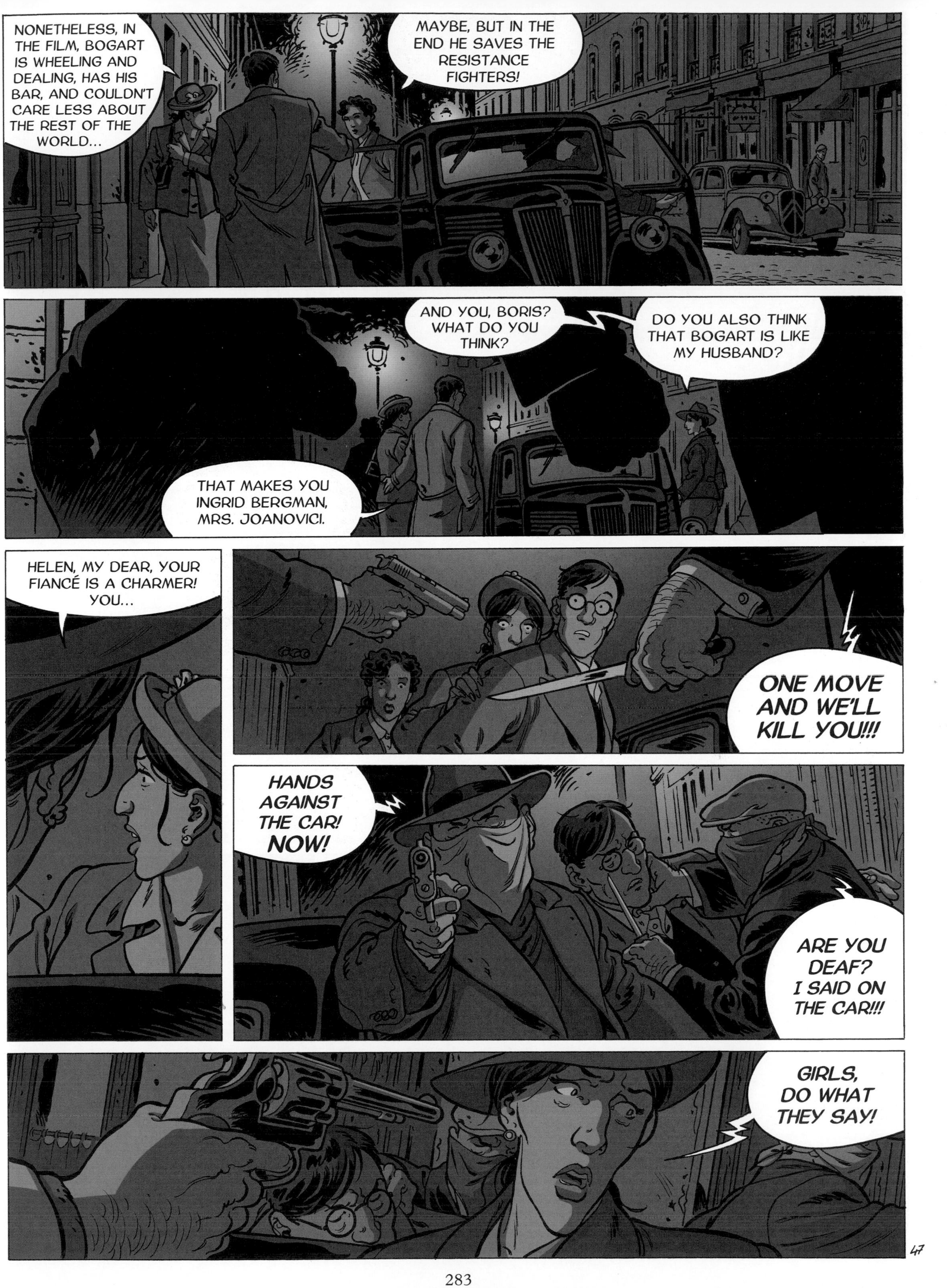
NONETHELESS, IN THE FILM, BOGART IS WHEELING AND DEALING, HAS HIS BAR, AND COULDN'T CARE LESS ABOUT THE REST OF THE WORLD...
MAYBE, BUT IN THE END HE SAVES THE RESISTANCE FIGHTERS!
AND YOU, BORIS? WHAT DO YOU THINK?
DO YOU ALSO THINK THAT BOGART IS LIKE MY HUSBAND?
THAT MAKES YOU INGRID BERGMAN, MRS. JOANOVICI.
HELEN, MY DEAR, YOUR FIANCÉ IS A CHARMER! YOU...
ONE MOVE AND WE'LL KILL YOU!!!
HANDS AGAINST THE CAR! NOW!
ARE YOU DEAF? I SAID ON THE CAR!!!
GIRLS, DO WHAT THEY SAY!
47

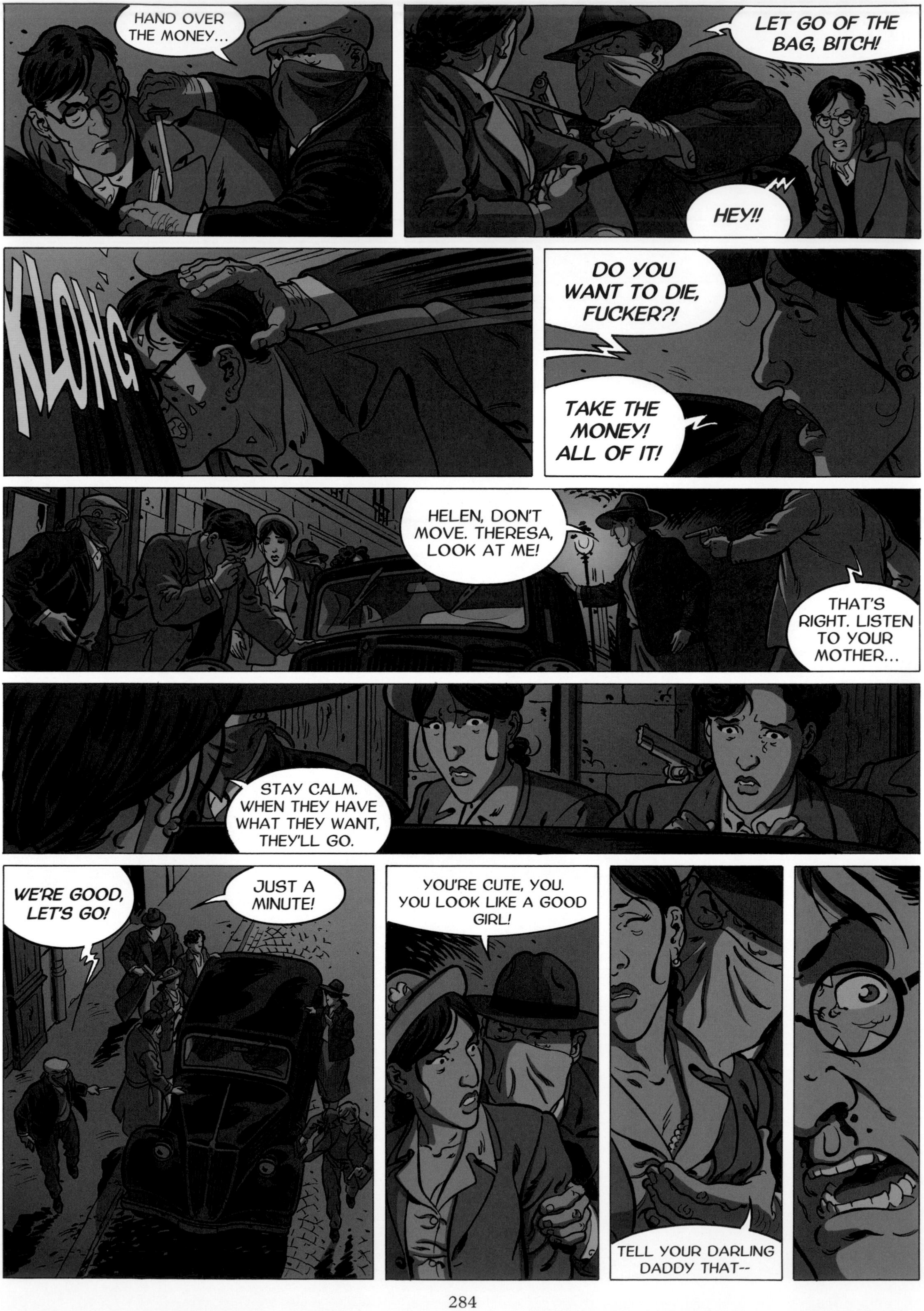
HAND OVER THE MONEY...
LET GO OF THE BAG, BITCH!
HEY!!
KLONG
DO YOU WANT TO DIE, FUCKER?!
TAKE THE MONEY! ALL OF IT!
HELEN, DON'T MOVE. THERESA, LOOK AT ME!
THAT'S RIGHT. LISTEN TO YOUR MOTHER...
STAY CALM. WHEN THEY HAVE WHAT THEY WANT, THEY'LL GO.
WE'RE GOOD, LET'S GO!
JUST A MINUTE!
YOU'RE CUTE, YOU. YOU LOOK LIKE A GOOD GIRL!
TELL YOUR DARLING DADDY THAT--
48

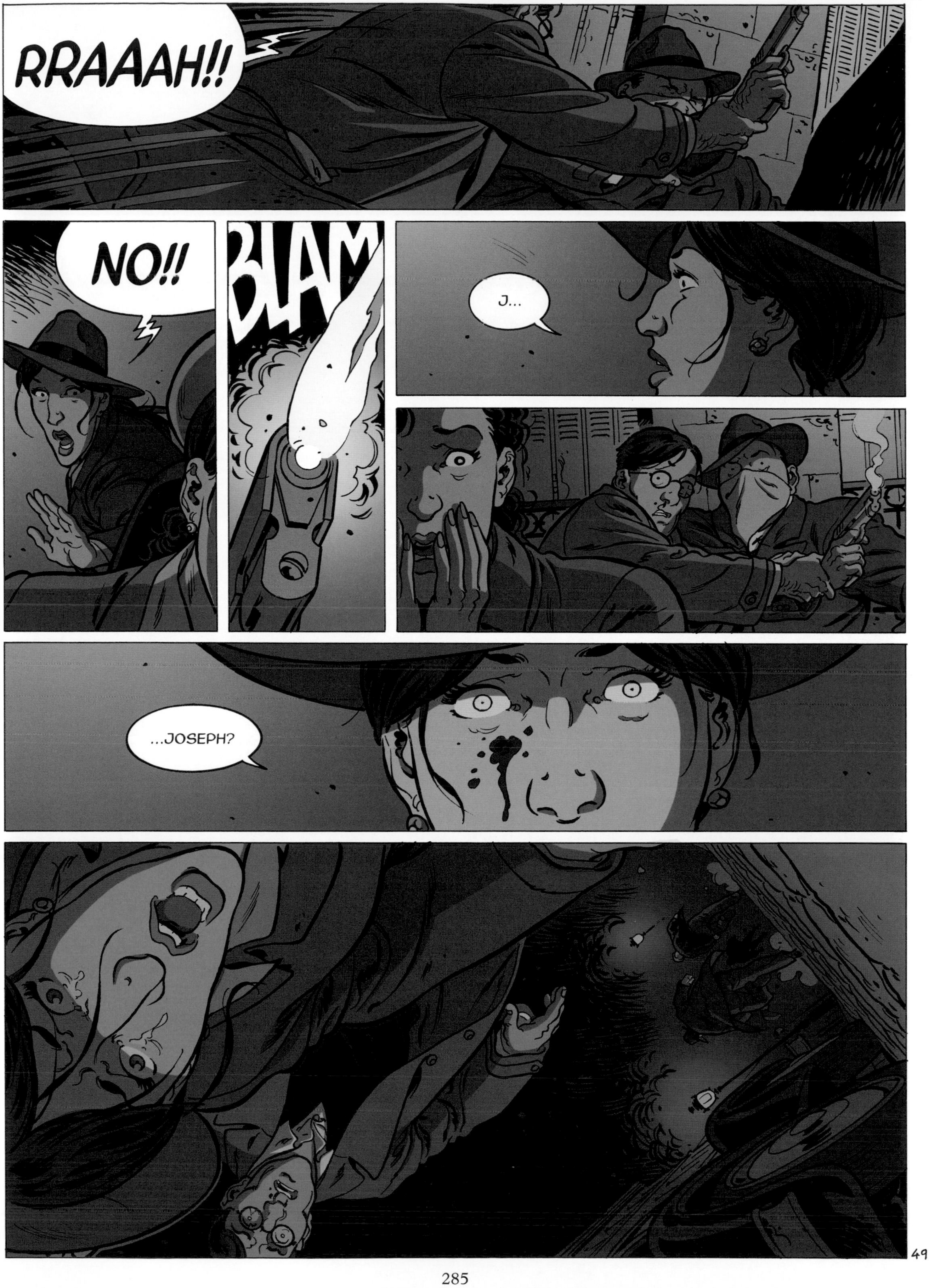
RRAAAH!!
NO!!
BLAM
J...
...JOSEPH?
49

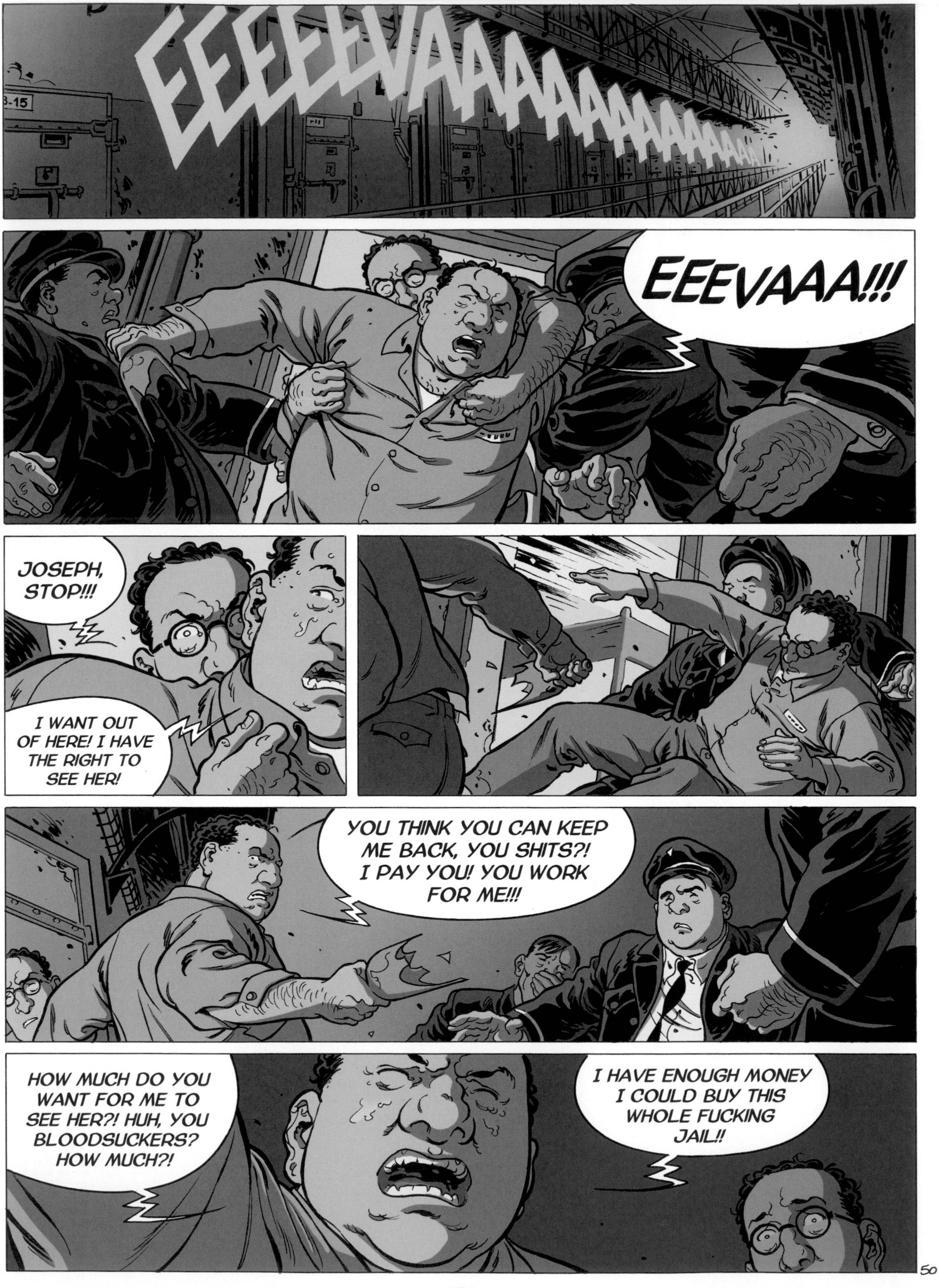
EEEEVAAAAAAAAAAAAAAA
EEEVAAA!!!
JOSEPH, STOP!!!
I WANT OUT OF HERE! I HAVE THE RIGHT TO SEE HER!
YOU THINK YOU CAN KEEP ME BACK, YOU SHITS?! I PAY YOU! YOU WORK FOR ME!!!
HOW MUCH DO YOU WANT FOR ME TO SEE HER?! HUH, YOU BLOODSUCKERS? HOW MUCH?!
I HAVE ENOUGH MONEY I COULD BUY THIS WHOLE FUCKING JAIL!!
50

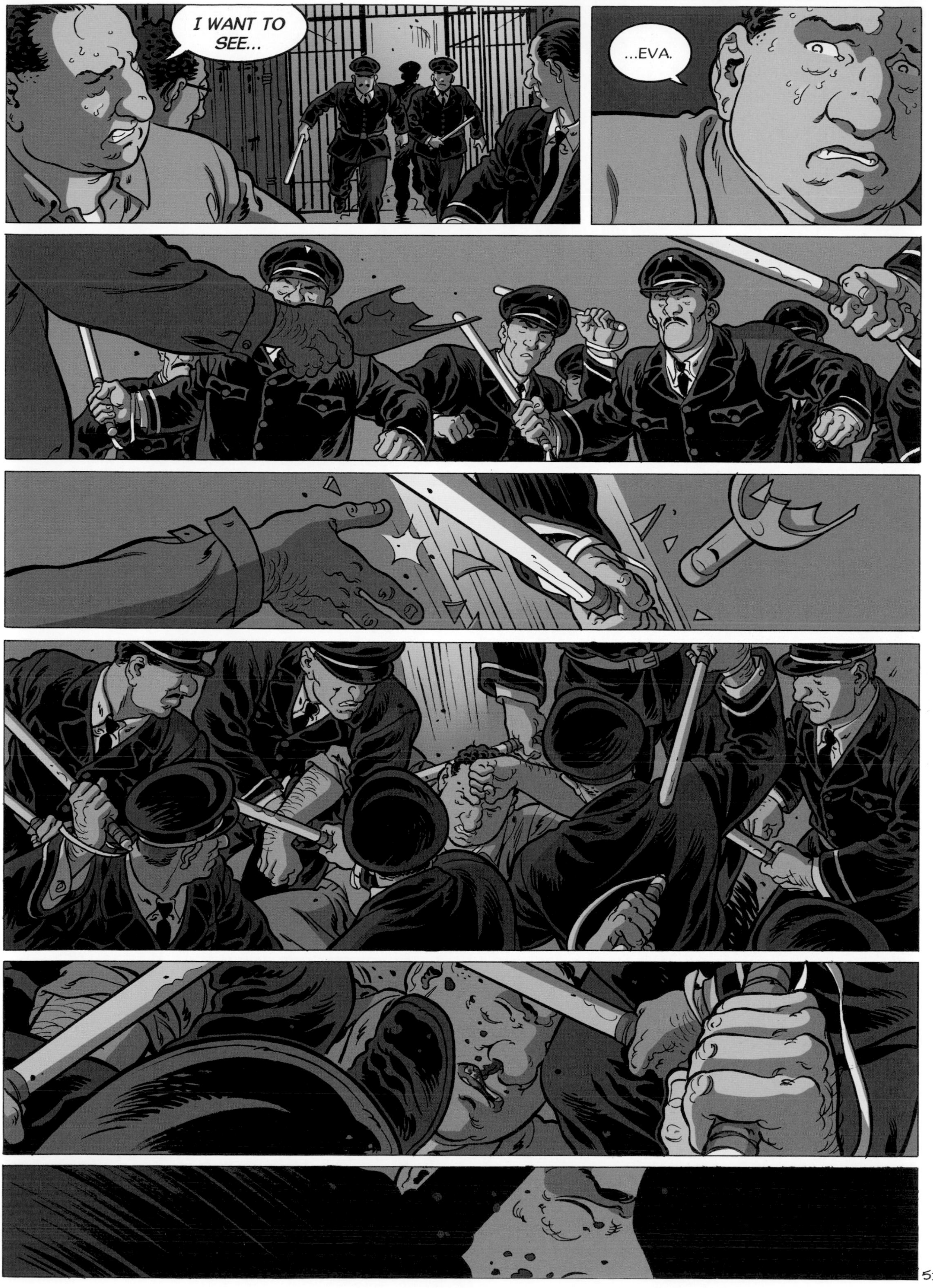
I WANT TO SEE...
...EVA.

51

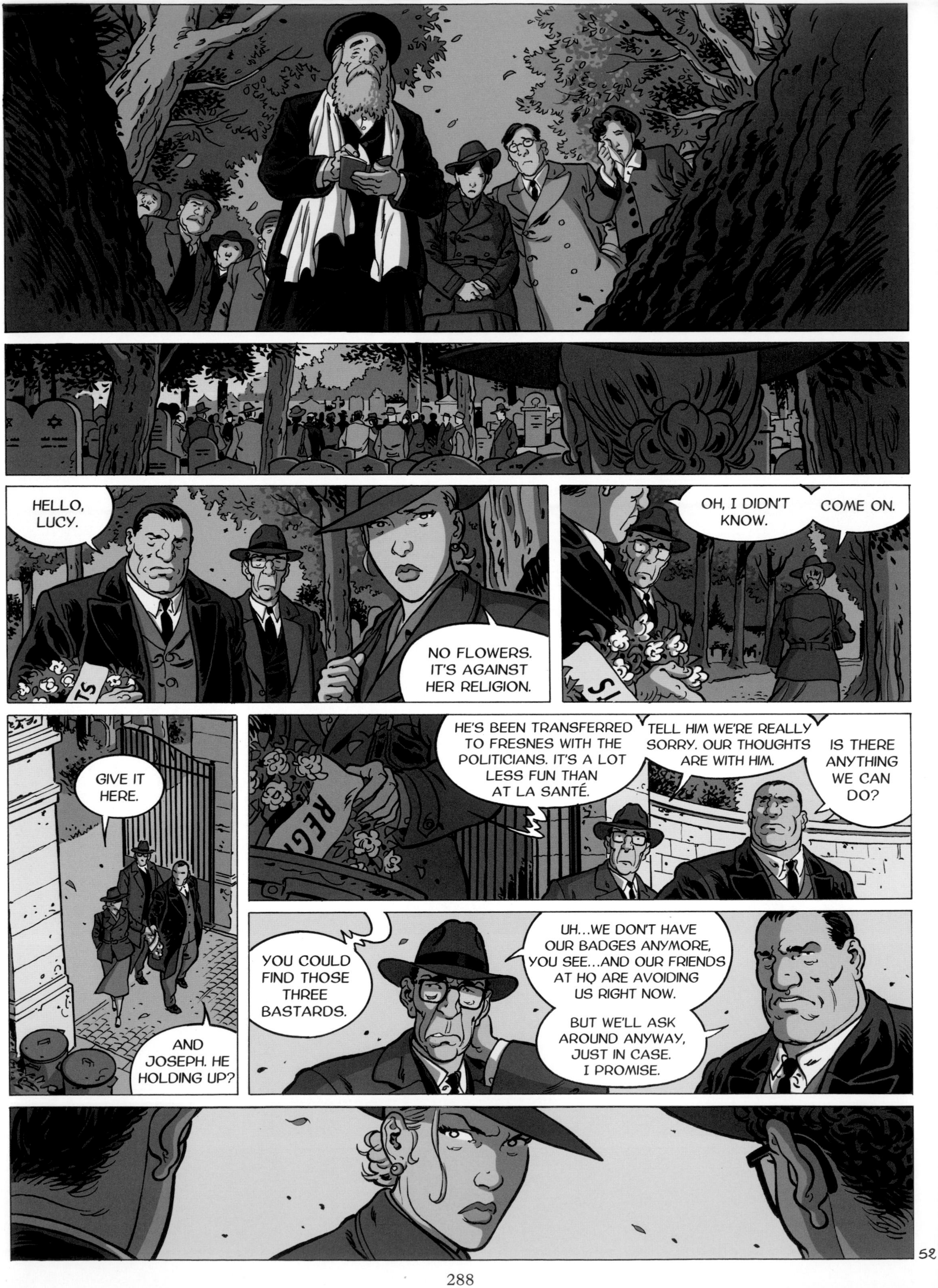
HELLO, LUCY.
NO FLOWERS. IT'S AGAINST HER RELIGION.
OH, I DIDN'T KNOW.
COME ON.
GIVE IT HERE.
AND JOSEPH. HE HOLDING UP?
HE'S BEEN TRANSFERRED TO FRESNES WITH THE POLITICIANS. IT'S A LOT LESS FUN THAN AT LA SANTÉ.
TELL HIM WE'RE REALLY SORRY. OUR THOUGHTS ARE WITH HIM.
IS THERE ANYTHING WE CAN DO?
YOU COULD FIND THOSE THREE BASTARDS.
UH...WE DON'T HAVE OUR BADGES ANYMORE, YOU SEE...AND OUR FRIENDS AT HQ ARE AVOIDING US RIGHT NOW.
BUT WE'LL ASK AROUND ANYWAY, JUST IN CASE. I PROMISE.
52

GOOD EVENING, YOUR HONOR.

MAY WE COME IN A MINUTE?

YOUR WIFE'S NOT HOME?

WE'RE SEPARATED.

WE HAVE GOOD NEWS FOR YOU, YOUR HONOR. THE JOANOVICI TRIAL STARTS IN TEN DAYS...

OH, "ECONOMIC COLLABORATION." I WISH THE PROSECUTOR GOOD LUCK.

...AND I JUST SPOKE TO YOUR SUCCESSOR IN MELUN. LUCIEN PIEDNOIR AND ANDRÉ FOURNET ARE GOING TO BE CHARGED WITH THE MURDER OF ROBERT SCAFFA.

GREAT. I'D SUGGEST A DRINK TO CELEBRATE...BUT THERE IS ONE GUILTY MAN MISSING, DON'T YOU THINK?

OH, I FORGOT...

WE JUST ARRESTED EVA JOANOVICI'S KILLERS.

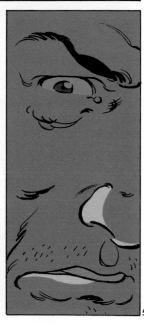

53

289

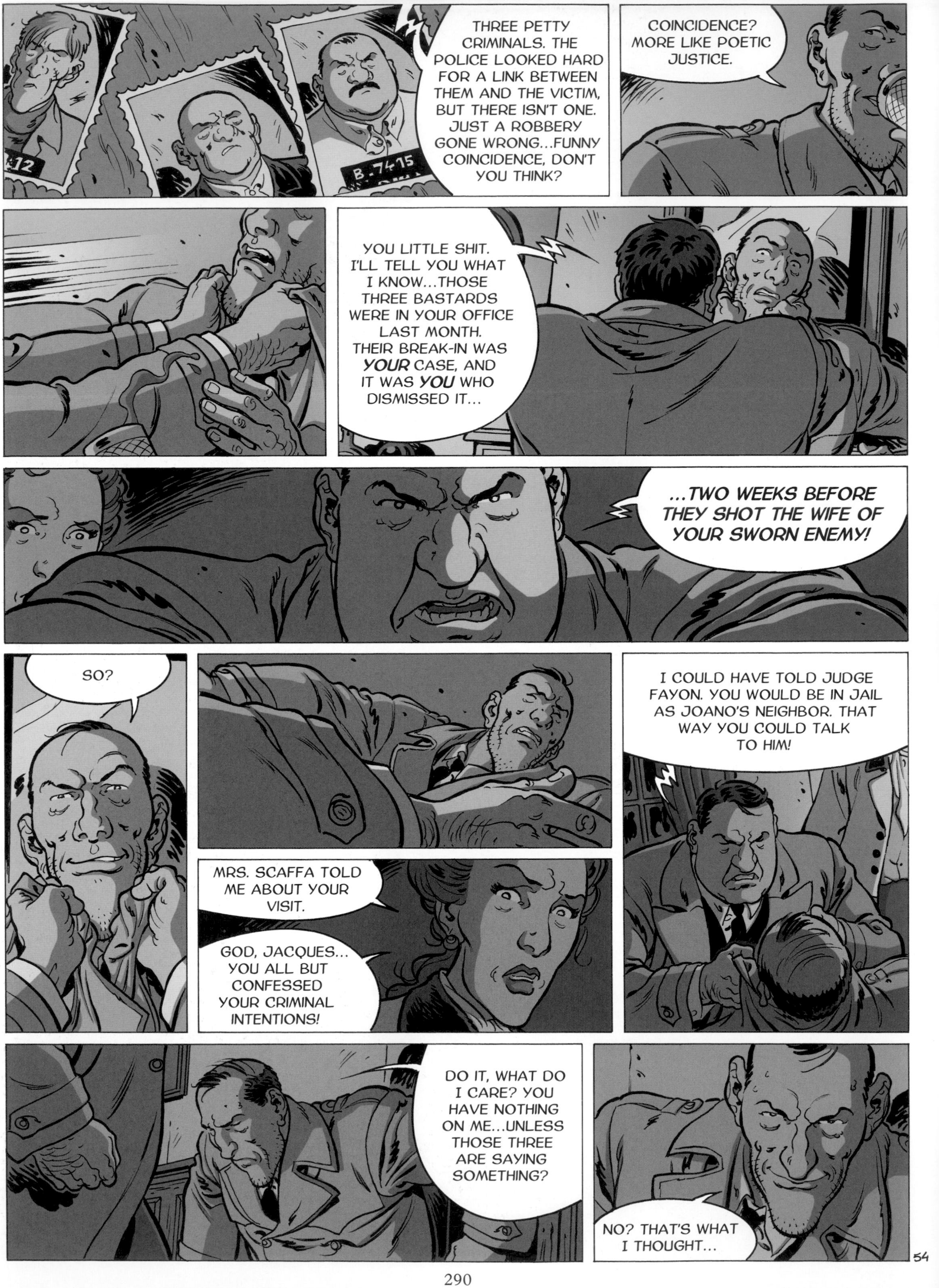
THREE PETTY CRIMINALS. THE POLICE LOOKED HARD FOR A LINK BETWEEN THEM AND THE VICTIM, BUT THERE ISN'T ONE. JUST A ROBBERY GONE WRONG...FUNNY COINCIDENCE, DON'T YOU THINK?
COINCIDENCE? MORE LIKE POETIC JUSTICE.
YOU LITTLE SHIT. I'LL TELL YOU WHAT I KNOW...THOSE THREE BASTARDS WERE IN YOUR OFFICE LAST MONTH. THEIR BREAK-IN WAS ***YOUR*** CASE, AND IT WAS ***YOU*** WHO DISMISSED IT...
...TWO WEEKS BEFORE THEY SHOT THE WIFE OF YOUR SWORN ENEMY!
SO?
I COULD HAVE TOLD JUDGE FAYON. YOU WOULD BE IN JAIL AS JOANO'S NEIGHBOR. THAT WAY YOU COULD TALK TO HIM!
MRS. SCAFFA TOLD ME ABOUT YOUR VISIT.
GOD, JACQUES... YOU ALL BUT CONFESSED YOUR CRIMINAL INTENTIONS!
DO IT, WHAT DO I CARE? YOU HAVE NOTHING ON ME...UNLESS THOSE THREE ARE SAYING SOMETHING?
NO? THAT'S WHAT I THOUGHT...
54

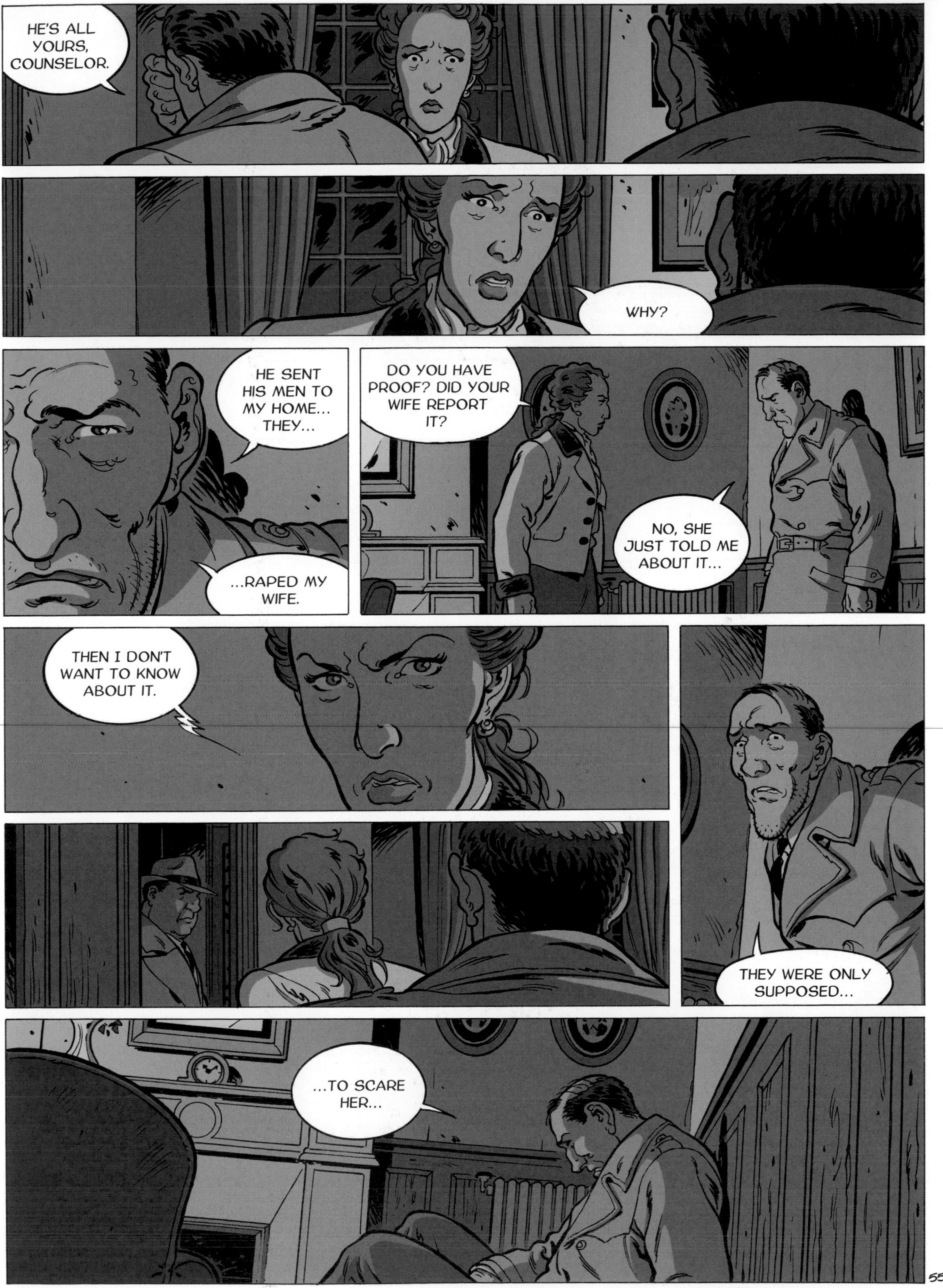
HE'S ALL YOURS, COUNSELOR.
WHY?
HE SENT HIS MEN TO MY HOME... THEY...
...RAPED MY WIFE.
DO YOU HAVE PROOF? DID YOUR WIFE REPORT IT?
NO, SHE JUST TOLD ME ABOUT IT...
THEN I DON'T WANT TO KNOW ABOUT IT.
THEY WERE ONLY SUPPOSED...
...TO SCARE HER...
55

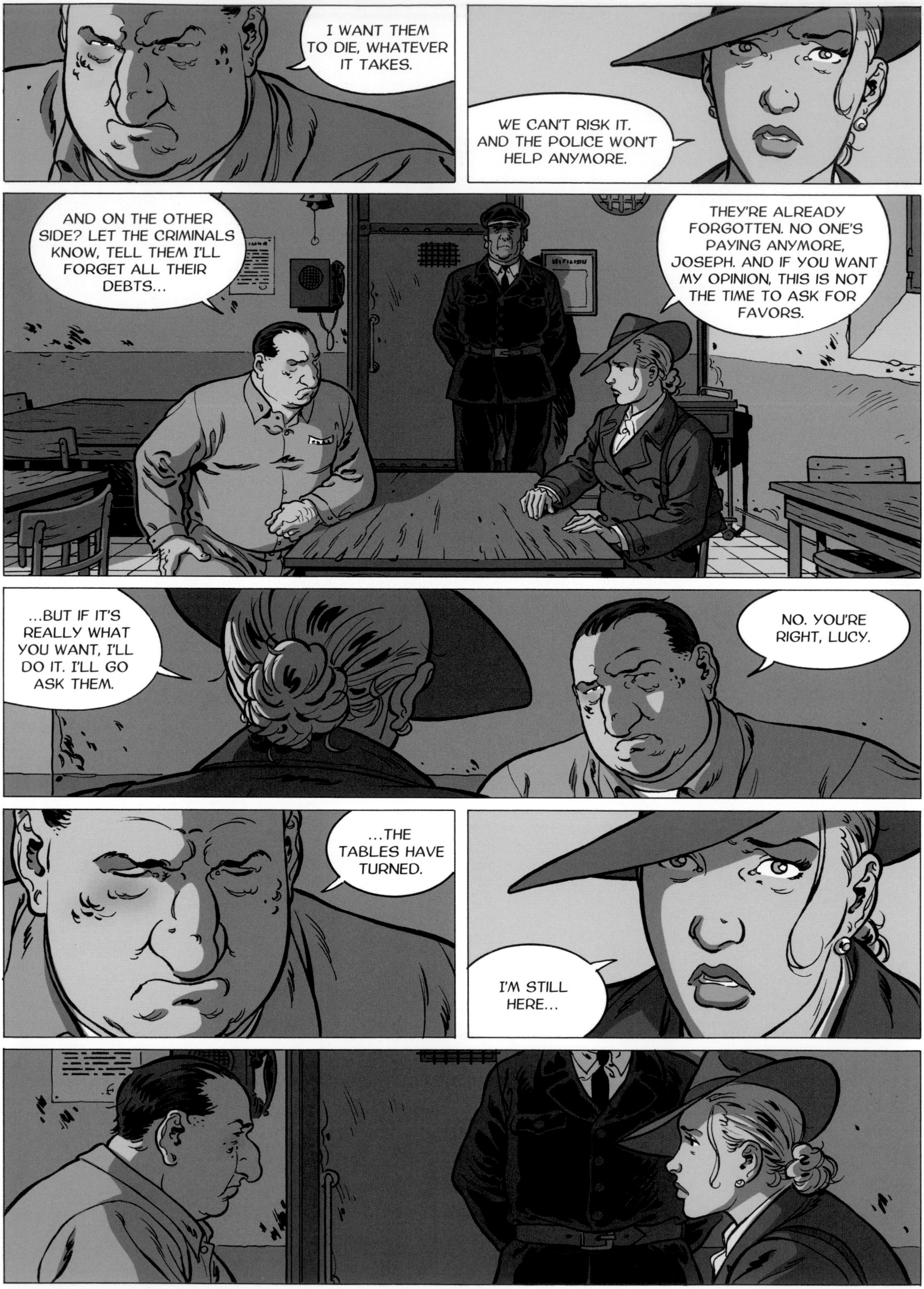
I WANT THEM TO DIE, WHATEVER IT TAKES.
WE CAN'T RISK IT. AND THE POLICE WON'T HELP ANYMORE.
AND ON THE OTHER SIDE? LET THE CRIMINALS KNOW, TELL THEM I'LL FORGET ALL THEIR DEBTS...
THEY'RE ALREADY FORGOTTEN. NO ONE'S PAYING ANYMORE, JOSEPH. AND IF YOU WANT MY OPINION, THIS IS NOT THE TIME TO ASK FOR FAVORS.
...BUT IF IT'S REALLY WHAT YOU WANT, I'LL DO IT. I'LL GO ASK THEM.
NO. YOU'RE RIGHT, LUCY.
...THE TABLES HAVE TURNED.
I'M STILL HERE...
56

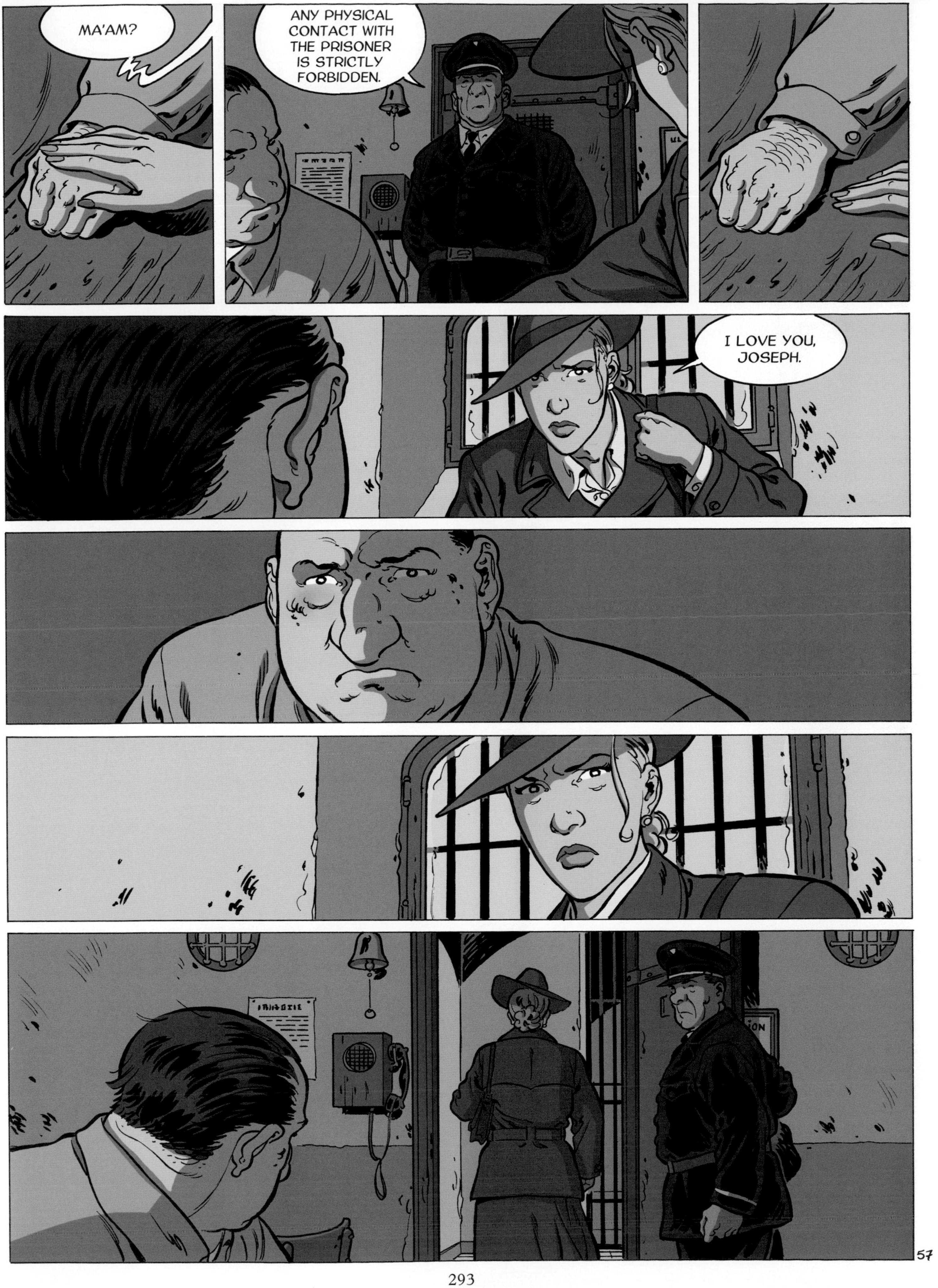
MA'AM?
ANY PHYSICAL CONTACT WITH THE PRISONER IS STRICTLY FORBIDDEN.
I LOVE YOU, JOSEPH.
57

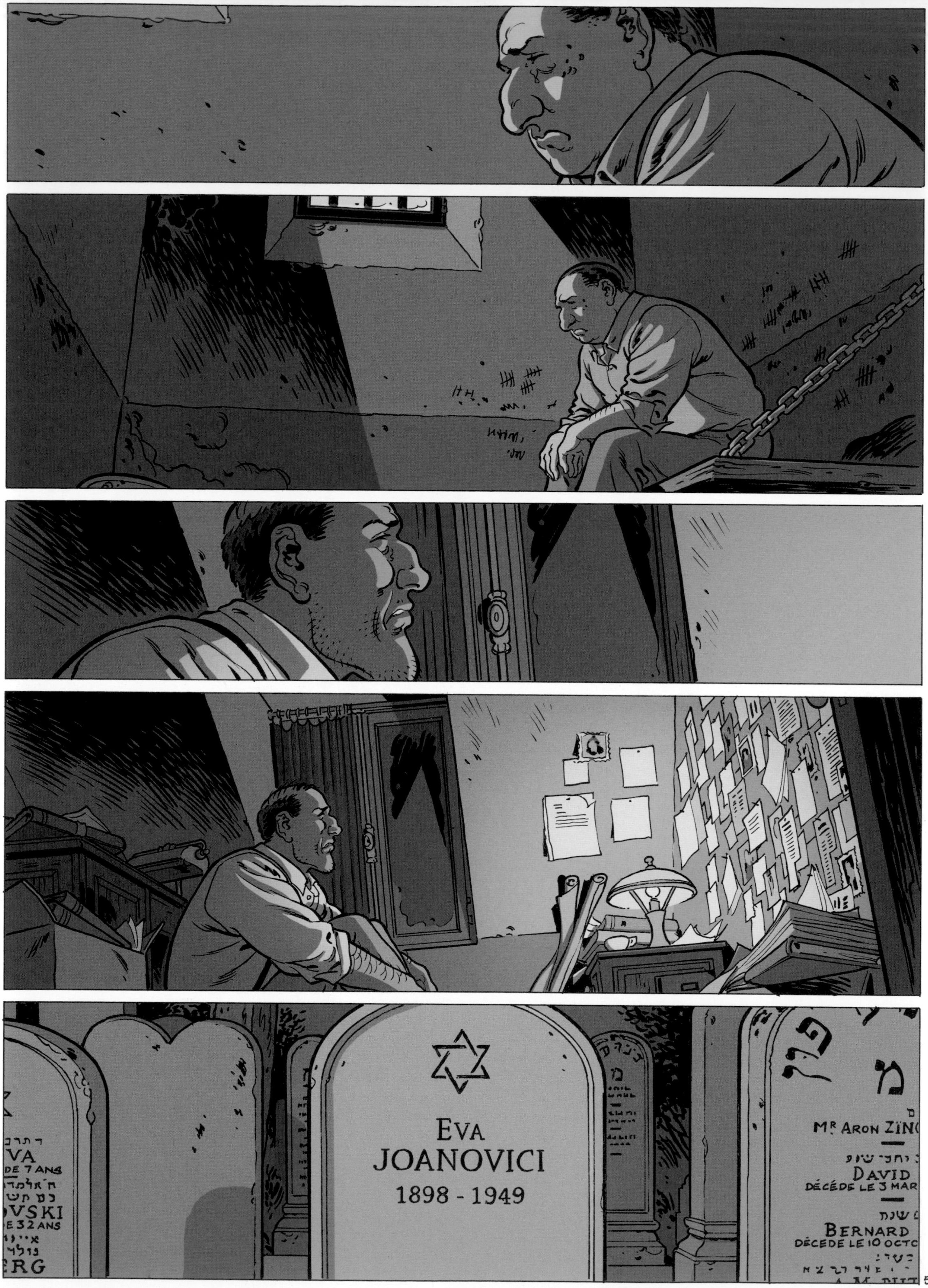
EVA
JOANOVICI
1898 - 1949
Mr ARON ZIN
DAVID
DÉCÉDÉ LE 3 MAR
BERNARD
DÉCÉDE LE 10 OCTO
VA
DE 7 ANS
OVSKI
E 32 ANS
ERG

58

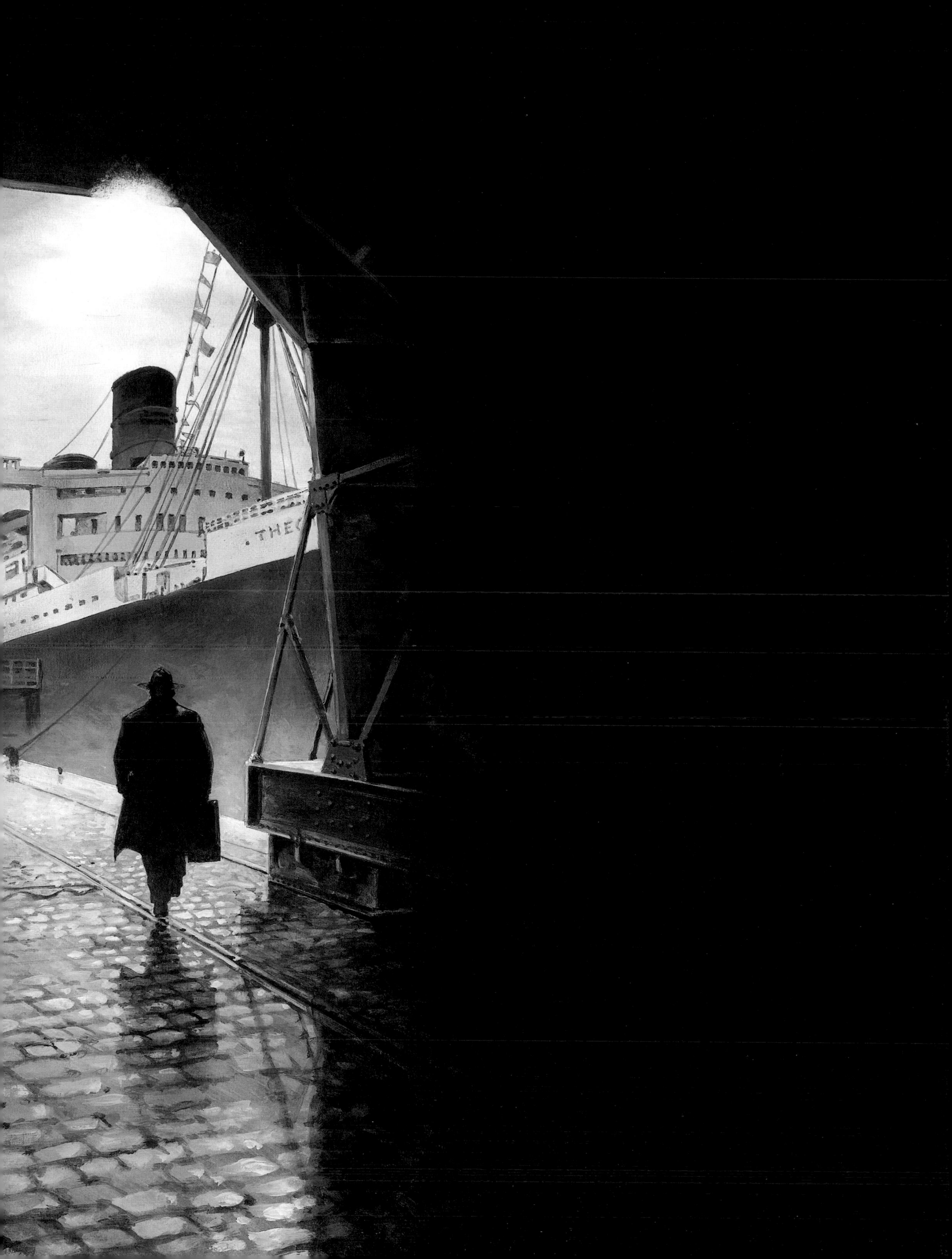

"No man is rich enough to buy back his past."

OSCAR WILDE

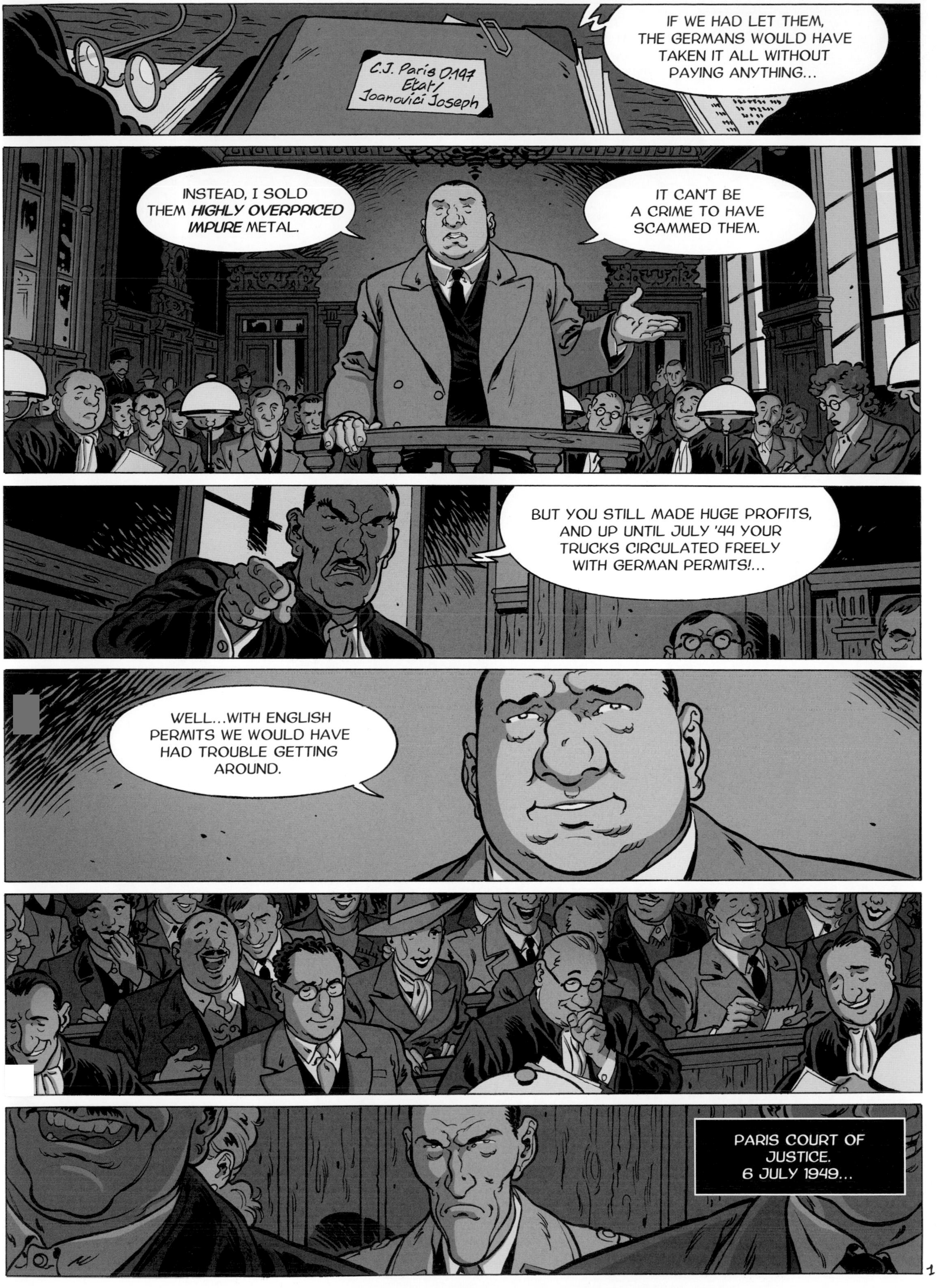
C.J. Paris 0.197
Etat/
Joanovici Joseph
IF WE HAD LET THEM, THE GERMANS WOULD HAVE TAKEN IT ALL WITHOUT PAYING ANYTHING...
INSTEAD, I SOLD THEM HIGHLY OVERPRICED IMPURE METAL.
IT CAN'T BE A CRIME TO HAVE SCAMMED THEM.
BUT YOU STILL MADE HUGE PROFITS, AND UP UNTIL JULY '44 YOUR TRUCKS CIRCULATED FREELY WITH GERMAN PERMITS!...
WELL...WITH ENGLISH PERMITS WE WOULD HAVE HAD TROUBLE GETTING AROUND.
PARIS COURT OF JUSTICE.
6 JULY 1949...
1

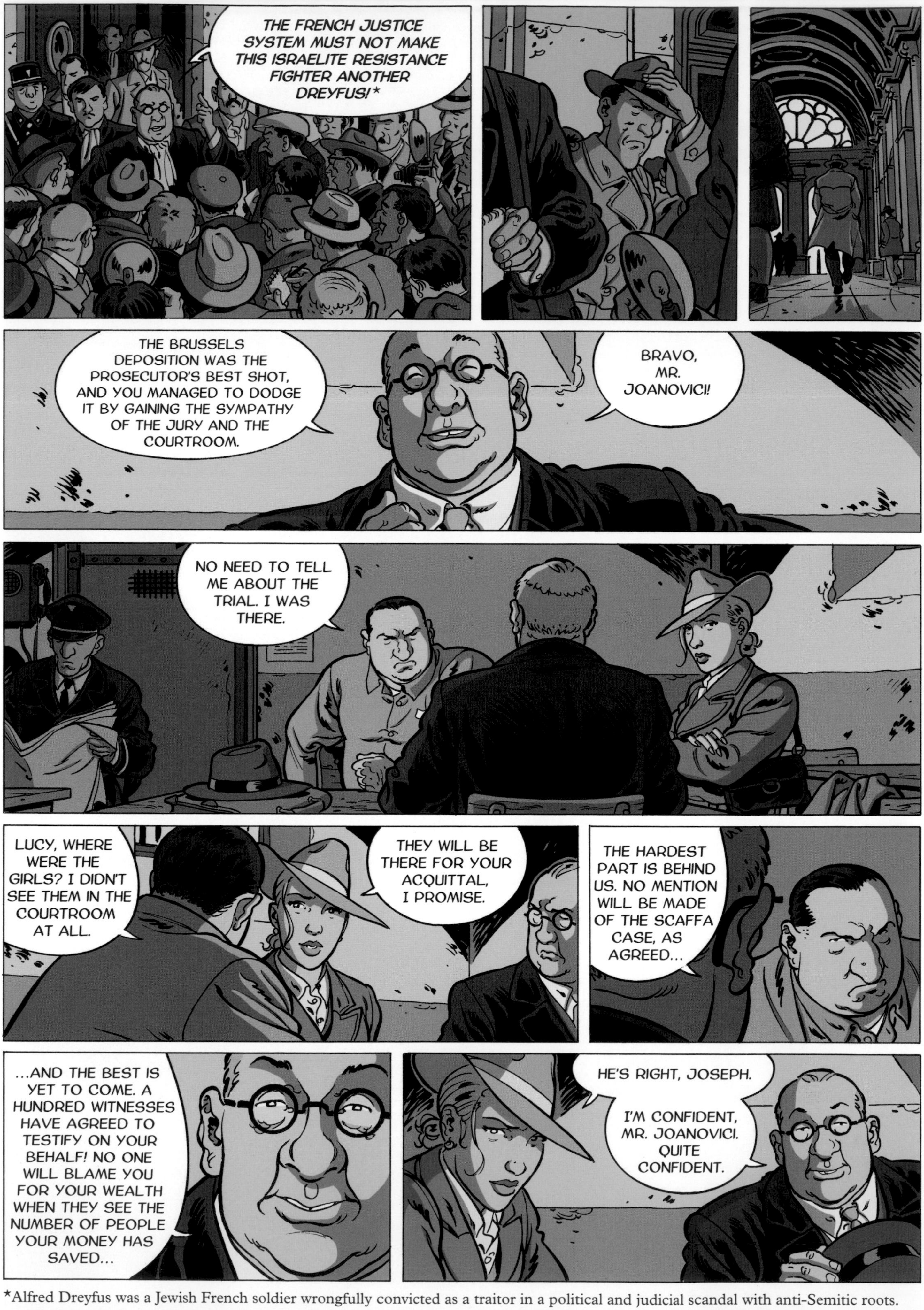
THE FRENCH JUSTICE SYSTEM MUST NOT MAKE THIS ISRAELITE RESISTANCE FIGHTER ANOTHER DREYFUS!*
THE BRUSSELS DEPOSITION WAS THE PROSECUTOR'S BEST SHOT, AND YOU MANAGED TO DODGE IT BY GAINING THE SYMPATHY OF THE JURY AND THE COURTROOM.
BRAVO, MR. JOANOVICI!
NO NEED TO TELL ME ABOUT THE TRIAL. I WAS THERE.
LUCY, WHERE WERE THE GIRLS? I DIDN'T SEE THEM IN THE COURTROOM AT ALL.
THEY WILL BE THERE FOR YOUR ACQUITTAL, I PROMISE.
THE HARDEST PART IS BEHIND US. NO MENTION WILL BE MADE OF THE SCAFFA CASE, AS AGREED...
...AND THE BEST IS YET TO COME. A HUNDRED WITNESSES HAVE AGREED TO TESTIFY ON YOUR BEHALF! NO ONE WILL BLAME YOU FOR YOUR WEALTH WHEN THEY SEE THE NUMBER OF PEOPLE YOUR MONEY HAS SAVED...
HE'S RIGHT, JOSEPH.
I'M CONFIDENT, MR. JOANOVICI. QUITE CONFIDENT.

*Alfred Dreyfus was a Jewish French soldier wrongfully convicted as a traitor in a political and judicial scandal with anti-Semitic roots.

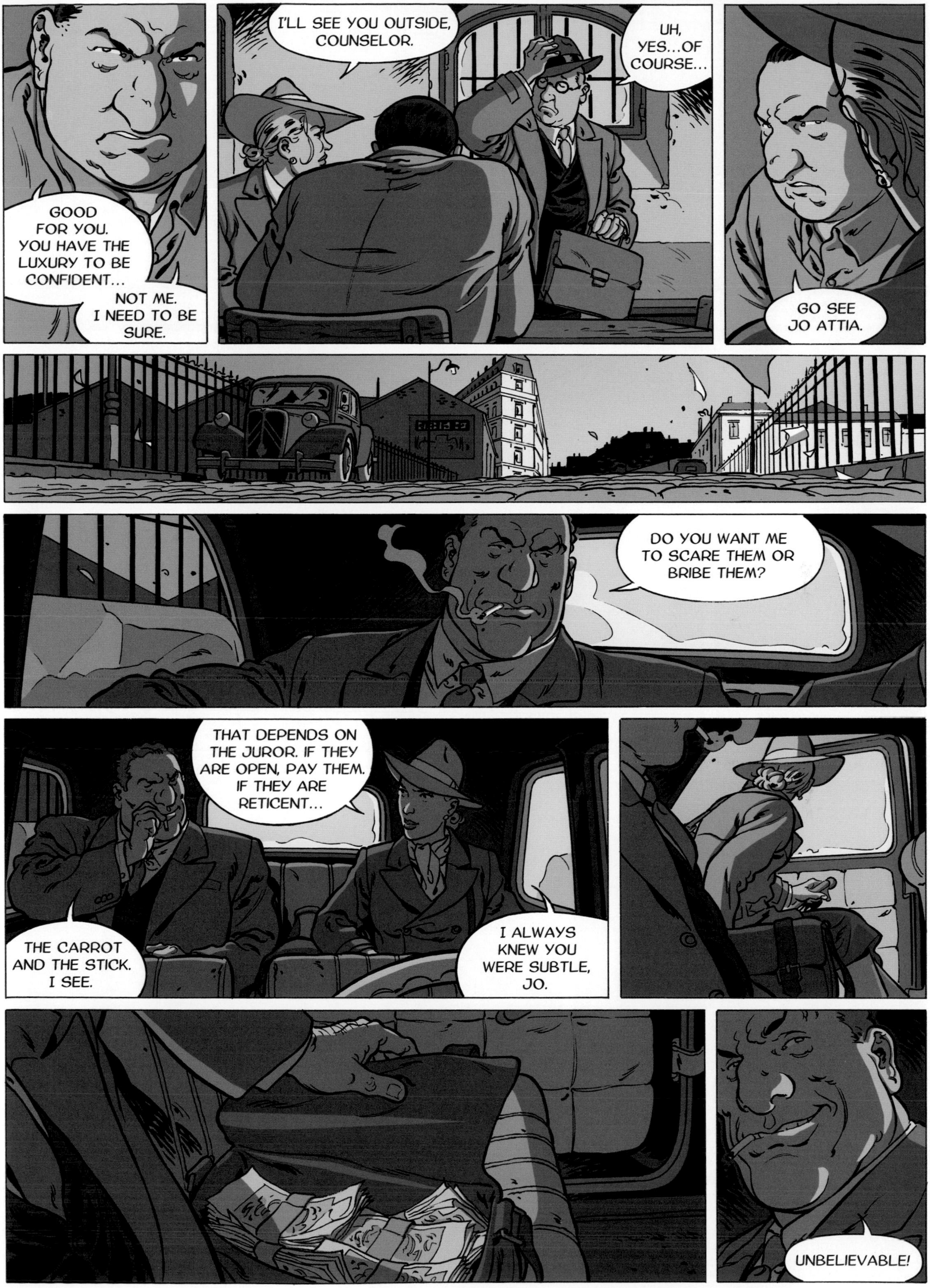
GOOD FOR YOU. YOU HAVE THE LUXURY TO BE CONFIDENT...
NOT ME. I NEED TO BE SURE.
I'LL SEE YOU OUTSIDE, COUNSELOR.
UH, YES...OF COURSE...
GO SEE JO ATTIA.
DO YOU WANT ME TO SCARE THEM OR BRIBE THEM?
THAT DEPENDS ON THE JUROR. IF THEY ARE OPEN, PAY THEM. IF THEY ARE RETICENT...
THE CARROT AND THE STICK. I SEE.
I ALWAYS KNEW YOU WERE SUBTLE, JO.
UNBELIEVABLE!

3

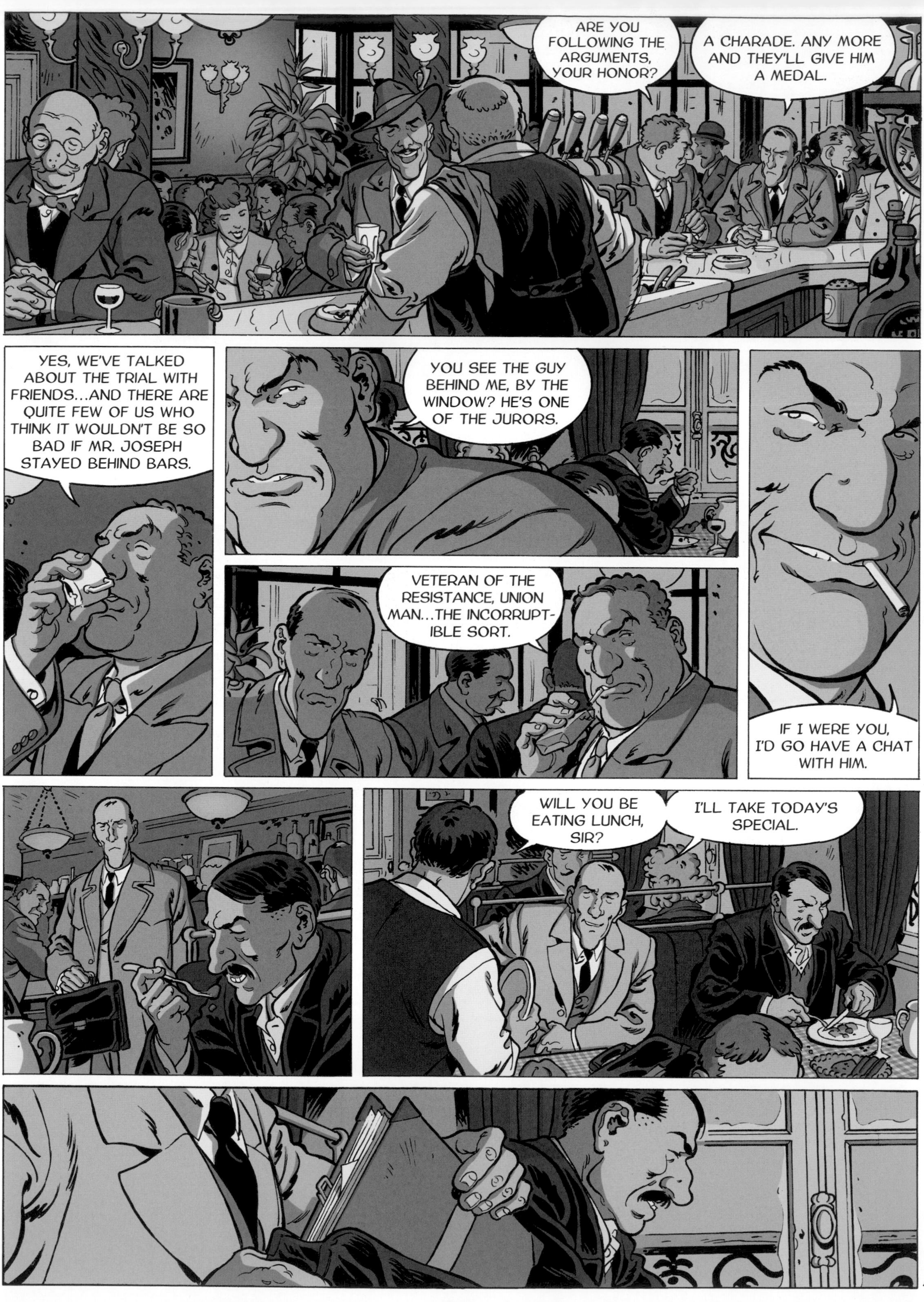
ARE YOU FOLLOWING THE ARGUMENTS, YOUR HONOR?
A CHARADE. ANY MORE AND THEY'LL GIVE HIM A MEDAL.
YES, WE'VE TALKED ABOUT THE TRIAL WITH FRIENDS...AND THERE ARE QUITE FEW OF US WHO THINK IT WOULDN'T BE SO BAD IF MR. JOSEPH STAYED BEHIND BARS.
YOU SEE THE GUY BEHIND ME, BY THE WINDOW? HE'S ONE OF THE JURORS.
VETERAN OF THE RESISTANCE, UNION MAN...THE INCORRUPTIBLE SORT.
IF I WERE YOU, I'D GO HAVE A CHAT WITH HIM.
WILL YOU BE EATING LUNCH, SIR?
I'LL TAKE TODAY'S SPECIAL.
4

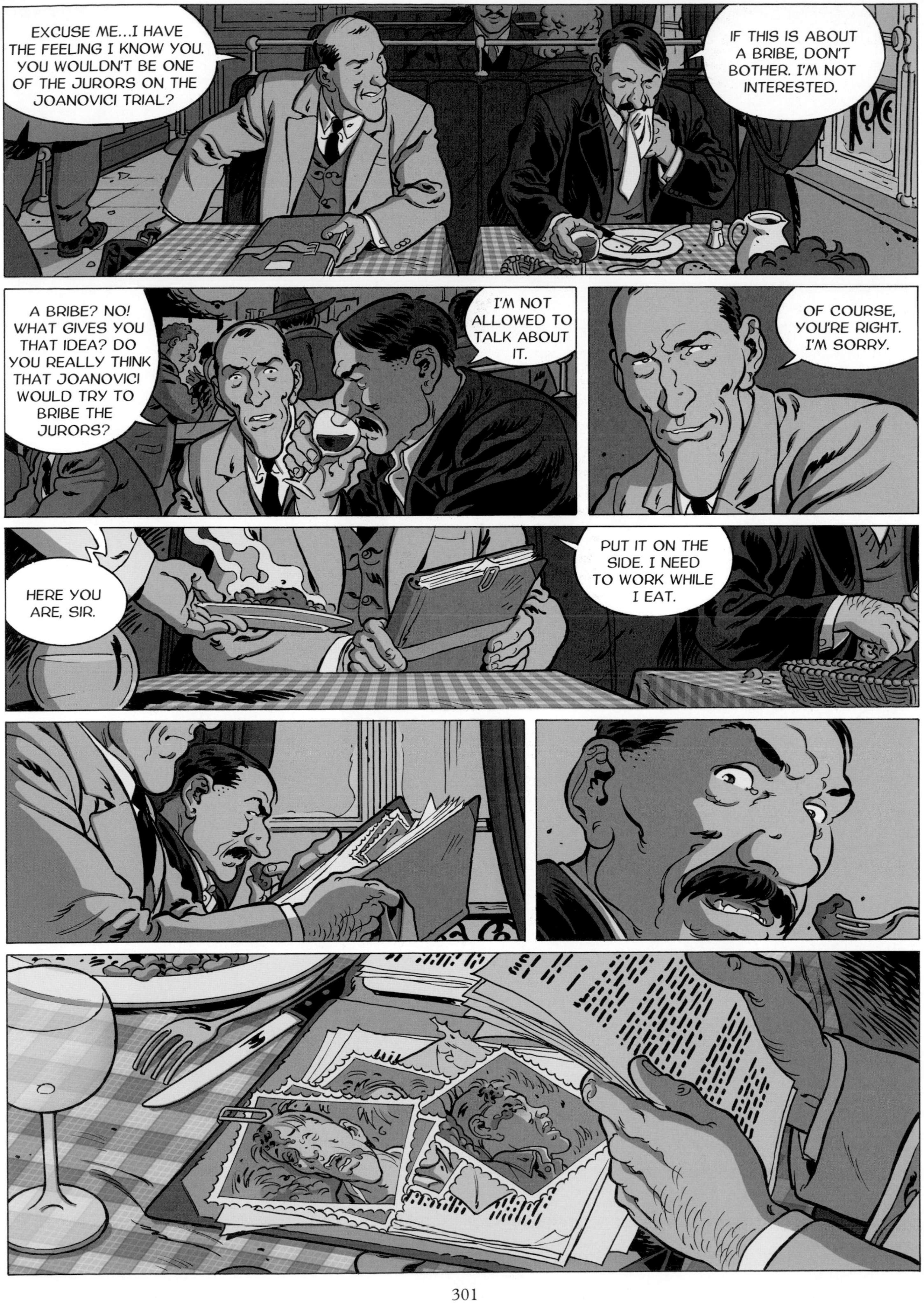
EXCUSE ME...I HAVE THE FEELING I KNOW YOU. YOU WOULDN'T BE ONE OF THE JURORS ON THE JOANOVICI TRIAL?
IF THIS IS ABOUT A BRIBE, DON'T BOTHER. I'M NOT INTERESTED.
A BRIBE? NO! WHAT GIVES YOU THAT IDEA? DO YOU REALLY THINK THAT JOANOVICI WOULD TRY TO BRIBE THE JURORS?
I'M NOT ALLOWED TO TALK ABOUT IT.
OF COURSE, YOU'RE RIGHT. I'M SORRY.
HERE YOU ARE, SIR.
PUT IT ON THE SIDE. I NEED TO WORK WHILE I EAT.
5

PERFECT.

EXCUSE ME, LUCY... WILL WE HAVE A MOMENT TO TALK TO HIM IN PRIVATE?

WE'LL SEE.

FOR OLD COPS, IT MUST BE FUNNY TO BE CHARGED WITH MURDER, HUH, PIEDNOIR?

HEY, FOURNET. I SEE YOU'RE HOLDING THE RECEPTION IN YOUR WIFE'S SALON. I'LL COME GET A TRIM ONE OF THESE DAYS.

DO WE HAVE TO PUT UP WITH THESE THUGS?

YOU KNOW WE DO.

DID EVERYTHING GO WELL?

PERFECTLY. I'VE GREASED ALL THE PALMS NEEDED.

EVEN SO, IT'S ALWAYS A GAMBLE, YOU KNOW...

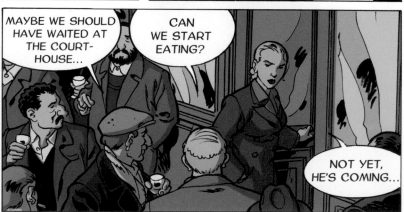

MAYBE WE SHOULD HAVE WAITED AT THE COURT-HOUSE...

CAN WE START EATING?

NOT YET, HE'S COMING...

6

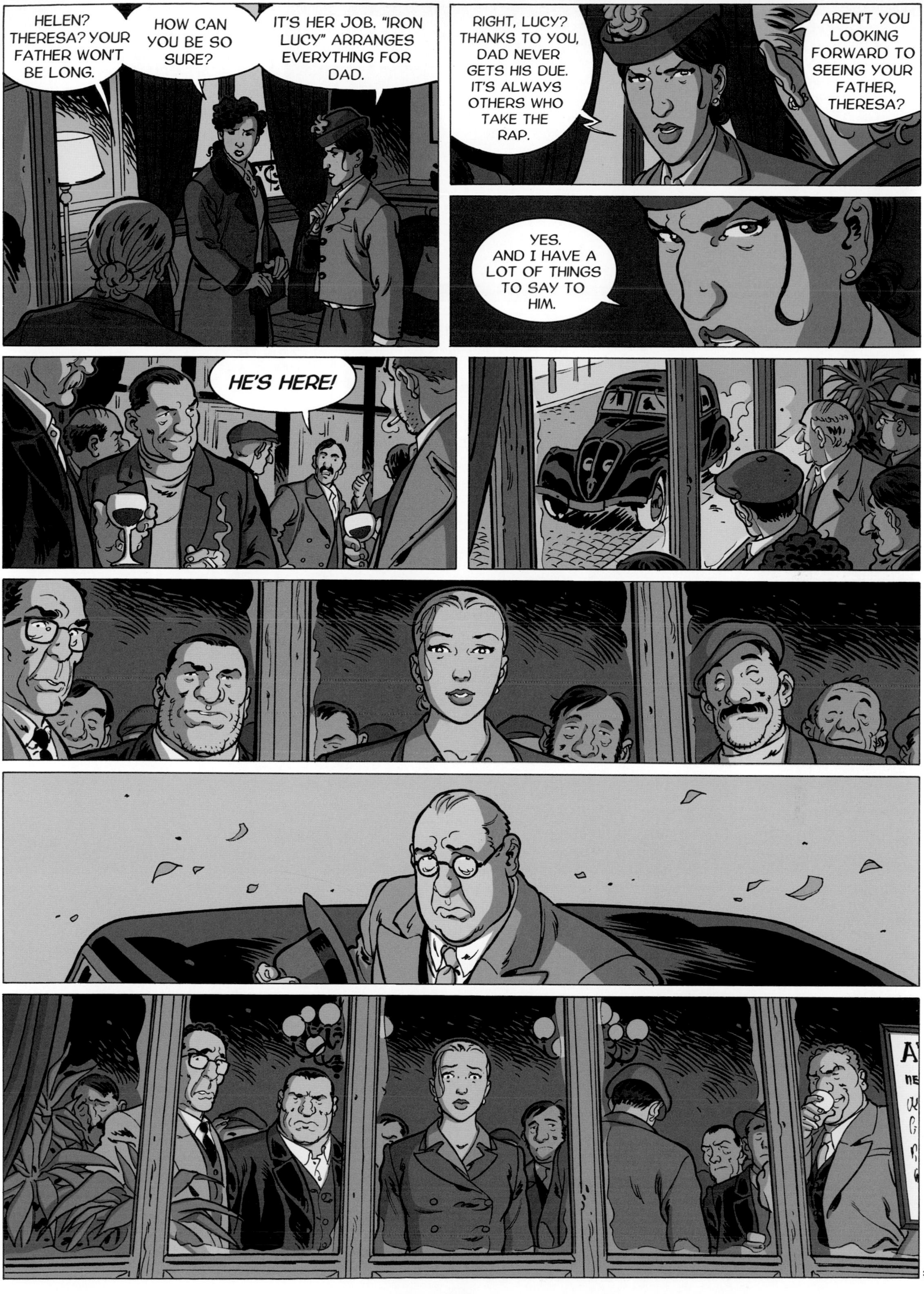
HELEN? THERESA? YOUR FATHER WON'T BE LONG.
HOW CAN YOU BE SO SURE?
IT'S HER JOB. "IRON LUCY" ARRANGES EVERYTHING FOR DAD.
RIGHT, LUCY? THANKS TO YOU, DAD NEVER GETS HIS DUE. IT'S ALWAYS OTHERS WHO TAKE THE RAP.
AREN'T YOU LOOKING FORWARD TO SEEING YOUR FATHER, THERESA?
YES. AND I HAVE A LOT OF THINGS TO SAY TO HIM.
HE'S HERE!
7

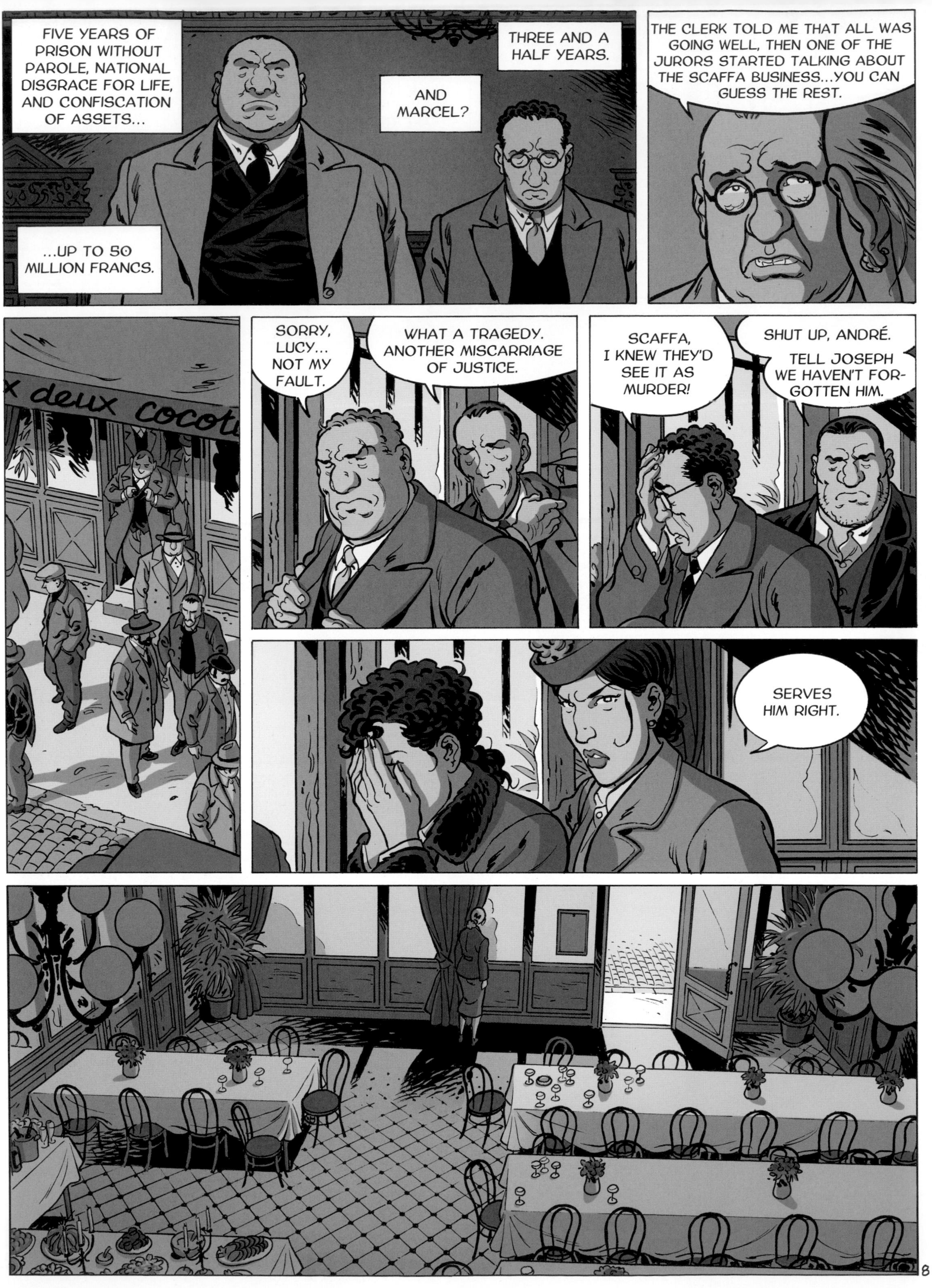
FIVE YEARS OF PRISON WITHOUT PAROLE, NATIONAL DISGRACE FOR LIFE, AND CONFISCATION OF ASSETS...
...UP TO 50 MILLION FRANCS.
AND MARCEL?
THREE AND A HALF YEARS.
THE CLERK TOLD ME THAT ALL WAS GOING WELL, THEN ONE OF THE JURORS STARTED TALKING ABOUT THE SCAFFA BUSINESS...YOU CAN GUESS THE REST.
x deux cocot
SORRY, LUCY... NOT MY FAULT.
WHAT A TRAGEDY. ANOTHER MISCARRIAGE OF JUSTICE.
SCAFFA, I KNEW THEY'D SEE IT AS MURDER!
SHUT UP, ANDRÉ.
TELL JOSEPH WE HAVEN'T FORGOTTEN HIM.
SERVES HIM RIGHT.
8

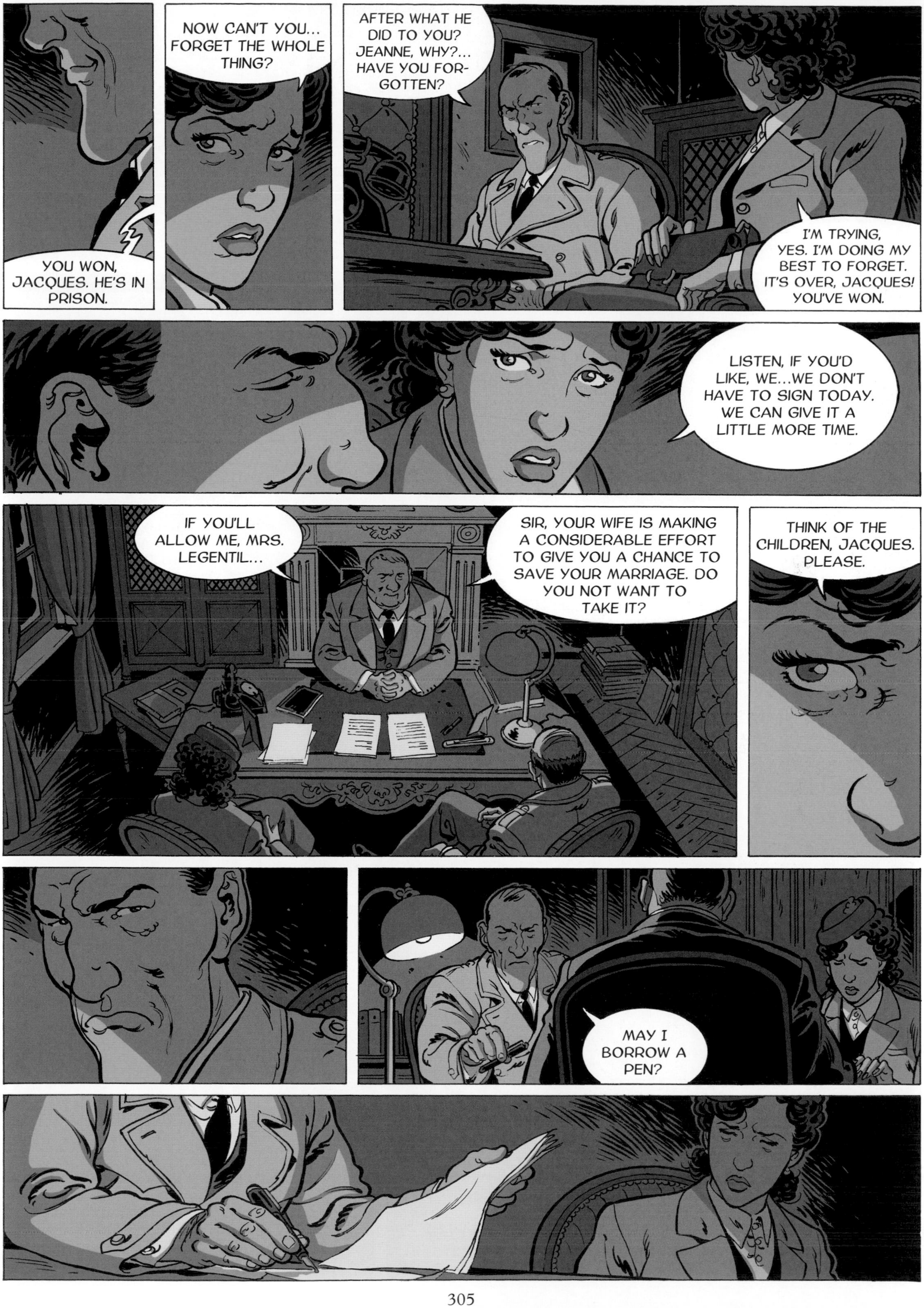

YOU WON, JACQUES. HE'S IN PRISON.
NOW CAN'T YOU... FORGET THE WHOLE THING?
AFTER WHAT HE DID TO YOU? JEANNE, WHY?... HAVE YOU FOR-GOTTEN?
I'M TRYING, YES. I'M DOING MY BEST TO FORGET. IT'S OVER, JACQUES! YOU'VE WON.
LISTEN, IF YOU'D LIKE, WE...WE DON'T HAVE TO SIGN TODAY. WE CAN GIVE IT A LITTLE MORE TIME.
IF YOU'LL ALLOW ME, MRS. LEGENTIL...
SIR, YOUR WIFE IS MAKING A CONSIDERABLE EFFORT TO GIVE YOU A CHANCE TO SAVE YOUR MARRIAGE. DO YOU NOT WANT TO TAKE IT?
THINK OF THE CHILDREN, JACQUES. PLEASE.
MAY I BORROW A PEN?

9

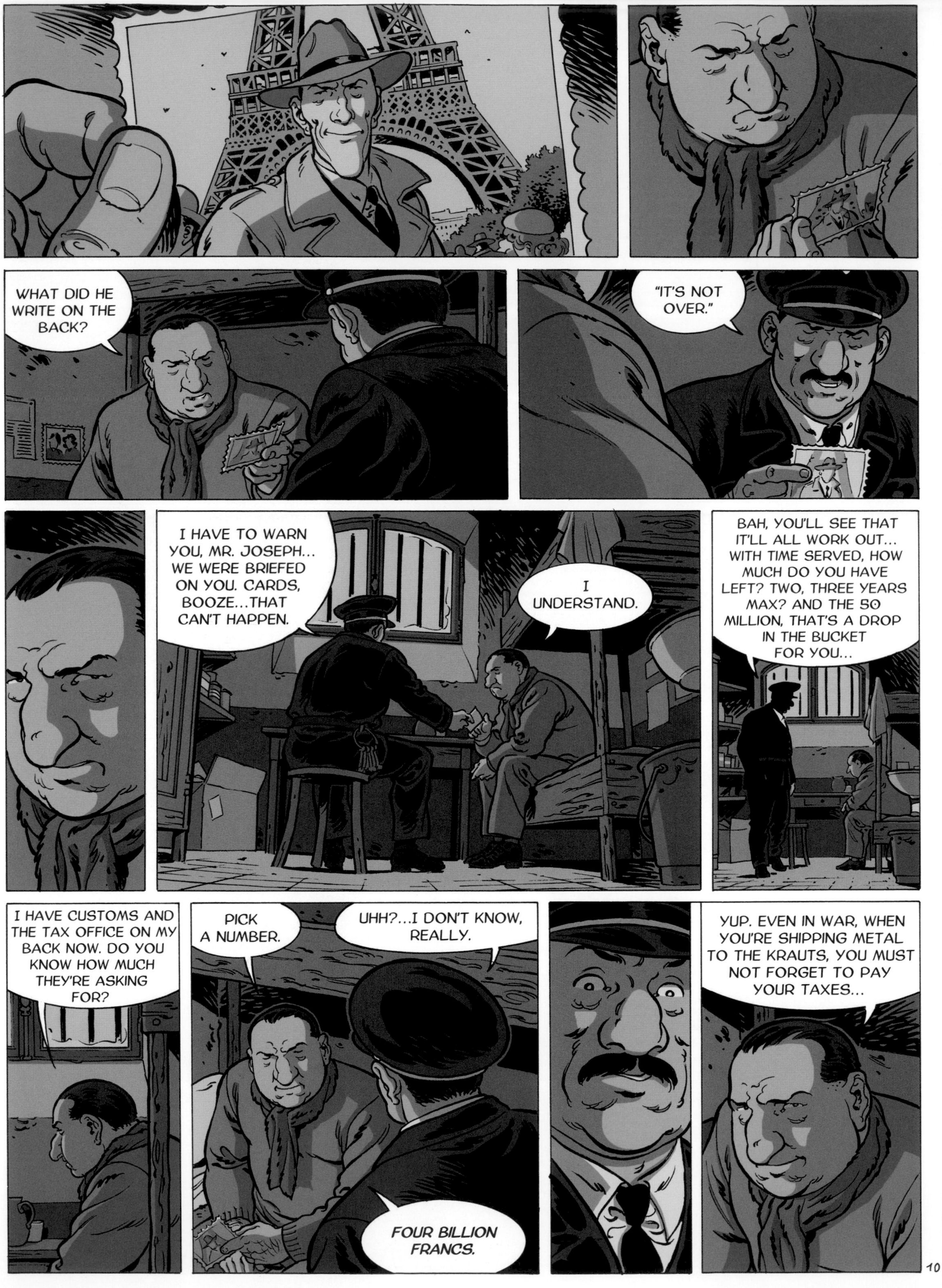
WHAT DID HE WRITE ON THE BACK?
"IT'S NOT OVER."
I HAVE TO WARN YOU, MR. JOSEPH... WE WERE BRIEFED ON YOU. CARDS, BOOZE...THAT CAN'T HAPPEN.
I UNDERSTAND.
BAH, YOU'LL SEE THAT IT'LL ALL WORK OUT... WITH TIME SERVED, HOW MUCH DO YOU HAVE LEFT? TWO, THREE YEARS MAX? AND THE 50 MILLION, THAT'S A DROP IN THE BUCKET FOR YOU...
I HAVE CUSTOMS AND THE TAX OFFICE ON MY BACK NOW. DO YOU KNOW HOW MUCH THEY'RE ASKING FOR?
PICK A NUMBER.
UHH?...I DON'T KNOW, REALLY.
FOUR BILLION FRANCS.
YUP. EVEN IN WAR, WHEN YOU'RE SHIPPING METAL TO THE KRAUTS, YOU MUST NOT FORGET TO PAY YOUR TAXES...
10

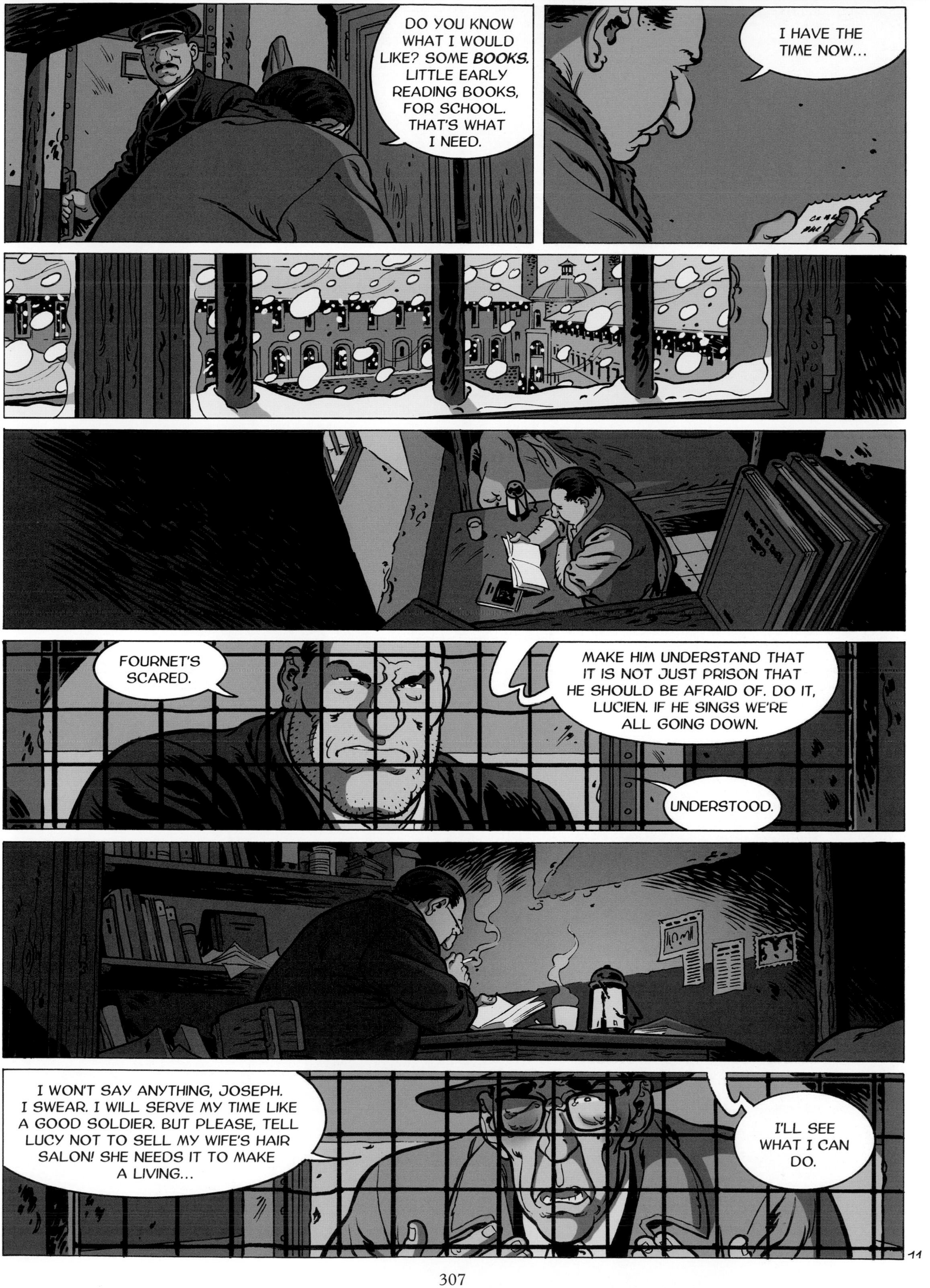
DO YOU KNOW WHAT I WOULD LIKE? SOME BOOKS. LITTLE EARLY READING BOOKS, FOR SCHOOL. THAT'S WHAT I NEED.
I HAVE THE TIME NOW...
FOURNET'S SCARED.
MAKE HIM UNDERSTAND THAT IT IS NOT JUST PRISON THAT HE SHOULD BE AFRAID OF. DO IT, LUCIEN. IF HE SINGS WE'RE ALL GOING DOWN.
UNDERSTOOD.
I WON'T SAY ANYTHING, JOSEPH. I SWEAR. I WILL SERVE MY TIME LIKE A GOOD SOLDIER. BUT PLEASE, TELL LUCY NOT TO SELL MY WIFE'S HAIR SALON! SHE NEEDS IT TO MAKE A LIVING...
I'LL SEE WHAT I CAN DO.
11

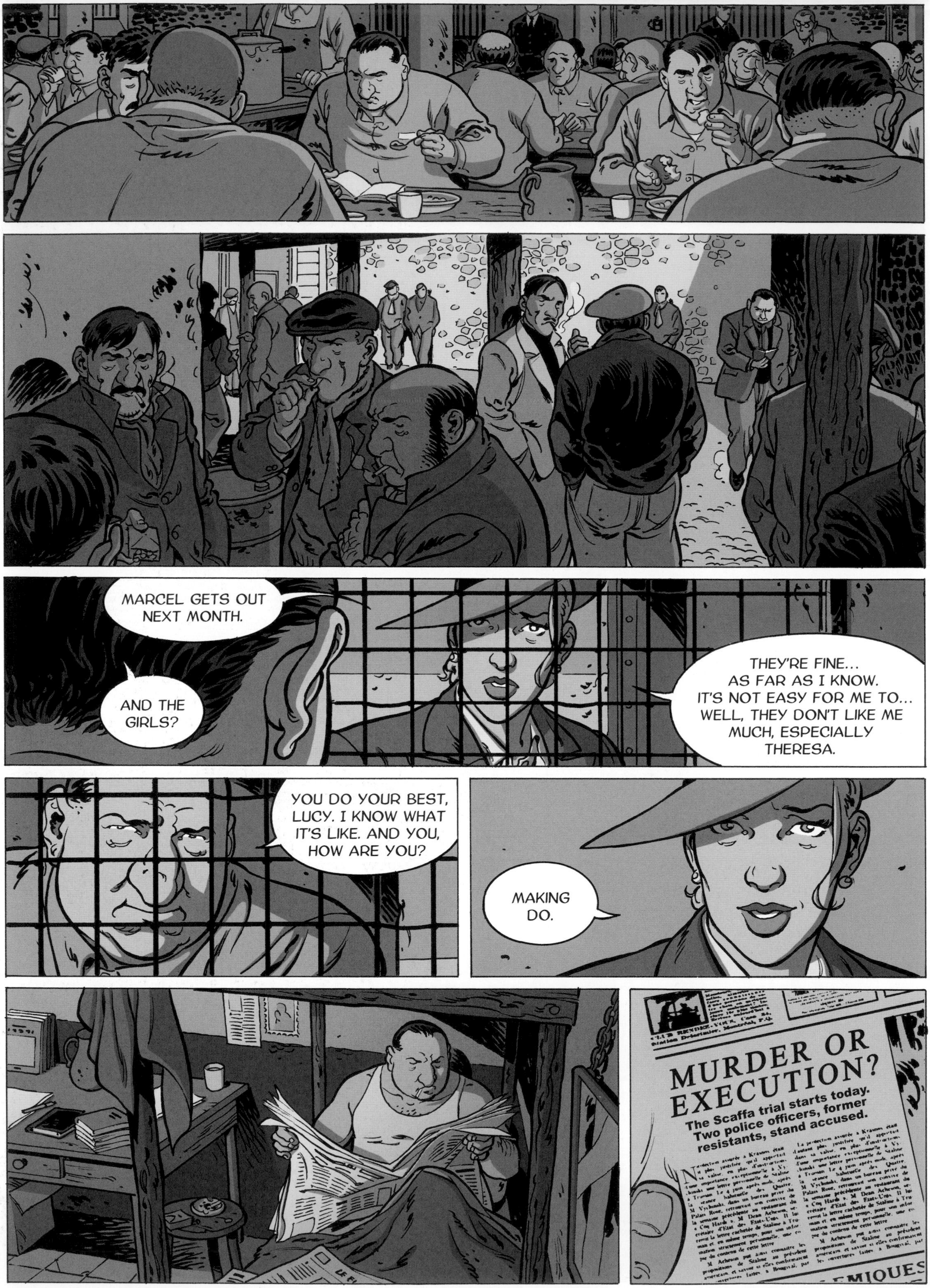
MARCEL GETS OUT NEXT MONTH.
AND THE GIRLS?
THEY'RE FINE... AS FAR AS I KNOW. IT'S NOT EASY FOR ME TO... WELL, THEY DON'T LIKE ME MUCH, ESPECIALLY THERESA.
YOU DO YOUR BEST, LUCY. I KNOW WHAT IT'S LIKE. AND YOU, HOW ARE YOU?
MAKING DO.
MURDER OR EXECUTION?
The Scaffa trial starts today. Two police officers, former resistants, stand accused.

12

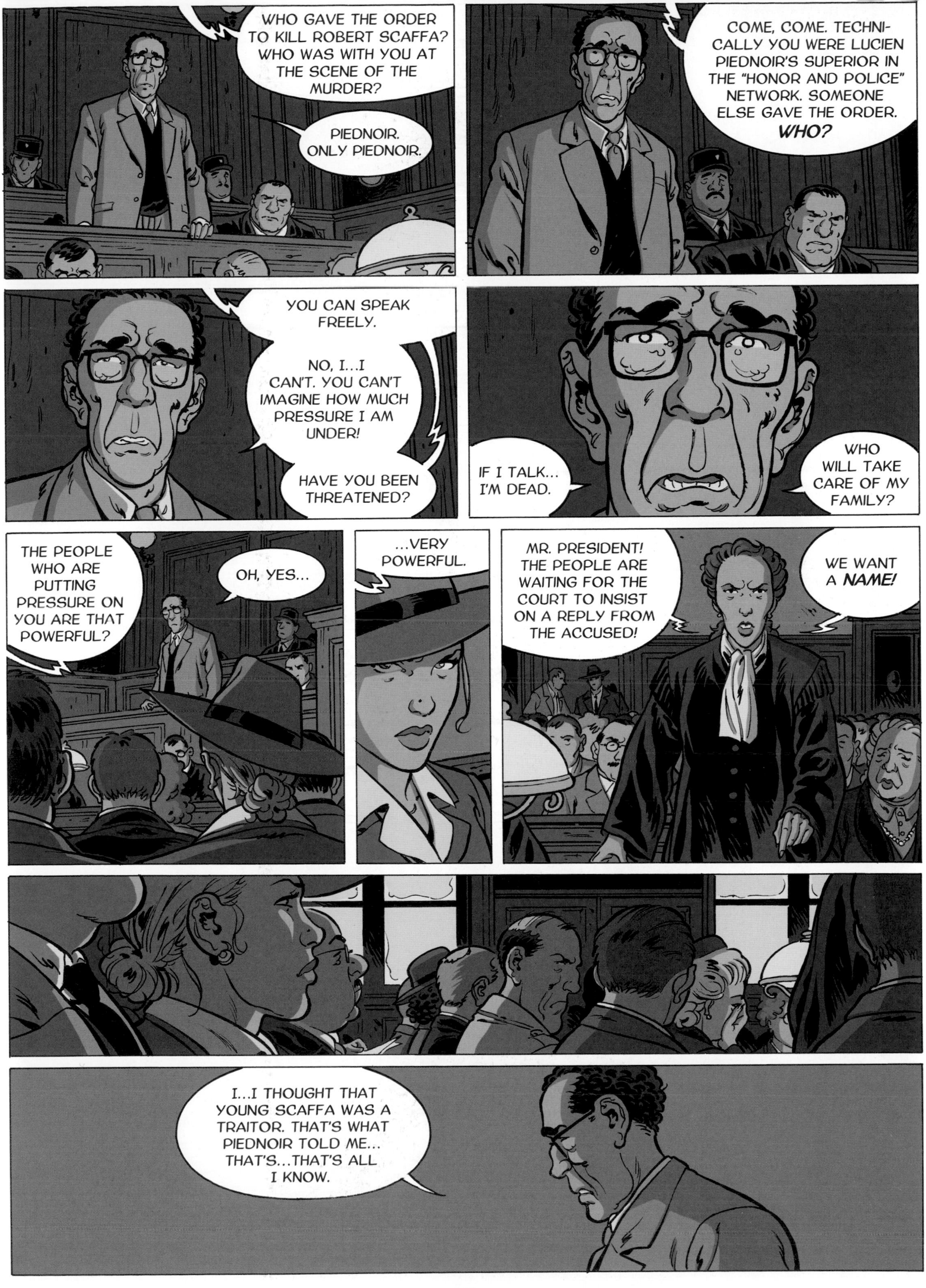
WHO GAVE THE ORDER TO KILL ROBERT SCAFFA? WHO WAS WITH YOU AT THE SCENE OF THE MURDER?
PIEDNOIR. ONLY PIEDNOIR.
COME, COME. TECHNICALLY YOU WERE LUCIEN PIEDNOIR'S SUPERIOR IN THE "HONOR AND POLICE" NETWORK. SOMEONE ELSE GAVE THE ORDER. WHO?
YOU CAN SPEAK FREELY.
NO, I...I CAN'T. YOU CAN'T IMAGINE HOW MUCH PRESSURE I AM UNDER!
HAVE YOU BEEN THREATENED?
IF I TALK... I'M DEAD.
WHO WILL TAKE CARE OF MY FAMILY?
THE PEOPLE WHO ARE PUTTING PRESSURE ON YOU ARE THAT POWERFUL?
OH, YES...
...VERY POWERFUL.
MR. PRESIDENT! THE PEOPLE ARE WAITING FOR THE COURT TO INSIST ON A REPLY FROM THE ACCUSED!
WE WANT A NAME!
I...I THOUGHT THAT YOUNG SCAFFA WAS A TRAITOR. THAT'S WHAT PIEDNOIR TOLD ME... THAT'S...THAT'S ALL I KNOW.

13

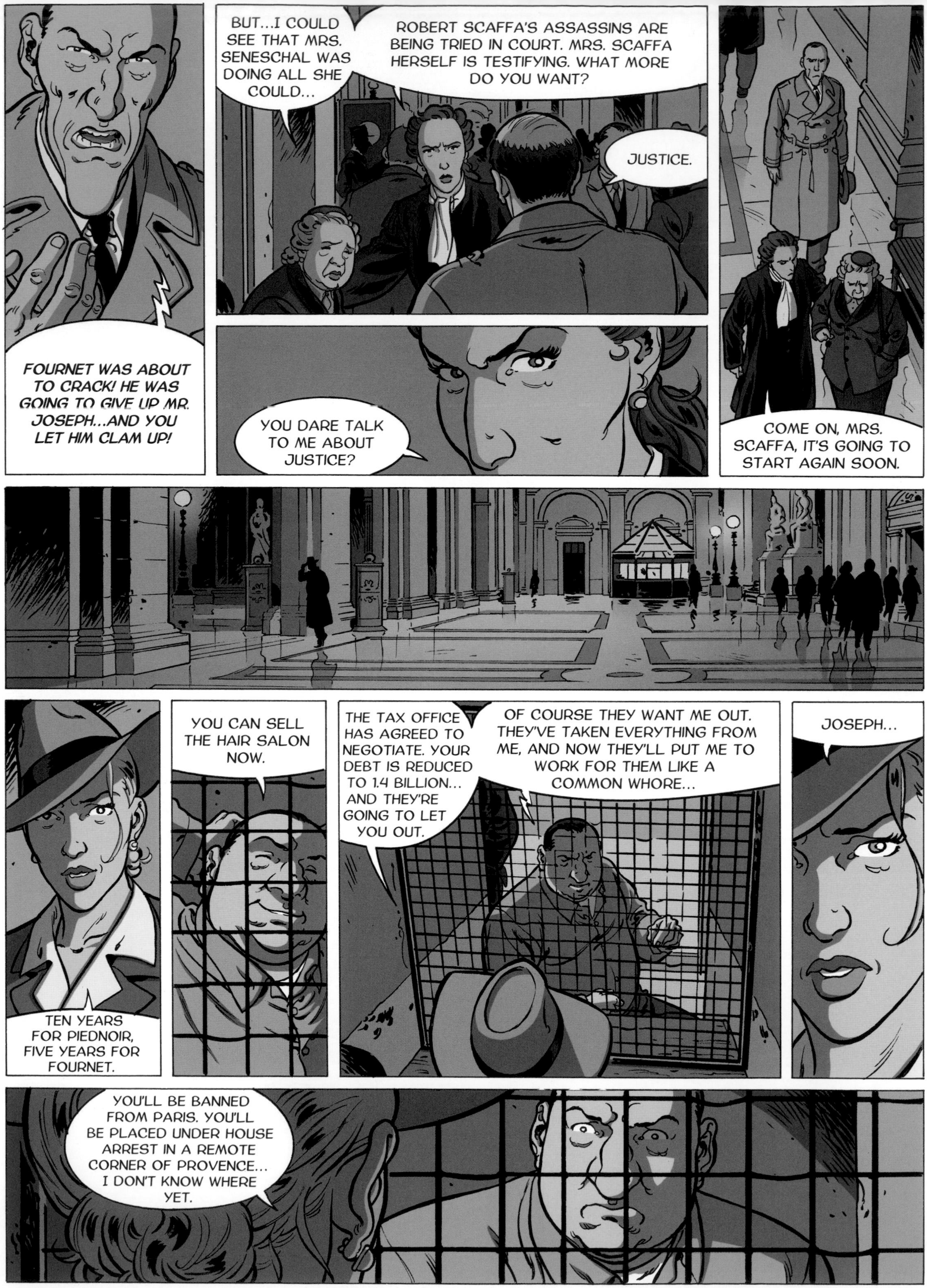
FOURNET WAS ABOUT TO CRACK! HE WAS GOING TO GIVE UP MR. JOSEPH...AND YOU LET HIM CLAM UP!
BUT...I COULD SEE THAT MRS. SENESCHAL WAS DOING ALL SHE COULD...
ROBERT SCAFFA'S ASSASSINS ARE BEING TRIED IN COURT. MRS. SCAFFA HERSELF IS TESTIFYING. WHAT MORE DO YOU WANT?
JUSTICE.
YOU DARE TALK TO ME ABOUT JUSTICE?
COME ON, MRS. SCAFFA, IT'S GOING TO START AGAIN SOON.
TEN YEARS FOR PIEDNOIR, FIVE YEARS FOR FOURNET.
YOU CAN SELL THE HAIR SALON NOW.
THE TAX OFFICE HAS AGREED TO NEGOTIATE. YOUR DEBT IS REDUCED TO 1.4 BILLION... AND THEY'RE GOING TO LET YOU OUT.
OF COURSE THEY WANT ME OUT. THEY'VE TAKEN EVERYTHING FROM ME, AND NOW THEY'LL PUT ME TO WORK FOR THEM LIKE A COMMON WHORE...
JOSEPH...
YOU'LL BE BANNED FROM PARIS. YOU'LL BE PLACED UNDER HOUSE ARREST IN A REMOTE CORNER OF PROVENCE... I DON'T KNOW WHERE YET.
14

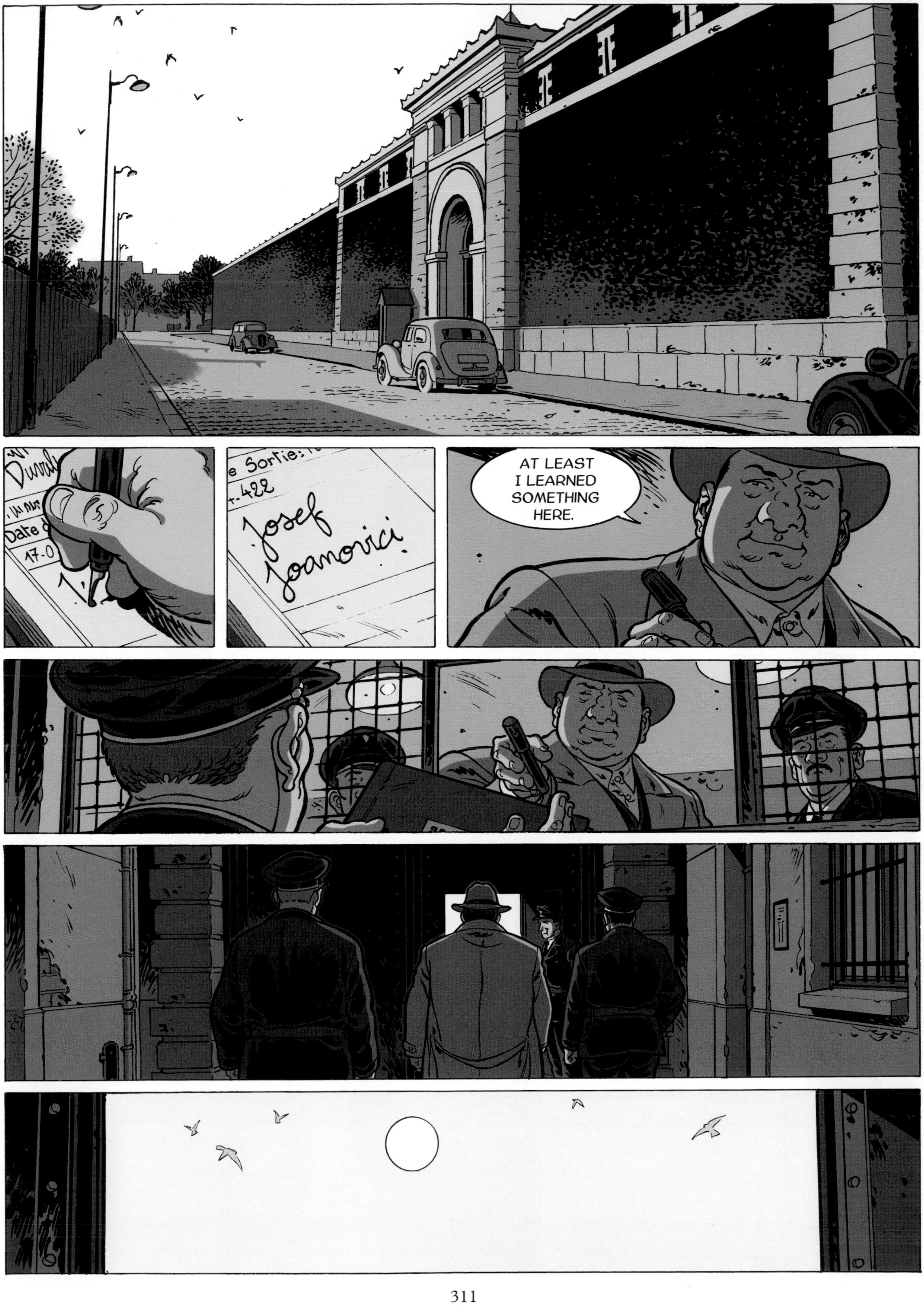
Josef Joanovici
AT LEAST I LEARNED SOMETHING HERE.

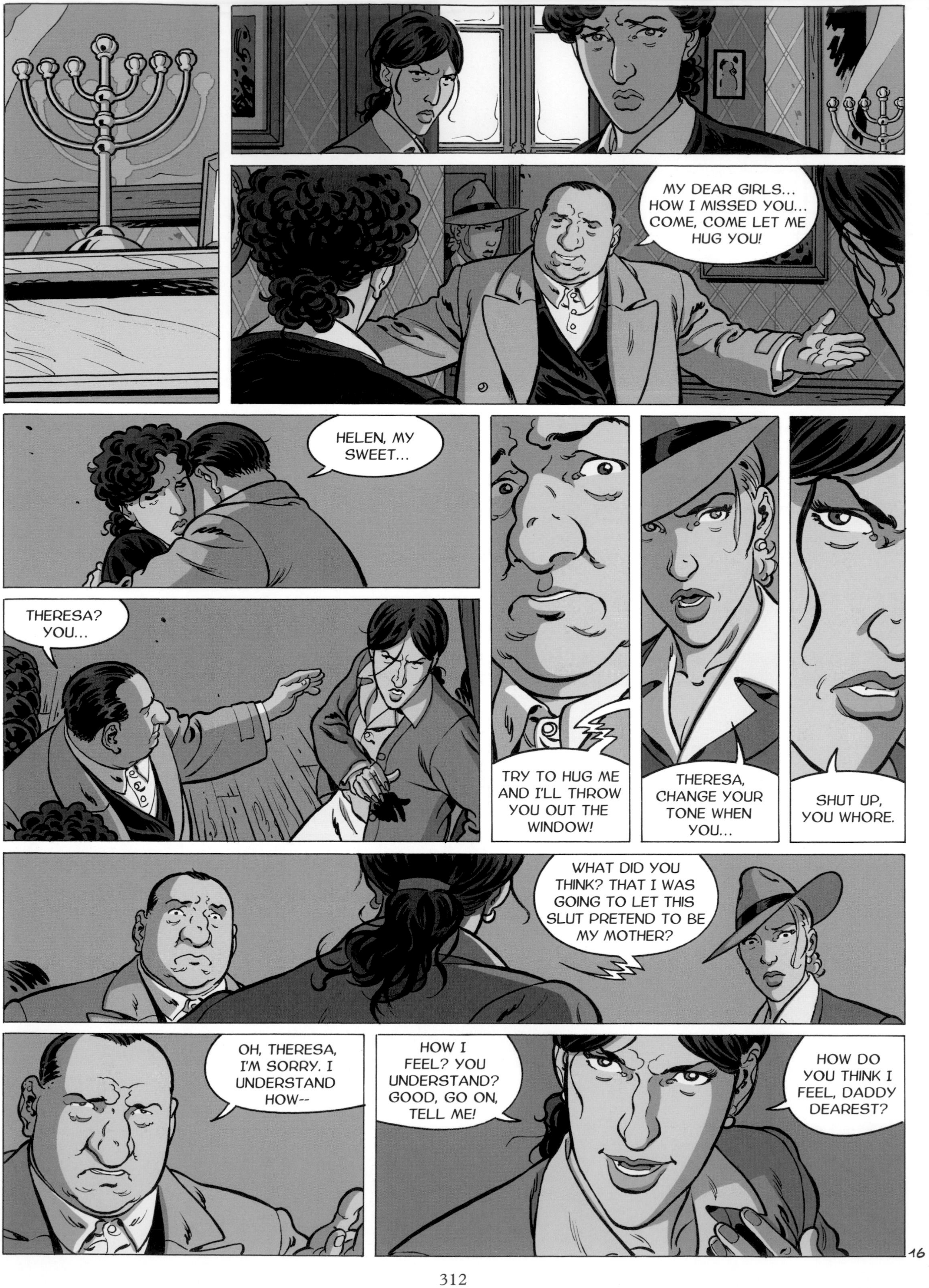
MY DEAR GIRLS... HOW I MISSED YOU... COME, COME LET ME HUG YOU!
HELEN, MY SWEET...
THERESA? YOU...
TRY TO HUG ME AND I'LL THROW YOU OUT THE WINDOW!
THERESA, CHANGE YOUR TONE WHEN YOU...
SHUT UP, YOU WHORE.
WHAT DID YOU THINK? THAT I WAS GOING TO LET THIS SLUT PRETEND TO BE MY MOTHER?
OH, THERESA, I'M SORRY. I UNDERSTAND HOW--
HOW I FEEL? YOU UNDERSTAND? GOOD, GO ON, TELL ME!
HOW DO YOU THINK I FEEL, DADDY DEAREST?
16

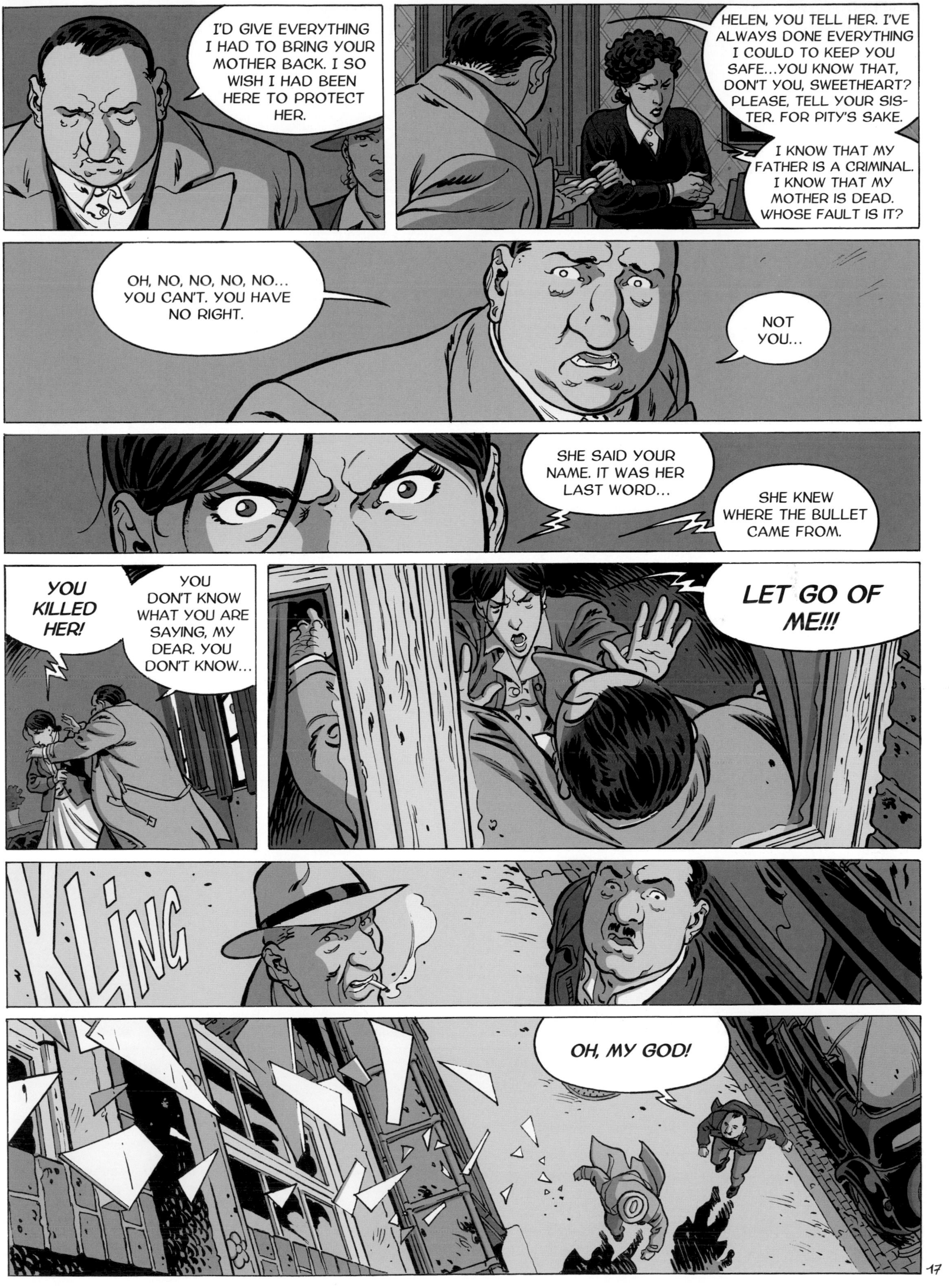
I'D GIVE EVERYTHING I HAD TO BRING YOUR MOTHER BACK. I SO WISH I HAD BEEN HERE TO PROTECT HER.
HELEN, YOU TELL HER. I'VE ALWAYS DONE EVERYTHING I COULD TO KEEP YOU SAFE...YOU KNOW THAT, DON'T YOU, SWEETHEART? PLEASE, TELL YOUR SIS-TER. FOR PITY'S SAKE.
I KNOW THAT MY FATHER IS A CRIMINAL. I KNOW THAT MY MOTHER IS DEAD. WHOSE FAULT IS IT?
OH, NO, NO, NO, NO... YOU CAN'T. YOU HAVE NO RIGHT.
NOT YOU...
SHE SAID YOUR NAME. IT WAS HER LAST WORD...
SHE KNEW WHERE THE BULLET CAME FROM.
YOU KILLED HER!
YOU DON'T KNOW WHAT YOU ARE SAYING, MY DEAR. YOU DON'T KNOW...
LET GO OF ME!!!
KLING
OH, MY GOD!
17

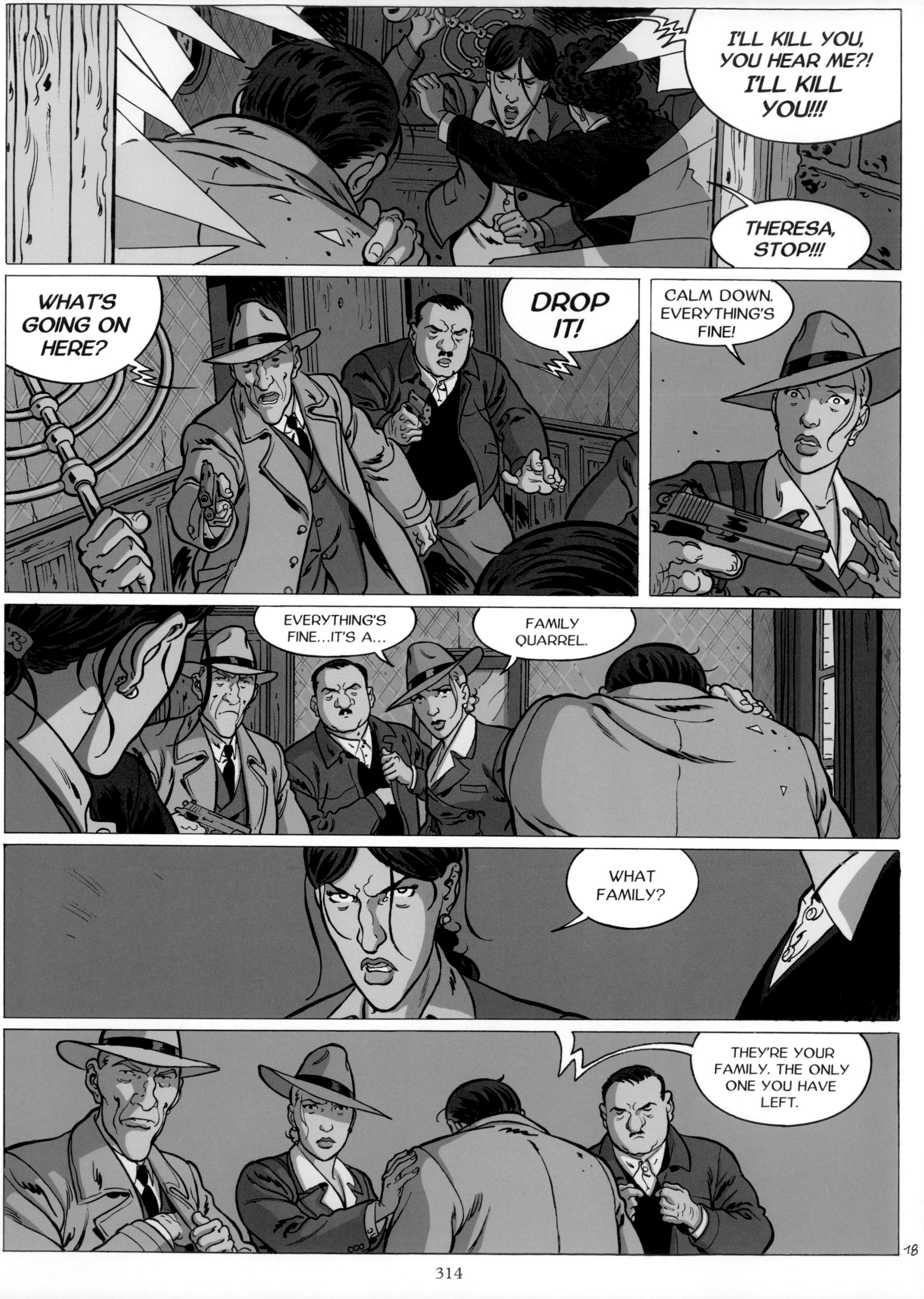
I'LL KILL YOU, YOU HEAR ME?! I'LL KILL YOU!!!
THERESA, STOP!!!
WHAT'S GOING ON HERE?
DROP IT!
CALM DOWN. EVERYTHING'S FINE!
EVERYTHING'S FINE...IT'S A...
FAMILY QUARREL.
WHAT FAMILY?
THEY'RE YOUR FAMILY. THE ONLY ONE YOU HAVE LEFT.
18

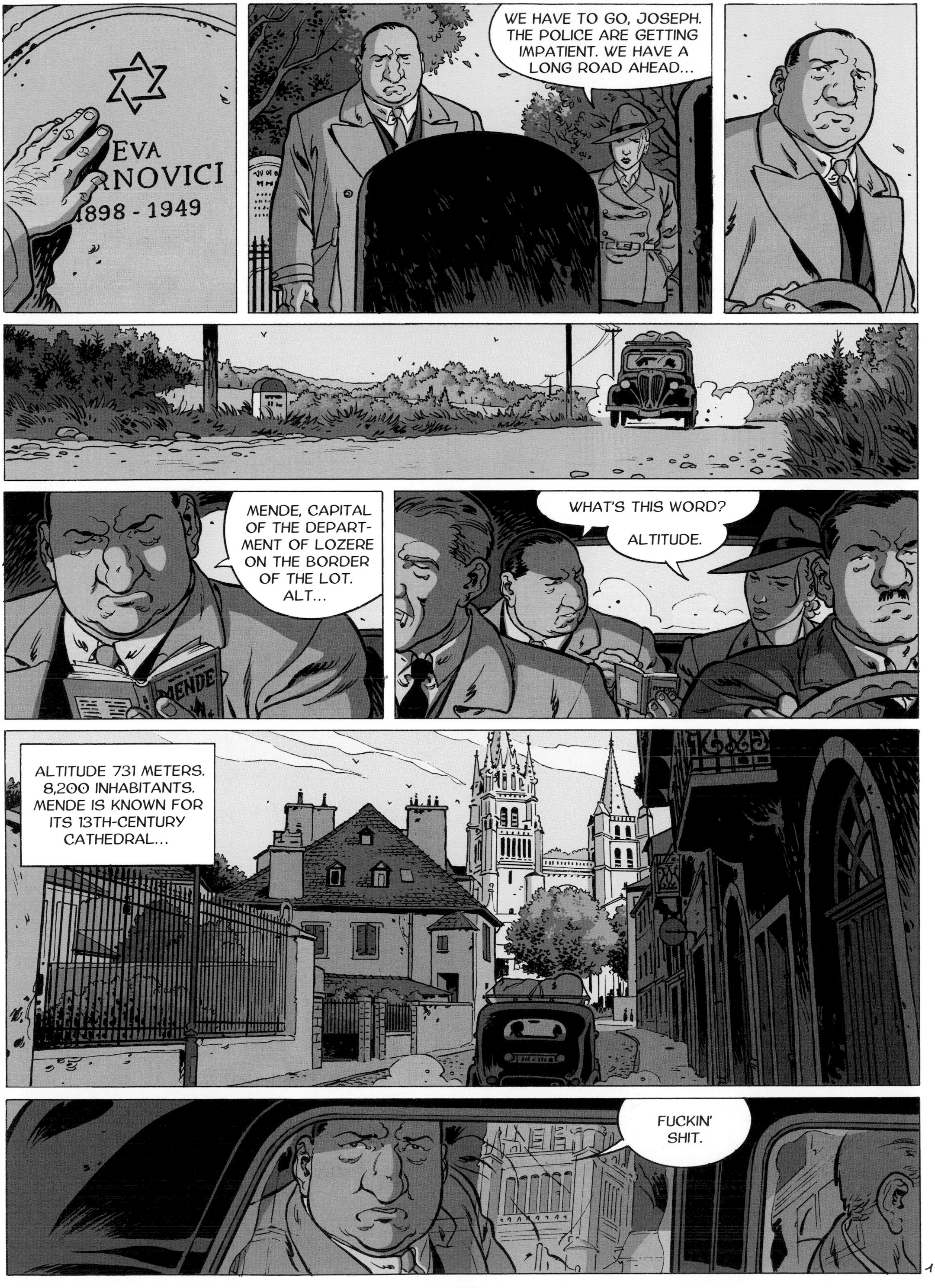
EVA
[...]RNOVICI
1898 - 1949
WE HAVE TO GO, JOSEPH. THE POLICE ARE GETTING IMPATIENT. WE HAVE A LONG ROAD AHEAD...
MENDE, CAPITAL OF THE DEPARTMENT OF LOZERE ON THE BORDER OF THE LOT. ALT...
MENDE
WHAT'S THIS WORD?
ALTITUDE.
ALTITUDE 731 METERS. 8,200 INHABITANTS. MENDE IS KNOWN FOR ITS 13TH-CENTURY CATHEDRAL...
FUCKIN' SHIT.
19

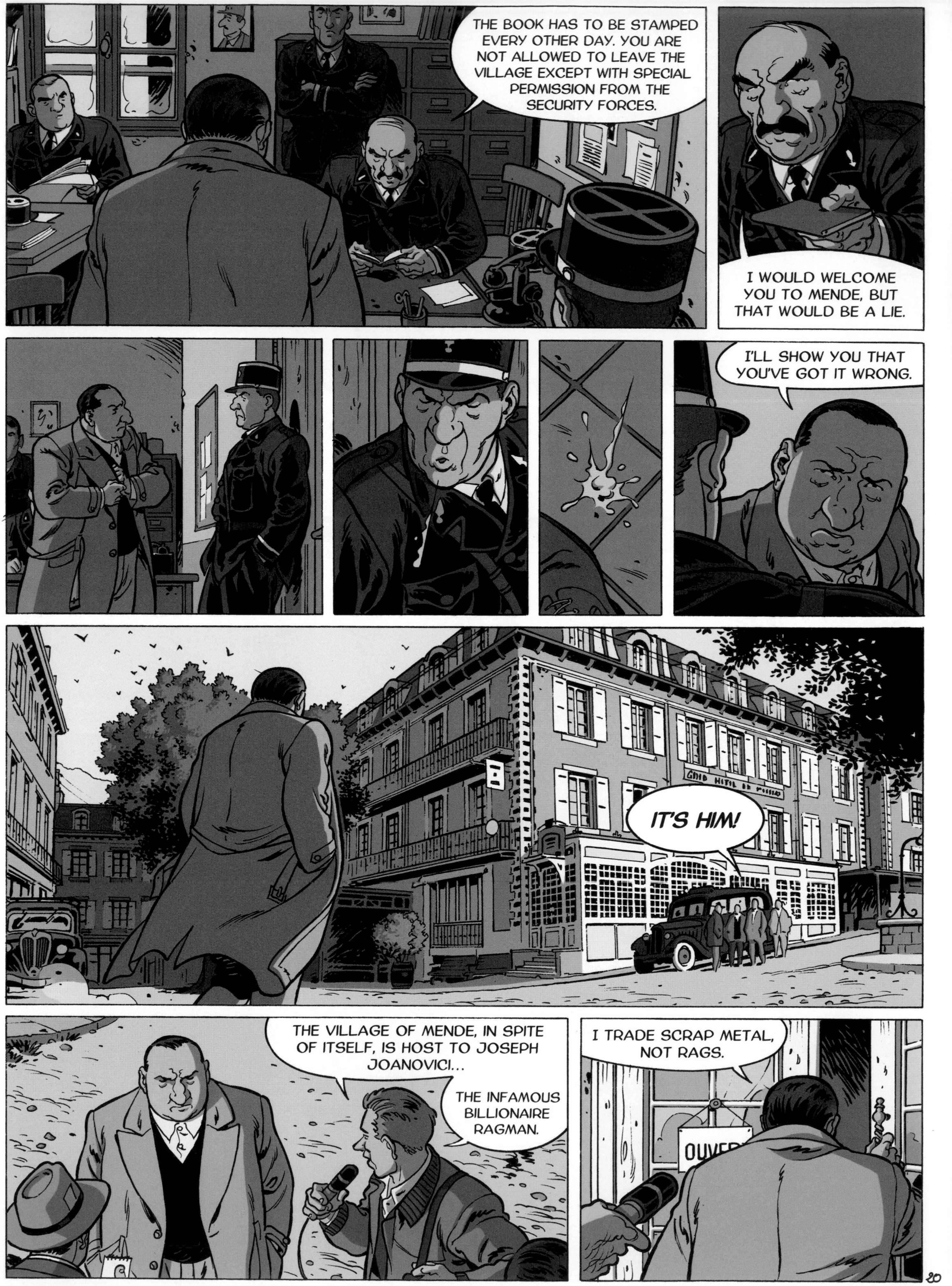
THE BOOK HAS TO BE STAMPED EVERY OTHER DAY. YOU ARE NOT ALLOWED TO LEAVE THE VILLAGE EXCEPT WITH SPECIAL PERMISSION FROM THE SECURITY FORCES.
I WOULD WELCOME YOU TO MENDE, BUT THAT WOULD BE A LIE.
I'LL SHOW YOU THAT YOU'VE GOT IT WRONG.
IT'S HIM!
THE VILLAGE OF MENDE, IN SPITE OF ITSELF, IS HOST TO JOSEPH JOANOVICI...
THE INFAMOUS BILLIONAIRE RAGMAN.
I TRADE SCRAP METAL, NOT RAGS.
20

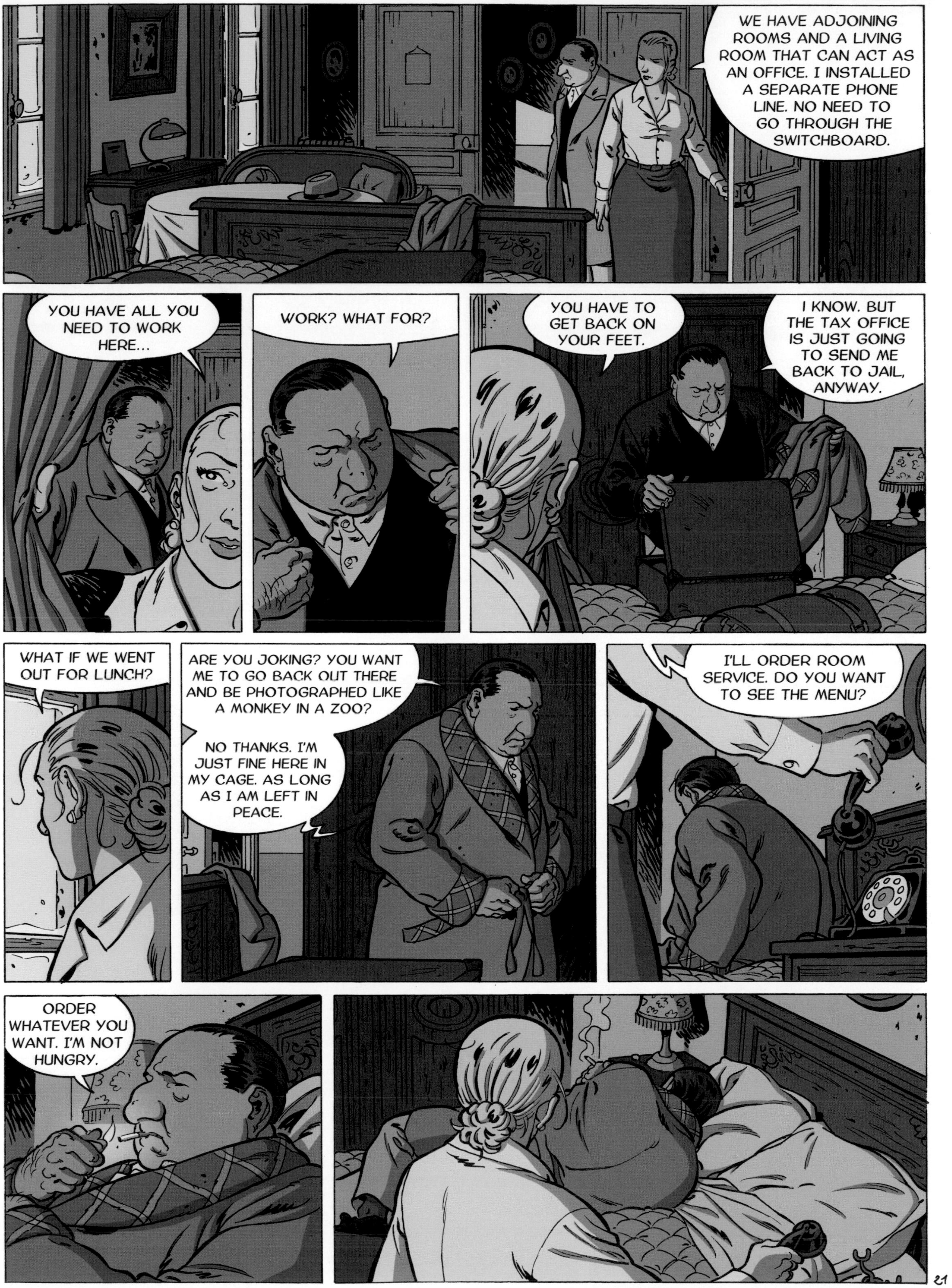
WE HAVE ADJOINING ROOMS AND A LIVING ROOM THAT CAN ACT AS AN OFFICE. I INSTALLED A SEPARATE PHONE LINE. NO NEED TO GO THROUGH THE SWITCHBOARD.
YOU HAVE ALL YOU NEED TO WORK HERE...
WORK? WHAT FOR?
YOU HAVE TO GET BACK ON YOUR FEET.
I KNOW. BUT THE TAX OFFICE IS JUST GOING TO SEND ME BACK TO JAIL, ANYWAY.
WHAT IF WE WENT OUT FOR LUNCH?
ARE YOU JOKING? YOU WANT ME TO GO BACK OUT THERE AND BE PHOTOGRAPHED LIKE A MONKEY IN A ZOO?
NO THANKS. I'M JUST FINE HERE IN MY CAGE. AS LONG AS I AM LEFT IN PEACE.
I'LL ORDER ROOM SERVICE. DO YOU WANT TO SEE THE MENU?
ORDER WHATEVER YOU WANT. I'M NOT HUNGRY.
21

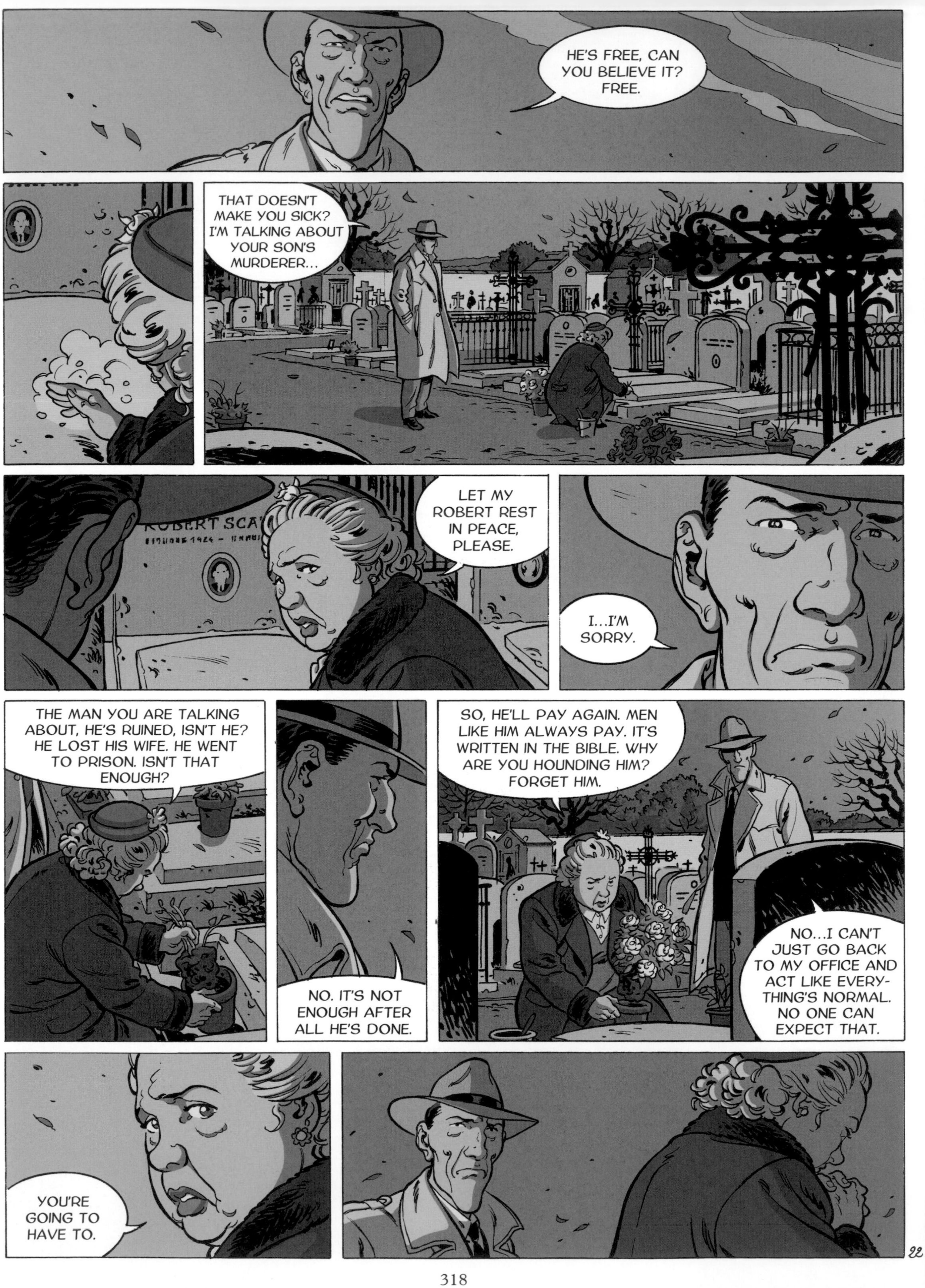
HE'S FREE, CAN YOU BELIEVE IT? FREE.
THAT DOESN'T MAKE YOU SICK? I'M TALKING ABOUT YOUR SON'S MURDERER...
LET MY ROBERT REST IN PEACE, PLEASE.
I...I'M SORRY.
THE MAN YOU ARE TALKING ABOUT, HE'S RUINED, ISN'T HE? HE LOST HIS WIFE. HE WENT TO PRISON. ISN'T THAT ENOUGH?
NO. IT'S NOT ENOUGH AFTER ALL HE'S DONE.
SO, HE'LL PAY AGAIN. MEN LIKE HIM ALWAYS PAY. IT'S WRITTEN IN THE BIBLE. WHY ARE YOU HOUNDING HIM? FORGET HIM.
NO...I CAN'T JUST GO BACK TO MY OFFICE AND ACT LIKE EVERY-THING'S NORMAL. NO ONE CAN EXPECT THAT.
YOU'RE GOING TO HAVE TO.
22

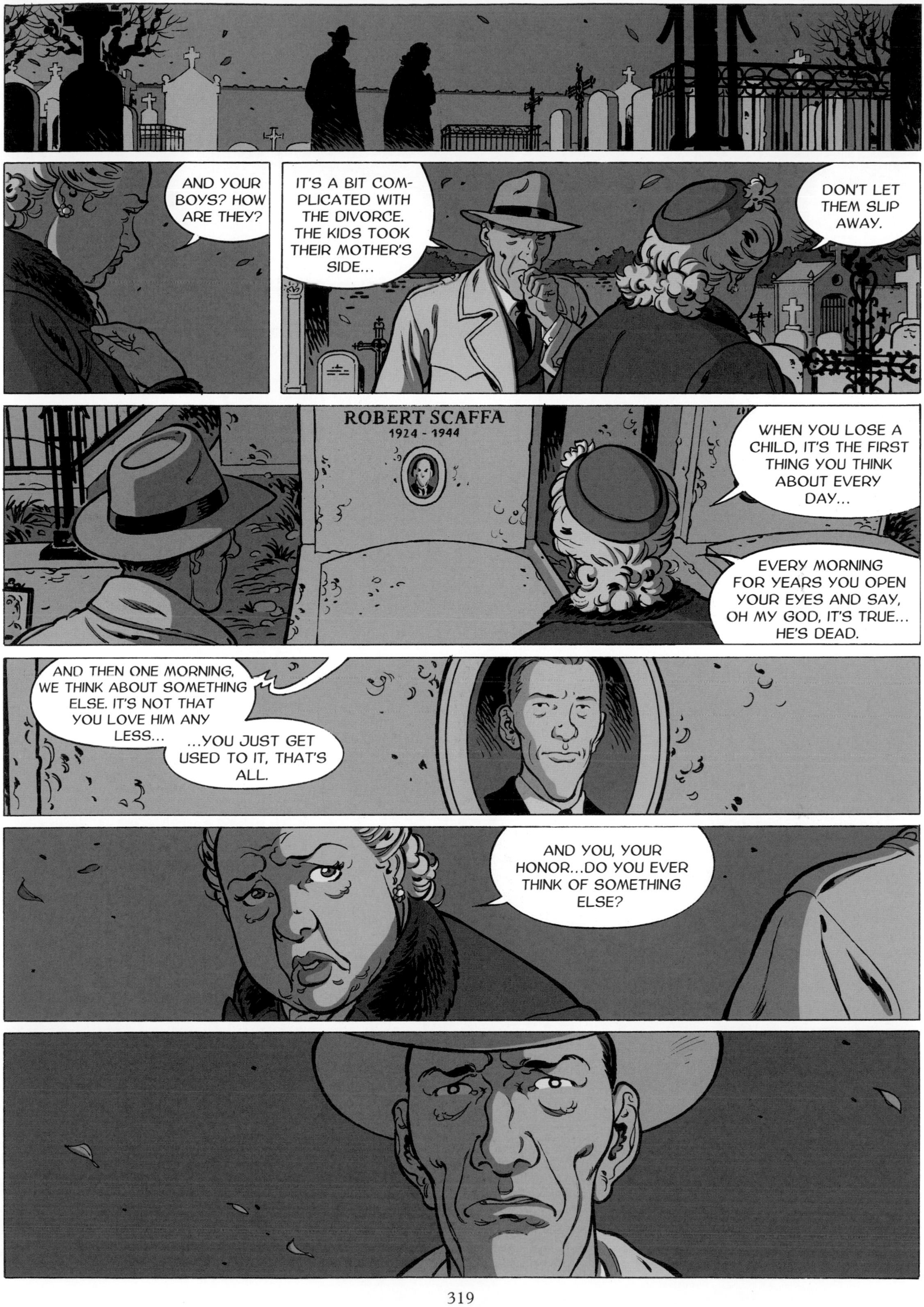
AND YOUR BOYS? HOW ARE THEY?
IT'S A BIT COMPLICATED WITH THE DIVORCE. THE KIDS TOOK THEIR MOTHER'S SIDE...
DON'T LET THEM SLIP AWAY.
ROBERT SCAFFA
1924 - 1944
WHEN YOU LOSE A CHILD, IT'S THE FIRST THING YOU THINK ABOUT EVERY DAY...
EVERY MORNING FOR YEARS YOU OPEN YOUR EYES AND SAY, OH MY GOD, IT'S TRUE... HE'S DEAD.
AND THEN ONE MORNING, WE THINK ABOUT SOMETHING ELSE. IT'S NOT THAT YOU LOVE HIM ANY LESS...
...YOU JUST GET USED TO IT, THAT'S ALL.
AND YOU, YOUR HONOR...DO YOU EVER THINK OF SOMETHING ELSE?

23

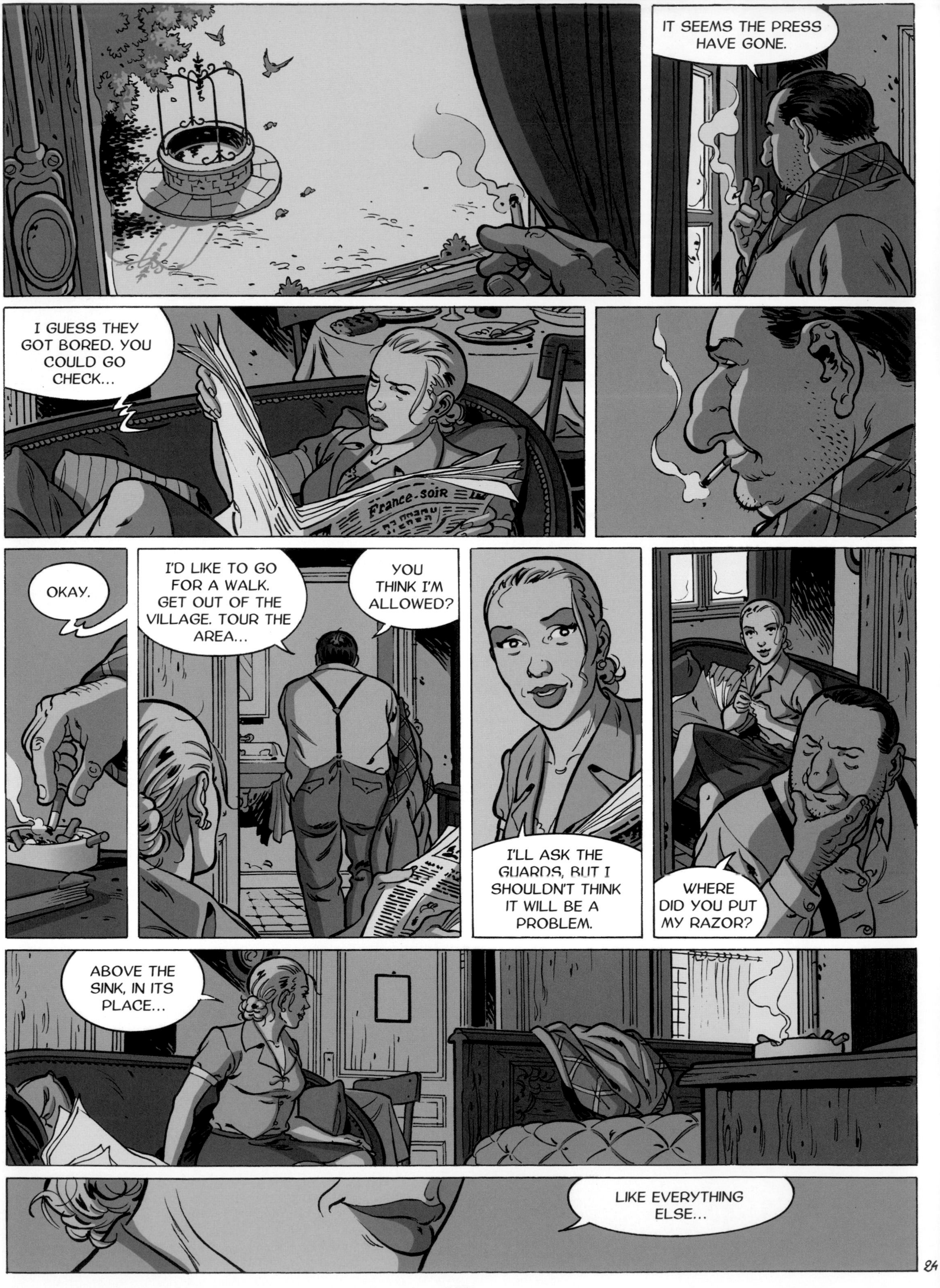
IT SEEMS THE PRESS HAVE GONE.
I GUESS THEY GOT BORED. YOU COULD GO CHECK...
France-soir
OKAY.
I'D LIKE TO GO FOR A WALK. GET OUT OF THE VILLAGE. TOUR THE AREA...
YOU THINK I'M ALLOWED?
I'LL ASK THE GUARDS, BUT I SHOULDN'T THINK IT WILL BE A PROBLEM.
WHERE DID YOU PUT MY RAZOR?
ABOVE THE SINK, IN ITS PLACE...
LIKE EVERYTHING ELSE...
24

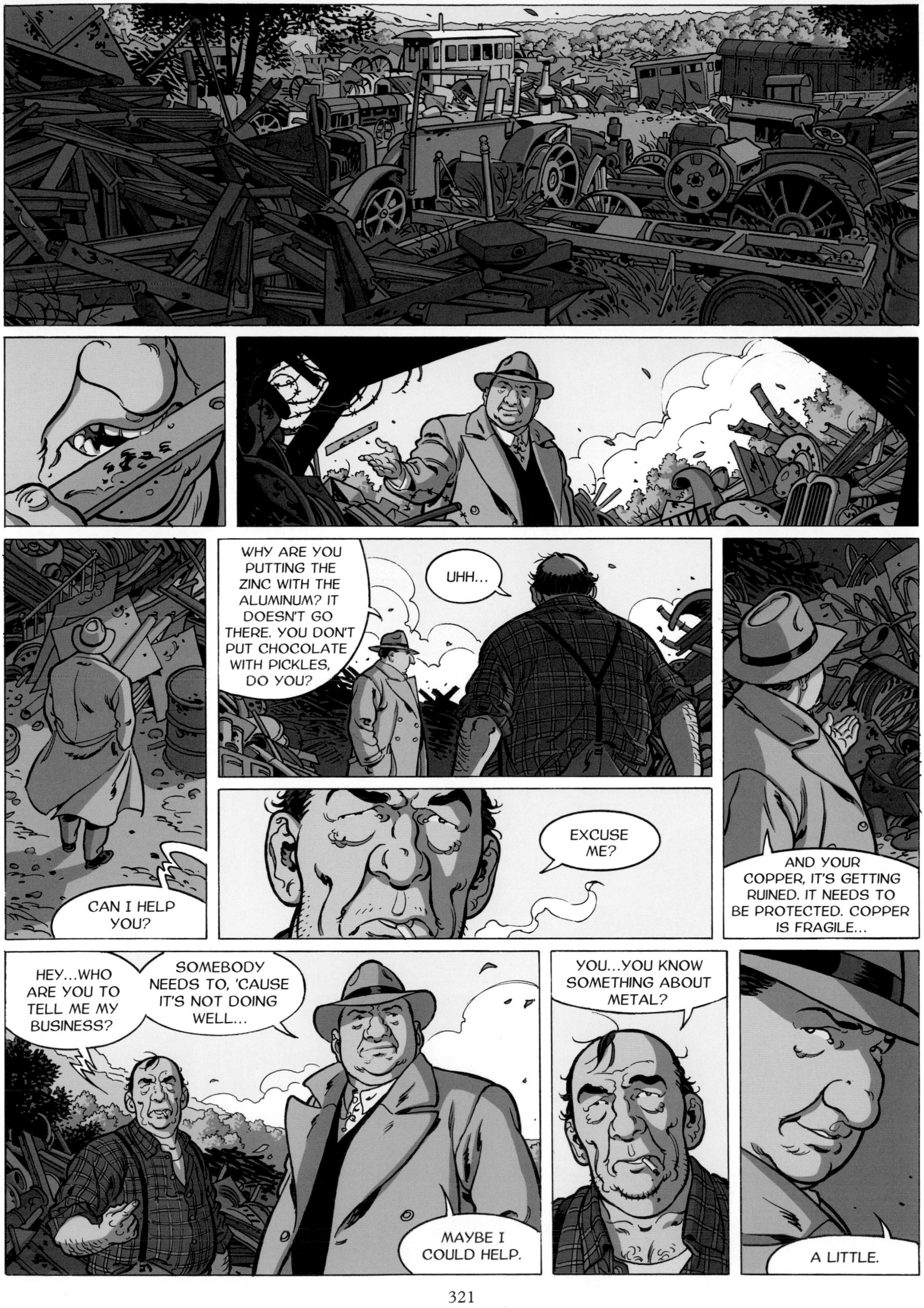
CAN I HELP YOU?
WHY ARE YOU PUTTING THE ZINC WITH THE ALUMINUM? IT DOESN'T GO THERE. YOU DON'T PUT CHOCOLATE WITH PICKLES, DO YOU?
UHH...
EXCUSE ME?
AND YOUR COPPER, IT'S GETTING RUINED. IT NEEDS TO BE PROTECTED. COPPER IS FRAGILE...
HEY...WHO ARE YOU TO TELL ME MY BUSINESS?
SOMEBODY NEEDS TO, 'CAUSE IT'S NOT DOING WELL...
MAYBE I COULD HELP.
YOU...YOU KNOW SOMETHING ABOUT METAL?
A LITTLE.
25

MARCUS AND LAZARD BANK, AT YOUR SERVICE.

MAY I PLEASE SPEAK TO ALBERT LAZARD? IT'S JOSEPH JOANOVICI.

JOSEPH? IT'S GOOD TO HEAR FROM YOU! YOU'RE BACK IN BUSINESS?

I'M HELPING A LOCAL GUY. HIS NAME IS MERCIER. I'M MAKING THE DEALS, HE'S DOING THE SIGNING...WOULD YOU BE WILLING TO FINANCE ONE OR TWO LARGE ACQUISITIONS?

IF YOU'RE BEHIND IT, I'LL FINANCE WHATEVER YOU WANT, JOSEPH. AS USUAL.

WE'RE GOOD?

WE HAVE THE FUNDS. NOW I JUST NEED TO SPREAD THE WORD...

HELLO, SIMON? HOW'S THE WEATHER IN SAINT-OUEN?

GREAT. GOOD. BEN, IF YOU SEE OUR FRIENDS FROM THE GOOD OLD DAYS, TELL THEM THAT JOSEPH IS BACK...I'M BUYING THE LOT. FERROUS AND NONFERROUS. YOU CAN REACH ME AT THE PARIS HOTEL IN MENDE, AT...

55-719.

55-719.

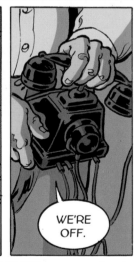

WE'RE OFF.

DIDN'T TAKE LONG...

HELLO?

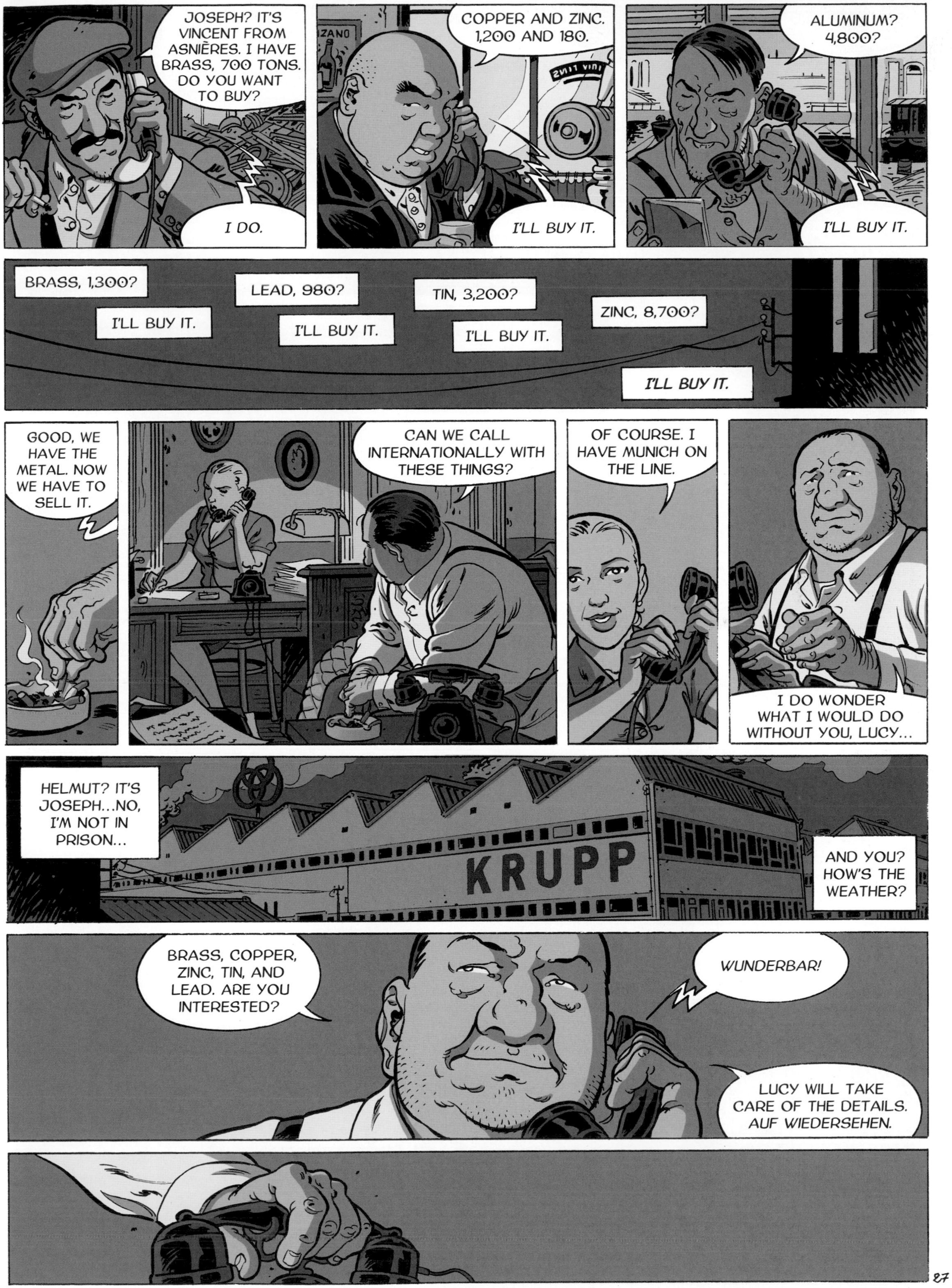
JOSEPH? IT'S VINCENT FROM ASNIÈRES. I HAVE BRASS, 700 TONS. DO YOU WANT TO BUY?
I DO.
COPPER AND ZINC. 1,200 AND 180.
I'LL BUY IT.
ALUMINUM? 4,800?
I'LL BUY IT.
BRASS, 1,300?
I'LL BUY IT.
LEAD, 980?
I'LL BUY IT.
TIN, 3,200?
I'LL BUY IT.
ZINC, 8,700?
I'LL BUY IT.
GOOD, WE HAVE THE METAL. NOW WE HAVE TO SELL IT.
CAN WE CALL INTERNATIONALLY WITH THESE THINGS?
OF COURSE. I HAVE MUNICH ON THE LINE.
I DO WONDER WHAT I WOULD DO WITHOUT YOU, LUCY...
HELMUT? IT'S JOSEPH...NO, I'M NOT IN PRISON...
KRUPP
AND YOU? HOW'S THE WEATHER?
BRASS, COPPER, ZINC, TIN, AND LEAD. ARE YOU INTERESTED?
WUNDERBAR!
LUCY WILL TAKE CARE OF THE DETAILS. AUF WIEDERSEHEN.
27

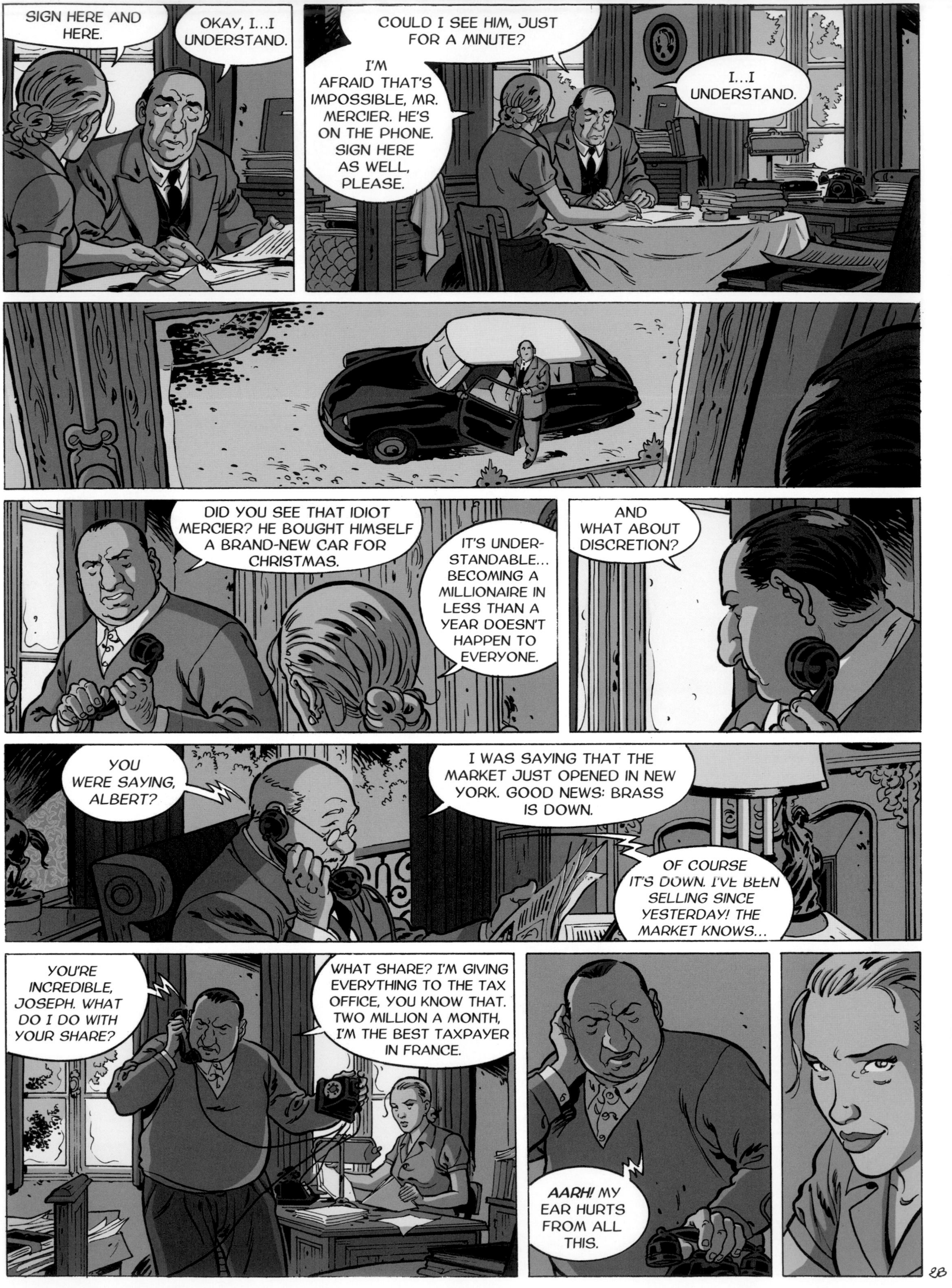
SIGN HERE AND HERE.
OKAY, I...I UNDERSTAND.
COULD I SEE HIM, JUST FOR A MINUTE?
I'M AFRAID THAT'S IMPOSSIBLE, MR. MERCIER. HE'S ON THE PHONE. SIGN HERE AS WELL, PLEASE.
I...I UNDERSTAND.
DID YOU SEE THAT IDIOT MERCIER? HE BOUGHT HIMSELF A BRAND-NEW CAR FOR CHRISTMAS.
IT'S UNDERSTANDABLE... BECOMING A MILLIONAIRE IN LESS THAN A YEAR DOESN'T HAPPEN TO EVERYONE.
AND WHAT ABOUT DISCRETION?
YOU WERE SAYING, ALBERT?
I WAS SAYING THAT THE MARKET JUST OPENED IN NEW YORK. GOOD NEWS: BRASS IS DOWN.
OF COURSE IT'S DOWN. I'VE BEEN SELLING SINCE YESTERDAY! THE MARKET KNOWS...
YOU'RE INCREDIBLE, JOSEPH. WHAT DO I DO WITH YOUR SHARE?
WHAT SHARE? I'M GIVING EVERYTHING TO THE TAX OFFICE, YOU KNOW THAT. TWO MILLION A MONTH, I'M THE BEST TAXPAYER IN FRANCE.
AARH! MY EAR HURTS FROM ALL THIS.
28

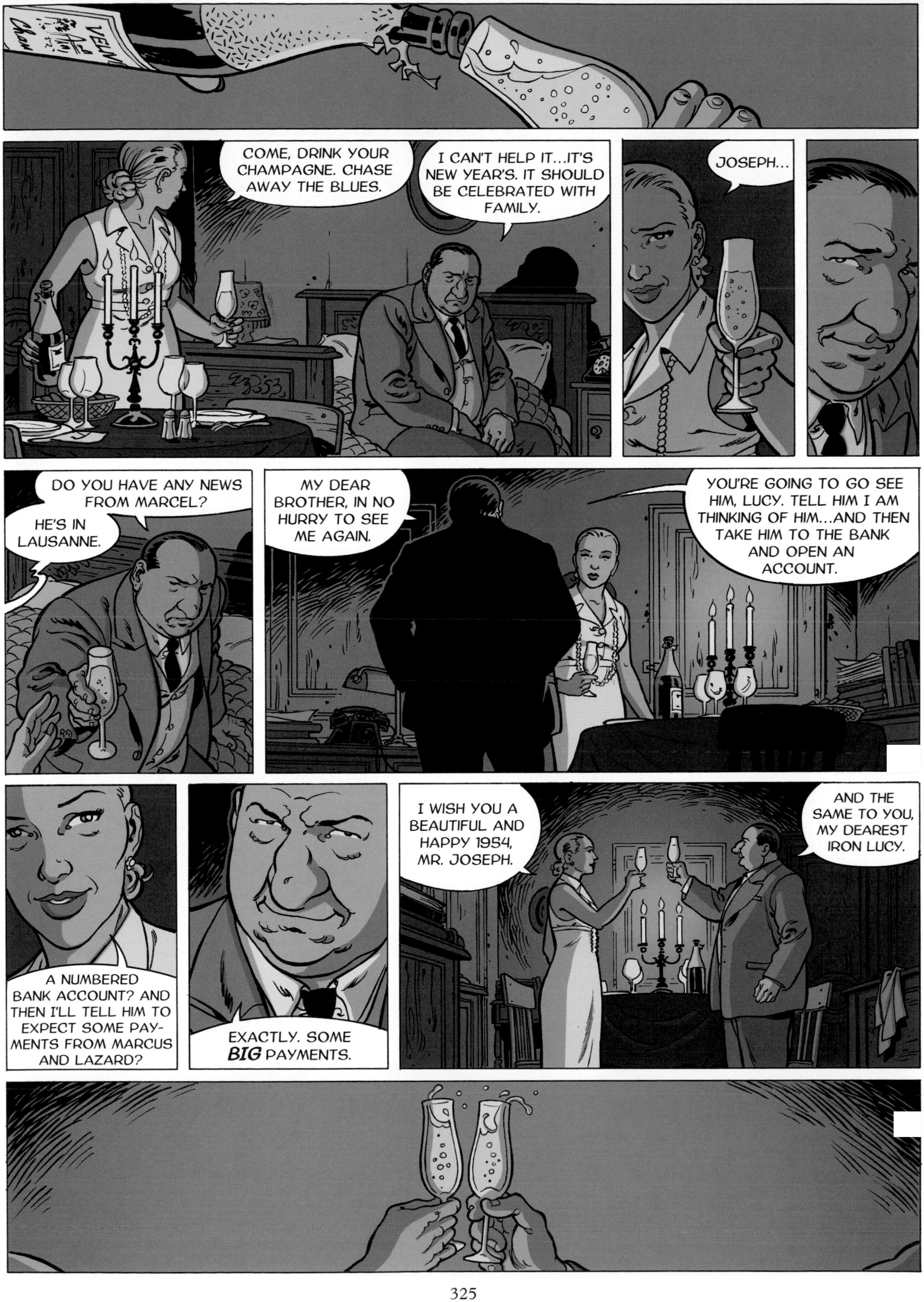
COME, DRINK YOUR CHAMPAGNE. CHASE AWAY THE BLUES.
I CAN'T HELP IT...IT'S NEW YEAR'S. IT SHOULD BE CELEBRATED WITH FAMILY.
JOSEPH...
DO YOU HAVE ANY NEWS FROM MARCEL?
HE'S IN LAUSANNE.
MY DEAR BROTHER, IN NO HURRY TO SEE ME AGAIN.
YOU'RE GOING TO GO SEE HIM, LUCY. TELL HIM I AM THINKING OF HIM...AND THEN TAKE HIM TO THE BANK AND OPEN AN ACCOUNT.
A NUMBERED BANK ACCOUNT? AND THEN I'LL TELL HIM TO EXPECT SOME PAYMENTS FROM MARCUS AND LAZARD?
EXACTLY. SOME BIG PAYMENTS.
I WISH YOU A BEAUTIFUL AND HAPPY 1954, MR. JOSEPH.
AND THE SAME TO YOU, MY DEAREST IRON LUCY.
29

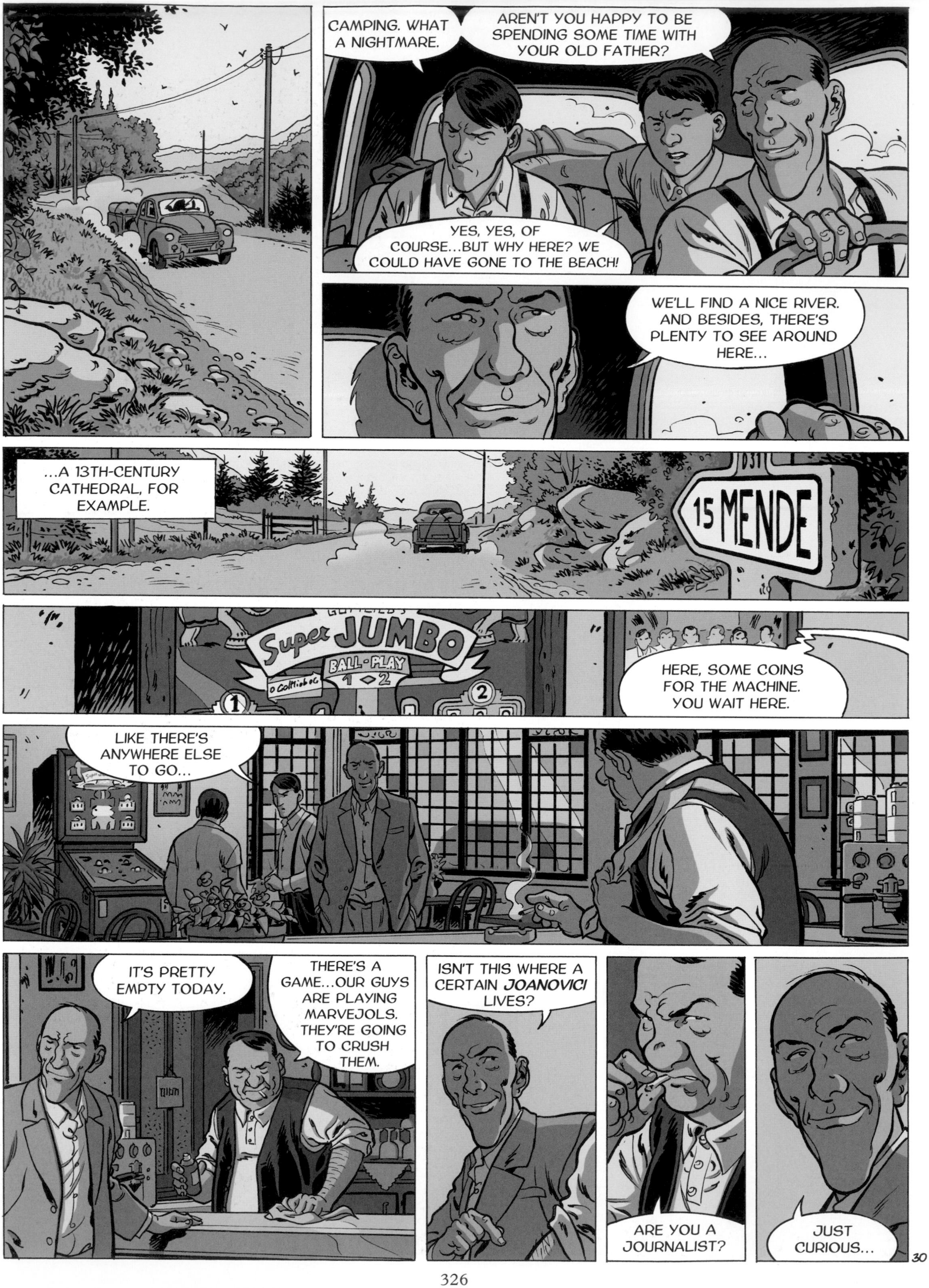
CAMPING. WHAT A NIGHTMARE.
AREN'T YOU HAPPY TO BE SPENDING SOME TIME WITH YOUR OLD FATHER?
YES, YES, OF COURSE...BUT WHY HERE? WE COULD HAVE GONE TO THE BEACH!
WE'LL FIND A NICE RIVER. AND BESIDES, THERE'S PLENTY TO SEE AROUND HERE...
...A 13TH-CENTURY CATHEDRAL, FOR EXAMPLE.
D31
15 MENDE
Super JUMBO
BALL-PLAY
1 2
HERE, SOME COINS FOR THE MACHINE. YOU WAIT HERE.
LIKE THERE'S ANYWHERE ELSE TO GO...
IT'S PRETTY EMPTY TODAY.
THERE'S A GAME...OUR GUYS ARE PLAYING MARVEJOLS. THEY'RE GOING TO CRUSH THEM.
ISN'T THIS WHERE A CERTAIN ***JOANOVICI*** LIVES?
ARE YOU A JOURNALIST?
JUST CURIOUS...
30

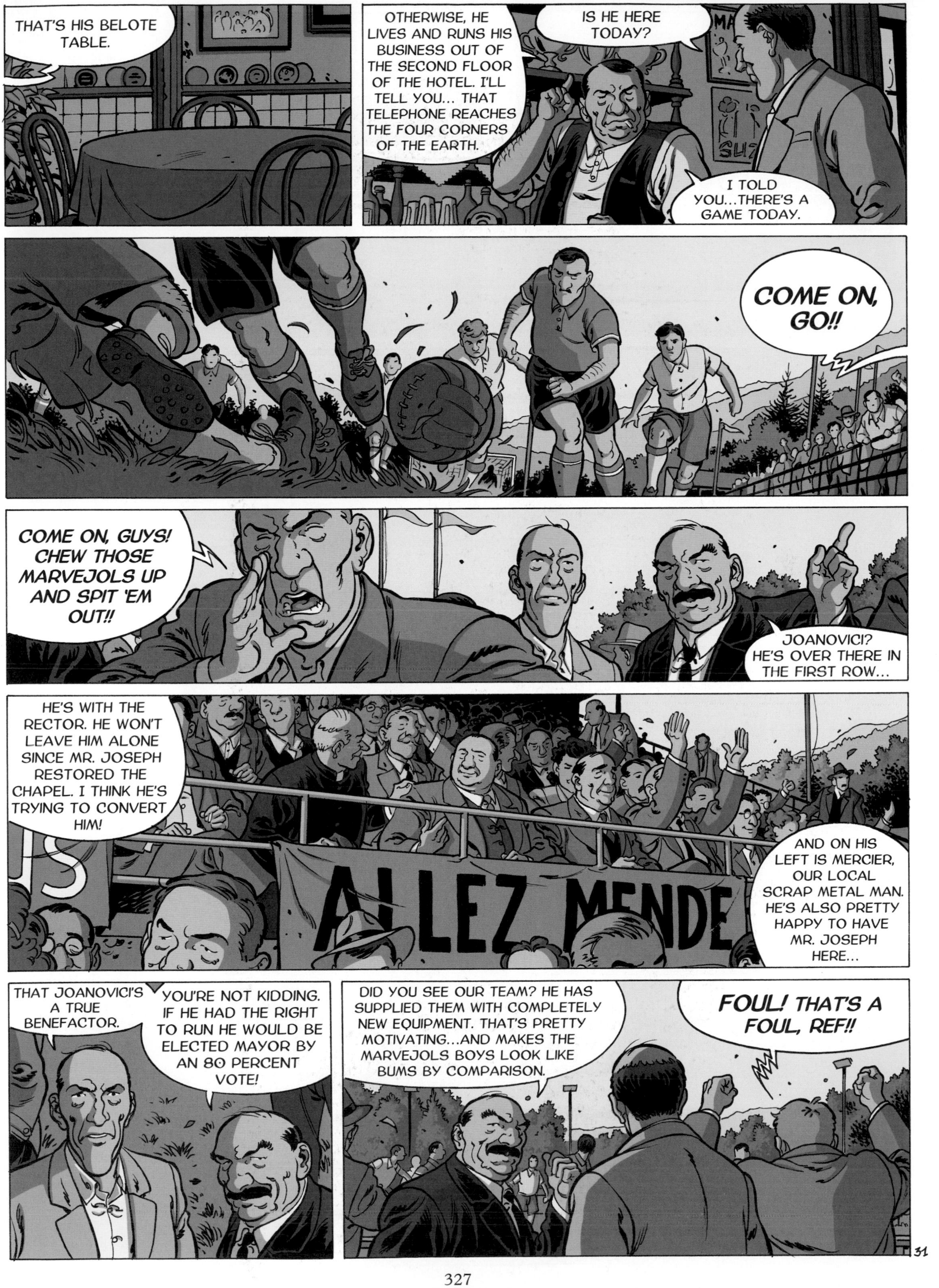

THAT'S HIS BELOTE TABLE.
OTHERWISE, HE LIVES AND RUNS HIS BUSINESS OUT OF THE SECOND FLOOR OF THE HOTEL. I'LL TELL YOU... THAT TELEPHONE REACHES THE FOUR CORNERS OF THE EARTH.
IS HE HERE TODAY?
I TOLD YOU...THERE'S A GAME TODAY.
COME ON, GO!!
COME ON, GUYS! CHEW THOSE MARVEJOLS UP AND SPIT 'EM OUT!!
JOANOVICI? HE'S OVER THERE IN THE FIRST ROW...
HE'S WITH THE RECTOR. HE WON'T LEAVE HIM ALONE SINCE MR. JOSEPH RESTORED THE CHAPEL. I THINK HE'S TRYING TO CONVERT HIM!
ALLEZ MENDE
AND ON HIS LEFT IS MERCIER, OUR LOCAL SCRAP METAL MAN. HE'S ALSO PRETTY HAPPY TO HAVE MR. JOSEPH HERE...
THAT JOANOVICI'S A TRUE BENEFACTOR.
YOU'RE NOT KIDDING. IF HE HAD THE RIGHT TO RUN HE WOULD BE ELECTED MAYOR BY AN 80 PERCENT VOTE!
DID YOU SEE OUR TEAM? HE HAS SUPPLIED THEM WITH COMPLETELY NEW EQUIPMENT. THAT'S PRETTY MOTIVATING...AND MAKES THE MARVEJOLS BOYS LOOK LIKE BUMS BY COMPARISON.
FOUL! THAT'S A FOUL, REF!!
31

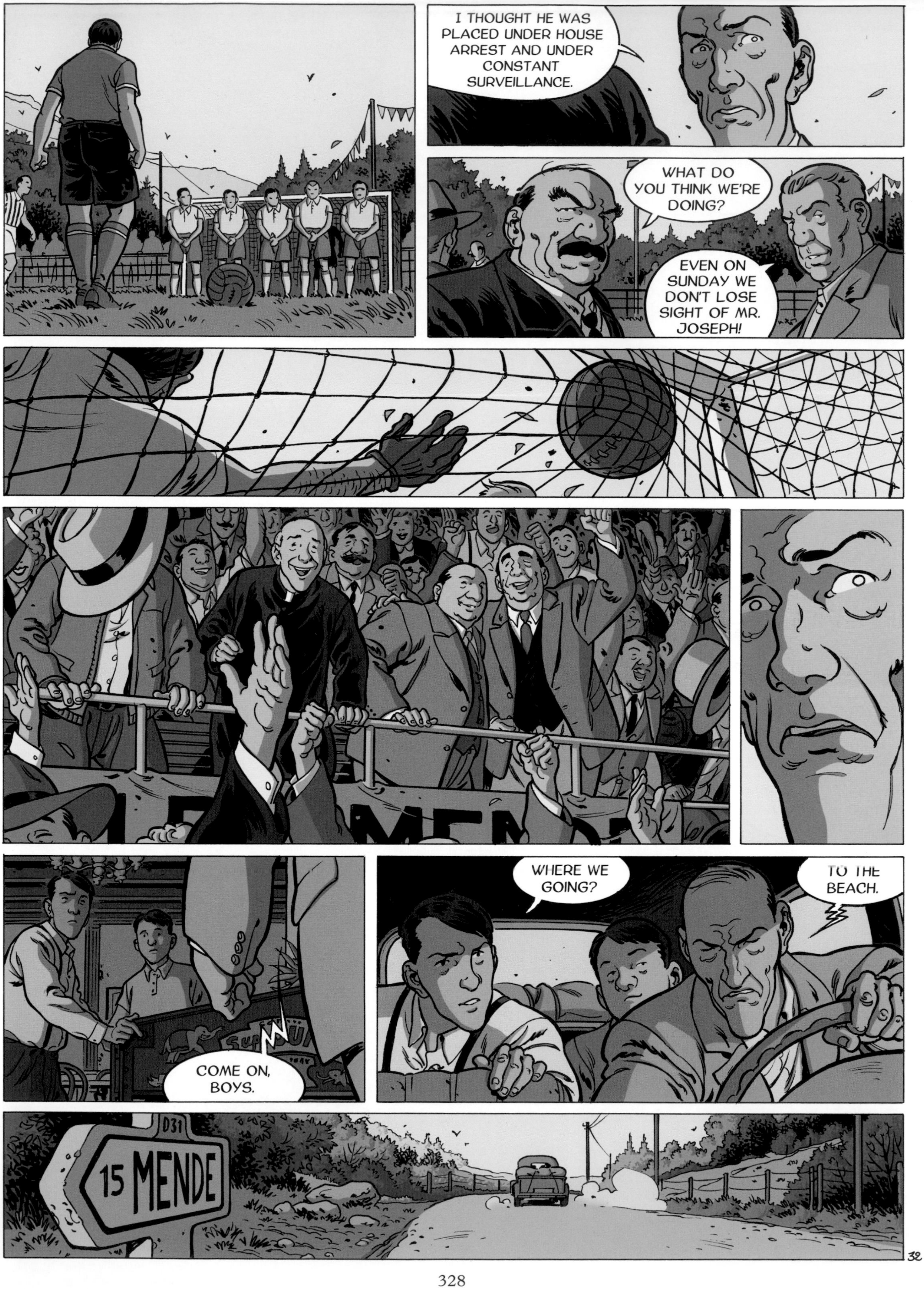
I THOUGHT HE WAS PLACED UNDER HOUSE ARREST AND UNDER CONSTANT SURVEILLANCE.
WHAT DO YOU THINK WE'RE DOING?
EVEN ON SUNDAY WE DON'T LOSE SIGHT OF MR. JOSEPH!
COME ON, BOYS.
WHERE WE GOING?
TO THE BEACH.
D31
15 MENDE
32

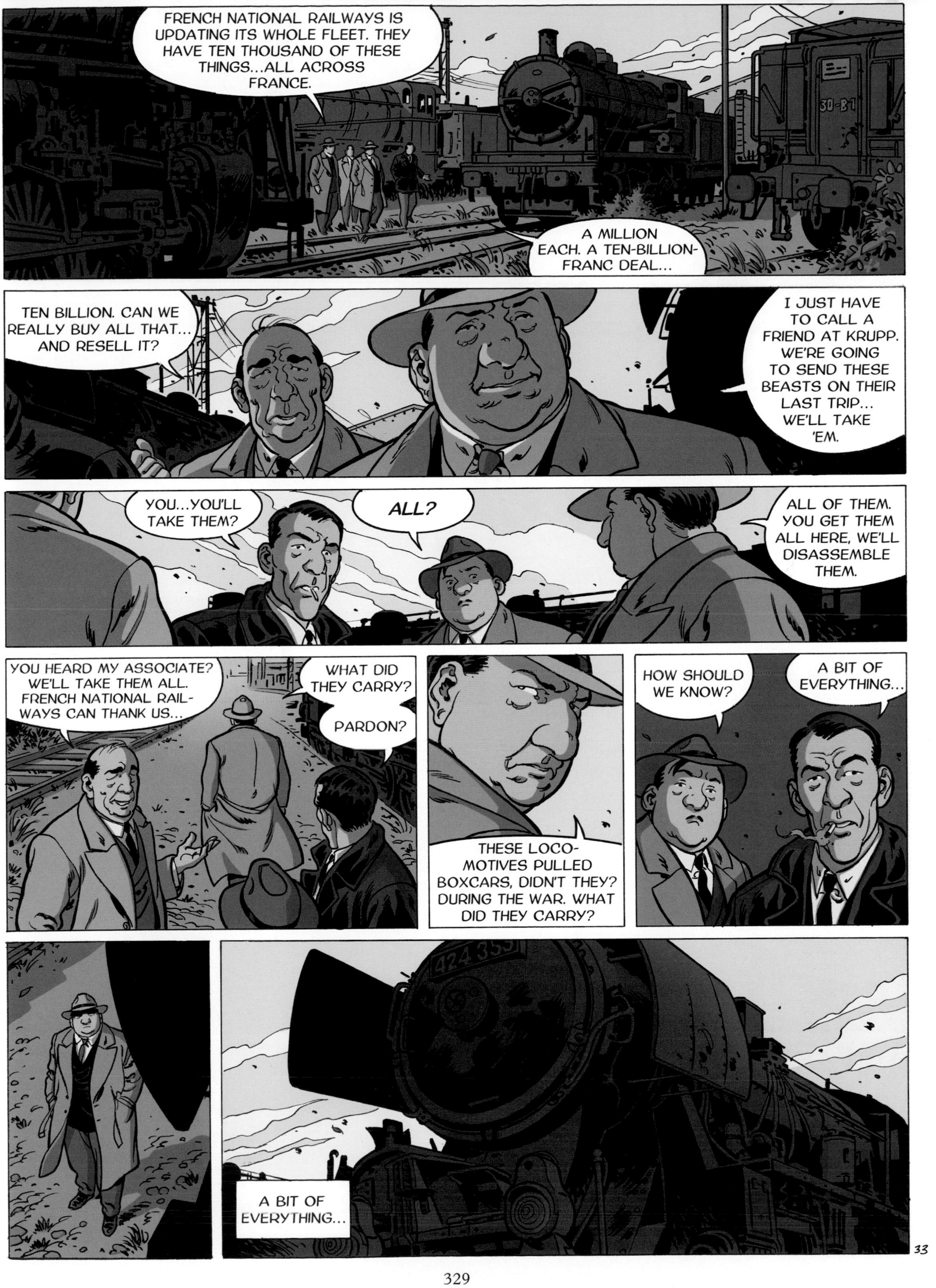
FRENCH NATIONAL RAILWAYS IS UPDATING ITS WHOLE FLEET. THEY HAVE TEN THOUSAND OF THESE THINGS...ALL ACROSS FRANCE.
A MILLION EACH. A TEN-BILLION-FRANC DEAL...
30-B1
TEN BILLION. CAN WE REALLY BUY ALL THAT... AND RESELL IT?
I JUST HAVE TO CALL A FRIEND AT KRUPP. WE'RE GOING TO SEND THESE BEASTS ON THEIR LAST TRIP... WE'LL TAKE 'EM.
YOU...YOU'LL TAKE THEM?
ALL?
ALL OF THEM. YOU GET THEM ALL HERE, WE'LL DISASSEMBLE THEM.
YOU HEARD MY ASSOCIATE? WE'LL TAKE THEM ALL. FRENCH NATIONAL RAIL-WAYS CAN THANK US...
WHAT DID THEY CARRY?
PARDON?
THESE LOCO-MOTIVES PULLED BOXCARS, DIDN'T THEY? DURING THE WAR. WHAT DID THEY CARRY?
HOW SHOULD WE KNOW?
A BIT OF EVERYTHING...
A BIT OF EVERYTHING...
33

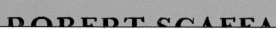

HÉLÈNE SCAFFA
1894 -1956

ROBERT SCAFFA

HAVE PITY, MR. JO...

...DON'T YOU HAVE THE THIRD ACE?

SOMETIMES THE ROAD IS LONG.

JOSEPH...

I'M FINISHING THIS HAND, LUCY...

OF COURSE HE HAS THE THIRD ACE! YOU'RE GOING DOWN!

JOSEPH!

FOUR TIMES IN A ROW IT'S RUNG AND THERE IS NOTHING BUT BREATHING AT THE OTHER END.

DKRIIIIN

DRR!

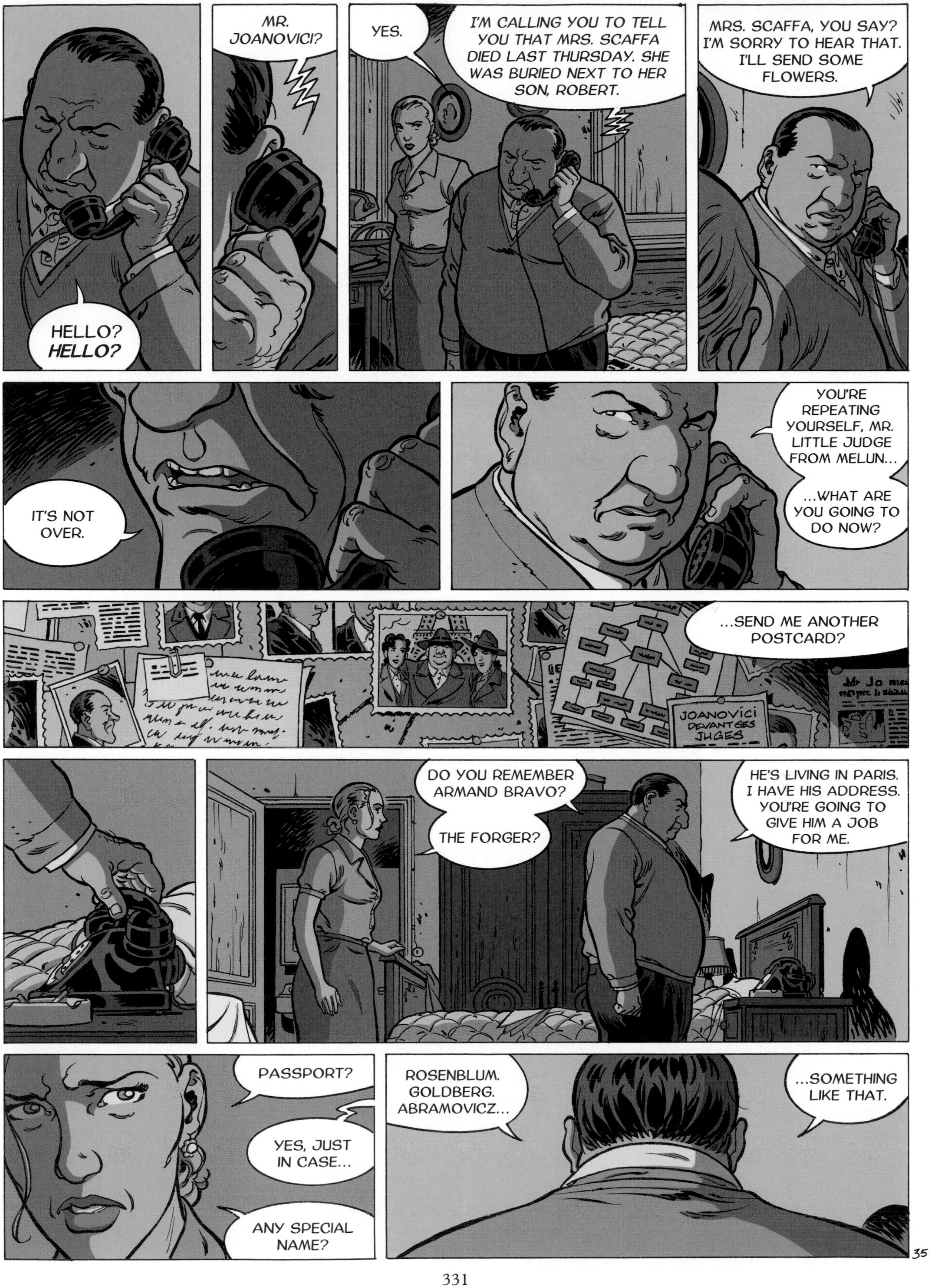
HELLO? *HELLO?*
MR. JOANOVICI?
YES.
I'M CALLING YOU TO TELL YOU THAT MRS. SCAFFA DIED LAST THURSDAY. SHE WAS BURIED NEXT TO HER SON, ROBERT.
MRS. SCAFFA, YOU SAY? I'M SORRY TO HEAR THAT. I'LL SEND SOME FLOWERS.
IT'S NOT OVER.
YOU'RE REPEATING YOURSELF, MR. LITTLE JUDGE FROM MELUN...
...WHAT ARE YOU GOING TO DO NOW?
...SEND ME ANOTHER POSTCARD?
Mr Jo
JOANOVICI DEVANT SES JUGES
DO YOU REMEMBER ARMAND BRAVO?
THE FORGER?
HE'S LIVING IN PARIS. I HAVE HIS ADDRESS. YOU'RE GOING TO GIVE HIM A JOB FOR ME.
PASSPORT?
YES, JUST IN CASE...
ANY SPECIAL NAME?
ROSENBLUM. GOLDBERG. ABRAMOVICZ...
...SOMETHING LIKE THAT.
35

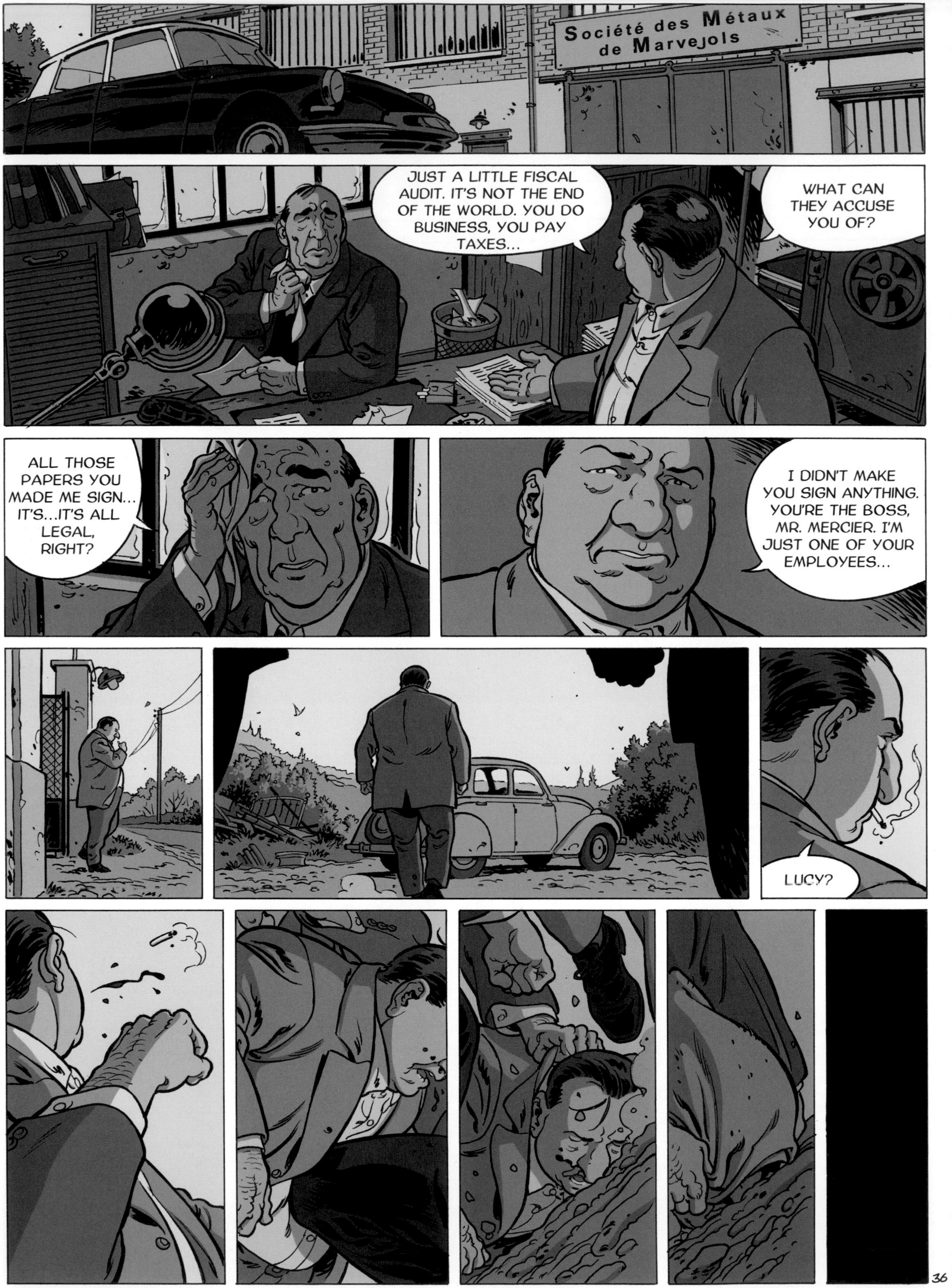
Société des Métaux de Marvejols
JUST A LITTLE FISCAL AUDIT. IT'S NOT THE END OF THE WORLD. YOU DO BUSINESS, YOU PAY TAXES...
WHAT CAN THEY ACCUSE YOU OF?
ALL THOSE PAPERS YOU MADE ME SIGN... IT'S...IT'S ALL LEGAL, RIGHT?
I DIDN'T MAKE YOU SIGN ANYTHING. YOU'RE THE BOSS, MR. MERCIER. I'M JUST ONE OF YOUR EMPLOYEES...
LUCY?
36

HELLO, JOSEPH.
JO? BOUCHESEICHE? WHAT ARE YOU DOING?
WE WERE HEADED TO MARSEILLE AND WE THOUGHT WE'D PAY YOU A VISIT...
IT SEEMS LIKE YOU'RE LIVING THE LIFE OF RILEY HERE. IT LOOKS LIKE YOU'VE MADE ANOTHER FORTUNE.
...AND YOU'VE COME TO TAKE YOUR PART? IS THAT RIGHT? YOU'VE WASTED YOUR TIME, GENTS. I HAVEN'T GOT ANY MONEY! THE TAX OFFICE TAKES EVERYTHING I EARN!
CLIC
WHO DO YOU TAKE US FOR, CIVIL SERVANTS? WE KNOW YOU, JOSEPH. WE KNOW YOUR TRICKS.
WE KNOW ABOUT MARCUS AND LAZARD. ABOUT LUCY'S LITTLE TRIPS TO SWITZERLAND. YOU UNDERSTAND? WE KNOW EVERYTHING. YOU'RE PAYING TWO MILLION A MONTH IN TAXES? WE WANT THE SAME.
I OWE YOU NOTHING...
...I'LL PAY YOU NOTHING.
YOU KNOW, JOSEPH. DEEP DOWN, I'M GLAD YOU'RE TAKING IT THAT WAY. IT'S GREAT. WE'RE GOING TO WALTZ DOWN MEMORY LANE, THE TWO OF US.
37

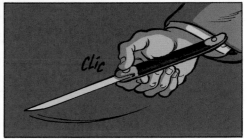

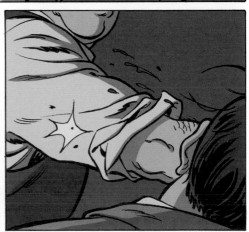

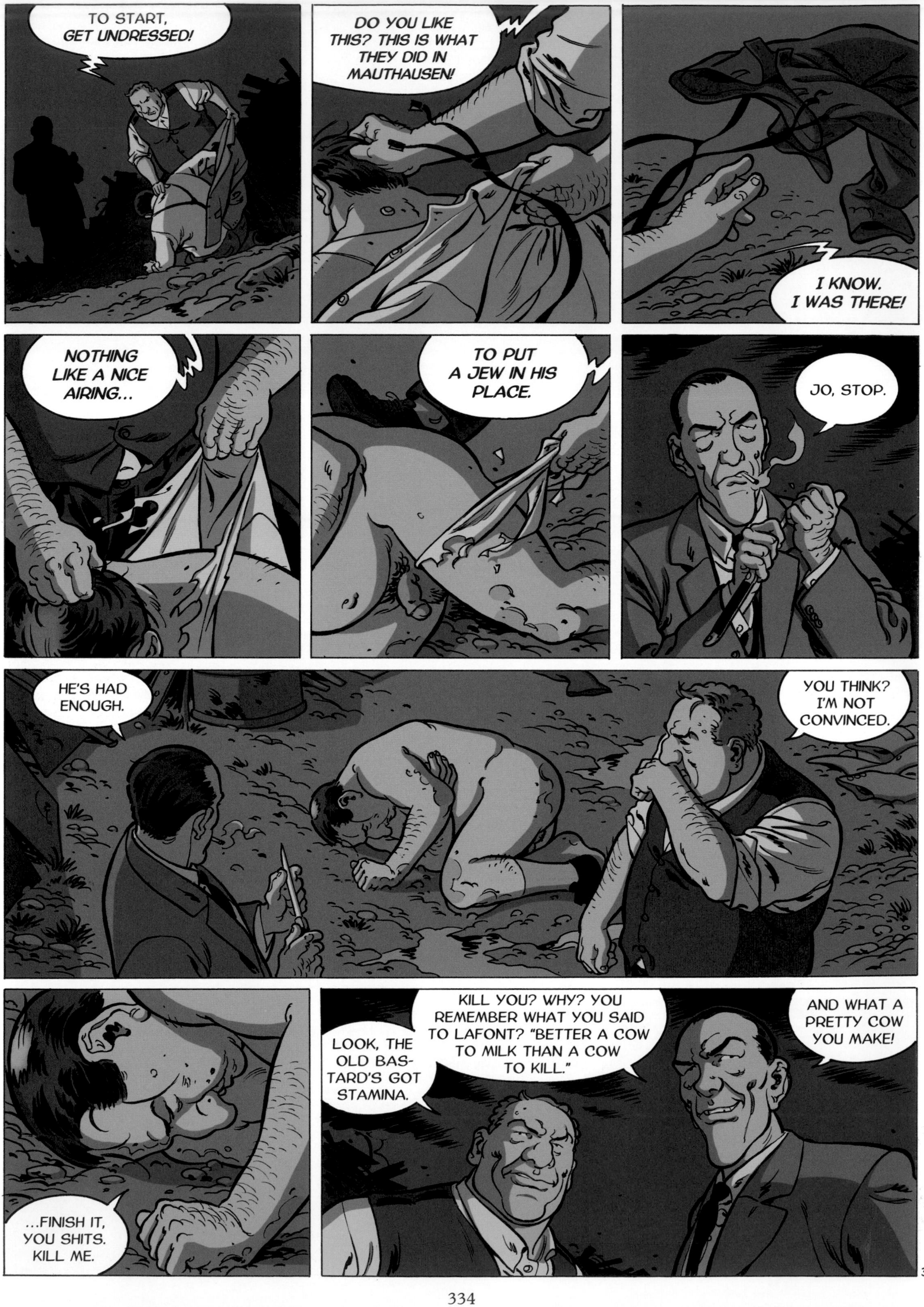
TO START, GET UNDRESSED!
DO YOU LIKE THIS? THIS IS WHAT THEY DID IN MAUTHAUSEN!
I KNOW. I WAS THERE!
NOTHING LIKE A NICE AIRING...
TO PUT A JEW IN HIS PLACE.
JO, STOP.
HE'S HAD ENOUGH.
YOU THINK? I'M NOT CONVINCED.
...FINISH IT, YOU SHITS. KILL ME.
LOOK, THE OLD BASTARD'S GOT STAMINA.
KILL YOU? WHY? YOU REMEMBER WHAT YOU SAID TO LAFONT? "BETTER A COW TO MILK THAN A COW TO KILL."
AND WHAT A PRETTY COW YOU MAKE!
38

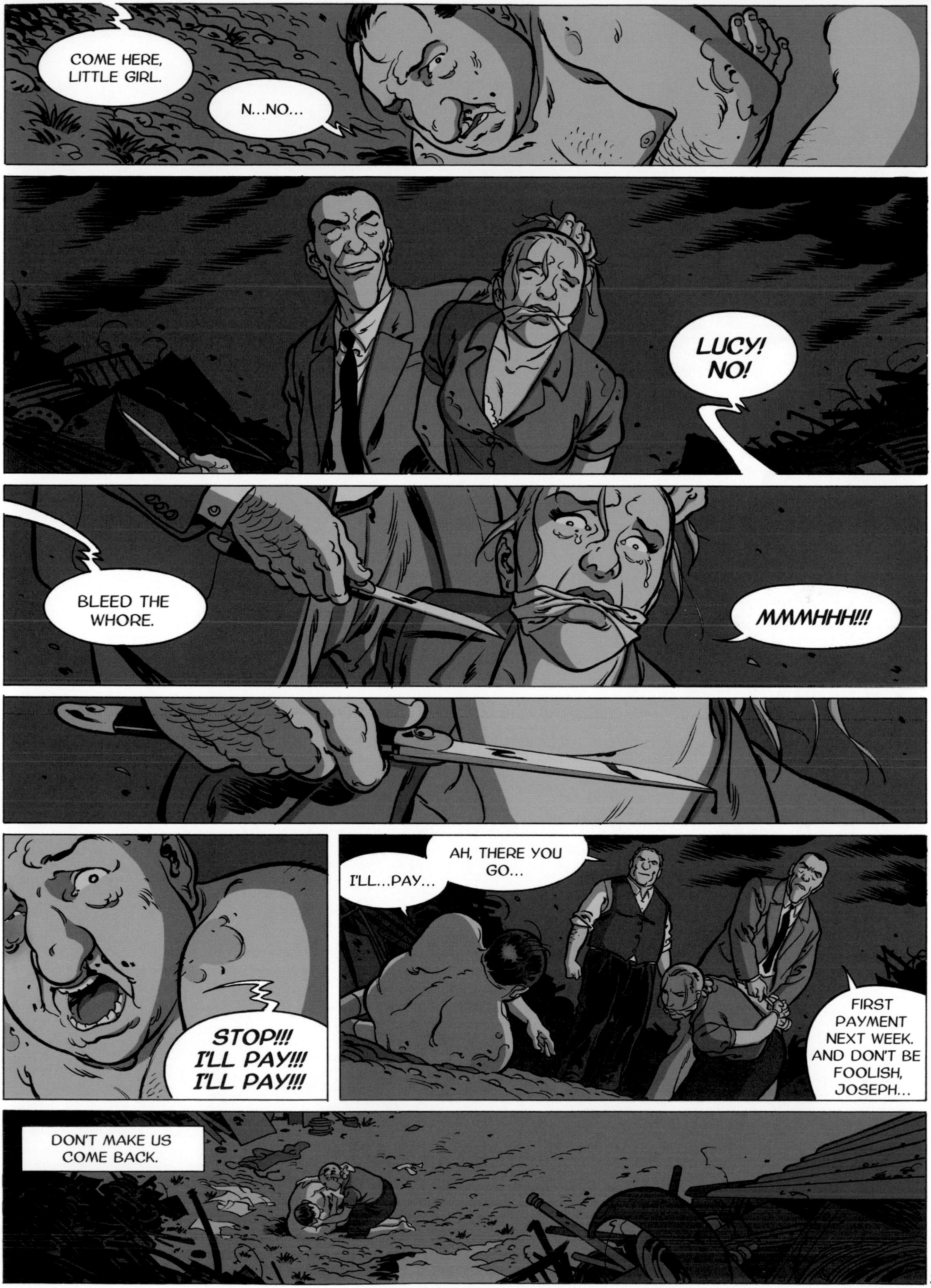
COME HERE, LITTLE GIRL.
N...NO...
LUCY! NO!
BLEED THE WHORE.
MMMHHH!!!
STOP!!! I'LL PAY!!! I'LL PAY!!!
I'LL...PAY...
AH, THERE YOU GO...
FIRST PAYMENT NEXT WEEK. AND DON'T BE FOOLISH, JOSEPH...
DON'T MAKE US COME BACK.

39

EVERYTHING'S FINE. HE...HE TRIPPED OVER SOME METAL. NOTHING SERIOUS.

M...MR. JOSEPH? YOU OKAY?

DO YOU WANT ME TO CALL A DOCTOR?

NO, THANK YOU.

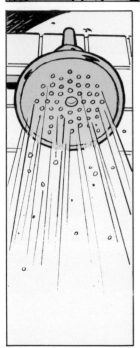

NEVER SAFE...

EV...EVA... SHE SAID...

I'LL NEVER BE SAFE.

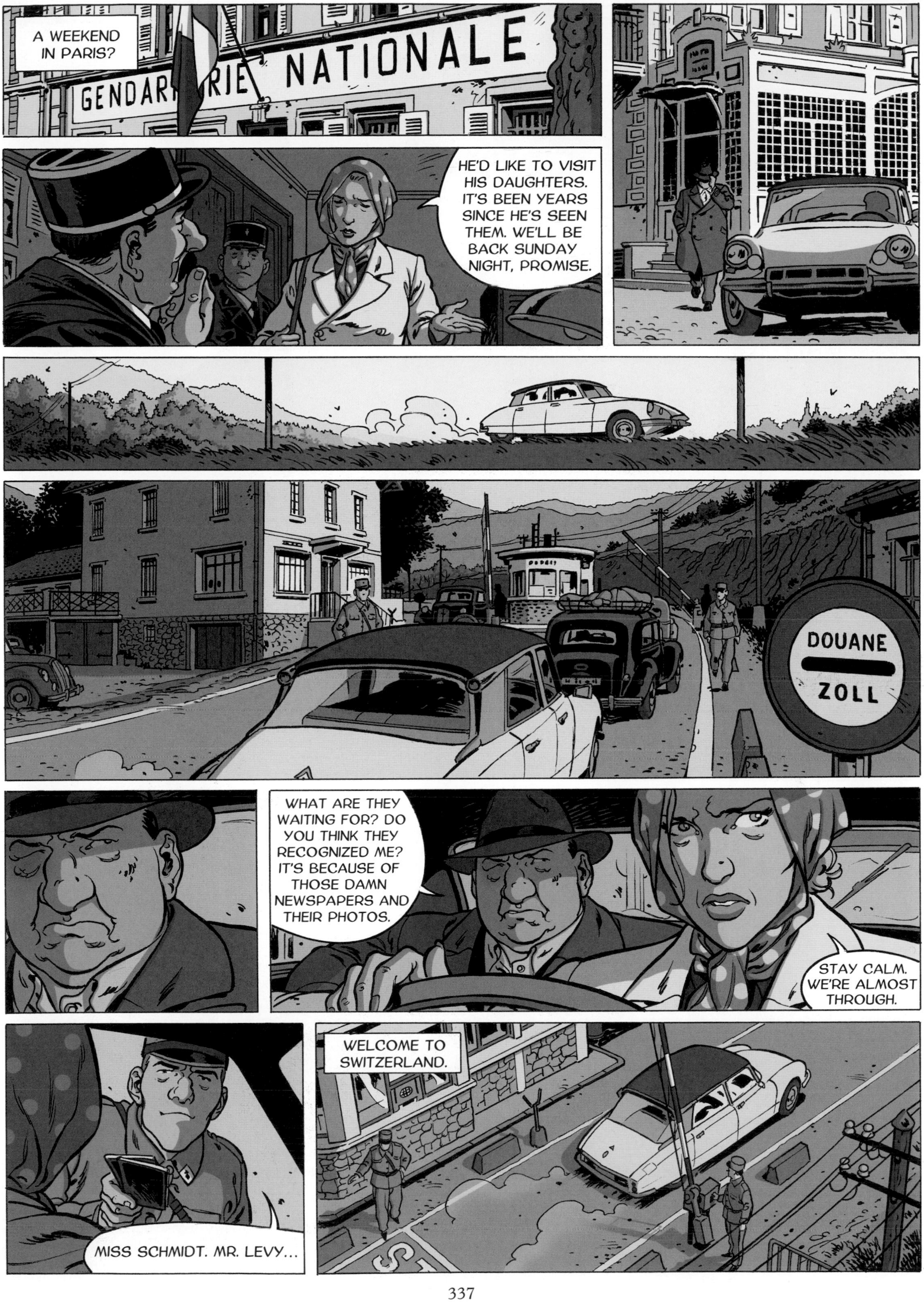
A WEEKEND IN PARIS?
GENDARMERIE NATIONALE
HE'D LIKE TO VISIT HIS DAUGHTERS. IT'S BEEN YEARS SINCE HE'S SEEN THEM. WE'LL BE BACK SUNDAY NIGHT, PROMISE.
DOUANE
ZOLL
WHAT ARE THEY WAITING FOR? DO YOU THINK THEY RECOGNIZED ME? IT'S BECAUSE OF THOSE DAMN NEWSPAPERS AND THEIR PHOTOS.
STAY CALM. WE'RE ALMOST THROUGH.
MISS SCHMIDT. MR. LEVY...
WELCOME TO SWITZERLAND.

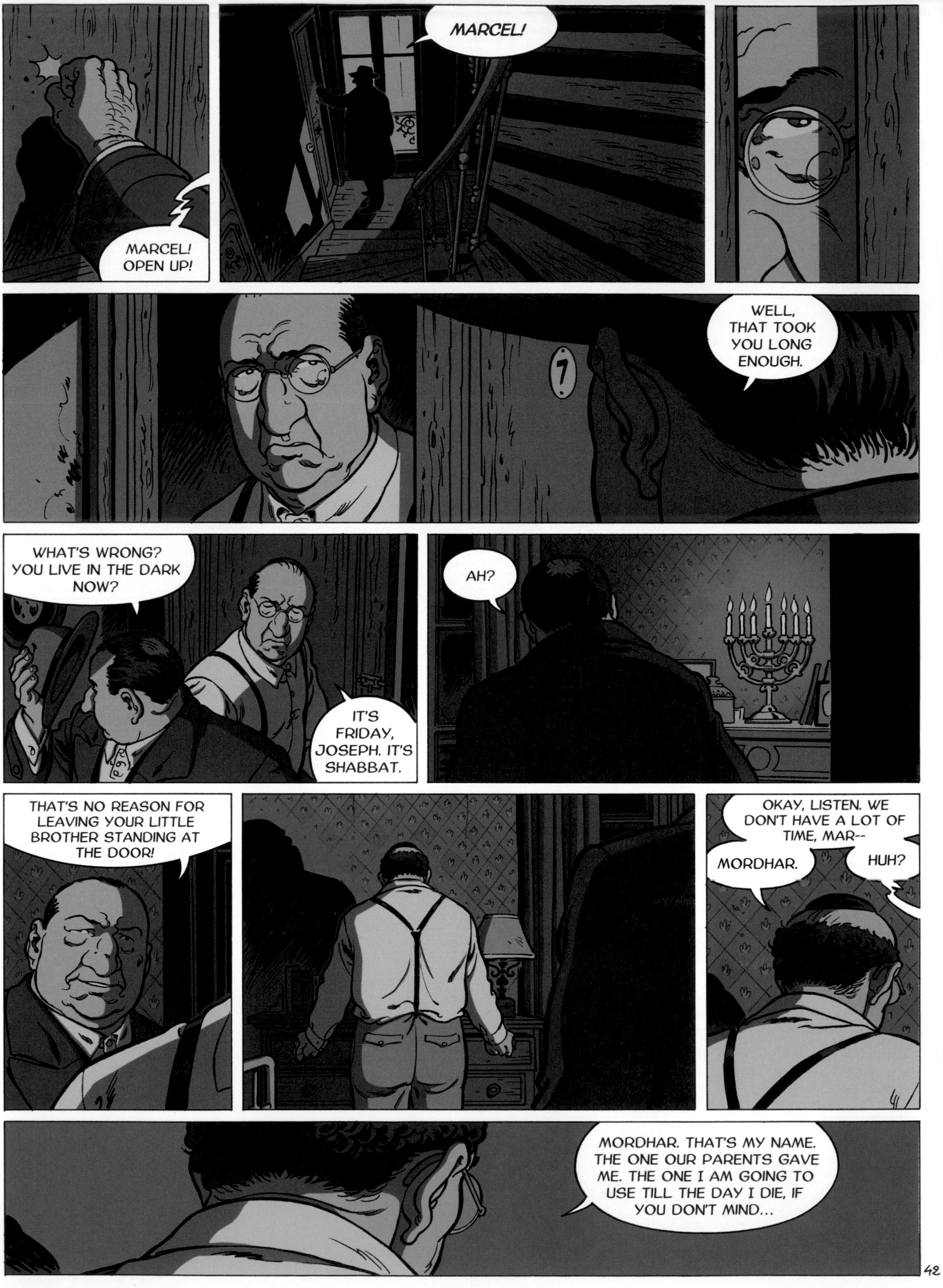
MARCEL!
MARCEL! OPEN UP!
WELL, THAT TOOK YOU LONG ENOUGH.
WHAT'S WRONG? YOU LIVE IN THE DARK NOW?
IT'S FRIDAY, JOSEPH. IT'S SHABBAT.
AH?
THAT'S NO REASON FOR LEAVING YOUR LITTLE BROTHER STANDING AT THE DOOR!
OKAY, LISTEN. WE DON'T HAVE A LOT OF TIME, MAR--
MORDHAR.
HUH?
MORDHAR. THAT'S MY NAME. THE ONE OUR PARENTS GAVE ME. THE ONE I AM GOING TO USE TILL THE DAY I DIE, IF YOU DON'T MIND...
42

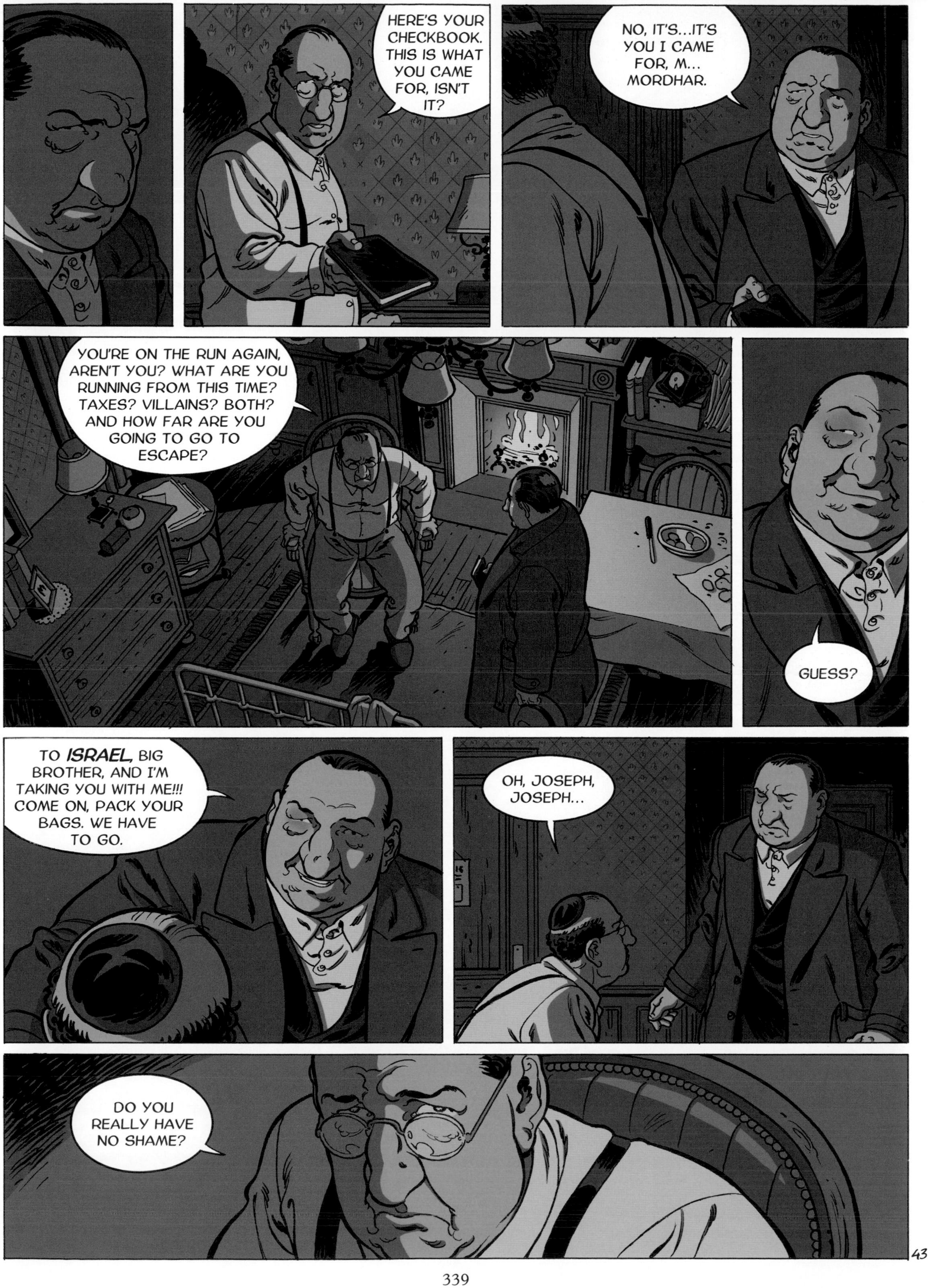
HERE'S YOUR CHECKBOOK. THIS IS WHAT YOU CAME FOR, ISN'T IT?
NO, IT'S...IT'S YOU I CAME FOR, M... MORDHAR.
YOU'RE ON THE RUN AGAIN, AREN'T YOU? WHAT ARE YOU RUNNING FROM THIS TIME? TAXES? VILLAINS? BOTH? AND HOW FAR ARE YOU GOING TO GO TO ESCAPE?
GUESS?
TO *ISRAEL*, BIG BROTHER, AND I'M TAKING YOU WITH ME!!! COME ON, PACK YOUR BAGS. WE HAVE TO GO.
OH, JOSEPH, JOSEPH...
DO YOU REALLY HAVE NO SHAME?
43

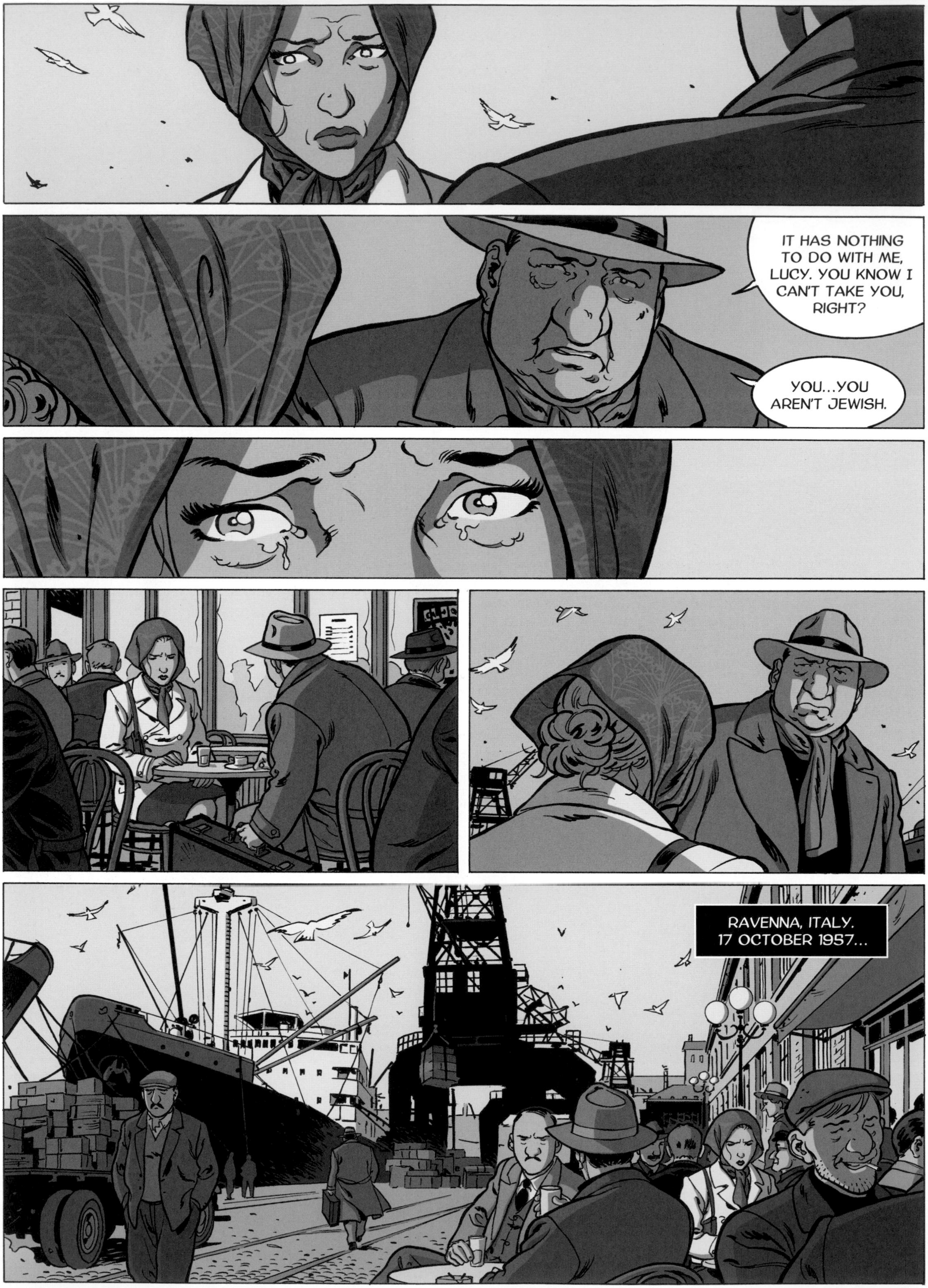
IT HAS NOTHING TO DO WITH ME, LUCY. YOU KNOW I CAN'T TAKE YOU, RIGHT?
YOU...YOU AREN'T JEWISH.
RAVENNA, ITALY. 17 OCTOBER 1957...
44

WE COULDN'T KNOW...HE SEEMED NICE ENOUGH. AND HE WAS HAPPY HERE. ASK THE RECTOR.

WHO'S GOING TO PAY MY PHONE BILL! A MILLION FRANCS!

I JUST SIGNED PAPERS, THAT'S ALL. I...I DIDN'T KNOW ANYTHING, I SWEAR.

MARCUS AND LAZARD ONLY GUARANTEED A FEW COMMERCIAL TRANSACTIONS. EVERYTHING WAS LEGAL...

NO COMMENT. LEAVE ME ALONE.

LUCY SCHMIDT, WHOM SCRAP METAL DEALERS AROUND THE WORLD NICKNAMED "IRON LUCY," WAS FINALLY LET GO AFTER THREE DAYS OF QUESTIONING...

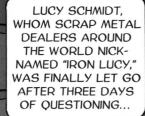

...BUT AFTER HAVING LOOKED AT HER PASSPORT, THE INVESTIGATORS WERE ABLE TO DEDUCE THAT JOSEPH JOANOVICI ENTERED SWITZERLAND UNDER A FALSE IDENTITY, THEN WENT ON TO ITALY...

...AND FROM THERE HE SET OFF FOR ISRAEL, WHERE HE WILL FIND SANCTUARY UNDER THE FAMOUS "LAW OF RETURN."

45

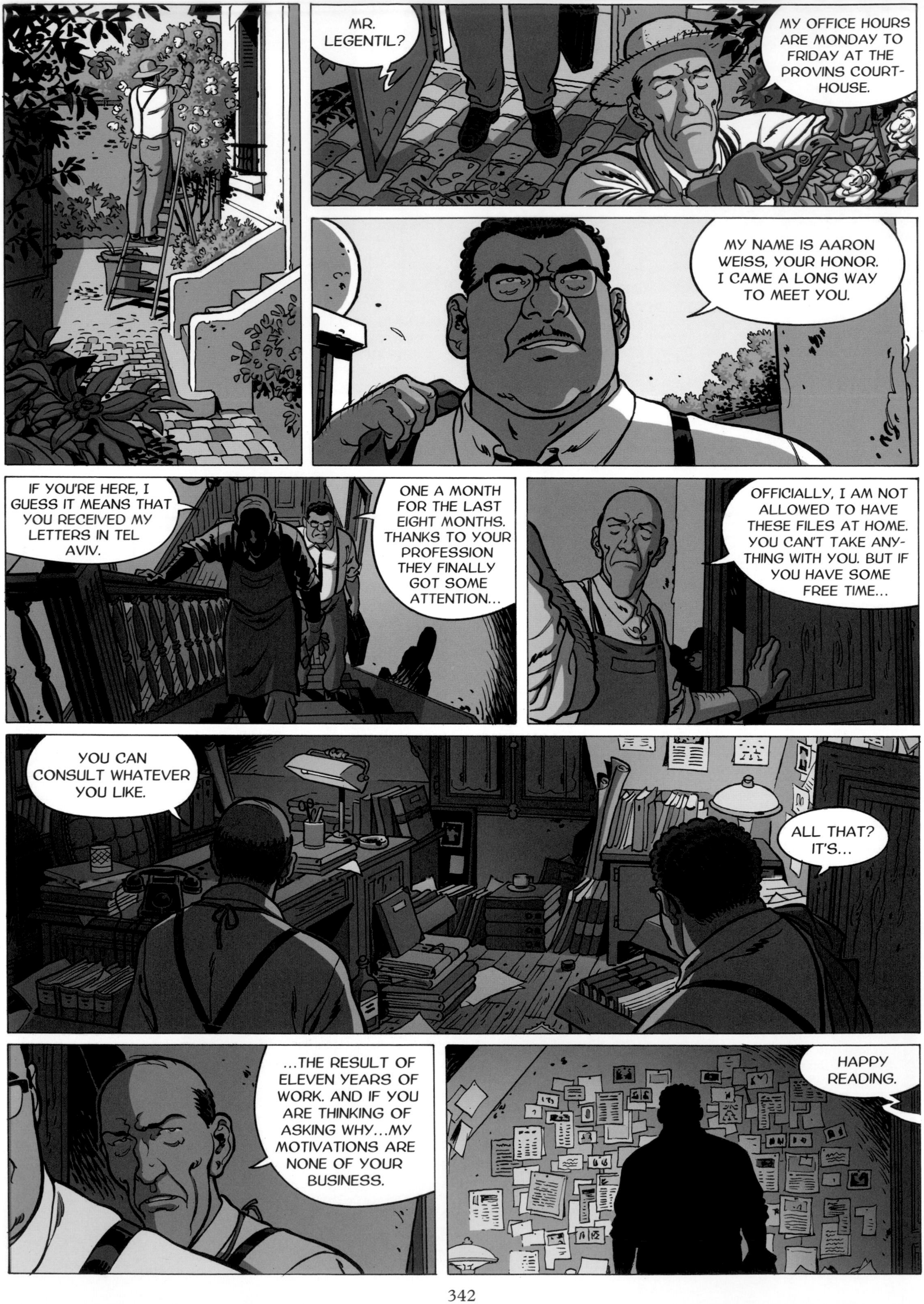
MR. LEGENTIL?
MY OFFICE HOURS ARE MONDAY TO FRIDAY AT THE PROVINS COURT-HOUSE.
MY NAME IS AARON WEISS, YOUR HONOR. I CAME A LONG WAY TO MEET YOU.
IF YOU'RE HERE, I GUESS IT MEANS THAT YOU RECEIVED MY LETTERS IN TEL AVIV.
ONE A MONTH FOR THE LAST EIGHT MONTHS. THANKS TO YOUR PROFESSION THEY FINALLY GOT SOME ATTENTION...
OFFICIALLY, I AM NOT ALLOWED TO HAVE THESE FILES AT HOME. YOU CAN'T TAKE ANY-THING WITH YOU. BUT IF YOU HAVE SOME FREE TIME...
YOU CAN CONSULT WHATEVER YOU LIKE.
ALL THAT? IT'S...
...THE RESULT OF ELEVEN YEARS OF WORK. AND IF YOU ARE THINKING OF ASKING WHY...MY MOTIVATIONS ARE NONE OF YOUR BUSINESS.
HAPPY READING.

46

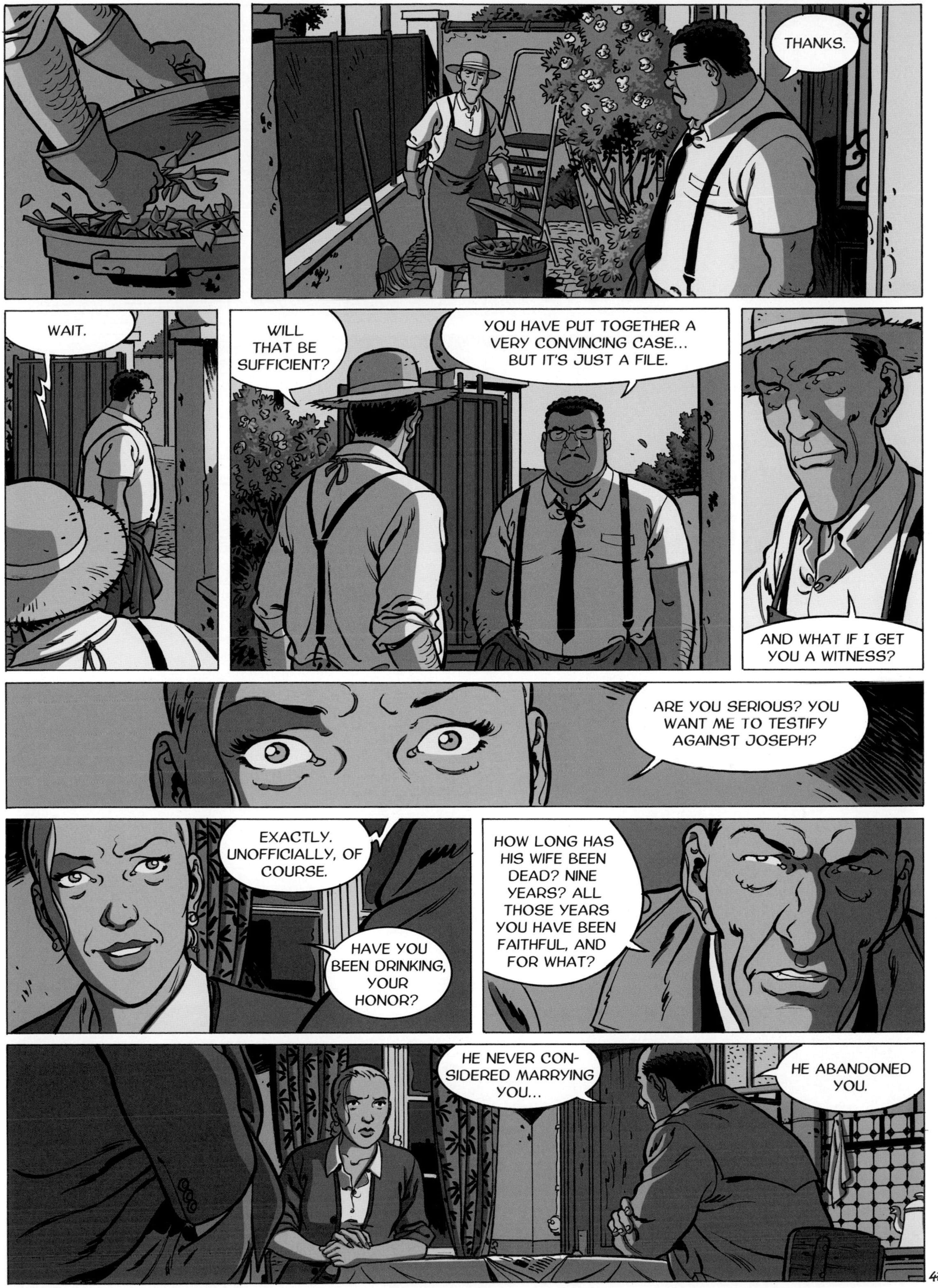
THANKS.
WAIT.
WILL THAT BE SUFFICIENT?
YOU HAVE PUT TOGETHER A VERY CONVINCING CASE... BUT IT'S JUST A FILE.
AND WHAT IF I GET YOU A WITNESS?
ARE YOU SERIOUS? YOU WANT ME TO TESTIFY AGAINST JOSEPH?
EXACTLY. UNOFFICIALLY, OF COURSE.
HAVE YOU BEEN DRINKING, YOUR HONOR?
HOW LONG HAS HIS WIFE BEEN DEAD? NINE YEARS? ALL THOSE YEARS YOU HAVE BEEN FAITHFUL, AND FOR WHAT?
HE NEVER CON-SIDERED MARRYING YOU...
HE ABANDONED YOU.
47

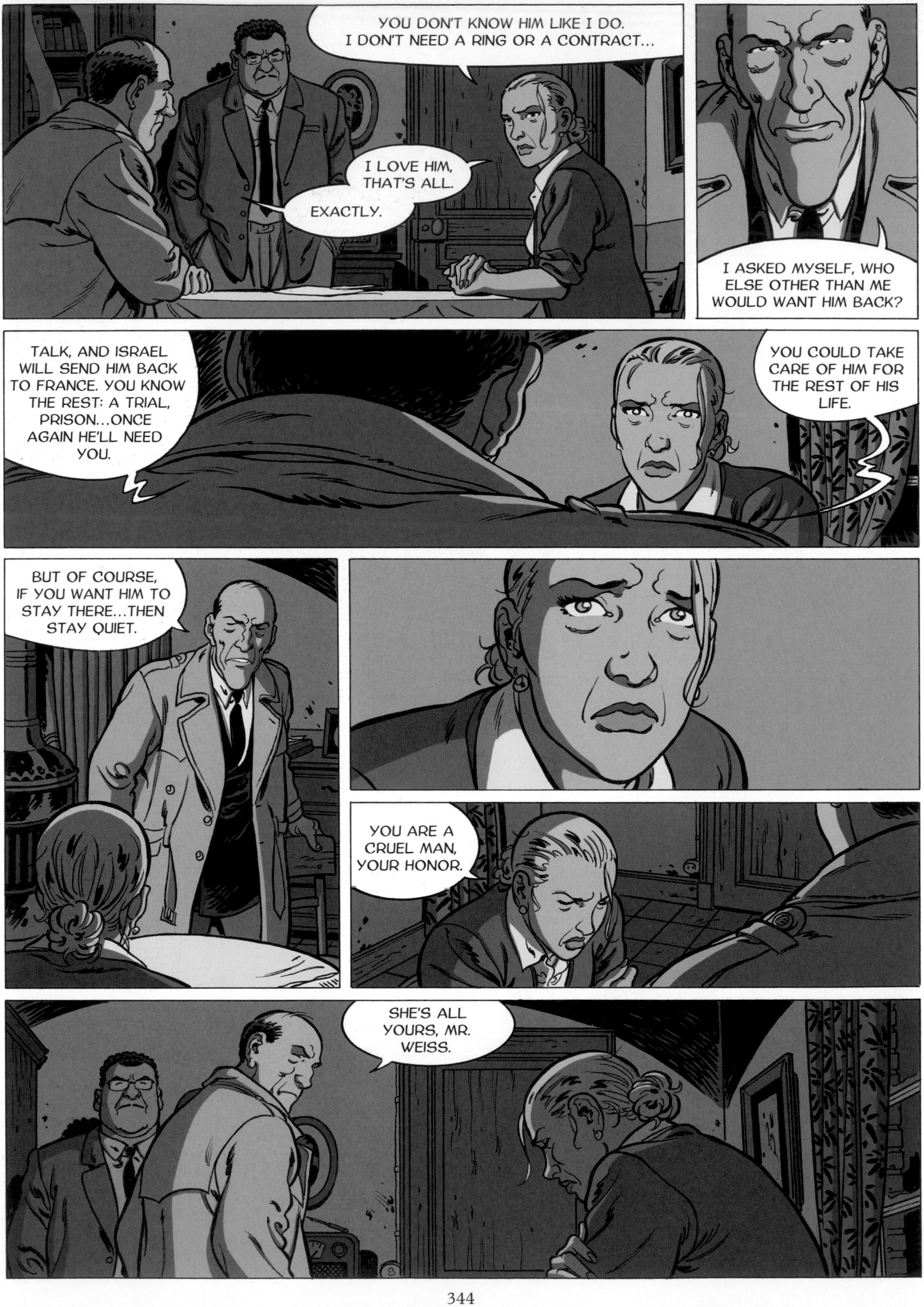
YOU DON'T KNOW HIM LIKE I DO. I DON'T NEED A RING OR A CONTRACT...
I LOVE HIM, THAT'S ALL.
EXACTLY.
I ASKED MYSELF, WHO ELSE OTHER THAN ME WOULD WANT HIM BACK?
TALK, AND ISRAEL WILL SEND HIM BACK TO FRANCE. YOU KNOW THE REST: A TRIAL, PRISON...ONCE AGAIN HE'LL NEED YOU.
YOU COULD TAKE CARE OF HIM FOR THE REST OF HIS LIFE.
BUT OF COURSE, IF YOU WANT HIM TO STAY THERE...THEN STAY QUIET.
YOU ARE A CRUEL MAN, YOUR HONOR.
SHE'S ALL YOURS, MR. WEISS.
48

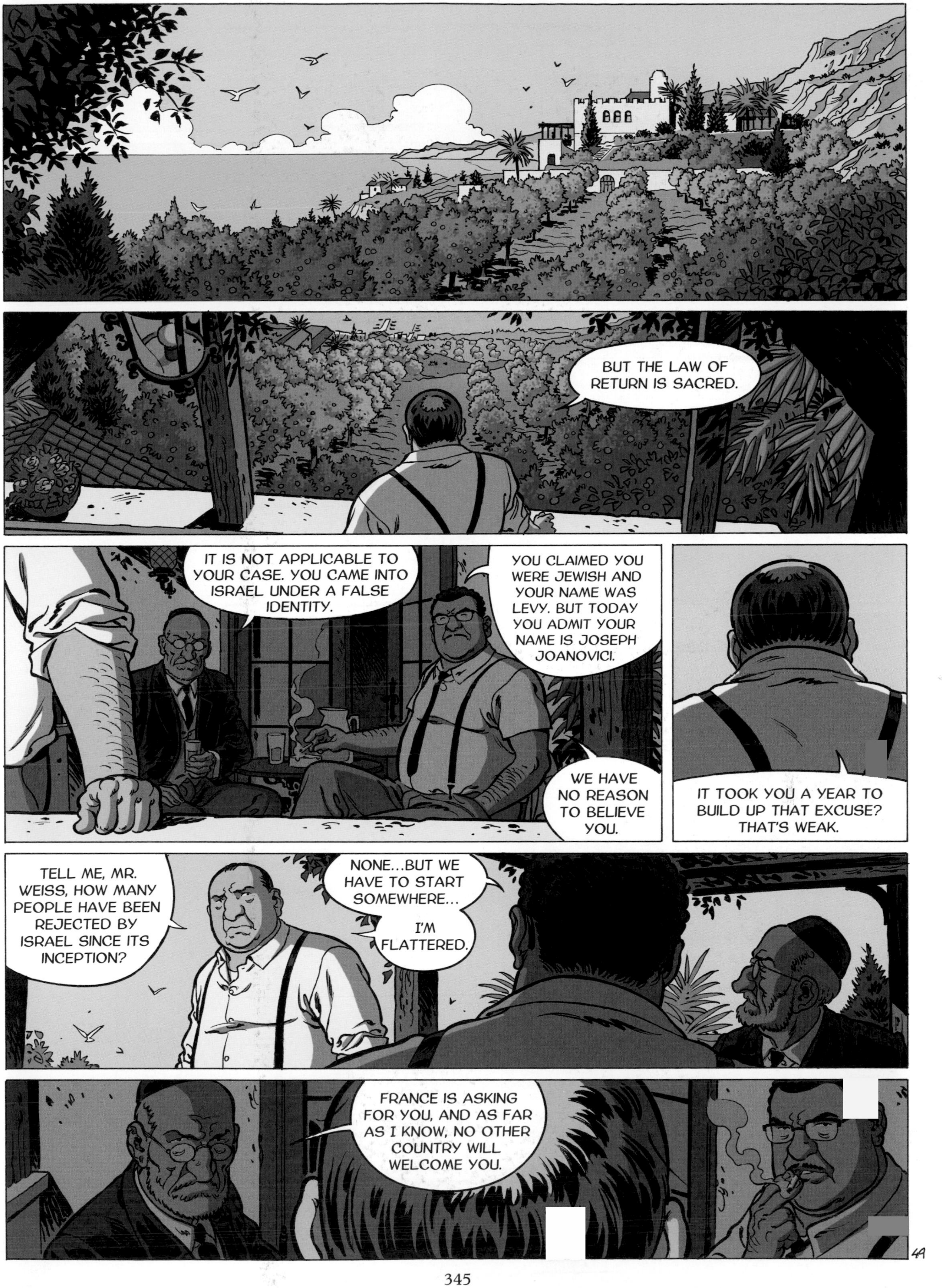

BUT THE LAW OF RETURN IS SACRED.
IT IS NOT APPLICABLE TO YOUR CASE. YOU CAME INTO ISRAEL UNDER A FALSE IDENTITY.
YOU CLAIMED YOU WERE JEWISH AND YOUR NAME WAS LEVY. BUT TODAY YOU ADMIT YOUR NAME IS JOSEPH JOANOVICI.
WE HAVE NO REASON TO BELIEVE YOU.
IT TOOK YOU A YEAR TO BUILD UP THAT EXCUSE? THAT'S WEAK.
TELL ME, MR. WEISS, HOW MANY PEOPLE HAVE BEEN REJECTED BY ISRAEL SINCE ITS INCEPTION?
NONE...BUT WE HAVE TO START SOMEWHERE...
I'M FLATTERED.
FRANCE IS ASKING FOR YOU, AND AS FAR AS I KNOW, NO OTHER COUNTRY WILL WELCOME YOU.

49

I DIDN'T COME EMPTY-HANDED, EITHER. YOU'RE SENDING ME BACK...BUT WHAT WILL YOU DO WITH MY MONEY?

YES, ABOUT THAT...

...YOU SIGNED A CHECK FOR $600,000 TO THE ASSOCIATION OF THE FRIENDS OF THE UNIVERSITY OF HAIFA.

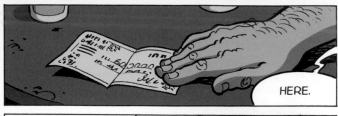

HERE.

THIS CHECK, AND ALL THE OTHER CHECKS YOU'VE SIGNED, WILL NOT BE CASHED. WE DON'T WANT THEM.

THE ASSOCIATION OF THE FRIENDS OF THE UNIVERSITY OF HAIFA HAS ALREADY INFORMED THE FRENCH AUTHORITIES OF THIS BANK ACCOUNT.

THE FRENCH TAX AUTHORITIES WILL PROBABLY REACH OUT TO THE SWISS...

YOU DON'T KNOW THE SWISS. THEY NEVER GIVE UP MONEY!

YOU'RE RIGHT. THEY WILL NEVER GIVE IT TO THE FRENCH...

...OR TO YOU.

DURING A CERTAIN PERIOD, THE SWISS BANKS KEPT MANY JEWS' MONEY. WHY NOT YOURS?

50

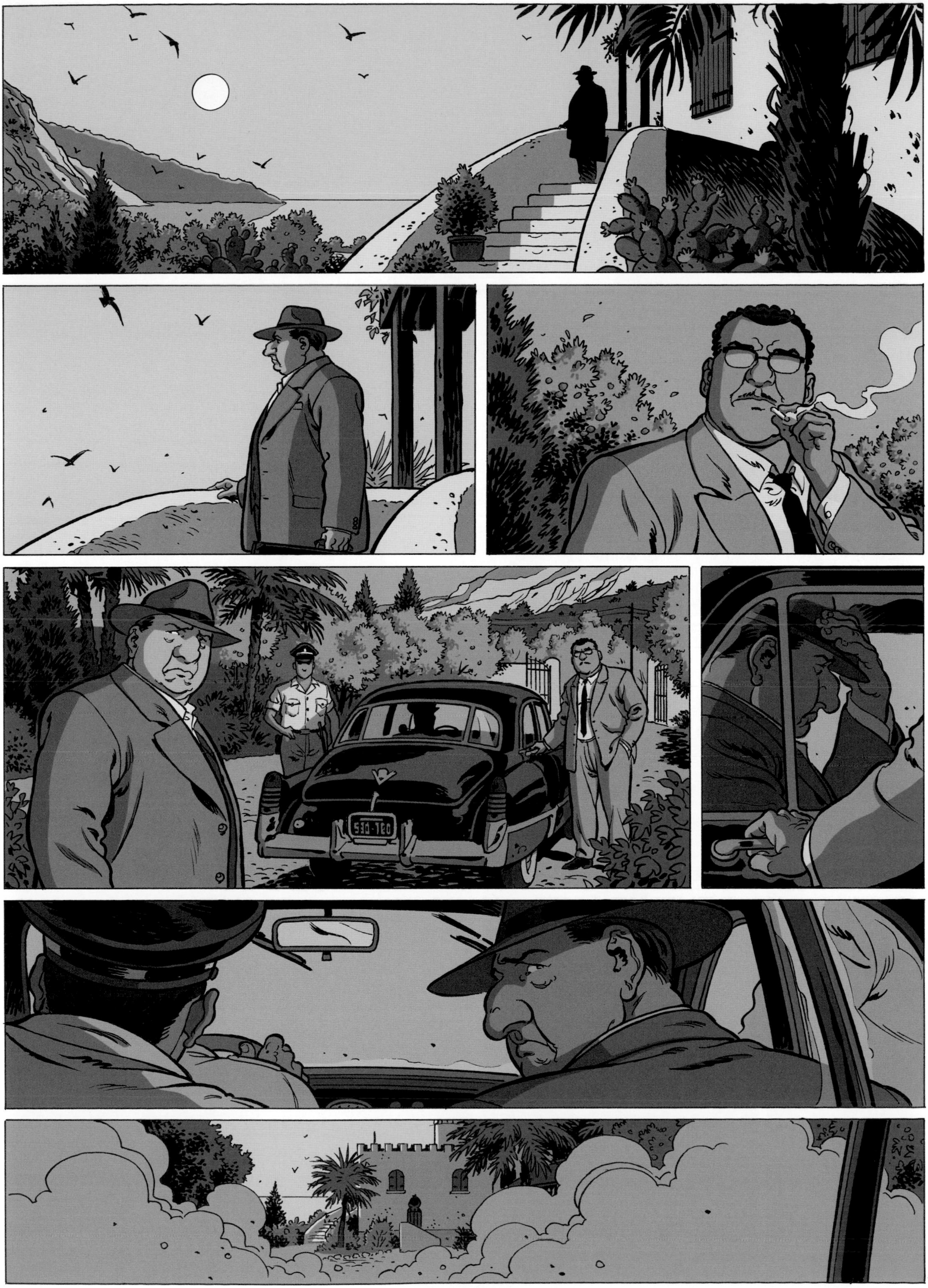

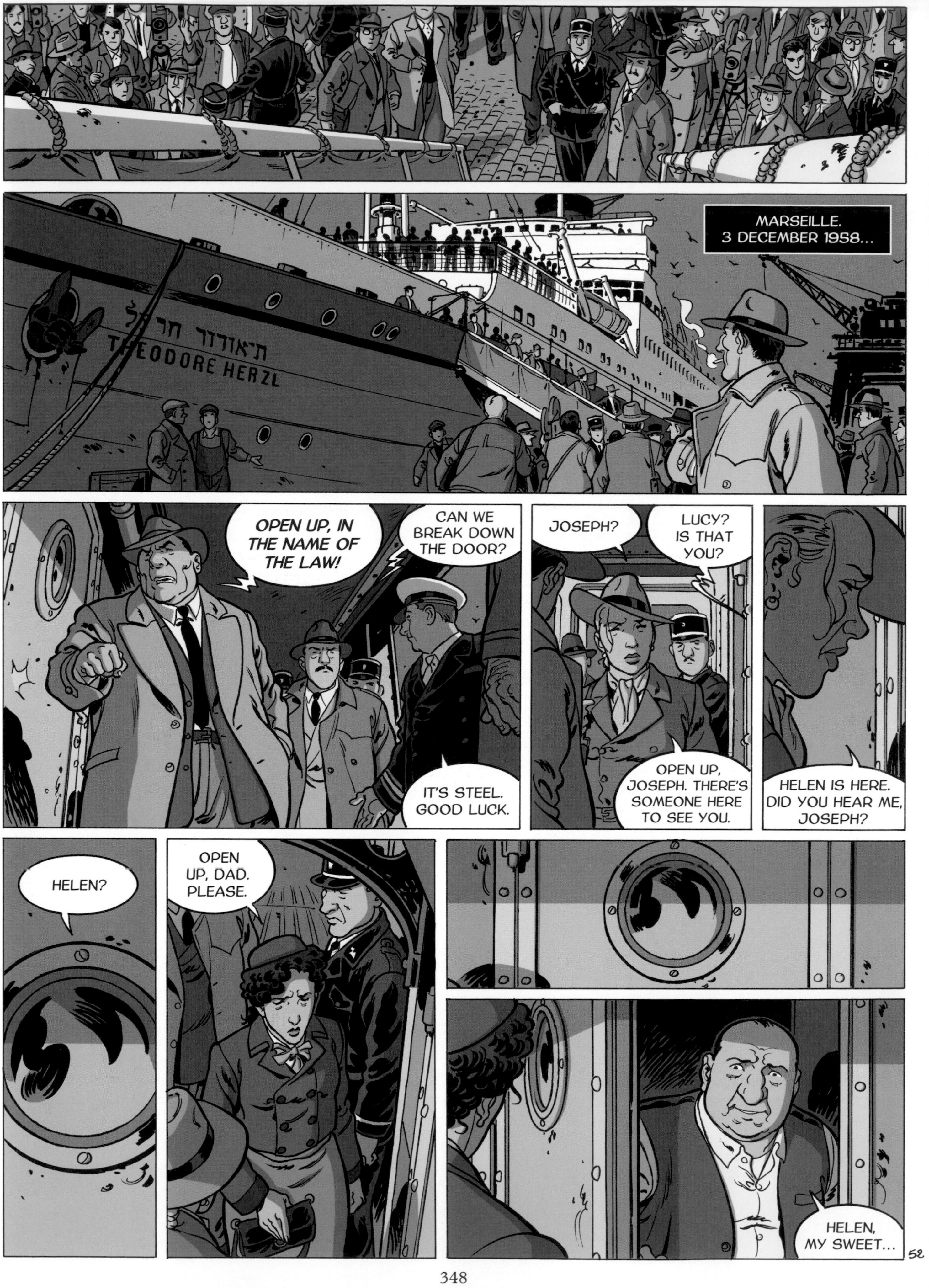

MARSEILLE.
3 DECEMBER 1958...
תיאודור הרצל
THEODORE HERZL
OPEN UP, IN THE NAME OF THE LAW!
CAN WE BREAK DOWN THE DOOR?
IT'S STEEL. GOOD LUCK.
JOSEPH?
LUCY? IS THAT YOU?
OPEN UP, JOSEPH. THERE'S SOMEONE HERE TO SEE YOU.
HELEN IS HERE. DID YOU HEAR ME, JOSEPH?
HELEN?
OPEN UP, DAD. PLEASE.
HELEN, MY SWEET...
52

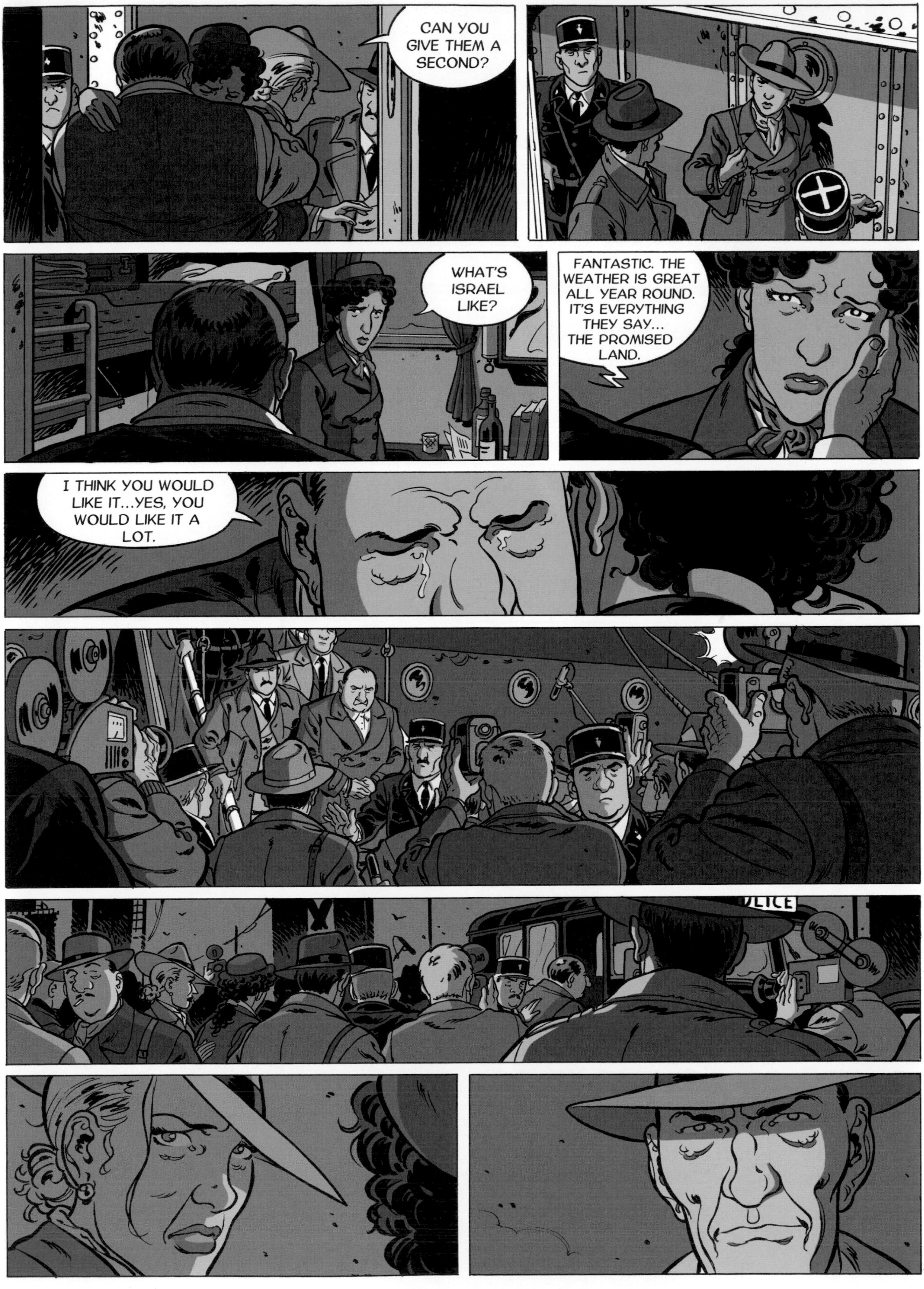
CAN YOU GIVE THEM A SECOND?
WHAT'S ISRAEL LIKE?
FANTASTIC. THE WEATHER IS GREAT ALL YEAR ROUND. IT'S EVERYTHING THEY SAY... THE PROMISED LAND.
I THINK YOU WOULD LIKE IT...YES, YOU WOULD LIKE IT A LOT.
OLICE
53

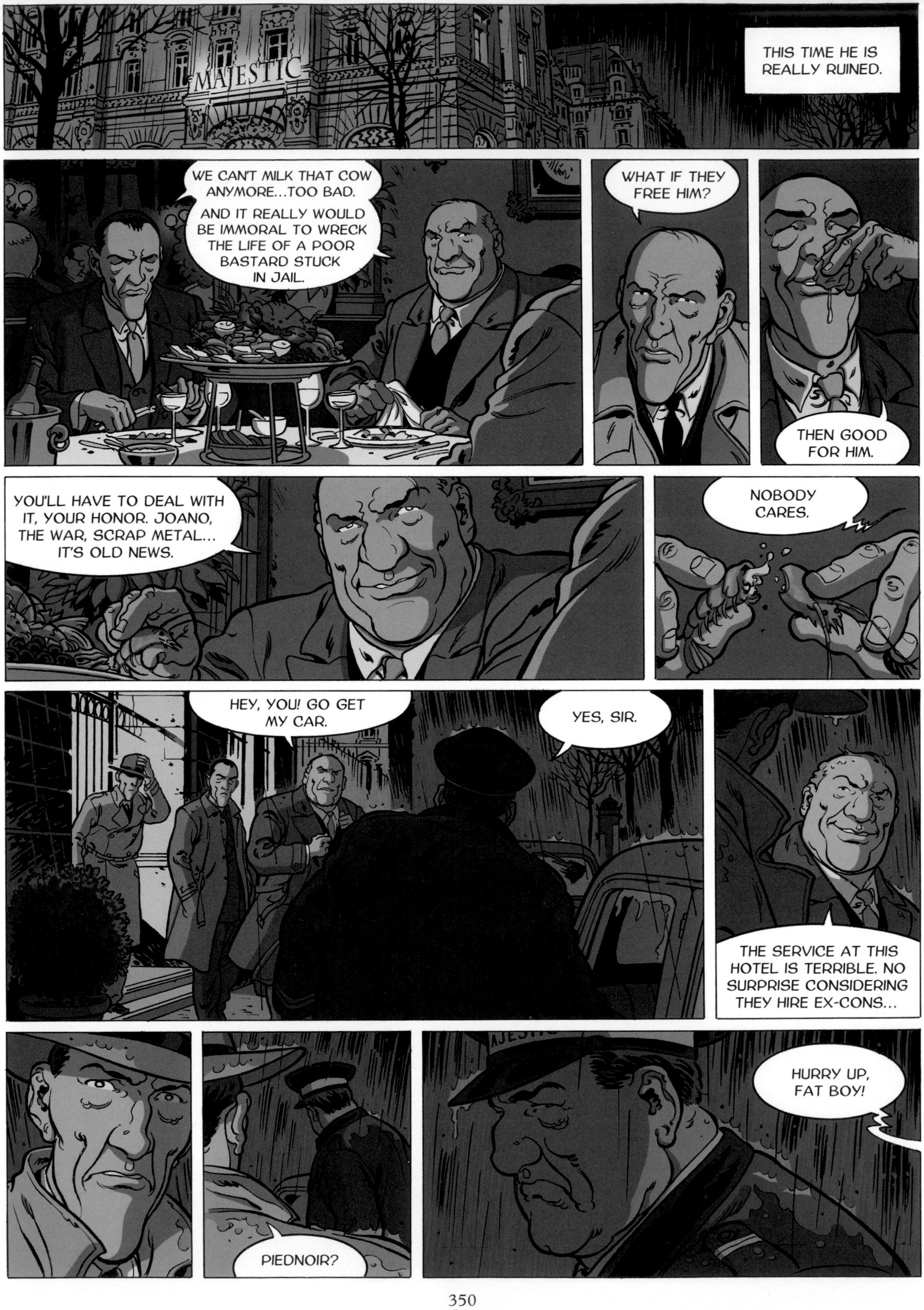
MAJESTIC
THIS TIME HE IS REALLY RUINED.
WE CAN'T MILK THAT COW ANYMORE...TOO BAD.
AND IT REALLY WOULD BE IMMORAL TO WRECK THE LIFE OF A POOR BASTARD STUCK IN JAIL.
WHAT IF THEY FREE HIM?
THEN GOOD FOR HIM.
YOU'LL HAVE TO DEAL WITH IT, YOUR HONOR. JOANO, THE WAR, SCRAP METAL... IT'S OLD NEWS.
NOBODY CARES.
HEY, YOU! GO GET MY CAR.
YES, SIR.
THE SERVICE AT THIS HOTEL IS TERRIBLE. NO SURPRISE CONSIDERING THEY HIRE EX-CONS...
PIEDNOIR?
HURRY UP, FAT BOY!
54

HE INSISTS HE WAS BORN IN 1905. BUT THAT'S NOT TRUE, IS IT? THIS MAN IS AT LEAST 70.

AND HE DRANK TOO MUCH, SMOKED TOO MUCH, AND LIVED TOO MUCH.

I DON'T KNOW. IF YOU SAY SO...

I AM GOING TO SUPPORT YOUR REQUEST FOR HOUSE ARREST. CONSIDERING HIS DETERIORATING CONDITION, IT'S THE ONLY HUMANE THING TO DO.

THANKS, I...

DON'T THANK ME. TELL HIM HE HAS TO EAT IF HE WANTS TO LEAVE HERE ON HIS OWN TWO LEGS.

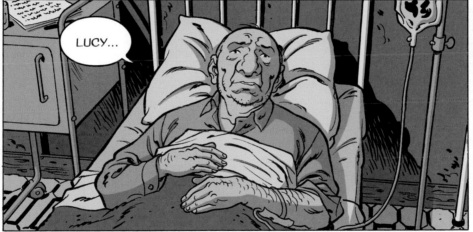

LUCY...

JOSEPH, YOU HAVE TO STOP THIS NONSENSE. THERE'S NO POINT. YOU'RE GOING TO KILL YOURSELF...

IT'S NOT FAIR, LUCY. NOT FAIR.

I KNOW, BUT THEY'RE GOING TO LET YOU OUT! YOU'RE GOING TO COME AND LIVE WITH ME, IN CLICHY...

IT'S...IT'S THERE. I WROTE IT ALL DOWN.

To the attention of General De Gaulle, President of the Republic of France

FOR YOU, LUCY. MAIL IT...

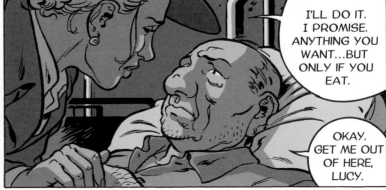

I'LL DO IT. I PROMISE. ANYTHING YOU WANT...BUT ONLY IF YOU EAT.

OKAY. GET ME OUT OF HERE, LUCY.

55

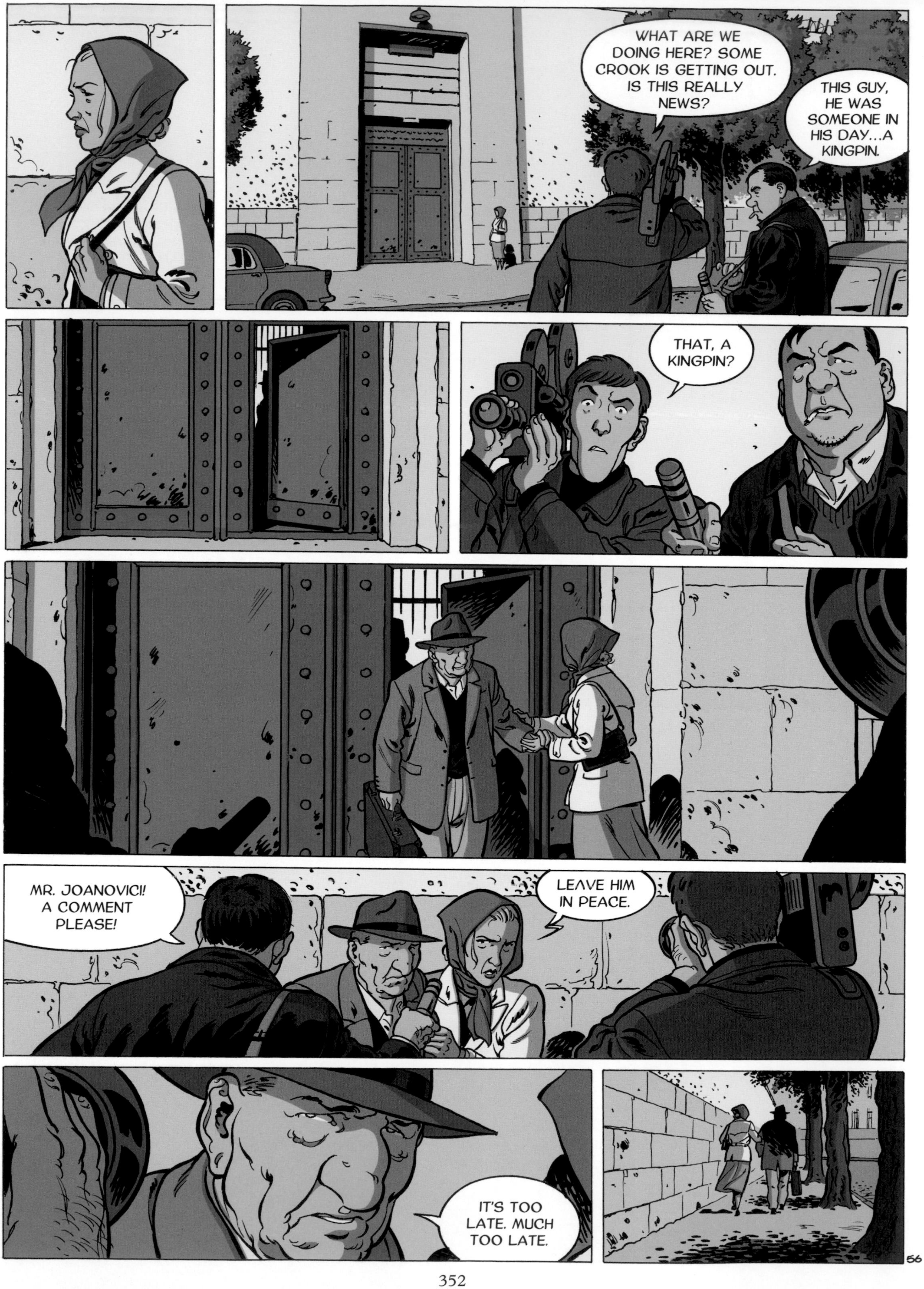

WHAT ARE WE DOING HERE? SOME CROOK IS GETTING OUT. IS THIS REALLY NEWS?
THIS GUY, HE WAS SOMEONE IN HIS DAY...A KINGPIN.
THAT, A KINGPIN?
MR. JOANOVICI! A COMMENT PLEASE!
LEAVE HIM IN PEACE.
IT'S TOO LATE. MUCH TOO LATE.
56

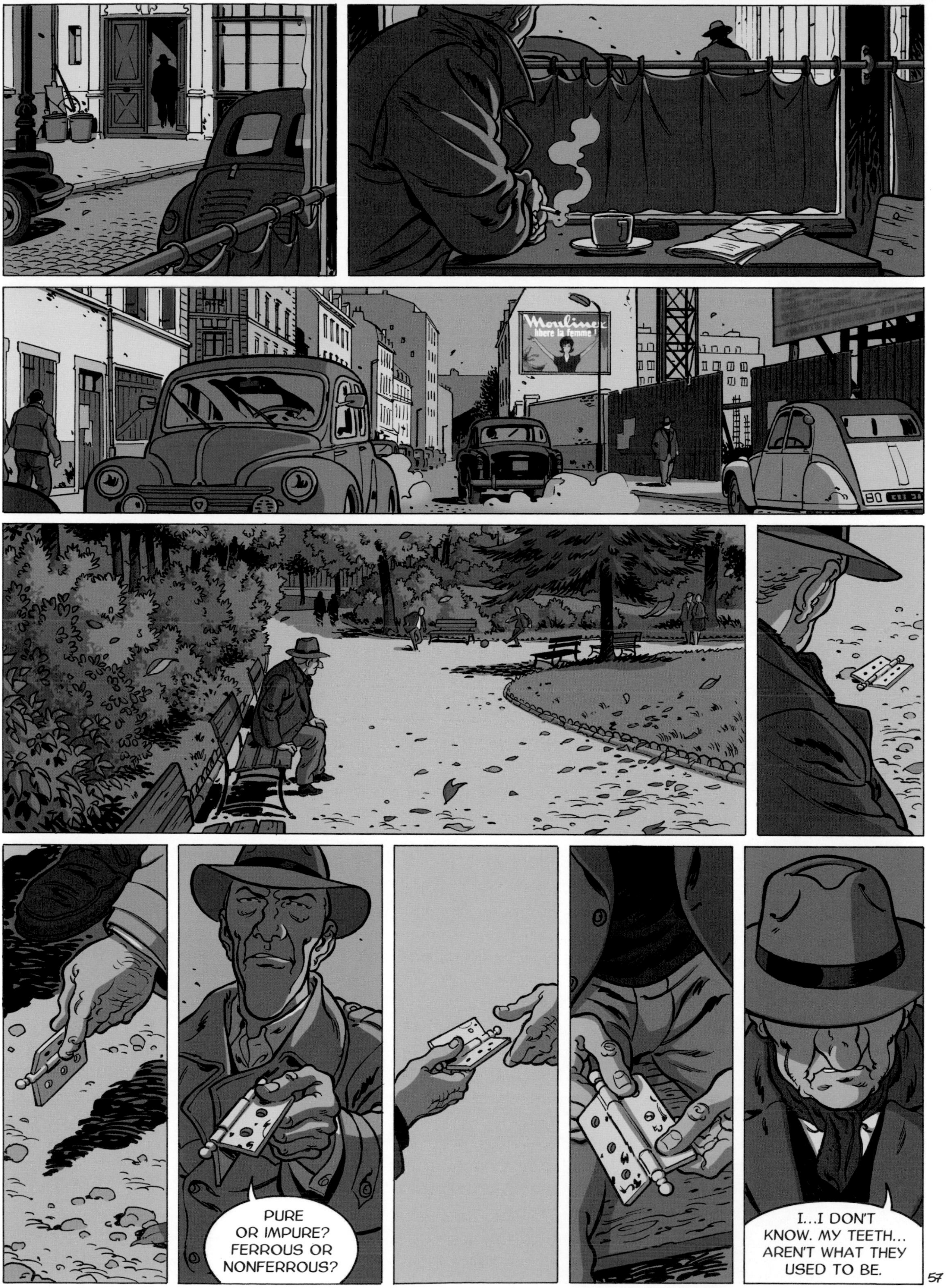
Moulinex
libère la femme !
PURE OR IMPURE? FERROUS OR NONFERROUS?
I...I DON'T KNOW. MY TEETH... AREN'T WHAT THEY USED TO BE.
57

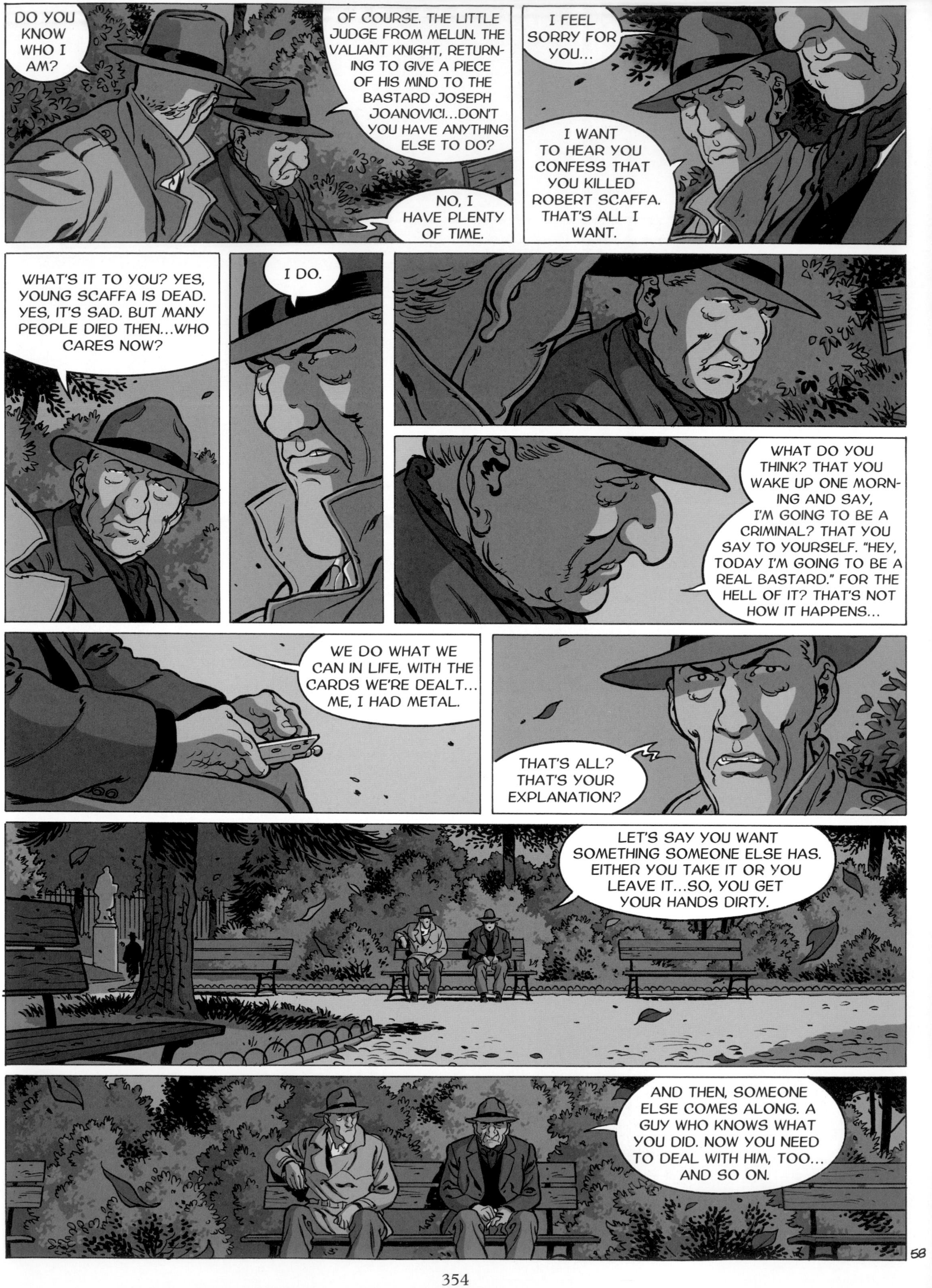
DO YOU KNOW WHO I AM?
OF COURSE. THE LITTLE JUDGE FROM MELUN. THE VALIANT KNIGHT, RETURNING TO GIVE A PIECE OF HIS MIND TO THE BASTARD JOSEPH JOANOVICI...DON'T YOU HAVE ANYTHING ELSE TO DO?
NO, I HAVE PLENTY OF TIME.
I FEEL SORRY FOR YOU...
I WANT TO HEAR YOU CONFESS THAT YOU KILLED ROBERT SCAFFA. THAT'S ALL I WANT.
WHAT'S IT TO YOU? YES, YOUNG SCAFFA IS DEAD. YES, IT'S SAD. BUT MANY PEOPLE DIED THEN...WHO CARES NOW?
I DO.
WHAT DO YOU THINK? THAT YOU WAKE UP ONE MORNING AND SAY, I'M GOING TO BE A CRIMINAL? THAT YOU SAY TO YOURSELF. "HEY, TODAY I'M GOING TO BE A REAL BASTARD." FOR THE HELL OF IT? THAT'S NOT HOW IT HAPPENS...
WE DO WHAT WE CAN IN LIFE, WITH THE CARDS WE'RE DEALT... ME, I HAD METAL.
THAT'S ALL? THAT'S YOUR EXPLANATION?
LET'S SAY YOU WANT SOMETHING SOMEONE ELSE HAS. EITHER YOU TAKE IT OR YOU LEAVE IT...SO, YOU GET YOUR HANDS DIRTY.
AND THEN, SOMEONE ELSE COMES ALONG. A GUY WHO KNOWS WHAT YOU DID. NOW YOU NEED TO DEAL WITH HIM, TOO... AND SO ON.
58

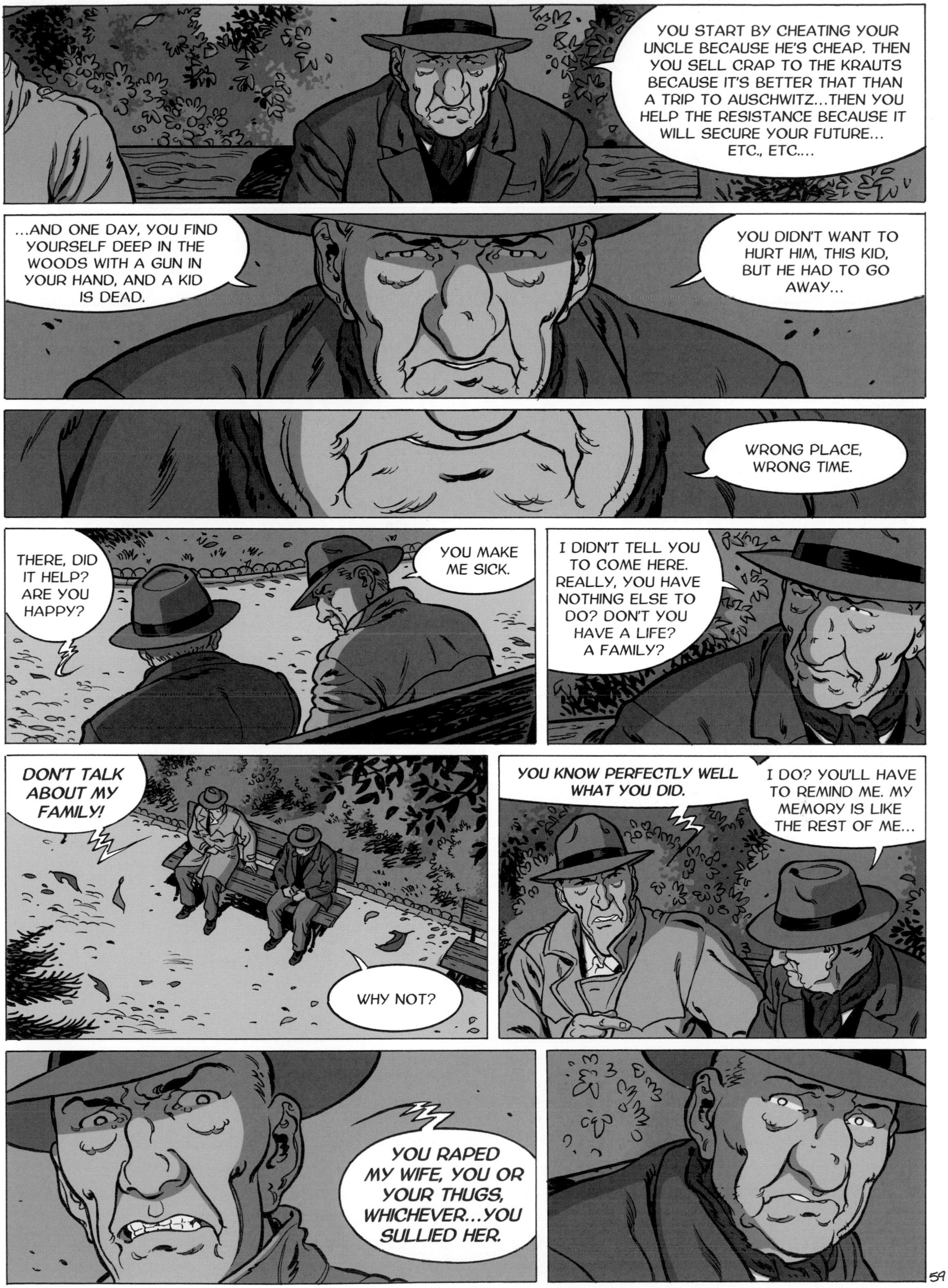

YOU START BY CHEATING YOUR UNCLE BECAUSE HE'S CHEAP. THEN YOU SELL CRAP TO THE KRAUTS BECAUSE IT'S BETTER THAN THAT A TRIP TO AUSCHWITZ...THEN YOU HELP THE RESISTANCE BECAUSE IT WILL SECURE YOUR FUTURE... ETC., ETC....
...AND ONE DAY, YOU FIND YOURSELF DEEP IN THE WOODS WITH A GUN IN YOUR HAND, AND A KID IS DEAD.
YOU DIDN'T WANT TO HURT HIM, THIS KID, BUT HE HAD TO GO AWAY...
WRONG PLACE, WRONG TIME.
THERE, DID IT HELP? ARE YOU HAPPY?
YOU MAKE ME SICK.
I DIDN'T TELL YOU TO COME HERE. REALLY, YOU HAVE NOTHING ELSE TO DO? DON'T YOU HAVE A LIFE? A FAMILY?
DON'T TALK ABOUT MY FAMILY!
WHY NOT?
YOU KNOW PERFECTLY WELL WHAT YOU DID.
I DO? YOU'LL HAVE TO REMIND ME. MY MEMORY IS LIKE THE REST OF ME...
YOU RAPED MY WIFE, YOU OR YOUR THUGS, WHICHEVER...YOU SULLIED HER.
59

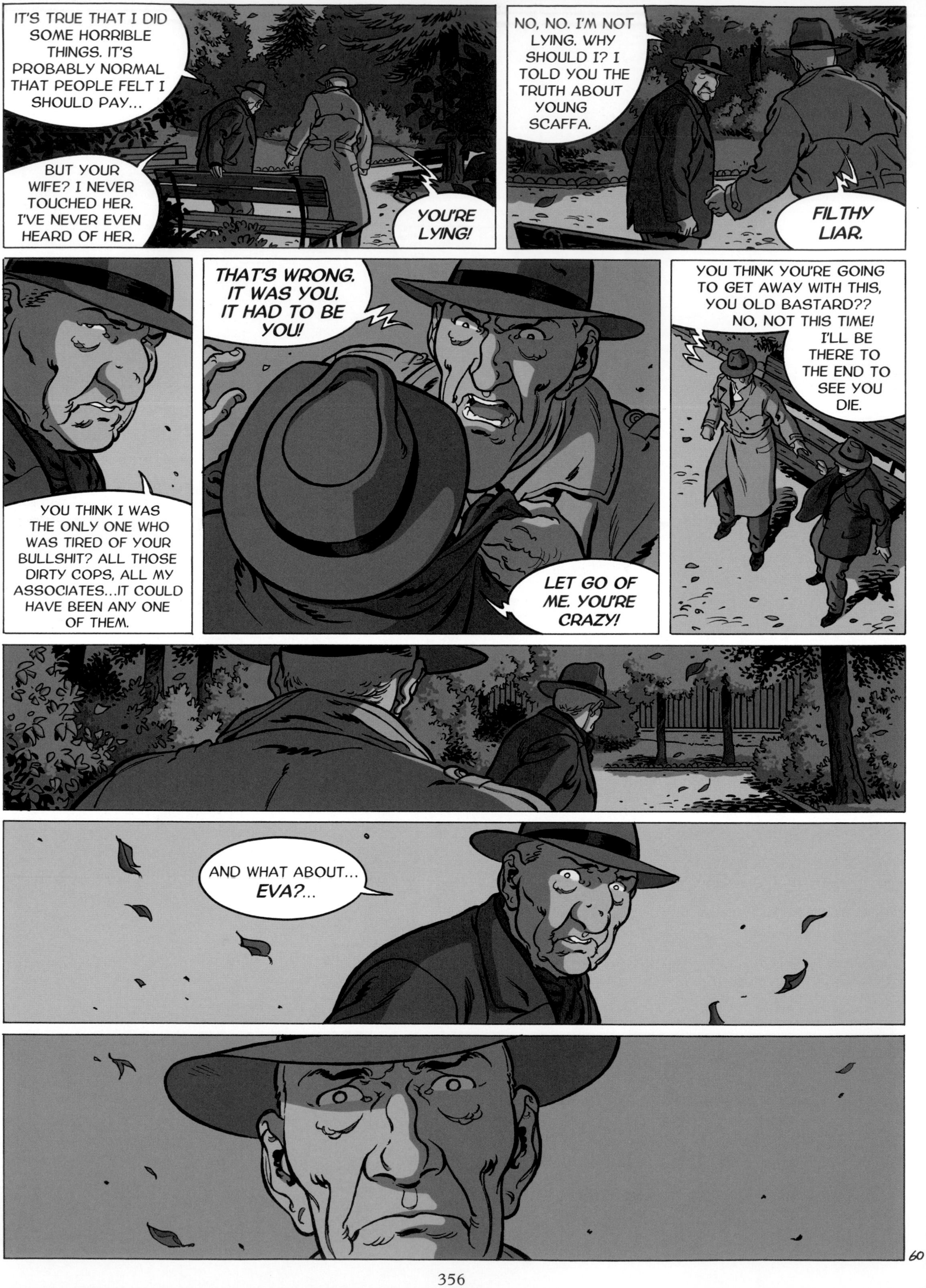
IT'S TRUE THAT I DID SOME HORRIBLE THINGS. IT'S PROBABLY NORMAL THAT PEOPLE FELT I SHOULD PAY...
BUT YOUR WIFE? I NEVER TOUCHED HER. I'VE NEVER EVEN HEARD OF HER.
YOU'RE LYING!
NO, NO. I'M NOT LYING. WHY SHOULD I? I TOLD YOU THE TRUTH ABOUT YOUNG SCAFFA.
FILTHY LIAR.
THAT'S WRONG. IT WAS YOU. IT HAD TO BE YOU!
YOU THINK I WAS THE ONLY ONE WHO WAS TIRED OF YOUR BULLSHIT? ALL THOSE DIRTY COPS, ALL MY ASSOCIATES...IT COULD HAVE BEEN ANY ONE OF THEM.
LET GO OF ME. YOU'RE CRAZY!
YOU THINK YOU'RE GOING TO GET AWAY WITH THIS, YOU OLD BASTARD?? NO, NOT THIS TIME! I'LL BE THERE TO THE END TO SEE YOU DIE.
AND WHAT ABOUT... EVA?...
60

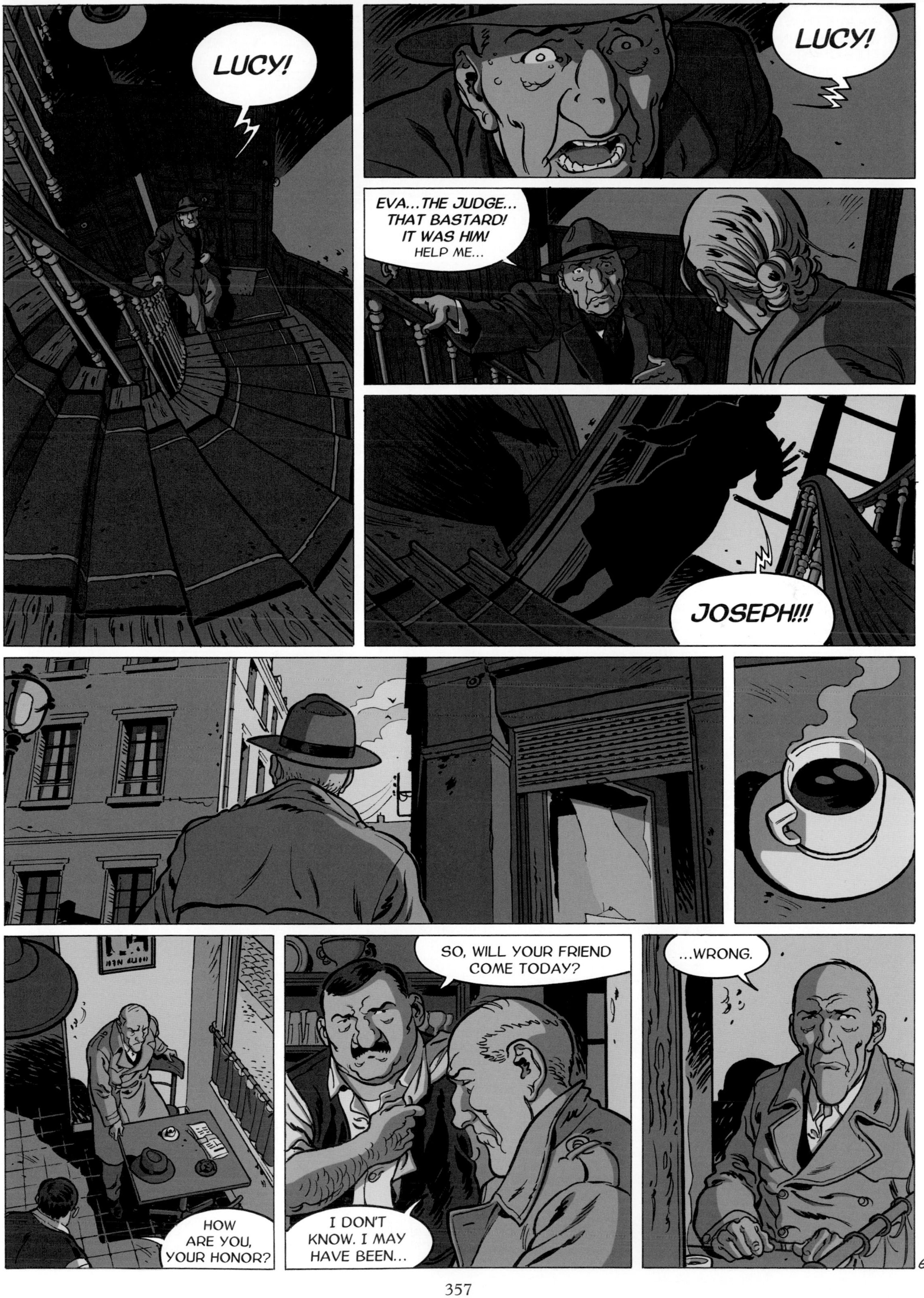
LUCY!
LUCY!
EVA...THE JUDGE... THAT BASTARD! IT WAS HIM! HELP ME...
JOSEPH!!!
HOW ARE YOU, YOUR HONOR?
SO, WILL YOUR FRIEND COME TODAY?
I DON'T KNOW. I MAY HAVE BEEN...
...WRONG.
61

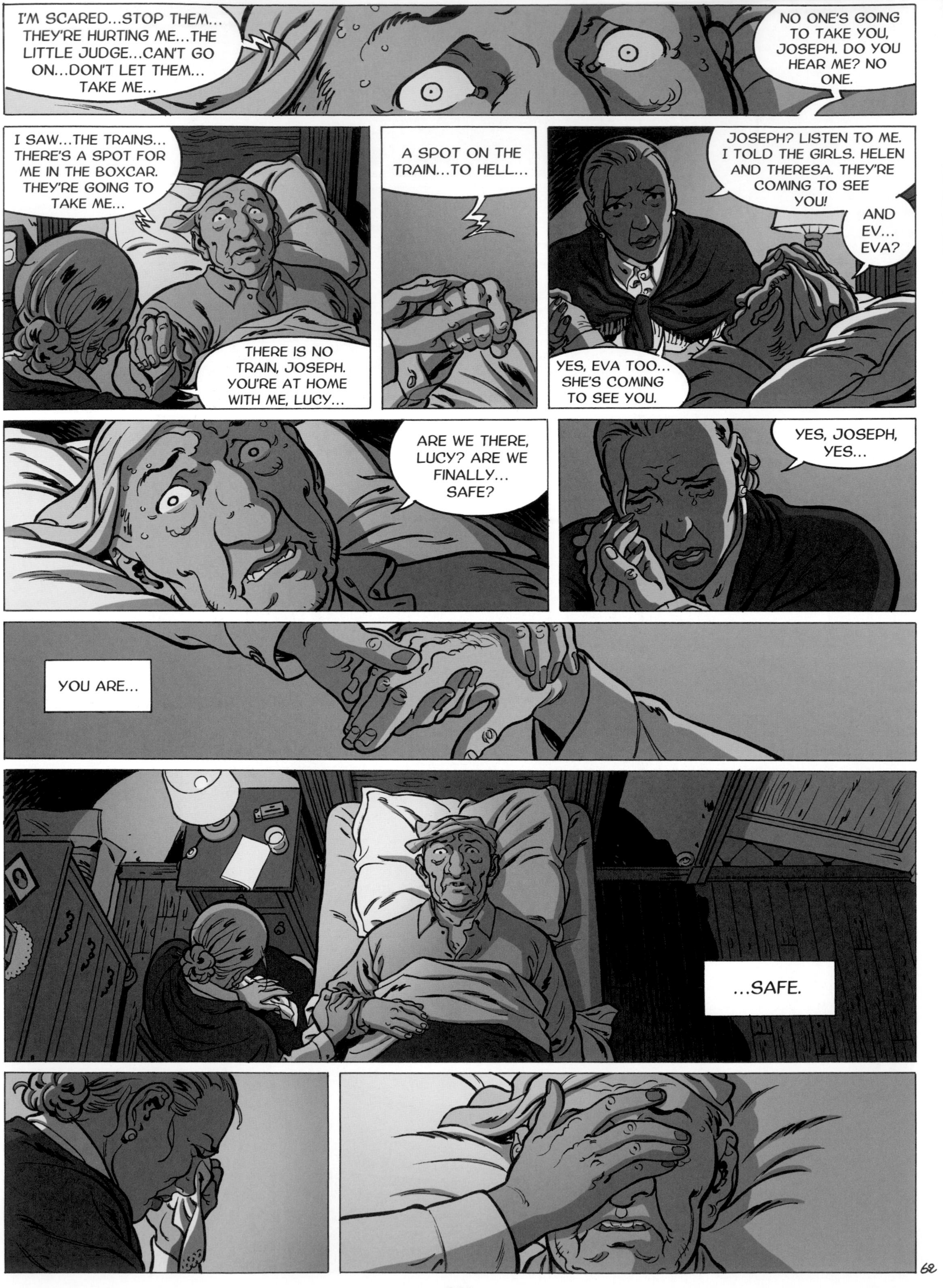
I'M SCARED...STOP THEM... THEY'RE HURTING ME...THE LITTLE JUDGE...CAN'T GO ON...DON'T LET THEM... TAKE ME...
NO ONE'S GOING TO TAKE YOU, JOSEPH. DO YOU HEAR ME? NO ONE.
I SAW...THE TRAINS... THERE'S A SPOT FOR ME IN THE BOXCAR. THEY'RE GOING TO TAKE ME...
THERE IS NO TRAIN, JOSEPH. YOU'RE AT HOME WITH ME, LUCY...
A SPOT ON THE TRAIN...TO HELL...
JOSEPH? LISTEN TO ME. I TOLD THE GIRLS. HELEN AND THERESA. THEY'RE COMING TO SEE YOU!
AND EV... EVA?
YES, EVA TOO... SHE'S COMING TO SEE YOU.
ARE WE THERE, LUCY? ARE WE FINALLY... SAFE?
YES, JOSEPH, YES...
YOU ARE...
...SAFE.
62

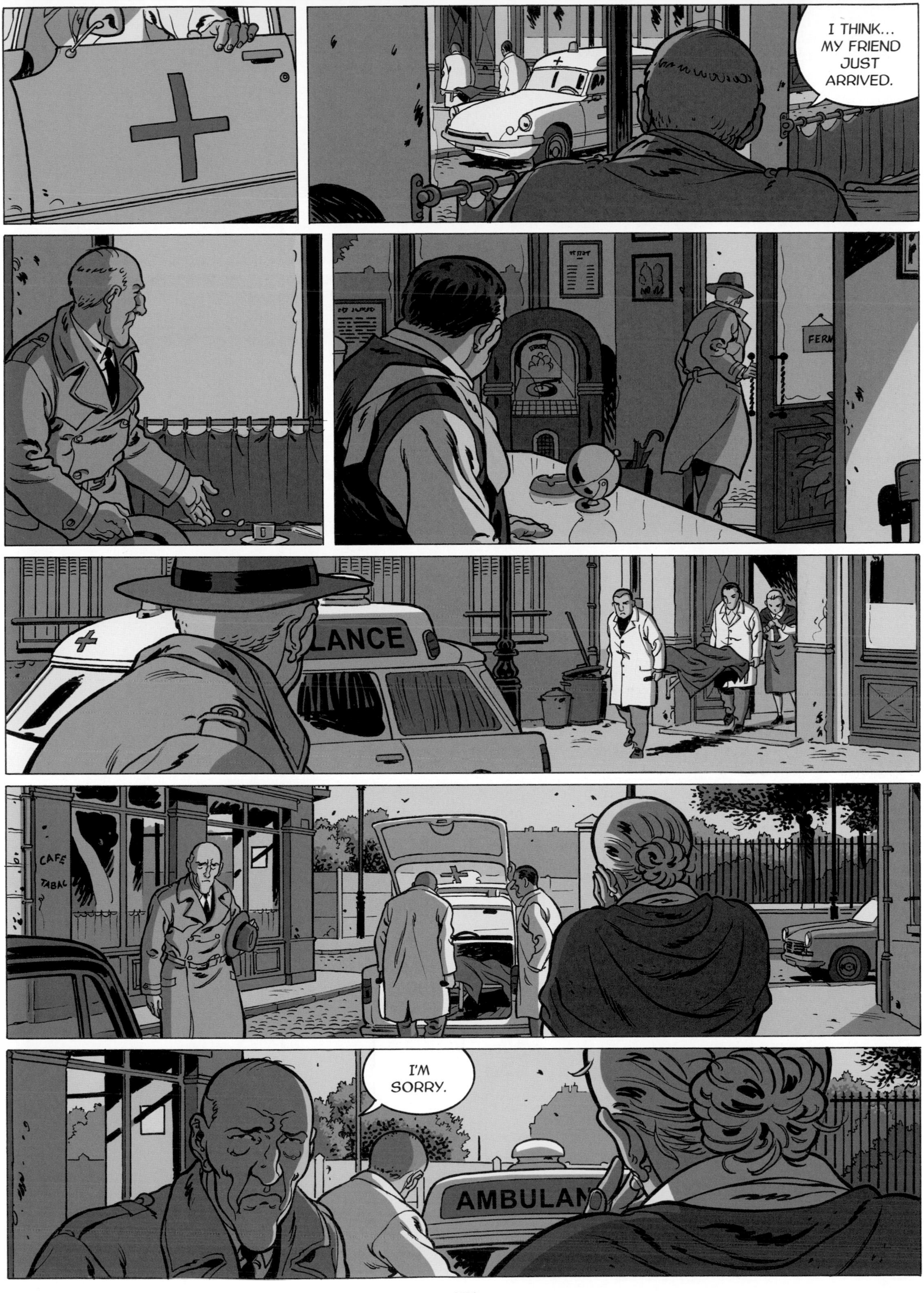
I THINK... MY FRIEND JUST ARRIVED.
FERM
LANCE
CAFE
TABAC
I'M SORRY.
AMBULAN
63

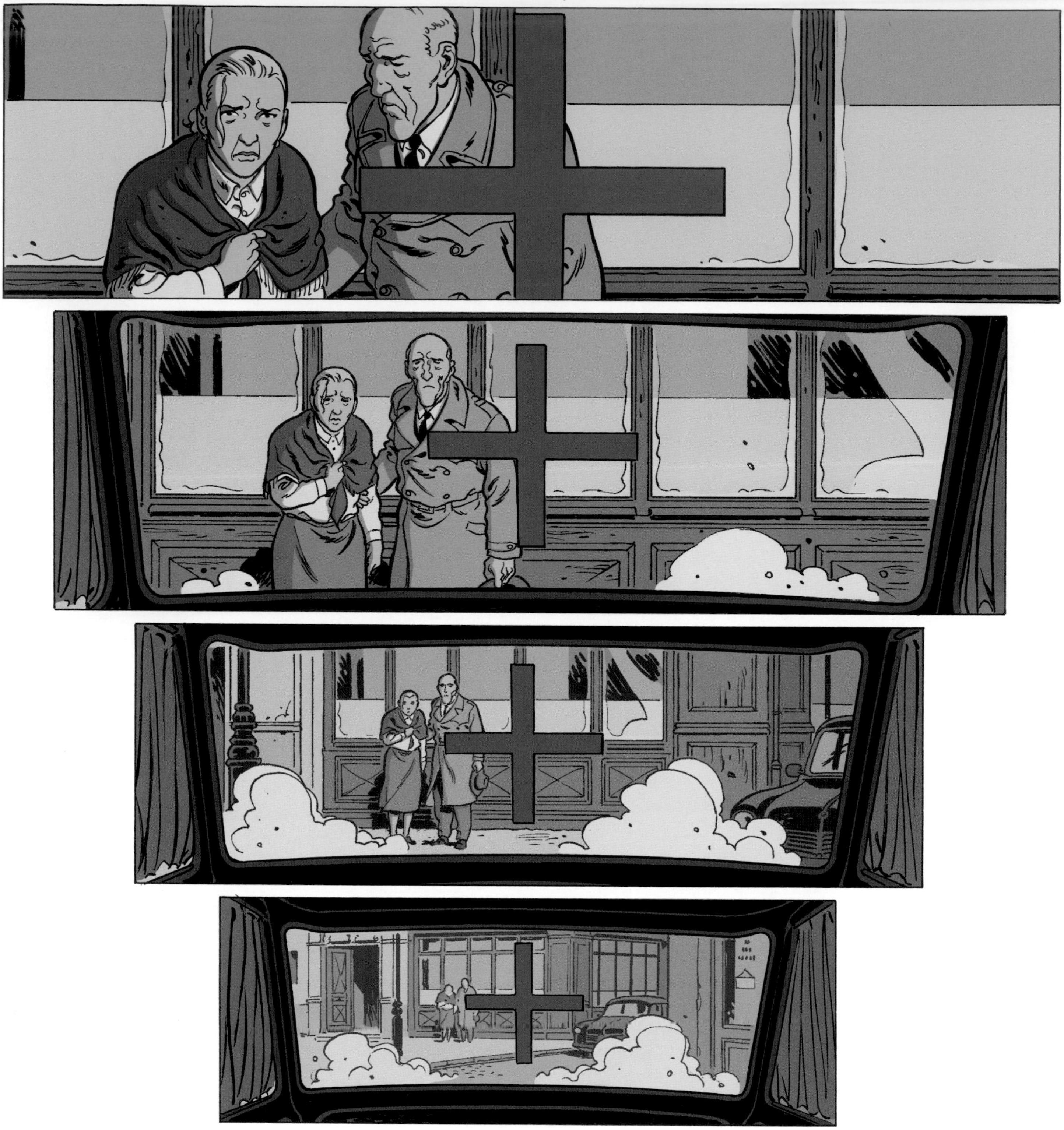

THE END

Born on May 31, 1976, **Fabien Nury** began his career as a copywriter and creative director in advertising. His meeting with comic writer Xavier Dorison was decisive. He decided to take the plunge and start at twenty-seven in his first scenario. Since then, Nury has scripted more than fifteen comics series, including *Once Upon a Time in France*, which won the Best Series Award at the Angoulême Comics Festival, and *The Death of Stalin*, which was adapted to the film with Steve Buscemi. Nury is also a television screenwriter and has created the *Guyane* TV series.

Sylvain Vallée, born in France on June 28, 1972, graduated in graphic arts from the Saint-Luc School of Brussels. He started as a cartoonist and a freelance illustrator in advertising. He published his first comic book at twenty-three and has worked on a dozen series with Glénat (*Gil Saint-André, Once Upon a Time in France*) and Dargaud (*XIII Mystery, Katanga*). He is now working on his first graphic novel, *Tananarive*.